THOMAS MANN
DIARIES 1918-1939

THOMAS MANN

DIARIES 1918-1939

1918-1921
1933-1939

Selection and Foreword by Hermann Kesten

Translated from the German by Richard and Clara Winston

Harry N. Abrams, Inc., Publishers, New York

. . . .

Publisher's Note

. . . .

The translation of *Thomas Mann: Diaries 1918–1939* was entrusted to Richard and Clara Winston in the summer of 1979. After the untimely death of Richard Winston at the end of that year, Clara Winston was assisted by her daughter Krishna Winston.

The publisher is greatly indebted to Michael Sonino and Russell Stockman for their thorough editorial work on the translation of the text, and to Mr. Stockman for his translation of the annotation and making of the index.

The publisher and Hermann Kesten wish to express their sincere gratitude to Peter de Mendelssohn for the invaluable work that resulted in the indispensable annotation. With his permission and that of the West German publisher of the original edition, S. Fischer Verlag GmbH, Frankfurt am Main, we excerpted the notes for our edition.

Library of Congress Cataloging in Publication Data
Mann, Thomas, 1875–1955.
  Diaries, 1918–1939.

  Abridged translation of his Tagebücher, 1918–1921,
1933–1934, 1935–1936, 1937–1939,
originally published by S. Fischer, 1977–1980.
  Includes bibliographical references.
  1. Mann, Thomas, 1875–1955—Diaries.
2. Novelists, German—20th century—Biography.
I. Kesten, Hermann, 1900–   II. Title.
PT2625.A44Z469 1982   838'.91203 [B] 81–22889
ISBN 0–8109–1304–6   AACR2

Designer: Samuel N. Antupit

© S. Fischer Verlag GmbH, Frankfurt am Main, West Germany 1977, 1978, 1979, 1980. English translation © 1982 Harry N. Abrams, Inc.

Printed and bound in the United States of America

Contents

....

Publisher's Note		*iv*
Foreword		*vi*
The Diaries	1918	*1*
	1919	*29*
	1920	*81*
	1921	*107*
	1933	*125*
	1934	*189*
	1935	*229*
	1936	*251*
	1937	*267*
	1938	*289*
	1939	*315*
Notes on the Text		*347*
Biographical Notes		*387*
Index of References to Thomas Mann's Works		*435*
General Index		*443*
Picture sections follow		*120, 216, 328*

Thomas Mann, one of the great novelists of our century, wanted to understand people completely. To know them better, he took the greatest interest in himself. Or rather, he constantly examined himself in order to portray others convincingly. To this penetrating interest we owe his stories, his novels, his biographical essays, some auto-biographical pieces, and—more than twenty-five years after his death—his diaries.

He kept diaries with certain interruptions from his schooldays in Lübeck until a few days before his death in Zurich. Surviving are the diaries from 1918 to 1921 and from 1933 to 1955. He wrote the entries for himself, without regard for posterity, yet through a clause in his will he offered up parts of them to posterity. Parts, for several times he destroyed portions of the record, including everything up until 1918 and from 1921 into 1933.

As early as February 17, 1895, Mann wrote his friend Otto Grautoff: "By the way, I am keeping especially warm these days. You see, I am burning all my diaries! Why? Because they were a burden to me; in terms of space and in other ways as well. . . . You think it a pity? But where could I store them if, for example, I took a long trip? Or what if I died quite suddenly and peacefully, in my sleep? It became awkward and uncomfortable for me to have such a mass of secret—*very* secret—writings lying around. All your letters and some ancient stories of questionable nature . . . sent their chemical components up the chimney. I suggest a similar cleaning to you. One truly gets rid of the past and can live cheerfully in the present and face the future without qualms."

In the entry for January 10, 1919, after he had read the finished parts of *Gesang vom Kindchen* to his wife, Katia: "She was very moved, and only objected to my depiction of our most intimate experiences. But it is these intimate things that are really the most universal and human, and besides, I do not have any such scruples."

On February 11, 1934, he noted: "These diary notes, resumed in Arosa during days of illness brought on by inner turmoil and the loss of our accustomed structured life, have been a comfort and support up to now, and I will surely continue with them. I love this process by which each passing day is captured, not only its impressions, but also, at least by suggestion, its intellectual direction and content as well, less for the purpose of rereading and remembering than for taking stock, reviewing, maintaining awareness, achieving perspective."

"Why do I write all this?" he asked in his entry for August 25, 1950. "Only so that I can destroy it in time before I die? Or is it that I desire that the world know all about me? I believe it knows more in any case—or at least its more perceptive people do—than it lets on to me."

When he decided not to return to Munich in 1933, he was extremely anxious lest these secret diaries fall into the hands of the Nazis and hopelessly compromise him. He was relieved when, with the greatest difficulty, they were brought to safety in Switzerland. Nevertheless, on May 21, 1945, he recorded he had just destroyed old diaries, "carrying out a long-held resolve . . . in the outside stove," that is, in the incinerator behind his house in California.

Once Mann was to wonder whether "the prayer-like communion in the diary" did not afford him a kind of protection.

Peter de Mendelssohn, editor of the German edition of the diaries, writes: "Certainly he wanted the world to know him, as well and as accurately as possible . . . therefore he stipulated that the parcels be opened and his entries read after the designated interval . . . and thus the demand was made that they become available to the general public. He did not shrink from self-revelation and self-exposure. On the contrary, these were the fundamental creative impulses behind his whole oeuvre."

Thomas Mann kept these diaries—some of which he destroyed and some of which he carefully preserved—absolutely secret while he lived and for a period of twenty years after his death. Even his wife and children were forbidden access to them, as were his friends and biographers. Yet he provided that after twenty years, they could be made available to the world. So sure was he of himself. So certain was he of his posthumous fame. So deeply did he feel that his manner of revealing himself, without scruple or reservation, was truly rare—if not unique—in world literature.

For in these notebooks he recorded everything; not so much his larger ideas as his smallest impulses, the most trivial details of his everyday life. He noted each headache, each stomachache, each medicine he took, each comfort and discomfort. He recorded the activities of his dogs and those of his six children, as well as what the children wore; he noted all the people he met and the ones who called on him (only rarely, to be sure, what they talked about); he described his homoerotic desires and temptations, sometimes noted that he had had sexual relations with Katia, the mother of his six children, and how things stood with them currently in this regard. He registered the progress of his work and the appearance of the household help; what he ate and drank; his digestion; when he had a haircut; his journeys and lectures and the reactions of audiences and critics; what he dreamed and occasionally his ideas and plans, and in detail his most banal perceptions and comments. He noted his daily walks; his every physical and psychic worry; each award and honorary doctorate; his sentiments and resentments; what he thought about revolutions and world wars and his dogs and his verses, the everyday and the unique and the constant and recurrent.

Of the sheer bulk of the extant diaries, the indiscriminate agglomeration of everyday details and personal reactions which characterize this unusual literary—yes, literary—work, on whose wrapping paper Mann wrote that these diaries were "without literary value," and which he therefore seems to have submitted to posterity simply as human documents—the American publishers decided to offer their readers a selection.

The selection I have here undertaken tries to preserve the curious character of these diaries, that is, to present the omnium-gatherum of a writer who held his own genius in no higher esteem than the supreme banality of a human existence.

I have never shortened a given entry. Instead I omitted entire entries, especially those containing tedious repetition. Yet I must reiterate that one deliberate artistic device in these diaries is their constant repetition of physical and psychological details and everyday happenings against a background of historical upheaval, throughout a life that was, after all, an adventurous one.

The notes are based almost entirely on the extraordinarily thorough and ingenious ones provided by the exemplary editor Peter de Mendelssohn for the German edition. I am convinced that Thomas Mann's diaries present the life of a genius with extraordinary immediacy, in spite of—even because of—their pedantic quality. It almost seems as though he were photographing his life, as though he were sketching a colossal portrait of the living Thomas Mann. So for this work of Thomas Mann's the exclamation again applies: ECCE HOMO.

Hermann Kesten   vii

THE DIARIES

1918

Back from Tegernsee since day before yesterday. The house without rugs and not yet cleaned. In the morning wrote to Major Endres about his Constantinople novel, to Martens about the *Betrachtungen*, and white lies to Adele Gerhard about her novellas, *Sprache der Erde*. Wet walk with Bauschan. Luncheon in the upstairs sitting room. Katia to see Faltin concerning her condition. He denies it, despite all indications. Mysterious. Bertram to tea. He is going to Elberfeld tomorrow, and brought his Nietzsche book, decorated with flowers and cleverly and allusively inscribed. Katia to Arcisstrasse. In the evening, read with emotion and feeling of being completely "at home" in Bertram's book, to which I am attached as it is so akin to my own.

Tegernsee is still vivid within me, with the bracing water, the boat, the reminders of the Lido at the beach, the visit to Bad Kreuth with Bertram, climbing the Hirschberg, the night in the shelter on the peak before and at sunrise with the south wind blowing. The departure from Villa Defregger ghastly. In the rowboat with the Fräulein, Golo, the new maid Anna, who carried the little one, crossing the turbulent lake with a storm threatening. I am curious about the adventure of publishing the *Betrachtungen*. Laughing up my sleeve, and expect almost anything. Glad that no travels are impending for this winter, and that in general we will not be leaving the Herzogpark house in the foreseeable future. Once it is put back in order it will be possible to live quite securely here, and I am prepared for everything; have gone through too much and anticipated too much for anything to really bother me. I'll finish *A Man and His Dog*, then, since I won't have to write a foreword for the 100th edition of *Buddenbrooks*, will proceed to work on *The Magic Mountain*.

I was wrought up to the point of exhaustion last night over the baby. The Fräulein on vacation, Katia out on errands, and I alone with the beloved little one, who had kicked off her covers. I removed her damp, cold things, but didn't know what else to do, and she cried loudly and alarmingly, probably sensing my helplessness. Was fearful of losing her trust. Afterward further irritation with the beastly cook. Shaky, tired, out of sorts. Better today.

Thursday, September 12

Worked on *A Man and His Dog* in the children's playroom. Letter to Loeb on questions of canine medicine.—The Kaiser's speech to the Krupp workers: read it with some emotion and sympathy, though also with amusement. Social humanitarianism, patriarchal: "Everyone has his duty and his burden, you at your lathes and I upon my throne." Tendency toward drama mixed with preacherly touches: the "ayes" demanded from the men. Schiller-like pathos: "I thank you! With this 'aye' I shall go—to the field marshal!" The whole thing very German in tone [and] spirit; old-fashioned in that it struck a popular note, not democratically demagogic. But the "German people" are the very ones to whom it is still easiest to speak in such terms.— Letter from Witkop in Freiburg; he is planning a monograph on me. Telephone call from Major Endres, happy over my letter; he talked animatedly, and asked permission, which I gave, to let his publisher quote me.—At table a visit from Mama; she seemed to me muted, fragile, and old, and her raptures over the little one struck a sympathetic nerve in me. After tea wrote letters, including one to young Herzfeld about the baptism. From seven to eight walked under overcast, sunset sky until dark, alone. The

3

park very picturesque. Claude Lorrain. In the evening, read with emotion the "Knight, Death, and the Devil" chapter in Bertram's book.—My room ready except for the rugs.—Katia's puzzling condition unchanged.

Friday, September 13

Blue-gray, stormy day. At breakfast, irritation with Katia, who took a skeptical attitude toward Bertram and the "importance" of his book, probably merely out of misunderstanding and wifely pride, since I had said we could be proud of his friendship. I know only too well how I meant it and mean it. I have too many followers whose adherence degrades me and unconsciously confirms all my own self-deprecation. Bertram is almost the only exception.—At work I cheered myself up; the episode in the veterinary clinic, the conversation with the guard.—Yesterday Dauthendey's death in Java was reported. Today a very pious, Christian announcement by his wife.—Speech of Vice-Chancellor von Payer presenting a peace program; curious how it will be received outside the country.—Bored myself after tea with a letter replying to Witkop. Nervous and tired. In the evening read in *Nietzsche*.

Saturday, September 14

Cool, blue-gold autumn day. But the work limping along.—Feel the *Nietzsche* to be a good, *moving* book, and the author a friend in the most comforting and virtually highest sense of the word. Sense of nostalgia reflecting on this mental landscape; survey of my own life. Deathly melancholy. On my afternoon walk thought once again how good it would be if I were to die now. Then feeling of love for the little one, and began experimenting in my mind with the hexameter poem. But also saw the thematic relationship between my future works and the domain of my reading: the romanticism of death plus affirmation of life in *The Magic Mountain*, the Protestantism of *The Confidence Man*. A sense of reaffirmation.—After tea, which [I] had by myself, a visit from the bookseller Berner.—I miss the rugs.—During my evening walk, came upon the little one, who was being walked in her perambulator on the allée. I brought her home and carried her up to her crib, full of love!—Long walk. The riverbank and the park were exceedingly beautiful as this gold-drenched fall afternoon passed into a theatrically romantic evening with a crescent moon in the sky, a milky mist floating over the meadows, and a fiery sunset beyond the black trees. Masses of thistles whose flowers are fading into fuzzy down.—In the evening, *Nietzsche*. In short, it is my book, treating of a subject that is far and away the most interesting to me—my central subject—and with a degree of intense devotion unique in literary criticism or history.

Sunday, September 15

Glorious, sunny, blue, warm, early-autumn day. Windows and French doors open. At breakfast read the Austro-Hungarian peace note to all belligerents, framed with considerable tact and human feeling.—My work consisted chiefly of revisions. Rested in the garden. Telephone call from Opitz, who is passing through. Correspondence in connection with the Rhineland lecture tour, for which I am asking 1,600 marks. Wrote to Cossmann and Walter. Warmly recommended the *Nietzsche* to Hofmiller. Outdoors, thought again about the hexameters. If only "Bauschan" were finished; but ennui and impatience only slow and paralyze my work.—Carried the little one about a good deal. Before nightfall, sauntered in the park during a golden sunset, with upset stomach from too much honey. In the evening, read the *Nietzsche* with admiration. His Germanism brought out most profoundly and ingeniously. Parallels to Goethe, who likewise, says the author, is German both where he is at his most sublime and his most earthy. *Faust — Zarathustra*; the rhymed *Sprüche — Scherz, List und Rache*. What lies between is—French. Heinrich quite *wrong* to cite the great Germans in support of his opinions.—The passage where my name actually appears in this book, set as it is on so high a plane, gives me a shock, though a joyful one, each time I approach it, even in anticipation. More mysterious, bemusing, and delightful to me are those passages—and they are plentiful—where the author has been mindful of me *without* referring to me by name.—Out of weakness and courtesy I have, I fear, written many dishonest letters of thanks for books received, and will, I fear, write many more in the future. This time I shall have the privilege of being truthful.—Tonight "winter time" begins again. I have turned back my pocket watch from midnight to eleven. Comical.

Monday, September 16

Not well. Abdominal pain from my large intestine; weak, out of sorts. Since this clear and pure late-summer weather continues, I was outdoors even before breakfast, after looking in on the little one. The Allied press comments on the Kaiser's Essen speech, Payer's address, the Burian note: repulsive and hopeless. What do they want? To drive out of us the experience of Goethe, Luther, Frederick the Great, and Bismarck, so that we can "adjust ourselves to democracy." I do not regret a word of the *Betrachtungen*.—Worked with difficulty and reluctance. Walk in the park; summery atmosphere. Rested outdoors after luncheon, and after tea called on Loeb, who prescribed pills for the intestinal irritation and gave me some medical terms for "Bauschan." Went to the post office and the pharmacy. Walked home in "winter-time" darkness. In the warmth of the summery evening the town smelled odiously of people. At home the rugs had been laid, but they must be rearranged. Read in *Nietzsche*.

Tuesday, September 17

Health improved. Worked more smoothly and cheerfully. Into town in white trousers on errands: pills, a collar for Bauschan, a few penholders.—Slept nervously during the night and gave it up early, largely, I think, out of excitement over the rugs.—Card from Bertram from Brückenau.—Afternoon in the garden. More Allied voices calling for "readiness for peace": nauseatingly heartless and hypocritical.—Very warm; the weather is bound to change.—I keep thinking of a political manifesto to be published internationally, something warm, humane, and well written that frankly and honestly [calls] a spade a spade on every point.—Beautiful pink late roses from the garden in my room.—Further occupied with "Bauschan" in the afternoon.—Evening walk without a hat in the darkness down to the ferry landing; the moon half concealed by clouds, the bats flying about while lightning flashes darted through a bright bank of

clouds off to the west.—Katia badly nauseated. Sympathy for her. Is going to Privy
Councillor Müller tomorrow. Her conviction that she is expecting convinces me too,
in spite of Faltin's denials. It would almost be even more worrisome if she were
mistaken.—Read *Nietzsche*. Stylistic preparations for a letter to its author.—A few
grapes for dessert this evening: a rare treat.—Am taking Loeb's pills containing strych-
nine and belladonna.—The Greco-Goethean element in *The Confidence Man*: "Such
exquisite and well-formed people sense in themselves a kind of apotheosis of the body.
From such a pinnacle of delight on the part of those who feel themselves to be divine
forms, the very culmination of nature, down to the contentment of robust farmers
and hearty subhuman creatures . . ." (Nietzsche).

· ·

Wednesday, September 18

· ·

Summer heat, silk suit. At midday read the newspaper in the park. Katia saw Privy
Councillor Müller. Result: uncertainty. Wait and see.—Not very well, eyes weak; from
the belladonna I suspect. Privy Councillor Pringsheim to tea. Superficial talk about
the dark political situation. The boundless confidence of the enemy. Clemenceau
horrible in the Senate, wallowing in noble triumph. France deciding how the "reconquered" territories are to be administered. Cool rejection of the Austrian note by
Wilson and Balfour.—Purely intellectual thoughts have a soothing effect after embittered brooding on the cheap humbuggery of politics. In connection with *A Man and
His Dog* and *Nietzsche*, thought how it is an ironical but sympathetic treatment of the
humanistic spirit that is really my stylistic element, or is becoming so more and more.—
Thunderstorm threatening.—Brief evening walk in silk suit, downstream among the
bats, which I am afraid of.—Worth noting that Marshal Foch is a Catholic, a romantic
militarist, pious, reactionary, probably royalist. He refers to the French victims of the
war as "martyrs." The enlightened enemy needs this type to be victorious.—The
demand that Germany pull out of occupied territories prior to preliminary negotiations, without any counterconcessions being made in advance by the other side—
outrageous.—After supper finished Bertram's *Nietzsche*. Gratifying to think that without *Tonio Kröger* and *Death in Venice* this book would not have been possible, neither
in certain of its specific turns nor certainly as a whole. Moving to see how it stands
as something dignified, prudent, magisterial, unassailable, irreproachable, yet brotherly
alongside my imprudent, untutored, stammering, and compromising artist's book. It
is incidentally profoundly musical, a series of variations on the theme of "ebb and
flow"—a great theme, the image of the world and of life, one might say. The critical
technique vibrant with lyricism and feeling. The recurrent quotations as parentheses
and leitmotifs. Admirable the sheer command of the material, the perspective over a
life's work that seems, after all, so fragmented; admirable the ingenuity with which
he presents associations. Clever, ingenious, and elegant his arrangement of the chapters,
each of which could stand by itself inasmuch as it is infused with his whole fascination
with the subject—with the Eleusis chapter as the crowning conclusion. Truly, I am as
proud of this work as if I had written it myself.—Stopping with the pills; I cannot
bear any poisons.

Cloudy, sultry. Completed, rather disinterestedly, the veterinary clinic episode in "Bauschan."—Invitation from Horwitz to give the opening address at this year's Intimate Afternoons. Declined.—Errands in town. Ran into Pfitzner on Maximilianstrasse. Chatted about *Buddenbrooks*, which his oldest boy has now read. About the war situation, pessimistically.—After luncheon wrote letters and read some of Rathenau's new book, *Zeitliches*. Clever, but not my sphere.—Lula to tea. Political discussions. Her lachrymose credulity contrasted with Katia's often harshly expressed skepticism. Embarrassing.—The little one in a long white dress, a pink rose in her waistband. I carried her about on the terrace for some time.—Very sultry, some rain. We escorted Lula home.—Continued reading Rathenau's *Zeitliches*. Edifying to read now in a fairly recent essay: "France is in danger of falling into our hands together with her ports and her capital."—He says, incidentally, that the passing of continental hegemony from France to Germany is confirmed by the disengagement of Alsace-Lorraine. Today France is making arrangements for the administration of "reconquered" territories. Are we then to believe that continental hegemony in the form of Alsace-Lorraine will once more pass to France, which even Rathenau calls a deteriorating state, dependent upon the protection of paid allies and practicing womanish policies? [. . .]

Last night I noticed a light through the closed glass door of the children's quarters, and since I had to wake Katia anyhow, as she had locked me out, we investigated. It turned out that Eissi was lying in bed with the light on and in a fantastic state of undress. He was unable to give any answers to our questions. Puberty games, or a tendency toward somnambulistic adventures as we already observed in Tegernsee? Perhaps both together. What form will the boy's life take? Admittedly, someone like me "ought" not to bring children into the world. But that "ought" deserves its quotation marks. All living things not only will their existence because they are alive, but *have* willed it or they would not *be* alive.

These mornings mere adolescents of young soldiers are drilling in the park again. Yesterday they were doing so under the command of an exceedingly bourgeois middle-aged lieutenant. So far they continue to obey, executing as one man the procedures prescribed by the system. The execution of the "Order Arms!" is charming, with the *delicate* return of their rifle butts to the ground as the third maneuver.—Rose early and walked in the allée in drizzling rain. Considerable drop in temperature, but the house is still warm. Worked on the rabbit-hunt episode. At noon into town in the rain. Picked up Bauschan's six-mark collar, which had had to be shortened, and put it on him at home. Early tea at four o'clock, and then with Katia to the Prinzregenten-Theater: *Parsifal.* Moved by the music itself. "The harmony of sweet tones." "I cannot distinguish between music and tears." The prelude has something mechanical about it, though, and at the same time a strongly authoritarian note. Beautiful colors on the stage. The tenderest and most moving part undoubtedly the foot-washing scene. Christian simplicity and, given proper distance from the stage, purity; whereas the Byzantine-domed temple scenes are overly pompous with ritual. The close is ultraromantic magic and not so powerful, in spite of its soaring highlights. The whole thing the

7

dream of an exceedingly high-flown, tired, and sensual old man. Pleasant buffet in the intermissions: vegetable soup, tomato sandwiches, red wine. Cigarette in the theater restaurant. Vulgar war profiteer's wife, large diamonds in her ears, picking her teeth with her stubby little finger after eating a twenty-mark portion of chicken.—Tired.

. . . .
Sunday, September 22
. . . .

Sunny autumnal weather. But did not go out before breakfast because I was holding the little one, who was crying.—Did not do any work as I wanted to finish the letter to Bertram. At noon in the park, where the greens are heavily mingled with yellows and browns. Leaves are falling too, and there is a chemical-autumnal smell.—Am reading *Indian Summer*, moved by the purity and sincerity of the language, the sublime decency of this mind.—In the afternoon napped in the garden.—Made arrangements for the beginning of December with Cologne, Bonn, Düsseldorf for 1,600 marks.— From six to half past seven read most of Grillparzer's *The Poor Fiddler* aloud to the three older children. The diction often reminds me of that of his countryman Stifter. In the beginning I also found a similarity to *A Man and His Dog*.—Before supper, walked for another half an hour, for the first time once again up in Bogenhausen.— The coming week will be very lively: Opitz will be visiting from Berlin and Reinacher from Strassburg; several evenings booked up with social affairs, a concert, and theater. So the story will have to be pushed ahead *par force*, since Martens assumes it is finished and is asking for copies.—Katia somewhat better this morning. After supper we chatted in my room about political affairs: about the young Flaubert, the coming socialist government, the possibility of the war intruding on our everyday life in a completely different way if national defense becomes necessary. It is true that even today Germany has not thrown herself entirely into the struggle.—Had very good pancakes for supper. Ended the day by reading *Indian Summer*. The engagement ceremonies and welcoming speeches at the end movingly droll and extremely heartwarming.—In Spain a new epidemic is raging, so the newspapers report: initial symptoms of influenza rapidly passing over into typhus. There have been many deaths.—

. . . .
Thursday, September 26
. . . .

Bright autumn day. Up early and went walking in the "Kurgarten." Wrote warm-heartedly on the rabbit hunt, which I finished. On going out onto the allée at noon I came upon the little one dressed in silk in her perambulator, accompanied by her two sisters and the Fräulein. They were off to pay a visit to Lula. In the tram, which I took with Erika, we met Katia. I rode with her as far as Isartor Platz, where we parted. Picked up Bauschan's now-engraved collar and then rode back. I came upon the dog on the allée, and while sitting on a bench I put the new harness on him, then took him walking in the park for half an hour.—Katia's condition has now been acknowledged by Faltin, but much time has been lost and much superfluous unpleas-antness endured if it is decided to terminate the pregnancy.—After luncheon, finished reading *Ivan Ilyich*. Rested in bed, then had tea alone, since Katia was at Arcisstrasse, and received a visit from Lieutenant Herzfeld on crutches. I carried his suitcase to the No. 9 tram, and we rode together part of the way. Then went to *Palestrina* at the Prinzregenten-Theater. Sat in a box on the right. During the intermission, with Cossmann and Frau Pfitzner in Walter's greenroom. Telephone conversation with Katia, *who told me that the "Betrachtungen" had arrived, along with a letter from Fischer.* So now we shall know.—In spite of my excitement and relief, I deeply enjoyed the music, which is so familiar and so dear to my heart. Picked Walter up after the performance and we set out on foot toward home. Found there the two copies of the book, and in addition, to my annoyance, the page proofs of Hülsen's Platen novel.—Fischer writes that the edition probably will not be sufficient, since already 3,000 copies have been ordered. Had raw eggs and punch for supper.

Saturday, September 28

Supper with Katia at the Löhrs' last night. I took them a copy of the *Betrachtungen*. Enjoyed the food and drink. Lula read us a lengthy political letter she sent to Dr. Endres that does credit to her cultivation. She also read his reply. I talked with Löhr about the dark future: about the effort Germany must make to modernize, democratize herself, sweeping away the old, romantic, imperial Germany, a task that can only proceed agonizingly and against the grain, meeting extreme resistance because the old Germany is much too deeply and firmly established in men's souls, is much too deeply identified, perhaps, with Germanism itself. Löhr gave me a book on German music by Von der Pfordten to look at. He praised it highly, but when I leafed through it in bed it turned out to be impossibly written. I was tempted to say of it, as a Frenchman would, that it was written "like a Boche."

Today the work again went along briskly, insofar as the word brisk ever applies. At noon, walk with Bauschan.—The political situation is assuming an almost helpless aspect. After severe military defeat, the Bulgarians have made their own cease-fire offer to the Allies. The beginning of the end? What will happen to Germany? *In* Germany?—The final four volumes of Carlyle's *Frederick the Great* have come from the publisher. Reading for these times?—After luncheon, dipped into the *Betrachtungen*, not entirely without approval.—Had tea alone, since Katia was seeing Privy Councillor Müller. She came back with written certification of the necessity to terminate, but first I must discuss the matter with Müller myself, so I made an appointment with him for Monday.—The withdrawal of Bulgaria from the German alliance appears to be final. Delighted speculation in England about the military effects (Salonika army) and the political ones (Turkey). Deeply serious articles in the German press. "National defense." "New men." "Unity above all dogmatic differences." What would the "Patriotic party" really like to see?—As I see it, either peace will come in a few weeks or an inconceivable catastrophe will descend on Germany.—Clipping sent from the *Berliner Tageblatt* with the "Unliterary Country" chapter reprinted from the galleys.— The evening walk calmed me. Read Gogol. A thing like the two Ivans' argument over the rifle reconciles one with life. It is desperate comedy, but that is the funniest kind. Wonderful, the profoundly melancholy conclusion after all the buffoonery. Gogol read the story aloud to Pushkin. Its tone is frequently the right one for *The Magic Mountain*.

A sixth child? There is no great difference between five and six, and after the war children will scarcely expect to receive economic provision for life. The right of inheritance will be curtailed to the vanishing point, property become altogether illu-

9

sory. Education is atmosphere, nothing more. Aside from Katia's health, I really have no objection, except that it will subtract something from the experience of "Lisa" (in a certain sense my *first* child).

Got to bed late yesterday; in wretched form today. Overcoming resistance, worked on the water birds. Odd hypocrisy of writing without enthusiasm; impermissible to let any difference show, and so one does it as one would if the enthusiasm were there, that is ne pretends to be enthusiastic with great effort.—Fischer telegraphed that the *Frankfurter Zeitung* wants to know which parts of the *Betrachtungen* have been printed before book publication. I telegraphed my reply. So the two great democratic newspapers are the first to show interest in the book. Ironic. But it is literature, even though antidemocratic.—What part will the book play? For it is possible that it will play a part. But it is also possible that its unreadability will prevent it from becoming noticed. Will the conservative press seize upon it?—Walk with Bauschan.—For tea, Frau D. Rauch. Finished reading *The Poor Fiddler* to the children and then Tolstoy's "Khodynka."—Evening walk.—Dipped into Carlyle's *Frederick*, about the Kunersdorf period, with thoughts about the present situation and doubts about *whether* we may legitimately apply the former to the latter.—Katia brought the little one in to say good night. Tenderness. Delight at her smile. Now she is sometimes taken from the garden toward the end of luncheon and brought to table, sitting on the suspect Fräulein's lap. Touching, when she sits up, the look of strain on her five-month-old face that is reminiscent of very old people. She seems much smaller and weaker when she sits. The unsteady little head whose warmth I so like to feel against my temple and cheek. I carried her around the dining room today and showed her things.—Erika seems to have a calling for domesticity and the role of a live-in maid. Today she made pancakes for our supper. Engaging in her household apron and frequently strikingly beautiful. Her mother secretly teases her about her indisposition, which came the other day for the first time.—Today, on my afternoon walk, thoughts of death and ideas for my will, beginning: "Premonitions, perhaps not solely the product of my wishes, induce me. . . ."—Count Eduard Keyserling and Georg Simmel have died, both in their early sixties. Do I have another twenty years?

I dreamed I [was] somewhere with Heinrich on the best of terms, and out of goodwill let [him] eat up a great number of cakes, small *à la crème* ones, and two pieces of torte, giving up my own share. Puzzled how this friendship relates to the publication of the *Betrachtungen*. I kept thinking this surely won't do, it is a totally impossible situation. On awakening, the feeling of relief that it was a dream.—In the morning mail an article by Krell about the book, along with a letter telling me that he had asked the *Rundschau* for the proofs and has written the article for them, but that they have now rejected it with diplomatic phrases. In addition, the young poet Zarek sent a volume of his stories, together with a letter of homage in which he says it is essential these days to stress "that a strong and vital youthful following has not sacrificed the spirit of beauty and of human dignity to the idols of politics." These young people believe in me, he goes on, and he is sending me his book "in reverence and profound gratitude" because he owes to me his commitment to intellectual and cultural dignity.—It almost seems as if I need not have written the *Betrachtungen* at all.—Better rested, I worked easily, and without the slightest resistance dashed off two pages. Then read Krell's article with profound physical excitement. Hard to understand why the *Rundschau* turned it down. Am inclined to think it is because of its lack of talent; but that may be unjust, for I nearly always find articles about me bad, especially when they are favorable. It is also possible that the periodical's political stance precluded its acceptance.—Dined alone before one o'clock, then by tram to Privy Councillor Müller, with whom I had a pleasant talk, though the results were hardly definite. He says he need not and would not wish to oppose a decisive wish of Katia's, if she has one, with a decisive prohibition on his own part. He does not want to shift the responsibility from himself entirely, but still it falls to us, in the final analysis to me. It would certainly be up to me to terminate the business. Back home talked with Katia. Then fitful rest.—Wind and rain. Wrote to Krell, to Hülsen declining his request, and did not go out again. After supper, telephone conversation with Dr. Faltin on the pregnancy question. Given Katia's moral scruples, he seemed very reluctant to undertake an abortion, and reinforced our resolve to let the matter take its course. I am content; I look forward to the new little life and believe that this is also the better course for Katia.—In the evening only read newspapers. To stiffen morale at the front, *Vorwärts* is forecasting all the horrors of possible anarchy and invasion. It is right to do so. But. . . . The Bulgarian collapse seems to be viewed as a military breakdown stemming from internal dissension. The retreat is being called precipitate and unnecessary. As far as we are concerned, it looks as though everything will hang in the balance during the next few weeks. Though internal conditions would be greatly altered, if we can hold out in the West until the winter we will probably come out of it with no more than a black eye, aided perhaps by antagonism between England and America. I said today that if America should decide the war, the future holds within its womb a European-American war.—Count Hertling is resigning, and with him also perhaps Foreign Secretary von Hintze. Still not a word about who is to succeed? I would be pleased if Bethmann were to return.

Friday, October 4

Prince Max von Baden appointed chancellor. Establishment of the new, democratic government in which the Social Democrats predominate. Formal peace offer and armistice terms from the "New Germany" are impending. Belief in "power" is being solemnly abjured—though Germany's enemies are steeped in that belief. The self-abnegation, remorse, and penitence are boundless. We now say that the enemy is in the right, admit that Germany needed to be reformed by such an enemy, and out of fear we declare ourselves reformed.—Lethargic, tormented, half sick. Tortured myself over the article and did not go out at midday. At tea that ass Von Delbrück. Letter from Leppmann saying that a new, expanded edition of his monograph is about to come out. Packed up copies of the *Betrachtungen* for him and for Pfitzner.—On the breakfast table this morning, a letter with Heinrich's handwriting. The sight of it dangerously assaulted my nerves, but it turned out to be nothing but a document for family signature concerning payments to Vicco.—The French translation of *Death in*

Venice proves to be a botch.—Evening walk. Nervously read a number of things at random: Meyer's letters, a shrewd but lachrymose pamphlet by Rathenau, Merezhkovsky on Dostoevsky.—Despairing and harried.

. . . .

Saturday, October 5

. . . .

Healthier. Drafted Keyserling article.—Walks afternoon and evening. Read the Meyer-Rodenberg correspondence; disappointing in its unimportance. Nothing but the emerging assertion of Meyer's conservative Germanism made any impression on me.—The culmination and worldwide defeat of this mentality and inclination is at hand. It is also my position. News by telephone from Arcisstrasse: Harden, who is here today, claims knowledge that the new government was established in response to a telegraphed request from the Supreme Army Command, since the western front can no longer be held and a government is needed that will be acceptable to our enemies as negotiating partners. Capitulation with surrender of Alsace-Lorraine is impending. "The greatest collapse in world history." Since the papers, even the Social Democratic ones, have said nothing to prepare anyone in Germany for the loss of Alsace, I refused to believe it at first. But at ten o'clock this evening the state of affairs was confirmed by Löhr. It is indeed true. Yesterday our armistice offer was sent to Washington via Sweden, along with our acceptance of all of Wilson's "Points," the Fourteen and the Five. Furthermore, England is more or less beaten at sea, he says. According to reliable sources, she cannot continue the war beyond next spring because of coal shortages and an inadequate number of freighters, also because her trade with America and Japan has been cut off. But we, defeated on land, are already done for, and can only hope that England and America will put a check on the French passion for vengeance, so that revenge will be "satisfied" with Alsace. He claims that the city is buzzing with rumors, and that it is shameful to hear how eagerly people are dividing up the territory of the Reich. Helgoland will be given up, likewise Posen and Danzig, the left bank of the Rhine neutralized. The newspapers are issuing extras saying that today's speech by the chancellor will consist of an appeal to Wilson. The noble Harden is supposed to have "talked about everything openly" in his remarks this evening in the Tonhalle, and was interrupted by "jubilation" at "surprising" passages.

Jubilation. In any event, the triumph of virtue is complete and Germany can grovel. It is certainly a bit painful that everything now hangs on the wisdom of a Quaker whether Germany obtains a peace that does *not* inject into her bloodstream undying outrage against the turn of events. In the interest of the German spirit and the preservation of its opposition to democratic civilization one might almost wish for this. But that is certainly not meant in terms of economics, and in this respect not in terms of any material self-interest on my part. My view is that the worldwide triumph of democratic civilization in the political sphere is an accomplished fact, and that consequently, if the German spirit is to be preserved, one must recommend the separation of cultural and national life from politics, the complete detachment of one from the other. The thrust of my *Betrachtungen* is against the fusion of the two realms, against the "politization" of Germany through the absolute domination, in the cultural sphere as well, of the victorious principle of democratic civilization.

Beautiful autumn day. Went out for a while before breakfast. Wrote one page. After shaving went into town, Walter having phoned and asked me to call for him at the theater office so he could pass along some political news. Plans concerning a *levée en masse* in case of devastating enemy demands. His discussions with the Bavarian war minister and correspondence with Rathenau; his desire that I back him up in his appeal to the latter. Agitation and depression. Mine is not the heroic stance. What I like about Hindenburg is that he refuses to play *va banque*, and has installed the "popular government" so that it can make peace. Provided it is acknowledged beforehand (and I assume that the world, too, will acknowledge it) that Germany is the real victor in this war—insofar as "war" is the proper word—there remains no other choice, and it is the only sensible and dignified choice, but to view things from the comic side and declare the victory of the virtuous Allies a colossal humbug (Three cheers for the president of the world!). One must also recognize the utter comedy of the fact that an American professor, of all people, had to come along with his Fourteen Points to set the world right. For the rest, all we can do is recognize and accept the political direction in which the world is moving, salute the democratic new world with good grace as a kind of world convenience that it will be quite possible to live with, assuming—and we may and must assume it—that Germany obtains raw materials and is treated in general according to her merits; and keep everything cultural, national, philosophical separate from politics and *free*, on a plane high above politics, something not in the least affected by democratic utilitarianism. This is the only viewpoint that is appropriate for me, and it is the one I advocated vis-à-vis Walter's feverish pessimism.

Letters from Frau von Térey (writing in anguish about Germany) and Bertram, who as a consequence of the *Nietzsche* has been offered a professorship at Bonn. A painful loss for me. At any rate he will still be in Munich this winter.—Went to the theater at half past six to join Walter, and heard, seated next to Consul General Bruckmann and his wife, a commemorative performance of *Die Schweizerfamilie* from 1809. Boring, though with a certain grace. Rode home with Walter in Frau Link's car to supper at our house, with presentation of the little one and political discussions. Declined to write to Rathenau.—At tea, from nervous tension, I unfortunately took an angry tone with Katia because of her weakness in handling the servants, especially the hedonistic and thievish Fräulein whom she does not dare dismiss.—I am calmer and more cheerful again, after having been very much disconcerted by the morning's conversation with Walter. One may well be curious to see how England will interpret and attempt to carry out the "Points": Freedom of small nations. Freedom of the seas. Disarmament. Inevitable that in actual practice less will be asked of the "victors" than of the "vanquished."

Sunday, October 13

To bed very late. Tired. Did little work, as I was interrupted by a visit from dear Dünzl. Walked far out of town. Slept in the afternoon. Letters to Bertram and Frau Térey. Short evening walk. Later finished reading the Russian essays with enormous approval, and then read here and there in the *Betrachtungen* for a long time (too long).—Germany agrees to the withdrawal of her troops and "assumes that Wilson's associates also desire a just peace and are taking the Points as their basis." There is terrible danger that the Allies, drunk with victory, will come up with a dictated peace that will either have to be refused immediately as unacceptable, and will lead to horrors like a last-ditch struggle or a revolution, or bring in its wake a latent state of war.

. . . .
Monday, October 14
. . . .

Slept better.—Great rejoicing in London! About the anticipated League of Nations? Or about what?—*Finished "A Man and His Dog."* Rode into town after shaving to send telegrams to Fiedler and Herzfeld regarding the baptism, which has now definitely been set for the 23rd. Had a haircut and heard that to his delight a soldier who wanted to return to the front was sent back home from the railroad station because no more men are being moved out. Word is going around the city that a hundred-hour cease-fire has already been arranged, but this proved to be a false rumor.—Had a variety of mail, letters of thanks from Pfitzner and Hofmiller, a note from Frank, who is engrossed in reading the book, a letter in support of me that consists entirely of a quotation from Flaubert, and so on. The first issue of a new Viennese illustrated, *Die moderne Welt*, a magazine for "Art, Literature, and Fashion." Disgusting.—Influenza is spreading again. The Fräulein has taken to her bed.—Katia's mother to tea.— My head felt hot and I thought I was ill, but ate supper with a good appetite and am probably just tired. Telephone conversation with Dr. Baumgarten, who is back from Berlin. The slackness and inertia there. The mood in the Deutsche Gesellschaft 1914— nasty jokes. Skeptical remarks about Wilson by the Spanish ambassador, though of course these are colored by Spain's hatred for America stemming from its experiences with idealism there, experiences that Germany will also have, I fear. I cannot even say that I "fear" it. From the bottom of my heart I hope the Germans learn a profound lesson from the thorough unmasking of these virtue-mongers of democracy. Perhaps this time they can be taught—for the future.—Read an essay by Marcks on Philip II, whose personality once again exerted a strong attraction upon me and induced vague dreams. Also did some thinking about *The Magic Mountain* once again, and the problem of its conclusion.—The little one restive, sickly, irritable. Probably teething, and was given Pyramidon.—Numbered the pages of the last chapter. The manuscript has swollen to 115 pages. Wondered whether this bulk was tolerable.

. . . .
Friday, October 18
. . . .

In the morning corrected the typewritten copy. Insightful letter from Bruno Frank about the *Betrachtungen*. Eissi still feverish. Took a walk at noon. Slept in the afternoon. Bertram for tea. Gloomy political discussions, then talked about the *Nietzsche* and the *Betrachtungen*. Letter of gratitude for the *Betrachtungen* from Leipzig. Invited to give a lecture in Bremen, also in connection with the book. People in Germany are still arranging public lectures on "the new books!" What is the real condition of this country? Men of the Bismarck generation sit around in despair, suddenly grown ancient in their grief. But the younger Germans appear to be scarcely troubled by the ruin. It is very strange. Yet it will be a material ruin, in all seriousness, and turn the Germans into a nation of helots *sans phrase*. The strength of Germanism will be smashed forever. Millions of German laborers are emigrating to Canada, where they are welcome as workers. Danzig is to be Polish! Prussia dwarfed by the lopping off of whole provinces. The dream of the old powers is at last being fulfilled: a completely impotent Germany in the center of Europe, working for others. The great majority of Germans seems not to be bothered by all this. A strange nation.—Word has it that the new production of *Madame Legros* has apparently vanished without a trace.—Yesterday and today have been reading Goethe's remarks on *Hermann and Dorothea* (in Gräf).

Monday, October 21

Cold sunny day.—Wilson's note to Austria in which the peace offer is rejected out of consideration for Czecho-Slovakia and Yugoslavia and their freedom and independence. Report that Congress has unanimously approved a credit of five billion dollars for armaments and maintenance of an army of five million men. Disarmament, peace, League of Nations, the end of power. Yes, what I now wish is for things to take a course that leaves no room for doubt, that *teaches* Germany, teaches her finally and once and for all, even though the chance of drawing any profit from such a lesson is to be prudently eliminated by the enemy for the foreseeable, not to say livable future.— Occupied myself with the manuscript. Extended walk in glorious autumn weather. After lunch, nervous attempt to improve some passages in the idyll, spots that since yesterday's reading strike me as lacking in poetic rhythm and have caused me much torment. Went to tea with Preetorius and Krell at Martens's, where I read aloud bits from *A Man and His Dog* that they liked very much. Preetorius is for having more illustrations, whereas originally we were going to have only a few. I walked there and back with Krell. Katia, who had been to Arcisstrasse, brought back the *Münchner Zeitung* with its article on the *Betrachtungen*; being political, it is not in the literary section and has been done by the editor-in-chief. As a matter of fact, the article strikes notes of emotional warmth such as I would never have expected. I felt rather stirred as I read it.—In the *Abendzeitung* there is the new note from the German government to Wilson. It contains nothing unexpected, and yet it will probably cause that universal judge some embarrassment. It seems to me that this scholar is gradually revealing himself more and more as a doctrinaire and ignorant fool, not least, but also not primarily by his note to Austria, the consequence of which is that neither the Czechs nor the South Slavs are now willing to negotiate with Vienna at all, and have dealt Austria its deathblow, though the disintegration of Austria is not really in the interest of the Allies inasmuch as the German parts of the country will thereby be propelled toward the Reich. Of course it may be that as a counterpart to the dissolution of Russia and Austria they are aiming toward the dissolution of Germany into its "nationalities" as well.—The humbuggery runs so deep that I refuse to be involved any longer, spiritually or intellectually. I don't wish to be impoverished, to that much I can testify.—Wilhelm II as a private individual going for walks by a Swiss lake in civilian clothes is also a strange notion. People are now talking about August Wilhelm as regent instead of the oldest grandson.

Brilliant late-autumn day. Began writing a lengthy answer to the Kammerspiele, but I tore it up in the afternoon, sending just a few terse lines instead. Brought down the old letters; compunctions about parting with them. They were taken away this afternoon along with the magazines. Received 500 good cigarettes from Fischer. Katia's mother for tea. I carried the little one down and she sat with us in her tiny chair; altogether touching. Letter from Emma Bonn about the *Betrachtungen*. Good article on Germany and democracy in the *Rundschau.*—It appears the announcement of armistice conditions is close at hand. Will there be an eruption of indignation? There will certainly be plenty of reason for it. Nevertheless, in all rationality, the only consideration must be to liquidate, one way or another, this impossible war in which Germany has truly preserved her honor. The rest will come as it may. A nation like Germany cannot be "annihilated." To be sure, the League of Nations and the end of politics is humbug. The French press is already fulminating against the union of German Austria with Germany, which would amply compensate for the loss of Alsace-Lorraine. The issue is not "justice" but power, and so will it be in the future.—The German Austrians have sent a note to Wilson.

In the morning began writing a prose draft of the poem "To My Youngest Child."—Took the tram into town and called on Jaffe, who spoke in awestruck terms about the sale of the *Betrachtungen*. Bought Hamsun's new novel, *Growth of the Soil*, and ordered a readable edition of *Luise.*—Ran into Krell, who claimed to have learned that if the armistice has not been accepted by next week a proclamation calling for "national defense" will be issued.—Came home on foot. An issue of the *Illustrierte Leipziger Zeitung* arrived, containing pictures and articles. The paper is all too obviously a vassal of heavy industry, and the contributions are disturbing in that they speak of the loss of the war in the conditional mode.—At tea, had the little one with us. A great deal in the paper about the impending armistice terms, which seem to be based on a desire for the war to continue or for Germany to be humiliated, the latter altogether unnecessary militarily. In any case, they display a fondness for harsh coercion and military force one would hardly expect of such exalted societies. Still, it seems that the French are nervous about new elections in England, since new elections in France would result in the fall of Clemenceau. The armistice terms for Turkey have already been officially released. They are fairly radical, and those for Austria will not prove to be much different. Finally, when the Bavarian border is threatened, Germany will learn what her terms are to be, i.e. when the Rhine no longer offers protection. And of what use will harsh armistice terms be then? Probably so we will grow accustomed to the spirit of the peace of Brussels.—Letter from Dr. Else Schöll about the *Betrachtungen*. In connection with the book, a long, long letter from a young lieutenant stationed in Posen; a rather confused and brooding gush of ideas about the fate of young people who have been through the war.—In Vienna the revolution is threatening to pass over into anarchy and bolshevism. The "Red Guard" being led by a Galician Jew who was once mentally ill. The assassination of Count Tisza in Budapest has a very tragic and, so far as the count and his ladies are concerned, a very noble quality. He was the epitome of Magyar aristocracy. The disintegration of Austria is proceeding rapidly. If only Germany will bear herself with dignity! But word has it that Scheidemann considers revolution unavoidable here as well. Perhaps out of fear of it, the press is urging the Kaiser's abdication. He is truly willing to make any concession. He is reported to have said, "Let the German people become the freest in the world!"

Thursday, November 7

Worked on the draft in the morning. Got down two hexameters. At noon went into town to get the copies, which again were not to be had.—Have caught cold.—At three o'clock there was a large demonstration on the Theresienwiese. No newspaper because of it, and no mail. All stores closed. A mass parade developed. Red flags. One soldier, carried about on the people's shoulders, delivering "speeches" at various spots. Cries: "Down with the dynasty!" "Republic!" Absurd rabble.—After luncheon read the first new issue of *Die Zukunft*, now being published again. Dripping with idealism, pacifism, and noble sentiments. Filthy buffoon! How is anyone supposed to believe *you* now, no matter whether what you say is believable or not?—Went to the Tonhalle with Katia in the evening for the Pfitzner concert. We met Hallgarten with young Paul Pfitzner and rode with them as far as Liebigstrasse, where we found no connecting trams running. Walked the rest of the way to the Tonhalle, where we first sat in the balcony, but then moved downstairs because of the draft. Sat with Berber, who had called me this morning, and who handed me a long, childish letter from a Fräulein Hoffmann in St. Gall, the daughter of the Swiss Federal Council member. Her letter excessively enthusiastic about the *Betrachtungen* and in general preoccupied with me. Apparently a friend of his, or likely enough his mistress. Many people wandering about on the streets, but no trams running, so that in spite of the crowds it was uncommonly quiet. Rumored that the mob threw gas grenades into the Türkenstrasse barracks, thus forcing the soldiers to vacate the building. Soldiers, incidentally, are said to have been ripping off their cockades, and in several cases we saw that this was true. The Walters, extremely nervous, sat with us for a while, but then left early. The concert was not overwhelming, though it had its beautiful moments: Haydn, Schumann, lovely songs by Pfitzner and Brahms, the *Oberon* Overture; but the singer was wretched. At the end we greeted Pfitzner and agreed to go to supper at the Vier Jahreszeiten, but did not keep our promise; instead went home with the composer of *Prinzessin Brambilla*, where I drank two glasses of punch with supper. Strange, ambiguous, uncertain mood in the city, under a clear but moisture-laden starry sky. Revolutionary, but peaceful and rather festive. Continual fireworks explosions, which I can still hear even out here at midnight. Somehow people are celebrating the dawn of a new age. Placards report the exchange of radio messages between the delegates and Foch, whose instructions sound rather brusque. The communications and transport workers have evidently gone on strike despite instructions from the Social Democrats.— No police were to be seen. Very cautiously, the authorities are letting people do as they will. Inasmuch as all this has any sense at all, and is not merely an "ersatz Carnival," as Berber put it, it is motivated by a drive toward separatism, or at least anti-imperialism ("Down with the Hohenzollerns!").—Shots are crackling constantly.

The firing went on until deep into the night, and began again in the morning. I took it too lightly after all. Awoke with a very bad cold. We learned of the night's "excitement" first by telephone from Katia's mother, then from the *Nachrichten*, which came late, and which carries two front pages, the first comprising an appeal to the people of Munich signed by friend Eisner. The "Democratic and Social Republic of Bavaria" has been declared, with "the moral force to obtain for Germany a peace that will preserve her from the worst." A "provisional Workers', Soldiers', and Peasants' Council" was convened in the Landtag during the night; the police commissioner has placed himself at its disposal. A founding national assembly is to be convoked as soon as possible, and all men and women "of age" will be eligible to vote for it. Strictest order, security of persons, and private property are "guaranteed" (by friend Eisner).— In Berlin an ultimatum from the Social Democrats has been delivered to the chancellor, demanding among other things the abdication of both the Kaiser and the crown prince by this afternoon. Scheidemann did not want this abdication. The demand is obviously being issued to forestall a revolution in Berlin, which is nevertheless bound to come.— As a counterpart to all this, Clemenceau's triumph in the Paris Chamber. Ovations for the "last survivor of the Bordeaux protest." One mob is the same as another, whether it celebrates or goes on a rampage.—We hear that at ten o'clock this morning the "fun" begins again. We have had a private warning (through one of the children's schoolmates, whose father is a policeman) that the sovereign masses may even visit Herzogpark. Distant shots can be heard. The revolution is favored with dry, frosty weather. The sun is breaking through. If it were to rain in torrents, events would probably grind to a halt.—Walter telephoned and asked us to make a call to Franckenstein for him, since his phone would not make the connection. Neither would ours, temporarily.—No mail. We are told that during the night the railroad station was also occupied by "insurgents" and that trains were stopped. What if there were an enemy air attack now?—Everything will settle down again one way or another, and we can go on enduring life as it was, is, and will be. Last night, while we were accompanying the composer home, I made a point of interrupting the political discussion and calling attention to the beauty of the humid, starry sky. Eternity puts one in a contemplative mood. Fundamentally, what is human is alien to politics. The little one is lying in her perambulator in the garden, shaking her silver bell and chattering. I seem to hear muted thundering from the direction of the city.—In any case, the revolution will become conservative the moment it is accomplished. Extremism then becomes the preventive and shield against whatever goes beyond the extreme, namely chaos.—

(*Afternoon.*) Bertram phoned at midday and promised to come to tea tomorrow. He identified himself as "Citizen Bertram." Said, of course, that Eisner by no means has the masses under control, and that looting was going on in the city. Above all, he reports that the distribution of foodstuffs has been interrupted. Anyone who had run out of bread would have got none this morning. (We received from our baker enough bread for two days, and we have some flour, so we can bake if we are not looted.) Katia, who went walking toward Bogenhausen around noon, spoke in front of the house with a young cyclist who was riding downstream along the Isar. He told her at length what is going on. He is a cook in the train station restaurant, which was totally looted during the night. The coolers, the wine cellar—nothing is left. And since there was nothing to do there he was told he might as well go home. A number of shops have been robbed, the Tietz department store looted; women were storming a furrier's. The barracks have been evacuated, the soldiers selling their weapons and uniforms and going home. Munich has no military left. What food supplies at the barracks had not been looted were confiscated by the "Council." The major skirmishes of the night took place first outside the Bayrischer Hof, to which several officers had fled, and where a number of them were shot, then in front of the Jahn Gymnasium at the barracks. It was machine-gun fire from there that I heard before two.—At noon I went walking with Bauschan on the allée, through the nearer park, and down Pienzenauerstrasse, where I talked to Frau Hallgarten. There I also read the posted proclamation of the "Council," with Eisner's signature, strictly forbidding looting as being disgraceful, and calling upon the workers to form a civil guard. News from Katia's father: lectures at the university were suspended on the arrival of Mühsam as a delegate from the Council. He summoned the students to the main auditorium and likewise called upon them to form a security guard to combat excesses. He said, moreover, that a hundred thousand Austrians are expected. (?) Someone shouted from the auditorium: "Now I can't get rid of the spirits I called forth!" Mühsam protested that he had not summoned any spirits.—Dull head cold, pain in my back, bronchial catarrh. In the afternoon I stayed dressed and only rested on the chaise longue, since Walter, pale and beside himself, had warned Katia of the approach of a "mob" that never, in fact, arrived. Katia and the children cleared out the pantry and hid threequarters of our provisions in various rooms of the house.—Now, after tea, I hear shooting again. "Demonstrations" imply a certain amount of discipline, but after they disperse at dark the fun will no doubt begin again, and things will take a very bad turn if the supply and distribution of foodstuffs does not start up again soon.—Telephone call from Vicco in Landsberg. Things still orderly there. He and the troops on duty. But he just heard that the business has also begun in Augsburg.—At the bridge this noon I saw a military auto with soldiers and a red flag driving toward Bogenhausen.—Read in the *Neue Rundschau* that a bolshevist putsch had been announced for Berlin for yesterday, the seventh, on the anniversary of the Russian Revolution. The telegraph office has allegedly been destroyed, but doubtless we will soon learn that what is going on in Berlin is no less exciting than events here. The "people" were shouting at the king: "Shitheel bumpkin!" and "Bloodthirsty tyrant!" (Very good.) It is not known for certain whether he escaped or has been captured in Leutstätten.

News from Arcisstrasse that the city is quiet, and that a directive from the city commandant has been posted, ordering bars closed by seven and streets cleared by nine o'clock. Telephone call from Krell: Mühsam is organizing the students only on behalf of the "Council." But on the other hand both Bruno Frank and Wilhelm Herzog belong to the Council. Both Munich and Bavaria governed by Jewish scribblers. How long will the city put up with that? Incidentally, it is said that Herzog has already expressed his frustration with Eisner, who is not nearly radical enough for him. Herzog himself, by contrast, is ultrabolshevistic, Frank *very* moderate. Krell greatly doubts that this rule of intellectuals can last long. The soldiers are showing distinct reluctance, he claims. Moreover, he describes the mood in the city as "depressed."—The evening edition of the *Nachrichten* appeared, as slim in content as the morning one; it is published under the aegis of the Council, utterly colorless, without opinions. The building has been occupied, and in order to keep the sparse news service going the editorial staff is carrying on under the supervision of the Council. The dictatorship is complete. And who is running it? Baumgarten told us recently that the president of the Hungarian National Council is a churchman who has used his own children as altar boys. Our own co-regent a slimy literary racketeer like Herzog, who let himself be kept for years by a movie star, a moneymaker and profiteer at heart, with the big-city piss-elegance of the Jew-boy, who would lunch only at the Odeon Bar, but neglected to pay Ceconi's bill for partially patching up his sewer-grate teeth. That is the revolution! The ones involved are almost exclusively Jewish. Military matters are in the hands of a Lieutenant Königsberger. In any case, the putsch was arranged beforehand, since Herzog had already been summoned the day before yesterday.— After supper Katia wanted to phone her parents. "Private calls are prohibited." "Since when?" "This minute." No military dictatorship could be more forthright. For the night everyone is locked in and left to his own devices. It is forbidden to go out; telephone communication is impossible.—

(*9:30* P.M.) Since the local dialing system still works, Walter phoned to say that word has come via Frankfurt that Wilhelm II, as was expected, has abdicated. Prince Max von Baden is regent, Ebert chancellor. Experts have been making reassuring statements regarding the course of things in Munich. Their opinion is that at present a capacity for organization exists.

. . . .
Sunday, November 10
. . . .

News of the spread of the revolution throughout the Reich. The red flag is waving from the top of the Royal Palace in Berlin. The desire in the air seems to be for a Greater German republic.—Flattering letter of thanks from the Union of German Scholars and Artists for my reply to the Scandinavian questionnnaire.—Telephone conversation with Bertram about the situation, including conditions in the enemy countries, to which we must now hopefully turn our eyes. I can say that my attitude toward future developments, if they really take the form I envision, is rather friendly, hopeful, receptive, consenting. I was never a "republican," but I have nothing against a German free state that includes German Austria, nothing against the fall of the dynasties and the Reich. The imperial idea, the imperial name, was, as Bismarck put it, a great recruiting force for German unification fifty years ago. It is my conviction that today we no longer need fear for the unity of the Reich even without the Kaiser. Today the Imperial House is a romantic vestige, and Wilhelm II actually played his role in an appropriately nervous, highly overwrought, and provoking manner. In practice it is really dispensable. I repeat to myself and others that the lack of resistance to a revolution proves its legitimacy and inevitability. I am content with the relative calm and orderliness with which, for the present at least, everything is taking place. The German revolution is after all German, though nonetheless a revolution. No French wildness, no Russian Communist drunkenness. It seems that things are moving from left to right, although presumably the social legislation will be radical. Bourgeois and objective elements are taking part. Krell, who visited me at noon, assures me that Herzog has already been turned out in the cold, and Professor Bonn, whom Katia saw, purports to know that Eisner no longer has much to say. Moreover, the moment that the bourgeois windbags of the Entente fall from power, above all Clemenceau, the moment the peoples begin to fraternize and the hate campaign against Germany subsides, with intellectually decent people giving the lie to the outrageous self-right-eousness of our enemies—at that moment my cosmopolitan benevolence will awake and I will bid the "new world" welcome. It will not be hostile to me, nor I to it.

Krell brought the check for 500 marks for *A Man and His Dog.* With the sun shining I again took a walk in the park. Duck and fruit tarts for luncheon. Read newspapers. In the *Frankfurter,* passed on by Katia's mother, Korrodi on "*Jean Christophe* and *Buddenbrooks.*" The latter he calls "the classic novel of the culture of Old Germany."—In the morning and afternoon I corrected the copies.—After my rest, word from Arcisstrasse that the armistice terms have been posted. They exceed all expectations. Withdrawal of the troops to thirty kilometers behind the Rhine. Occu-pation of Cologne, Coblenz, and Mainz. Surrender not only of munitions, but of so much railway stock that it is doubtful whether anything would remain for non-military use. Surrender of several battleships and 100 submarines, and so on. Will that be accepted? It must be, and yet perhaps today it need not be. What is the deadline? The news arrived belatedly. If it is true that the Italians are going home, that the English are mutinying, that France is in revolution—then these terms may still be fulfilled, insofar as they can be fulfilled, and possibly under protest. They are mean-ingless so far as the peace is concerned. Social revolution might preserve Tyrol and Alsace for Germany. Clemenceau's principle of guarantees and securities is meaningless in a new world. What does Metz signify even if it goes to France? What do strategic borders mean? They will hold a referendum in Alsace and it will stay with Germany. Will the "victory" blind people to the fact that Clemenceau, that vestige of Bordeaux, is at least as obsolete a piece of furniture as the German Kaiser? The danger is America, with its assured republican majority, its fresh troops, its colossal vanity, and its anti-quated social conditions.—Took short evening walk. Meanwhile Bertram had tele-phoned to express his disgust with the "terms," and to tell me that an acquaintance on the Council assures him a radio telegram has been posted at the Landtag saying that revolution has broken out in Paris and Clemenceau has been overthrown. At supper, anxious talk about the "terms" and the spirit behind them. They are demanding 5,000 locomotives and 100,000 rail cars. Later, just as I was about to start on Ponten's novel, *Der babylonische Turm*—an original work, I am told—H. von Weber phoned. He reports that wild shooting has broken out on Unter den Linden in Berlin; monarchist officers are defending several buildings against the "Red Guard." Also the bolshevist-communist Spartakus group is becoming dangerously active, has seized the *Lokal-Anzeiger* and is proclaiming its program calling for all power to the Workers' and Soldiers' Councils without elections or a national assembly. Since the revolution in Paris is probably taking a bolshevist turn as well, Weber says, we must fear its further spread, must begin a counteraction and back the government with the power of our pens. Vague proposals. For the rest of it, Weber also believes that the Allied terms will not be realized. The *Norddeutsche Allgemeine* has been renamed *Die Internationale,* its appearance otherwise unchanged. (Leppmann's piece on the *Betrachtungen* will no longer be allowed to appear.)—Later spoke with Krell about the same subject. Mühsam is said to be secretary of the Munich police, and is arresting everybody who formerly arrested him. The twenty-two-year-old Minister of War Königsberger has been dismissed because he took too vulgar and insulting a tone with an aged general. Eisner, though with the best of intentions, is frantically making ridiculous appointments. Herzog is returning to Berlin. At present he is staying at the Vier Jahreszeiten, and is spending this evening with Preetorius. (!)—This evening the populace is milling about the placards detailing the "terms" in disbelief and horror.—Before supper I took the copies to Krell, who is passing them on to Preetorius, Martens, and the Writers' League.

. . . .
Tuesday, November 12
. . . .

The little one's fever is gone.—Cheered up in the course of the evening yesterday. The Schöll sisters came to supper. Frank phoned after nine o'clock. He reported enthusiastically about a note from Eisner to the Allied governments and peoples, and told of a placard posted in the city assuring that the Allies would provide for Germany's food supplies during the cease-fire. Amusing stories about the behavior of our revolutionary W. Herzog on the crucial evening, his entrance into the editorial office of the *Münchner Neueste Nachrichten*, hat on his head and with his arms folded. We invited Frank to have supper with us tonight.—Immediately afterward came a call from Krell, likewise from the Theater Club. He too was full of the Bavarian government's note. The postscript to the terms guaranteeing Germany's food supply may well be a result of the news they are getting over there about our revolutionary countercurrents and events. He added that he has read the greater part of *A Man and His Dog* and is enchanted. The landscape description, he commented, something new for me, is altogether original thanks to its humorous tone. He thinks it amazing how my whole being is present in this work, just as much as it is in the 600 pages of the *Betrachtungen*. His remarks made me feel good, and distracted me from political matters so that I felt a great sense of relief. The assurance of food supplies will presumably have the effect of averting bolshevist terror; the humiliation of being fed by outsiders is impersonal enough, heaven knows, and our bolshevist-fearing enemies are not helping us out of "mercy," but know very well what they are doing.—Appointment with Krell for this afternoon at Martens's.—I was talkative, escorted the two ladies to the tram, and went to bed in good humor. Read in Ponten's novel for a while.

Up early today. Eisner's note disappoints me. I find no particularly humane sentiments in it, and intellectually it seems to me insignificant thanks to the moral wretchedness with which it casts the guilt for the war and all guilt for what happened during the war on the German "governments and sovereigns," from whom we are now liberated, and only berates these. This is abject and revolting. It is a slap in the face of all higher truth, and is tantamount to a complete acceptance of our enemies' sanctimoniousness and self-righteousness, which is, moreover, merely official. For among the French and English peoples are those of more discriminating and honorable conscience who know that these two powers are not "guiltless"; we have to assume as much, for there is no other explanation for the rumors about the flight of Poincaré and the overthrow of Clemenceau—though such rumors need not be true. Eisner's way of thinking and speaking also sanctions the fictitious opposition between the German people and the German government that the enemies once used as an instrument of war, and that they have now abandoned, insisting that the people must atone for the misdeeds of their masters, since they gave them their full approval. The truth is that the German people went into this war with enthusiasm once they believed it had been forced upon them, confident that they would win it and be able to organize Europe along German lines. This heroic struggle, in the course of which prodigious feats were accomplished, was lost thanks to terrible military and political mistakes and to the German mentality, which is profoundly unsuited for such a struggle, and it is ending in incredible catastrophe. This outcome should not break the morale of the German people to the point of disgusting self-betrayal. Rumor has it that Hindenburg, even now still a national hero, took flight yesterday with the Kaiser to Holland. Everyone believes it, and yet not a word of grief or gratitude accompanies him. This is revolting. (In fact Hindenburg is still at his post at headquarters, working in the service of the Republic.) My attitude toward the Greater German social republic that appears to be forming is completely reconciled and affirmative. It is something new, something appropriate to the German spirit. The positive result of this defeat is that it places Germany in the forefront of political evolution. The social republic is something well in advance of and superior to the idea of the bourgeois republic and plutocracy of the West; for the first time France will be forced to follow Germany's lead politically. If this was the underlying goal in the German war, it would explain the pioneering quality and initiative (in spite of everything) of Germany's conduct of it. Perceptive Frenchmen have become aware of this during these years, and have been reminded of the France of the Revolution. Even now there is no need for the Germans to lie crushed and submissive to what Lloyd George has called the "dramatic verdict of world history," which is something entirely superficial. There was too much worship of success after 1870; we must not now make too much of it once again. In this respect the Eisner note is lacking to a lamentable extent in dignity, in an incorruptible sense of justice. Those who have dictated the "terms" are by no means heroes of humanity blessed by world history, but rather bourgeois imperialists, devotees of power politics, and stupid, revengeful devils. The Berlin note to Branting, which was published simultaneously, is, though more sober, better than the Munich one, because it keeps clear of the question of war guilt altogether, and simply points with angry and accusatory earnestness to the physically murderous significance of the demands, so brazenly excessive in the present situation.

The flight of Wilhelm II had been in preparation for several days. It was accomplished in ten automobiles. He was in civilian dress. Ten generals accompanied him, as well as members of his court. The palace where he is "interned" is surrounded by a wall and a moat.—Karl of Austria has abdicated. The Democratic Republic of German Austria has declared itself a component of the German Republic.

Rainy weather.—After writing this I put together the huge insured parcel of signed galleys for Leipzig, sealed it, and felt a sense of accomplishment in doing so.—The meeting at Krell's was canceled.

Night of unrest, but it passed without incident. Last night we again heard automobiles driving by. These belonged to residents of the neighboring villas who were taking their prize possessions and fleeing with them into the city. Military patrols were marching about all night long. Also the increased strength of the guard is to be maintained for the present, we hear.—Extremely ominous announcements and prospects for the near future. The loss of ore shipments from Alsace-Lorraine and Upper Silesia means unemployment for millions. The coal miners are demanding wages of fourteen marks for an eight-hour working day. Food production and distribution are about to break down. Internal self-destruction proceeds apace under the socialist government. Salvation will come from the French and Americans marching in and restoring order, arranging things in Germany according to the wishes of Western Europe. I confess that I scarcely object to that any longer. The "Reich" is done for. A democratic-socialist Reich is idiocy. Clemenceau extremely amiable toward Eisner because he sees him as an ally in the destruction of the Reich.

Did not feel like working, but wrote to Térey and briefly to Wassermann, who would like to have the *Betrachtungen* sent to him.—Only a half-hour noon walk, in bad weather. Restless during the afternoon. Letter to a young Berliner who wrote me enthusiastically about the *Betrachtungen.* At tea, Frisch, who then stayed on until eight o'clock amid stimulating political discussions. Likable man. Am tempted to participate financially in the *Neue Merkur.* No evening walk. In the *Nachrichten*, Quidde against the "revelations," Foerster for them. Foreign opinion has it that the German people have changed institutionally but not morally. We should not lend support to such shameless self-righteousness. Though so far as the *conduct* of the war is concerned, I now see to my humiliation that it was waged by Germany without seriousness and morality. The day war was declared Wilson reduced steel prices by half. Whereas here. . . . The morale of the people and their self-respect were undermined by every possible means.

Last night, while waiting for the looters, began reading Hamsun's *Growth of the Soil* with my former pleasure at his special tone. Shall continue.—Many military patrols have again been seen in the neighborhood, as early as late afternoon.

Eisner is being severely criticized in the Berlin press for his "ultimatum" to the Foreign Office. The *Berliner Tageblatt* sneers, *Vorwärts* reproves him. Suspicion is being voiced that Eisner wishes a separate favorable peace for Bavaria. Would it not be a politic idea, incidentally, to trick the Allies by first allowing Germany to fall apart, then permitting the separate states to conclude their own individual peace agreements with more favorable terms? The disintegration would most probably prove to be a mere episode.—I hear shots.

Dark, wet day. Worked on the draft and considered a division into "cantos." Walked with Bauschan in splashing slush. Two more issues of the *Europäische Zeitung* arrived; politically I find myself actually much in accord with it. There can be no doubt that the future belongs to the concept of socialism, even of communism, *as* an idea—in contrast to the old democracy represented by the West, which incontestably has no part in the future. Probably Germany ought to take the new idea for its own, outwardly as well as inwardly.—No nap in the afternoon. Dr. Brantl for tea; I gave him a copy of the *Betrachtungen*. Much talk about the catastrophe, the inhumanity of militarism, don't you know, and so on. In the *Nachrichten* an effete article by Martens on Heinrich's *The Patrioteer*. So that has now come out and is marching toward glory. Incidentally, word has it that the author is personally avoiding a triumphant attitude. People are surprised at his moderate, anti-bolshevist stance. They shouldn't be. Naturally he disapproves of bolshevism, not only as a method but as an idea as well, the reason being that he is nothing but an old-line democrat of the Celto-Romanic, Wilsonian stamp, and basically regards the bourgeois parliamentary republic as the framework within which humanity can achieve infinite progress.—Accompanied Brantl.— The bourgeois press is working with systematic zeal for the removal of Eisner. I don't know whether it is acting intelligently, but at bottom its conduct probably expresses a populist resentment against the government of Jews.

Sunday, December 1

Did not get up until nine o'clock. In the *Nachrichten* the address Heinrich courageously delivered in the "Council." France and Wilson! Glorification of the republican virtues. "The empire of the Kaisers." "We sons of defeat." "The Republic." "Justice." When will he have had his fill of it?—Worked on the draft somewhat. Walk, colder. Shortly after luncheon, napped, then to town at 4:30 for the founding meeting of the Munich Political Society 1918 in the rooms of the Automobile Club at the Preysing-Palais. Spoke with Gleichen, Frank, Martens, Dr. Funk, Kassner, Baumgarten, and others. The last-named spilled the news that Friedenthal insinuated I put him up to moving for my "rehabilitation" with the proposal in the Writers' League. When I objected, he drew back and said he had exaggerated, that Friedenthal only meant that anyone who wanted to "join up" again needn't think it would be all that easy. No less objectionable. Thus the realm of action. Even a first step leads into these miasmas. Came back home and won't go again. But still it gave me a shock and upsets me.—I did not even stay for supper, but ate soft-boiled eggs at home with Katia. Afterward read Hamsun.

Sunday, December 8

Holm sent me Cossack stories by Gogol that he has newly translated.—The first issue of a magazine "for Order and Justice" arrived (editor: Dietrich Eckart) containing the seductive idea of nationalizing the entire banking system.—Card from Brandenburg inviting me to a lecture.—Worked on the draft, but without spontaneity. Tired, depressed. Periodontitis on one of my front teeth. Will have to begin the protracted and repugnant procedure at the dentist's.—Rather warm, filthy weather. Walked with Erika while Katia went with Klaus to the Pinakothek to see the Grünewald Isenheim

Altarpiece, which will now become French property.—Belligerent exchange of telegrams between the Organization of Transportation Officials, calling for the national assembly, and Minister Hans Unterleitner.—At five by tram to the Bernsteins', where their daughter performed some music with Pfitzner. Heard part of a Beethoven sonata that seemed almost arid compared to the Schumann that followed; only the latter really aroused my interest. Splendidly expressive accents, romantic sonorities. In addition to the Pfitzners and their children, Frau Piloty and General Schoch's wife were there. I stayed on with the latter and the Bernsteins for some time, engaged in musical and political talk. Walked home.—Bruno Frank has been announced as a speaker for the first open meeting of the Political Council. This little confidence man with the dimple in his cheek will talk on "Revolution and Humanitarianism." Oh yes, oh yes. Anyone who knows what is good for him goes along.

Friday, December 20

In the morning, occupied myself briefly with the poem. Had a sitting with Schwegerle. After tea, letter to Duke Adolf Friedrich von Mecklenburg, whose wife, the charming little Feodora, has died. Other correspondence. At seven went to the Club, where I met Martens, Kassner, Rilke, Frisch, Bonn, and others. The artist Renner, who served with Vicco in Landsberg, introduced himself to me. Sat at table beside Oppenheimer, the brother of the political economist. Afterward, parliamentary discussion on "war guilt," German self-recrimination, etc. Stimulating. Was tempted to take part, but refrained, since what needed to be said seemed to me too ticklish. Principal speakers were Brentano, Bonn, and Editor-in-Chief Müller. All too political, not moral and psychological. No writer spoke. I was absorbed in admiring an elegant young man with a gracefully foolish, boyish face, blond, refined, rather frail German type, somewhat reminiscent of Requadt. Seeing him unquestionably affected me in a way I have not noted in myself for a long time. Was he a guest in the club, or will I meet him again? I readily admit to myself that this could turn into an experience.

Sunday, December 29

While I was working on the poem (laboriously) a registered letter arrived from Frau Förster-Nietzsche, along with a document concerning the prize established by Consul Lassen, awarded to me for the *Betrachtungen*. The statement (obviously intended for the press) is badly written. Mixed feelings.—The little one somewhat better. Her ear is being treated with hydrogen peroxide—itself half a hexameter for my poem, "its dull, muffled roar numbs her hearing"—so that she rolls her eyes and appears to fall asleep. Carried her about for some time and entertained her with the potbellied rolypoly doll, which I set dancing on the table. Her cold is greatly hampering her, but still she made several attempts at talking: "Dada" and "Gaga." The Fräulein is leaving us; I said goodbye to her at noon before taking an hour-long walk. Warm wind, also rain. After tea, began to write to Frau Förster-Nietzsche, but hadn't the energy. Melancholic and out of sorts. Evening walk. Ebers for supper, who spoke about Frau von Schnitzler's salon, where he has encountered Heinrich, Hausenstein, Rilke, and other such celebrities. . . . Realized that I live a solitary, withdrawn, brooding, peculiar, and sad existence. Heinrich's life, by contrast, is very sunny just now.—Dipped into Tolstoy's diary of his old age. Find much in it strongly repugnant. Thoroughly agree with other things. "The main purpose of art . . . is this, that it tell the truth about the soul, revealing and giving expression to all the secrets that one cannot say in simple words. . . . Art is a microscope that the artist focuses on the secrets of his own soul, and that then *reveals to men the secrets common to them all.*" Very good.—*The Confidence Man*, for example, means exactly this.—Made some good decisions yesterday with regard to the new beginning of *The Magic Mountain.*

1919

Slept badly. The poem in the morning. Too prosaic. Fine springlike weather. Extended walk. Nadoleczny with the little one; met him in the entry hall. He said he was satisfied; the baby really does seem normal and cheerful now, and has amiably accepted the new Fräulein despite her ugliness.—Since the first, have been reading the *Frankfurter Zeitung* again.—After tea, letter to Witkop. At half past seven, Richter for supper. Conversation about the pending tax on "war profits," the property tax, etc. Katia came back from Arcisstrasse relaying the remarks of a certain Cohen, a shrewd businessman who recommends that people go out and buy everything their hearts desire. Good; my heart desires a Phonola or some similar machine. We agree that it would be a good idea to talk to a lawyer about financial arrangements. We ate and drank well, pleasant evening. Richter had a car come for him from Schwabing.— Radek, the bolshevist agitator, is in Berlin, working there for a joint war against the Allies. Perhaps that is less insane than what our bourgeoisie is doing. It is probable that it would bring about the socialist world republic that would relieve Germany of her burdens—or could do so if the peoples of the Allied nations were not scared off from the idea of communism by another hate campaign like the one against "militarism." But it would become clear that England, France, and America have been the representatives and advocates of the bourgeois age throughout this whole revolutionary war since 1914, and that their entire wartime ideology has consisted merely of remnants of the ideology of the bourgeois revolution of 1789.—Again I stressed that our revolutionary withdrawal from the war was an egotistical, un-European, and internationally tactless course of action, because in so doing we pushed the enemy governments into a position of triumph most destructive to the general cause. The disintegration of the English and French front was far advanced; our premature revolution disturbed this process in the most irresponsible way, leading to an absurd but striking victory of the one side, and weakening socialism in the Allied countries to the point of impotence, not only its strength but also its will. Perhaps Germany has once again shown herself to be the "procrastinator par excellence"—once again, moreover, out of "conscience." For what was at stake was the "salvation of her own soul" or "slackerism," as Dehmel has written.

After yesterday's evening reading the children wanted me to write in their scrapbook a critical review of their theatrical performance on Sunday. I carried out the assignment to everyone's satisfaction.—The day had brought a rather long letter from Frau Förster-Nietzsche. Today a package containing a letter and a number of books arrived, and at first glance I was thoroughly confused by it, for the letter read like a lampoon. But it was meant as a joke, and when I looked over the books in the afternoon they proved to be highly intelligent. They touch on the ideas of the *Betrachtungen*. Author: Christoph Flaskamp.—Wrote more than twenty hexameters.—Went to Gosch!—Katia to tea at Lula's. After tea I went to Nadoleczny to have my ears cleaned. On the way I saw a placard announcing that Liebknecht was shot while attempting to escape from his captors. Word has it that Rosa Luxemburg was murdered by the populace.— Walked home. There I had the little one with me in my room for some time.—Read newspapers. Gratifying to read Count Brockdorff's note on the way the French supervisor of the economy, Martin, is behaving in Mainz. The French national character is disgusting.—In Wassermann's novel the moral is beginning to become a bit too evident, but the cinematic quality continues; festival barn-burning in Hungary!

Friday, January 17

The shooting of Liebknecht and the murder of Rosa Luxemburg by the rabble are confirmed. Revolted.—Worked on the poem. Katia and the little one kept me company as I was getting dressed this noon. Went for a walk in the park again at last.—Rested in bed after luncheon, then endless, wet, and freezing tram ride to Krecke's clinic to see Dr. Loeb. He looked very pale, but he continues to improve. Political chat. In addition to his wife, another lady and a Herr Majer were there. Afterward went to Arcisstrasse for tea. Came home with Katia. Letters: from Consul Lassen, among others. Reading: the newspapers and two issues of *Die Zukunft* with impressive articles by Rathenau.—Telephone conversation yesterday with Krell: Preetorius will be unable to work for a long time. *A Man and His Dog* is to appear without illustrations.

Monday, January 20

Excessive burden of correspondence has characterized the past several days. By the way, my former method of keeping this diary makes no sense. Will henceforth enter only matters worth noting.—All sorts of professors have been writing letters to me and sending me their work. A letter from the writer Ponten delighted me. Yesterday elections to the national assembly were held and there was a party in the evening at Marckses'. He owns beautiful Hofmanns, Kalckreuths, and Liebermanns. I had come to a dead halt on the poem, but today it again flowed tolerably well, even though I had drunk a good deal of wine yesterday and got to bed late. Today a copy of the propaganda leaflet from the Berlin *Heimatdienst* arrived, with my contribution. My last sitting with Schwegerle. Continued reading Wassermann's "film." An article by Paquet in the *Frankfurter Zeitung* interested me tremendously; about "proletarian culture" in Russia. The materialistic, positivistic, rationalistic elements in all political idealism have become completely clear. Intellectuals who refuse to subscribe to communism must go hungry, must flee; Merezhkovsky, Andreyev. The tyranny must be dreadful. After all, revolution and culture! Since politics has taken over, people are complaining about the degeneration of poster art. The Berlin election posters are supposed to be wretched, while well into the war years it was quite a different story. *The Prince of Homburg* and *The Maid of Orleans* have been banned. Yet Heinrich declares that now, at last, thought and art are going hand in hand with government. There is no longer any other word for him: idiot.

Saturday, February 8

Bitter cold, blue sky. Splendid. A veritable St. Moritz day. In the morning prepared for the evening reading and took care of several letters. On the balcony in the afternoon. Once again put on full dress, and just before seven went with Katia by car to the Women's Club, Finkenstrasse, where the reading was held. The auditorium crammed and very hot. It seemed to me that I was not reading well, but the hunting chapter from *A Man and His Dog* went over very well and held the audience for more than an hour. After the intermission I read the "School Sickness" section from *The Confidence Man.* This is perhaps the most remarkable thing I have written, but the book as a whole can hardly be kept at such a level. After the reading, a brief gathering in the upper hall of the club with the Willichs, Lula, Ida Beer-Walbrunn, Frau von Bissing. I spoke to Endres, Hoerschelmann. Then back home with Katia; changed, and had supper.—The performance will be repeated on the 22nd.

Monday, February 17

Thirty-four lines of verse. A record. Went to Gosch. Letters from Bertram and a lieutenant colonel's widow (the latter about the *Betrachtungen*). After tea, during which we had the little one with us on the settee, we were treated to a "festival" by the two younger children, one they have been preparing for weeks, consisting of a puppet show, refreshments, and dancing. The refreshments amounted to a quantity of stale bread and cake they had been hoarding, along with lukewarm barley coffee and candy.— When I returned from my evening walk, Katia greeted me with the news that according to an announcement Dr. Loeb was cremated today. He must have died on Saturday. Although not unexpected, stunned and sorrowful.—At luncheon I was ridiculously depressed because I learned from Katia that her mother had been extremely displeased by my prisoners-of-war letter. Bertram, who had very strong things to say about the behavior of the French in Alsace, was delighted with it. I sent him the "Zuspruch" and took care of other correspondence.—Read newspapers. Wilson's repulsively unctuous speech about the blessing of the League of Nations and the non-return of the colonies to Germany, which (in contrast to Belgium, France, England) has shown itself to be unworthy. New armistice conditions with a short deadline; they are of such a nature that Count Brockdorff has handed in his resignation, which apparently is not being accepted. The conditions represent a British compromise proposal between the French and American positions, and apparently they are to be followed before the preliminary peace by a second phase including radical disarmament and simultaneous supplying of food. Disgusting, disgusting. And comical. What a swindle the whole thing is.—Amusing bit of correspondence from Munich in the *Frankfurter Zeitung* to the effect that I have completed a new story titled "Bauschan," in which "a hunting dog falls into the hands of a non-hunting master."

Tuesday, February 18

Insufficient sleep, and am quite shaky. In the morning, also had to write the Reich Central Office about the fee, since a request for permission to reprint has come from Hamburg. Nevertheless I managed another twenty lines.—Eliasberg to tea. Pleasant. Gave me some fine books.—In the evening, *The World's Illusion.* The sex-murder affair utterly unreal, it seems to me.—General disenchantment with draft for the League of Nations, which in fact leaves nothing to be desired in its lack of imagination and intelligence. Telephone conversation with Dr. Endres, who expects street fighting in the very near future, since the Spartakists want to prevent the Landtag from meeting in order to keep Eisner in power.

Friday, February 21

In the morning took care of the proofs for the *Münchner Neueste Nachrichten.* In between, a visit from Mama. Afterward worked on the poem. Katia burst into my room with the news, which she had just learned by telephone, that Eisner has been assassinated by a Count Arco. Shock, horror, and disgust with the whole thing. What will the consequences be?—Short walk with Katia and the children along the Isar in serene, mild spring weather.—There have been several of these senseless bloody crimes. Eisner's murderer—some say he is a member of a student corps, others that he is an army officer—was promptly shot in turn by the minister's secretary. A Spartakist poster brands him a tool of the bourgeoisie, and summons the workers to a meeting on the Theresienwiese. Armed men forced their way into the Landtag, which had just assembled for the first time, and fired shots. Minister Auer was severely wounded; a Center deputy and a general, it is said, were shot. Defense Minister Rosshaupter, pale as death, was seen being taken away by soldiers, under arrest. Planes are circling over the city, dropping leaflets telling of the events and urging everyone to keep calm and to stay off the streets after seven o'clock. The situation is confused and dangerous. Still, level-headed elements seem to be somewhat in control. The fact that Auer too is wounded may be politically favorable, as it might have a quieting effect. Perhaps the gravity of his condition is even being exaggerated. The idiocy of Arco's deed at this moment must be immediately obvious, but many people are delighted by it. Our boys' schoolmates applauded and danced when the news came.—Theaters etc. closed. Presumably my reading tomorrow will be canceled.—On the balcony in the afternoon.—Telephone conversation with Endres about the situation.—Katia to tea with Erna Hanfstängl.—So I did not go out again.—The bullet, it is said, was extracted from just below Auer's heart, and the doctors are hoping to be able to pull him through.—Telephoned Martens. The Spartakists have occupied the newspapers; we have a soviet government *à la russe.* Calamitous food situation feared, and the relationship to the rest of the Reich is problematical.—Fräulein Willich telephoned; presumably the reading cannot take place, but there is no way to definitely cancel it. She confirmed that a search is on for aristocrats. In her neighborhood, soldiers forced their way into the residence of Count Moy.—After supper, great turmoil here in Herzogpark. Many automobiles driving around, shots. Several calls from Frau Walter, of course. The soldiers, obviously convinced that there is a plot, are searching for weapons. They called on the Marckses and on Baron Rummel, who treated them to wine. Around 10:15, stupendous explosions of hand grenades in the immediate vicinity. Presumably the front gate of a house being blown apart because it was not willingly opened. After that, wild screaming. Katia and I on the balcony in the darkness. Quiet followed. Agitated. I do not think they will be coming to us. They seem to be concentrating on military officers.—In the *Frankfurter Zeitung,* interesting correspondence from 1887 between Bismarck and Salisbury on the subject of European politics.

Saturday, February 22

Did not sleep badly. Was told that a good deal more firing went on during the night. Levien is said to be at the head of the government. No mail, no newspapers. Also no trams running. But the telephone works.—Yesterday wrote to Bab and Preetorius.— A few lines written on the poem. Stuck where I got to the military godfather and a

Front and back covers by Emil Preetorius for the deluxe edition of A Man and His Dog. 35

political ditty is called for. In a quandary.—Took a walk; lukewarm, rainy, dirty.—Telephone conversations with Martens, Schwegerle, Walter. An eleven-man government has been formed, consisting of Majority Socialists, Independents, and Communists. Levien and that awful Sauber are at the top. The militaristic, wartime expedient of protective custody is being practiced with a vengeance. Many aristocrats are said to have been arrested, military officers, industrialists, even Prince Leopold, and further arrests are pending. Auer is alive. It was Professor Sauerbruch who operated on him, but he wants it kept a secret. The ruling group is pretending that a reactionary plot is indeed at work, one supposedly begun with the sailors' uprising, and of which the killing of *both* Socialist leaders was the continuation, with the goal of making Prince Leopold king. They allege that Auer, too, was shot by reactionaries, for at the time of the shooting someone was heard shouting "Vengeance for Eisner!" Also [a] Center deputy was shot. The populace, at any rate, is convinced that there is a royalist conspiracy. Whatever happened, we now have bolshevism. The arming of the proletariat has been announced. Looters, however, have been threatened with death, and yesterday's house searches, in the course of which some looting took place, are said to have been completely "spontaneous." Security guards are on duty. Ours is stationed in the Jahn Gymnasium, and we have the telephone number from Walter. Last night's hand-grenade explosions were from a skirmish between soldiers and looters.—It is not clear whether the soviet republic has been officially proclaimed and the Landtag dissolved for good, or whether the present situation is only temporary. If it is the former, it would mean separation from the Reich and a delay of the peace treaty. Possibly the movement will spread to the rest of the Reich. That would mean first of all a prolongation of the blockade.—Rumor has it that the archbishop has been murdered. But the tolling of bells this morning may have been for Eisner, however unfitting that would have been.—I was able to sleep in the afternoon. After tea, began a letter to Wassermann about *The World's Illusion*. Dipped into Landauer's *Aufruf zum Sozialismus*; its argument against Marxism is quite good. But in human practice things turn out differently, and Auer and Ebert are solid men. The present rulers in Bavaria may be also, incidentally. When God places someone in an official position He usually provides him with a little caution, sense of responsibility, and conservatism to go with it, especially in Germany. I rather think that things will not take too Russian a turn.—It is quiet outside.

. . . .

Monday, February 24

. . . .

Still no mail this morning. I wrote a new prose draft for the political passage having to do with the second godfather, but the length is disproportionate, and the question of what can properly be said about these matters when everything is so obscure and ambiguous greatly disturbs me. Moreover there is a contradiction between the hexameter form and brooding reflection. The form demands clear, healthy thoughts.—A heap of rather inconsequential mail arrived after all: printed matter, things from Keyssner and Hellpach, a trivial piece by Frau Térey from the *Pester Lloyd* about Rolland and me, etc.—Session with Gosch. The trams were running again. Arrived home very late for luncheon. Slept in the afternoon. Went walking in rainy weather soon after tea in order to be back by the curfew hour (seven o'clock). Read issues of the *Frankfurter Zeitung*.—The political situation is beginning to seem less extreme. The Majority Socialists have put a stop to the arming of the workers. The Spartakists have already left the government again and are in the opposition. The soviet system has not been proclaimed, and there is talk of convoking the Landtag. By the way, Cabinet Ministers Timm, Hoffmann, and one other cannot be located. Auer's condition is considered hopeless. Young Count Arco, on the other hand, who seems to be an utter booby, will apparently escape with his life, presumably only to forfeit it to justice. The murder of the archbishop was a myth. But in the course of the attack on the Landtag one senior official and Center Deputy Osel were killed.—Last night in bed I finished reading the extant canto of Goethe's *Achilleis*. The dialogue between Athene and Achilles at the end delights me and encourages me greatly. Hexameters must always deal with ideas that can provoke a response such as this:

> What you say is worthy and true. In your youth there is wisdom.

Achilles' speech on the warlike destiny of man, who would seem to deserve peace and more pleasurable occupation as recompense for the brevity of his life—all this is excellent, imbued with a somber fatalism as it explains this inequity by referring to the story of Pandora:

> Then it was determined, the inescapable sorrow.

And the hexameter itself speaks out against such brooding:

> Let us leave all of that aside for now! All that we say,
> Wise though it well may be, is bound to our mortal vision,
> Never affords us a glimpse of vast unfathomable futures.

Wednesday, February 26

Stormy, springlike day. While I was finishing the draft of the passage in need of rewriting (now it will work, I think), Eisner was buried amid the tolling of bells and heavy firing from the direction of the city reminiscent of New Year's Eve. Frau Dr. Hallgarten and her son were there. She tells me the funeral was dignified. I hear that Heinrich spoke also, as had seemed likely. He probably did so on behalf of the Political Council, using all the language that is in the air these days, as is only appropriate when paying last respects to a political humanitarian.—Walked. After luncheon, began reading Hefele's *Das Gesetz der Form*, and also looked into Goethe's plan for his *Achilleis*, delighted with his intentions. I feel completely the attraction that the material had for Goethe. His inability to carry it out must be viewed with the same regret that we feel over his unrealized plan to treat the theme of the Wandering Jew, described so temptingly in *Dichtung und Wahrheit*. The psychological or pathological motif (Achilles, knowing that he is going to die, falls in love with the Trojan woman and in his passion "clean forgets" his own fate) is fascinating, and incidentally has a somewhat Kleistian tone. Which is to say it seems modern. How at home I always feel in the Goethean sphere; how it gladdens and stimulates me. If I manage to get to *The Confidence Man* I will be able to live and work entirely in that realm.

The Reich Cabinet has declared that the Councils will not be tolerated as political factors anywhere. Lot of good that will do. We shall now have the opportunity to taste a degree of unfreedom here that would never have been thinkable under the *ancien régime*. The mail, telephone, and telegraph are going to be censored. Censorship of letters is already in force. Letters abroad (only abroad?) containing unfavorable reports on our situation are being confiscated. It is said that foreign bourgeois newspapers will no longer be admitted. Controls have been imposed on the newspapers here, incidentally, in a malignantly comical way: the *Bayrische Kurier* must publish atheistic articles, the liberal papers, radical socialist ones. The state of emergency is being continued for the present, with the curfew set at such an early hour that I must do without my evening walk. The 100 hostages remain in custody. The Soldiers' and Workers' Council rules absolutely; there is talk of convoking the Landtag only "if circumstances permit." How long can this tyranny last? On the other hand, one cannot foresee how it is to end, since all power is in the hands of the Revolutionary Socialists. The Reich government will be unable to do anything. At best any corrective will come from the Bavarian Majority Socialists. The sole independent newspaper is the *Post.*—Fräulein Willich telephoned; the reading will take place on Sunday morning. Fine with me.—At last began a letter to Vitzthum. Before supper, took a brief walk up and down in the dark part of the allée. Read further in Hefele's *Gesetz der Form*, which was recommended to me by Dr. Bernhart. But cannot make much of it.—Katia spoke enthusiastically to me about Tolstoy's folktales, which she is reading aloud to the children and says I must read.—Today was a holiday, strictly enforced. No trams. Strollers along the Isar as though it were Sunday.—The wind has died down. The sky this evening was clear, moisture-laden, starry.

- -
Thursday, February 27
- -

A few lines of verse. Had not thought I would be held up this way now, so close to the end. I must cut it short. A long treatise on the questions of the moment would be wholly misguided.—Wet snow. Went to Gosch, who tried the bridge on satisfactorily.—Yesterday thought about *The Magic Mountain* with pleasure and hope, thanks to the contact with the pure, productive Goethean realm. Want to read his *Campaign in France* at night before going to sleep. Good to take the most important impressions that will be of benefit to my work directly over into sleep.—Tea guests: the Mhes, Dr. Bülau, and the student Brünger. Moderately entertaining. Hope these nice people found it worth their while; they stayed until seven and may have been arrested. Not only has the curfew not been lifted or extended to a later hour, but according to announcements it is to be enforced even more strictly. Sessions of the Congress of Councils. Military measures in the city. Spent all day reading nothing but newspapers. In the *Neueste*, a compulsory account of Landauer's memorial address at the funeral, with many quotations from Eisner's poems and a long account of the ceremonies. The Wagner music seems to have been cut for lack of time. Heinrich too had no chance to speak, which I deplore, for on this occasion literature should not have been placed too far toward the end of the program.—In the *Frankfurter Zeitung* a feeble, poorly written article by Eulenberg to the effect that nobody should be blamed for nationalistic failings during the war, and that there is a great sense of pride to being a German Republican. I was tempted to answer him that for the first time in my life my sense of freedom is suffering, and that I cannot take a walk in the evening. Incidentally, he complains that even among intellectuals there is far too little understanding for what has been achieved.

The dishonesty of our pretentious, moralistic new masters surpasses everything. They deny that any looting has taken place. They insist that someone crazed with grief shot Auer, whereas in that case, unlike the case of Eisner, there really was a conspiracy and an assassination plot.

Worked on the versification of the precarious passage. Went to Gosch, who installed the bridge temporarily. It pinches and wobbles.—Had an appointment for tea with Martens at the Club. Took the tram into the city just before five. Leaflets being dropped from planes. Many people gathered in the Odeonsplatz. I met Krell, who had already been to the Club and informed me that the streets were to be cleared and the trams halted, since street battles were presumably impending. Rumor that the Central Council had been dispersed by a few soldiers who had burst in armed with hand grenades. Mühsam, Levien, and Hagemeister, the leader of the conspiracy against Auer, have supposedly been arrested. Walked home with Krell. Katia's mother, who had come for tea, hastened to return home.—Rumor too that Minister Hoffmann is traveling around the country rounding up troops with which to march on Munich. Hatred for the radical literati seems to be deep and widespread.—The janitor at Arcisstrasse, who also works at the Landtag, maintains that the story about the dispersal is a false rumor. The three Communists were actually arrested, he says, but were released after twenty minutes.—Martens, on the telephone, believes bloody decisions are coming.—Shots from the direction of the city could be heard during the course of the evening.—I wrote to Frank about an anthology of stories. As for politics, I added: "I make no bones about my dislike for the alliance of the radical literati with the rabble, and hope that solid people will win out."—Distracted. The wobbly bridge makes me uncomfortable. Read without pleasure. In Hefele's book I was moved most by the letter to Erasmus. Leafed through a new essay of Rathenau's. Depressing in every respect. Must I allow myself to be told everything as the bitter truth? It hardly gets to the bottom of things. And the mixture of economics and religiosity is not to my taste either.

Saturday, March 1

In very bad mood, anguished and depressed. After working briefly on that bothersome passage in the poem, went to Gosch, who took a long and painful time to refit the bridge, then temporarily restored the partial so that I will be able to read tomorrow.— Haircut.—The political situation seems somewhat more relaxed. A compromise has been concluded over the shouted protests of the Communists; the soviet republic has been rejected. But Berlin seems once again to be in a state of high tension. Düsseldorf freed from the Spartakists by a military coup.—Müller-Hofmann and his wife, née Huch, to tea. Likable people.—Maurice Muret sent the *Gazette de Lausanne* with an attack by himself on my prisoners-of-war letter. I ought to answer it.—In the *Neueste*, the "Bauschan" fragment "Awkward Encounter."—Was able to take my evening walk again. Later read here and there in Goethe's *Conversations*.

At eleven o'clock last night, heavy cannonade and machine-gun fire. Meaning uncertain. Possibly an attack by troops from outside. Today we heard that there had been an attack on the Stadelheim prison—unclear by whom and for what purpose.—Dressed first thing in the morning, and after making my preparations soon after breakfast went into the city for the reading, which was to begin at half past ten. It went gratifyingly well; the hall again full, a branch of lilac placed on the lectern by an unknown hand. Once more the audience very much liked the hunting chapter; the "School Sickness" not so well matched to the temper of the times.—Splendid weather. Black hordes of humanity. Walked home, and was back just in time for luncheon. On the way bought theater tickets for Katia and myself. During the meal a lovely basket of hyacinths was delivered, from an unknown lady in gratitude for my reading "Bauschan." Rested in bed in the afternoon. For the children's tea, Fräulein Dr. Schöll, who had also been in the audience. Then with Katia to the Residenz-Theater: *The Beaver Coat.* So human.—Card from Bertram: the English have refused him permission to go to Bonn and he will be returning to Munich. Letter from young Zarek in Davos. Frisch, who sent the *Neue Merkur,* is very insistent about the poem. Anxiety.—In the evening, read the sensible article on political matters by Frisch in the *Merkur.*—Explosions of hand grenades.—Privy Councillor Dyck told Katia's parents how pleased he was with the fragment of mine published in the *Neueste.* This little work will possibly be a great sentimental success. But the poem is another matter. It is after all too private. And Katia thinks the line "Shoulders of flute-playing women, Nile valley shoulders" impermissible.

Worked on the poem. I like the Pandora passage. To Gosch. The Hallgartens for supper. The card on the lilac branch I found on the podium bore, we discovered, a theme from *Die Meistersinger.* Frau Hallgarten thought that stupid, but she is incomparably more stupid.—The definitive armistice conditions beyond belief. Aside from all the humiliations, annual tribute of ten to fifteen billions for thirty to fifty years, etc. It is almost silly. These leaders are truly no less dunderheads than ours were. And Muret wonders at my scorn. The role of Wilson: desperate and tragicomic. He is still trying to seem superior while it is plain that the "Armistice" is merely a device for putting over the most arrogantly imposed peace. But one must assume that all this is meaningless.

Too late to bed yesterday. Not enough sleep. Bertram critical of the meters, and I suffered tortures correcting the proofs. Deeply and painfully out of sorts, in fact despairing. Somewhat better after my afternoon rest. The little one to tea. Picked up the Walters and went to the Odeon with them, where I met Bertram. Brahms Violin Concerto, Hugo Wolf Serenade, a Schumann symphony. Back home by tram with Bertram. The two of us ate a cold supper, Katia keeping us company, then worked on the metrical rough spots, which were settled in a reasonably satisfactory manner.

"Wohl liebt' ich sie" (with the abbreviated "liebt' ") will simply have to stand. Bertram did not leave until twelve.—Walter mentioned an article on the *Betrachtungen* in the *Wiener Journal* by Egon Friedell; very warm, but at the same time hailing Heinrich. We should consider ourselves fortunate to have two such fellows, he says.—Yesterday there was an Eisner memorial at the Odeon, at which Heinrich spoke. He said that Eisner had been the first intellectual at the head of a German state, that in a hundred days he had had more creative ideas than others in fifty years, and that he had fallen as a martyr to truth. Nauseating. I did not hear about the main thing he said until Bertram told me, namely that Eisner had deserved the honor of being called a "literatus of civilization." *Not* nauseating. . . . In the greenroom, portraits of the martyr and a heap of red streamers.

Monday, March 24

Katia still in bed. [. . .] The cough looser.—Letters from Fischer (about the deluxe edition of *Death in Venice*), Baumgarten, Keyssner (who sent a good article against Foerster), and the student Trummler (Werkbund).—Worked on the conclusion of the poem. Canceled appointment with Gosch and went walking. Invited Bertram to the reading on Thursday.—Changeable weather.—At tea, the baby wrapped in Katia's quilt.—Business letter to Richter about the 10,000 marks and the *Death in Venice* edition, for which I am asking ten percent royalty and 4,000 marks guarantee.— Deeply upset by the world news. Resignation of Count Károlyi and proclamation of a soviet republic in Hungary. An agreement with Moscow and deployment of Russian troops. Communist demonstration in Vienna. In Italy the entire Socialist party has gone over to communism. All this in response to Allied imperialism, which is concentrated in Paris and is nurturing imperialism among the Poles, Czechs, Rumanians, and South Slavs. In Budapest, in Vienna, even in Hamburg and Bremen (in the behavior of the sailors there) the mixture of Spartakism with *nationalist* feelings is unmistakable. I am nearly ready to retract my wish for that pack of "victors" to learn a lesson from the effects of their baseness toward Hungary. Rejection of the peace terms by Germany! Revolt against these bourgeois windbags. Let us have a national uprising now that we have been worn to shreds by the lying claptrap of that gang—and in the form of communism, for all I care; a new August 1, 1914! I can see myself running out into the street and shouting, "Down with lying western democracy! Hurrah for Germany and Russia! Hurrah for communism!"

Tuesday, March 25

Katia up again until afternoon. Beautiful mild weather. Letters from Ponten and Engel, the editor of the *Berliner Tageblatt*, who asks me for assistance for Zarek, suffering from tuberculosis.—*Finished the poem* and numbered the lines. There are 977. So this odd little undertaking too has been accomplished and thus a new book finished, the first since the *Betrachtungen: Herr und Hund. Gesang vom Kindchen. Zwei Idyllen.*— Went to Gosch. On the tram met Hallgarten, Klose, and Löwe.—The little one at tea by Katia's bed.—Began a longish letter to Baumgarten about the *Betrachtungen*. Evening walk. Began studying the book about world freemasonry, pencil in hand, in connection with Settembrini. For now I am beginning to turn my thoughts back to

The Magic Mountain, in which a whole world, a polyphony of themes, attractions, and ideas opens up for me once again. At night before going to sleep I am reading Ponten's *Die Insel*; decidedly gifted.

Sunday, March 30

In my exhaustion, forgot to note that yesterday the Hermes-like young dandy who made an impression on me several weeks ago attended my reading. In conjunction with his slight, youthful figure, his face has a prettiness and foolishness that amounts to a nearly classical "godlike" look. I don't know his name, and it doesn't matter.— Colossal snowfall during the night and today; everything thickly blanketed. It continues to snow tonight with rather an air of disaster.—Two letters about the *Betrachtungen*. One of them, pleasant to read and worth answering, from a Protestant theologian, professor, Ph.D., and pastor, the other from a woman who lived for a long time in Paris.—Slept a bit later than usual. Breakfast with Katia, the little one beside us. The 300 cigars I ordered for 257 marks arrived from Frankfurt.—By tram to the Odeon for the dress rehearsal of the Akademie concert. Waited for Walter with his sister-in-law and children, who came by car, and went up with them. Chairs were set up for a young protégé of Walter's and me, since the house was sold out. A Mozart symphony, lucent and gracious. Piano concerto by Chopin, heroic, sentimental, nobly sweet, and frivolous, played by the earnest, likable Frau Sandra Droucker. The Seventh Symphony of Beethoven, with the extremely brilliant slow movement marked "Allegretto."— Rode home in Walter's car.—After luncheon, discord with Katia. "Fault" on both sides. She disturbed me after I had just begun to rest in the chair, extremely tired, and unfortunately I could not conceal my annoyance. Slept. At tea the matter seemed settled.—The Danzig affair is exciting, the German refusal to permit Polish troops to land there a blessing. But by querying the Allies the way has been left open. Turbulent scenes in the French Chamber in connection with events in Hungary. Attacks on the government. Protest against military intervention in Russia. Confused blend of avarice and fear in France. At the moment they fear a German-Austrian-Hungarian-Russian alliance.—Katia has given up on Faltin and is turning to Ammann.—Sent photograph to Sweden.—The evening walk strenuous because of the unshoveled piles of snow. Did not get far.—At supper Katia cut her finger badly. Luckily I had gauze bandages close at hand. Considered whether or not she should have the delivery at the Red Cross hospital. Tenderness.—Continued with Hamsun's novel. Very tired.

Monday, March 31

Blue sky, thick blanket of snow; looks like a beautiful January day. No mail all day. God knows why. Got ready for the "Museum." Difficult walk in mild air. Yesterday the *Frankfurter Zeitung* sent Hermann Keyserling's *Travel Diary of a Philosopher*, an enormously fat volume, but seemingly rich in content. The only worry is that I should be devoting myself entirely to *The Magic Mountain*.—At five o'clock went to Nodoleczny about my ear, which is still itching and draining. Walked home through the Englischer Garten amid drifting snow. Katia had gone to see Ammann, who found everything in order and expects the delivery at the end of April. After our belated tea, correspondence. After supper Katia sent for Frau Köckenberger.—Continued with

Hamsun. Wonderful. I was struck by the folksong quality in the man's conversation with the woman who has committed infanticide: how she lies, first saying she wanted to fetch juniper by the brook, then changing it to birch twigs. His moralistic nature-conservatism, hatred of the city from which all evil comes. Life's drolleries; the way Axel makes up with Brede, who wanted to have him killed, so that his savior Oline will not have too great a claim on him. Admirable.

Tuesday, April 1

[. . .] Incessant heavy snowfall; the garden bench is completely buried, so that it has disappeared. Complained at the post office because the mail again did not arrive. Transportation breakdown. Fresh vexation with Katia at breakfast over excessive consumption of butter. Needless and regrettable. But it is clear that this sort of thing always happens when I am overtired for some reason, worn out and therefore irritable. Human failures always have physical causes; knowing this should act as a check, but the depressed state itself prevents the needed presence of mind at the decisive moment.—Wrote to Professor Anfrommel in Heidelberg about Protestantism and Germanism. Looked through my manuscript once more and got it ready to take along with me.—

Saturday, April 5

Toward evening felt ill again, and temperature rose to 38.2° Celsius. Took bicarbonate of soda, chest powder, and aspirin. Slept well. Constipation relieved after breakfast.— In the news, ominous developments. We are on the point of declaring a soviet republic here, to be allied, moreover, with the Hungarian and Russian soviets. I find Bavaria terribly comical, and see all this as little more than mischief, but I would like to see the Allies forced to swallow it, and I almost love communism insofar as it is pitted against the Entente.—On Löhr's advice Katia is going to the bank with checks to withdraw 10,000 marks.—Blue skies, mild weather, with snow still on the ground.— While I stayed in Katia's bedroom, Erika played with the little one.

No fever. Studied freemasonry all day. Toward evening, visit from Katia's mother. In the evening paper more definite reports on the proclamation of the soviet republic, which is to take place this evening, it seems, "without bloodshed, without unchecked nationalization, and with respect for all property."—News that the Kurt Wolff-Verlag has bought the G. Hirth publishing house and will move to Munich in the fall. Their slogan: "Publishers of the new generation of writers." Which is a lie.—Cigarette tastes bad. The catarrh hangs on obstinately.—The bank was only permitting withdrawals of up to 5,000 marks. A lively scene there. There is also said to be a good deal of bustle in the city, but quiet, expectant. No one expects riots. Who would be fighting? The garrison will not protect the Landtag. The citizens are unarmed and fatalistic. The leaders seriously believe that the proletariat in the Allied countries will follow. *Dubito.*

Up early. The front page of the *Nachrichten* covered with the proclamation of the soviet republic. Today a general strike and "national holiday." Rapprochement with Hungary and Russia, break with Berlin. Red Guard. Nationalization of the press. Plans for expropriation. The tone is sharp, yet it is clear that what is involved are protective measures on the part of the Majority Socialists, as was the case at the time of the first revolution, though this time going far enough to bring in the Communists. But I am counting on a fourth and totally radical upheaval before reaction sets in. It may be assumed that the rest of Germany will follow, and if radical socialism in Germany assumes tenable forms, the proletariat of the Allied countries, which will no longer have anything to hope for from the capitalist exploitation of Germany, will have no choice but to do the same. We must recognize that capitalism has been judged and found wanting. It is no longer permissible to speak to the workers about the identity of their interests with those of capital. Such an identity existed and still exists in the "victorious" countries, but it has been condemned by the times, intellectually discredited, and despite all the materialistic crudity of their concept of revolution the proletarians have gone beyond this kind of solidarity; they do not give a damn about "economic reconstruction." In the other countries they have not yet come so far, but they will have to follow, and instead of a solidarity of interests with native capital they will adopt solidarity with foreign comrades of their class.

Very warm, sunny, rather windy spring weather. Only patches of snow remain, otherwise dry.—Letter from Lassen, who wants to distribute 1,000 copies of the *Betrachtungen* among the German student population and later 500 more at Scandinavian universities. Wrote to Fischer about this, also about the advertisement and other matters, and sent him reviews. Letter to Preetorius about the hundredth edition and about "Bauschan."—Walked for an hour and a half with Bauschan.—In the *Rundschau*, an excellent and gratifying essay on Bertram's *Nietzsche.*—The Frankfurt cigars very poor, hardly enjoyable. Also ordered cigarettes, which I can scarcely manage to dig up here.—Grolman sent a scholarly work on Hölderlin.—After luncheon, newspapers. Unable to rest. Very warm.—No more newspapers will appear before tomorrow evening.—The business with Amann is affecting me strongly, especially his glib, tactless, and nasty way of treating the fraternal conflict, this leading motif of what is an intellectual work. "Heinrich Mann is reported to have said: 'What will become of my ideas?' " Shameful.—Correspondence in the afternoon. Stopped a municipal official from sending me his "Allegorical Interpretations of Natural Events." Inquired of his superiors about the whereabouts of my debtor, the former sergeant. Short evening walk.—News from the city: the university has been closed, the rector and senate deposed. A leaflet from the Independent party denounces the elements behind the proclamation of the soviet republic for their opportunism. The Independents will cooperate only if their highly radical demands are met. If not, then. . . . The situation was clear to me. The fourth revolution is imminent.—An even stricter state of siege has been imposed. Curfew at eleven o'clock. Why exactly?—Read all sorts of things in the *Rundschau*. Very tired.

Toward evening, sore throat and long-lasting, tormenting cough that kept me awake until two o'clock. Am hung over today from lack of sleep, and feverish.—Since the editorial staff of the *Münchner Neueste Nachrichten* has refused to collaborate, the paper is being issued entirely by the new government. Talked on the telephone with Ludwig about the new regulations regarding housing. Withdrawals of 100 marks daily from bank accounts are permitted. Valuables, jewels, and the like may not be removed, thus Katia's mother will probably lose her pearls. The decrees are being signed by the former student Toller, from East Prussia, who once sent us eggs.—After breakfast, cleared out my storage shelves somewhat, unpacked the manuscript of *The Magic Mountain* and took a first look into the material once again. I spent some time on what has been written, which I shall probably rewrite completely for objective and subjective reasons. A new beginning must be fashioned. The first chapter will probably remain unchanged, except for expanding the section on the piously conservative "Spanish" grandfather. Regaining control of the material will be no easy task.—Was supposed to go to Gosch, but because of the windy weather decided to stay indoors all day. Until luncheon, read with fairly critical feelings here and there in the *Magic Mountain* manuscript. The subject matter is distinctly ticklish and requires tact. Every detail must be examined to see whether it only touches upon the verge of aestheticism or oversteps the limit. Once again I came upon fascinating motifs. The theme of "time," with which I want to start at once, and the theme of "forbidden love."—In the afternoon, soon after assuming a horizontal position, tormenting cough once more. Head heavy; tired, in bad humor. Depressed by Katia's condition. She is extremely hoarse.—Frisch sent a check for one thousand marks as fee for the *Gesang vom Kindchen*. It will take me ten days to cash the check (100 marks a day).—Since the weather had calmed, I took an hour's walk anyhow after tea, and when I returned I wrote some letters.—Schwegerle reports that the bronze cast of my bust is at his studio.—This evening, finished the book on freemasonry, which after all cannot furnish me with much that is new.—The *Münchner Neueste Nachrichten*, edited by Socialists and Communists, carried greetings from the Budapest soviets to the Bavarian soviets. Lenin particularly inquired about what was being done about real estate, and will have to be informed that properties under a thousand acres are exempt from confiscation.

Saturday, April 12

Sniffles and cough. Studied the accumulated notes. It may be thanks to my stuffed-up head, but just now I cannot summon up anything that could be called enthusiasm. Will the whole business strike me as being futile and obsolete, so that the constant restraint of disenchantment dogs my progress? In any case, the whole story must be clearly presented as a "tale from long ago"; certainly there is inherent in it ample satire of the preceding epoch—more than in *The Patrioteer* it seems to me. Still it will have a similarly old-fashioned effect, if only because of the pathological undercurrent.—Last night finished Hamsun's *Growth of the Soil*, a splendid work and, though completely apolitical, one in profound contact with all the present yearnings: glorification of the solitary farmer, of rustic self-sufficiency; hatred of the city, industry, commerce; ironic treatment of the state—all this is communism poetically perceived, or better: humanely poeticized anarchism. And for all the cleverness of his technique there is nevertheless simplicity in it, goodness, health, humanity. A spirit that is doubtless the spirit of the future—which is to say the present—and one lacking in my own prewar endeavor. "Bauschan" and *Gesang vom Kindchen* are closer to it. *The Magic Mountain* and *The Confidence Man* will be historical long before they are finished. But ultimately it will simply be a matter of picking up again and producing my daily quota.

Anger and sorrow over the children's behavior: Klaus gorging himself on snacks five minutes after he had been firmly forbidden to, so that I struck him roughly. Erika had taken Katia's gold penholder to school without permission and lost it there. Depressed.—Took an hour-and-a-half walk in mild, overcast, windy weather, and thanks to it had better appetite.—Telephone conversation with Endres, who warned me about some crackpot, clearly deranged, who wants to bring me his manuscript. Informed me that Augsburg is already negotiating with the Bamberg government, and that the only reason troops are not being sent is because they are confident of a rapid, *nonviolent* collapse of the soviet regime for economic reasons.—Katia's mother to tea, to whom I gave the page proofs from the *Merkur.*—Went out a bit more before dinner, though there was a nasty west wind. In the evening, finished reading the story "Miriam" by young Borrmann in Königsberg; for all its highly intellectual window-dressing I found it rather dubious and confused. Then a profound and lovely short novella by Sologub, *The Kiss of the Unborn.*—Persistant cough.—Since yesterday Katia sleeping on the third floor. Hope the delivery is soon, and that it goes smoothly.

. . . .

Sunday, April 13 (Palm Sunday)
. . . .

Severe coughing at night. Slept propped up by three pillows. In the morning, occupied myself with the *Magic Mountain* notes. While I was at this, Richter and Krell telephoned that during the night the soviet government was overthrown and that the Hoffmann administration is in control. The Councils have partly fled, partly been captured by soldiers.—Walk at noon. After luncheon, read Sologub's *Light and Shadows.* At six o'clock to the Odeon for the *St. Matthew Passion.* Was introduced to Madame Reinhardt in the greenroom and spoke with Braunfels. Sat all the way up front on a folding chair. During the intermission Katia's mother said some kind things to me about the *Gesang vom Kindchen.* Skirmishes in the vicinity of the railway station between government and Council troops were reported, so that a good many people left. Nothing of this could be heard in the auditorium, but heavy firing and even cannon fire had worried Katia earlier. Erika is visiting a friend in the city and spending the night there. Klaus, who sang in the boys' chorus, joined me with his friends Hoffmann and Richard Hallgarten to walk home in the rain. Absurd that little Frau Hallgarten is going to Berne as a delegate to the women's conference. Such a vapid little brain.—Gave *Peter Schlemihl* in the Pantheon edition to Lotte Walter, who has just been confirmed. Was not very attentive during the *Passion.*—For the time being I welcome the overthrow of the soviet government. Everywhere there are people who believe that it will come back, that "it" is inevitable, and to a large extent I share that belief. But there is a great difference between theory and practice, and I loathe irresponsible "revolutionaries" who are a disgrace to intellectual life like these fellows who have run their course for the time being. I would have no objection if they were shot as noxious vermin, but we had best be careful not to.

Rain, unexpected. No newspapers. Some foreign mail, but local mail not being delivered. Protracted general strike. Telephone service stopped.—Worked on the material.— Visit from Katia's father, who said that military intervention should not be expected, that Epp and his forces are in Jena but Hoffmann will not allow them to enter Bavaria.—Rested soon after luncheon, had tea just after four, and then walked in wind and pouring rain across the Englischer Garten to Preetorius's. In his pleasant studio, Michalski and former Labor Secretary Thomas spoke of their evolution toward communism. In the audience were Wolfskehl, Landshoff and his wife, Dr. Oldenbourg, Erich von Kahler, and others. For a time I was troubled by coughing and had wet feet, but listened with close attention and good intentions, without taking much part in the discussion. It went on quite late. Already a quarter to nine by the time I reached home by the same route. Katia depressed and cross; received my halfway affirmative report in that mood, which produced discord. My doubts and my abhorrence of a tyranny by the materialistic and rationalistic spirit of so-called proletarian culture are lively enough. But nothing is more certain than that the old social and economic order is over and done with, and that the social revolution especially means the denial of what needs to be denied, namely the Allied victory.—Heavy firing. Bell ringing, which probably signifies an alarm.

Thursday, April 17

In bed yesterday, continued with Sologub. Again neither mail nor newspapers today. The trams also do not seem to be running, but now the telephone is functioning. No news can be obtained. My attitude toward affairs very uncertain, but my personal wishes are for the "Whites" to march in and for the restoration of the bourgeois order.—Bertram said that authorized looting was carried out on Leopoldstrasse yesterday with the aid of furniture vans. Alois Ludwig reports that he had been denounced, that the soldiers who came to search knew all the places in the house where stores of food were hidden, and confiscated them. Confiscation of linens and clothing also in the offing, he maintains. Today safe-deposit boxes in banks are to be "examined." Key-holders are supposed to report for that purpose.—Even if there is to be a "White" victory, grave disorders are to be feared, looting by the retreating Reds, etc.

Meanwhile I am pondering *The Magic Mountain*, for now at last the time is right for resuming work on it. During the war it was too early; I had to stop. The war first had to clarify itself as the beginning of the revolution, and not only did it have to end, but the end had to become recognizable as only a pseudo-end. The conflict between reaction (affinity for the Middle Ages) and humanistic rationalism is by now entirely historical, prewar. The synthesis appears to lie in the (communist) future. What is new consists essentially of a new conception of man as a mind-body entity (abolition of the Christian dualism of soul and body, church and state, life and death)— a conception that already existed in the prewar period, incidentally. It is a matter of perspective vis-à-vis the renewal of the Christian *civitas Dei* in humanist guise, a human City of God somehow imbued with transcendence, that is to say oriented toward the mind-body unity. Both Pastor Bunge and Settembrini are equally right and wrong in their viewpoints. Sending Hans Castorp into the war thus means sending him into

47

the beginning of the struggle for the new after he has thoroughly savored its components, Christianity and paganism, in the course of his education.

Hülsen reports that Dachau is in the hands of the Reds. He says there are enough provisions in the city to last for several weeks, because the confiscations brought in a great deal. Henceforth rationing will be handled in the Budapest fashion, with the propertied classes receiving a minimum. Neat. Student Toller is reported to hold the high command on the Red front. Delicious.—The troops driven out of Dachau were not those of Epp, but parts of the Munich garrison loyal to the government that had withdrawn to the town. Officers and 700 enlisted men have been captured. But word has it that strong forces are supposed to be stationed near Pfaffenhofen. In the city, placards have been posted that partly defend the Communist leaders against all and sundry slanders, and partly fulminate against the "parasitic bourgeoisie." Wood and coal are being distributed to proletarians only. Airplanes have dropped leaflets announcing a ban by the Bamberg government on all participation in the revolutionary tribunal.—Went for a walk at noon. Before luncheon, telephoned Martens and talked about the situation. Read some in the *Mittelalterliche Weltanschauung* and slept very well in the afternoon. On my walk, after witnessing a sensually exciting spectacle, thoughts about the motif of forbidden love in *The Magic Mountain*.

Katia's mother to tea. The baby present. Conversation naturally about the situation and prospects. Frau Pringsheim has jewels at the bank worth at least 300,000 marks, which she has to consider as probably lost. But the time for examination of her safe-deposit box does not come until Tuesday. The prospects for our fine linens, also there, are likewise not very good.—An airplane passed overhead and was shot at; firearms crackle, rattle, and bang all over the city. Absurd!—Incidentally we have no butter left, and I am running out of cigarettes. Basically I do not believe this regime will last more than a few days longer. Negotiations with Bamberg are said to be already under way.

Hail showers.—Fine evening walk in the twilight through the park with Bauschan. Later studied the *Mittelalterliche Weltanschauung*. Quiet; no shooting and no Epp bugles.

. . . .
Friday, April 18 (Good Friday)
. . . .

Quiet hangs over the city. Mail arrived, local as well as from Berlin, but evidently outside newspapers are not being delivered. The agency sent an item about the Museum evening from the *Münchner Zeitung. Velhagen und Klasings Monatshefte* came, with Strecker's review of the *Betrachtungen* followed by a hatchet job on *The Patrioteer*. Kindnesses of this sort have a soothing effect, but only on the nerves, and are quite dubious even at that. The level of criticism is not high.—Brandenburg has sent a "proclamation" dealing with theatrical matters.—Wrote to Strecker and Kuckhoff, among others. After luncheon, *Mittelalterliche Weltanschauung*. After tea began reading "The Ass's Skin" aloud to the little ones. Was interrupted by the Ludwigs, who called. Around seven walked into the city; with no trams, but crowded with people, it had the air of a quiet Sunday. Called for Hülsen at the Hotel Leinfelder. Martens came along. Was told that the general mood is very depressed, especially among the lower middle class, the shopkeepers, etc. No resistance being offered; the chances for the communist government improving daily. We ate at the Scholastika Restaurant. Miserable and embarrassing bickering at a nearby table between Bavarian and Prussian patrons. Ate two omelets at five marks each. Conversation about the situation, the future, the prospects for literature. Financially, plans are to confiscate twenty-seven percent of the capital assets of Bavarian citizens, including the gold in safe-deposit boxes, which confiscations will be credited to the owner however. In foreign policy: Danube federation, Bavaria seceding from the Reich and uniting with Hungary and German Austria to form a bolshevist bloc. The Red Army was going to advance on Augsburg for the purpose of obtaining provisions, but the Bamberg government is now willing to supply Munich with food. A White Guard is being recruited, but with what success is unknown, and fighting spirit on the other side is evidently low. All the same, an attack by the Reds might prove dangerous to them. The *Münchner Neueste Nachrichten*, under another name, is to be transformed into a major communist newspaper. Martens, revolutionary as he always was, is holding himself in readiness to handle the features department. Professor Jaffé, on the other hand, is saving himself for a return of the previous regime, and expects a turnabout soon. The prevailing opinion is that this may well take place, and communism collapse once more but return again later.—About Heinrich. Repeated postponement of his *Brabach* play; no one has any faith in it. The affair with Toller, who compromised him in the most tactless [fashion], resulting in his being served with a summons. Heinrich has written two new plays, one of them a Napoleon drama, *Der Weg zur Macht*. Hmmm. Steinrück's comment that Heinrich is no dramatist is true; even *Madame Legros* does not prove the contrary. But he is also no novelist; rather he is the type of European literary man who today carries more weight than either dramatists or novelists. I did not have the presence of mind to say this.—Wretched tales being disseminated by Halbe. His pleasure at my being unnoticed at Wedekind's funeral. Utterly wretched.—We all walked home together, joined by Krell from the Max Monument on. Katia was still awake and I told her about it. Continued reading Sologub.

Saturday, April 19

Some city mail. Katia thinks she may expect the baby to be born today or tomorrow [. . .]. On the point of beginning to write, I worked on the material.—Report that the Hotel Regina has been occupied by proletarians. No one can gainsay our new masters' sense for the fantastic. The luxurious suites of that tourist-industry palace housing the poorest of the poor—delicious! The question is when it will be the turn of private houses.—Long walk.—Sent the *Merkur* to Krell.—From Freising, Berner has sent a copy of the *Tägliche Rundschau* with a further article by Strecker about Heinrich and me. First half wallops *The Patrioteer*. Now this is too much. Yesterday I sent him a letter rebuking him for his evaluations and comparisons.—At tea, Katia's mother. The director of the Regina Palace told her that the official notice about the proletarianization of the hotel is untrue. The hotel is continuing to operate. It is true that there are but few tourists however. So they lie.—Latest report: a leaflet from Bamberg reads "Citizens of Munich, hold out! Our troops are on the way!" Perhaps that would be a relief to our rulers. After long disputes, so we hear, the trams are running again today in order to bring in money; they cannot pay their bills.—Rumor circulating that the preliminary peace treaty was signed with the exclusion of Bavaria. Also Bavaria will be excluded from food shipments for the time being. This allegedly was printed in the Augsburg newspapers. The victory at Dachau is an outright fraud.

At the mayor's request Dachau was evacuated by the troops garrisoned there so as to protect the town.—After tea, read "The Ass's Skin" to the children in the presence of the ladies, which amused me greatly. It seemed to me that the earlier parts of *Royal Highness* were unconsciously influenced by it.—Wrote a few lines to Hirschfeld thanking him for the latest novel he sent. Then went out for only a short walk. In the course of the day, spoke on the telephone with Professor Ammann and Frau Köckenberger. Katia had a hot bath before supper, but there were no further signs of progress.—In the evening read *Mittelalterliche Weltanschauung*. Heavy firing and bell ringing, but the latter may have been for Easter.

Sunday, April 20 (Easter Sunday)

Beautiful warm spring day, but it clouded over in the course of the morning. No progress with Katia. My cold is improving very slowly. Last night in bed after my bath, tormenting, long-lasting coughing again.—Today no mail or newspapers at all. Under the soviet government the Sunday peace is perfect.—*After an interruption of four years I have begun to work on "The Magic Mountain" again*, i.e. I resumed with a new foreword to the first chapter and mean to expand it by adding the figure of Grandfather Castorp in a section called "Of the Christening Basin." Since revisions are needed in many places, will probably recopy the present text onto the good paper I have become accustomed to from the manuscript of the *Betrachtungen*. The new foreword announces the time theme, which was not done before. Moreover the new chapter is enriched by the addition of the motif of the christening basin as a symbol of history and of death. The vessel has already been used in the *Gesang vom Kindchen*, and thus it has autobiographical and unifying significance.

At noon a visit from Katia's mother. A lady in the city, someone she does not know, indicated to her with remarkable certainty that "by Tuesday everything will be different." Belief that change and liberation will come soon seems to be very firmly entrenched in the people's heads; our milk woman also said something along the same lines with absolute conviction.—Went walking with Bauschan in the interior of the park. The spring already fairly far advanced. The shrubs are budding, the grass has turned green. In particular, the bright yellow-green leaf-buds of one specific bush are quite swollen. On the way home I met the four older children in black velvet suits. They had been to the Aumeister restaurant and had eaten tomato soup. They were carrying primroses that they had wrapped in wet handkerchiefs to keep them fresh; the handkerchiefs, in turn, they had tied to the ends of sticks.—Good holiday dinner: double-smoked pork and Sachertorte. Afterward, continued to read in the *Mittelalterliche Weltanschauung*. Economically, the fundamental idea of ascetic transcendentalism assumes a wholly socialist-communist character. Remarkable to see with what ironic tolerance, typically enough, the pure idea of the City of God is adapted to all the realms of inadequate human reality. There is also something timely in all this.—Rested well in the afternoon. Tea with the three little folk, the baby so poignant, as always.— Read the latest "Notices from the Executive Council." There is a great sense of the need for public order. The threats and measures against looting, illegal requisitioning, etc. (evidently there have been many such cases), sound draconic. The system's basic militaristic undertone emerging sharply; prime necessity the creation of a strong army. They say that Churchill has called upon the Reich government to combat communism jointly with the Western Powers! This is an appeal to our hatred of the Allies—and in my case it scores a certain success. Highly interesting, the theories of the Russian Communists on the international situation. Contradictions and separate-interest factions within the Allied bloc. Incompatibilities. The "League of Nations," so far a paper creation, will merely play the role of the capitalists' Holy Alliance to repress the workers' revolution. The revolutionary proletariats of all countries are called upon to wage a struggle against the ideas of the Wilsonian League of Nations, which is branded an alliance for robbery, exploitation, and imperialist counterrevolution. I cannot conceal my sympathy, despite my repugnance toward a class tyranny such as never remotely existed before—in my lifetime. The role of France: "Since finance of capital in that nation has taken a predominantly usurious form, industry being weakly developed and the productive forces completely shattered by the war," France's interest "is directed toward preserving the capitalist regime by desperate measures: barbarous pillaging of Germany, direct subjugation and thievish exploitation of the vassal states, and pressing for the payment of loans made by the French Shylock to Russian tsarism." This is Russian Christianity speaking. The word "usurious" in connection with French interest-bearing loans is a giveaway. Usury is felt to be Jewish—which it is, after all. Russia has *medieval* feelings about capitalism, and knows how to communicate its views to the world.

Toward evening not well, probably stomach. Walked up and down in the allée in the dusk. Supper with the children. Klaus very sweet. I gave him *Master and Man* in the Insel edition, and Erika an issue of *Velhagen und Klasings Monatshefte*. Went on reading the *Mittelalterliche Weltanschauung* with keen interest.

Monday, April 21 (Easter Monday)

I awoke at six o'clock to the sound of footsteps overhead, and realized that labor had begun. Katia in the bath. It started right after midnight. Frau Köckenberger has been here since early morning. I lay down again, got up at seven. Though earlier the pains had been coming in such rapid succession that Katia expected the baby by eight o'clock, they had slowed down again. I telephoned her mother. Walked on the promenade, waiting for Ammann. Then took tea and zwieback upstairs. The mail: a most unpleasant laudatory piece on the *Betrachtungen* by Strecker in the *Tägliche Rundschau*. Having arrived meanwhile, Ammann came down while I was eating, and I plied him with breakfast. We chatted until half past nine and I showed him the pictures. Then he went upstairs again. Slow progress. Injections.—Ten-thirty. Wrote to Mama. Ammann again came down and sat with me for a while. It is going very slowly. The dilations are extremely painful and Katia is suffering a great deal. Her mother came down shaken and Ammann spoke of morphine, but it is otherwise calm.

(*After luncheon.*) It is over; a healthy boy was delivered. The impatience through these very hard, frightful hours; especially unnerving the wait in the allée for the cab bringing the assistant with the instruments, for the total fruitlessness of the extremely painful first stage of labor from eight o'clock on made it necessary to resort to forceps. Even Ammann seemed impatient. Then the operation was quickly accomplished. Erika reported to me that it was a "lad." Katia wept violently after the anesthesia, which was alarming but no surprise. Then calm. A charming scene: the children's congratulations, Erika in the van, bringing the baby to the bed. He seems to be the type of Katia's twin brother. Sat for a long time by Katia's bed. Bade goodbye to the doctors. Luncheon with Katia's mother and Frau Köckenberger. Great relief. For Katia's sake

very glad the baby is a boy, as it unquestionably gives her a psychological lift.—
Spoke angrily to the maid Josefa, who balked at having to take the midwife's utensils
back to her, since no porter was available.—Short rest. The Löhrs to tea with their
daughter and Bertram. (Katia had a good appetite, ate gruel with egg for lunch, tea
and cake in the afternoon, jam omelet for supper.) Conversation about conditions.
Visits to Katia. Short evening walk with Bertram, who then stayed for supper. Erika
doing nicely as deputy housewife. Conversed about the ideas in *The Magic Mountain*,
which Bertram spontaneously applauded from his vivid sense of the subject's intellectual attractions. My thoughts about a future synthesis of Christianity and humanism,
a new mind-body humanity that may even now be coming into being, and that
Nietzsche too hailed in a way.—Bertram handed me a beautiful and costly present for
Lisa, whose first birthday comes on the twenty-fourth, a mother-of-pearl letter opener
with gold ornamentation. With it was a thoughtful poem that I read with emotion.
He left at ten o'clock.

Tuesday, April 22

Up early. Katia was suffering from cramplike pains in her diaphragm that became very
bad toward morning, but subsided after application of camomile compresses. I prepared
her breakfast with the help of Erika, then had my own and did some necessary
telephoning. Katia's mother reports a leaflet from Bamberg dropped in great quantities
yesterday: "People of Munich, we know what you are going through. Hold out! Help
is near." Today a demonstration strike and "military review." Klaus and his friend
Marcks have gone into the city to see it. The trams have stopped running. Telephone
worked only in the morning. There are persistent rumors that the water supply will
be cut off, but it has not happened yet. The city is said to be encircled by "White"
troops. I wanted to go to the registry, but forebore because of the circumstances. Sat
for a long time in the lying-in room while the baby skillfully drank from the breast
for the first time. Read Bertram's birthday poem to Katia.—After a very cold, clear
evening the sky this morning was again fair, but soon it clouded over and snowed.—
No mail of course.—Visit from Katia's mother just before noon. Went for brief walk
in winter suit and overcoat. Tea at Katia's bedside after I had rested nervously. Not
feeling well. Headaches. Spent the afternoon in the lying-in room on the third floor
and read Katia "A Fallen King," the Lagerlöf story that I had read before and hold
in high regard. Walked before supper for half an hour in biting cold. After eating,
visited Katia again, who was just taking the baby to her breast. He nurses adroitly
and vigorously. Katia inspected his sex, for the thought crossed her mind that we were
lying to her. Was completely convinced and obviously happy. As far as I am concerned,
it should be noted that I cannot summon up a fraction of the tenderness for the boy
that I felt from the first moment for Lisa—which might seem surprising.—Krell sent
back the *Gesang vom Kindchen* with a courteous and gratifying letter that I read to
Katia.—In the evening, read the *Mittelalterliche Weltanschauung* as I had done in the
afternoon.—Krell also sent an essay on property by Wassermann that I read during
my supper; it seems to be intelligent, just, and reasonable.—On the eve of the baby's
birth I read in bed Sologub's story dealing with the Khodynka disaster, which for
sheer horror makes Tolstoy's account pale to nothing.

Wind, hail, and gusts of rain, then snow. Katia not bad, objectively, but weak and inclined to melancholic forebodings, thoughts of death.—I was tired and numb; made no progress. Arranged to call on Schwegerle to see two portraits of Hamburg senators by Trübner. Need the costume for Old Castorp.—At noon Katia's mother was with her. We were expecting Ammann, but he did not come. Walked. Afternoon, slept. Ammann came while we were at tea and stayed until half past seven. Lula joined us. Conversations about the situation, which has profoundly embittered the Old Bavarians. General von Kneussl is in charge of the government troops moving against Munich, and they are gearing up carefully, since failure would spell doom. The general impression prevails, however, that the communist regime is collapsing of its own accord. People no longer seem to be afraid of it, for the *München-Augsburger Abendzeitung* intends simply to start publishing again. This morning the word was that the leaders had fled, but there seems to be no confirmation of this. They are sharply divided on the issue of the banks. Leviné and Axelrod want to confiscate safe deposits, Toller and others are against it. In Budapest the soviet government is said to be on the verge of collapse since the Rumanians are marching on the city. Ammann, like Löhr, is not sleeping at home, but keeps changing places every night for fear of being taken as a hostage. Lula is moving into the Carolinum with her daughter. Looting is expected during the critical hours of the interregnum.—Before supper, went walking in the slush of the allée.—Finished looking through Eicken's *Mittelalterliche Weltanschauung* once more, a brilliant book that has provided me with many stimulating suggestions.— In the evening, stories by Chekhov. Pleasant, but really unsatisfactory and pointless. Mean to turn to more serious reading and take up Goncharov's *A Common Story*, whose pedagogic tone should stimulate me.

Wednesday, April 30

Worked on the grandfather. Summoned to the housing office. Subject: billeting. It may well come to that. Considering taking in two girls, friends of Erika's whose parents live in the country and who need a place to stay in town.—Katia has back pain. At noon, her mother.—I am rather tired and cross. Walked in cool but not unpleasant weather.—After luncheon, alarm, perturbation, and rage prompted by the maidservants and Klaus, who were holding down his little brother together and tickling him so that he screamed for help and cried. Indignant because violent tickling is among the things I find most repugnant and outrageous. Scolded the boy loudly and told off the maids.— Heavy gunfire.—Bertram for tea at Katia's bedside. Talked about bolshevism and my ambiguous attitude toward it. Afterward read the first chapter of *The Magic Mountain* to him, with the new introduction and the grandfather insertion so far as it is written. He liked the new material by far the best. Discussion about the strengths and weaknesses of the chapter and the quality of the whole thing as distinctly a novella with the scope of a novel, the only proper term for it being a "tale."—Plan to install Bertram as a nominal resident of the house.—Erika brought home a leaflet from Bamberg she had picked up, unequivocally promising the liberation of Munich and bringing news from the outside world. The strike in the Ruhr is reportedly over, the rest of Germany quiet. The Italian delegates, not content with the Brenner frontier, have left Paris over Fiume, which Wilson refuses to cede to them. Whereupon England has also announced her withdrawal from the conference on the grounds that she cannot approve any peace that leaves an ally unsatisfied. According to Bertram, France has taken possession of the Saar coal mines; the region is supposed to be placed under the League of Nations for the time being, and after fifteen years will itself decide whether it wishes to belong to France or Germany. Danzig is to be neutralized.—Hatred and disgust. How can one help but go over to communism lock, stock, and barrel when it has the tremendous virtue of being hostile to the Allies? To be sure, communism is marked by disorder and cultural Hottentot-ism, but in Germany it would scarcely remain that way for long.—After supper, composed with Bertram a telegram of reassurance to his mother in Elberfeld. It is to be sent by way of Wassermann in Vienna.—Abandoned Meredith's novel and began reading a Turgenev story, "Jakov Pazynkov," in my handsome new edition.—Katia's mother telephoned that she had seen a placard saying there was fighting at Starnberg, and that "the Prussians" (the "Whites" are of late demagogically referred to as Prussians) wreaked havoc in that area.—Countless artillery explosions in the distance.

Thursday, May 1 (12:00 noon)

Erotic night. But one may not wish for calm *quand même.*—National and "worldwide" holiday. Katia's mother telephoned in the morning to say that the white flag is waving from the Wittelsbach Palace and that the Reds capitulated at four o'clock. Turned out to be incorrect. There is not yet any talk of surrender, and the gunfire continues at intervals. According to Katia's mother, who came around noon, there is tremendous excitement in town. During the night, hostages held in the Luitpold Preparatory School were killed and mutilated. Their names are not known; there are said to have been ten of them, some townspeople and some aristocrats. A placard declares that the Factory and Soldiers' Councils abhor and reject this "bestial deed," but this is only a reaction to the placards reporting the acts of the "Prussians" in Starnberg. Tremendous rage among the bourgeois population. All red armbands have suddenly vanished. The Councils declare themselves to be behind the "government" of Toller and Maenner, the more moderate Communists. The fighting is said to be continuing, toward the north it would seem, for there is a barricade near the ferry on the way to Föhring. Count Bothmer, the writer, is said to be among those murdered. The liberal Count Törring is also mentioned.

Worked on the first chapter. Am constantly bothered by the need to give it a fictional, "synthetic" form. But the need for exactitude overpowers the former one and determines what is essential.—Complained again, with Katia's mother present, about the dreadful behavior of the children and the housemaids.—Cannon fire.

(*6:00* P.M.) All afternoon, strong cannonade and machine-gun fire. Nevertheless I slept a little after a three-quarter-hour walk through the park at noon in windy, cold weather with gusts of snow. Went as far as the ferry, where no barricade was to be seen. Before tea, telephoned Krell for news. The city is almost entirely in the hands of government troops that arrived in the course of the afternoon and were greeted warmly by the populace. They are Prussian and South German units in steel helmets, good-looking, and well disciplined. They met with hardly any resistance. The gunfire was relatively insignificant; the touted heroism of the Reds evidently amounted to nil. The only fighting took place around the Palace of Justice and the Stachus. There is still some firing from heavy and light artillery. A reactionary volunteer corps composed of students is said to be "acting up," firing into the city and terrorizing the populace. The first step will be to establish a military dictatorship over the city, and it will be Prussian until the Bavarian Free Corps, countless units of which are said to be forming, has been assembled. Lieutenant General von Möhl, the Bavarian commander, is signing leaflets calling for the capture of the ringleaders, who have probably absconded with public funds. In the morning we were told as a certainty that Privy Councillor Döderlein was among the murdered hostages, but this too has not been confirmed. On the other hand, one of the victims was Count Moy, the former adjutant to the king. Two titled ladies were also among them, which is particularly repugnant. The bourgeois newspapers will be out again by tomorrow evening. All this news came from Martens, who telephoned it to Krell after an editorial conference.—The Munich communist episode is over; there will scarcely be much desire left to try it again. I too cannot resist a feeling of liberation and cheerfulness. The pressure was abominable. I hope those scoundrelly heroes of the "masses," who have on their conscience the brazen, criminal stupidity of murdering hostages, can be seized and given over to exemplary judgment. The slaughter of the women is the most repulsive thing of all. Count Moy was a pleasant, obliging, totally nonpolitical, and unaggressive gentleman; his murder is moronic.

(10:30 P.M.) Krell called back to inform us that no one must be seen on the streets after seven. Anyone who disobeys risks being shot. He heard about the murder of the hostages from Hans von Weber. Privy Councillor Döderlein was killed for certain; also Lindpaintner, Stuck's stepson, Count Arco, a Countess Arco, and the Prince and Princess von Thurn und Taxis. The rest of the bodies were so mutilated as to be unrecognizable!—If only the bestial murderers and those who egged them on could be apprehended.—Read Katia a few Chekhov stories. After supper Frau Eliasberg telephoned in great turmoil, relating that her husband had been arrested as a Russian, accused of having served the communist regime, and was now being held at police headquarters. She asked for Endres's telephone number. I gave it to her, soothed her, and asked that she or Endres let us know if we might offer bail if needed, but heard nothing more.—Finished reading "Jakov Pazynkov," which is an homage to Romanticism and a little on the sentimental side.—There is a small armed camp on Mauerkircherstrasse. Machine guns and an artillery piece have been set up. Cannons are still being fired frequently in the city.

Monday, May 5 (evening)

Slept badly, but calmer and more serene today. Started over once more and intend to continue in this vein.—At noon, visit from Privy Councillor Pringsheim, who expressed bitterness about *Black Flags,* which he has just read. Longish walk in cool weather. Katia stayed in bed for luncheon but got up at half past four for tea. Bertram came, and the Löhrs with their daughter. Comments that the liberation of the city took place in the nick of time. What we went through would have been only a beginning.—Discussed the cultural situation with Bertram, the necessity for a cultural front against all kinds of fanatical extremism, not only antinational elements, but also those dangerous to the world at large. We have been peering into an abyss, we agreed. The Entente is hateful, but the West has to be saved from the horrors of a mass migration from below.—Little Michael was in the dining room for the first time. A remarkable little face, at the moment somewhat miserable and jaundiced. After the Löhrs left, Katia went back to bed. I took a walk with Bertram from seven to eight, as far as the sunken ferry, and had supper with him. We talked about Hebbel, his nationalism and conservatism, his psychological casuistry and his prose, which I am not familiar with.—After Bertram left I looked in on Katia, then read with interest the evening paper, which is highly "militaristic" in content. A proclamation by the Möhl command calling for the elimination of the loutish type of soldier meets with my full approval. Incidentally, Löhr said that a good deal of neat "cleaning up" by summary court-martial has been going on, which is certainly nothing to regret. To my gratification the red flags have vanished from the city; the Residenz, the War Ministry, etc. At the Siegestor a military band was playing *Deutschland, Deutschland über alles.* The Epp corps marched in with splendid discipline, amid great rejoicing. Katia's mother feels it is again too "militaristic," but I am quite in sympathy and find it is considerably easier to breathe under the military dictatorship than under the rule of the *crapule.*

Monday, May 12

Warm. Rain and thunder. Forged ahead with the writing. A number of issues of the *Frankfurter Zeitung* belatedly delivered; a great deal of mostly uninteresting mail. Telegram from the *Illustrierte Leipziger Zeitung*; protest against the Entente peace. Questionnaire from *Der Spiegel* about bolshevism, etc.—Eissi's hair cropped close with a side part; handsome.—Katia had an unlucky day: lost the key to the linen closet in which the basket of keys is kept, so that we were without tea, butter, sugar, etc. The children lost a good bread knife that they were bringing back from the repair shop.— For tea, Frau Pringsheim. Wrote to Witkop. Walked for only half an hour before both meals.—In the evening, read the newspapers, as I also had in the afternoon. Hard to decide to what extent the horrifying way the newspapers have of discussing conditions represents political tactics and to what extent it is genuine. Certain comments are undoubtedly seriously intended, such as that of a Social Democratic delegate who has returned from Versailles and proclaims, even considering the consequences, "Don't sign!" At any rate, the solidarity of the proletariat seems to be standing the test no better now than in 1914.—It sometimes happens that on my walks I find myself reciting with pleasure passages from the *Gesang vom Kindchen*—admittedly always from the first half. I am now convinced that the baptism section drops off seriously.

Tuesday, May 13

Slept fitfully. The "peace," the sentencing of the Kaiser, etc., gnaw at me considerably. Nonetheless, more attentive while at work than I have been the past few days. Letters from Fischer (about Lassen's purchase of 1,000 copies of the *Betrachtungen*) and Ponten. Interview about bolshevism by the *Chicago Tribune* arranged through the Union of German Scholars and Artists. Long cablegram!—At noon into town. Had my hair cut and shampooed by the agreeable assistant at the Vier Jahreszeiten, then from the main post office telegraphed the *Illustrierte Leipziger Zeitung*: "The Allied Peace betrays the idiocy of the victors." Then to Gosch, who tried the bridge once more. Unfortunately it pinches, cuts, and tortures me.—Richter urged me by telephone to ride out to Feldafing with him on Friday. Wrote letters to Lassen, Fischer, and others. Brief evening walk. Evenings in bed I am continuing to read *Virgin Soil*.—Quite out of sorts.

Sunday, May 25 (evening)

Worked on the first chapter of *The Magic Mountain*.—Shaved. At twelve o'clock the student Günther Weitbrecht came by appointment. Calling to thank me for the *Betrachtungen*. Law student, but heart not in it. Studying in Tübingen, son of the proprietor of a well-known Hamburg bookshop. Nice North German boy with attractive blue eyes. Took him with me on my walk, in glorious spring weather, and enjoyed hearing his young voice. He was genuinely grateful to me and wishes to write.—In *Simplicissimus*, a satire on Heinrich's flight with his family from Munich during the soviet republic in a car that Friedenthal obtained for him. Had already heard the story from Bertram. When I discussed it with Katia at tea I recalled the unforgettable scene from my youth when Heinrich ran away from Papa, already deathly ill, who had come out onto the landing. I, however, stayed to talk with him, and Papa thanked me for it on his deathbed.—Wrote letters in the afternoon. Merry scene, the children playing with friends on the small lawn. After supper, read the *Süddeutsche Monatshefte* on the war and Germany's collapse. All the misery of it gripped me again.

Tuesday, June 3 (evening)

Cloudy, cooler. Began writing my speech for the Pfitzner celebration but was interrupted by Cossmann, phoning to say that the affair is postponed to the eighteenth. Bother.—Walked with Bauschan. During luncheon Katia's father phoned to tell her that her grandmother Dohm died on Sunday. She has already been cremated.—Ponten has sent his study on Greek landscape, Krell his article on the *Betrachtungen* that has now been published in *Der Wagenlenker*. Read some of the things in the latest *Rundschau* and in Shaw's wittily cogent book *Peace Conference Hints*, likewise sent by Fischer. It was written *before* the beginning of the conference, and his predictions in the event that Wilson should fail are amusingly dour. Dehmel's war diary also came. A letter from Herzfeld.—Katia melancholic.—Leviné condemned to death by the summary court, despite a letter from Harden eulogizing him as a devout Christian; the style and content of the letter have evidently greatly irritated the public. I am providing young Trummler with a written testimonial that ought to protect him from further arrests. But I cannot summon up much sympathy for Leviné's brand of brutal idealism that rides so roughshod over reality.

Friday, June 6

My forty-fourth birthday. Cloudy, alternately sultry and cool, without rain. In the morning Katia and Erika were already there when I came downstairs, had put up wreaths and heaped up gifts. Katia had managed to find a great many sweets. A convenient little lighter, a wallet for coins and bills, and a Thermos bottle delighted me. A fine gugelhupf that Mama had made stood on the table. Erika brought Lisa down in gala dress, with a wreath of daisies on her head and a bouquet in her hand. A congratulatory letter from Fiedler.—In the forenoon I wrote letters to Bertram, Ponten, and Johst. Took short walk. After luncheon, read in the *Frankfurter Zeitung* the document signed by Delbrück, Max Weber, Mendelssohn, etc. concerning war "guilt." The children at tea. A great deal of cake and rich torte. Afterward, took care of more letters and then went walking again. Supper very cheerful: chicken and rice, Sachertorte, and Moselle wine. Katia and the children in their best clothes. Klaus, wearing a very tight suit he has grown out of, had a giggling fit when the conversation turned to a seventeen-year-old girl who already has a baby. Was she still going to school, I asked. No, she had left. Because she had a baby? At this Klaus coughed up his wine. Afterward, in my room, had guessing games. Everyone was convinced that Golo had eavesdropped at the door; he betrayed himself by his obviously hypocritical reasoning. His deception really quite comical.—Touching congratulatory letter from Privy Councillor Marcks, whose wife and son also have their birthdays today. "For our Fatherland so urgently needs every ray of sunshine and every bit of guidance for the future. Your life is just such an illustrious guide. . . ." Good Lord.—This year has netted *A Man and His Dog* and *Gesang vom Kindchen*. I must be content with that. May *The Magic Mountain* require nothing significantly more a year from now! Yesterday Katia's misfortune, her disorganization in misplacing and looking for things, gave me fresh stimulus toward *The Confidence Man*.

. . . .

Saturday, June 7 (evening)

. . . .

Moni's birthday. Her presents were heaped up where mine lay yesterday on the corner table in the dining room. Cloudy, warm, hazy-damp June day. Showers. Clearing toward evening. Continued reworking the second chapter. Have realized that only by copying with close attention and making improvements will I really recover the whole thing and once again have all the threads in my hand. Katia's father to tea. Telegram of congratulations from her mother, from Berlin. Took care of some correspondence. The garden is very pretty in its first luxuriance and freshly tended, with lawn mowed and paths raked. After luncheon I sat under the chestnut tree for a while. It was too wet to lie there. In the evening, read in the *Nachrichten* a pretty little story of a childhood Whitsuntide by Martens; sent him a note of appreciation. Before going to sleep, am reading Péladan's *Le Panthée*. Much too French. A good deal of it ridiculous, and the sentimental voluptuousness is not my cup of tea. His romanticism, antirepublicanism, cheering and likable. But there is something absurd, ignorant, about his passion for Wagner.—It seems to me that there are some fine spots among Hatzfeld's poems, but I have difficulty relating to lyric poetry, at least by contemporaries.

. . . .

Whitmonday, June 9 (evening)

. . . .

Very warm day. For the first time we breakfasted under the chestnut tree. Walter, to whom I sent the *Gesang vom Kindchen* yesterday, telephoned and spoke highly emotional words of praise, which gave me great pleasure and buoyed me up, for I had slept badly and was droopy.—Reworking the second chapter. I thought the first still needs improvement; it will be necessary to show how Hans Castorp is intellectually bound by his own time, reveal his mental and moral lassitude, lack of faith, and hopelessness.—At noon, visit from the Walters, who came to see Michael. We sat in the garden and Walter repeated his warm praise of the poem, which he has now read three times, once aloud to his wife. His response to it is by far the most favorable I have had so far.—After luncheon it looked as though we would have a thunderstorm, so I went to bed. But the weather cleared. At five to the Walters', with whom we had tea in the garden along with Dr. Pixis, the widowed Frau Hoch, and the actor Dysing. Pixis defended the execution of Leviné, which of course is one point of view. We are concerned about the reconciliation of all classes. There was also talk about young Toller and his affair with Mme. Durieux. After our return home Katia had a visit from Frau Pfitzner. I went for a leisurely stroll for another hour in the lush park, here and there coming upon lovers lying in the grass. Supper on the veranda. Continuing to read Péladan's novel, which I now find more fascinating. Certain romantically tinged digressions analyzing contemporary life, such as the passage on the role of love in our era, are good. In general, his antidemocratic attitude is pleasing, except where his pronounced antimilitaristic ideas come to the fore. Under the present circumstances these sound almost like an obsession, but may be explained by his hatred for the state and the army, which he considers to be its sole instrument.

Sunday, June 15

Blue and lovely. I worked on the speech, taking only a short walk. The newspaper, which resumed publication yesterday afternoon, was delivered late. The absurd comedy of the peace drags on. Japan has intervened, threatening an alliance with Russia and Germany. Italy once again on the outs. Answer to Germany postponed.—I sprinkled the children with the garden hose, much to their delight.—Telegram from Steegemann in Hannover, who would like to publish the *Kindchen.*—In the garden in the afternoon. Balzac. At tea, visit from Löhr with daughters.

In the afternoon and evening, hordes of people walking in the park. Wound my way between them in order to get quite a way out, then read *Birotteau*, sitting on the grass until sunset. Supper on the veranda. I told Katia about the charming episode that occurred recently during the third act of *Der arme Heinrich*, how Walter threw glances at me from the podium to call my attention to the monks' chorus. This is the sort of thing one could not have dreamed of as a young man newly arrived in Munich. Katia, infected by a certain complacency on my part, spoke of our splendid situation in general. There is something touching about two such melancholy people spurring each other on to enjoy their bourgeois comforts.

Balzac entertains me hugely. He belongs among the titans of the novel. I cannot follow the financial affairs, and yet he has a breadth of sympathy like Tolstoy's, though not so humane. The French fascination with society puts me off, but is nevertheless amusing. He spawns characters; he is irresponsible both as artist and as thinker, and in fact may be quite unimportant.

Persistently lovely weather; blue, dry, warm enough for silk suit. Corpus Christi, no mail or newspapers. Took up *The Magic Mountain* again and worked on the first chapter, which I expanded by adding several things that put the whole on a decidedly grander scale. In this connection I reflected that the ethical difference between capitalism and socialism is trivial, since for both it is *work* that is regarded as the highest principle, the absolute. It will not do to pretend that capitalism is a parasitic and unproductive mode of life. On the contrary, the bourgeois world knew no higher concept or value than that of work. Socialism raises this ethical principle to official status, making it an economic principle, a political and human standard against which individuals are measured, so thoroughly that nobody asks why and how work should possess such absolute dignity and consecration. Or does socialism lend new meaning and purpose to work? Not so far as I know. Is work a faith, an absolute? No. Intellectually, morally, humanely, religiously, socialism stands no higher than capitalist conventionality; it is merely a prolongation of it. It is just as godless, for work is not divine.—At noon, visit from the architect Ludwig and his wife, who are leaving Munich. Katia and I walked with them, then I turned back at the bridge and walked into the park, where I read Balzac on the grass.—Frau Herms to tea.

(*Evening.*) I wrote to young Weitbrecht about sympathy with the past and the future. Children's games in the garden. The little Herms boy and Professor Salz's infant daughters were there. Lisa sat on her pillow on the grass and took part in the games with touching laughter and attempts at talking. I picked her up and carried her for a stroll along the allée, which I had not done before, until her evening porridge was ready. With thunder in the distance, Katia and I walked in the park before supper. The sky clouded over, a rain-laden wind began to blow, and we ate indoors. But the storm has not yet broken. I continued with the Balzac adventures.

Brisk and beautiful. Am in the accustomed state after an erotic night: partly subdued, partly more relaxed and refreshed. Continued with the third chapter, inserting pages from the first manuscript after all, as recopying the whole would really be a waste of time. Walk. Letter from a "state director" and Reichstag deputy Winterfeldt about the *Betrachtungen*. Letter from Bertram. Afternoon in the garden; newspapers and rest. The reservations and conditions proposed by the national assembly rejected by the enemy. After tea wrote to Fischer, having extended our contract for another six years, until my fiftieth birthday that is, and the publication, I hope, of my Collected Works. Card to Herr von Winterfeldt.—Richter for supper. Afterward we stayed on the veranda by the light of my lamp from Tölz, drinking the last bottle of our Bordeaux. From Arcisstrasse a report that placards are now posted announcing *unconditional signature.* So be it. Arrangements with Richter concerning another sojourn in Feldafing, which I have tentatively set for the beginning of July.

It impresses me deeply and mysteriously to see how great a role the problem of time plays in Spengler's philosophy of history. This has preoccupied me as a fundamental motif of *The Magic Mountain* since 1912 or 1913, when Spengler was still at work on his book. I added details such as the special physical and psychic relationship between grandson and grandfather just before I began reading the *Decline*, prompted by the book's reputation, but also by a foreboding that it would be somehow pertinent. The experience once again confirms what I take to be my unusual sensitivity, linking my solitude sympathetically with all the more profound thoughts and insights of the times. The fact that around 1912 the problem of "time" became acute for philosophers and dreamers and entered into their creative work may be related to the historical upheavals of these present days, at that time still deep underground.—I am less and less inclined to reject the possibility that Spengler's book may mark an epoch in my life in somewhat the same way that I was affected twenty years ago by *The World as Will and Idea*. I cannot always follow it, and don't worry about that; it does not prevent me from eagerly absorbing the a priori, familiar essence of the book.

Yesterday evening visited, with Katia, Dr. Endres and his wife, who are celebrating their tenth wedding anniversary. The Löhrs, Geffckens, the old widow Heigel, and Public Prosecutor Endres were there. I was tired, nervous, and extremely depressed; once again cursed my amiability. There was a punch made of bilberry wine which, of course, has given me painful constipation.—Rain, cold. Long walk after work. Quite chilled in the afternoon; slept. We had Lisa at tea. Fischer announces new editions of the *Betrachtungen* and again invites me to Glücksburg.—Moving letter several folio sheets long from a Berlin neurologist about the *Betrachtungen*; humanely and intellectually probably more penetrating and passionate than anything that has been written to me concerning these matters.—Letter from the Frankfurt bookseller Niderlechner.— I want to look over the hunting chapter from *A Man and His Dog* before I read it for the students.

(*12:00 midnight.*) Early supper. Then went to the "Neues Theater," where Professor Kutscher and his students had gathered in the reading room on the top floor. Hatzfeld and Brandenburg were the only people I knew. Opposite me was an elderly gentleman in uniform, a doctor if I am not mistaken. Read the hunting chapter, *légèrement.* Hearty applause. Kutscher made a speech in my honor, concluding with a request that the audience express its thanks with a standing ovation. Inscribed the guest book, sat around for a time, and left at half past ten. Took the tram home, where I looked in on Katia. The children still up, having just come from a concert. Had a snack.—Have given up reading Balzac again; too much ado about society. In the evenings, am reading *Martin Salander*, which I scarcely know.

Friday, July 4 (evening)

Wrote my testimonial for Toller's play that I read last night. Overburdened with letters. Furious at the outrageous behavior of the housemaids. Depressed, tired.

Saturday, July 5 (evening)

After a stretch of very cool, in fact downright cold weather, suddenly today is sultry, summery. In the morning, wrote to the Berlin neurologist in order to catch my breath. I am suffocating from all the letters I owe, my nerves being destroyed by the world's pressures and importunities. I'll also have to say something about Keller for Zurich.—Walk in the sultriness. Afternoon nap in the garden. For tea, Klaus Pringsheim and family, who arrived at Arcisstrasse yesterday. Thunderstorm, which cooled things off somewhat. Read diligently all day in Spengler's book, which elicits my astonishment and admiration.—In the morning Katia fended off a youth who wished to enlist me for his magazine "for surmounting class conflict." I brusquely turned away another on the telephone. Ernst Bischoff of the Berlin Foreign Office wants to see me "semi-officially." Correspondence, public and private demands are piling up. If I go out a few evenings in a row and get to bed late I become desperate.

Sunday, July 6 (evening)

Very warm. Went further through the third chapter and incorporated much of the old manuscript. Read Spengler in the park. Very tired, depressed, and under the weather. Spent the afternoon in the garden. Frail. Katia with the children to Arcisstrasse, where they played music for eight hands, which I would have liked to hear. But my desire to participate in anything stands at about zero, my unsociability is enormous. After tea, wrote to Alberts and Bertram. Then sauntered about outside, since the threatened thunderstorm had receded. The trip to the seashore recognized as a necessity and much on my mind. At supper Katia told about a visit her brother paid to Harden. Harden again complained bitterly about my standoffishness, and mentioned as a certainty that I would be elected to the literary section of the Berlin Academy of Arts along with Hauptmann, Dehmel, and Kerr (drama, poetry, and criticism). Curious. It would be interesting, and at the same time it evokes thoughts of death. Moreover, Kerr will manage to block it. The case of Heinrich is very odd. Once again his hour has passed, in spite of his Odeon eulogy for Eisner. But ever since I read about Haenisch's plan I have been considering whether I should not refuse in Heinrich's favor, i.e. accept only on condition of his being admitted simultaneously.—Reading Spengler.

Wednesday, July 9

Rain and thunderstorms these days. I was much under the weather, inclined to head-aches and heart palpitations. Forced myself to produce a letter about Keller for the *Neue Zürcher Zeitung.* Klaus Pringsheim and his wife had supper with us last night. Katia and I at Arcisstrasse for tea today, where there was a great deal of talk about their son's fateful deficiencies. Fischer's letter from Glücksburg came today; I am expected there, and am beginning to make my preparations. The trip is problematical, but I am going to take it.—Katia highly vexed and disgusted with the housemaids, reactions that I shared. She does not look well, worries me, urgently needs a vacation too, but is indispensable here.—The Academy affair seems to have fallen by the wayside already, owing to a refusal and warning issued by Dehmel, who is already frail. So be it! Continued with Spengler, an intellectual "novel" of the first rank. The artistic element all very exaggerated, systematic, and arbitrary, but everywhere brilliant and fascinating. The paragraphs on Michelangelo, for example, are for me something like an introduction to the art of painting. Along with this, before going to sleep, have been reading *Salander*, which in turn piques my appetite for *Der grüne Heinrich*.— Read in the *Frankfurter Zeitung* an interesting article on Don Carlos of Spain, referring to a book that I intend to order.—Discussion of the "trial" of Wilhelm II continues; locally also about that of Mühsam and his comrades. The jargon-ridden politician's tone of the man repels me.

Thursday, July 24; Glücksburg, Strandhotel (afternoon)

On the birthday of my poor little Katia, whom I love just as I love my six children, I am again making an entry. I have been here since early Tuesday, the 15th. Stayed over Sunday in Berlin, where I went to tea at Frau Rosenberg's in the Tiergartenstrasse and remained for a good supper, shared by two young people who also live in the house, one a student, the other in the Foreign Office. Next morning shared a cab to the Lehrte station. Extremely time-consuming departure and journey in an over-crowded train to Hamburg (including my getting off by mistake in Wittenberge). From Hamburg a seven-hour ride in a local train, which I managed to survive some-how, to Flensburg, where I went directly to the station hotel and spent the night. Came here by steamer early next morning. Cordial welcome by the Fischers, who had been expecting me on Monday. Before they met me, renewed my acquaintance with Herr Satz; after thirty-five years as I figure it. "At that time the hotel was managed by a Herr Satz."—"He stands before you!" Inquired after "Hanni," whose eyes of those days I think I recognize dimly in his otherwise ugly sisters, and who was here for one day himself, a black-bearded man. He has been a businessman in Hamburg, but owns a house here and wishes to return home to live. It is all quite strange. In addition there are the air, the scents, the colors, the dialect, the physical type of the people. Tonio Kröger, Tonio Kröger. It is the same every time, and the emotion deep. The Kirsten shipbuilding family from Hamburg with their two sons in wide trousers, one of them with a head like Armin Martens's.

The former naval officer Schellong, a Gerhart Hauptmann type. His wife sarcastic, North German, anemic; a touch of Lula. The children's nursemaid pretty; Hamburg with a dash of overseas. Lovely sail on the Förde with Schellong, Frau Fischer, and Tutti. Went to the clubroom in the Kurhaus as guests of the rather suspect, somewhat stupid Baron Schenk, who wears an air of melancholic bachelordom. Kirstens = Hans Castorp.—Swam in the ocean three times. Long letters to Katia, who forwarded the mail. Sent her a cake. Disposed of other essential mail with many postcards. Moved from a rear room with a balcony looking over the garden into one in front, this one facing the small beach, the front yard with tables, and the ladies' bathhouse. Went with the Fischers into Flensburg this morning. Sent Katia another cake and bought her cocoa. Gave Tutti Fischer a pocket knife. We returned in the rain on the over-crowded steamer in time for luncheon.—Rum toddy, the rum in a small bottle, with a heated glass and hot water to be mixed to taste. The weather variable; much rain, always damp, continually cool, even cold. In the evenings there is sometimes reading aloud in the Fischers' room. I read a legend-like novella of Reisiger's, a problematic work, to great praise. Fischer a good man; his wife often shows a bad streak of obstinate stupidity. Their little girl touches my paternal feelings. Tutti as pleasure-loving as Erika, decent and kind so far as I can judge. The days have passed quite rapidly. The food is simple but wonderful, with an unpretentious solidity, so tasty that one is at first truly astonished. Mother Satz, the good Frisian woman, is interested in "poets." Copied excerpts from her poetry scrapbook for me.—Yesterday finished the first volume of Spengler's opus with intense interest. The most important book!

. . . .
Thursday, July 31; Glücksburg
. . . .

[. . .] Wrote in Tutti Fischer's album this morning. Satisfactorily, I felt. Letter from Frank. Registered letter from Katia with all sorts of enclosures concerning the *Betrachtungen* and other matters. Peter Pringsheim back from Australia after a forty-eight-hour rail trip at government expense. The sea voyage frightful because of influenza. Twenty dead thrown overboard without the ship's even stopping. He himself in good condition, tanned, otherwise hardly changed; nationalistic and "reactionary" in his thinking, like all those outside the country. His parents, Katia, and the four children at the station with flowers. I am sorry I missed it. Wired warm greetings yesterday.— It appears that I will be changing rooms once more day after tomorrow, moving up to the fourth floor and somewhat extending my stay. Am continuing to read Keyserling. The weather continues cloudy, strong southwest winds with occasional glimpses of sunlight. Today I went swimming again out of love for the sea and the purity of it. But I shivered, and the churning water was full of seaweed and jellyfish. In the afternoon, chocolate at Bethien's and a second inspection of the house and garden that Fischer has his eye on. For dinner, large tender steaks with potatoes, then cold roast, sausage, and hardboiled eggs in addition. Late visit to the Schellongs, in the garden. Before supper sat on the beach. Early end to the day. Bored. I constantly watch with yearning the Kirstens, who own large properties here. Today saw the young people playing ball on their sweeping lawn. [. . .]

. . . .
Monday, August 4; Glücksburg
. . . .

Last night simultaneous games of roulette and dominos in the dining room. Afterward Frau Fischer sang Brahms and Wolf in a well-trained voice. Up later today. Had the barber come, then breakfasted with the others. The Fischers' daughter has recovered. On our walk together in Glücksburg I bought her a doll she had taken a liking to. Letter from Monika. Card from Walter, and telegram from the Excelsior confirming room reservation.—The storm persisits, but the wind seems more favorable, and there have been many sunny intervals. When I came up from luncheon I found the chambermaid still cleaning. She left, and when she returned she brought a telegram, forwarded from Munich, for which there was an additional charge of three marks. Litzmann in Bonn informing me, already on the 28th, that the philosophical faculty has awarded me with an honorary doctorate on the occasion of the university's centenary. I had the bellboy send off a telegram of thanks, and am making no effort to conceal my pleasure. We went to the Ruhetal for tea, in the course of which I told Fischer about the telegram. Jollity and much use of my new title. Plans for celebrating with champagne. We drank chocolate in the garden and walked home by a roundabout way through the delightful countryside. I get along well with Flake, who is a good young fellow. This morning I went for a walk with him alone, and we discussed the obligatory questions of the times in a friendly way and with kindred feeling. For this evening we have been invited to the Schellongs for a tea punch. The socialist Breit-scheid will be there.

Friday, August 15 (evening)

Holiday. Assumption. The fine weather continues, but somewhere there must have been a thunderstorm, for it was cooler.—Continued to revise the fourth chapter; the Pribislav episode is good.—Walk. In the garden during the afternoon. Bertram for tea with Glöckner, who kept calling me "Herr Doktor" with delight and great formality. He talked about the gathering of the George circle in Heidelberg, the strongest impression of his life. About George and Platen. The latter, I remarked, wholly lacking in the sacerdotal manner and without pretensions of being anything but an "intinerant rhapsodist." Political matters: the impending famine in Europe, in Germany first of all. Only a question of months before we will be unable to pay for the importation of foodstuffs. But the masses will no longer want to work elsewhere either. I said that it is a matter of attitudes. The world no longer wants all of that, is casting it away. We spoke of Hamsun, the Nobel Prize winner, and his novel of the soil as a worldwide symptom.—Evening walk with Katia, who loves me dearly and to whom I am infinitely grateful.—Read Keyserling, skipping somewhat.

Sunday, August 24

Another fine day yesterday, fresher. Katia sent a special-delivery letter about bread, which is in short supply. Gave instructions about a package for her. Much correspondence afternoon and evening. Stomach not in order. Today a change of weather, rainy but warm. Katia telephoned. She is "unwell"; that is one less thing to worry about. Wrote away on *The Magic Mountain*, a new section, not feeling well. For dinner to Arcisstrasse, where I gave Peter Pringsheim a copy of the *Betrachtungen*. Napped in the piano room and stayed to tea, to which C. von Pidoll had been invited. Music afterward: *Meistersinger*. Darkness of impending thunderstorm. Felt very odd, seriously suspected appendicitis; miss Loeb, wondered what other doctor to turn to. Thoughts of death; morbid, sensitive mood. Left at seven o'clock and, since the rain had let up, walked home from the Max Monument, which rather did me good. Went to see the children, spent some time at little Lisa's bedside, since she was still awake. Deep affection and great tenderness.

Saturday, September 13

To the Löhrs' for supper yesterday evening. Jof keenly aware of the importance of the honorary doctorate from Bonn University, and he impressed it upon me. Overwhelmingly tired. Slept after brief reading in *Martin Salander* with the chaise longue pillow under my back, and found myself in the same position when I first awoke at six o'clock.—Short, hot days. The sun is fierce, but night falls before seven, though today nightfall brought scarcely any cooling relief. Went for a brief stroll into the park in the darkness. The promenade and the path along the river are disfigured by a small railroad track being used in construction work on the "Central Isar."—Today introduced the phenomenon of simultaneous daylight and moonlight into *The Magic Mountain*. Horrible letter from that frightful "Jane" Mann; I passed it on to Lula, disavowing any connection with her. Congratulations from Paul Ehrenberg, which touched me. I loved him, and [it] was something akin to requited love. . . . In the afternoon began reading the second volume of Blüher's *Rolle der Erotik in der männlichen Gesellschaft*.—Katia has made an appointment for our neighbor, Dr. Hermanns, to have a look at me.—The baby Lisa touching when she says "porridge" and "baba." Erika and Klaus pleasant and charming.

· ·
Monday, September 15
· ·

Yesterday Bertram for tea and supper. I read to him from the third chapter of *The Magic Mountain*. Friday, will be going with him and Glöckner to hear *Parsifal*. Evening thunderstorm. Very warm again today. Proofs of the Fischer edition of *A Man and His Dog*. After dinner yesterday, over black coffee and liqueurs, visit from Frau von Térey; today from G. Hermann, the author of *Jettchen Gebert*. This afternoon Dr. Hermanns, who examined me and stayed for a late tea. He diagnosed affection of the vagus nerve, wants to undertake a metabolism test, recommends some kind of sport such as fishing. Might well do as a family doctor. Read the *Neue Merkur* and the newspapers. The coup of that silly Garibaldi imitator and buffoon D'Annunzio in Fiume.

· ·
Wednesday, September 17
· ·

Morning occupied with the *Magic Mountain* manuscript. At 10:15 into town in glorious weather. Had a shave, bought throat lozenges, and proceeded to Jaffe's, where I inaugurated the new reading room by reading from *The Magic Mountain*. Read the third chapter in rapid tempo, from the breakfast to the Settembrini scene, amusing the audience greatly. The reading met with decided success, which made me very glad and restored my appetite and courage for the whole enterprise, which is after all distinctly outmoded. Present: Bertram and Glöckner, Katia, Dr. Mannheimer, Eliasberg, Hoerschelmann, Frau Godwin, among others. I also talked with several strangers, among them a doctor who knows Davos as a patient. Jaffe rapturous. Katia and I headed home on foot with Bertram and Glöckner in summery warmth, cutting through the Englischer Garten after taking leave of them.—Restive in the afternoon. Sent the Pfitzner speech to Cossmann. Went walking in the dark. In the evening read Blüher. One-sided, but true. As for myself there is no doubt in my mind that "even" the *Betrachtungen* are an expression of my sexual inversion.

· ·
Friday, September 19
· ·

Five o'clock at the Prinzregenten-Theater: *Parsifal* with Bertram and Glöckner. Center seats. Extremely powerful impression: emotion, admiration, and the usual intrigued mistrust. Never was a work of art so naively contrived a product, a compound of religious impulse, sheer lasciviousness, and sure-handed competence that comes across as wisdom. The aura of sickness: I feel "hopelessly at home" in it, I said to Bertram. Whereupon both of us, as if speaking with one voice, exclaimed: "Why of course, it's *The Magic Mountain*."—The two friends walked me home in a light rain.

Sunday, September 21

Very cool, rainy. Went walking in my slicker at midday. After tea, read some of the proofs for the Fischer edition of "Bauschan." Continued reading *St. Petersburg* in the evening. Mannered and bizarre.—Katia reported her brother Peter's having said at home that we have an "ideal marriage". . . .

Tuesday, October 21

Beginning September 29, two-week stay in Feldafing, mostly alone with the housekeeper Piokarska since Richter is off traveling; food excellent, worked on *The Magic Mountain*, feeling tranquil, though at times the solitude seemed unreal. Visits from Ponten and Professor Uhde-Bernays. With Richter I visited the architect Behr, his Budapest wife and siblings. Enviable property by the lake near Tutzing. Eskimo dog, white, that howled; I found him very funny. Behr an original type, who as an interior decorator has traveled abroad a great deal working in great houses and at royal courts, and has made a lot of money. Large collection of antiques. Sailing with Richter; outing to Ammerland with one of the women friends always around him. Returned to Munich on Saturday of the second week with some pages of new manuscript, finding the house completely unheatable in the intense cold. Only managed by wearing the quilted vest and my bathrobe. Then iron stoves were delivered. My room disfigured by the huge pipe.—Heaps of mail, extremely busy. Official induction, perforce, into the "Citizens' Guard," to which I donated 100 marks.—With Katia to the Kammerspiele; alone to the Goethe Society at Jaffe's, where Count H. Keyserling spoke. Next afternoon he visited us with his wife, a granddaughter of Bismarck's, gluttonous and talkative.— Learned that next time Bertram is to speak on the *Betrachtungen*.—Privy Councillor Clemen sent his two-volume illustrated book dealing with the Germans' protection of works of art in Belgium etc.; he also commented on the *Betrachtungen*.—Many proofs to read: Pfitzner speech, the *Palestrina* essay in brochure form, the "School Sickness." The conclusion of the Fontane essay had to be revised for Fischer's Fontane book. While still in Feldafing I attempted to make some drastic cuts in the "baptism" in *Gesang vom Kindchen* with moral support from Richter, which is something I need when cutting. Improved. It seems to me that I have removed the embarrassing aspects, that the whole is better rounded out. In suspense about the reception of the little book.—In Feldafing I finished reading *St. Petersburg*, then *Jungfräulichkeit*, a work of Ponten's youth. I began Strindberg's *By the Open Sea* (brilliant and horribly uncongenial) and finished it here. In the past few days have read Ponten's *Der Bockreiter*. Very good. Am pleased that the publishers have used my praise of Sinclair and Ponten.—Cold autumnal weather; sleet, fog, little sun. Stowed away the coal bought at an outrageous price from "de Bertol."—Pleasant work on *The Magic Mountain*; am approaching the examination. The scene with the directress mysteriously obscene. "Mercurius" amused me.—In politics, the Baltic affair, the Entente's outrageous request that Germany participate in the blockade of Russia. Grotesque, cynical. The whole thing is such a farce; I prize my head and my heart too much to devote thought to it. The value of the mark is still sinking in foreign exchange. On the other hand it is said that economic morale shows signs of recovery.—Day before yesterday, visit from Hatzfeld. The Kestner Society wants *more* of *The Confidence Man.*—Today distinctly unwell; undone by chest powder and freshly baked bread. Flatulence and heartburn at night. Ill, discomfited, and without appetite. In the morning had only tea and one zwieback, and did not attempt to work.

Thursday, November 6

Warmer. Rain and wind. In town, bought among other errands a wedding present for Eva Bernstein and Klaus Hauptmann, a ruby-glass vase that I had filled with chrysanthemums. Ordered a pair of boots from Henneberger for about 280 marks.—Very calm and polite reply from Fabricius; gratifying. Tickets for Dr. Freytag's premiere tomorrow. Did not go out again. Frank here for supper, who earnestly warned me that Guenther is an outrageous swindler. Conversation about Spengler and Schopenhauer, about theater, the spread of anti-Semitism, etc. Stimulated. In the newspapers, editorial comment on the projected ten-percent surtax on intellectual vocations. Can hardly believe it. Is the workers' republic a form of the culture state? Problem.—After Frank left, ugly incident with Katia concerning another thousand marks for one of her brothers. After mild objections on my part about such large expenditures, she brought up the hated Feldafing-Richter matter, and, on learning from me that Richter had declared our down payment of 10,000 marks to the tax office, flew into a rage. She was as angry with me as with him, and probably rightly so, for I had received this information from Richter without giving it a second thought, accepting it as an accomplished fact, without even considering or for that matter knowing that Katia had failed to declare the payment herself, so that now we may well have trouble with the authorities. Still, Katia's anger can be traced to the weak condition of her nerves, which was demonstrated by the fact that she reproached me for my recklessness in the Richter affair as opposed to the difficulties I was making about the loan to her brother. Lamentable incident. Depressed and shaken. It is quite clear that Richter acted selfishly and ruthlessly to the point of impropriety. We will have to take steps to extricate ourselves from the Feldafing involvement. Even the business with the art works seemed fundamentally wrong to me and not something for me to get mixed up in, for it does not become me to allow myself to be drawn into the Bachstitz orbit in which Richter lives and breathes. I suspect, by the way, that Richter regards the publication of the deluxe edition of *Little Herr Friedemann*, for which according to his statement my fee is to come to roughly 4,000 marks, as a kind of return favor and compensation for his exploitation of me in other business matters. I must consider this further, so as not to be over-hasty in either my actions or my words.

Friday, November 14

Frost. The central heating turned on; pleasant and comforting. Finished the fourth chapter of *The Magic Mountain*, with the examination scene and Castorp's admission.

At noon, visit from a hard-of-hearing artist from Hamburg who sketched a portrait of me, not much of a likeness. Did not go out until evening. After tea and again after supper, read all the newly written material to Katia. Settembrini's doctrines questionable in the artistic framework. But they are also questionable intellectually speaking, because, though not taken seriously, they are the only positive element morally, the only counterpoise to the vice of death. On the other hand, the novel's intellectual humor is based on this contrast between the mystique of the flesh and political virtue. Incidentally, I admit to myself that I have now brought the book to the same point at which *The Confidence Man* came to a halt, and not by chance. Actually I have emptied my bag. Fiction must now take over. *Incipit ingenium.*—Good critical letter from Professor Boll in Heidelberg on Spengler. Enthusiastic letter from Judge Friedmann about the *Gesang vom Kindchen*, the earlier edition. Tickets sent by the dancer Edith von Schrenck and by Wandrey.

Sunday, November 23

Yesterday, while I was at the opera, the premiere of Heinrich's *Brabach* took place at the Residenz-Theater. During breakfast today Katia's mother reported on it by telephone. Enough.—At eleven o'clock took the No. 30 tram, whose runs are soon to be suspended in the face of outraged opposition, to Jaffe's, where Spengler gave a talk on Goethe as thinker. He spoke in a rigorously schematic manner that exposes the strong strain of modern sentimentality within his "platonic" aspirations. Overcrowded auditorium. I talked to the Bruckmanns, Von der Leyen, the Hattingbergs, and Seif. Left with Endres and his brother, the prosecutor, walking in the rain. Outside the Feldherrenhalle, a demonstration of nationalistic students. Songs and cheers. While I was listening to Spengler, Katia was at Oestvig's Wagner matinee with the two oldest. The crowd nearly tore him to pieces. The poor boy gave encores to the point of total hoarseness.—Very tired, slept in the afternoon. Tea in Katia's bedroom. Afterward, visit from two gentlemen and two ladies, a deputation from the Society for Artistic Culture, offering me an honorary membership. I suppose it can be accepted. Wrote to Hofmiller, Preetorius, the Goldenbergs, etc. Walked only as far as the mailbox. Warm wind, rain. In the evening began reading Kassner's *Zahl und Gesicht.*—Have decided to say no to the invitation to Vienna. Cannot impose that on myself now, especially if I am even to consider going to Switzerland.

Tuesday, November 25

Sexual excess, but although the nervous excitement long delayed sleep, it has proved intellectually rather more beneficial than otherwise.—Continued with the Fontane book (on *Effi Briest*). Went for a walk. Slept in the afternoon. Katia at Arcisstrasse. Definitely canceled the Vienna visit and felt relieved. Also wrote to Viereck in New York, among others. Walked for a while in the evening.—Heinrich has written Mama that he now has many enemies in Munich, hence the hissing, but that there was also "impassioned" applause requiring "fifteen" curtain calls. Horrible. His friendship with that wretched Elchinger, which has netted him a crawlingly deferential notice in the *Nachrichten*. Horrible.—In the evening, read three chapters of Hofmannsthal's *Frau ohne Schatten*. It must be strange and voluptuous to fantasize like that, and the desire and courage to do so does not exactly point to sterile exhaustion. Something heartening about it for me.—Ready for my bath.

- -
Thursday, December 4; Vienna
- -

Rose at 8:30 and stayed in my room until nearly noon. Rainy weather that later cleared. After breakfast wrote Bertram. S. Trebitsch sent his new book and later telephoned to invite me for luncheon tomorrow. On the whole the invitations so far have not been accumulating as I was told they would, whereas the Walters declare that they are "overbooked."—Walked a little, went into St. Stephan's where there was organ music, then headed toward the Stadtpark. Ate luncheon at one o'clock in a modest and likable restaurant next to the Hotel Tegethoff for 35 kronen. Returned to the Imperial and rested badly; too nervous. Telegram from Katia about her own and Eri's recovery. I dictated a telegram telling of my arrival yesterday to Heller's secretary.—Ordered tea at four o'clock, but it never arrived. Ate a sandwich, and at half past four went to the rehearsal, which dragged on until after nine. In the course of it I went back to the hotel once more to telephone Trebitsch. I have to cancel tomorrow's engagement on account of the dress rehearsal, which begins at 10:30 in the morning, after which I am to dine with Frau Direktor Baumfeldt, the pretty Jewess with the Japanese eyes whose acquaintance I made in Heller's office, and Dr. Rosenthal.—The play, or rather the perfomance, tormented me of course as always, but still it stirred me in that it recalled to me many inner experiences of that time. I had the feeling that even then I was developing the *Betrachtungen* and the conflict with Heinrich. And in fact the work is not lacking in contemporary relevance. None of the actors is bad, nor is any one of them particularly good. The Giovanni, something of a Moissi imitator, is not without charm; in street clothes (uniform), by the way, more than in costume. Frau Wagner doesn't know what to make of the symbol of Fiore, which gives me a guilty conscience. The length of the thing threatens to be catastrophic. They never got to the end of the third act because Onno had changed clothes and left so as not to miss the last tram to Hietzing. In Lorenzo's dressing room, made new cuts with Rosenthal that further distort the whole. The opening performance is scheduled to begin at five. Returned to the hotel pretty well unnerved. Had a supper of a sandwich, sausage, and smoked meat without anything to drink. For the sake of the producers and the actors, who admire the work with the simplicity of theater people, I hope that the fiasco will prove relatively mild. As for my own feelings, it is clear that nothing could have been more unnecessary or misguided than this trip; I should have followed my better judgment and stayed at home. A waste of money, time, and nerves; things would have to take a miraculous turn before I could change my mind about this.

- -
Friday, December 5; Vienna
- -

Extremely out of sorts this morning. Room service not functioning, felt neglected and poorly treated. The rest of the day I was kept fairly breathless. Went to the dress rehearsal at 10:30. Was handed a letter from Musil. Was sketched for the *Morgen*, etc. Moved to see the dedication and faith the directors and the actors bring to the play. The sets attractive, none of the actors bad. The second act may give pleasure. But the length, the length of the thing! The new cuts, which Klitsch (Lorenzo) studied until four in the morning, make very little difference. Once more it will be a tiresome *succès d'estime*. The rehearsal ended about three. Went with Rosenthal to Dr. Baumfeldt's, where luncheon was nearly over. Engaging man, charming wife. Very good meal with coffee and liqueurs. Accompanied by Rosenthal back to the hotel, where I discovered all sorts of mail and rested a bit. At around six went to tea at Heller's in the Kohlmarkt, where there were hordes of people. Auernheimers, Ginzkey. The one-armed Wittgenstein played. The Walters. Reunion with the ladies I traveled with from Salzburg to Vienna. Afterward went with the Walters, Spieglers, and others to a café. From there to see the Hofmannsthals in their attractive mansard pied à terre. The ladies not there as they were off at the opera. Conversation with Hofmannsthal on the window seat in the stairwell. Then supper in the studio with him, his wife, his daughter, and Müller-Hofmann. To bed at eleven.

Saturday, December 6; Vienna

After breakfast a visit from the journalist and Concordia man Löwy. I let him persuade me to stay and lecture on the 11th, since on the 12th I will have an express connection by way of Passau-Regensburg. Visits from Musil (about the magazine) and O. Brüll. Nervous, harried. Am waiting for Trebitsch, hoping he will have a calming effect.— Half-hour tram ride out to Hietzing (Schönbrunn) and luncheon with Jacobson in the elegant Trebitsch home. Rode back with Jacobson. At the hotel, shaved and dressed.— Just before five to my box in the theater. Excellent production, though the first act was disturbed by many late-comers. Sense of great goodwill on the part of the audience; there were already calls for the author after the second act, but I remained in my box because I didn't know the way to the stage. At the end, full, warm applause and many curtain calls for me, both with the actors and alone. Elation, congratulations. Thanks to the actors. The charming little Steinböck delighted by his success as Vannino. Dinner at a restaurant with a large group. I drafted a telegram to Katia and entrusted it to Heller. By cab with the Hellers to Dr. Baumfeldt's, where the same group was assembled. Cake, wine, tea, liqueurs. Sat next to Frau Wagner (Fiore). Frau Rosar of the Burgtheater. The French friend who asked for the play for Paris; extremely impressed. At half past eleven, left with the Hellers and Frau Wagner, with whom I chatted on the way.—At the end of the second act, which turned out especially well, I had vivid memories of the time in Utting before my engagement, when I was staying alone with Mama and writing the last scene, so pleased with the ending that I inscribed it specially into my journal in violet ink.—Relaxation and contentment.

Sunday, December 7; Vienna

Slept restlessly. After breakfast called up the Walters and met them in the hotel café, along with a lady I did not know, a friend of Mahler's. Through the Walters was invited to luncheon at Karpath's, the music critic's. Visit from Albert Heine (Burgtheater) whom I went to meet in the lobby. Walter continued talking with Heine, as I had a visit from Dr. R. Strauss, a likable man who sat with me for quite some time.—Read the *Neue Freie Presse* with the announcement of my forthcoming reading; dawdled. Then met Walters again in the lobby and together we went to Karpath's, a bachelor who keeps a good table—insofar as such a thing is possible here these days. Turkish coffee and liqueurs. Talk of musical life. I was treated with great deference. At the end Walter sat down at the Bösendorfer and played Viennese waltzes. Back at the hotel I rested on the chaise longue, changed, and went out to a coffeehouse, where I had a very expensive cup of hot chocolate and a pastry and felt uncomfortable. Walked a bit, and after seven made my way to the theater, where I went backstage and greeted Frau Wagner and little Steinböck, who wants me to inscribe something into his copy of *Fiorenza*. Took a seat out front and watched from the scenes between Fiore and Lorenzo to the end, especially interested by the conversation between Lorenzo and Savonarola, and captivated by the latter's vision ("Am I chosen"), which Klitsch spoke very well. Many empty seats in the theater; ticket prices too high. Rosenthal assured me that the house will be full again by tomorrow; Sunday bad for attendance. Moreover it seems that the Volkstheater seriously intends to continue the run. At the end I went backstage again and took several bows with the actors and by myself, people shouting their praise. Then went with Rosenthal, a pleasant but highly nervous man, to Gause's, where I had a bit to eat. We talked about the theater and about things that seem to be the wave of the future: astrology, physiognomy, graphology. Back to the hotel at 9:30, where the desk clerk delivered to me Musil's collection of novellas, *Vereinigungen*, inscribed with a quotation from *Death in Venice* as a dedication.

. . . .

Monday, December 8; Vienna

. . . .

After breakfast wrote to Musil. Called Schnitzler, whose unlisted number I had got from Rosenthal, and arranged to have dinner with him on Wednesday. Letter from Specht, informing me that he will be bringing his "life's companion" with him tomorrow. A copy of *Fiorenza* arrived, probably from Steinböck.—Fine sunny weather.— I am counting the days, for I am constantly on edge. The waste of time and the return trip make me anxious.—Decided to send copies of *A Man and His Dog* to Klitsch, Onno, Frau Wagner, and Steinböck, as well as to Rosenthal.—Went out to the Hellers'. They had asked me to come, and strongly urged me to repeat my reading on Sunday, this time in the large hall of the Musikverein. I was nearly persuaded. Attended Mass at the cathedral afterward, then went to Gause's restaurant, where I ran into the Walters. We had a pleasant meal together; I particularly liked the rice pudding with chocolate sauce. Chatted about theatrical matters and personal ones, health. Back to the hotel, where a charming letter from Steinböck awaited me, and a copy of *Tristan* for autographing. Rested a bit. Then over to the Musikverein to look at the large auditorium (through the greenroom into the director's box); an imposing hall, very striking, richly gilt, accommodating roughly 2,000. I immediately decided not to read in it. Arrived a bit late. Then sat next to Frau Walter and Frau Heller, greeted Dr. Rosenthal. Firmly declined a second reading in that en rmous hall. Walter and Rosé gave a remarkably beautiful performance of the *Kreutzer* Sonata. The huge audience very responsive. There followed the Brahms Horn Trio with its romantic atmosphere. Spoke with Rosé outside, also with his wife and son, an admirer of mine who also hopes to be a musician. Then to the Akademie-Theater—by various byways as I had lost my bearings somewhat—where I stood to watch the second act. It seemed to me that the production was beginning to slide; flubbed lines, some ad-libbing, a general coarsening. However the house was full and attentive.—Back to the hotel, freshened up, then with the Walters to Spieglers'. Pleasant evening. The cellist Buxbaum; marvelous comic. Much laughter. His wife had been to *Fiorenza*. Oestvig had also been at the theater and phoned Walter about it. Good food. Red wine and cigars. Left late. After one by the time I got to bed.

Tuesday, December 9; Vienna

After breakfast wrote something in little Steinböck's script and caught up with these notes for yesterday. Heller telephoned: yesterday's performance a tremendous success, ticket sales also, the house really sold. Definitely declined the Musikverein reading and made reservations for Saturday via Salzburg.—Visit from Müller-Hofmann, with whom I spoke on Hofmannsthal's behalf about the magazine.—Then a visit from the young writer Marilaun.—Shaved between calls.—At noon Müller-Hofmann returned to take me to the Hofmuseum. Brueghel! Velazquez! Vermeer! The Velazquez portrait of the Infanta reminded me of little Elisabeth. The Brueghels most impressive. A great narrator. The purposiveness, precision, the human density and variety filling every corner, together with the scurrilous and the grotesque, the pervasive uncanniness— how could I not stand in awe!—Back to the hotel. Rosenthal telephoned and invited me to the Baumfeldts' for this evening. Repeated that with yesterday's full house the mood had been superb. He was sorry I was not there.—Specht and his lady friend were waiting for me in the hotel dining room, although I had intended to go out somewhere with them. We ate, talking about music and the *Betrachtungen*, for 67 kronen per person, without soup, and I paid only for myself. I felt justified in doing so since he had brought his companion of his own accord, but still it was possibly shabby of me.—In my room, a telephone call from Heller, who had Rosenthal with him. The reading is now to be repeated on Friday afternoon in the middle-sized concert hall under the auspices of the Urania Society, and my extra expenses will be covered. Pleased to have something to do on Friday. Thinking of reading the *Kindchen* before a more intimate group on Thursday.—Napped from four to five, nervously as usual. Then had tea and rum and some pastries sent up. Went out and walked for an hour along the Ringstrasse for the air and the exercise. Bought a chocolate bar for 37 kronen. Passed the Burgtheater, which I will attend tomorrow perhaps. Changed at the hotel and went down to the lobby. It was full of Italian officers and lit by open flames in hanging metal vessels that had to be refueled with some sort of fluid. Waited for Rosenthal, who took me to Baumfeldts'. Dinner in the salon with only the few of us. The lighting is always very subdued, as there are penalties for consuming too much electricity. People therefore confine themselves to one or two rooms, with a candle here or a lamp there for illumination. Talked about *Fiorenza* (which Klitsch and Onno would cheerfully perform every evening) and about theater in general. Our host has written a play about the stock market. The relationship between literary social criticism and democracy.—Very good steaks, pastry horns with poppyseed filling, good bittersweet liqueur, imported cigars. Once more there was talk of holding the second reading on Sunday evening in the large hall of the Musikverein, but I hope nothing comes of it, for I am extremely anxious to leave. The party ended at eleven. Rosenthal saw me back to the hotel, a quite likable man. Read newspapers in bed.

Yesterday evening when I returned to the hotel I met the Walters in the lobby, along with the singer Dr. Schipper, who had just arrived. He had been charged 15 kronen for a cup of tea, and was full of indignation at Vienna. The Walters left early this morning for Berlin; I said good-bye to them last night.—The *Neue Freie Presse* is now brought to me each morning, and today it contains a lengthy article by Auernheimer about *Fiorenza*; good on its contemporary relevance, but lacking insight into its poetry. Yesterday Rosenthal and I discussed the plan of publishing a shortened performing version of *Fiorenza*.—Heller phoned about the programs. Tomorrow: *Kindchen* and *The Confidence Man*. Friday: *The Magic Mountain*.—Letter from Löwy, very flattering.—Telegram from Katia: wishes me well, everything all right at home. Bertram will be in Munich until the 17th.—Visit from a Dr. Leo Stein of the *Neues Wiener Tagblatt*. A pleasant young man of German-Bohemian background; we talked about political and cultural matters. He tells me there is a virtual epidemic of syphilis in Vienna.—Heller phoned again to invite me for tomorrow. A portraitist has made an appointment for tomorrow noon.—Wrote to Fischer (about the performing edition) and to Auernheimer.—At 12:30 took the Ringstrasse tram and the No. 40 out to the villa section and Sternwartstrasse, where Schnitzler lives. At first alone with him in his study; later joined by his wife, son, and little daughter. Salten arrived for dessert. Then came Beer-Hofmann and his wife and a Dr. Kaufmann, a philosopher. Was told many nice things about "Bauschan" and the *Betrachtungen*. Spoke with Beer-Hofmann about his *Jacob's Dream*. Much talk of politics and related issues, with Salten expressing deep bitterness concerning the revolutionaries and the present government. Also talk about the fate of Wilhelm II. About psychic pain. Had tea at five. Then left with Beer-Hofmann and took the No. 41 tram to the Burgtheater, where Schnitzler had arranged to have a ticket waiting for me with the stage doorkeeper. I wanted to see Heine playing the Pope in Müller's Galileo drama. The play somewhat coarse but effective, the production good. Schott, who plays my Piero de Medici, played a young prelate. Engaging delivery and appearance of the actor who played the young Milton in the last act. Beautiful theater, music between the acts. Came somewhat late, but was let in. Afterward walked in cold wind to Gause's, where I had supper for 40 kronen. At the hotel I arranged with the desk clerk for a telephone connection tomorrow. Salten is sending me tickets for his dress rehearsal tomorrow in the Burgtheater. Schnitzler gave me Egyptian cigarettes.

Was bothered during the night by that gum infection. Pressed the button earlier than usual, at eight. The maid and the bellboy very attentive. They came simultaneously, the latter delivering as usual the *Neue Freie Presse*, in which there is a glowing review of yesterday evening's reading. Dressed before breakfast and wrote out something from the *Gesang* in Löwy's artists' album. Also took care of other autographs. Now eager to pay the week's hotel bill that I found in my room last night, no more than I expected, and to begin to get organized for my departure before leaving for the dress rehearsal at the Burgtheater.

Arranged for a car at six tomorrow morning. Walked to the Burgtheater, where I saw many familiar faces without knowing all of their names. Spoke with Frau Rosar,

Trebitsch, Jacobson, the Schnitzlers, various gentlemen from the Concordia, etc. Three one-acts by Salten; pleasant and with an air of genuine experience of life. I deeply enjoyed the acting, slow-moving but polished and professional. Went to Gause's to eat and spent another 40 kronen. Then to the hotel, where I quickly had to shave and change. Found a farewell and thank-you letter from Löwy. After 3:30 to the Musik-verein, the greenroom of the middle-sized hall. Visits from Brüll, then Frau Baumfeldt, the attorney, and Rosenthal. The affair in a way unsuccessful, lacking excitement, at least for me. Restless coming and going in the hall. The reading from *The Magic Mountain* took an hour. I then had to dismiss the audience with only a few words, since the hall was required again for an evening performance. I then had to take repeated bows, called back by a small group of enthusiasts. Wrote a number of autographs, mostly for women, but also for several men. Farewells. Onno came and complimented me on my reading. Was a bit servile toward Frau Baumfeldt. Rosenthal once more accompanied me back to the hotel. Sincere and deeply-felt farewell from him.—Had tea and pastries. Received my passport from Heller and tipped the hand-some young messenger 10 kronen, at which he smiled radiantly. To my annoyance I found I left a portion of the manuscript of *The Confidence Man* in the greenroom; hope I get it back.

Now eager to pack, then plan to have supper with Musil and be up tomorrow at five. Hope to be home by tomorrow evening and thereby conclude my notes on this mad junket.

Monday, December 15; Munich

Saturday morning, without breakfast, taken together with a Russian-Viennese-Munich business director by cab to the Westbahnhof for 160 kronen. Had time for breakfast there, which was to be the only meal of the entire journey, a more strenuous, both-ersome, and tedious day than I had anticipated. Extreme cold, excessive standing in line and waiting, particularly in Salzburg. Local train the rest of the way. Only in the evening did I manage to get a bit of sausage and bread in Rosenheim; until then I had nothing but chocolate. Arrived in Munich close to midnight. Checked my baggage and walked home in cold and fog. Katia already asleep, but got up to welcome me. Ate a generous supper, with tea. Comfort of homecoming. Katia in fairly good health, everything all right with the children. Mountains of mail that I looked through until four in the morning. Then five hours' sleep.

Yesterday, Sunday, went with Katia to the station in the morning by cab to collect my luggage. Extreme cold, but beautiful weather. Unpacked before luncheon. Slept soundly through the afternoon. Bertram came to tea, then the Ludwigs. Evening walk with Bertram, who then stayed for supper. Talked about his mother, who, horror of horrors, is suffering from dog worms, *echinococcus*.—Talked much about my trip during the day.—Considerable mail about *A Man and His Dog*. An amusing letter of tribute from little Hoerschelmann.

Today still very cold. Up at 8:15. Lisa at breakfast. Now sometimes calls me "Tommy." Composed various telegrams.—Strange to sit at one's accustomed place in the clear-minded state of morning and recollect the unreality of travel.—On my study table a bouquet from Frau Dietz for *A Man and His Dog*.—Among the books that have come is Fischer's Fontane book, including my essay that Martens wants to reprint in the paper. Phoned him in the morning and reproached him for failing to mention the

Vienna performances in the *Nachrichten*. Meeting arranged for Thursday. Worked morning and afternoon trying to clear up the accumulation of mail. After lunch a parcel of books newly bound by Göhr, the first such batch in five years. Put them on the shelves, though there was barely room. Took walks at noon and again in the evening; very cold, ground lightly dusted with snow. After supper sat with Katia, and with the help of this diary recounted the Vienna stay day by day. Afterward read some of the proofs for the deluxe edition of *Gesang vom Kindchen*.—A clever commentary on Heinrich by Blei in *Die Rettung*.—Sent 20 kronen to the Hotel Imperial in Vienna for the chambermaid, whom I could not find when I left; the unpaid tip weighed on my conscience.

Wednesday, December 17

Worked hard on the article all morning. Then into town to the telegraph office, to Zechbauer, and to the barber's. After luncheon read the *Süddeutsche Monatshefte*: Count Reventlow on the war and what led up to it. Entirely correct in its way. At tea, Katia's mother, whom I told all about Vienna. Then wrote five letters and took a short stroll outdoors. After supper read, or rather skimmed, Keyserling's new essay *Was uns not tut*. He would accord a dominant role to philosophy in the establishment of a synthesis of mind and spirit. Decidedly astute and true. I am considering writing an open letter to him for Grossmann's magazine.

Friday, December 19

After breakfast occupied myself with Count Keyserling's two short pieces. Then into town to the Progress office where I started dictating the Fontane article. Bought collars at Arnold's, size 39, the 40s having become too large for me. Seven marks fifty apiece. After luncheon read an article by Boy-Ed on the subject of Beethoven's deafness. Also the writings of a privy councillor's son killed in the war. Katia to tea in Arcisstrasse. Wrote three longish letters. Evening walk in snowstorm. (At noon frozen slush in town.) After supper read the *Neue Merkur* (Pannwitz on Hofmannsthal's story) and the *Rundschau* (Kerr on Palestine with all his clever nastiness and "exultant" smugness).—Eliasberg sent a new book of Russian love stories.

Sunday, December 21

Spent the morning correcting the typed manuscript. Then with Katia to the Odeon; Verdi Requiem in a very beautiful performance under Walter. Spoke to him in the greenroom, where we left our wraps. Impression: The unattractive aspects of Christianity as an abject and servile religion of the lowly. Its greatness: The pessimistic cult of death and the grave, which embraces a whole ethical world, one that survives in Bach's Protestantism (*St. Matthew Passion*) but was wholly unknown to classical antiquity. Verdi's work has strong Italian national characteristics, despite which it is truly great music. What is fascinating is the interweaving of the obsession with death with a strong, sensuous affirmation of life. Naiveté, heavenly mandolins.—Privy Councillor Marcks gave us a lift home.—Afternoon nap. For tea a very tasty brown cake made with cocoa. Elisabeth with us. The children off to their dress rehearsal of *Minna von Barnhelm.*—Sent the typed manuscript to the *Berliner Tageblatt*, requesting acknowledgment of its receipt by telegram. Wrote a reassuring letter to Mama. Wrote the publisher of *Die Gartenlaube.*—Major thaw, wet, windy. Took an evening walk. Read in Keyserling's work in the evening. Our lights are flickering, the lines whipped by the storm.

Monday, December 22

Spent the morning reading further in the Keyserling articles. Took a walk, with slush and mud underfoot. Began reading, with approval, Spengler's *Preussentum und Sozialismus.* Afternoon nap. A low, green-tiled stove has been placed in my bedroom. Henneberger brought my new 280-mark boots and tried them on me. Wearing them, I went with Katia at 7:30 to the Marckses', where some twenty people were assembled to see the children put on their quite praiseworthy performance of *Minna von Barnhelm.* Golo as the Lady in Mourning was eerily funny, especially after the play was over. He easily made the most remarkable contribution of the evening. Genuine pleasure at the good sense and charm of the play. Peter Pringsheim here for Christmas. Sympathy for young Hallgarten, who suffers from weakness of the stomach and was in severe pain. We left at eleven and had a second supper at home.

Tuesday, December 23

Slept late. Rain and wind, huge puddles. Wrote a letter to Fischer congratulating him on his sixtieth birthday. Then into town, where I looked for light-colored summer boots, but without success. The stove being hooked up in the bedroom and the pipe fitted; much dirt and hammering. I napped in my study. Peter Pringsheim to tea. Took my walk in rain and wind. Continued with Spengler's *Preussentum und Sozialismus.* His use of Nietzschean diction strengthens the effect for me of his "brilliant constructions" (he uses this term once in describing Marxism). But quite apart from his constructions and antitheses, from his whole intellectual apparatus that is, my sympathy with the simple sentiments of his work (which I had already recognized in his major book) often approaches rapture.—Little Elisabeth broke Katia's tortoiseshell brush. Her dismay over the accident very touching and amusing.—I am giving Erika a copy of *Buddenbrooks* for Christmas, and have written my dedication into a two-volume copy from the 103rd to 112th printing.—Now for my bath.

Wednesday, December 24, Christmas Eve

Stormy night, lashing rain. This morning, began an open letter to Count Keyserling. Short walk in the rain with Bauschan, who is clearly ailing, sad to say. The symptoms are loss of appetite, droopy sadness, trembling of the head, twitching, and whimpering. We are hoping that what he has is nothing too serious like a brain infection. Will have to take him to the veterinarian.—Continued with the Spengler, a virile, magnificently skeptical piece of work that strengthens heart and soul.—After my nap, dressed with some care. Katia in a fever of preparation. Tea somewhat later than usual. My presents to Katia: an umbrella, writing paper, a good pair of boots, and a Kodak camera. Also the deluxe edition of *A Man and His Dog.*—At half-past six Katia's mother and Peter, who supervised the lighting of the tree. The four older children sang in the dimly lit study. Following old custom, we then moved into the entrance hall. I went to get the little ones, carrying little Elisabeth in my arms. She was deeply impressed by the lighted tree, then overjoyed by her toys and soon lost in play. The older children also very happy, showered with presents as in prewar times. I received a traveling tea-making kit with various accessories, underwear, handkerchiefs, many jars of preserves, cigarettes, some very good photographs of Katia with the six children and of Lisa by herself. Golo and Moni recited poetry. A late dinner, with roast goose, chocolate cake, Moselle wine, and French champagne. Everything seemed truly lavish. After Katia's relatives left, the children stayed up late. Erika said her favorite present was my book. Eissi very pleased with the works of Hauptmann. Eleven-thirty. The Christmas bells are pealing out over the city.

· ·

Thursday, December 25, the First Day of Christmas

· ·

Rain, wind, with intervals of dark-blue, stormy sky. Heller wrote a cordial letter about the effects of my sojourn in Vienna, and requested a picture.—The *Berliner Tageblatt* telegraphed that the Fontane article will appear in its New Year's issue.—The children playing in the entrance hall. Wrote letters. Telephoned Dr. Gruber, who came to have a look at Bauschan. He diagnosed a lung infection and promised to send a proper veterinarian. The poor animal is visibly quite ill; hot nose, gaunt, difficult breathing, trembling, and all the while so trustful and good, seeking our help.—With Katia and the children to Arcisstrasse, where we had our luncheon in the well-heated former boys' bedroom. Coffee and liqueurs in the library. Golo not feeling well. I am also under the weather, since I had trouble falling asleep last night thanks to heart palpitations and headache (from the tough goose). Left before three in order to be able to speak with the veterinarian. I came upon him in the entrance hall where he was examining poor Bauschan. Youngish man with duelling scars and a title of Doctor. Diagnosis: distemper. At the moment going around in an especially virulent form that affects even older dogs. Festering lung infection, but certain nervous symptoms (which I too had observed) also suggest that the brain and spinal cord are involved. The prognosis is grim. It was decided to take him to the animal hospital, since inhalation treatment is indicated. There the doctor will also make a referral. I will have to get used to the thought of losing the dear animal. Fed him sausage in the warm spot where he likes to lie.—Went to bed and napped. Then made myself tea and ate some stollen with applesauce.—Took care of some mail, then dressed in dinner jacket and went to the Löhrs', where there was a small party with the Pringsheims, Vicco and his wife, [and] the Endreses. Moderate supper. Tired. Vicco's horrible wife next to me at the table; terrible boredom. Later in the evening a young actress, recently engaged by the National Theater, recited Chinese poetry and some of Rilke's; good diction, but otherwise stereotyped delivery.—By the way, reciting poetry realistically is a wretched custom. It grew late. Home through rain and storm. One o'clock.

Fog. Slept late. Wrote some on the open letter, then went on foot to the animal hospital, where I did not stay in the waiting room but had the attendant take me straight to Bauschan's cage. He was standing up, very thin. He recognized me and lifted his paw. His nose is wet with mucous, which he licks, thereby reinfecting himself. The kidney infection seems to stem from this. The attendant made pessimistic remarks. I tipped him five marks and left after a melancholy interval. Paid a good-sized bill at Prantl's and came home on foot through lifting fog and gentle dampness.—I am depressed at being held up once more by the article.—Last night I decided to discontinue reading Emma Bonn's novellas; they are kitsch pure and simple. After dinner I continued looking through Kassner's book on physiognomy, but it is too detailed and precious to offer much for me. I put it back on the shelf. Slept a bit. Worked again after teatime, then shaved and changed into dinner jacket.

1920

Somewhat ill, had to watch myself at mealtimes. After a frugal breakfast, almost finished the article; only the final paragraph lacking. Young Lipmann came to join me on my walk. Discussed cultural matters. The latest crop of young people is reacting against Expressionism, returning to form. *Death in Venice* is very much the order of the day. "I am a grandfather!" The real underlying need, however, is for new spiritual values, a turning away from nihilistic demoralization, from bolshevism of every kind.— J. Brüll sent from Vienna a third scrapbook of newspaper clippings. Also the cultural section of the *Neue Freie Presse*, containing an essay on Hofmannsthal's novella *Die Frau ohne Schatten* and the *Gesang vom Kindchen* together. Keyserling sent an essay on Spengler. Just right. Letter of thanks from Wandrey and other mail.—Napped. Dr. Endres and his wife to tea, which was served in my room. I read to them and Katia the open letter to Keyserling, as much as I have finished. The candles on the Christmas tree were lit for the last time and the tree taken down. Had our evening meal in the entrance hall, heated now by the iron stove. Afterward we had a tea punch as a belated New Year's celebration for the children. I read them the hunt chapter from *A Man and His Dog*.—Troubling telephone conversation with Lula, who wanted me to recommend something for her to read, but nothing "painful." She is tearful, enjoying her misery. I full of anger and disgusted sympathy. It seems her surgeon is her lover, and she intends to rendezvous with him in the country. Or perhaps she only makes that appear to be the situation in her hysterical dejection.

Thursday, January 8

Last night finished the Saltykov, reading in bed. Possibly the most intensely bitter and gloomy thing ever written. An orgy of suffering at the end; by the conclusion Judushka is no longer detestable, his suffering is so great.—Today returned to *The Magic Mountain*. Decided in the course of the night to change the order of Chapters One and Two, an intention that Katia approved when I told her about it at breakfast. Changes will be necessary. In any case the Hamburg chapter has been a thorn in my side. Must be rewritten.—All sorts of mail.—The weather before noon remarkably lovely, half springlike, with blue sky while snow still lingers on. Katia and I took a walk for nearly two hours in the farther reaches of Herzogpark, and discovered the reason behind all the clearing and digging that has been going on there; they are building a navigable canal.—Feel better, but still not normal. Napped badly. Had tea in my room by myself and then took care of correspondence. In the afternoon the weather changed abruptly, a west wind sweeping in, damp. Headache. Read the *Rundschau*, containing Hauptmann's latest verse play. The articles mostly unpleasant and confusing.—A correspondent for the *Corriere della Sera* telephoned asking if he might call tomorrow.

Tuesday, January 20

[. . .] A dark day, snow flurries. Central heating on since yesterday. Wrote two pages of dialogue. Prinz phoned to hear more about Bauschan, of whose death he had learned from Friess. He seems serious in his intention to publicize the fact in the foreign press, and spoke of sending the story over the wires, though this has not as yet proved opportune.—Went for a short walk. Read the newspaper after lunch: Clemenceau's defeat as a presidential candidate is some satisfaction at any rate. Then Bekker's reply in the *Frankfurter Zeitung* to Pfitzner's polemic, which by and large does Pfitzner no harm.—Rested poorly. After tea, while Katia was off with her mother visiting her brother's ashes, I tried to write the open letter to Elchinger, but was too tired and wrote to Bertram instead, informing him of Bauschan's death. Took another walk. After supper, went on with *Crime and Punishment*. Letters: from Niderlechner in Frankfurt and from Privy Councillor Goetz in Strasburg and Berlin about *A Man and His Dog*, including more on the *Betrachtungen* and an invitation to give a reading for students in Jena.

· ·
Wednesday, January 21
· ·

Wet snow. In the morning, began writing the open letter for the *Münchner Neueste Nachrichten*. Went out for a while after shaving. Dr. Helene Herrmann sent her long essay on *Effi Briest*, which is excellent. Browsed through it after lunch. Katia reported a depressing air of crisis in town. The price of bread has doubled, the value of the mark is down to eight centimes, and a silver mark coin fetches eight paper marks. This reflects the German acknowledgment of how we are seen by other nations—as is wont.—Before tea, a to-do over the copies of the *Frankfurter Zeitung* borrowed from the Hallgartens; they had disappeared in the children's quarters. Everyone denied all knowledge of them, but I insisted on their being produced. They finally turned up in the children's bathroom, probably brought there by the perfidious Golo.—After tea, without going out again, I finished the open letter to Elchinger, including one vigorous passage influenced by Dostoevsky, relating to the national necessity for a religious ideal transcending individual prosperity.—Wind, snow, hail. Erika off to the Pfitzner concert. After supper, read the letter to Katia with the children present. Katia very approving. I wonder whether the newspaper will print it.—Went on with *Crime and Punishment*.—Erika reported a scandalous incident at the university: Max Weber spoke out against Count Arco, was booed out of the hall, and when he reappeared he was greeted with such an uproar that the rector, since called in, had to cancel the class. The antirevolutionary, nationalistic mood of the students is basically gratifying to me, although Arco is a fool and the individual proponents of that mood are boors.—I congratulate myself on having written the letter in one day.

· ·
Tuesday, February 10
· ·

From Wednesday, January 29, until early today I stayed in Feldafing and Polling. I forgot to take this diary along. Katia was with me for the first five days, during which we had bad or indifferent weather. Clear frost set in on the day of her departure, and only today does it appear that it will be replaced by foehn. Richter was away until after Katia left. The highlight of the visit: Richter's superlative Gramophone, which I put to continuous use, either alone or with Katia or Richter. The *Tannhäuser* Overture. *La Bohème*. The finale of *Aïda* (an Italian *Liebestod*). Caruso, Battistini, Madame Melba, Titta Ruffo, etc. A new theme for *The Magic Mountain*, a rich find both for its intellectual possibilities and its narrative value.—Pleasant stay, Frau Piokarska managing the household and doing the cooking. Many walks. Had lunch with

Bruno Frank in his newly acquired little house. Went with Katia to dinner at Fräulein Bonn's. Visited her again for tea with Richter, and met her brother from London. Worked on *The Magic Mountain* every day (the scene with Settembrini's visit with Hans). Wrote letters. Early last Saturday, after a week and a half that is, went to Polling to visit Mama. Return to the old familiar place, so appealing and wreathed in nostalgia. Mama concerned and affectionate, full of complaints about both Heinrich's wife and Viktor's. Went for a walk in the dark and lost my way. Up at seven, and before breakfast and sunrise, with the moon still high in the sky, went for a walk in the icy cold (yesterday). The frozen countryside before daylight, with the quarries and the mountain range locked in snow, seemed like a lunar landscape. Sense of the pure country life; piety something sensual and physical (the pastor in *The Magic Mountain*): "The religious man thinks only of himself."—In Polling, too, I worked further on the scene and took care of correspondence. Detailed answer from Hofmannsthal concerning the magazine. Articles from the *Svenska Dagbladet* and *Gewissen* about the two idylls. Report that a "Berlin man of letters," in all probability Herzog, has decreed that the two pieces are "beneath discussion, as far as his taste is concerned."—Deferential letter from Stefan Zweig, to whom I sent the manuscript of *The Hungry* for his collection, at Eliasberg's suggestion.—Settled matters with Richter regarding *The Blood of the Walsungs*. Will receive 10,000 marks for it.—Roughly 4,000 marks from Copenhagen for translation rights to *Tristan* (Frau von Mendelssohn).—Elster agreed to 1,000 for the facsimile edition.—Spent evening rummaging through old family mementos, photographs, letters, etc., since the light was too dim for reading. Mixture of familiarity, tedium, and sadness.—Finished *Crime and Punishment* while in the country, as well as sections of Wolynski's book on *The Brothers Karamazov*, and began Philippe's *Marie Donadieu*. Too much of the female element. Somewhat the same complaint with Musil's short stories, which did not particularly appeal to me.—On the political scene, the extradition business, a major stupidity on the part of the Entente. Massive patriotic demonstrations in Germany. Gratifying for me that the worst of our national miseries are over. The backlash is powerful. The impotence of the Entente in the extradition matter is glaring.—While in Feldafing, read the proofs of my open letter to Keyserling.—Woke at six this morning in Polling, breakfasted, and went with Mama to the station. The trip not bad, browsed through Hackländer's fairy tales and the newspaper, smoked some of the good cigarettes that I found in Weilheim for 30 pfennigs. Arrived at ten. Carried my suitcase to the tram myself, resting frequently, and left it at the pub on this end. Reunion with Katia, who has lost weight recently, and with the children. Little Elisabeth was lying in bed, and upon seeing me cried "Tommy! Tommy!" Second breakfast. Glanced through the mail. A large and beautiful reproduction of Brueghel's *Winter* sent by Dr. Strauss from Vienna. Until lunchtime, unpacked and put things in order. Katia to tea at Helene Raff's, with Muncker, etc. Officially, I am "not arriving until this evening." Took care of some mail, wrote these notes.—In the country my zest for *The Magic Mountain* was renewed, partly thanks to the rest, but also thanks to new ideas about the material.—Sent my British contract regarding *Royal Highness* to Fischer, asking if we should not bring it up again.—Have very much turned against the journal proposition. According to both Frank and Richter, Guenther is impossible.—My first evening stroll to the Maximilianeum and into Bogenhausen. This evening read the *Neue Rundschau*. Under the pseudonym of Linke Poot, Döblin ridicules a passage in my "Old Fontane" in which I speak of Fontane's plan for a Likedeeler novel. He is quite wrong. Perhaps I will set him straight.—More miscellaneous mail came.—Ready for my bath.

[. . .] Letter from Dr. Else Schöll about *A Man and His Dog*. Another from Stockholm concerning Swedish translation of the *Little Herr Friedemann* stories.—Brought the visit scene to a close. Went walking along the brook. After lunch read one of two novellas that young writers are hoping to dedicate to me, a good description of battle from the recent war. Ate too much stollen at tea. Wrote letters. After supper, read in Bloch's book *Vom Tode*.

Today again mist and sunlight. Tired. Seeing Heinrich unnerved me. I was upset and talked too loudly during the intermission.—Wrote one page more. Waiting with somewhat irritated impatience for Boehm's answer to my query concerning X-rays.—Into town, where I finally bought that jacket at Bamberger and Hertz, paying for it by check. Then bought a wristwatch nearby, which I have long desired; 375 marks, also paid by check. Afterward, as excited as a child, lit a cigarette and ran into the Pfitzners, with whom I talked about Vienna, his polemic, my idylls, and so on. He invited me to his next symphony concert.—In high spirits at luncheon, even frivolous. Erika brought a grateful letter from her religion instructor, Pastor Merz, who will perform the baptism here at home.—Katia not feeling well; has back pains, fears it is flu.— Not well rested, tired. In the afternoon paper a long, tedious review of my *Two Idylls* by Kutscher. He lectures me something awful about the *Gesang*. Am sending the clipping to Bahr and to Bertram.—The deluxe edition of Goethe's *Tagebuch* arrived, published by the Phantasus-Verlag.—With Katia and the older children to the Vier Jahreszeiten for a sonata program by Walter and Disclez. Beethoven, Pfitzner, and a modern Russian. The Scherzo in the Beethoven struck me, Pfitzner was closest to my heart. The Russian was sonorous, polished, melancholy, and perfumed. Rode home with the Walters.—After dinner read the Goethe *Tagebuch*. Civilized morality. Then read further in Pannwitz. "Greuel der Völker" is excellent.—Kept singing the final phrase of *Aïda* all day.—Once more late to bed.

[. . .] Fine sunny day. Went on making physiological notes for *The Magic Mountain*. Went walking. Rested a while after luncheon on the balcony. Then to the hospital on the left bank of the Isar (Ziemssenstrasse), where I was taken to Boehm, whom I had met at a party at Ceconi's. Was outfitted with a white hospital smock and taken into the X-ray laboratory, where I watched while a resident and his assistant took various pictures of lungs and one of a knee joint, both men and women. The doctor also showed me a series of photographic plates (diseased lungs and a stomach ulcer). Let me see the bones of my hand on the screen. Invited me to come whenever I wish to watch. X-rays are scheduled for four o'clock every day, except Saturdays and Sundays.—From the hospital to Arcisstrasse, where I had tea. Then with Katia and her mother to the Hoftheater, where I picked up the tickets for *La Bohème* that Walter had had held for me. The love scene in the first act was charming. Otherwise scarcely moved. The dramatic framework is dreadful—ridiculously sentimental and implausible.

Spoke with Falckenberg, who commiserated with us on the death of Bauschan, which he had learned of "from the newspapers," and with Borns. Walked home. After supper read the paper, the *Auslandspost*, and Grossmann's *Tage-Buch*, which though not of the highest quality is thoroughly entertaining. In it are excerpts from Keynes's book on Versailles (Wilson!), whom Pannwitz calls, to my delight, "the old washerwoman of the ocean."—Late!

Sunday, February 29

Sparkling springlike day. Slept late. Wrote a bit further. At noon took the four children for a walk. Afternoon on the balcony reading an excellent essay in typescript, *Metaphysik und Geschichte*, by Dr. Baeumler, Berlin, an open letter to me dealing with *Palestrina* and my *Betrachtungen*. Stimulating, fruitful stuff, which I find thoroughly congenial. After tea I sent the manuscript on to Cossmann, recommending it to the editors of the *Süddeutsche Monatshefte*. I would be delighted if it were to come out as a pamphlet. Took care of some more letters and walked only as far as the postbox. This evening continued to read *The Idiot*.—Katia has a cold.—Invitations going out to a large late tea at our house next Thursday.—Yesterday the *Nachrichten* printed an item from *Vorwärts* with the brazen falsification that the Erzberger trial is representative of the cultural situation of the Wilhelmine period as portrayed by Heinrich Mann in *The Patrioteer*. Really a fine piece of impertinence to try and identify someone of Erzberger's political stripe, that merry king of profiteers and true product of the Republic, with the Kaiser's era. The reference to Heinrich is characteristic. A talented writer, desiring to be a democratic society novelist, presents a counterfeit image of the German state as something comically republican, and then the Republicans attempt to justify themselves on the basis of this "satire". . . . Things are mightily confused in Germany.

Wednesday, March 3

Yesterday evening and today, read further in *Royal Highness* in the English translation with great enjoyment. The style seems comfortable and authentic.—Today again a wonderful day, fresher than yesterday. Wrote a page. Walked. After tea wrote to Mama, to London, and to Fischer. Took evening walk in mist and moonlight. Klaus Pringsheim writes of pending negotiations with America over motion-picture rights to the novels. They offer $4,000 and $2,500, a fortune in our currency. For the moment, however, all we have is a three-month option. Thus I am now strongly in favor of a weakened German currency.—This afternoon and evening read various interesting and stimulating things: in the *Tage-Buch* a letter of Dehmel's to the pacifists, excellent, highly gratifying; in the *Neue Merkur* a very good article by Lion on Germany and France. A harrowing novella by Döblin, *Predigt und Judenverbrennung*, compared to which the torture scenes in *Ulenspiegel* seem utterly innocuous. Also an article on the religious element in modern art, obviously by a Catholic churchman; discriminating, objective, good. Also an epistemological critique of Einstein's theory (which, incidentally, has been analyzed by Flammarion and largely rejected by him); it deals again with the problem of time, one that today assumes a real urgency, and that I anticipated in my conception of *The Magic Mountain*, just as I had anticipated the political antitheses leading up to the war. My satisfaction at my seismographic sensitivity in more than one respect in those days is diminished, even nullified, by sorrow in the recognition, constantly absolutely confirmed, that this novel as well as *The Confidence Man* should have been finished in 1914. Its merits have been vitiated by the abnormally rapid course of events.—But are seemingly more fortunate writers faring any better? Heinrich's views, though they shine ever so brightly at the moment, are basically undermined already by recent developments. His Western leanings, his worship of the French, his pro-Wilson stand, etc., are already outdated and worn. Truly there is no point upsetting one's digestion by jealousy.—I often think about Dr. Baeumler's piece; I would very much like to see it appear in print.

. . . .

Monday, March 8

. . . .

[. . .] Abrupt change in the weather, dark, snow squalls, cold (0° Celsius). Wrote a page and a half. The mail came at noon. Went into town to Hönn, the bookbinder, a likable man who is binding three copies of the deluxe edition of *A Man and His Dog* for me. Selected some attractive papers. Returned home wet with snow and frozen. After lunch read here and there in the *Tage-Buch.*—On the tram the driver told me about a farmer who had had three French prisoners of war assigned to him. The three recently came back to his farm and asked to be taken on again; they said no one gave a hang about them in France. Anger at the French is very strong among the populace. The people are saying "In the next war we won't take any prisoners."—At teatime Katia's mother, and later Dr. Hermanns. Made a third or fourth attempt at a letter to the *Post* in connection with the Author's Evening, only to tear the letter up again. Wrote a short answer to J. W. Harnisch.—Long registered letter from the editor of the *Kultur-Korrespondenz*, raving about the *Betrachtungen* and begging me for a contribution. I will probably decline, explaining that I have spoken my piece and must leave it at that while I turn to other projects.—Katia better.—Went out again for a while; snow a foot deep, branches bowed down, heavy going in wind and sleet. For supper, excellent cutlets. The two big children to Strasser's concert with Katia's mother. The snow and bad weather are reported to have gotten still worse. Read a very funny, grotesque piece in the *Rundschau* by L. Hermann about a Communist rally in Berlin, at which I [laughed] heartily.

. . . .

Friday, March 12

. . . .

Wrote one more page. An hour's walk. Cold. Katia able to come to meals. Read *The Idiot.* Slept. At five o'clock young H. von Gleichen came to call, with the request that I come to the Berlin meeting of the Union of German Scholars and Artists at Whitsun and [talk] on the awakening of German self-awareness. Asked for time to consider.— Katia's mother to tea upstairs, the two youngest present.—Took care of letters, including one to Federal Councillor von Bühl, who had sent me his article. Also thank-yous for letters about *A Man and His Dog.*—Colonel von Hemmer, who headed the general staff of Bothmer's army during the war, wrote me a letter full of enthusiasm for the *Betrachtungen.* Gleichen also told me that the book is being read with great fervor. He suggested my talk might [be] a restatement of the book's argument, which further developments have confirmed and strengthened.—Took another walk. After supper, sat at Katia's bedside. She had me massage her body, ribs, and breasts, so that I became greatly aroused. *The Magic Mountain* will be the most sensual book I have written, though in a cool style.—This evening, read Dostoevsky's political-literary writings.

Saturday, March 13

In Berlin a counterrevolutionary overthrow without a struggle. Kapp proclaimed "dictator" and Lüttwitz minister of the Reichswehr. The former government has fled, the National Assembly and the Prussian Diet are dissolved. Learned of this during a visit from Mama, which interrupted my work. Endres had telephoned. I do not care for Kapp at all; but doubtless it is true that the previous government had already made too much of a mess of things. Noske's troops were unwilling to fire on the advancing forces and were withdrawn.—Outdoors for only a short while at midday. Katia once again out of bed for tea. A curious episode with a so-called Count Henkell von Donnersmarck from Kattowitz, who had been recommended to us this morning by a "Baron Soden," and who then put the touch on the architect Ludwig for 250 marks for food. Our suspicions rose during supper, when we determined that the Bogenhausen bridge, where supposedly his "auto" had been stopped by a patrol, had not been barricaded at all. Much telephoning with the Ludwigs, where the imposter had turned up on a bicycle, and with the local precinct and police headquarters. An experience, highly interesting in connection with *The Confidence Man*, but unsettling and disturbing.—In the evening, walked as far as the Maximilianeum. Wintry weather, starry sky. After supper, read the paper for the latest news from Berlin. Tension and worry. Will the announced general strike spread to Bavaria, and Kapp's regime quickly crumble?—The Bavarian Reichswehr has declared its autonomy and its loyalty to the government. Does this mean the disintegration of Germany? Will the Entente intervene? But why should the French step in? I fear the moment is badly chosen, although the Erzberger case prepared the mood for such an operation.—Ready for my bath.

Sunday, March 14

Wrote one page of "Sudden Enlightenment." Interrupted by a visit from a police officer, come to take notes on the fraudulent count. Mama with Katia. In response to a telegram from his wife, Heinrich left for Prague in a cloud of dust with his little girl, out of fear of the "Rightist element." One of the Munich papers, doubtless a Centrist one, recently carried a satire on the conflict between his luxurious way of living and his adulation of the poor in his works, the very poor whom he now dismisses as being "Rightist."

Wanted to take a walk, but ran into Moni with little Elisabeth, who took possession of my walking stick. So I stayed with the children until lunchtime.—Afterward, continued with *The Idiot.*—Katia out of bed all day, except for breakfast.—The air milder; sunny, but still wintry.—Richter telephoned from Feldafing to get the latest political news.—Napped in the afternoon. Was invited to tea at Gleichen-Russwurm's, the only other guest being a young baron. Political discussions. They expect good things of the new government in Berlin. Matters here will be decided within the next two days.

Today troops marched out of the Türkenstrasse barracks, singing and waving black, white, and red banners. They would certainly be at the disposal of anyone ready to take action. Negotiations with Epp are supposed to be in progress. Gleichen suspects that the English would prefer a conservative government in Germany. He also believes that American money might be involved. He would not consider the disintegration of Germany such a misfortune. I, too, would prefer it to the centralized Republic, which is a lie. Highest esteem for Lenin, the only true man in the world, a Ghengis Khan, the incomparably more powerful antithesis of poor Woodrow Wilson.—Took another walk as far as the Maximilianeum. After supper talked with Ludwig by telephone. The bogus count is a mentally unbalanced young man from a good local family, and last night he confessed the whole prank to his doctor. The psychiatrist got in touch with Ludwig. The sick man's father is going to call on Ludwig. His mother, who is herself psychologically unstable, is inconsolable. The patient is shattered, must go back to the mental institution. A strange case.—Tonight read Bertram's *Nietzsche* with undiminished love and affinity.

. . . .
Monday, March 15
. . . .

General strike. No trams. The Bavarian ministry has resigned. General von Möhl is the state commissar. Berlin without electricity. According to a special issue of the *Nachrichten*, which Katia's mother brought us at noon, there is general opposition throughout the country to the Rightist coup. The Democrats in coalition with the Socialists. The obvious vulnerability of the new Berlin regime.—Wrote another page on the scene in the X-ray room. The 1,000-mark payment for the *Tristan* facsimile came, along with letters from Grolman et al., and a parcel of books from Hellerau (Claudel). In the afternoon a short stroll near the house. Keyed up by the political unrest. My afternoon nap disturbed by the sound of carpenters hammering. A. Ludwig to tea. Plans to move to Meran. (Nonsense.) Took care of a few letters. Then to the Walters', who drove me to the concert at the Odeon in their official car. The Ninth Symphony. The mystery of musical genius, incomparable, untrammeled, beyond human ken. At the same time, in this case, a touching love for humanity, however disunified by "fashion." Walter, already exhausted from *Tristan* and the final rehearsal, was quite broken at the end, but in a state of exaltation. Was tremendously applauded. Drove home with Frau Ivogün.—From Frau Endres we hear that Kapp has already resigned, with the stipulation that new elections take place in two months and that the chief ministries be staffed by professionals. I am glad if something is achieved on the political plane, assuming good sense and order were followed and the conservative ideal is not compromised.

. . . .
Tuesday, March 16
. . . .

Overcast; chill, raw wind. The political scene murky. The general strike still on, no newspapers, no trams, schools closed. News of Kapp's resignation premature.—Wrote further on the X-ray laboratory scene. Took Klaus and Golo for an hour's walk around noon. Afternoon nap. [. . .] After tea wrote at length to Bertram. Went out again, in cold, windy weather. Citizens' Guard everywhere about.—Katia suffering from a sinus cold; Hermanns came to see her in the morning. I had him explain the X-ray plates.—

Endres called after supper. The Berlin government seems unable to hold on much longer. Hindenburg trying to mediate, have Ebert and Kapp enter into negotiations, Lüttwitz withdraw his troops from Berlin. Both impossible. In Munich the Landtag in perpetual session. It is vacillating between Kahr and Winterstein as heads of the government. If it is the latter, the Socialists will take part. Evidently the situation is less critical here than in Prussia. But all these developments strengthen the possibility of secession. In any case, this was my first reading of the situation and is, I am tempted to believe, the direction matters will take in Germany. The disintegration of the Reich is unavoidable, and is a necessary step toward the realization of a Greater Germany. The French would be freed from their nightmare, understanding would be possible at last, a new peace concluded with the individual German states, and the Versailles provisions cast aside. German-speaking Austria and the Tyrol to be annexed to Southern Germany. Prussia to develop independently, in line with her own character and taste. The "Reich" will once more be an idea, a dream, a hope. Possibilities for a greater imperial Germany relegated to the background until some future date.—Continued reading *The Idiot*.

Wednesday, March 17

Overcast and chilly. Endres phoned after breakfast: Kahr has formed a new government with the Socialists excluded. Questionable whether that was wise. It throws the Socialists together from now on. The strike, the transit stoppage continue. Wrote a page of the "X-ray" in some uncertainty, for I have not experienced all of it. Bought a toothbrush at the pharmacy and took a walk. Saw the bridge barricaded and guarded by units of the Citizens' Guard.—Letter from Supreme Court Justice Dietz about the *Betrachtungen*.—Katia still has sinus condition.—After lunch, *The Idiot*. Napped. Katia's mother to tea, bringing a bulletin put out by the strike leaders. According to it, Kapp and Lüttwitz have already resigned and are asking for amnesty. As far as Bavaria is concerned, the crisis is resolved in that power is being transferred to civilian hands (Winterstein) and a new government formed, one which will continue to include the Center parties and the Democrats, with a churchman taking over the Ministry of Education. One clear success of the coup has been to force out the Socialists. The Independents can scarcely count on the revolution-weary masses, and have reason to fear a powerful backlash if they take any steps. The strike over. Trams have been running since five o'clock.—I read aloud the scene with the directress and the examination scene. Katia's mother amazed at their vividness.—Took a walk as far as the Maximilianeum. The bridges still under guard. Eight o'clock curfew. The Pfitzner concert postponed until Friday.—This evening continued with *The Idiot*.

Thursday, March 18

Had to make corrections in what I wrote yesterday on the basis of information given me by Hermanns over the telephone. At noon, errands in town, since the trams operating again. Bought a pound of pralines for 24 marks. Went to Jaffe's, where I bought some more books by Philippe. What made the strikers give up was a lack of money. The rumor that Bauer had called for a general strike untrue. Several parts of the country have gone bolshevist. In Berlin, Lüttwitz is supposed to have placed his troops at the disposal of the old regime; Kapp said to have fled the country.—Rain.—My April 22 trip to Augsburg postponed because of the printers' strike.—After lunch read *Marie Donadieu*, which I had begun in Feldafing. I finished *The Idiot* last night before going to sleep.—Afternoon nap. After tea, letterwriting. Went to the Marckses' for dinner, where the other guests were Preetorius and an engaging young North German aristocrat. Stimulating conversation, partly on the subject of the occult. Left at 11:30. Rain.—Katia's cold still bad. Hermanns came to treat her.

Monday, March 22

The day dedicated to the Zurich currency matter. Woke early, and right after breakfast went on foot to the Progress stenography office where I stayed from 9:30 to 12:00, dictating the "Arrival" chapter, but managing to finish only a bit more than half of it. Drove home, rested a while in my study after lunch, and at 3:30 went back by cab for more dictating. The driver demanded ten marks, which was probably excessive. I gave him eleven. Dictated until 5:30, finishing the chapter. Worried about whether many of the details are aesthetically acceptable. Took the tram home in pleasant weather, had late tea with Katia in her room, then wrote the letter to Korrodi that will accompany the manuscript, commenting on the content of the story, and began correcting the typescript.—The newspaper carries reports of the collapse of Kapp's undertaking, which proves to have been so poorly planned that it could not possibly have won support at this juncture. Also a report on the movement of the extreme Left.—After supper went on with *Marie Donadieu*. The scene with the woman and the two so very different men is superlative; the one between mother and daughter utterly charming and very French; Maupassant might have done something similar.—Yesterday I read Bahr's essay on Stifter. Bertram's is better.—Katia improved, should be up tomorrow.

Tuesday, March 23

A brilliant sunny day, with hoarfrost in the early morning. I finished looking through the dictated typescript and dispatched the parcel to Zurich. The film people came at 11:30 and took pictures of me (in my study) and with the children (Klaus, Golo, and Lisa) in the garden. Katia out of bed. Strolled a while in the garden with her, enjoying the sunshine, then took a walk by myself. After lunch telephoned Richter in Feldafing to let him know I would come tomorrow. (Heard the Gramophone in the background.)—Bought a new dog for 750 marks from the policeman who recently offered to get me one. A small shepherd by the name of Lux, who seems to be of friendly disposition, good-tempered and alert.—At teatime Katia's mother and Frau Hallgarten. Wrote a bit.—Went walking with Lux, whose name should perhaps be spelled "Luchs."—Katia worried about Klaus, who, it turns out, ferreted about in my study while we were gone and read Wedekind.—Finished *Marie Donadieu* in the evening. The final scene, with its victory over "woman," highly erotic and at the same time French, Christian, and antifeminist all in one—masterful in a restrained way. On the whole, many subtle strengths in the book.—The older children, off at a performance, came home at 10:30. Lux barked like a good dog.

Awoke at home in Munich before eight and after breakfast busied myself assembling and packing what I would need. Fine day. This done, I went for a walk with Katia and little Elisabeth from 11:00 to 11:30 on Mauerkircherstrasse. Had a beefsteak at 11:30 and said goodbye to Katia with mixed feelings, for I could not help suspecting that she resents my going away, though this feeling is partly due to her illness.—With our maid Elise, who helped with the suitcase and rucksack of food, to the Starnberg station, where I ran into Alfred Kaufmann and was soon joined by Frank. Enjoyable ride with the two of them. Parted from them in Starnberg, and then proceeded by steamer to Possenhofen, where I was met by little Fanny. Came here. Greeted by Richter, who had put on a Beethoven record by way of welcome. The dog Fakir. Unpacked and rested for half an hour. A young baroness from the neighborhood came to tea, which was served in the sitting room. The usual political discussions. Then Gramophone music. New record: *Parsifal.* Later a twilight walk with Richter. After the generous supper, music: Wagner, Beethoven, Verdi, and Puccini. Cherry brandy.— Overtired. Eleven o'clock.

Friday, March 26; Feldafing

Mild weather, light rain, then clearing. After breakfast thought about the further course of the novel and wrote a few lines. At eleven with Richter to Tutzing, where we visited Frau von Prittwitz in her beautiful house on the lake. A charming lady of the aristocracy, her speech interspersed with bits of French. She invited me to visit with Katia. The lounge quite splendid, with a view of the lake. Walked home by the main road. Had a pastry at the bakery. After luncheon read some Péladan, then tried to nap but without much success, since I had had coffee and Fakir was barking at various workmen. After tea wrote a long letter to Wassermann. Took a walk as far as the Hotel Elisabeth. Then Frank came to supper as my guest. Later I read aloud the X-ray scene from *The Magic Mountain.* Then Gramophone music. The reading seemed to make no particular impression, which deepened my sense of tiredness.—In the newspaper, postscripts to the Kapp episode. Colonel Bauer has been in touch with the Independent Socialists, who showed themselves not disinclined to join with the Conservatives in dealing the death blow to parliamentarism. But even if it is necessary to preserve the bourgeois republic, inasmuch as we cannot survive economically for the time being without the support of Western capitalism, it is nonetheless stupid to adopt the Western view of the men who attempted the coup. In actual fact, Germany is now even spiritually under the domination and tutelage of the Entente. The good wishes and the benevolence of the American note naturally deeply affecting.

Saturday, March 27; Feldafing

Read Péladan in bed last night until 1:00. Not feeling well, flatulence. Unrested and strained. Was greatly displeased with Frank yesterday. He behaved tactlessly toward Richter, who is a noble and original character in his way, and he also damaged part of the Gramophone mechanism.—Came down to breakfast around nine and found Richter already up. Apparently today is his birthday (also Heinrich's), as I was made

93

aware by cake and flowers. He is going into Munich at noon. I overheard a telephone call in which he ordered wine with all the self-indulgence of a moneyed bachelor. Said good-bye to him, since I would probably not be back from my walk before his departure. So now I am alone here, and the week ahead is dedicated to solitude and stillness. The day is extraordinarily fine.—I wrote only a few lines, tired and nervous from the novelty of being alone. Received a letter from Eliasberg, who sent along an article by his dead brother. Took a good two-hour walk without an overcoat; warm foehn weather. Had my noonday meal in the main room and afterward read the newspapers and the *Auslandspost*. Lay down in the afternoon, may have slept. After tea wrote to Musil and Eliasberg; walked to the station before supper to mail the letters. Afterward listened to music for a long time; played Beethoven while still at table. Later in the evening read Péladan. French always does inspire me greatly.— Ready for my bath.

Thursday, April 8

[. . .] Up at 8:30 and wrote somewhat further after breakfast. Walk at noon. Bushes and trees are swiftly greening; the air is mild. Lisa over her fever. After lunch, in the garden. Looked at my open letter to Keyserling in the *Tage-Buch*, read the newspaper. Took my rest outdoors. The gardeners busy with the spring grooming. Katia to tea at Arcisstrasse. Met her at the Kammerspiele, where we saw the old Spanish play *Don Gil of the Green Trousers*, handsomely staged by Falckenberg. The actors, however, lacked talent for comedy. Sybille Binder thoroughly charming. After supper glanced through Sologub's *The Little Demon*.—Lux has run away several times. The second time he was brought back by a boy who found him on Königinstrasse, to whom I gave five marks. This evening I had the dog in my room, where things took such a turn that I had to clean up afterward.

Sunday, April 11

Warm and overcast with a likelihood of rain. Wrote some passages descriptive of landscape and the seasons. Dr. Hermanns with Katia. The test came out negative, the results relatively favorable. For the present, rest, milk, sun-lamp treatments; in May she should probably go to Kohlgrub. Took Lux walking; he is adjusting nicely. After lunch, in the garden. Have begun reading *The Wedding Trip* by De Coster. After tea wrote to Mama about Regensburg, the 6,900-mark piano, Katia's health. In the evening took Klaus to a performance by Hardt in the Schmidt Auditorium. Remarkable evening. Hardt did readings from Heine, Kleist, Wedekind, Walser, Morgenstern. Then he did impersonations of Wassmann, Wegener, Moissi, Schildkraut, Bassermann, and Pallenberg with fantastic accuracy. I went backstage afterward. Horwitz asked me to write a few lines about the performance, since no one was there from the press. Regretted that Katia had not come along, for she would have greatly enjoyed the impersonations. This evening, when we were discussing our relatively fortunate situation, she said to me, "For your second wife, you must marry someone rich; then *we'll* have even more kopecks." I was reminded of the Kleist anecdote about J. S. Bach, who (as am I) was accustomed to let his wife attend to all practical matters. When he was asked for instructions at her funeral, he replied, sobbing, "Ask my wife!"—

What is remarkable is that the educated classes still cling to their fashionable, revolutionary, pacifist attitudes. Hardt's program, predominantly revolutionary, was well received precisely because it pandered to these preferences. The intellectuals are still raising the cry for justice, even though the proletariat is earning thirty-six marks a day and the middle class is going hungry because of such high wages.

Monday, April 19

[. . .] Made little progress, since this is a very tricky spot. Letter from Sweden concerning the translation of *Little Herr Friedemann*. Note from Korrodi, who is prepared to pay immediately (350 francs = roughly 4,000 marks), despite the fact that the chapter cannot appear for another three weeks. Other matters. Took only a short stroll at noon. Some varied reading after lunch, then went to bed. The Litzmanns from Bonn to tea, along with Bertram, with whom I later took an extended walk. Weather overcast and cool. He stayed to supper; in the afternoon he was suffering migraine, but felt better in the course of the evening.

Tuesday, April 27

[. . .] Up at 8:30. A page and a half more. An hour's walk. Weather cloudy, cool. After lunch read Ponten's prize essay on the spiritual renewal of the world, with which I was not completely satisfied however. Rested in bed. Bertram and Glöckner to tea— his last visit until summer. From 6:00 to 7:30 I read aloud the truly successful sections from *The Magic Mountain* dealing with the first measurement of Castorp's temperature and the X-ray. Great impression on the two friends, who later discussed the passages with me at length. My hopes were not disappointed. We did not go out again before supper, for which both stayed. Discussed the seemingly inescapable economic catastrophe we are facing.

Thursday, April 29

Yesterday finished reading Balzac's *Girl with the Golden Eyes*, impressed by his audacity and greatness.—Overcast today, rather raw weather. Peat fire in my room. Wrote roughly two pages more on the October morning meeting of the cousins with Mme. Chauchat.—In the course of my noon walk I fell to thinking of *Der Ring des Nibelungen* with the most rapt emotion—ultimately overcome with a wave of rage at Heinrich and his wanton political blabber against Wagner. Feelings of hatred.—After lunch read the typescript of Ponten's story "Die Fahrt nach Aachen." Found it moving and admirable. Napped in bed, but interrupted by the delivery of the liqueur from Tegernsee, which had to be paid for. After tea wrote to Ponten, only to tear up the letter, which had become too discursive, and begin another, shorter one. Evening walk down the Isar. During supper Katia had to give the boys a scolding for their bad behavior. I, too, chimed in.—When anyone seems on the verge of tears, Lisa says "Don't cry! You're *so* good!" (patting them affectionately).—This evening attempted once again to read Jean Paul (*Titan*), but cannot tolerate baroque lyricism. Mean to read some small pieces by Jammes that were sent by Rheinhardt, who translated them.

Yesterday and today cool and rainy. Bad state of mind; made no headway with my writing. Oppressed, disconsolate. The whole thing impossible. The recent sections have to be rewritten. No pleasure in the ideas, and no capacity for working them out. Paralyzed. In the foreword to my edition of Baudelaire there is something about the mind's being the divine principle in man and the soul the infernal principle—which bolsters my position somewhat.—Yesterday wrote several important letters. Today's mail brings none of the things I am waiting for, neither the answer from Fischer nor news from Korrodi about the chapter from the novel.—Yesterday after lunch Hatzfeld came to see me with the manuscript of his novel, which had been turned down by Cassirer and which he wanted me to read and recommend to Fischer (Heimann).— Yesterday evening a shattering episode. Katia found Klaus's diary lying open and read it. Though there was nothing overtly wicked in it, it revealed such an unhealthy coldness, ingratitude, lovelessness, deceitfulness—to say nothing of the callow and silly literary and radical posturing—that her poor mother's heart was deeply disappointed and wounded. Katia wept over the boy as she had some years ago when he lay at death's door. Myself sick at heart, I attempted to reassure and comfort her. I will never play the infuriated father. There is nothing the boy can do about his nature, which is not of his own making. Also I refuse to believe that he is totally lacking in decency. Without doubt much of this is simply tasteless showing off.—Both of us are still shaken by the experience.—Katia went to Rieder to have her lungs X-rayed.— Walked for an hour in the rain, out toward Bogenhausen.—Katia back in time for luncheon, upset by Rieder's rudeness.—Wrote letters after tea. Katia came in with cheering news about the talk she had with Eissi, which reassured her. He also wept bitterly. I think it did him good to realize we were aware [of] some of the difficulties faced by young people. At supper he still appeared chastened, but then, since I pretended not to notice, he let himself go again.—The rain stopped; I went out for a breath of air. This evening read the *Allgemeine Zeitung*, with an article about me by Elster, and the *Auslandspost*; new articles by Rathenau, who says much that is true but whose self-satisfied, prophetic air makes an unpleasant impression.

I have been here since Monday evening, having left Munich after teatime in a thunderstorm. Fairly nervous and tired, I was taken by auto to the station. Traveled with W. Speyer. The Expressionist Georg Kaiser gave me a cold stare before getting into the next car. Richter was here to receive me, and we discussed the Pniower affair during dinner, Richter being the first person to agree with me on the matter. He left the next morning. The three or four days since then have passed quickly. The weather has been sunny and summery; thunderstorms in the distance, though today one came quite close, causing me to stay indoors for my rest. I woke at about 8:00 each morning, used the rubber tub I had brought along, had breakfast out of doors, either in the garden house or the "grove," also doing my writing in one place or the other. The work has gone well, calmly and effortlessly. I am in the midst of Settembrini's exposition on the "Sociology of Suffering," a comic bit of rationalism.—Twice I have gone rowing on the lake at midday, the first time toward Tutzing with an east wind causing the water to be slightly choppy. Rowing with the wind is more fun, since one has the impression one is moving faster. At any change of course little waves begin to lap and slap at the bow. It was quite warm; I wore neither jacket nor vest and even removed my suspenders. Since I was wearing no undershirt, only my shirt, my back was exposed to the breeze, a most pleasant sensation. For overcivilized people the natural verges on voluptuousness.—The second time I headed for Possenhofen through haze and over mirror-smooth water. One morning, when the key to the boathouse was unobtainable, I sat by the path on the shore. Have been taking Fakir for walks in the afternoon; at first I was somewhat afraid of him because of his size. Yesterday we took an extended excursion as far as Erling, two hours. I prefer the path along the railway embankment as before.—Evenings, and after lunch as well, have played the Gramophone, for which I have an almost sinful passion, and to which I have assigned an important role in *The Magic Mountain*. The parallels between the novel and *Carmen* came to me in connection with the emotionally tinged current craze for Piccaver's recording of "La fleur que tu m'avais jêtée." Soomer's performance of "Wotan's Wrath" is magnificent. Burrian renders the "Was, da sie mich gebahr—ihr Liebesber-*ge—war*" passage from *Tristan* superbly. I especially love the *Martha* record of Battistini. Flotow's melodic line is so natural that hearing it one can always predict how it will proceed.— All sorts of mail yesterday and today. Yesterday I telegraphed the *Vossische Zeitung* asking them to return the manuscript, since they apparently intended to keep me dangling. Doubtless they wish to spare their professor. My "fellow culprit," Dr. Zillmann, wrote suggesting we proceed jointly, which I will avoid.—Fred wrote, asking me to contribute to the Altenberg publication that he is putting together. Assured me, to my surprise, that Altenberg often spoke in enthusiastic terms to him about me.—Read Turgenev's *Faust* to the end, and am sampling some stories by Count Alexei Tolstoy.—Frau Piokarska is taking good care of me.—Damp, with persistent light drizzle. I am planning to go to the station with Fakir to meet Richter, who is due back. Not settled whether I will stay here over Whitsun or not.

Tuesday, May 25; Munich

Yesterday, Whitsun Monday, in Feldafing, where I spent the morning in the garden house revising my recent pages. Then, in lovely weather down to the lake; sailed with Richter, Fräulein Häuser, and "Sepp" from Starnberg in the direction of Seeshaupt. Enjoyable, lovely outing. I could see the lakeside house where Katia and I spent the second summer after our marriage. We had a hearty meal at the inn, then set our course for Tutzing, going across the lake, since the wind had veered and was blowing toward the north, and had tea on the terrace of the Hotel Simson. Then, since it was entirely becalmed, had to have the skipper row us home. Back at Feldafing, found Prof. Uhde-Bernays and his family at the house. Played the Gramophone for the children. Supper with Richter and Fräulein Häuser. Richter's confession that he feels himself alien to bourgeois society, to which I offered by way of conclusion that he was "not at all a bad sort." A touchingly solemn glance from him. Farewell concert. I went upstairs early, finished packing, and read a bit more of A. N. Tolstoy's novellas in bed.

Up this morning at 7:00, shaved, and got myself ready. Warm, oppressive weather. Had breakfast with Richter in the garden house and went to the station with little Fanny. Two trains from Garmisch, neither very full. Waited for the second and was in Munich by about 10:30. A cab home, where Katia greeted me in the garden, remarking how tanned I was, and how my face had filled out. She herself does not look well. Kohlgrub absolutely essential. Had some breakfast, and was sitting in the garden reading the mail, mostly letters from readers, when I was frightened to death by a false cry for help from Moni, and ran to see what was the matter. After living in the self-indulgent ambience of a bachelor household, now pressed by troubles and vexation; the inside of the house seems poorly cared for, the tax declaration is due, and even with considerable chicanery we will owe some 20,000 marks. Katia, at the end of her patience, gave one of the housemaids a tongue-lashing; there has been friction with the Walters on account of the children, since Grete smashed up one of the bicycles, Klaus is in love with her, and so forth.—Reunion with Lisa in the bedroom. I was tender with Erika, whom I found tanned, strong, and beautiful, and showed affection toward Klaus, whom I hugged and told to be of good cheer, even if "life isn't always easy." I believe puberty is giving him problems.—Unpacked and put things away. Right after lunch went upstairs and lay down. Tea with Katia on the terrace. She had been to the tax office. The newspaper disgusting as usual. Katia wants to persuade me to vote in the upcoming Reichstag elections—for the Democrats, moreover, by way of supporting the middle class. At most I would vote for the German People's party. But given the situation in Bavaria, where the moderate parties have no prospects and the choice lies between the Socialists and the Catholic parties, I will remain on the sidelines.—Sultry, silk suit, cloudy, thunder. Lisa is practicing going up and down the stone steps in the garden.—We are invited to the Löhrs' for dinner.

. . . .
Wednesday, May 26
. . . .

Vicco and his wife were supposed to have been at the Löhrs' yesterday, but since he is still suffering from his nicotine poisoning they begged off. Löhr, coming straight from arbitration proceedings concerning the promotion of employees at the bank, had to go back to work by nine. We learned of the death of Henry Haag, who drowned himself in the Elbe. The news was passed on to Löhr officially, and in the coldest possible manner.—[. . .] Today a very warm summer day. Did some writing, changing once more the section from the "encyclopedia of suffering." Into town, where I bought a straw hat for 55 marks and had my hair cut. At Honsell's, ran into W. Seidel, just back from America. I was wearing the remade summer suit for the first time and the 500-mark boots that had just been delivered; took pleasure in the quality and elegance of my clothes.—Rode home with Walter, who invited me to *Der Corregidor* and to *Oberon*.—At table, obviously for my sake, Klaus made an antiradical remark. I was touched by it.—In the garden; then storm, quite local but violent, with a few re-sounding thunderclaps. I spent the time resting a bit longer on my bed. For tea, Katia's mother, joined later by her father as well. Wrote several letters. Born, whom I mistakenly caused to be turned away at the door, brought his color illustrations for *Death in Venice*. I find them stiff and unattractive.—Took a short walk in the damp, invigorating air. At supper, discussions with the children about socialism, during which Katia showed herself to be critical and negative. That is poor pedagogy. Most important to me is the children's confidence, which is only compromised by such behavior.—Erika and Klaus are both reading *Royal Highness*, discussing the characters between themselves.—I have begun Keller's *Zurich Novellas*, which I had not read before; find them somewhat tedious.—Katia packing for her trip.

Sultry, showers, then sunny summer heat. Weary, troubled mood, caused in part by forebodings about the economy and in part by uncongenial reading matter (Flake's journal). Gloomy thoughts about the uselessness of my writing, the minimal response that it elicits.—Wrote on a bit, but without hope or any clear view of where I am headed. To Gosch at noon, who has several things to do on my teeth. Bicycled, ending up with a ride through the park. Katia still occupied with preparations for her trip. We had an earlier teatime with Gerta Marcks, who will be looking after things here in Katia's absence. After Katia said her good-byes I accompanied her to the station. The train left at 6:00 (Murnau-Kohlgrub). I stayed until it pulled out and waved a cheery farewell. Katia worried about her mother, who is feared to have stomach cancer.—To the Künstlerhaus for a meeting of the Pfitzner Association, where the members wasted a great deal of time in artful discussion of the superfluity of such an organization. Thiersch, Busching, Hallgarten, Courvoisier, Löhr, Bruckmann, and others. I took no part in the discussion (although I was tempted to say something about the relationship between Walter and Pfitzner). Left with Hallgarten and rode home with him. First supper on the veranda with Fräulein Marcks. Klaus and Golo off to sing in the *St. Matthew Passion.*—Read the *Neue Merkur,* which contains a story by Reinacher that I recommended to them.—Not a word from the *Vossische Zeitung,* which I find outrageous.

Sunday, June 6

My forty-fifth birthday. In the morning wrote to Katia. At breakfast, gifts in the dining room. A splendid rucksack, sweets, paperbacks, socks.—Election day. Even old Nurse went off to cast her ballot, leaving Bibi bawling alone in his playpen. I soothed him and cheered him up. I had long ago decided not to "exercise my franchise." This afternoon attended to more letters. For dinner Privy Councillor Marcks with his wife, son, and niece, also Katia's parents. The table decorated with roses. Our manservant waited on table and was paid 10 marks. Good food, except for the fish, which was somewhat far gone. Moselle from Arcisstrasse. Two bottles of sparkling wine at 64 marks a bottle. Coffee. Fräulein Marcks sang some Schubert and Brahms. Privy Councillor Pringsheim played *Tristan,* but not very well. My in-laws brought cigarettes, sweets, a cigarette lighter that doesn't work, and a silver paper knife. The evening went pleasantly enough. The Marckses' niece, a confirmed Berliner with a government job and a salary of 1,200 marks a month, is off on a business trip to Budapest. Eissi very free with her at table, under the influence of the champagne. Marcks and I conversed quite a bit about politics. At table he had some intriguing things to say about the medieval ban on lending at interest, which, however, could not be enforced. Calvin gave it sanction, thereby ushering in the bourgeois age that is now in its last gasp (Pastor Bunge).—I had expected my father-in-law to deliver a little speech, and was prepared with a response, but no speech was forthcoming.

Monday, July 5

The Hallgartens came to dinner Saturday evening. Discussion of the horrors of economic and social conflicts.—Yesterday, Sunday, a morning walk with Katia, Erika, Klaus, and Moni as far as the Aumeister, where we had a snack. In the evening a change of weather; thunderstorm and sudden drop in temperature. Feeling very bad, pale, congested, anxious, nauseous. Felt better once in bed, however, and slept rather well. Tired today, but went on writing on the physiology discussion and then went into town on errands. Cool, sunny weather, contrary to expectations.—Letter from Bertram, who is embarking on his trip to Scandinavia at Lassen's expense. Fantasies of meeting up with him in Lübeck and sojourning on the North Sea.—Yesterday began a long letter about *Death in Venice* and my relationship to homoeroticism to the poet C. M. Weber (Olaf), who had sent me his poems by way of Seidel.—This afternoon attended to other letters. Arrangements for the fall tour to Bonn, Cologne, Elberfeld, and Barmen.—These past days have read Brandes's *The Romantic School in Germany* with keen interest. Staggered to discover ideas in Novalis that had come to me as I penetrated into the world of *The Magic Mountain*, unaware that they might have occurred earlier to others. Looking forward excitedly to the dialogues between Bunge and Settembrini. The latter must find the views of the other man obscene, and feel himself obliged to intercede gallantly in order to protect the innocence of Hans Castorp. Does this finally lead to the challenge to a duel?—In love with Klaus these days. Germ of a father-son novella.—Intellectual ferment.

Sunday, July 11

Crisp, sunny day. I made revisions in the manuscript, wrote a bit more on the letter about German style. Then out on my bicycle, along the Isar as far as the Flaucher (or should it be Pflaucher?), where I rested on a bench for a bit. Crowds of Sunday promenaders. Hosts of brightly dressed cyclists, clubs sporting banners and scarves. Working-class sports festival. On the way back, the roads blocked here and there by their gathering partisans.—Before and after lunch, in the garden reading Lion's chapter on Venice in the Rococo age. A brilliant work.—After tea, read my last two scenes to Katia, who found them highly satisfactory. For the Sunday afternoon scene I will adopt a technical change she suggested. After 7:00 we went out once again, with Golo and Moni. Eissi, who at the moment enchants me, has sent a story to *Simplicissimus*, an impossible one, of course, and intends to send another to the *Rundschau*. A folly from which he must be dissuaded.—Went on with *Lost Illusions*.

Wednesday, July 14

No writing yesterday morning except on the letter to the German teacher, which I may possibly give to the *Vossische Zeitung*.—A 1,000-mark honorarium for the deluxe edition of *Gesang vom Kindchen* arrived.—At noon by cab into town, where I bought a bicycle at Schad's as a present for Katia's birthday; 1,525 marks.—Katia's mother's birthday. Katia and the children there to tea. After tea I wrote to Elchinger in regard to *Weltliteratur* (the jubilee number) and to Lion concerning his chapter on Venetian philosophy. For dinner to Arcisstrasse, where the majolica and the bronzes are once more on display. Good food, followed by fruit and champagne. Reading of birthday letters. Home by tram at 11:00. Rencontre with Katia, [. . .] I am not entirely clear about my thoughts in this respect. It can scarcely be a question of actual impotence, but more likely the customary confusion and unreliability of my "sex life." Doubtless this stimulation failure can be accounted for by the presence of desires that are directed the other way. How would it be if a young man were "at my disposal?" Be that as it may, it would be foolish to let myself get depressed by a failure whose basis is hardly new to me. Far better to treat the matter lightly, with humor, detachment, and self-confidence, since these are the best "medicines."—A letter from Fiedler about the situation his essay on Luther has put him in.—The *Allgemeine Biologie* by Hertwig has come.—Lisa, irritable and feverish after her vaccination, has a rash.—This evening we are off to Feldafing. I packed up my work, etc. after breakfast.

Sunday, July 25

From Thursday the 15th to Friday the 23rd in Feldafing, the first four days with Katia, and with Richter there part of the time. Intense heat. Rowing, swimming in the lake, and listening to the Gramophone. With Katia and Feuchtwanger at Frank's for dinner. Pitch black coming home. Very poor mood for working. No progress at all on *The Magic Mountain* except for a few preparatory notes. Struggled with a letter about the teaching of style that I had thought to send to the *Vossiche Zeitung* and had started several times but abandoned out of disinterest. Katia left on Monday. On Tuesday, to my surprise, a visit from Eri and Eissi, who bicycled out with Richard Hallgarten. Am enraptured with Eissi, terribly handsome in his swimming trunks. Find it quite natural that I should fall in love with my son.—Lovely, pastoral summer day with the children; chicken for lunch in the "grove," then rowed toward Tutzing. They returned from the train station while I was eating supper, since they hadn't had enough money for the express. Left again at ten, after I had played several things for them on the Gramophone.—The weather during the whole stay quite summery, hot, interrupted by mild storms. I came back Friday evening on the very fast new train—the 8:11, in Munich by 8:45. Short conversation with the attractive young man in white trousers sitting next to me in third class. Very pleasurable. It seems I am once and for all done with women? Greeted everyone after riding home by cab, for which I paid 20 marks. Eissi was lying tanned and shirtless on his bed, reading; I was disconcerted.—Yesterday was Katia's birthday. Gifts in the morning, including her new bicycle. Took Eissi along on a brief midday walk and talked with him about the essay question. Katia's parents here for chocolate. In the evening a garden party at Dr. Mannheimer's, where Kerner's *Totengräber* was performed in the open air. Admirable little work, well presented. Unique Romantic tone. The technique entrancing, thanks to the impression that in such a fashion one might capture the whole of life. Unassuming and yet quite daring. Spoke to a number of people, all of them men incidentally, with the exception of a creature at the end who "got to know" me. Came home on foot. To bed very late and tired.—Finished the pedagogical article today; read it aloud to Katia and Klaus in the garden. Will send it to the *Vossische*. To tea Adele Gerhard, who stayed late. After dinner read Dostoevsky's *Honorable Thief* and a translation of Perrault's "Fairy." Golo cried helplessly over Emelianushka.—In Feldafing I contracted with the Madrid society about *Death in Venice* for only 750 marks, which was dumb of me.

- -
Tuesday, July 27
- -

Yesterday and today revised the last section. After lunch yesterday, bicycled to the Progress office to dictate the pedagogical article. Yesterday evening read a story of Eissi's steeped in Weltschmerz. Sat by his bed and commented on it, accompanying my criticisms with tendernesses that I believe he took pleasure in. In the evening wrote a letter of sympathy to Frau Ganghofer on the death of her husband.—Tired and lethargic. Sent off the article to the *Vossische Zeitung,* though I find it weak and illogical. Rain. Hardly went out. Born and his wife to tea. He showed me some of his prints. Bertram sent a picture postcard from above the Arctic Circle. I inscribed dedications for the facsimile edition of *Tristan.* Am reading the book on physiology lent me by Hermanns.—Katia has a bad cold.—Richter's deluxe edition of *Little Herr Friedemann* arrived during the last few days.

- -
Wednesday, July 28
- -

Rain. The river swollen. Wrote on, beginning the new section with the onset of winter. At noon to Salzer to get stronger lenses prescribed. Read in the physiology book. Not well rested, disturbed by Katia's coughing. After tea, letter to Stefan Zweig regarding his "Dostoevsky." Annette Kolb, whom I did not much care for, to dinner. By the way, she thought Klaus takes after me. She had high praise for a French novelist by the name of Proust, or something like that. Escorted her to the tram.

- -
Sunday, August 1
- -

Katia in bed. Wrote further (a humorous passage). Rain. Did not go out at noon, but sat by Katia's bed and talked with her about "incest," specifically a father's physical love for a daughter who resembles her mother in her youth; a highly natural situation, I explained.—After lunch read in the writings of Pannwitz, principally the pamphlet on Nietzsche.—Dr. Rosenthal from Vienna to tea. Stimulating conversation, walk. In the evening read a good, heartening article in the *Merkur* on the end of Expressionism, then went on with Hertwig's book on physiology, which once again reveals the poverty of our knowledge regarding the actual life process. We do not even know why the stomach does not digest itself. The usual explanation, namely that the living protoplasm possesses a specific resistance to the gastric juices, rings hollow when we confront the mystery of life.—The stronger glasses are serving me well. But my eyes have stood up remarkably, considering my age; the lenses are below normal strength.

- -
Sunday, October 17
- -

Yesterday morning did some writing. In the evening to the Eliasbergs' at 8:30, where the gathering was entirely Jewish: the Borns, the Rheinhardts, the Meyers, the Feucht-wangers. Frau Eliasberg's dolls not bad. On Saturday afternoon a meeting relating to the Nietzsche Society at the Musarion Verlag, with Wölfflin and Bertram present. Toward the end I became quite fervid, and spoke of the unification of Europe by means of the German spirit, and of cosmopolitanism as being the genius, essence, and destiny of the German national character.—Yesterday went by tram from the Eliasbergs' to the station to pick up Katia, who came in from Oberstdorf at around 11:00. Met her, then took a cab home, where the four older children were waiting up for us. Katia very happy. Little repast with champagne. Much recounting and then to bed. I heard some noise in the boys' room and came upon Eissi totally nude and up to some nonsense by Golo's bed. Deeply struck by his radiant adolescent body; overwhelming.—[. . .] This morning, after breakfast with the whole family, wrote letters: to Wiesbaden about a reading there, and to Klagenfurt (Carinthia) about the outcome of the referendum, mentioning Dr. Endres's name. At noon Katia and I accompanied Katia's mother through the Englischer Garten. After tea read Dostoevsky to Katia and the children. A short walk with Erika. It began to sprinkle, the weather changing abruptly; the lovely autumn seems to be over.—Read Kahler's essay *Der Beruf der Wissenschaft*.—Grateful to Katia for her unwavering love for me even though she no longer awakens my desire, and I am not able to give her pleasure, that is the ultimate sexual pleasure, when I lie with her. The serenity, love, and equanimity with which she takes this are remarkable, and thus I need not be too deeply affected myself.

Tuesday, October 19

Strange outcome of yesterday's reading at Steinicke's, to which I went by tram in a cold north wind with the children and Eva Löhr, who was visiting them, while Katia, who had been at Arcisstrasse, came straight from there. Met the shockingly stupid and tasteless Dr. Kemmerich, who attached himself to us and followed us up to the cloakroom. A dense crowd at the ticket table. The hall packed, even around the podium and to the side of it. The Eliasbergs, Herbert Eulenberg, among others. I was in bad form, did not manage to deliver the introduction as I had prepared it, at least not at the beginning. I then read the scene with the directress to a rapt audience that laughed appreciatively at every opportunity. When I left the platform for an intermission there was no applause. I returned, read the examination scene, and again at the end of it there was not a trace of applause, the first time such a thing has happened since I began giving public readings. It was a combination of chance, misunderstanding, the "refined" character of the audience, the confusing arrangement of things. Obviously nearly everyone had enjoyed himself. My entourage disconcerted. No one said anything about what I read except for Kemmerich, who prattled inanities. I, too, was confused. The organizers, who had reason to be pleased with the proceeds, thanked me. I came home with Katia and the children through the Englischer Garten. It was a painful affair for me because of the presence of the children, relatives, and friends. Later in the evening I had heart palpitations, had difficulty falling asleep, and was awakened early by the commuter train. The fatigued, nervous, distraught, and foggy state that I have been in for weeks (the long readings have been particularly hard on me) was scarcely improved by this senseless occurrence. My thoughts are now turning toward the approaching Rhineland tour. I fear the strains of it, but it may also bring encouragement. The winter will be abnormally busy for me. The central question in my mind is the fate of *The Magic Mountain*.—We heard from Wassermann, who is for a short time in Munich.

Yesterday continued revising *The Magic Mountain*, which must be pushed forward a bit. Bicycled to Nadoleczny to have my ears attended to.—Proofs of *Blood of the Walsungs*. Reading the *Don Carlos*.—With Katia this morning to the open rehearsal of the *Missa Solemnis*. The Walters, the Viennese countess, Erb, and others. Remarkably impressed by the appearance of Princess Gisela, an Imperial Highness inasmuch as she is descended from Karl V. The expectations aroused by Walter's talk fulfilled at best sporadically. In order to enjoy music I need to have heard it *often*, know it *thoroughly*. My chief impression was of a remarkably handsome young man, Slavic in appearance and wearing a sort of Russian costume, with whom I established a kind of contact at a distance, since he noticed my interest in him immediately and was obviously pleased by it.—Very cold for the past few days. Fur coat. Afternoon on the balcony. Katia out for the evening at the Hallgartens', along with the Kurt Wolffs and Count Kessler. I declined despite their urging. Read Mahler's letters to Walter in copies that Walter and his daughter have made.

Most of the month of November was taken up by the Rhineland-Westphalia trip: Mühlheim (stayed at the home of the young Buller couple, he a manufacturer); Duisburg (Mahler's Second Symphony); Bochum (the Mummenhoff family); Dortmund (matinee at the Stadttheater, dinner with the Maurachs at the Fürstenhof); Elberfeld-Barmen (stayed with the Bertrams, a moving experience); Düsseldorf; by way of Hagen to Lüdenscheid (both ways by car, staying with the young manufacturer Noelle and his mother, a man who was pleasingly deferential and who aroused warm feelings); Essen (staying with Dr. Hessberg; presented with huge bouquet on the podium); then Bonn-Cologne for a whole week, where I stayed with the Litzmanns: endless parties and testimonials, addresses to students at both universities, excursion to the Siebengebirge region, the Drachenfels, considerable time with Bertram and his colleague Langhammer. The last reading on the 20th in Wiesbaden. Day trip home from there on the 21st.

At home took up *The Magic Mountain* again. Hans Castorp's acts of charity. Overwhelming amount of mail to take care of that had accumulated during my three-week absence; books, letters, etc. Soon it was December. From the 9th to the 12th a three-day stay with Katia in Berlin for the meetings on orthographic reform. Sleeping car. Hotel Excelsior. Conference at the Ministry of the Interior. Visited the Rosenbergs in Matthäikirchstrasse. Saw Katia's brothers. Two evenings in the theater: three Russian plays at the Kammerspiele, and at the Grosses Schauspielhaus *Danton* by Rolland, impressive. The whole episode quite successful. Luncheon with Fischers discussing business matters.

On my return took up my normal existence. Worthy of mention: an evening at Kurt Wolff's, Luisenstrasse, with a reading by Hardt. Introduced to Princess Pilar and her brother Adalbert. (A few days later heard Hardt read my *Wardrobe* at Schmidt's.) The large benefit tea at Löhrs' for the African colonists. Evening party here at home, with readings by Reisiger and Ponten.

Just before Christmas the Litzmanns from Bonn were frequent guests. Gave several readings from *The Magic Mountain*, starting from the beginning. They are coming once more tomorrow evening.

Odd jobs: an article on the Editiones Insulae for the *Nachrichten*, which appeared in the Christmas edition, and *Children's Games* for the Christmas edition of the *Vossische Zeitung*.

The holidays followed the usual pattern, dimmed somewhat by an ear infection of Elisabeth's and my own influenza-like condition from which I am still suffering.

Took on the job of writing an introductory piece for the Russian issue of the *Süddeutsche Monatshefte* that Eliasberg is editing. Payment: 1,000 marks.

After the holidays, took steps to secure a passport with Switzerland in mind. Would like some time in Feldafing and Polling before that.

Reading has been rather fragmented for some time. Have now begun Pontoppidan's *Kingdom of the Dead*, which fascinates me.—Correspondence with Prof. Curtius about his book *Wegbereiter*, and about the *Revue de Genève*, which wants me to contribute something, and means to publish *Tonio Kröger* and a study on me. Further foreign editions in the offing, namely Italian and Spanish ones. (*Death in Venice* will have just the right tone in Spanish.)

The weather during the big tour was mostly favorable, also while we were in Berlin. For the past several days it has been warm and damp.

Friday, December 31

Yesterday the Litzmanns to supper again. Another long reading from *The Magic Mountain*, to the end of Chapter Three. The evening grew late. Today at noon into town to see about the passport and attend to other errands. Had to show my doctoral diploma to the police. Bought a fancy lorgnette.—The warm spring weather continues.—A great number of books have been arriving again these days: a large monograph on Strauss by Specht, another on Romain Rolland by Stefan Zweig. I glanced through them this afternoon. The high-minded, pallid, humanitarian personality of Rolland still strikes me as insipid. Presumptuous of him to call himself the disciple of Tolstoy, Wagner, and Goethe.—Long letters from Bertram and Eltzbacher. There is to be a party at Arcisstrasse to ring out the year, with the Löhrs, Professor Fehr, the Schölls, and Pidoll. When I came back from town I installed the new calendar. It seems rather a long time since I last did so. A year *is* long after all. One way or another, 1921 will see the completion of *The Magic Mountain* and open up unknown new paths in my life.

1921

Yesterday, New Year's Day, the children put on a theatrical performance at the Hallgartens'. *As You Like It*, in which Erika was quite entrancing. Later on chatted with Wölfflin and Marcks for a while.—Slept late this morning. Took care of mail and did very little work, as in the past few days. At noon, in utterly springlike weather for which my winter overcoat is much too warm, went out with Klaus. We met Endres and his wife and walked with them through the park as far as Prinzregentenstrasse. To tea at Paul Ehrenberg's in Schwabing, having walked through the Englischer Garten. There was music, and I read the first chapter of *The Magic Mountain* and some sections of *A Man and His Dog*. The affair went on for a long time, until 9:00 o'clock. The company consisted of the painter Tragi, who played the accompaniments, his daughter, his son-in-law, and the Bodensteins. Walked home, where we had only beer and sandwiches for supper. A strange encounter between Erika and Fräulein Kleinsgütl, somewhat disturbing.—Called up Feldafing to say I will be coming out there tomorrow evening in order to write the Russian article.

Sunday, February 6

From the 16th of January to the 3rd of February a tour through German-speaking Switzerland. Winterthur: Stayed at Colonel Bühler-Kohler's, a well-to-do family, attractive son. Baden, Aarau, Berne: Harry Maync, a walk with two students through the lovely old town the morning before my departure, the arcades, the patrician houses with their gardens on the river; encounter with Weese at the station. Zurich: Evening at the Hottingen Club, very splendid; Korrodi's dinner speech, Ermatinger. Basel: The editor Dr. Knuchel and his wife, Professor Joël, the surgeon Iselin; stimulating evening after my reading from the *The Magic Mountain*. Zurich again: Return to Zollikon to Faesi's; luncheon with Prof. Sieveking and Reiffs; Dr. Trog; reading to a capacity audience in the handsome main auditorium of the university. Solothurn: The pharmacist Pfaehler, climbed the tower; majestic Baroque-Renaissance church, magnificent early-Renaissance-style Town Hall; reading at the freemason-like "Potters Association," with so-called "death tribunal" afterward at which I was interrogated. St. Gall, Lucerne: Forest Inspector Burri, an original little fellow; stayed at the Hotel St. Gotthard; solitary steamer excursion to Weggis in the loveliest weather; the Pilatus. On the 30th of January left Lucerne for Davos, passing the Walensee with its view of the Churfirsten, then from Landquart up into the snow-covered mountains. Dreamlike. Dreamlike too revisiting a real place that I have long since transformed into a landscape of the mind. Was met at the "village" by Platzer and taken by sleigh to the Kurhaus. After lunch went to the ice carnival. Pictures taken with Niddy Impekoven. In the evening I was a guest at the ice sportsmen's banquet, then saw Impekoven dance at the Kurhaus. On the 31st a morning walk by myself. After lunch a sleigh ride with Platzer to Mondstein under overcast sky. Mozart concert afterward. Evening spent in the Kurhaus café. On February first, attended a bobsled race and a children's affair at the skating rink. That evening, gave a reading in the music room of the Kurhaus. The audience included people taking the cure, Dutch and English. The café afterward. On the second, climbed the Schatzalp with Platzer. Cold foehn. Got up above 2,000 meters. To the west the blue sky almost black. Took a bad fall during the descent. Called on Jessen. After lunch went to the pharmacist Lang's for coffee with Platzer and Dr. Wolfer, owner of a sanatorium. By way of finale, a walk to the former Philippi Sanatorium. Looked long and hard—as indeed I had done throughout my stay. Tea with Platzer and his aunt. On the third, departure at 6 A.M.; coffee in Klosters, then Landquart, Sargans, Rohrschach, Lake Constance, Lindau. Express train to Munich. Arrived at 10:30, met by Katia.

The usual correspondence to be taken care of. Yesterday already made revisions in *The Magic Mountain* on the basis of notes I had taken. Käthe Rosenberg visiting. This morning at the Odeon; open rehearsal of Mahler's *Das Lied von der Erde.* Deeply moved. Supper at Arcisstrasse with Katia, her cousin, and Frau Rosenberg.

The Russian issue with my introduction has appeared. Eliasberg phoned to say it has made quite a stir. The Hungarian socialist *Neue Zeitung* intends to review it, and Merezhkovsky plans to write a letter to me or the editor. Very pleased.

Already busy making preparations for the Thuringian tour. Have also made firm arrangements with Halle. Invited to visit Privy Councillor Colmers in Coburg.

. . . .
Wednesday, February 23
. . . .

Returned to Munich yesterday morning. Traveled to Coburg on the 11th; met at Lichtenfels by Privy Councillor Colmers and his wife, who took me by car to their home where I would be staying. Went to the theater; a high-flown, overdone drama by Wildgans, the leading man a Munich actor by the name of Putz, with whom I was greatly taken. Later I made his acquaintance at the Colmers' and spoke flatteringly to him. Next morning visited the hospital. White doctor's smock. Two goiter operations; greatly impressed. Made the rounds. The Hohenlohe-Langenburg family to tea (the princess is a Royal Highness). The princesses' albums. My reading in the evening attended by Duke Karl Eduard, who was highly entertained. I stayed on through the 13th. Visited the duke at his castle. Was driven to another castle in the neighborhood and shown through it. Departure on the 14th; by car to Lichtenfels, thence by an inconvenient sequence of cold local trains to Gera, where I was met by Frau Litzmann. Hotel. Reading attended by the prince, the princess, and the crown prince; conversation afterward with the latter. Spent the night at the hotel. Next morning with Frau Litzmann to the castle at Krossen, Privy Councillor Litzmann having met us at the station. A novel experience for me to stay in that old, rambling ancestral seat, most of it now closed off, with its immense collections of Asiatic art. Gigantic bedroom with canopy bed. In the evening Elizabeth von Heyking read a novella aloud. On the 16th to Weimar. Hotel Fürstenhof; quite awful, like all hotels in these provinces. Frau Förster-Nietzsche was in the audience at my reading, and sought me out afterward. Before my departure on the 17th I had breakfast with her, along with Dr. Öhler and his wife. A half hour alone with Frau Förster beforehand. She spoke of Nietzsche's last years. All in all a remarkable impression. Family resemblance in the eyes. The oddity of his strikingly good manners even in advanced stages of his paralysis.—On to Halle. Hotel Stadt Hamburg, awful. Met by Frau Litzmann, who is frighteningly, hysterically in love, and who went with me as far as Naumburg the next day. Met old Vaihinger after the strenuous and unrewarding reading. Spent some time with Katia's cousin Dietrich von Rohrscheidt and his wife. On the 18th to Jena, where I was met by Professor Naumann. To tea at his home, along with Eugen Diederichs and his wife and Prince and Princess Georg von Sachsen-Meiningen. Reading at the Rosensälen (*A Weary Hour*). Afterward we repaired to the picturesque tavern where one pays the bill *à discrétion* at the cigar counter as one leaves. Seated next to the congenial Prince Georg. Still later, more conversation at the Naumanns'. On the 19th, a walk with Naumann and Diederichs. Visited the university, with its glorious mural by Hodler of the 1813 student uprising, a monumental evocation of young, idealistic, and militant manliness. Back to the Naumanns' at noon, where I rested for a time in the children's room before boarding the train for Berlin. Evening arrival, Hotel Excelsior; mix-up about my "reserved" room. Had tea with rum at supper in the lounge. Delight at the running hot water. Telephone in the room. On the 20th (Sunday, Election Day) was at the Rosenbergs' at luncheon, where I found Peter and Klaus, Klaus's wife, and Professor Hans Rosenberg. Had a brief rest there, then went on to tea at Gerhards' on Wilhelmstrasse. Back to the hotel. Olga Prings-heim called. With Dr. Elster by car to the Werner Siemens Gymnasium for the reading. The auditorium packed and overheated. Read the "Thermometer" chapter from *The Magic Mountain* and also *The Railway Accident*. The ovations virtually frenetic, shat-tering. Throngs of people wanting autographs afterward, paying homage. The lady who cuts silhouettes. Afterward a reception at the Elsters'. Walked back to the hotel with Elster. On the 21st was fetched by Dr. Francke (of Sybillen-Verlag). Conference at 11:00 A.M. with Fischer about the essay volume and the Collected Works. Breakfast at 12:00 on Motzstrasse with the people connected with *Gewissen*. Afternoon in the hotel, where I was informed by telephone that my sleeping-car ticket had been deliv-ered. Otherwise I would have gone to the Deutsches Theater to see *The Maid of Orleans*. Hasty preparations for departure. At 5:00 by cab (60 marks) to Klaus Pringsheim's out in Charlottenburg-Westend. Tea there together with Heinz Prings-heim and his wife. Took the subway back into town, supper at the Rosenbergs', then to the Anhalt station. A First Lieutenant Meyer had bribed the conductor and rode as far as Wittenberge solely in order to be able to talk with me for half an hour in the sleeping-car corridor. Handsome young Westphalian; hope he got his money's worth. As pleasant and easy a return journey as one could imagine, though to be sure it cost nearly 500 marks. Sumptuous breakfast in my compartment, including eggs and pastry supplied by the Rosenbergs. Arrived here at 10:50, in fine weather. Brought dolls from Berlin for the younger children. The usual mountain of mail. Frightful letter from Frau Litzmann, which I read to Katia. Embarrassed at how I am to treat her and her husband. Read up on the Georg Kaiser trial, also Endres's article about the Russian issue. Will certainly not finish Jaeger's *Kranke Liebe*, which I began reading on my trip. A repellent, joyless work that offers me nothing artistically.—Clear, cold weather. Despite all the burdens and distractions, the main thing now is to put together the essay volume and push on with *The Magic Mountain*.

Tuesday, March 1

In the past week, blessed by fine late-winter weather (usually took my afternoon nap out on the balcony), I pushed ahead with *The Magic Mountain* (sports events and the Schatzalp) and worked my way through piles of correspondence. Also signed several hundred sheets for the deluxe edition of *Blood of the Walsungs*, Heine already having done his. Have not yet managed to do any work on the essay volume.—In a novel everything depends on one's keeping the ideas present at all times, holding fast to the fine strands and motifs, in short forgetting none of the threads one has begun to spin.— We attended Ponten's reading at the Museum and greeted him afterward. He strikes me as being too full of himself. We also went to an evening party at H. Ebers's in Schwabing, where Seidel read some rather poor stuff. I paid a sick call on Walter, in bed with gallbladder trouble, and chatted with him for an hour. Today at noon Trummler and two of his friends from the Werkbund came by to pick me up for a walk. The three youths spoke of their plans for building a sort of monastery for young men, complete with refectory and cells. Their pedagogic ideas derive from Goethe and Jean Paul. I feel sympathetic to their good German traditions. Their values and dreams have nothing of Western European political radicalism about them.

The London Conference has begun. Highly uncertain what it will produce; anything, the wildest of things, is possible.—The children's Fräulein, old Emmi, a rather hangdog and dirty creature, left today. Tomorrow we have a new governess coming, today a new cook. Little Elisabeth, delicate and spoiled with tenderness, has become extremely self-willed, refuses to eat or to go to sleep when the whim takes her. Concerned.—I have been reading here and there in Uexküll's *Theoretische Biologie*. Noted that interest in biological questions, even of the newer, less mechanistic, anti-Darwinist sort, disposes one to be conservative and rigid in political matters. Something similar can be observed in Goethe. Have also begun to read *Barthli, der Korber* by Gotthelf. The lightening episode in it made a great impression on me yesterday evening.—Privy Councillor Vaihinger sent me someone's essay on the theme of illusion in my works. Another essay also arrived, this one on the *Betrachtungen*.

. . . .
Friday, March 4
. . . .

The Künstlerdank (Elster) sent the Berlin reviews, and in gratitude has made me an honorary member.—At tea the foolish young Count Matuschka.—Attended with Erika the evening of readings by Klitsch in the Bayrischer Hof. Spoke to him. Astonishing gifts, but tendency toward Viennese jollity.—The cinema episode in *The Magic Mountain* is taking shape.—Visited Schwegerle's studio at midday to see his relief of Pastor Evers from Lübeck.

. . . .
Monday, April 4
. . . .

Another brilliant spring day. Spent yesterday evening at Martens's together with Ponten, Seidel, and the monocle-wearing writer from Pienzenauerstrasse. To his own naive delight, Ponten read aloud from a work in progress. There was a woodruff-flavored bowle that disagreed with me, so that I had to ask for tea. The rather fruitless talk dragged on until after one o'clock. In the cool night walked home with the monocle-wearer through the Englischer Garten. Before falling asleep read in Frey's *Spuk des Alltags*. Wrote a bit further today. Helbling, the young literary historian from Zurich, came by to join me on my walk; brought chocolates. We talked about Switzerland. This afternoon he sent over a copy of his dissertation, "Die Figur des Künstlers bei Thomas Mann"—comprehensive, and critical of me, whom he conceives of as a late bloom and end of a line. Remarkable that he includes a chapter about my connections with the Stefan George sphere.—On the balcony.—Hermanns found Katia improved, but prescribed more rest. Katia and I came down hard on Klaus for his laziness and conceit. It is one's duty, after all, not to shirk displaying the unpleasant emotion of anger now and then, however much one is inclined to out of self-respect.—

112

Illustration by Thomas Theodor Heine from the deluxe edition of Blood of the Walsungs.   113

Bertram and Glöckner to tea. We sat with Katia in her bedroom, where I read "The Dance of Death" from near the end of Chapter Five. At about 7:30 we went out for a stroll. Supper with the two friends and the children, including the new governess, Fräulein Frenzel. Bertram played the piano afterward. I served port and tea. The celebration of Heinrich's fiftieth birthday at K. Wolff's seems to be still on. Fancy invitations appear to have been sent out promising a program of old Italian music and recitations: a sonnet in his praise, excerpts from his works; opera stars, fanfares and flourishes. *Habeat, habeat.* How satisfied with the world he must be!

Friday, May 13

A party yesterday evening at the Hallgartens'. The children put on a play as a farewell to Gerta Marcks, who is being married and going to live in Rostock. Amusing. Conversed a good deal with Marcks, at his instigation. Back home Katia and I embraced. I feel deeply and warmly grateful toward her for the goodness with which she accepts my sexual problems.—Today renewal of summer's glory; was not especially tired. This morning, wrote out the revised text of my statement. Went to Gosch, then bicycling.—A new housemaid of a better sort.—Katia's mother to tea; she is having heart trouble. She took a look at *Blood of the Walsungs.* I read aloud the statement, which goes off tomorrow to Cotta.—A volume of the big Nietzsche edition came from Musarion Verlag. Other books. Read the *Auslandspost.* Am basically satisfied by the ratification of the ultimatum.—Displeasure with Erika for her improper behavior toward Katia, which was over by evening however.

Thursday, May 19

Finished the article on Ungar yesterday and read it to Katia in the garden in the afternoon. Bicycled along the Isar to have a look at the canal now under construction, and was greatly impressed.—Summery heat, occasional thunder.—Today a very warm, fine day. After breakfast in the garden, into town for a motion picture preview on Sonnenstrasse. I was in a receptive mood, finding much I honestly liked in the first and longer film. What captivated me in a philosophic sense was the simultaneity of things, of differing aspects of life, the sense of "meanwhile." There ought to be a film made with the title *The Fullness of Time.*—Purchased a few things and came home on foot in the heat. A certain Herr Uriel Birnbaum from Vienna sent a book of his poems, along with a longish, clever essay in the vein of the *Betrachtungen* on the theme of Austria, Germany, and the Jews. Jewish conservatism, very good. Napped in the garden. Ponten came to tea and was agreeable, as he usually is. I shared the letter with him. He walked with Katia and me to the Hoftheater, which was presenting Courvoisier's opera *Die Krähen,* together with his ballet *Der Zaubergeiger.* Neither was especially pleasurable. We spoke with Gulbransson during intermission. It is as sultry as at the height of summer. In the evening mail a long, politically slanted article from *Le Temps* about the *Betrachtungen.* What it comes down to, though of course it is never said in so many words, is the question of the Ruhr.

[. . .] This morning I came up with ornamental titles for a number of sections in *The Magic Mountain*. At midday I read in the woods—*Colonel Chabert*, which I have just begun—faithfully accompanied by Lux in his new collar. While I lay under a tree he stayed close beside me. Ate hungrily. Continued reading *Chabert* all afternoon in the garden. Later, at the piano, studied Don José's aria from the piano score so I can sing it for myself. To dinner at Walters', who had also asked the owner of Philharmonic Hall in Berlin and his wife. Too much shouting and laughing. Lotte sang a few things later, and at my urging Walter played Viennese waltzes with great artistry and brilliance, so that the evening was profitable after all.

Tuesday, May 24

Awoke yesterday at nine, and spent the morning determining the section titles up to the end of Chapter Five. Read some in the park at noon, the *Neue Merkur* with several interesting things, particularly an essay on a new book of Freud's that I found stimulating in that it confirms certain historical tendencies. The end of Romanticism, of which I am still a part, expresses itself in all kinds of ways, including for example a weakening and dying of the sexual symbolism that is virtually identical with it (*Parsifal*).—At about three Ponten dropped by, finding me in the garden, and instead of leaving soon, as he had intended, he stayed on, talking about artistic matters, until nearly 6:30. He then had tea with us, still conversing about art; this was not bad in itself, but it robbed me of any chance to rest. At 8:00 the Wassermanns came and had dinner with us on the veranda. I went to bed in a state of exhaustion, with a headache that has returned today. After breakfast, composed an angry telegram to Fischer, demanding that they return the book materials. Wrote in a similarly impatient tone to Cotta, and somewhat more delicately to Frank about the French checking. Everyone makes me wait, while I never make them do so.—Nevertheless wonderful summer weather day after day. Correspondence with Ida Boy-Ed about Baltic beach resorts.

My health is most worrisome. With a bad head and stomach I walked to a bench in the Kurgarten, where I suddenly felt so nauseated that I hardly knew how I would get back home. Then I lay in the garden, half dozing. Felt terribly ill again at lunch. Only by resting afterward on the chaise longue did I recover to a degree, although my head still aches and my nerves are ready to snap, as I observed when little Elisabeth fell on the garden path and hurt her lip.—Letter from Fischer that crossed with mine, saying that the proofs of the book are on their way and that the volume will come to 400 pages. He mentioned a new printing of *Frederick the Great and the Grand Coalition*, which is nonsense, and totally counter to our agreement. I again became angry, and fired off a telegram of protest.—In the garden the whole afternoon, reading Balzac's story *Adieu*.

Tuesday, May 31

On Sunday I went through [the] sections of *The Confidence Man* and *The Magic Mountain* that I am to read on the second; was genuinely surprised at the comedy and wit of the military examination scene. Incidentally, it will probably be more effective to read the "Hippe" section rather than "Analysis."—On Sunday evening Reisiger was here at the house, and read from his translations, which led to a discussion of Whitman's homosexuality.—Yesterday, Monday, I heard from Frank that he was ill; it will be at least five days before he can deliver the manuscript. So I have no choice for the moment but to turn my attention to the lecture, which in fact preoccupies me almost totally. I am eagerly reading on in the Tolstoy biography, pencil in hand; will then go on to Goethe, first having another look at Bielschowsky. Mahrholz's book about autobiography might also be useful. Yesterday read a fine little play about Ulrich von Hutten in manuscript. It was written by Schöne in Magdeburg, an agreeable talent, the author of the recent *Affenkomödie*. Got off a letter to him this afternoon. In addition wrote to Director Skuhra in Vienna, responding in detail to his recent literary suggestions, and to Uriel Birnbaum regarding his letter and the package of books. Nothing else of importance.—Was impressed by the Salzburg plebescite in favor of Austria's annexation to Germany.—Yesterday was cool and gray. The storm system that had been with us for several days has now passed. This morning very fine, bright, fresh. The garden with its freshly sanded paths gives me pleasure.— Renewed inquiry from the organizing committee of "Nordic Week." Now I must accept, since I can no longer conceive of the seaside holiday with Katia without Lübeck and the lecture. Too bad that *The Magic Mountain* has to be put aside again, but one must take life as it comes.—Wrote to Lübeck about possible subjects for the lecture. Bicycled for an hour and a half. In the afternoon sat out in the newly groomed garden reading the Tolstoy biography. Visit from Cossmann after tea in connection with the advance printing and his literary plans for the *Süddeutsche Monatshefte*. Discussed the problem of German culture. Humanism not German, but absolutely essential.—Later played with the children in the garden. Made sand pies for them.

· ·

Friday, June 3
· ·

Yesterday evening went very well. The hall was packed, and the audience, in which young people, students, pleasant faces predominated, was clearly interested and receptive. Supper afterward in the Witter Weinstube with the Wassermanns, Pontens, and Martens. Heard from the latter that the Swedes are sounding out opinion in Germany concerning the Nobel Prize, for which I am being considered. Negotiations with Rikola-Verlag. Annual royalties of 15,000 marks. As much again or even more for the deluxe edition.—Later on with the Wassermanns in the Hotel Marienbad. Discussion of the Jewish problem. Katia and I walked home at a late hour. Once in bed, was awake until nearly 2:30 reading Frank's novella to the end. Was absorbed and impressed.

Today very warm. Made notes and outlines for the lecture. Went into town and spent money. On the tram met Katia, Walter, and his daughter. He is about to take a trip to Malmö.—The *Vossische Zeitung* appeared with my article. Telegram of thanks from the publisher. Letter from Fischer in response to my last angry note. Strained relations.—Afternoon in the garden reading the *Auslandspost*. Katia's mother to tea. A glowing review of my reading in the *Nachrichten*—not by Sinsheimer, naturally.

My forty-sixth birthday. All in all, I must say that my state of mind is better and brighter than on recent birthdays.—Very warm and humid. Katia gave me my presents before breakfast, chiefly an elegant and obviously practical water-heating apparatus for the washstand. Letters, congratulations. A moving note from Mama. The two little ones wearing crowns of flowers. Little Elisabeth recited a short poem Katia had written. I then rode into town, where I met Martens and the people from the Rikola-Musarion publishing house at the notary's office on Karlsplatz. There were documents to sign and business details to be negotiated. The meeting dragged on. Then walked with Martens through the Englischer Garten, and was told that my statement has already appeared in the *Berliner Tageblatt.*—Windy, overcast. Spent the afternoon in my room resting on the chaise longue. Occupied with the French reviews of the *Betrachtungen;* a new one just appeared in the *Revue de Genève,* which was sent me by Mme. Maury. Should write and clarify my position, but fear I will not get around to it.—An advance of 1,100 marks from New York for the rights to *Little Lizzy.*—Katia's mother to tea. Then [with] Katia, the children, and the governess to the Hoftheater to hear *Carmen.* Unfortunately Moni, who has been unwell for some time, had to stay home. Thought the whole production unsatisfactory except for Frau Reinhardt. Luise Willer was miscast, the José common. The conductor was a very young assistant by the name of Böhm; likable. I was very tired, nervous, and irritated by the precocious chatter of the children and the governess's little lectures as she showed off her cleverness. Supper also something of a failure; the champagne was warm and therefore undrinkable. Telegrams from Litzmanns and from Björkman in Lübeck.

Wednesday, June 8

Another lovely day, not too warm, with blue skies. Spent the morning making notes. At eleven went with Katia to Kurt Wolff's for the Tagore lecture. Select audience. Confirmed in my impression of him as being a refined old English lady. His son brown and muscular, a virile type. I was introduced to Tagore, said "It was so beautiful," and pushed Katia forward: "My wife, who speaks better English than I." He probably did not realize who I was. Björnson, Princess Pilar, Prince Adalbert, quite nice. I was captivated by two young people, strangers to me, handsome, possibly Jewish.—Afterward with Katia to the Tietz department store, errands. Bought strawberries on the street. Read Tolstoy in the garden after lunch. Heard about the suicide attempt and present grave condition of Frau Schwegerle. The young Rheinhardts to tea. Little Frau Rheinhardt sang songs by Debussy, Zemlinsky, and later some old Italian ones. I then read aloud the "Research" section. Rheinhardt, as a medical man, raised various objections. In the evening, continued with Tolstoy.—The new water heater was installed.

Sunday, June 26

Loveliest, summer-like improvement in the weather since yesterday. Wrote some more of *Goethe and Tolstoy,* not without enjoyment. Yesterday Wandrey came to [tea]. Discussed Spengler, Stefan George, the pedagogical influence of the latter, his stamp on people close to him. Also talked of Blüher, whose book on Christ he recommends as something that would intrigue me. In the evening to the Deutsches Theater to see Pavlova, who did not impress us especially. Some of the variety acts excellent. Was interested in a young man who sat in front of us, a modern type with such a pleasant face. Had a cold supper at the theater.—Very tired, naturally, and did not work at my full strength today. After tea a visit from Carl Ehrenberg, who wanted to play us parts from his opera, the text of which I had read. The work seems to have something.—Constipated for days now. Have taken no walks.—Have begun rereading *Wilhelm Meister's Travels.*

Saturday, July 16

Very hot days. For exercise evening bicycle rides, sometimes alone, sometimes with Katia; yesterday to Englschalking on a very dusty road. The usual letters, people wanting to visit etc. The day before yesterday we had Hedwig Schöll to dinner, who played music with the children, then some Debussy and Chopin. Anxiety and anger concerning Golo, who was missing from 3:00 to 10:00 and was greeted sternly when he came home.—Every day after breakfast, in the garden for three hours of good and interesting work on the lecture which, except for its dreadful length, is making good headway. Yesterday I read Katia what I have written and I thought it quite good, though far too long. Still hard to see how it can be condensed for the podium.—This afternoon the sky clouded over, there was distant thunder, and it cooled off somewhat. I have let Mama know I will be in Polling Monday evening.—Letter to Vitzthum. Correspondence with Fischer on the problem of the *Betrachtungen*, which I too would like to see in a one-volume format; above all I would like to see it reprinted soon. They are considering having Heilborn, the editor of *Das literarische Echo*, undertake the abridgment.—Long walk up the Isar.—Corrected proofs of *Rede und Antwort.*

Tuesday, July 26

Very hot. Only shirt and silk jacket until evening. Several telephone calls with Katia. Various business matters for me to attend to, including a visit from the supervisor of the housing office in connection with the possibility of compulsory billeting. Completely reworked the lecture in the forenoon while the gardeners were busy with the garden, one of whom, young, beardless, with brown arms and open shirt, gave me quite a turn. Spent the remainder of the day thinking out further plans, feeling listless and somewhat ill from lack of exercise. A wealth of thoughts on education, the importance of enthusiasm, love, dedication. Read in *Wilhelm Meister's Travels.* Astounded at the truly Goethean aura of *The Magic Mountain.* The lecture will in this sense be an appropriate, full-fledged counterpart to the novel. An hour's walk before supper, which somewhat stimulated my appetite. Took care of a great deal of mail; letters to Eliasberg, Ida Boy-Ed, etc.

Monday, August 1

Slept fitfully. Wrote further. As always lately, the work exhausts me terribly. Bad stomach. Phoned Katia, who is due back with the children tomorrow. L. Hardt came to tea, and read me some prose pieces by a Prague writer, Kafka. Certainly unusual, but otherwise somewhat tedious. Went walking with him, annoyed and prevented from breathing deeply by the smoke from the train. In the evening finished *Norm und Entartung,* an important work from the George orbit, and probably deeply imbued with truth and life. I cannot think of a better positive position in response to the hopelessness of a progress-oriented civilization and intellectualized nihilism than this doctrine of bodily purity and the strong state. This despite the fact that I feel myself condemned by such a doctrine.—The heat today less oppressive.

Saturday, September 17

In the interim Katia and I took our summer trip, from which we returned last Monday, the 13th. Left on Sunday, August 7, taking the sleeping car to Lübeck. Met there by Bertram. Went into town with him and visited the Mengstrasse and Beckergrube houses. The architecture of the marketplace: Lübeck and Venice. The area around the cathedral. Tea in the café opposite the "Purgatory" on its west front. Along the Upper Trave back to the train station, then traveled on with Bertram through Travemünde and Niendorf to Timmendorf. Arrived at the Villa Oda, where we spent two weeks, Bertram staying with us for the first eight days. His departure delayed for a day by migraine. Good conversations with him on our evening walks. Mornings I worked on *Goethe and Tolstoy* out on my balcony. Read aloud in the woods. Justice Hasenclever our neighbor at table. Katia's accident and injury. East wind. The surf. Swimming. Blue sailor's cap. The exquisitely formed young athlete from Hamburg, still more boy than man, a glorious, enchanting sight, especially when he ran. Knowing I would not be able to see him anymore made departure difficult. Via Hamburg to Wenningstedt on Sylt. In Hamburg a wretched hotel overnight, all that was available. Passed by Husum, crossed the coastal sea of reeds. Met on the island by Katia's cousins. First view of the North Sea from the top of the steps leading down to the beach. Attractive room in Haus Erika right behind the dunes. Stayed a week on the island. The wicker beach shelters from which one steps directly into the powerful surf. Enraptured by the sea. The great, soft wind. The waves like beasts of prey. Glorious carpets of foam. Visits to Westerland and List, where we climbed the fantastic shifting dunes. Amazing impression. Visit to Jacobsohn's Friesian-style house. Plans for buying property. Dinner at the Dunes Hotel, luncheon with the Rosenbergs. Read them *Goethe and Tolstoy.* Object of curiosity in Campen and Wenningstedt. Complicated trip, the embarkation sheer torture. Returned by way of Watt on overcrowded train to Hamburg. Arrived late in the evening in Lübeck, going to the Burghaus, where dear old Ida Boy-Ed had prepared a cordial, most gratifying welcome. Week's stay in the city. Delivered the lecture on September 4 at the Johanneum. The crowd and the heat tremendous. Great honor accorded me during the event, as during the entire visit. The bust in the Behn house, which the museum director Heise took us to see. The Nolde exhibit in the Katharinenkirche. The *Dance of Death* in St. Aegidian's. Visits to the relatives. Festival theatrical offerings. Dinners and suppers. Warm feelings toward Senator Vermehren and his wife, and toward Neumann, the mayor. The Marienkirche. Laid a wreath in the cemetery. Interviews with Swedish and German journalists. Old school friends. The plan for restoring the Mengstrasse house. Departure on the morning of the ninth for Berlin. Stayed on Matthäikirchstrasse; pleasant. Tea at Kysers'. In the evening *The Weavers.* Attended a rehearsal of *Herod and Mari-*

amne at the Deutsches Theater on the tenth. My lecture that evening in the Beethovensaal. The hall packed, the audience respectful. Hundreds of people spoke to me, flowers for me and for Katia. Party afterward. The Fischers, the Hülsens, Born. The racy Frau Kainer. Next day a conference with Fischer and Heilborn concerning the *Betrachtungen*. Luncheon at Bondis' in Grunewald. Tea at Klaus's in Charlottenburg. In the evening, *Kean*, with Bassermann in the title role. Dinner at the Russian restaurant. On the last day discussions with Fischer, Greiner, and Kayser at the office. Collected Works, foreign rights matters. The Frenchman on the staff of the *Nouvelle Revue Française*. Breakfast with the Fischers at the Adlon Hotel. Back home with them in their car. Evening departure for home in a sleeping car.

Just now extremely tired and worn out. Katia weighed down by household and maid problems, I by the sheer insolubility of the problem of abridging the *Betrachtungen*. Working at that. Crushing correspondence. Have decided to hire a secretary.— Peter Pringsheim here. He has been here at the house, and we were invited to Arcisstrasse today for luncheon.

. . . .

Thursday, September 22

. . . .

Yesterday began writing a letter to Frisch on the Jewish question to be used in the *Merkur*. Continued with it this morning and afternoon. News yesterday of the terrible explosion in Oppen near Ludwigshafen. This evening a gathering at the Löhrs': Ambassador Count Zech and his wife, née Bethmann-Hollweg, and Baron Egloffstein. The late chancellor used to read *Buddenbrooks* aloud to his children in the evening.— Yesterday and today took my afternoon nap in the garden. For several days have been trying to read a Hungarian novel, *Sárarany*, but find it boring. On the other hand have developed considerable interest in the writings of Franz Kafka, recommended to me by the monologist Hardt.—Klaus and Erika are preparing themselves for the performance of Pfitzner's *Palestrina* by studying the libretto. I gave them each a copy of my pamphlet.

. . . .

Friday, October 28

. . . .

Ten days at Feldafing. Bertram with us the evening before my departure. Read aloud the article on the Jews. Katia objected, and I grew annoyed and upset. Frisch and I debating back and forth whether to drop the whole thing or make cuts; ultimately decided on the latter.—In Feldafing foehn at first, then, after an interval of rain, fine crisp autumn days. I invited Martens to visit me, having been moved by the passage in his autobiography in which he describes me as a young man. He stayed for three days. Lunch at Fräulein Bonn's. Spent two evenings at Frank's, who read aloud a fine story. Walks to Tutzing. Played the Gramophone as usual. Great stillness and solitude. Worked my way into the sixth chapter of *The Magic Mountain*. Countless letters. Correspondence with H. Simon in Frankfurt about a planned Goethe week with Hauptmann, Harnack, Einstein, and me. Left early yesterday in order to accept an invitation to dine at the Hotel Continental with the Viennese financier Kola. Martens and Director Skuhra also present. Sumptuous dinner, wonderful Haute Sauternes. The billionaire not especially impressive. His career seems to have had an American cast ever since his start as a small-time newspaperman. He spoke of the rather modest

Thomas at age thirteen, with his sisters Julia (left) and Carla and his brother Heinrich (right).   A1

A2   *Thomas's mother, Julia, née da Silva-Bruhns.*

Thomas's father, Thomas Johann Heinrich Mann.

A3

The home of Katia Mann's parents, Alfred and Hedwig Pringsheim,
A4   *on Arcisstrasse in Munich.*

The music room in the Arcisstrasse house. A5

. . . .

Top: *The Hotel Schatzalp in Davos, Switzerland.*

. . . .

Bottom: *The Waldsanatorium in Davos. Both served as models for the "Berghof"*
A6   *sanatorium in* The Magic Mountain.

. . . .

The Mann house at 1 Poschingerstrasse, Munich, where Thomas Mann lived from 1914 to 1933.

A7

A8   *Thomas Mann's study in the Munich house.*

number of millions of pounds sterling that would put Austria back on its feet.—Today made vigorous headway with the writing. Using the graph paper again, which makes writing easier. My ideas about pre-publication revised as a result of conversations in Feldafing; I am now thinking of simultaneous publication in Prague, Zurich, and Berlin. The technical problems, having to make copies for the journals and the translator, loom large.—The *Betrachtungen* question settled in favor of a one-volume edition.— This afternoon word came of the death of Frau von Rohrscheidt. Katia to tea at Arcisstrasse. After taking care of letters I went there by car to offer my condolences.— Will be presenting *Goethe and Tolstoy* soon at the Vier Jahreszeiten. Posters up already. Cards to Ponten, Martens, and others.—Was highly stimulated by my reading of Turgenev in Feldafing. I then began the new novel by Hanns Johst, *Der Kreuzweg*, with its blatant stylistic imitation of Heinrich's writing.

Sunday, November 6, to Sunday, November 13

Sojourn in Zurich. Stayed with the dear Hanharts. Read in the Tonhalle and delivered the *Goethe and Tolstoy* in the main lecture hall of the university. Party at the Hanharts'; the Faesis (with C. F. Meyer's daughter), Korrodi, the Reiffs, the Sievekings. Mornings in a white smock at the Polyclinic. Two nice evenings at the theater: *Liebestrank* and *Strom*. A long walk with Dr. Hanhart. Home again Sunday evening, tense and exhausted, with 700 francs. Cashed the American check for 92,000 marks, of which my share amounts to roughly 70,000. The reading at the Vier Jahreszeiten netted about 4,000 marks.—Books and letters.—Began reworking the "Walpurgis-Night" section. Today started an article on Martens's autobiography for Korrodi. Korrodi has agreed to pay 100,000 marks for the serial rights to the novel.—The Wassermanns came for tea and will be here tomorrow evening for dinner. I am writing this on Thursday, November 17. On Saturday we shall have the Hofmannsthals with their daughter and B. Björnson and his wife here for luncheon. This afternoon went with Katia to see Marcks to congratulate him on his sixtieth birthday. Afterward with Katia to the Deutsches Theater to hear Battistini. We sat in 200-mark seats, for which, admittedly, we had only had to pay the 40-mark tax. The audience made up of profiteers. They laughed at the singing of the woman who shared his recital and literally whistled her off the stage so that she did not return. Battistini ancient but still a great artist, musical and stirring. Enormous success.

Sunday, November 20

Since Zurich the weather had turned cold, changing to rain after my return. Since yesterday, however, it has turned colder again.—The social life was strenuous and I was exhausted. Yesterday morning I wrote my answer to the international questionnaire from *Politiken* on the salvation of the world, then finished the article on Martens's book for the *Neue Zürcher Zeitung*. In the afternoon, after luncheon with the Hofmannsthals and the Björnsons, I dictated for two hours.—Very upset today and out of sorts. My depression also manifests itself in the form of very poor digestion. Katia in bed with a cold. I went with Erika to the Residenz-Theater, where Wassermann gave his lecture on "Integrity." He said many good, commendable things that the audience found inspiring. The final question remains one of conscience, whether it behooves us to fight; him against "the word," me against "democracy."—The new Fischer editions have arrived: *Rede und Antwort* and *Buddenbrooks*, each in the binding of the Collected Works. Attractive. Nevertheless I am not at all pleased with the new book; even in the preface there are three mistakes. I am also suffering both physically and psychically from the fact that all No. 4 underwear is now too small for me, No. 5 too big.—Acid stomach and constipation.—There was a reception for the Wassermanns and their friends in the hotel lobby. His success was of the same sort as my own at the Vier Jahreszeiten; this is the sort of thing that lifts people's spirits. More than art, it directly contributes to spiritual renewal. What havoc has been wrought by the "revolution," by politics, programs, and "committed humanitarianism."—The Hofmannsthals left last night for Berlin. They are returning in ten days, and have invited me to see *Der Schwierige* with them.

Thursday, December 1

Slowly recovered from the deep depression that followed the overexertion of my Zurich visit. Have begun enjoying life again; the icy gray winter mornings and my work on *The Magic Mountain*, for the sixth chapter of which I am about to finish the first section, "Changes." In a reasonably restored state I went with Katia to the theater a couple of times, the Kammerspiele. Saw *The Miser* in an impressive production and a few days later a two-act play by Turgenev, more novelistic than dramatic, with the excellent actor Goetz in the leading role. The program also included Chekhov's humorous one-acter, *The Bear*, also excellently done. The acting delighted me.—A number of copies of *Rede und Antwort* arrived. I put together a list of people to whom copies should be sent, and am packing a few each day. Fischer wrote encouragingly about the book. I have been reading in it, and clearly my mental state is better, for I no longer find it so unsatisfying. Countless letters received, written, dictated. Curious business with Frisch concerning my noticeable absence from the narrative issue of the *Merkur*. I have promised to write for him a summation of the discussion between Curtius and Gide on German-French relations. I also promised the *Prager Presse* a little piece for their Christmas or New Year's issue.—The weather continues to be dry and cold, very hazy, so that all kinds of infections are about. One of our servant girls has been in the hospital for a long time now.—Reading: Hamsun's new novel, *The Women at the Pump*, with extreme pleasure; Witkop sent me his *Kleist*, about which I wrote him appreciatively; and countless other books have arrived.—At noon today with the Litzmanns to look at the new house on Pienzenauerstrasse. This evening we are having the Walters here. Tomorrow evening dinner at the Löhrs', where I have promised to read from *The Magic Mountain*. I am to read on the fifth in Bamberg.—Proofs of the new printing of the *Betrachtungen* have been arriving; I read them without pain, often with approval. Also there is to be a new edition of *Death in Venice* separate from the Collected Works format. My income this year will amount to 300,000 marks.

1933

Last night I was able to sleep surprisingly long and well, thanks to a harmless calcium preparation we learned about from the Nikisches. I took breakfast in bed, as has been my custom of late, then dashed off a few lines to Suhrkamp concerning a censorable phrase about nationalism in the Wagner essay. Why provoke these beasts at this moment?

This morning—but this is typical of mornings—I was free of the morbid dread that has oppressed me for hours on end these last ten days, during which my nerves have been strained and exhausted. It is a sort of fear-ridden, intense melancholy such as I have previously experienced, to a milder degree, when parting from material things. Recently this feeling reached a crisis one night when I had taken refuge with Katia. From the character of this crisis it is clear that what is involved is the pain of leaving a long-familiar situation, the awareness that an era in my life has come to an end, and the recognition that I must find a new basis for my existence. Despite the rigidly set ways of my fifty-eight years, I view this necessity as spiritually beneficial and I affirm it. It is also an opportunity—more stimulating than depressing—to throw off those obligations I had assumed in the course of the years out of social considerations, out of a "sense of responsibility" or "vanity" or what you will, and with one wrench tear myself free from the "snares of this world," to concentrate hereafter on my own life. This pledge of a new beginning I began to fulfill yesterday afternoon when I dictated to Katia the explanation for my resignation from the executive committee of the Writers' League.

Erika has been with us since Monday evening, and it is doubtless no mere accident but rather one of those "blessings" of my life that my two favorite children, my oldest and youngest daughters, have been at my side during this time.

Eri brought with her innumerable stories of idiocies and atrocities in Munich, arrests, brutal treatment, etc., which add to our perturbation and disgust, rendering even more emphatic the warnings contained in letters from Scharnagl and Löwenstein to the effect that recognizable members of our family had best not return to Munich. Today Erika is driving to the Tyrol to pick up Therese Giehse, who has taken refuge there. The two of them will stay in Switzerland. As for Katia and myself, the plan so far continues to be—though we must wait to hear from Reisiger—that tomorrow or the day after I will go to stay with him in Seefeld while Katia and Medi return to the Poschingerstrasse house for the present and see to the needed arrangements and technicalities. While I was writing this, Katia came to me with the new idea of accepting the invitation of the Werfels after all, and sharing their house in Venice for a time. An attractive prospect, though the friendship between the German and Italian governments and my own *Mario* argue against it.

My worries about the passport, which expires on April 1, seem about to be allayed thanks to the presence here of Dr. Feist and his personal connections with "the Party" (some sort of caretaker relationship).

Yesterday evening we bade farewell to the Nikisches, having first shared a bottle of Haute Sauterne in our customary evening haunt, the ladies' salon, before a last game of Casino. The fine little people, whom I must consider true friends and loyal adherents, were very glad to have run into us and to have shared this period of intimacy. They parted from us with genuine sorrow, there being more room in their hearts than in our more troubled ones for such emotion.

The series of sunny days still continues up here. Today, as well, the skies turned clear, though the early morning was cloudy and a reversal in the weather bringing foehn was anticipated.

After dressing I met Katia at the ski slope and we took a walk together under the most brilliant blue sky.—Curiously wishy-washy and flaccid letter from Willy Haas of the *Literarische Welt* in the wake of our correspondence. He stopped just short of using the phrase "glorious times."

Had lunch alone with Katia, Medi having gone off on an outing. Afterward sat on the balcony and read some good things in the *Rundschau* by Hermann Heller and Kessler. Wonderfully beneficial their higher perspective after a diet of the crudely journalistic.

Erika brought me a quantity of reading matter, including the issue of *Corona* containing my Goethe lecture. She also brought the manuscript of the third *Joseph* volume together with my materials. Bertram's little book of poems; loftily depressing, decent yet revolting.

In the village this afternoon with Katia to have passport photos taken. We debated where I should go next: Seefeld? Innsbruck? Zurich? All sheer fantasy until an answer comes from Reisiger.—Had tea as usual in the Old India, without Medi, and read in the *Neue Zürcher Zeitung* about Falckenberg's arrest, Gerlich's death, and other horrors. Back in the hotel, visited Eri on the fourth floor. She had driven back with Frau Giehse and had heard new stories from Munich about murders and atrocities, on top of the usual political outrages, brought on by the outbreak of the Days of National Freedom. Ugly mistreatment of Jews. The despair of this idiot Hitler at the anarchy and the disregard of his prohibitions. Count Arco's confession that he planned to assassinate Hitler. The archbishops of Vienna and Munich conspiring to form some kind of Danube confederation.

Frau Giehse discounted the rumor that the horrors are abating in Munich. The wisdom of Katia's returning once more called into question, though her presence on Poschingerstrasse is essential on many counts. Discussion with her about this and about household rearrangements, which should not be undertaken hastily, either in regard to selling the car or giving notice to the servants. New nervousness, uncertainty, and anxiety.

. . . .

Thursday, March 16

. . . .

Since yesterday the aspect of things has once more undergone a significant change. Plans will have to be altered. Reisiger telephoned in the evening from Seefeld. He will not be staying there, since Austria on the whole is sinister and to be avoided, as Therese Giehse had indicated. This confirmed what we had already secretly been thinking. Which seems to leave Switzerland, and in fact after all our deliberations the choice seems to be for me between Lenzerheide, at the house of Hanna Kiel, and Zurich, where we would be near the Franks. The worst of it is that at the moment both places frighten me.

Though I slept tolerably well, from the time I awoke this morning my nerves have been in a bad, anxious state. I feel a rush of fear at the thought of being separated from my family, although I am ashamed of the feeling. Despair at my ability to survive after the destruction of even this tenuous *modus vivendi.*

Nervous crisis while talking with Katia, after which I felt somewhat calmer however. We decided that for the present we should not separate, but should go together tomorrow to Lenzerheide and postpone Katia's trip to Munich, the more so since her safety there could not be guaranteed. Decided to entrust Feist with the most essential business in Munich.

Pleasant letter from Bermann Fischer about my situation, also about Gyldendal Forlag and Jespersen and Pio, who are competing for the Danish rights to *Joseph*.— Letter from Østergaard, the Danish translator of *The Magic Mountain*, about the same matter.

Friday, March 17

This morning better and calmer than yesterday, despite the fact that I slept fitfully and woke early. I had a bath and then breakfasted in bed. In the course of the day yesterday we worked out our plans fully and settled on what to do for the time being. Instruct Golo to go to Munich. Medi also to go back there and return to school, despite even sharper warnings that the Franks have sent from Lugano, which neither we nor the child believe to be valid. After Lenzerheide our next stop will be Lugano, the Park Hotel. Discussed moving the household with Katia, which should not be undertaken hastily. Her parents to be informed through Medi. Possibly entrust Frau Kurz with the task of giving notice. Feist, who was treated brutally by Eri, was given the tasks of renewing my passport, sending along my fur coat, and arranging for the transfer of money to Switzerland.

We had tea for the last time at the Old India, along with Eri and Medi. Bought stationery and toilet articles. Back at the hotel we packed our suitcases again. After dinner, once more spent the evening with Dr. Richter, together with Eri, Feist, and the young man from Ostrau in Moravia who wants to go on the stage. Talked about setting up house eventually in Locarno or Zurich. Discussed the brazenly sadistic propaganda plans announced by the German government, the heralded crushing of public opinion and imposition of total uniformity, eliminating all adverse criticism and crippling any opposition. The disgusting modernistic twist, the psychological opportunism in view of what is actually cultural, intellectual, and moral regression. The boldly modern, fast-moving, futuristic approach put to the service of an antifuture, a philosophy devoid of all ideas, a mammoth advertising campaign for nothingness. Horrible and base.—The sociable evening did me a great deal of good physically.

Learned that the *Tage-Buch* and the *Weltbühne* have been banned. Concerned about the *Rundschau*. The trend of the country is undoubtedly toward stifling as much as possible all organs of education; witness Papen's actions against the primary schools. Obviously they are not in favor of learning or of any kind of thought, but prefer to see the masses mired in stupidity, the better to impose mechanistic uniformity with the aid of modern techniques of psychological suggestion. The worst form of bolshevism translated into *German* terms, but distinguished from the Russian variety by the absence of any ideas.—

Falckenberg, who had been arrested as a "Bolshevik agent," is said to be free again. The Kammerspiele urging Frau Giehse to return; they need her.

Yesterday morning at 11:30 departure from Arosa. Overcrowded train, deeply depressing newspaper reading. Eri, driving to Chur with Therese Giehse, visited with us in mid-journey. The heavy foehn hard on the nerves. Lunch with Eri and Frau Giehse at the Steinbock in Chur. I drafted my answer to Academy President Schillings, giving neither a clear yes or no to the declaration that came before I left on my trip, but explaining my reasons for resigning. Farewell from Medi, who was going on to Munich. Tears. Leavetaking from Eri and Frau Giehse, who were proceeding by car for Zurich and Berne. Met by a car from Lenzerheide. Bags loaded in it, then the drive up here, altitude 1,450 meters, over some spectacular stretches of highway. Anxious. Welcomed by Fräulein Kiel. The house small, but not without charm were we in better shape psychologically; beautiful landscape with half-frozen lake. Unpacked in our little rooms. After tea, walked to the village, where I sent off the letter to Schillings and the telegram to Wassermann, who had inquired from Vienna about my situation with regard to the Academy. The road icy in patches.

Dinner with Hanna Kiel, simple but pleasantly cultivated. Smoked afterward and chatted in the company of two girl skiers, one of whom is amusing, boyish, almost attractive, in spite of her puffy and heavily powdered upper lip.—Exhausted. Peppermint tea.

In bed read a story by Leskov in the *Corona*. Slept until half past five this morning. After awakening, increasing perturbation and feeling of despair amounting to a crisis, with Katia looking after me from eight o'clock on. Horrible sense of frenzy, helplessness, twitching muscles, almost a shivering fit, and feared losing my rational faculties. Comforted by Katia, and with the help of Luminal and compresses, I slowly regained a certain calm and was able to take some tea and an egg. Cigarette.

The Hungarian-Swiss doctor, who recommended staying here for a few days and prescribed a sedative. The morning passed quickly while I stayed in bed, dozing. Mild air, snow, some sun, and brighter than yesterday. Light lunch with Katia in the downstairs room, still in my dressing gown. Our hostess off in Zurich. Then back to bed again. Medi telegraphed her safe arrival.

Katia into the village to request the call that had come from Döblin in Zurich and to arrange things with the Park Hotel in Lugano. We have decided to go there on the 23rd, since beauty, comfort, and companionship beckon; the Franks, the Hauptmanns, possibly also the Fischers.

Tea with Katia at my bedside. Discussed the future, trying to achieve a certain degree of confidence.

Especially disturbed by the decision of the dictators to have the Reichstag elections serve merely as a guide for the representation of the people in the various states. What will the hopelessly duped Bavarians say to that? The haste and the naked force with which the propaganda victors are exploiting their victory and seeking every means with which to safeguard that victory—and they are the ones who denounced the shortsighted harshness of the victors at Versailles! The domestic Versailles is more horrible than the outside one. Will there not have to be an effort to revise it? The defeated forty-nine percent of the German population has been no less mercilessly maltreated, no less humiliated, rendered desperate, and spiritually ruined than was Germany during those four war years. That, in fact, is the principal significance of all this. They want to annul not only the domestic consequences of the defeat, that is to say all progressive, socialist measures, but also to establish a new state of mind, as though the war had been won rather than lost. But the defeated elements want to take retribution for their defeat on their own countrymen, in the vengeful, despotic style of a Clemenceau.—

Döblin's call came from Zurich and Katia went over to the neighbor's house to let him know how things stand.—He approved of my statement and recommends staying clear of Munich for a month. Is setting up a colony in Strasbourg. Expects surprises and battles in Germany.

Eri also called. Zurich apparently teeming with emigrants.

Dictated letters to Katia: to Bermann Fischer, Reisiger, the Danish translator. Gyldendal offers a 1,000-mark advance for *Joseph*.

Letters from Suhrkamp, Steiner, and Käthe Rosenberg, which we read while having dinner. Mood more stable.

Sunday, March 19; Lenzerheide

Yesterday evening I took one Adalin tablet with my peppermint tea and before bedtime a Phanodorm tablet. Slept excellently and faced the day in a far more stable frame of mind. Spruced up very comfortably in the bathroom. Katia and I had a pleasant breakfast downstairs, beginning with orange juice. The maid Martha, from Berlin, somewhat slow and casual, but friendly and eager to please.

Many snow flurries yesterday. Today brighter and colder, and the landscape sparkles with the new snow.

At breakfast we discussed the banning of Bruno Walter's concerts in Leipzig and Berlin. What will the world think of this display of childish barbarism and dogmatism! Katia heard on the radio at the neighbor's house yesterday a wild diatribe against the Center party, "which purports to be a Christian party," and "for fourteen years has been acting as an accessory to the Communists." Nowhere in the world or in history has more idiotic demagoguery been waged. There is something hellish about this technique of using every word to achieve the maximum stupidity, all the while trampling underfoot all that we know to be true and decent.

I observe a certain pleasure in giving Evil its head now that it is in power, in this "Go on, go on! Show what you can do! One of these days you will be judged, no matter how much you try to stifle judgment now."

I refuse to apply the term "historical," as Schillings used it in his Academy declaration, in reference to this monstrous phenomenon, the frenzied consummation of a counterrevolution we have been caught up in for the past fourteen years.

I transcribe here my reply to Schillings: "I cannot give the desired response to the declaration placed before me. I have not the least intention of working against the government, and as far as German culture is concerned I believe I have always served its cause and will try to do so in the future. But I have come to the decision to disengage myself from all official duties that I have accumulated over the years and to pursue from now on my private concerns in complete retirement. I therefore request, Honorable Herr Präsident, that you accept my resignation from the literary section of the Prussian Academy of Arts."

I am considering sending similar messages to the German Academy, the PEN Club, the Rotary Club, and also the League of Nations committee.

To judge from their speeches, the Nazis seem in no way eager for an accommodation with the Catholics that would guarantee legal passage of their Enabling Act. So will they simply go ahead with it illegally? The Communist party is not banned, but its duly elected deputies are not permitted to take their seats; after this nothing can come as a surprise.

Katia spoke with Medi by telephone last night. She was received most cordially at school, by both teachers and fellow pupils. No incidents at home, no inquiries. Golo is due back there today from Göttingen. I am now somewhat reassured about my old diaries and papers, which were among my chief worries at first—typically enough.—

—Shaved in the bathroom before coming to table, and then walked with Katia down the road as far as Valbella and the next hamlet. Bright foehn weather. Fresh white snow combined with mild spring air and strong sunlight. The valley is lovely, and in summer, with its lake and open footpaths, it must be an attractive place to stay, its tone civilized by the presence of the shops in the village and the large, elegant hotel.

We had a simple, healthful lunch at one and then rested on the balcony. I was badly exhausted again but revived after lying down and dozing. Read a bit in *War and Peace*. Set out after three on a walk to Lenzerheide, where I bought cigars at the hotel. Back home again at five in time for tea in the dining room. Then, lying on my bed, dictated a number of letters to Katia.

. . . .

Monday, March 20; Lenzerheide

. . . .

Yesterday evening after dinner I sat on the corner bench and read a manuscript, a childhood narrative by young Kieve, a friend of Moni's. Not bad.

Very tired, as is Katia. We both took Adalin with our peppermint tea. Somewhat restless sleep, but not worrisome as this is usual in the high mountains. This morning everything bedecked with snow. Heavy snow flurries. Clouds drifting through the valley.

When we came down for breakfast after dressing we were met with fresh shocks and upset, for the serving girl had listened to the radio last night and reported that a Socialist delegate in Munich named Auer (or Bauer) had shot a police officer and his companion; clearly an act of all-too-understandable despair and fury, but one that could well bring about the banning of the Social Democratic party in Bavaria just as it has been already in Baden. Moreover announcement of the national celebration being prepared for tomorrow on the occasion of the opening of the Reichstag, one designed solely to befuddle the people: much pealing of bells, banners, paeans to freedom. It is all too stupid, low, and loathsome. Once again we were utterly filled with horror and bitterness. Katia concerned about the children, though I soothed her by convincing her that they are not affected by such events. She phoned Erika, who intends to go to Munich for a day but is still postponing the trip. She had heard nothing new, by the way. Hanna Kiel is due back this afternoon.

Mail from Munich. Copy of *Europa* with the Wagner essay as abridged and translated by Bertaux. Letter from Bonnet concerning the Madrid meeting. Two letters from Signora Mazzucchetti—one from Milan, the other from Innsbruck—thanking me for my communications from Arosa. In the earlier one she urges a quick return to Munich; in the second, after talking with Germans in Innsbruck, she anxiously warns against it.

Speeches by Papen and Goering side by side in the *Vossische Zeitung*, the former calling with statesmanlike concern for order, restraint, and conciliation, for a "German" revolution rather than a "Bolshevik" one, the latter foaming at the mouth and defending the atrocities. "Marxism" should not only be rooted out, but the very word forgotten, so that no one will know what it is. Claims he and his cohorts have already managed to forget it.

Went for an hour's walk before lunch in the hot sun and foehn. Rested afterward on my bed. Around four went with Katia to Lenzerheide in chillier wind. I had my hair cut and ran into my Bulgarian doctor at the barber's. The barber brought out an old issue of the Swiss magazine *Er und Sie*, containing pictures of Klaus and Erika. Bought cigars and cigarettes. We had tea in a pastry shop.

Light frost on the way home.

We have canceled our reservation at the Park Hotel in Lugano and intend to go to Montagnola on the 24th instead. Katia spoke on the telephone with Frau Hesse and with Golo, who gave a reassuring account of things in Munich, where he and young Köster have moved into the house. Medi tells us that she is rehearsing the Horst Wessel song at school in preparation for the huge celebration of freedom and patriotism. Call from Feist in Munich. My passport is actually in order; he will bring it up to us here tomorrow.

We are breathing somewhat easier, although we shudder anew whenever we think of how justice has been bound and gagged so that only terror and chicanery have any say. Even today the Communist party is not banned, but its leaders and its well-meaning members are being tortured in prisons: the writer Ludwig Renn, for example, and Thälmann, the chairman of a legitimate political party that extends all over the world, and in Russia is the ruling political and social force. It is incredible. And moreover it is being perpetrated by individuals who are far more "bolshevist" than these decent members of the German Communist party.

Tuesday, March 21; Lenzerheide

Yesterday's evening mail brought a letter from Katarina Godwin about the last executive meeting of the Writers' League. There was no signature, and the letter was at first barely comprehensible, then very comical and scorn-provoking. Friedrich, who had not yet received my letter of resignation, wanted to "depose" me. Grotesque, wretched business. Although most of those present remained passive, a number of different positions were taken. Honest indignation on the part of Fräulein Godwin.

Dinner with our hostess, with drowsy conversation afterward while I smoked. Adalin with peppermint tea. Some *War and Peace*, then slept until 5:00 or 5:30. During the night a snowstorm from the north. Everything buried under a heavy cover of snow; sun, persistent fierce wind. The danger of catching cold is considerable, especially in the morning with the unheated bathroom, little water, and the cold staircase.

Was the first one down to breakfast, then joined by Katia and Fräulein Kiel. Wrote afterward to Frank in Lugano and sent him Godwin's letter. Great deal of mail. Books of no importance, letters from Reisiger (in Seefeld), Maril, and Jespersen and Pio (contract for *Joseph*). Issues of the *Neue Zürcher Zeitung*: removal of Jews from legal and medical positions, concentration camp in Munich for Communists and Socialists. Those being held in "protective custody" are treated properly. Gerlich and Aretin were not denied spiritual counsel. (!)

Because of the harsh wind we went only as far as the post office in Valbella, where we telegraphed Fischer to accept the offer from Pio. The 1,000-mark advance will be welcome.

Indignant that Strauss has taken over the concert from which Bruno Walter was barred. Furtwängler conducted the government's command performance of *Die Meistersinger* on this day of jubilation. Lackeys.

The strange phenomenon of an imaginary "historical moment," an unmotivated victory celebration replete with bells, Te Deums, flags, school holidays, and whatever else they can think of, staged by command of the people, the government, or the Party. Who has been conquered? The inner enemy—who after all made it possible for the national uprising to take place. Idiotic. But if only that were all it is, and it were not compounded with so much base, murderous malevolence!

Stupid decree from Hindenburg at the opening of the Reichstag, which is supposed to represent at last a reawakened, more militant people. Why more militant all of a sudden?—The formation of a government in Bavaria has been postponed pending the outcome of the Reichstag negotiations concerning the Enabling Act, which above all would provide for the local governments' being structured along precisely the same lines as the Reichstag. If the agreement with the Center fails to materialize, which the National Socialists apparently do not even want, the government will proceed to rule in a commissarial-dictatorial style. Under such circumstances my return to Munich would certainly be delayed. I only want to go back in order to calmly put our affairs in order and prepare for our move to Switzerland.

—Coffee after lunch. Chilled and not well rested. Went to bed and napped. Between 4:00 and 5:00 I walked with Katia to Parpan in a cruel north wind. The air filled with swirling, driven snow. It is still snowing now out of a gray sky.

Tea with Fräulein Kiel and Frau von Morgen, back from her ski tour deeply tanned, with her boyish voice and unfortunate puffy upper lip.

A memorable feature of the stay has been the family of chow dogs with the pups Pooh Bear and Lilli, remarkable animals resembling lions or bears, a thick-furred, pointed-nosed breed of wild and tender disposition, the bitch a tawny yellow like a lion, the puppies black with deep purple tongues as though they had been gobbling blueberries.—

—Feist arrived, who in his hopeless fashion did not wait for my passport but came on up here without it, probably hoping to find Erika with us. He swears that the letter his telegram had promised will be here tomorrow. He paints an optimistic picture and characterizes the situation as not at all risky for me, which is also foolish and uncomprehending. A letter from Katia's mother presents a totally different view; friends have been urging her to warn me strongly against an early return. Dr. Bernstein called on her expressly for this purpose. He has been a witness to the typical goings-on at the Writers' League. I am curious to see whether some decent concluding statement will be forthcoming from that quarter.

—The passport must still be signed by the "political review officer" of the police passport division, a formality delayed by the national holiday. I wonder.—

I have been thinking of sending a letter to the Bavarian Reichskommissar, emphasizing my ties to Germany and asking for a guarantee against harassment. Now it seems friends in Munich have had the same thought and have urged Feist to suggest it to me.—

—In recent days my need for literary activity has found outlet in letters, such as the one to Signora Mazzucchetti and today's to Bruno Frank, and also in these diary notes. That helps me somewhat, but it is not good enough.

The return of my passport still delayed. Katia is very doubtful that it will be renewed. Apparently it is being held up in the "political division"; no action is being taken on the request for an extension. This leads one to surmise the worst. What would a refusal accomplish? Into what corner do the authorities mean to push me by leaving me without a German passport? Am I to be forced into expatriation, and do they then plan to confiscate my house and possessions? I have the feeling that some such malice and wickedness is being hatched.

Yesterday evening with the ladies. Later Feist joined us. Bach and Handel recordings played on the small and somewhat wheezy Gramophone. A call from Bruno Walter from the Hotel Baur au Lac in Zurich. In overshoes and coat, hurried over to the house next door to take the call. Friendly exchange concerning the horrors and our personal plans.

A frosty night, minus 16° Celsius, they say. Sunny. Slept fairly well, bathed. Fräulein Kiel off skiing with little Frau von Morgen. At breakfast one of these necessarily unresolved talks with Katia about Germany and the terrifying side of its character. She then went out with Feist to do some skiing.—

—Besides the newspapers, which make me quail, the morning post brought the page proofs of the Wagner piece; working on them kept me from *Joseph*. It is a rich work, incorporating all the themes of my life.

Frau Mahler-Werfel wrote concerning their Venice house, which she puts at our disposal for the spring.

Walk with Katia. Alone with her at lunch. We have decided to go to Montagnola tomorrow, even without the passport, which is not immediately needed. In the course of the day we considered whether something could not be done with the help of the League of Nations.

Out on the balcony after lunch. Then with Katia to Lenzerheide, where we bought envelopes for mailing the *Wagner* proofs.

The suitcases were brought out and we are packing up again. Perturbation at the impending departure.

Monday, March 27; Lugano, Hotel Villa Castagnola

This provisional, uncertain journeying from place to place continues, while our homeland is barred to us by hostile, malevolent, threatening forces.

We arrived here on Friday at six in the evening and were met by the *padrone* of the little Hotel Bellevue in Montagnola, who drove us back in his car after the business with the luggage had been straightened out—by mistake Katia had sent home the Lugano luggage claim check instead of the Munich one. The hotel, run in ingenuous Italian style, quite nice and with a lovely view, but its isolation, its primitiveness, and its meagerness oppressed me. My nerves reacted at once with an attack of anxiety, and it was a good thing that we could spend the very first evening with the Hesses in the lovely, elegant house given them by his Zurich patron, Bodmer. They have a refugee staying with them, Wiegand, a Social Democrat from Leipzig. Wine and conversation. Back at the hotel, poor bed, the warm water ran cold. We did not open the suitcases that were delivered next morning.

Frank, who is living at the Palace Hotel, drove up on *Saturday* and took us back

135

to Lugano. Visited his wife at the hotel; she was on the point of leaving by way of Milan and Verona for Munich, there to arrange things and liquidate their holdings as Katia means to do shortly. From there with Frank to see the German consul, a friendly old man, entirely of our mind but in no position to do anything about our passports. We have no choice but to simply let them expire and cast ourselves upon the mercy of other countries.—We visited the Villa Castagnola and looked at rooms there. In the padrone's car to the Hesses' for lunch. Good food with Haute Sauterne and coffee. I rested in the library, and at four o'clock the five of us took a long walk through mountain forests and villages, quite enchanted by the ideal, delicate landscape offering itself in the hues of Romantic paintings, at once magnificent and fragile, a meeting-place of North and South, with snow-capped mountains, the lake, small hamlets, serene and grandiose, *trop meublée*, and for me something quite new and exciting.

Artless *pranzo* at the Bellevue, then from eight on spent the evening once more at the Hesses'.

Yesterday, *Sunday*, after having our breakfast downstairs, we informed the padrone of our "temporary" departure. Collected our luggage and had it brought here to this quiet, elegant, but secluded hotel, complete with lovely grounds, European cuisine, etc., all of which I find soothing inasmuch as it represents a level to which I am accustomed.—Went back to visit with Frau Hesse in her elegant study and to borrow the rubber tub, since we have no bathroom here. We were then driven back down by the friendly, attentive, and understanding padrone and began moving into our connecting rooms looking out on the garden. Unpacked and arranged things until lunch. In the dining room, met and exchanged greetings with the Fuldas. Afterward rested in bed (fitfully), and at four o'clock went out with Katia into the Sunday air of the town. Noisy athletic contest at a sports field with a large parking area, many spectators, much shouting. Through the city park or botanical garden with its exotic and semi-exotic flowers, oaks, etc. Tea in a crowded café frequented by natives. Walked on up into town, climbing many steps up to a church with a fine facade, richly colored inside, Byzantine-Romanesque style, with a peaceful courtyard flanked by a stately building with a doorplate reading "Monsignore X, Arciprete." Returned by way of an unlovely industrial quarter, surrounded by throngs of returning sports fans.

Asked for stronger lighting in our room. Dictated letters to Katia. We wrote to Monternach in Geneva to ask about the possibility of a passport through the League of Nations. Also to Fayard in connection with the publication of the Wagner essay and the royalty arrangements with Bertaux.

Shaved and dressed. Dinner in the dining room; the company quiet, unaggressive, ladies, old people. Trout, pheasant, pudding with zabaglione. Afterward with the Fuldas in the otherwise empty game room, smoking. Several hours discussing the unspeakable and horrible situation, focusing at the end on what has been happening at the Academy. Fulda's broken state, his grief and wounded feelings as a German Jew. He is seventy-one and without hope. The talk did him good. I gave him the *Wagner* proofs. Animated, endless discussion of the criminal and revolting insanity, the sadistic pathological character of those who have come to power through the use of the most demented and shameless means in their thirst for absolute, unchallenged domination. . . . Two possible ways they might be overthrown: an economic catastrophe or a foreign policy disaster. Intense desire for this; prepared to make every sacrifice, share any suffering. No personal ruin would be too high a price to pay for the ruin of this common scum! It was left for the Germans to stage a revolution of a kind never seen before; without underlying ideas, even against ideas, against everything nobler, better, decent; against freedom, truth, and justice. Humanity has never seen its like. Accompanied by vast rejoicing on the part of the masses, who believe that this represents their true desires, when in fact they have been duped with insane cunning though they cannot yet perceive it—and the sure conviction of those of a higher level, and even conservatives, nationalists (Kardorff), that the whole thing is headed toward a terrible debacle.

The grotesque and crude swindle of the Reichstag fire. It appears that the alleged culprit, Van der Lubbe, is to be "publicly executed" without so much as a trial. Thus absolute power claps silence on what is universally known to be a brazen and criminal lie. This to the accompaniment of pealing bells and loud exultation. The Germans preen themselves on being a great people once more. The war, the defeat, might never have happened; their consequences have been nullified by a false war that called itself a revolution, conducted in mimicry of Allied propaganda against its own people. Revenge of the very types who lost the war. This type is given a new lease on life, while the nobler elements in Germany are condemned to the agony of spiritual homelessness. Concentration camps everywhere filled with "prisoners of war."

I took Adalin with camomile tea, then Phanodorm. Fell asleep very quickly and woke up, thoughts racing through my mind, at 5:30 in the morning on *Monday*. Got up at eight, bathed in the tub, and had breakfast in Katia's room while the maid tidied up my own. Then wrote these notes while smoking cigarettes.

—With Katia into town to do some shopping. We ran into the Fuldas and Frank. Back to the hotel by tram. Packed up copies of *Wagner* after lunch. Rested. Went for a drive with Frank at 3:30. Found ourselves on a closed road and had difficulty making our way back. Looked at a beautifully situated villa high on a slope that is for sale for 95,000 francs. Back in town for tea at the Café Huguenin. Met Frau Massary. The Bavarian prime minister, Held. Frank reported that those in power in Munich are making overtures for the future to the Bavarian People's party. Convinced that the character of the Bavarian people, their strongly Catholic nature, will prevail in the foreseeable future and make life in Munich possible again.

Back home dictated letters to Katia: to Bonnet, Bertaux, the Agence Littéraire Internationale.

My mood somewhat more confident, less anxiety-ridden. Inclined to take things more lightly under the influence of my contact with Frank, who is somewhat of an easygoing worldling. I can hardly welcome this change in my attitude, even though it is necessary and desirable from the standpoint of my health.

Word of organized protests in America and England against German anti-Semitism, effective enough to have caused the rabble in control in Germany to counter with cringing lies. Symptom of cultural subservience. The dictators' hatred of every sign of "intelligence" and restraint.

Tuesday, March 28; Lugano, Villa Castagnola

After dinner yesterday, with the Fuldas again in the game room. He has the touching and somewhat wearisome garrulity of Polonius. His wife good-natured, as is he; he has already read halfway through the Wagner essay and showered it with praise.— Katia telephoned Munich; all is well at the house, but there are letters from Golo and Katia's mother on the way that warn against Katia's even visiting Munich. The information on which these warnings are based is still unclear. Fulda is convinced they would not dare to lay hands on me. He feels they have had to come down a peg under pressure from abroad. The question raised in the House of Commons whether it was true or not that Germany is expelling her thinkers and poets.

Misery of refugee journalists in Prague, Zurich, etc. Schwarzschild wants to continue publishing the *Tage-Buch* from Prague, to serve the Diaspora of intellectuals and the German-reading public abroad. That will be very good even though it will be unavailable in Germany.

I tried a small glass of a winelike soporific the Fuldas use, and in addition took Phanodorm. Felt too tired to continue reading Tolstoy and slept wonderfully well. This morning I still feel traces of the drugs in my limbs.

The weather has cleared. Blue skies and cool temperatures. I am enjoying my room, cheerful and well arranged with its view of the palms and cedars in the garden and its good soft bed. We unpacked the large box of lighter-weight clothing we had asked Frau Kurz to send, none of which I can wear now except for the coat.

Keen appetite at breakfast, then smoked a little cigar while taking care of some writing.

Went with Katia at 11:00 to the Postplatz, where we boarded the bus for Montagnola. Clearest of days, with a touch of the South. Rode up to the Hesses'. Lunched with them, Herr Wiegand still there, then were shown Hesse's private suite. Sat out on the terrace, rested. Then tea and a walk. The perfect, exquisite, Romantic landscape. The southern effect of the stone walls in the blue-white light. Recalled Hesse's previous house with its almost tropical garden.

Came back on the 6:30 bus from the post office, after Katia had picked up mail for us at the Bellevue, including corrected proofs of the *Wagner*. Wiegand, leaving for Italy, came on the same bus.

Walked from the Postplatz to the hotel, where I finished a letter to Fiedler that I had begun in the morning. After dinner, with the Fuldas in the salon. They claim that their friend Dr. Ilgenstein would be able to take care of my passport. Unlikely in view of the inability of the consul to do so, who certainly wished us well, but all the more urgent since Katia has been newly warned through her mother and Golo by a well-informed friend in Munich that she herself must not think of returning, since they have been confiscating the passports of wives in order to force the return of their husbands.

Discussed with the Fuldas the horrors in the German newspapers. The *Berliner Illustrierte* full of photographs glorifying the regime! Outside reports of atrocities and the Germans' feeble denials. The demonstrations abroad against anti-Semitism and the Germans' holding Jews as hostages. The government's call for boycotts and pogroms. Threats against Denmark. Neighboring countries distrustful and arming. The breakdown of the so-called Four-Power Alliance. Financial mismanagement and animosity of Jewish high finance. How much longer?

Quotas for the number of Jews in the academic and legal professions based upon their percentage in the total population. They are being accused of being ungrateful "for the hospitality extended to them by the German people." The government intends to treat them like other aliens and will put no obstacles in the way of "opposition movements." Threats to the press to also maintain a "passive" position.

In the *Vossische Zeitung* an excerpt from my *Wagner* with a very fine introduction. They selected the passage on nationalism, of all things, so as to protect themselves—and their readers—"intellectually." But how long will the government tolerate such friendly notice being given either me or my work?

The sunny weather persists. The maid is tidying up my room during breakfast. Telephone conversation with Dr. Ilgenstein about the passport. Agreed on a time for his visit.

We are expecting Erika this evening. She is on her way to the Riviera. Annoyed with Klaus, who wrote a rude letter to Dr. Friedrich without my authorization.—

Letters to Bertram, Dr. Löwenstein. Chilly inside our rooms, but later, when Katia and I walked as far as the Monte Bré Kurhaus by way of the path with the many steps, it became very warm. Slept on the bed after lunch. Received Dr. Ilgenstein at 3:15, a somewhat ceremonious and pompous man. Had tea with him in the hotel garden; summer suit, glorious afternoon. Talked about the impossibly extreme state of affairs in Germany. With Ilgenstein to see a lawyer, Van Aken, whose partner is a member of the Berne legislature, about the passport business. Pleasant house, charming mother from the Rhineland. Tea was served, and I was assured by the lawyer that I will obtain an international passport either through him or through Monternach, for whose answer we should wait.—

Took leave of Ilgenstein and looked in on the attractive Hotel Seehof to make a reservation for Erika and Therese Giehse, but during our subsequent walk they arrived already and took accomodations at our hotel. I was in my room writing when Erika came in. Great joy at seeing her. Her Swiss cabaret project has not entirely fallen through. She came down here just to see us, and tomorrow is returning to Zurich, where she has a circle of friends.

Dinner for the four of us at an unfamiliar table. Then were joined by Frank and Speyer, and spent the evening with the Fuldas in the salon. Drinks and conversation. The perfidious hostage system in Germany. Whether the systematic economic boycott of the Jews will be enforced seems to depend on the "good behavior" of the foreign press, but simply the threat of such a thing represents a new provocation to world opinion.

Mail for me. An article from the Basel *National-Zeitung* on conditions in Germany, making the point that if I were in Germany I would be in the Dachau concentration camp by now.—A fairly long letter of appeal from Kiefer in Basel; his flight following the mistreatment of his son, his reports from Geneva. Isolation of Germany, whose economic prospects appear to be very bad. Nevertheless people expect the regime to last for years unless conflagrations outside Germany hasten events, as Van Aken, for one, predicts. Unlikely that there will be any slackening of tension inside Germany in the near future. On the contrary, there will be bloodshed; the signal for it, an assassination, will be staged with the same unscrupulousness as everything else. Advises that I abandon the country with my family.

Ullstein has stopped the sale of Feuchtwanger's *Josephus* because of the author's alleged involvement in the dissemination of stories of anti-Jewish atrocities in Germany. How long before censorship is directed against books? Doubtful whether Fischer, who has published Trotsky, will be able to continue his business in Berlin.

Thursday, March 30; Lugano

Slept quite well without artificial aids after reading some in *War and Peace*. Glorious morning, except that our west-facing rooms are somewhat chilly early in the day. I

139

mean to read the corrected proofs of the *Wagner*, of which both Frank and Fulda spoke enthusiastically yesterday evening.

Erika and Frau Giehse think that I look better, as do the Hesses. In fact I have become calmer here, have less of a tendency toward anxiety attacks; a certain adjustment to the situation has taken place, and I recognize that in spite of all the agony I am still able to speak of my characteristic good fortune, inasmuch as Katia and I were outside the country when the catastrophe struck. A precipitate flight over the border would have been more terrifying. The problem of the Munich household will be solved one way or the other and a new base, perhaps a small house near Zurich, can certainly be set up before too long. The realization that returning to Munich is impossible and not even desirable for perhaps a year must be assimilated and accepted.

A visit from Katia's parents is under consideration. Katia would like to have the children, Golo and the little ones, here for the Easter holidays. Yet these accomodations are expensive, and I would not like to be on the move again so soon. We must first try to arrive at some arrangement here.

The vile slanders against Braun and Severing; rumors, idiotic charges of "embezzlement," confiscation of property, wretched, cold-blooded economic strangulation. The dismally loathesome vindictiveness of the whole thing. The helpless despair of the Deutscher Klub in Berlin under the chairmanship of that witless criminal Papen.—

Corrected the *Wagner* proofs. Then a fine, bracing walk up the mountainside with Katia and Eri. Talked about the future, Zurich, a little household to be established there, the extent to which our Munich possessions can be incorporated—it will have to be in only a limited way. How to arrange being together with the children for the Easter holidays. Bibi's trip to Italy. Golo, too, could only be here briefly; it is only Medi who would be spending any length of time with us. Later on the children will transfer to schools in Zurich. We wish to establish a temporary residence there without attracting attention.—Plans for going to Madrid in May in the Buick, Erika doing the driving if she is free, otherwise Hans, whom we will have to keep on till then. We will then have the car for our new life in Zurich. Cheerful things to contemplate as we walk on this lovely day and look down at the lake. A sense of new confidence and of spiritual recovery.

Lunch for four. I then sent my laundry out and rested for an hour. Finished my letter to Bonnet of the "Coopération," describing the uncertainty of my situation and raising the question of opening the discussion with a prepared lecture.

At 4:00 Eri drove us to Montagnola to the Hesses', where we had tea and again went on the same lovely long walk we recently enjoyed. Were late getting back to the hotel for dinner, where Frau Giehse was waiting for us. Afterward with Fuldas in the salon. The senile prattle of the old man. Mail for me: Bertolt Brecht praising me for my "message," with which the honor of German literature had been saved; from the Foyer the texts of the speeches at the Wagner dinner; also letters from Annette Kolb and Ida Herz. Read the *Vossische Zeitung* with deep perturbation.

· ·

Friday, March 31; Lugano

· ·

Hesse has lent me his Insel edition of *War and Peace* in place of my wretchedly translated Reclam edition. Before going to sleep I spent some time reading on in the first volume. Slept badly thanks to my preoccupation with things in Germany, the boycott and the hostage business, the insane arms build-up, the stupidity and vileness.

New surge of depression. Took Evipan at about five o'clock and then was able to sleep. Katia was up with me and left the connecting door open.

Another glorious morning of misty freshness. But my nerves are taut again and under more strain than during the past few days. I finished correcting the proofs and sent them to Fischer. Letter from Paul Ehrenberg, who is in financial straits and had not considered my own situation. It shook me to see his handwriting again. . . .

Erika drove us around the lake to Paradiso and [?]. Charming spot, high, crowned by a chapel with sun-warmed walls. After lunch I lay on the chaise longue reading *War and Peace* with pleasure. Rested somewhat, then had tea with Katia on the terrace of the Hotel Müller. Mild thunderstorm, beautiful multicolored sky.

Back home, dictated letters: the reply to Paul Ehrenberg, then one to Kiefer, one to Mrs. Lowe-Porter concerning *Past Masters*, etc.

In Breslau all Jews have had their passports revoked. In Munich, and evidently elsewhere as well, the systematic boycott of all Jewish-owned businesses has been instituted even though propaganda from abroad has died down. The proprietors are expected to pay employee wages as before. Idiotic inconsistency of their vileness, since the "movement" stops short of attacking the Jewish banks. An article in the *Neue Zürcher Zeitung* also gravely points out the economic self-destructiveness of the policy. Rabid threats by Goebbels in his paper against anyone who dares to oppose the "organization." The *Völkischer Beobachter* raves against the *Deutsche Allgemeine Zeitung*, which now pretends to know better, but which time and time again was accessory to the crime. The fools who helped to fatten this monster!

Katia is urging her parents to come to Switzerland and move their collection to safety.

Saturday, April 1; Lugano

Yesterday new reports from Munich. Everyone leaving the country must carry a certificate of political reliability. Katia anxious to have the children here, that is to have Golo bring Medi to us. Telephoned him yesterday evening and again this morning.—Idiotic wickedness in the conduct of the Jewish boycott; business establishments must remain open and employees be paid, yet the public is prevented from entering them. Those who do so nonetheless are photographed and denounced. Yellow marks on all Jewish shops. It is too incredibly ridiculous and insane.

After dinner, at which we drank Asti, we spent the evening as usual with the Fuldas in the salon. The women phoned Munich and Berlin, also Frau Giehse, whose brother is being held in protective custody while her mother is on her deathbed. I received a letter from Knopf about the essay volume.—Fulda's lamentations and Jewish despair tragicomic. By the way, he keeps coming back to the *Wagner* with the utmost admiration.

Before going to sleep read Tolstoy for a good while. It was half past twelve before I turned off the light, but by five-thirty I was awake and did not really fall asleep again. Erika came at eight to say good-bye. She is returning to Zurich, commissioned to look about discreetly for a small house for us. We have decided that we soon ought to find a temporary base in Switzerland, specifically near Zurich, unobtrusively taking rented quarters so as to escape this expensive hotel existence. It would be desirable if we could continue to draw our own money from Germany. I have begun to adjust to the thought that I will not be returning to my accustomed life in the foreseeable future—besides, it would not be the old life anymore, but a hateful and perilous new one. I am much concerned about having my papers sent here, old diaries etc.

Bermann Fischer telegraphed that he would be passing through Lugano this afternoon. It appears he cleared out of Berlin with the children, leaving in a cloud of dust, as Frau Fischer reported by telephone from Rapallo in great agitation. "Do you know whether passports are still being issued to Jews?" The grotesque conversational style of these times. Old Fischer is taking many sleeping pills.

Thunderstorm during the night. Today everything veiled in rain, but mild. We watched from the balcony and the window as Eri drove off. She will be back in about ten days.—

Worked on the *Joseph* manuscript. Katia, back from the railway station, reported on the brief talk she had with Bermann Fischer, who is deeply perturbed, having left a Berlin full of turmoil and bewilderment. A madhouse. Everyone in confusion as to where he stands, what applies to him, what does not. The boycott business is supposed to have originated in Munich and to be distasteful even to Goering.

With Katia to the Crédit Suisse, where we collected money transferred from Munich. Then looked in on Frank at the Palace. His wife is still not back; he does not have any inkling why. He drove us back home.

Read Tolstoy after lunch. At 3:45, the weather having turned clear, went walking with Katia up to the Monte Bré Kurhaus where we had tea. Met the elderly English globetrotter. Once home again, wrote to Ida Herz.

Visit from the engineer Franco Ender, who owns the villa we looked at the other day, a Social Democrat who wanted to arrange an interview, but I declined. Handsome young man of a southern type; with his new young wife and baby he gives the impression of being a charming human being. Doubtless his chief reason for coming was to establish personal contact. My presence here is known, having been reported by the Ticino newspaper.

After dinner I read "The Coat of Many Colours" to the Fuldas.

Finished the letter to Ida Herz.

Katia telephoned Poschingerstrasse. Golo has not yet been able to obtain the necessary certificate of political reliability because no one at the office knew who was to receive them or even who was to issue them. He is planning to cross the border at Baden.

The trains from Germany are long and crowded.

. . . .

Sunday, April 2; Lugano

. . . .

We arrived here a week ago, and I cannot help feeling gratitude for the friendly and solicitous way we have been treated.

Clear, cool morning. Wind from the north. Somewhat short, but for the most part refreshing sleep. Awakening early, I thought about the spiritual condition of people in Germany: this Privy Councillor Oskar Wassermann, for example, director of the Deutsche Bank, who announces to the outside world that all is well with the German Jews, and who speaks of a revolution that in the light of its unparalleled magnitude is proceeding with the greatest possible discipline and moderation; or the Social Democrat Wels, who explains that he is withdrawing from the Second International because of some angry foreign declaration; or this Democrat, Professor Hellpach, who not only is at no loss for words, but who writes reverential articles on the "new heroism" and the like. What is all this? Fear? Forced acts of submission? Or a wave of feeling that has overwhelmed everyone inside the country and is stronger than the forces of humanity or reason? In any case, it can only end disastrously as it did after the mass frenzies of 1914. Nevertheless one does not feel wholly comfortable in the company of these exiles, types like Kerr, Tucholsky, etc. Hauptmann, too, is remaining outside the country; but I find greater solace in Hermann Hesse, whose self-imposed exile is based on sound moral principles. How strange that no one in Germany feels my outrage and disgust at the truly swinish methods by which this "people's movement" won its victory! Is my role merely that of an Erasmus vis-à-vis a new Lutheranism? Great revolutions, with their excess of terror and passion, generally inspire sympathy, compassion, and awe in the rest of the world. That was and is the case with the Russian Revolution, just as it was with the French Revolution, before which no living soul in the world could remain unmoved. What is wrong with this "German" one, which has isolated the country, bringing down upon it nothing but derision and loathing? Which has caused not only the Kerrs and Tucholskys to flee the country, but also people of my own stature?

Katia spoke on the telephone with the Franks after breakfast. Frau Frank has returned by plane without a clearance. The confusion seems to be indescribable. No one knows what is what. A fundamental sense of depression and helplessness, despite the nationalistic, anti-Jewish festivities and all the banners. The feeling is widespread that the half-mad leaders like Goebbels, whose wild rantings on the radio alienate the world, are increasingly losing control of the reins, that bloodshed is imminent, and that a military dictatorship capable of maintaining order is on the horizon. Hitler, who has long been a mere puppet like Hindenburg, of course, is supposed to be in a fairly desperate state of mind—just as his conservative allies have been for some time. By the way, so far as I am concerned, a cautious, somewhat shamefaced silence must be maintained. I am not being denounced, my resignation from the Academy caused no rejoicing. My absence seems to exert a certain dampening effect, is a cause of slight embarrassment. It seems they would prefer to have me there, in some circles at least—whose sentiments, to be sure, would not protect me from arrest were I to return tomorrow.

Thus it was very foolish and frivolous of Bertram to write, as he did on the picture postcard received from Friedrichshafen today, that nothing would, and nothing "dare," stand in the way of my homecoming. Vicco's long letter yesterday from Bolzano also showed an inadequate intellectual grasp of the situation.

Frau Frank brings bad news about our chauffeur Hans, who naturally has been thoroughly corrupted and represents a dangerous element. We must definitely get him out of the house.

On tenterhooks worrying whether the children will call to say they managed to get across the border today.

Short walk with Katia at noon. Had coffee on the terrace after lunch, though lately it particularly disagrees with me. Read Tolstoy in my room and had a short rest. Then with Katia into town, where we had our tea at an outdoor table at the Café Huguenin. Visited the Franks at the Palace Hotel, where we met Frau Massary and her sister. Long talk about the usual matters. Many people in Germany count on the Reichswehr's stepping in and establishing a military dictatorship, especially if there should be an economic collapse—which seems almost inevitable. In Munich there seems to be an inclination to come to terms with the People's party and form a government with it, perhaps under Epp. People in Munich are saying that with the advent of such a government there will be a strong desire for the return of persons like myself. That I would be sitting in prison on my second day home just now is a virtual certainty.

Lovely afternoon, picturesque light on the mountains. But a brisk north wind and haze. The park and the lakeside promenade crowded with people. I am glad we have a week ahead of us before another Sunday.—

Brooding over how to shorten the Egyptian section of *Joseph* already done.

. . . .
Monday, April 3; Lugano
. . . .

Another brilliant, fresh, sunny morning. After breakfast it is very pleasant to smoke and, with the balcony door open, to sit down to some light literary work such as these diary notes or letters. But it is high time this vagabond existence of upheaval and turmoil was put behind me and I found my way back to work on the *Joseph*. Nonetheless, this arduous holiday experience has not been wasted. I often see it in relation to the Faust story that will come after *Joseph*, with which I "would achieve something highly original."—

Yesterday before dinner I dictated business letters. We eventually left the game room because of the presence of others and settled ourselves with the Fuldas in a corner of the large salon. Dr. Löwenstein from Munich, who is staying at the Paradiso. Agitated conversation over beer about the "revolution." Bermann Fischer phoned from Rapallo to express his confidence. Apparently he has had reassuring news about the status of the publishing house. New arrangements were also made with Frau Hesse. Then, to Katia's great joy and reassurance, a call came from the children in Zurich. They made their escape at the last moment, for today travel restrictions were put into effect all over the country. Medi left school on the pretext that I was ill; she, who had been so eager to return, expressed her great relief at being away from Munich, for it has been terrible. She and Golo were spending the night at Eri's hotel; they are now on their way to us.

Yesterday evening I went on reading Tolstoy so avidly that I was over-stimulated. Resorted to Phanodorm after one, which gave me peaceful sleep until seven or eight.

The passport business at a standstill; no answer from Geneva, so we are having another appointment with Van Aken.

Wrote a rather long letter to Vicco. At noon with Katia into town, where we bought some fine shoes. Back by tram.

After we had lunched on the terrace Dr. Van Aken arrived, and we discussed the question of a Nansen passport. He also made suggestions about protecting our German holdings. Einstein's were confiscated, and probably the same threat faces all those who do not return.

Later with Katia by car to the railway station. Had a talk with Prime Minister Held, who is just back from Munich and gives a bleak account of conditions there, but believes that a coalition with the People's party is in the making. Feels German anti-Semitism might be curbed by the threat of lifting the agreed financial moratorium.

The train arrived; I greeted Golo and took Medi once more into my arms. The hotel bus brought us all home, where the children were shown to their rooms. I rested a while, then we all walked with Dr. Löwenstein, who called for us at 3:30, up to the Kurhaus Monte Brè, where we had tea. Discussed events and the financial measures to be adopted. Considered "mortgaging" the Munich property to a Swiss, to Helbling for instance. We sat with the children under an awning and watched the sunset, then walked home by roundabout paths. I walked arm in arm with Medi once more. She told me about Marie Kurz, who understood the situation perfectly well and wept as they said farewell. "You won't be coming back." This continues to move me deeply.

No more time for correspondence. I dressed, we had dinner with the children for the first time, and spent the evening with the Fuldas. Medi brought all sorts of mail, including a letter from Professor Heuser concerning Golo's prospects, which are quite slim, and my tour. Article in the *Nouvelles Littéraires* about the Wagner lecture.

Wednesday, April 5; Lugano

Letters to Reisiger and Dr. Knoche. Worked on the manuscript. At noon, with the sun already too hot, walked with Katia and Golo out toward Gandria. In the afternoon we were taken in a Barbay's car to Montagnola. Very warm day, which cooled off rapidly by evening. Tea at the Hesses' in the dining room. Then inspected the changes in their garden. Later a game of boccie on their well-tended court: Hesse, myself, our wives, Golo, Medi, and a painter who was visiting. We walked back to Lugano by way of Gentilino.

After dinner Dr. Löwenstein, who sat with Golo and us in a corner of the salon to discuss what precautionary measures we should take with regard to our Munich securities. Then talked with the Fuldas, whose apprentice lawyer son has been temporarily suspended from practicing. Discussed dictatorship as the governmental form of the twentieth century, and how the concept has been discredited by the crude nonsense in Germany that is an insult to the entire world. The dictatorship is in impossible hands, and even if there can be no return to parliamentary democracy these people are bound to fall. What disappointment this unhappy nation will have to swallow, now so intoxicated and seemingly blissful! The stock exchange is in turmoil. Either economic developments or a crisis in foreign relations will break the regime's back. But what will be done with this idolized scarecrow Hitler, whom millions worship, if the conservatives and the Reichswehr take over? Even if his regime were swept away he would have to be installed as president, for to depose him and clap him in prison would be too much for the German heart to bear.

Hitler's gang cannot fulfill its promises. Its achievements are bound to remain distinctly minimal. Therefore it must all the more hold the masses in thrall. Celebrations and banners. The communist issue has served its turn. The fuss over the Jews will subside in the face of indignant protests from outside. What then? There will be assassinations, the scenario as crude and full of swindle as before. What matter if the higher elements see through it; the important thing is to hoodwink the masses, inasmuch as the intelligentsia no longer plays any role. Whoever speaks out is lynched. The question is what kind of life the intelligentsia will adopt. And since all its avenues of influence are cut off, how will it register its criticism, at least for history?—

—Copies of the *Rundschau* with the Wagner essay have come. Was asked to give lectures in Locarno, but declined.

Katia got up earlier than usual, since Medi was going on an outing into the mountains with Frau Hesse, and Golo was leaving. We said good-bye to him at 8:30. When and where we shall see each other again remains uncertain.

Again a summery day with a cool morning. Had breakfast by myself. Toward noon went to the barber nearby to have my hair cut. Spent some time in the garden before lunch reading the *Rundschau*. In the afternoon had tea with Katia at the Belvedere, overlooking the lake. Misty, cooler. Back home, dictated a host of letters, the most important to Motta, but also to Bonnier, Knopf, etc. Korrodi would like a section of the *Joseph* for the Easter issue. Promised him the pyramid episode, which Katia is copying.

Walked about in the garden with Medi before dinner discussing the future. Talked about a stay in the south of France.

After our meal I sat alone reading in a corner of the large salon. Unwell, stomach overfull. In the *Rundschau* an unappealing story by Broch. Interesting piece (for my *Faust*) by Huxley about Lawrence and his letters.—The others joined me later, including Dr. Löwenstein, who is going back to Munich. Bruno Frank informed in a curt note that he has been stricken (probably along with all the other Jews) from the membership list of the Rotary Club. (!) A new indication of the state of mind in Germany. Very sinister. My resignation is settled. The only question is whether to comment on the absurdity of the club's action.

Korrodi has told Erika that Katia would be in particular danger in Munich, since she is known for her outspokenness. Denunciation?

Erika's Zurich plans momentarily disrupted, since Therese Giehse, whose brother they are holding prisoner, is being prevented by elements in Munich from taking part. She has to go back. We are expecting Erika, who is driving to France to meet up with Klaus and write the children's book.

Anecdotes about the theater. Phanodorm.

Fine cool day. Intestines and stomach somewhat disturbed. Eumydrin, am being careful.—Letter from Frau Fischer about her arrival and Wassermann's problems with his first wife, which further upset me.

Telephone conversation with the man in Locarno whose offer I declined. Last night with Prof. Joël from Basel. Our subject was Kiefer, but he reminded me of his earlier suggestion that I move to Basel, which has taken on new meaning today. The idea must be considered. Arranged for another meeting with Joël.

Thinking about compressing Joseph's journey through Egypt. Walked with Katia toward Gandria. After lunch read an article in the *Rundschau* about Jünger's book (thought of my Faust story) and went on with Tolstoy. At [?]:15 by tram to the Hotel Bellevue au Lac with Katia and Medi. Tea with the Joëls. Discussed the situation over tea and during the slow way back. The problem of Basel. An expensive place to live. But highly attractive as an intellectual milieu and European center.

Erika back again with Frau Giehse. Cocktails with Eri on the hotel terrace. Dressed for dinner. Welcomed Therese Giehse in Katia's room; she is determined not to return to Munich, even though her brother is being treated as a hostage. The five of us at dinner. Afterward in the main salon with the Fuldas, the Franks, and Speyer. Separate and general conversation. New and pleasant vistas opened up by Fulda's suggestion that we choose the South Tyrol, Bolzano for example, for a longer stay. It could be conveniently reached via Milan. Venice not far away. Places in the mountains to go to during the summer. Not far from Munich, thinking of Katia's parents. Medi's desire and right to be in school pose one difficulty.

New excitement. New alternatives.

The news that in Germany they are beginning to clamp down on intellectuals; not only the Jews, but all those suspected of being politically untrustworthy and opposed to the regime. One must be prepared for house searches. Fresh anxiety about my old diaries. Imperative to bring them to safety.

Every evening am reading Tolstoy at bedtime. Always powerfully gripped by it. Only extreme sleepiness makes me put down the book, and such sleepiness comes quickly, though without any assurance that it will last through the night.

Saturday, April 8; Lugano

After breakfast wrote to Golo, giving him full and exact instructions about sending my papers and other materials kept in the cabinet and writing desk. Sent him the keys.

They say they have seldom had such persistently lovely weather here. Another clear day, cool in the morning. Katia down to see Erika at the Seegarten.

There I found the three ladies having breakfast in the garden. Went with my two for a walk to Gandria. The sun very warm.

After lunch, Tolstoy. Brilliant description of the Battle of Austerlitz.

The Munich Rotary Club has sent me the very same letter they sent Frank, dryly informing me that my name has been stricken from their membership list. It came unexpectedly. I would not have thought this would happen. Shock, amusement, and amazement at the thinking of these people, who are expelling me, the "jewel" of their organization, without a word of regret, of thanks, as though it were the most natural thing in the world. What is going on in the minds of these people? How did they arrive at the decision to expel us?

I rested on the bed, slept for a bit. Then Erika drove us to Chiasso in uncertain weather, which later cleared up. We had intended to cross the border and pay a quick visit to Como, but were unable to do so because Medi had not brought her passport along. A nice young official, proud of the discipline and precision that set Switzerland apart from Italy. Drove back by way of Capo Lago, where we had tea in a cold wind. Crazy proprietress from Lower Bavaria.

Urgent letter from Lewisohn in Paris about the brutal treatment accorded the Jews in Germany. Demands some explanation for the American people, who have turned against all Germans and are once more disposed to believe all the old wartime propaganda. A foolish demand, stemming from ignorance of the terrible significance, ferocity, and frenzy of what is taking place in Germany, and of the consequences that would follow even the mildest show of dissent.

Agonized talk with Katia about developments, for example the states' being stripped of all their rights in favor of the Reich—this Reich. Everywhere regional governors are being appointed by the Reich, with the chancellor assuming the title in Prussia. My pessimistic belief in the irreversibility of all this, even the disenfranchisement of the Jews. The world will have to become accustomed to a situation in Germany that, though German, and uncannily characteristic and willful, is a phenomenon of world psychological processes corresponding to the situations of Russia and Italy. It is my private belief that it is here to stay, and, despite all sorts of crises, that nothing is going to get better, that I will be remaining outside—but perhaps ought not to be allowed to.

—Knoche sent the requested dental information.—Heard from Signora Mazzuc-chetti.—The Agence Littéraire Internationale concerning the *Sketch of My Life.*—Sympathetic note from Gilbert Murray in Milan.—Touching letter from Vicco in Bolzano.—Ida Herz reports on her business and the nervous toll exacted by the ferocious victory celebrations.—Prof. Peterson answered from Baltimore about the Käte Hamburger matter; he has heard some "frightful-sounding" news from Germany, which he considers exaggerated.—

After dinner, music in the salon, to Medi's great delight; Fulda has commented on her "charming seriousness." Gathered in the game room. The usual conversation, with Erika and Therese Giehse present. Differing opinions over the duration of the present state of affairs in Germany. I cannot share the opinion that it will soon blow over. There is nothing to take the place of what is now in the saddle, and a governmental and social cataclysm like this one, with all its attendant savagery, injustice, wickedness, and pathology, cannot be reversed. Disappointment, disenchantment, despair, are not sufficient countervailing elements. The parallel with the war, though certainly obvious, is also beside the point in this situation. Despite all the insane hatred of communism, the system has much in common with it, and it is possible, even probable, that it may very well develop into a sort of national bolshevism. All sorts of things are possible. But that the betrayed and besotted people will rise up in "civil war" and sweep it all away is beyond my hope. This war has already been underway for a long time, taking forms as new as those of the "revolution"; and what will it set in place of what we have now?

During the war the fulfillment of the German "ideals" of 1914 miscarried, and Germany was "democratized" as a result of her defeat. In actual fact the "German Revolution" is the war of revenge, merely internalized. While the revolution carries with it certain international risks, such as moral isolation and cultural disrepute, these only confirm its claim to being a purely German solution that must not be thwarted; the movement thus holds all kinds of prospects. No one can force Germany to return to democracy. The only question is whether the basic human components in a country with Germany's traditions will not gradually win out against the villainous radicalism of the "new spirit." Hitler has handed down this "gospel" with regard to the press: "The right to criticize carries with it the obligation to tell the truth." Of course the "truth" as he means it is not truth in the humanistic sense, in the spiritual sense. Truth and justice are aspects of absolute spirit, of free conscience, and according to the writer Ernst Jünger absolute spirit, that is to say truth, is nothing more nor less than "treason." This seems an exceedingly profound, new, and revolutionary doctrine, but it is only another version of the slogan from the beginning of the war: "Whoever doesn't lie now is a scoundrel."—

Sleeping pill. Tired, dispirited. Finished the first volume of *War and Peace* before going to sleep.

Slept tolerably well. Cool, changeable weather now. Erika and Therese Giehse left in the Ford this morning, headed for Milan and the Riviera, where they plan to meet Klaus. I said my good-byes to them from the balcony. Shattered by still another parting and uncertainty about when I shall see them again. Perhaps in Bolzano.— Medi to an outdoor concert in Lugano.

Cannot force myself to work energetically on the novel. I "work" on these jottings.

More letters, noteworthy among them a fine communication from the conductor Gustav Brecher of Leipzig about the Wagner essay. A pleasure.—A remarkable letter of apology from some anonymous "personage" who counts on being recognized—in vain. He is inwardly moved to deplore the present trend, when "friendship has been trampled underfoot." No idea who it can be. Nevertheless remarkable, and also a symptom of the times. A letter in English from one A. P. Saunders of Hamilton College, Clinton, in regard to *Goethe and Tolstoy*.—

The relaxation I felt here the first days seems to have vanished. My nerves are again strained, overwrought. In any case, we will stay here until after Easter and wait for the visit from Bermann Fischer. The unresolved passport business constantly worries me. Am waiting for Motta at least to give me an idea of where the matter stands.—

Frau Frank, depressed and needing to talk, visited Katia. I found the two of them on the terrace. Strolled along the quai in the Sunday ambience to the Palace Hotel, where we talked with Frank and Speyer. Frank astonished and delighted on his own account by my expulsion from the Rotary Club. We met Medi returning from the concert with an acquaintance.

After lunch read the Brecher article. Had a short rest, after which Signora Mazzucchetti arrived. We sat on the terrace for a while, then went to the Belvedere for tea. Hotel guests from Milan and Germany. The feeling in Italy about "Germany" almost as bad as in other countries. Mussolini: "Cet Hitler est un singe." He is supposed to have remarked about Croce's most recent book that "he was entitled to write it, but what angered me was that he dedicated it to Thomas Mann." He is not very well informed. At a dinner he took issue with someone and exclaimed: "Thomas Mann is in no way a representative of Germany. He has done nothing that would allow him to call himself so. Stefan Zweig—that is another story!"—That would not go over well even in these parts.

Discussed the question of *Joseph's* being published by Mondadori. I would like to have them do the Wagner essay, and I gave a copy to Signora Mazzucchetti as she was leaving.—

Then took a walk with Katia. Very hazy, but still no rain. Back at the hotel I wrote to Brecher, whom I would like to quote on the jacket band. Since he has already been removed from his post, it can do him no further harm.

After dinner, conversation and card games with the Fuldas in the large salon. Casino and Patience.

Remark made by Prime Minister Held in the café: "They commit one idiocy after another." A new ordinance, by virtue of which students belonging to nationalist organizations are exempt from written examinations. "Antigovernment workers" can be summarily dismissed from their jobs to make room for Party members and receive no unemployment compensation. One should expect a general uprising in the near future, prompted by rage and despair. I wish I could believe it.

Overcast morning, with clearing likely. Yesterday evening I was in the proper mood for recasting the journey through Egypt. Made a start on a new version.

Another letter from Paul Ehrenberg, to whom I am lending 800 marks.

Into town at noon.

In the afternoon a lovely walk to Gandria, where I read a long letter from Reisiger while we were having tea on the terrace at the steamboat landing.

After dinner sat with the Fuldas and Adrienne Thomas in the salon. In the *Völkischer Beobachter* a proposal by a doctor to have the Jews sterilized. What a cheery official newspaper.

The *Frankfurter Zeitung* speaks out against the dogmatic racial policy, not without a certain courage to be sure (courage that here and elsewhere is always confined to this single point), but then hails the radical centralization of power in the Reich as a great historic act, even though it expresses little reverence for historical tradition or "ethnic identity." The thousand-year-long fragmentation of the Germans eliminated in a single stroke. But will not all sorts of other fragmentation appear in its place? Heretofore it was considered un-German, Marxist, and insensitive to strip the German states of political power and individual sovereignty. But in a speech to workers Minister of the Interior Goering falls into that very same Marxist groove. What a farce! But for all that, might not something deeply significant and revolutionary be taking place in Germany? The Jews. . . . It is no calamity after all that Alfred Kerr's brazen and poisonous Jewish-style imitation of Nietzsche is now suppressed, or that the domination of the legal system by Jews has been ended. Secret, disquieting, persistent musings. Come what may, much will remain that in a higher sense is repellent, base, and un-German. But I am beginning to suspect that in spite of everything this process is one of those that have two sides to them. . . .

I am spending the mornings rewriting the journey.

Motta and the Ministry in Berne have failed me on the passport request. Letter to Ambassador Müller in Berne.

Yesterday dictated a series of long letters, after which we went into town to have tea and discuss the matter of Basel with the Joëls. I answered Lewisohn and wrote to Gilbert Murray about Golo. The manuscript went off to the *Neue Zürcher Zeitung* the day before yesterday and Korrodi thanked me for the "magnificent chapter," which did my heart good.

This morning had Wüterich treat my bad toe.

At 11:30 in Ludwig's car to his beautiful place near Ascona. Others there were Remarque and his wife, the old Count Wolff-Metternich, Ernst Toller, and, later, Secretary of State Abegg. Breakfast, tour of the house and garden, and animated conversation, almost entirely about political matters. Abegg's optimism. He finds it inconceivable that the regime will last, is counting on the Reichswehr and the Veterans Association. Ludwig, however, sees the Germans as finding psychological gratification in all this, and I consider that the only effective means of toppling the leadership would be war. But that will be carefully avoided.

Abegg argues against Bolzano, in contrast to Ludwig.

Back at the hotel, a variety of mail, including a letter from Annette Kolb and cards from Bertram, who is in Locarno, through which we just passed, and "hopes to see us again in Munich." After dinner I wrote a card to him, without insisting that he visit us. Also wrote to Schickele in Sanary.

Abegg told stories of looting and mistreatment of Jews by bands of Storm Troopers. The mayor who registered the arsonist of the Reichstag as a member of the National Socialist party has "disappeared." Am curious to learn what the dogs will do with him. What a hodgepodge of betrayal, criminality, and base humbug the whole thing is!

Yesterday in the *Frankfurter Zeitung* Furtwängler's highly discreet but nevertheless admonitory letter to Goebbels on cultural policy, and the idiot's lengthy reply. The complacent and empty language of these new rulers, such as that phrase of theirs about "restored national honor." If that is what they mean by honor! In the evening with the Fuldas, Frau Klöpfer, and Goetz, author of *Gneisenau*. Thunder and rain.

Easter Monday, April 17; Lugano

Restless night. Recurrence of the tendency toward irritability and anxiety. The passport matter at a complete standstill. After breakfast dictated to Katia letters to Motta, Ambassador Müller, and Mayor Seitz of Vienna.

Wrote dedications in the Fuldas' copies of the Wagner essay and *Tonio Kröger*.

Beautiful day. The two youngest carefree and spruce as they set off for a concert in town.

Letter from Heinrich in Nice, full of hatred for the criminals and scoundrels now in power in Germany. His Berlin assets have been confiscated, his Munich home "sequestered."

Letter from Bonnier, who wants to publish the Wagner essay in book form.

With Katia to see the Franks at the Palace, where we sat together on a bench in the sun and mostly discussed the baseness of that radio broadcast about my Wagner essay. In today's Germany such a broadcast amounts to an act of murderous denunciation.—Talked of the passport disaster and the question of clearing out the Munich house, which would be desirable but very conspicuous and final.

After lunch said good-bye to the Fuldas.

Headache, some sleep. In the afternoon to the Hesses' with the children.

Wednesday, April 19; Lugano

Yesterday, after I had done some writing, the Munich situation took a turn for the worse, with a manifesto against me appearing in the Easter issue of the *Münchner Neueste Nachrichten* under the title "Protest by Munich, the Wagner City." It carried many signatures. Bruno Frank brought us the dastardly document. Stricken with disgust and horror; the shock lasted all day. It strongly confirmed our decision not to return to Munich but rather to devote all our energies to the plan of settling in Basel.

In the afternoon another conference with the lawyer Becher about deeding the house to the children. He drove us into town, where we had the notary Antonini witness our signatures on the application for such a procedure.

Afterward we went to the Palace Hotel to see Frank about the Munich protest against me, and to discuss the requisite reply.

At night, a combination of Adalin and Phanodorm, thanks to which I slept until 5:30, though no more after that.

Today after breakfast I wrote my reply, which turned out quite well. Frank came and helped tone down my calm and dignified letter even further.

With him, his wife, and Speyer to see Frau Massary in Bissone, where we had lunch.

Back home Katia typed up the reply for the *Frankfurter Zeitung*, the *Neue Freie Presse*, the *Deutsche Allgemeine Zeitung*, and the *Vossische Zeitung*. We sent it off.

Tea in the main salon. We expected the Bermanns from Rapallo, but they did not arrive.

Composing the letter had a calming and salutary effect on me.

The week's international developments, especially the speeches in the British House of Commons, have been so disastrous that even the Munich cultural agitation can hardly stir up the powers that be to any strong action against me.

Thursday, April 20; Lugano

Nervous perturbation, feeling unwell. Fitful, oppressed, and poorly slept.

The Bermanns never turned up yesterday. They are now due tomorrow evening. Bermann is in Zurich, where it is hoped he can make some useful business arrangements. He wrote that the firm has foreign exchange rights for its authors, which would be most beneficial for us. Will such rights not be withdrawn?

Cold and rainy. I did some work and we then went into town with the children to make some purchases for them. Korrodi sent proofs of the "Pyramids." Schickele wrote at length, also about our coming to Sanary, which he recommends. As a result of his persuasion and his offers, the plan has taken on a new reality for us, and we have almost decided to go. We should first set up things for the autumn in Basel, and in conjunction with the trip arrange for Katia to meet her parents either in Zurich or in Basel.

New deliberations on the fate of the children, since Katia is reluctant to let them return to Germany. Where then? To Zurich? Should they remain on vacation until the autumn?—When the embassy returns my passport, one way or the other, I must take it to the consuls here.

A fine letter from Stefan Zweig about the *Wagner* protest. Much mail yesterday and today, including letters from Keyserling, Wassermann, Käte Hamburger, Witkop, and a letter about Golo from Mrs. Murray, writing on behalf of her husband who is in Greece.—

After lunch a good nap. My stomach is rather bothersome as always when my nerves are under strain. The Chianti is too constipating, at least the red. Today I had tea with my lunch.

The abrupt change in the weather and the resulting cold are astonishing. In the afternoon we went walking with the children, had tea at the Belvedere and looked at the suite on the top floor, which, with its view of the lake from all the windows, holds considerable attractions. But summer in Lugano does not tempt us much.

Telegram from Erika and Klaus that they will be here tomorrow. Surprise.

Dictated a series of letters, including one to Korrodi in connection with Käte

Hamburger and the Munich to-do. Löwenstein, in Milan, attributes the whole thing to "intimidation and psychosis." The former especially has undoubtedly played a major role. I am fairly certain, for instance, that the critic Berrsche admires my essay. By the way, the whole university remained silent, as did Preetorius and others. . . .

—The events in Germany are constantly on my mind. Later on, when I have liquidated my affairs there, I will surely write about this. The return of barbarism, in olden times introduced by primitive peoples from elsewhere, now introduced by deliberate choice as "revolution" with the help of a youth strongly conditioned to think in simplistic terms. The expulsion of middle-class, humane intellectual elements, chiefly in the guise of anti-Semitism, and the reduction of all questions to racial and national terms, more thoroughly and terribly than ever before. I could have a certain amount of understanding for the rebellion against the Jewish element were it not that the Jewish spirit exercises a necessary control over the German element, the withdrawal of which is dangerous; left to themselves the Germans are so stupid as to lump people of my type in the same category and drive me out with the rest. Essentially this is, as the Munich matter shows, the hatred of the simplistic-minded for any subtlety, which they feel to be antinational and galling to the point of arousing murderous rage. This revolution boasts of being bloodless, but it is the most hate-filled and murderous that ever was. Its special character, no matter what one imagines, does *not* consist of "idealism," joy, magnanimity, love—emotions that have always been compatible with many blood sacrifices made in the name of faith and the desire for a better future. Instead we have hate, resentment, vindictiveness, baseness. It could be far bloodier and the world would nevertheless regard it with respect if it were finer, brighter, more noble in spirit. As it is, the world indubitably despises it and the country is isolated. But this regime lacks any feeling for moral imponderables. To them, cleverness consists in believing *only* in power politics, and the action in the House of Commons is taken to be only a ploy of some sort. This is the greatest stupidity of all.

A most moving letter from Max Mohr to the *Münchner Neueste Nachrichten* protesting the Munich swinishness. Although there is of course no possibility of its being printed, Katia and I are deeply gladdened and encouraged by this manifestation of simple integrity.

Sunday, April 30; Rohrschach-Hafen, Hotel Anker

Yesterday in Zurich in pouring rain to the little Jew Tennenbaum—recommended to us by the Franks—who received us hospitably and discussed our financial problems with us. New possibilities proposed for transferring our money. Acute nervous exhaustion. At four o'clock the little man accompanied us down the crowded Bahnhofstrasse, where a parade was to take place in honor of the hundredth anniversary of the founding of the university, and saw us to our train.

Two hours later we were here, after a troublesome change of trains at the Rohrschach station. Reunion with Golo. Checked into the hotel. The three of us at dinner. Golo's account of the confiscation of our automobiles and of a search of the house "for weapons." Uncomfortable sensation caused by proximity to the border and our impressions of the general mood here. Later on the lawyer Heins and his friend Frau Walter, who came by car and brought the trunks packed by our housekeeper Frau Kurz. We sat together in a corner of the dining room and brooded at length over the question of going back or staying away. At 11:00 we broke up, and I slept in a moderately good bed until 5:00, when I woke up suddenly seized with panic about the suitcase containing the diaries; was then able to sleep a while longer with the help of half a sleeping pill.

Very nervous this morning, frightened and shaky. The three of us at breakfast, then serious and depressed discussions. Afterward a long meeting with Heins in the same corner of the dining room. Continuation of our thinking aloud. The alternatives that present themselves are either returning or declaring war and removing what we can of our possessions. Katia however agrees with me in coming back to a middle way, namely deeding some things to our children and disposing of other things wherever possible, since I do not wish the psychic burden and other consequences of an open breach and the confiscation of our capital. There is discussion of the possibility of speeding up the acquisition of Swiss citizenship. The house problem, the transport of some of its furnishings. My manuscripts, two paintings, and the bust of Medi will be taken care of by Heins. The Gramophone can be shipped to Basel by Koch.

Having come to a reasonable temporary conclusion, we took a walk with Heins after eleven up into the surrounding country, in the sun and the moist air from Lake Constance. The five of us had lunch at one in the dining room. In half an hour we will depart for Basel while Golo returns to Munich in the car with Heins and Frau Walter. The fiction of our imminent return is to be maintained. Heins and his law partner are to look into the matter of the misplaced suitcase; evidently some foul play there. On Tuesday they will telephone me in Basel to let me know. My fears now revolve first and foremost almost exclusively around this threat to my life's secrets. They are deeply serious. The consequences could be terrible, even fatal.

The positive result of the past days was the phone call from the French consul in Lugano informing us that the Quai d'Orsay was being most accommodating and that residence permits for France are assured us.—

(*Basel, 9:00* P.M.) Rohrschach will remain one of my worst memories.—Pouring rain, thunder, sultriness. A difficult, nerve-wracked, and care-ridden journey, with spells of anxiety that gave way to immense fatigue. Katia and I sat holding hands a great deal. She more or less understands my fears concerning the contents of the suitcase. We had to change at Zurich. There we met Dr. Helbling and his family. At about 8:00 we arrived here, still in heavy rain, and were driven to the Hotel Drei Könige, where we took a too expensive double room with bath. Mail arrived: a telegram from Feist, the *Wagner* contract from Bonnier. We had supper in our room: ham, eggs, and tea. The hotel is very good, its well-run ambience having an immediate effect on one's spirits.

Talked on the telephone with Tennenbaum in Zurich about business matters. Tomorrow is a holiday, so we will not be able to accomplish much. Katia wrote to Pierre Bertaux, who is supposed to go to Munich, and to Heins about his efforts in connection with the suitcase, which might entail applying to some government agency.

. . . .

Wednesday, May 3; Basel

. . . .

Yesterday evening we again crossed over to Spitz and had dinner outdoors overlooking the Rhine. Afterward we settled down in the salon of the hotel, where I read this and that in the *Neue Rundschau* and drank linden-blossom tea.

Slept better, as did Katia. The morning was very overcast and rainy, but now it seems to be clearing up.

A letter from B. Croce came yesterday, along with an issue of *Critica*.

At dinner Katia and I again discussed the question of expatriating or returning. Since living on capital deposited in Switzerland is against German law, returning will soon become impossible, by autumn at the latest. But before that we will have to come to a decision, in the face of the threat of having all our property confiscated if we stay away. This can hardly fail to happen, and we must consider how we are going to respond. It already seems too late to withdraw our liquid assets, since Golo has reported "difficulties" at the Feuchtwanger Bank. I am the one who has prevented us from taking definitive action here; what motivated me was less a question of returning to our accustomed life than the thought that Germany, even a Germany wracked by confusion, is a tremendous country, whereas Switzerland—but Switzerland has great advantages.—

Telephone call from Fräulein Joël while Katia was out. Prof. Schmalenbach will be by in the afternoon to take us in his car to look at houses.

At 10:30 went out with young Andreae. Looked at an attractive modern house in the St. Albans settlement.

Had lunch with Frau Burckhardt-Schatzmann, lovely old patrician house, along with Herr von der Mühll and his wife, née Burckhardt, and Annette Kolb.

Rested somewhat, then picked up by Prof. Schmalenbach, in whose house in Riehen we had tea. Then went to see a house which was thought suitable for us, but which I found horrible; it would rent for 3,000 francs.

I was not feeling well, and the impression the house made on me of a ghastly and dreary déclassé existence so aggravated my state that back at the hotel my nerves collapsed, bringing on tears.

Wrote briefly to Ida Herz, who is living at Poschingerstrasse and has packed my *Joseph* library and sent it on here to Dr. Bernoulli. Katia telephoned Bernoulli's wife.

Talked on the phone with Pierre Bertaux in Sèvres, who is going to drive to Munich to see Golo, and will perhaps bring out some money.

We stayed in, had tea and eggs brought up to our room.

After the good weeks in Lugano this confused transitional state has once more stirred up my anxieties. There are moments when I fear my nerves will give way completely.

News of the arrest of all German union leaders. A new blow, which was prepared for the day after the "Day of Labor."

In Berlin and Cologne another twenty-nine professors suspended, among them Katia's brother.

Friday, May 5; Basel

[To the Joëls' for dinner] where we met Vollmoeller, whose house on the Rhine became a possibility in our house hunting. A most relaxing and refreshing evening with the elderly brother and sister. There was also much talk of an old property belonging to landed gentry, the Wenkenhof, which is highly recommended to us and represents the best of Basel tradition. The wealthy owner must see to various improvements.—We went home on foot; I was very tired, but could not fall asleep without Phanodorm.

Today clear warm weather. After breakfast I began packing. Ida Herz has sent the list of the *Joseph* reference books. Expressions of sympathy. Interesting letter from Meier-Graefe about a house in St. Cyr.—

Summerlike warmth. Visit from Dr. Hirsch, from Munich, who brought me greetings from Vossler. The latter, too, has had his house searched.

We went out and took care of some errands. Then a visit from W. Kiefer, who lives in Hüningue, across the border on French soil.

We looked up Vollmoeller's house on the Rhine and found it remarkably appealing and atmospheric. It would be good to live there a while. In general, Basel is going to great trouble to have us settle here, and [?] will surely exert pressure on the owner of the Wenkenhof to do his part.

Luncheon with Annette Kolb on the terrace in Spitz. Later on at our hotel we said good-bye to this odd person, who is going to Ireland via Paris.

Back in our room I smoked and rested. Katia began the mighty task of repacking, storing in camphor those things that are to stay here over the summer.

After tea we returned once more to the ever-debated problem of getting money out of Germany—for which it will soon be too late. My moral right to the half of the Nobel Prize money that remains in Germany is indisputable—vis-à-vis a state that is ignorant both of justice and decency. The money was not earned in Germany; it was a gift from outside. If it is lost, it will be my fault for shrinking from the ultimate step that would exclude me from Germany for good. The disgusting thing is that, do as we will, and in spite of our acting with the greatest circumspection, loyalty, and restraint, it is almost certain that all our Munich property, the house, the furniture, and the library, must be given up for lost.—

I finished packing my trunk. We have plenty of time. It is only 5:30, and our train to Mulhouse does not leave until 10:00. At Mulhouse we will be given a sleeping car, which we will not have to leave until 2 P.M. tomorrow when we reach Toulon.

· ·

Monday, May 8; Les Roches fleuries

· ·

Yesterday went on an automobile tour with Erika and Therese Giehse through Hyères and Toulon to Sanary and Bandol. We visited Schickele, presented ourselves at the Hotel Bandol, looked at houses, then all had lunch at the Meier-Graefes'. Later I rested in the boudoir of the lady of the house while Katia went to look at houses in St. Cyr. Went to see others with the windbag of an agent. The choice narrows down to three, of which the one here is by far the most pleasant and reasonably priced. The terrible drawback is its distance from friendly colleagues. Theater, Schickele. Then drove home, first stopping in Toulon, where we wanted to make a call to Bertaux in Paris, but could no longer get a connection. Dinner in the dining room of the Grand Hotel (no appetite, exhausted and nervous), then sat together in the lobby. Erika was coughing, and sent to the pharmacy for some medicine. Then drove the rest of the way home, and after lingering a while went to bed very tired.

Today blue skies and strong wind from inland. Strained nerves. The essential thing would be to settle the matter of the house, to install ourselves, and return to a regular life. Everyone recommends that I write a letter to the "governor," General von Epp in Munich, in the hope of arriving at some arrangement regarding our financial holdings and furniture.—

Yesterday I heard Bibi play the violin; was impressed by his skill and talent.—

More about the abominations and scurrilous deeds in Germany and even outside the country. The fatal "accident" of young Mendelssohn, who was probably mistaken for Remarque.

Schickele and Meier-Graefe warn us strongly against Basel because of its proximity to the border and to the influence of National Socialist propaganda. Inwardly turning away from this plan. Beginning to think about Berne.—

Katia keeps trying unsuccessfully to reach Pierre Bertaux by telephone; he is to leave tomorrow for Berlin to see Golo. I stayed out in the windy sunshine with the children in front of the hotel, went to see Erika, who is hoarse, and had breakfast in her room with Klaus, Therese Giehse, and Annemarie Schwarzenbach. Waiting, not knowing what to do.—

—A twenty-minute walk with Katia to the house that is her favorite on this coast. Found the woman with the key and were shown through. Quite satisfied, and we decided to rent the tasteful and thoroughly congenial property. But on our way back doubts arose again about whether setting ourselves up in a house for three months with a German maid makes any sense. Back at the hotel we discussed the matter with the children. It is probably better to preserve a mobile and only provisionally settled existence, moving into the Hotel Bandol where Katia's parents could be made comfortable, and where friends are nearby. We can stay four, six, eight weeks, and still be free to go elsewhere in the summer, to Biarritz or Arosa. The decision to settle down here in a house for a long period, a year, would be too hasty in every respect.

Telegrams to Schickele, to Meier-Graefe, and to the owner of the house.—

After lunch had a good nap. Afterward a wretched tea on the veranda of the nearby bar.

Over the telephone commissioned Schickele's son to make arrangements in Bandol.

Back at the hotel Katia and I drafted the letter to General von Epp, which is in any case an interesting step to take, though I myself do not have any hope of success from it. Katia dictated it to Erika, who typed it.

I read Tolstoy in the garden; the air turned very crisp, but the sky is completely clear and the wind has abated.

Tuesday, May 9; Les Roches fleuries

Yesterday before and after dinner the letter to the governor was typed and read through. I read it once again this morning, and it satisfies me as a clarification of my personal situation and attitude, even though I do not in the slightest believe that it will bring about an accommodation. The answer is much more likely to be immediate confiscation of my property, or possibly either hostile silence or cool rejection of my version of the facts.

Slept fitfully, lying awake or half awake much of the night. Sunny morning. It promises to turn very hot today.

Yesterday on the telephone young Schickele mentioned an item in the *Frankfurter Zeitung* on the "reorganization" of the Academy. All members with any European sympathies have resigned, even Pannwitz, also Mombert. To be sure, Ricarda Huch and Hauptmann are staying in—he, this man of the Republic, friend of Ebert and Rathenau, who owes his stature and his greatness to Jews. On the "Day of Labor" he allowed the swastika flag to be flown from his house. Perhaps he thinks himself Goethean in his firm opposition to everything common. He likes to converse with intelligent people, with tyrants. (He has also visited Mussolini.) I hate this idol whom I helped to magnify, and who magnificently rejects a martyrdom that I also feel I was not born for, but which I am driven to embrace for the sake of intellectual integrity.—

157

We came to the conclusion that we would have been too hasty in committing ourselves to the little house for the summer, where the climate might prove difficult to tolerate, and where too many responsibilities would have been involved. The plan now is to move to Bandol tomorrow. I strongly hope that while I am there I shall hear some news from Frank about the suitcase, and thus attain sufficient peace of mind and sense of security to be able to work. For midsummer we will be free to go either to the seaside or to Lenzerheide. Actually the thought once more goes through my mind of returning to Munich in the fall, now that I have written to Epp, even though on sober reflection I know that to be impossible.—

Spent the larger part of the morning reading Tolstoy, lying on a reclining chair out on a little balcony above the garden. Then went down to the small beach and returned with Katia and the children to have our lunch. Afterward talked about a house near Zurich, for at the moment that city is uppermost in our thoughts.

Rested a little. Later we took the younger children for a walk away from the sea and up into the mountains, where many of the terraces are thickly planted with daisies. Could not determine what their purpose might be.

The walk tired me greatly. Back home, insignificant mail forwarded by Schickele, whose son has volunteered to drive us to Bandol tomorrow.

Golo wrote from Berlin, where he went in haste as he was under threat of being taken into protective custody. He is bitter about the theft of his little car.

Decided to have my favorite pieces of furniture, the desk, the armchair with footstool, and also the phonograph removed from the house, and later shipped to wherever we are. Bernheimer to collect the furniture, Koch the phonograph.

Wednesday, May 10; Les Roches fleuries

After dinner, which disgusted me, no doubt owing to my overtired state, we had a visit from E. A. Rheinhardt, who is living in Lavandou. Sat and chatted in Katia's room. I felt very sluggish.

The night was troubled. Good reliable Phanodorm was no match for the howling storm and the terrible itching of my mosquito-bitten hands. My mind kept dwelling on the decision, the letter to Epp aside, to have Bertaux bring out the 90,000 marks that are available, but naturally not before Golo and Moni are out of the country. As for the furniture and the phonograph, instructions must be sent off later today.

The wind has abated, the sky is somewhat overcast with foehn. We are once again on the point of moving. The trunk, hardly touched, must be put in order and the overnight bag packed again. We are taking the 10:30 bus to Toulon, where we change for Bandol.

It is now established that the chauffeur Hans must have passed on information about the suitcase; according to the shipping firm there is no other way that the Brown House and the political police could have known that it was sent. Wretched lout.

They parked Golo's little car, stripped, on Poschingerstrasse, right before his eyes, obviously as a provocation. What a government! Does loyalty to it make any sense?

I breakfasted this morning with the young people in Les Roches. At 10:30 the bus came, our many bags were taken on board, and off we went to Toulon. The old vehicle had a tendency to stall. In Toulon the luggage was transferred, with people in the street good-naturedly lending a hand. A townswoman helped me carry my trunk. The Toulon-Bandol bus overcrowded. Arrived here. A good deal of mail, including a customs notice which apparently refers to the suitcase.

A letter of greeting from Paul Valéry, who was attending one of the meetings of the Comité in Madrid, and wrote during a speech by Pinder, who quoted me.—Letter from Knopf, and several messages of support for me.

We lunched in the large, tasteless dining room. Our rooms have loggias, and I am writing out on mine. But I find everything in this cultural milieu shabby, rickety, uncomfortable, and beneath my accustomed standard.

Unpacking and putting away our things was very strenuous, since along with the usual luggage we also had the summer clothes and supplies of underwear that Frau Kurz had sent. I then gave my strained nerves a rest, had tea and arranged letters while Katia went to the post office to send off the carbon of the letter to Epp with an accompanying note.

Though the hotel's garden separates it from the street there is nonetheless considerable noise from passing cars.

Tuesday, May 16; Bandol

Heinrich arrived to have dinner with us. First sat together at one of the outdoor cafés along the harbor. Discussed the situation.

Wednesday, May 17

Yesterday and today worked on the novel. Wrote on a bit. Arrival of Ilse Dernburg. Tea in the hotel garden with her and the three Schickeles as well as Heinrich and Katia's parents. The usual conversations.

Notice from Toulon that the suitcase has arrived.

Ilse D. brought advice from Berlin not to attempt any illegal steps with regard to the money, but to take the newly imposed tax and embargo into account and apply for expatriation. I agree with this.

The international situation very tense. It is to be hoped that the German *canaille* will be defeated on the armament issue.

Short drive with the Schickeles to look at the Goëland Hotel. Too cramped, too small, even though tasteful, and the cooking aromas are not good.

Dr. Heins disapproves of the letter to Epp, since he has steadfastly maintained the fiction of our return. He intends to make overtures to the general. Bermann Fischer for his part will also do something in Berlin in connection with our passports.

The article Erika brought from the *Völkischer Beobachter* about the new Academy is thoroughly stupid. On the other hand, they seem to be taking a more careful attitude toward me in Berlin: Rust apparently deplored my resignation from the Academy, and the *Berliner Tageblatt*, a Leftist newspaper, paid homage to me.

Must record that this period has been a bad one for sleep. Last night I again had great trouble falling asleep, partly because of a coughing fit that recurs in connection with my present cold—which is not serious, however, and is running its course.

Took Luminal. Began reading George Bernard Shaw's *The Adventures of the Black Girl in Her Search for God*. Bermann Fischer recently sent me the proofs.

Slept late in the morning and had to hurry down to breakfast, since Katia was driving to Marseille with her cousin to go to the consulate and attend to various other duties.

Discussion yesterday evening with Heinrich about the possibly justified social core of the German "movement": an end to parliamentary parties, the proletarianized petty-bourgeois masses uniting to bring about socialism. The partly stolen, partly ragged and outdated garment in which this is being clothed. The incredible contradictions. Wiegand wrote from Levici about their burning the works of Sigmund Freud in Dresden as a demonstration against the "soul-destroying over-valuation of drives, for idealism." What ignorance and mendacity in the phrase "soul-destroying over-valuation"! When it is precisely such drives that the anti-intellectual movement holds sacred. They might well want to protect drives from dissipation, that makes some sense, but it is idiotic to be protesting against their over-valuation at the same time. A disgruntled but well-meaning petty bourgeoisie is forever at odds with the barbaric, dynamic, and irrational aspects of the movement.

A leisurely start, writing letters to Hesse and Reisiger. Took a short walk before eating, in the course of which I found a lovely woodland path, and was glad for the appetite with which I polished off a lunch consisting of hors d'oeuvres, noodles, roast veal, cheese, and strawberries.

The sky clouded over and some raindrops fell. But now the weather has settled down again.—

Coffee at the Réserve with Katia, Heinrich, the children, and Feuchtwanger. Young Schickele came to invite us for a drive with his father. We were taken through Sanary and La Seyne to the fortified harbor of Toulon and had a look at its installations. The countryside rich with picturesque views suggestive of modern painting, perhaps largely a matter of the light.

Katia's visit to the German consul in Marseille surprisingly successful; her passport now also covers the children. No difficulty, although they were fully aware who the father was, and even showed respect. It almost seems as though they would be prepared to extend my own passport there.

Diebold in Frankfurt sent a story of his "with deepest respect." The dedication is somehow painful.

The big children phoned from Paris and will perhaps drop by here again before heading for Zurich.

In the *Dépêche*, Toulouse, an article by Heinrich on the rule of the losers in Germany.

We talked about some of the more disgusting aspects of the system, their frank acknowledgment that they are lying, as when they issue denials of their own misdeeds, referring to them as "intended for export," while they go right ahead carrying out their atrocities. Or when objections are raised against the flagrant corruption of some of the trials against "Marxists," their answer is: "We still need these trials."—The contempt shown for one another by the party bosses. The fraud of the infallible

Führer. Hitler's entourage calls him "the cork," because he bobs along on the surface of any stream. Goering a sick bloodhound, who has just had his official residence refurbished to the tune of 98,000 marks ("for the benefit of German craftsmen") and has given orders that all death sentences be carried out, sentences long postponed inasmuch as the Republic was considering abolishing the death penalty. All possible penal reforms have been totally crushed by this criminal. Privy Councillor Max Planck's attempt to talk to Hitler, who answered him, "I am not an anti-Semite. It is very regrettable that the Jews have this unfortunate identification with Marxism. . . ." He has a different lie for everyone.

The economic misery and ruin justify the most pessimistic outlook. The forecast is for inflation and bread coupons. The wishful thinking of exiles, to be sure, but it is truly only a natural human desire that these scoundrels, who have brought the country to such a pass, should receive their just and terrible punishment.

Tuesday, June 6; Bandol

My fifty-eighth birthday.

Yesterday in the course of the evening my depression somewhat got the better of me. I left the table and had some dinner sent up to my room. Later, however, I spent some time with Katia and Heinrich in the music room.

During the night repeated coughing fits caused by nerves; the resurfacing of the question of our immediate future was preying on my mind. But was able to fall asleep again.

The sky overcast and disposed to rain. Katia and the children with birthday greetings. The children had been up early to fetch carnations for the breakfast table, pastries, and a torte. Katia had set out a bottle of liqueur and one of eau de cologne for me, as well as a briefcase sent by Ida Herz. The children had breakfast with us while we once more discussed, with no conclusion, the question of staying here or leaving.

Letters of congratulation from Fiedler and from Alfred Neumann. Telegrams from the Franks, the older children and their friends, the Bermann Fischers, and Knopf. Ilse Dernburg brought carnations.

I began a letter to Schwarzschild about his magazine.—Visit from Frau Marchesani, who lunched with us.

In the afternoon we took the bus to La Ciotat, where we had coffee at the casino and were strongly tempted to stay when we saw the lovely houses set in gardens along the shore. Came back to the hotel late. Champagne was ordered, and the children performed the Vivaldi concerto. We ate birthday torte and drank champagne and stayed together longer than usual, with Golo displaying good knowledge of politics as we talked.

Thursday, June 8; Bandol

Letters from Mrs. Lowe-Porter, who sent along the foreword to *Past Masters*, from Bruno Walter, writing from Zurich, from R. G. Binding (offended and stupid), from C. G. Heise (about the *Wagner* business, at some length), and from Bermann Fischer, who urgently advises against Knopf's ideas, since he is trying to arrange things in

Berlin through the Ministry of Education and we must not spoil his chances. As he depicts the situation, Hitler-Goering-Goebbels represent the "moderates." My private conviction is that no good can be expected from this crew, for myself [and] for all of us.

Goering dines daily with his entire "staff" at Pelzer's. The way these fellows *revel* in their positions, having made it to the top by means of lies and criminal acts.

I finished my letter to Schwarzschild, though by now I see no point in sending it. On the one hand, it does not satisfy me as a first public statement, while on the other it would run counter to Bermann Fischer's and Heins's plans.

In the afternoon with Heinrich and Katia to visit the Feuchtwangers, who received us in their new home on the ocean between here and Sanary; very pleasant, practical, and roomy. Herr Pinkus from Berlin.

Later Schickele came for us and took us on a lovely drive by way of Le Beausset, the magnificent road winding through a gorge with Saracen castles on the heights above.

In the evening I read aloud the letter, which led to a prolonged discussion of our situation. Klaus sulky because he has been forbidden to participate in a Paris emigré cabaret for fear it might jeopardize the attempt to get out my books. He overestimates the liberating effect of such a venture, which I myself would not have forbidden.

. . . .

Sunday, June 11; Bandol
. . . .

Agitated days. A new confrontation with our problems brought about by Knopf's desire to hurry the publication of *Joseph*. Correspondence and telephone calls (yesterday evening) with Bermann Fischer in Lugano. Decision to pave the way for fall publication of the first two volumes, appearing everywhere simultaneously, accepting the possibility that the chaotic state of affairs will block the publication of the German edition.

Bermann's efforts at the Berlin Ministry of Education that might lead to an obligation on my part to return. . . . Fear that Bermann wants to involve me in the firm's being "conformed."

Yesterday and today wrote only letters.

Heinrich has moved into his little place, where I visited him this noon.

We met him and Ilse Dernburg at the Réserve, which we have come to appreciate as an attractive café, quiet even on Sundays.

Various things being done at La Tranquille, where we will be moving tomorrow. But no news from the maid Maria, who, it seems almost certain, is being prevented from leaving Munich to join us.

. . . .

Saturday, June 17
. . . .

Last night I dreamt that Rolland had died, and that I was delivering a very earnest eulogy beside his coffin, furious about the German crimes.—

The mistral has abated; clear, blue skies. In the morning I went on arranging the text and composing titles. Spent a short time at the bathing beach at noon.

After lunch a headache and in the afternoon some fever.

Heinrich and Ilse Dernburg to tea.

Discussion with Katia and Golo about selling our German gold bonds deposited in

Switzerland at a sixty-percent loss, as advised by both the Zurich banker and the financier Tennenbaum, before they drop even further. The decision must be made for reasons of safety. We determined that we still have the sum of two hundred thousand Swiss francs remaining to us, and I took a certain [pleasure?] in imagining it as a million French francs. Selling the bonds is "illegal," of course, but the longer I stay out of Germany I am in any case becoming ever more illegal myself—and how illegal are those people who started it all by robbing me? Moreover I am throwing them half of my assets and the house to boot.

Bermann told Golo in Basel that he was prepared to risk the "illegality" of paying me my royalties on the *Joseph*. Under these circumstances I can hardly succumb to seductions from abroad for the time being.—

The National Socialist *Berliner Tageblatt* has published, so I hear, another lamentation over the Academy's losing me. Golo brought us an astonishing article from this very paper about the *Wagner* matter. In the light of this, I cannot think that publishing the little book at this time could constitute a provocation. Must write to Bermann in this regard.

Heinrich stayed for supper, after which my fever disappeared. At nine the Schickeles and the Meier-Graefes came, five people, six including Heinrich, and we had a sociable evening like those back home in Poschingerstrasse, with sandwiches, pastries, tea, and wine, and increasingly animated conversation about things in Germany. I read "The Coat of Many Colours," which they seemed to like, although no one said anything particularly perceptive about it.—Midnight came, and when the guests had left we cleaned up together.

Friday, June 23

Heins has sent his long petition to Epp, for which Paul Stengel is to act as intermediary, putting in his own word for me as well. Where will it lead?

Bermann called from Paris. We discussed the first volume, the edition of 10,000 copies, my payment and how to secure it. I persuaded him to visit.

Letter from Katia's mother, reporting that an American has offered to rent the Poschingerstrasse house for 400 marks a month, which would cover our costs. We might even ask for more.—

Finished preparing the fair copy of the first volume, complete with introduction and subtitles, so I can send it to Fayard. It is, to say the least, an original book that has a character of its own.

Composing subtitles for the second volume.

At noon out among the cliffs.

After tea dictated numerous letters. Then a walk with Katia.

The three youngest children back at suppertime from Marseille, where they had driven with the Schickeles.

Le Temps carries an article about the "disorder in Germany," the dissolution of the Veterans Association, and all other organizations and parties. The anarchy to which the article refers consists principally in the reign of lies, disavowals, contradictions, and stupid, false babble. They deny that there is a dictatorship; instead they use the phrase "Germanic democracy." The government claims to be "rooted in the people," and pretends that it is the fulfillment of the people's will, etc. Dictatorship, they claim, goes against the will of the people. Hence the definition. Along with this, they proclaim the reign of a "noble minority," and everything that is not related to the Storm Troops is forbidden, suppressed, dissolved. The state and the people are made synonymous with the Party, so that any anti-Nazi forces outside the country are branded "enemies of Germany."—In Bavaria a move against the People's party, which is under suspicion of having had a hand in the Austrian resistance to National Socialism. The Austrian government banned the Party after the recent acts of terrorism. Will Dollfuss be able to maintain himself? He has outside support, but what good can such support ever do inside the country? If Austria could fend off Hitler it would be a significant defeat for him. But I doubt that it could happen.—

In the quiet of the evening I thought about my life, its pain and difficulty from early on as well as its favors, thanks to certain lucky aspects of my character. But I believe that ultimately I shall become quite tired of them, and not only of them but also, in contrast to the metaphysical hopes and longings of my youth, of life in general. Enough, enough! When one finally says that, one does not mean one's own "individuation," but rather the whole thing—out of the probably accurate perception that not much ever changes. The meaning of the phrase "weary of life" is not personal, it is all-encompassing.—

The coolness of the weather is astonishing, especially for this part of the world. My catarrh refuses to go away.

Monday, July 3

Vain efforts to get back to creative writing. Lacking the necessary serenity and energy. "What is the point of this nonsense?"

The weather warm and still. Schwarzschild's *Neue Tage-Buch* has come and I read it eagerly, but was somewhat disappointed. The piece by Dollfuss reveals the man's insignificance.

Bad case of nerves, gloomy and heavy spirits.—To tea with the Meier-Graefes, Ilse D., and Heinrich, who read us two sharp and hard-hitting pieces against the German regime, one in German, one in French. Thereupon a discussion of politics; Heinrich's account of a reception in Berlin at Bernhard's shortly before the take-over especially struck me. François-Poncet was the only one there who seemed to have no illusions about what was in store. His parting remark, "Should you be crossing the Pariser Platz one of these days, my house is at your disposal," was what decided Heinrich to leave.—

In the *Frankfurter Zeitung* a strange article by Pfitzner, in which he defends himself against charges in connection with the *Wagner* business and publishes our respective letters of June 25—not to my discredit; but that he uses the term "scum" for those who protested against that vulgar denunciation—that calls for some reply. It would give me the opportunity to make the simpletons who signed the protest see the implications of their action.

Thursday, July 20

For exactly two weeks nothing noted here. Our life goes along on its accustomed way under ever clear skies and in the midday hours blazing sunlight, yet the heat is by no means unbearable. A day of storm, which apparently served the same purpose as a thunderstorm, even lowered the temperature considerably, and the evenings are always fresh, so that when we are home alone I enjoy sitting in a wicker chair on the little veranda outside my study. I sit there for long periods, smoking and watching the stars come out.

Erika has been here for several days to be with us for Katia's fiftieth birthday. We plotted the celebration together.

Social life with the local residents continues: the Schickeles, the Meier-Graefes, Heinrich (and his lady friend), Jordan, Erika's women friends who live in "La Jeanne," which we visited yesterday in Eri's Ford; a charming, cloistered spot some twenty minutes' drive from Sanary. One pleasant memory is the sociable evening in our garden, at which I read "The Great Hoaxing" with apparently profound effect. On such occasions I always have the feeling that I am cheating and deceiving my audience because I am not presenting them with the unsuccessful parts, the doughy, inert passages, but rather a "prize bit," suppressing the rest so that it seems that the whole is at the same level. Such trickery is implicit in any sampling. Moreover, during the reading the selection emerges as much better and more effective than I had taken it to be, and thus it is permissible to conclude that the parts I conceal are also proportionately not as bad as I imagined them to be.—The "Scenes of Nazi Life" that Heinrich then read at my urging are not successful.

I have finished the reply to Pfitzner's article and have read it aloud several times, both here and at the Schickeles'. The comments it elicited varied greatly and confused me. Erika was dissatisfied with the melancholy, conciliatory tone of the piece— although the language is such that it would be almost a miracle if it were to appear in Germany. I am very curious about the outcome. Presumably at the very morning hour that finds me writing this they are cudgeling their brains at 90 Bülowstrasse, Berlin, for I gave up on the increasingly hopeless *Frankfurter Zeitung* and decided to send it to the *Neue Rundschau*. The question is, will they risk taking it? Should they do so, it will be the first message from me to appear inside the country, placing the blame on the Munich blockheads for my expulsion and my not returning, describing the encroachments officialdom has made against my property, and thereby foreshadowing what is in store politically. Nonetheless the piece exhibits so much resignation and mildness that it might lead to an appeal for my return. The contradiction is that I would not consider doing so. Nevertheless it is just this contradiction that intrigues me. I know there are elements in Berlin who regret my staying away; I want to feed this sentiment and make it vocal, perhaps in the form of a public demand for my return and a disavowal of the Munich dunces—at which point I could set forth the additional and actual reasons for my refusal to return.

Many discussions with Erika about my situation and attitude, which I concede seem oblique and unclear; but this is a natural consequence of the uniqueness of my situation. Bermann, the S. Fischer-Verlag, which needs to have me if it wants to remain in Germany, will be bringing out the first volume of *Joseph* in the fall. They are speeding up the printing of the book, and I have devoted a number of mornings to reading the proofs of the first half, deciding in the process to make no cuts, but to leave the dough in the dumpling, come what may. To be sure, Bermann has an understanding with Querido, and, should the book encounter difficulties in Germany, Amsterdam will take it over. Nevertheless Bermann is anxious for it to appear in Germany, for reasons that are bound to arouse bitter disappointment in emigré circles. Bermann wants me to deny my advertised status as a "regular contributor" to the

Amsterdam *Freie Presse* (yesterday's phone call from Berlin). I had no such thing in mind when I gave him my basic, general, and non-binding assent. Any such disclaimer would make for bad feeling and give a distorted picture of my position. I warded off Bermann's irresponsible attempt to catch me unawares. He gave me to understand that possibilities existed for putting my affairs "in order" and that the intermediary needed my "power of attorney," but I emphatically refused to grant any such power. In that context, the denial he asked for what not seem to be so very "essential," and even though my staying out of Germany speaks eloquently enough, this hedging between decisiveness and prudence, of which my essay is doubtless an expression, is no longer possible. The whole exercise becomes pointless because with the beginning of September the grace period for withdrawing funds comes to an end, and we will receive a summons to return or face confiscation of our property if we disobey. My Munich belongings, movable and stationary, the fine house with all its irretrievable contents will be taken away, and I will be deprived of my citizenship *cum infamia*. Other severe shocks are in the offing for me, but I have my public answer ready and have good arguments on which to base it. Precisely in view of these pending developments, my reply to Pfitzner is right and important, because it has been couched in such a way as to put the enemy in the wrong, both in human and national terms. That, at any rate, was the instinct that guided my brief.

In spite of this, Erika's passionate urging that I not present a blurred picture of my views and my position has made an impression on me, and the public rejection that the required denial expresses weighs on my mind. It will be necessary to write a decisive letter to Bermann, one that would clarify my intentions and fend off any constraints on my freedom.

There is no question of returning; it would be impossible, absurd, senseless, and fraught with terrible danger to life and freedom—that much is clear in my mind, even though I have so far tried to delay any clear and *voluntary* break on my own part. The situation depends on our acquiring Swiss citizenship and establishing ourselves in Zurich in the fall. To be sure, we are somewhat intrigued by the possibility of an elegant place in Nice belonging to an American-Belgian couple, admirers of my writings, that has been offered to us for the winter through Kurt Wolff. Tomorrow Katia will drive down with Erika to have a look at it. Spending the winter in Nice under such agreeable conditions would make sense, as it would postpone matters, but it would mean prolonging this transitory and undecided life style, which also affects one's inner state; a more forceful solution would undoubtedly be to settle in Zurich following the attainment of Swiss citizenship; Zurich is more natural, more familiar territory for me, and I could have part of my familiar framework of furniture, books, the phonograph, etc., brought there—sacrificing the rest.

Apart from the article and the proofs, a good deal of correspondence during these two weeks. A long handwritten letter to Bruno Walter in Semmering about his professional plans and my own situation.

My health passable except for spells of nervous prostration and depressive fatigue. Constant anxious awareness of Katia's appearance and the signs of worry and perturbation in her face, which, though not surprising, are heartrending.

Continuing to read *Witiko*. A further reading experience: an excellent essay by Trotsky on National Socialism.

The national holiday from the 14th to the 18th; fireworks in Sanary that I saw from a distance. Drove to Bandol on the 18th to participate in the local merry-making with the Meier-Graefes, the Schickeles, Katia, Erika, and the children. The fireworks gave me great pleasure.

Several messages of sympathy from Germany. Aid solicited for Kiefer in Basel, Fräulein Hamburger, Dr. Beidler. The bookseller in Bandol asked me to autograph French translations.

In the afternoon drove to St. Cyr with the Schickeles to have tea at the Meier-Graefes', where we met Aldous Huxley and his wife. They drove us back home.

Wednesday, July 26

The great heat continues. Further work on the novel. Letters from Mrs. Lowe-Porter and the editors of a new German magazine, *Der Monat*, published in Prague. Fresh proofs, the greater part of which I read this afternoon in the garden. Except for a few disturbing aspects the book pleases me greatly.

Charming Eva Herrmann had lunch with us.

The climate is basically marvelous. Of course the heat and the force of the sun are now at their height, but the afternoons cool off quickly and refreshingly. I sleep under the sheet.

I distinctly feel that my inner state has improved, although I in no way count on a sudden change or improvement of the situation in Germany. But I have grown calmer, have become used to this exile, this separation from my accustomed Munich home, and look toward the future with some confidence, whether its setting be Nice or Zurich. To wish to return to my accustomed former life would make no sense, since it is not there to be reclaimed. To be sure that life was in many ways conducive for me, designed for one who has difficulty adjusting to change, and at first it was a powerful shock to be cut off from it. Yet the person who knows suffering has less reason to cling to accustomed conditions than the "happy" one. For him change is more welcome, and it would be sheer sentimentality to cultivate homesickness for the forfeited Munich existence. It was not entirely happy, for it had its troubles, and wherever trouble is present one's sense of attachment is naturally mitigated.

By now I feel more contempt than horror for events in Germany, steeped in lies and truly miserable as [they] are. The eradication of "socialism," Thyssen's economic dictatorship, the rule by fear of the revolutionary Storm Troops, the perjury of those dear little chaps concerning the mistreatment of prisoners—all this is little more than lamentable. One has given up searching for adequate words with which to describe one's loathing. As for the revolutionary achievements that are supposedly being secured for the next hundred years, one can see with the naked eye from a thousand miles away that they are a fraud, especially the "unity of the nation." How long did this unity last in 1914? And unity was far more genuine, far less coerced back then. Today two-thirds of the nation are living as the Rhinelanders did under the occupation. The occupation is to a large extent in a mutinous state, however, and the drunken lust for power and high living, limited as it is but to a few, is severely curtailed by worries about it.

Am deeply curious to see what will have happened by spring. They are arming madly, and the world knows it. The fact that the world looks on without intervening gives an impression of impotence and fatalism, and above all shows how much the Treaty of Versailles has lost authority and validity. As I see it, war is unlikely, but precisely if it does not come the imposed and "conformed" unity of the nation will soon reveal itself to be a fiction. I have the feeling that I can wait it out, and can also regard the various threats aimed at me from Germany with far more composure than I did a short while ago.

Very fine late-summer days with an almost full moon.—The *Neue Rundschau* came, and I looked through it in the evening. A lead article by C. Schrempf approving the national excesses, describing them as justified by economic history. Binding translates an oration of Pericles honoring those fallen in battle, this without capital letters—*harmonisé*. I am especially interested in the exchange of letters between Liszt and the Comtesse d'Agout, since it ties in with my discussion with Beidler.

A thoughtful way must be found between the often hysterical outrage of the emigré journalists and the supine attitude of German authors ready to cooperate in the "reconstruction." I very much question Schrempf's argument that the ruling principle should be the defense of national security, and that "should Germany achieve the requisite armed parity *in good time* and *in proper measure* (?), we can rest confident that for the remainder of the century a European war would be most unlikely." He adds that any war would be a war of despair, not of hope.—An essay full of half-truths, meant to justify events. Basically a piece of historical servility. The only comfort in the midst of all this groveling is the pamphlet by the theologian Barth. Another theologian, Dibelius, though more subservient, nevertheless sets out to defend Prot-estantism against the state and National Socialism. Only in this sphere and from this quarter does it seem possible to maintain a certain resistance, a modicum of integrity.

The Prague newspapers full of the murder of Lessing and the indignation it has aroused. The German press treated it with acquiescence.

Went to tea at the Golls', who live nearby, then went for a walk with them, in the course of which we met the Schickeles, the Meier-Graefes, and the Simons.

A letter from Hermann Kesten in Sanary.

Up early and went swimming. Privy Councillor Saenger arrived during my working period. As expected he was concerned about the announcement of my association with *Die Sammlung*, which poses a risk to the Jacob volume, and could shake the Fischer publishing house to its foundations. Many hours threshing over the matter both before and after lunch, with interspersed discussion of conditions in Germany and the world's attitude to them. It seems the threat is felt strongly everywhere. But whether they are ready to pull themselves together for the necessary response is questionable, even unlikely, despite Germany's feverish rearming. Many other subjects discussed, the whole miserable business. As far as my own affairs are concerned, I discover that interest in the books is extraordinary, the demand strong; thousands of advance orders have been pouring in. For many people it would be a source of satisfaction and comfort to see someone vilified by the Nazis achieving a new artistic success. I showed myself to be possibly accommodating by dictating a telegram to Bermann; it went off at once and committed me to nothing.

Curious statement by Suhrkamp, the editor of the *Rundschau*, that the thing will end with the partitioning of Germany. So that is what they are thinking—and writing—inside the country.

Telegram from Erika that a fine, suitable house has been found, furnished, at the reasonable rent of 550 francs per month. Dilemma: the insecurity and cultural dependency of Switzerland and the silence I would have to observe as a condition of my stay, which would not even lessen the risk there. Heinrich's warnings, which Saenger largely echoed. We are still waiting for a letter from Erika, for word from Nice, and for the Swiss entry visa.

Thursday, September 7

The habit of a morning swim from the landing (where the water is still and clear) has become dear to me.

Went on with the writing, doing better than yesterday, when I was interrupted.

Phone call from Saenger, who had spent a sleepless night in noisy Toulon.

Reading that detestable Prince Rohan's *Europäische Revue*—a quite unbearable activity, poison to the nerves, outrageous and at the same time depressing, actuated by self-torture and the rather feeble desire to hear the other side and come to understand its "way of thinking." At any rate the *Revue* does not speak of a "revolution," but rather of a "national counterrevolution," which the editor and his contributors hail, however, as a great awakening that should serve as a model to the rest of Europe. That the political picture should change over a life span of sixty years is not surprising. Why should this arouse hatred and abomination in me? "Fascist" authoritarian methods with national overtones are beginning to supersede old classical forms of democracy everywhere. Why make a special German mystique out of that? And why must Germany insist on representing itself as the leader and savior of the world? After the antidemocratic upheaval in Russia and the one in Italy—which is intellectually insignificant—Germany comes up with one of her own, which represents the seizure of power by the impoverished and hate-filled petty-bourgeois masses, the class that constitutes its most debased stratum as far as mentality goes. So this is already the third in the series. What distinguishes it from the others? Is the world supposed to be healed by the filthy mysticism, the muddled philosophy of life with which this movement is decked out? Because current changes in political technique and method of government assume the form of a murderous cult of racism and war whose moral and intellectual level is lower than ever before in history? Vindictiveness and megalomania combine to form a threat to the world beside which prewar imperialism was innocence itself. Moreover, this prince with the soul of a waiter assures us that Germany will organize Europe as peacefully as she achieved power internally "in accordance with the Constitution." But this is the only nation in Europe that does not fear and abhor war; rather it deifies it, has nothing less in mind in all that it has done in the past six months, has prepared for nothing less than war, which perhaps it does not consciously desire, but which its background and nature dispose it to desire. The program—partly conscious, partly unconscious—is clear: first vanquish the "enemy within," that is to say all those elements that resisted war (at the same time a way of taking revenge on its own people for having lost the war), and then—.What comes then no one knows; it cannot be predicted, and they deny that it is what they want. But secretly they hope for it, long for it as their beloved Chaos—a love that entitles them to political dominion over the entire world—that is what they are arming themselves for with all their might.—This cannot be denied; it is the simple truth. But, according to the *Europäische Revue*, whoever entertains such notions is simply no longer capable of "taking the leap from the dead past into the dynamic future."

Katia feverish again and in bed part of the time. Worried.

Annette Kolb to tea, whom we last saw in Basel. After supper Golo drove me to St. Cyr to the Meier-Graefes', where we again met Annette along with the Schickeles. Our host read aloud two stories about artists. Discussed the questions hanging over us, also the matter of the *Sammlung*, which seems to be a blow to the Fischer publishing house and a serious danger for the Jacob book. What is more, Klaus has played a trick on us by including Heinrich's article in the first issue.—I told them about the card I had received today from Munich, signed "a National Socialist" and warning me "never to set foot on German soil again." The handwriting, typical of a petty shopkeeper, is telling. I also read them some passages from Barth's pamphlet. Had an attack of anxiety.

Have begun rereading *Don Quixote*, and intend to finish it this time.—Did not get to bed until 1:30.

Katia in bed with fever and backache.

Did little good work; upset, irritable.

Napped in the afternoon.

Letters from Lewandowski about the Holland tour and from Stybel in Tel Aviv about the Hebrew translation of the Jacob volume. Answered the latter after tea and gave instructions to have the corrected proofs sent there.

In the *Prager Mittag* a highly questionable statement by Joseph Roth aimed at publishers who have remained in Germany. In part tasteless, in part denunciatory. The emigré alcoholic contingent.

Evening walk with Medi.

In the evening read a Franconian Nazi newspaper that was sent to me for some mysterious reason, containing a speech by the "Führer" about culture. Astounding. This man, a typical product of the lower middle class, with a limited education and an acquired taste for philosophizing, is truly a curious phenomenon. No doubt at all that for him, in contrast to types like Goering and Röhm, the main concern is not war but "German culture." The ideas he presents, haplessly and in a truly pathetic style, constantly repeating himself and making dreadful solecisms, are those of a hard-working but hopelessly limited grade-school pupil. They might be touching if they were not so frighteningly presumptuous. Never before have the men of power, the men of action in world affairs, set themselves up in this way as the preceptors of their people, even of mankind. Neither Napoleon nor Bismarck did so. Rather they created a certain order, a foundation shaped according to their vision, upon which the higher life of the spirit, the arts and sciences, could thrive or not. They took political measures to promote what aspects of this cultural life seemed useful to them, rigorously suppressing what went against them. But never would they have spoken *ex cathedra* to proclaim a cultural theory for the nation or to outline a cultural program, although they were far better qualified intellectually to do so than this poor lout. To be sure, they as yet had no notion of the "totalitarian state," which provides not only a power base but a base for everything, and even dominates culture—culture above all. This state knows what culture ought to be, and reduces it dictatorially, sweepingly, to a few feverishly self-taught concepts based on terribly spotty reading. The totalitarian state is, among all other things, the state of Plato, in which the philosophers *rule*—at least *one* philosopher, a simple laborer whose head has been set spinning by the times, and who has been brought to power by the calamitous disorder of the day, a man who confounds his hysteria with artistic sensibility, his inner confusion with deep thinking, and without the least doubt or compunction undertakes to impose upon a people with an intellectual tradition as great as Germany's his own thickheaded opinions. National Socialism is a philosophy. . . . When one recalls the modesty and respect with which the trade-union man Ebert approached cultural matters, one has to recognize what a dreadful course democracy has taken since those days.

Sunday, October 1

Slept well and woke up at 8:30 to another lovely autumn day. Church bells ringing.

From morning on we waited for our visitor from Munich, but up to now, at noon, he has not arrived. Bothersome since Katia wanted to go look in on Erika, whose health needs tending.

I finished the long "Arrival" section, which still needs to be subdivided, and I now have to wait for the books to come before I can proceed. The books stored in Basel must also be sent for.—Stopping on page 1056 of the manuscript.—

Katia could no longer be detained from driving down to Zurich to see Erika. I am staying in so as not to miss the lawyer's arrival.

I took a short stroll in front of the house and came upon two motorists, one of whom identified himself as Bumann, Heins's lawyer partner. He had driven here with a friend in place of Heins, who has had his passport revoked, he alleged, to keep him from having any contact with us. An unpleasant and disturbing development. Without asking any more for the moment I sent the man away until 2:30, and am bracing myself for the worst.—

Bumann returned at 3:00, a youngish, typical Munich type, and with Golo also present we had a three-hour conference with him, drinking coffee and smoking. Our view of things is clarified to the extent that we are now sure that the Party police, who were ostensibly only acting for the revenue office and feigning disinterest themselves, stepped into the case again as soon as it appeared to be taking a peaceable and legal direction. Astounding reaction on the part of the Party police official when Heins remarked that the revenue office was only concerned with getting its money: "And what about us? Do you think we don't want anything?" What appears to have happened is that the Party police do not acknowledge the legal claims of the revenue office, and wish to proceed with the confiscation in their own interest. They are blocking payments to the revenue office, forbidding such payments, so that no release of the sequestered properties can take place.—We were surprised to discover that Heins has known about the 60,000 marks spirited out through the French embassy for a long time; he must have heard either from Bermann or that idiotic Feist, who so long delayed sending out the best of the books in his care that it is now too late.— We also learned that the question of my having to forfeit my citizenship only arose when my name appeared on the contributors list of *Die Sammlung*—and in fact the question is still unsettled. But in Munich, where my position is viewed in light of the *Wagner* protest, they plainly expect it to be revoked, and see no reason to reach an arrangement with me when they can presumably take everything I have.

Talked about things in general in Germany, the compensatory nature of the uplifting national holidays, the sense of oppression, suspicion, intellectual barrenness. This young native son of Munich repeatedly declared that if only he had money outside he would clear out, and the sooner the better.

Later on spoke among ourselves over our belated tea about the unlikelihood of coming to any satisfactory arrangement about the property. The need to have Koch quickly ship my furniture that is presently stored in Badenweiler, and the radio-phonograph. Must speak to Tennenbaum.

—The base mendacity of the people currently in control of Germany is astounding. They confiscate our autos by presenting an order signed by a high-up official of the Party police. Later, when we urge them to buy the car that has meanwhile been half driven into the ground, they scratch themselves behind the ear and explain that we are right, confiscating a car is a fairly revolutionary thing to do, and that they might consider buying it. But if you take them at their word and go away, you find them maintaining a few days later that they never said any such thing. The political police had nothing to do with it; the Storm Troopers acted without authorization. No, they never received any letters from your lawyer, and so on. This is how they act in both large matters and small, even in foreign affairs. Such lies, disclaimers, and assertions that they never said any such thing—God have mercy!

—Their barefaced cynicism: when the "victors" take over the Social Democratic newspapers the editors are dismissed without warning or compensation. Their contracts still have half a year to run, and they demand to be paid their salaries as is their legal right. So they are hustled off to a concentration camp, where soon enough all such demands for justice are knocked out of them. "We've softened them up. There won't be any further complaints." (Smirking, self-congratulation.)

—Their idiotic cunning: "Don't think we're so dumb as to believe your bank account contains only 4,000 marks."—Admirable!—They take it for granted that they are rightly regarded as being very stupid, and they are full of suspicion and feelings of inferiority.

—The simple rule of force, which makes a mockery of all legality. A Nazi wants someone's apartment and has an eviction notice sent. While the victim's lawyer is working on the wording of his defense, the Nazi sends Storm Troopers to confiscate the apartment anyway. The situation is only complicated by the fact that the owner of the apartment also occupies a position in the Party. It is always possible that he also requests a detachment of Storm Troopers and that the apartment turns into a battlefield.

It is highly probable that some high-placed Party police official wishes to have my house, and that therefore a settlement with the tax officials is being thwarted.—

—The utter irresponsibility in matters of civil rights, in defiance of the right to one's honor, which in the wording of the law comes even before the right to life itself. The far-fetched corruption trials that have driven so many to their deaths, of which now and again one proves to be so utterly unfounded that it has to be thrown out— a miscarriage of justice that would put an end to any public prosecutor's career in any constitutional state. But Germany's prosecutors no longer run this risk. All responsibility rests with the person defamed. The public only learns of his "corruption," which is proclaimed far and wide; any denials they feel obliged to register are hidden in fine print. The accusers have an easy time of it, for they are free from any responsibility for the honor of their fellow men.—

Before dinner I walked a bit in the direction of Zollikon with Katia. Afterward Bumann and his school friend, another Munich attorney, were back at the house again and we entertained them in the living room. The chance to visit and talk freely they visibly enjoyed, and they stayed until midnight. I talked chiefly with his corpulent thirty-year-old lawyer friend, a clever and humorous Munich type who knows how to make himself agreeable, and who reminded me of H. L. Held, also of Therese Giehse. Much talk about German reality: its absurdity, its baseness, its abysmal taste, its illogic, mendacity, and intellectual poverty in its welter of contradictions—yet for all that its historical importance. To be sure, any thinking person immediately notices the half-educated and reactionary materialism of the racial doctrine. But this notwithstanding, the role of Jewry in Germany has played itself out. In practice, what any cheap street-corner intellectual would call the "liberal humanitarianism of the nineteenth century" is over and done with. That Jews with honorable war records are still allowed to practice at the bar does not alter much. People are reluctant to take legal action in any case, much less with a Jewish lawyer. Ministers of justice make a show of proclaiming the full equality of this category of lawyers, but this is merely a "tactical" gesture, a concession to civilized opinion, a way of satisfying the world at large and giving lip service to ethical standards of earlier days. In the next breath, every pure-blooded German lawyer is prohibited from forming a partnership with a Jewish colleague.

—Spoke of the concordat which the Church has chosen in preference to a barren and dangerous martyrdom, and which, by the way, has caused great pain, disillusionment, and bitterness among the honest clergy and German Catholics. Nevertheless the churches are open, and everyone attending them is expressing opposition to the "totalitarian state," which in its secularity and materialism is truly "Marxist"—regardless of its idiotic hatred of "Marxism."

—The wild farrago and muddle-headedness of the "movement," which imitates anything in sight, no matter how incongruous. The honor guard of Storm Troops posted like statues in front of the Feldherrenhalle is a direct and unabashed imitation of the guard the Russians keep in front of Lenin's tomb. It is the "ideological" arch-enemy they are imitating—as they do in their films—without reflecting, perhaps without even being aware of what they are doing. The similarity in style, the *style of our time*, is far stronger than any rational differences in "ideology."

The seething discontent of the rank and file, who see themselves cheated out of a few really first-class pogroms and of socialism. The rivalry and discord among the "leaders"; Goering, strutting about in his fantasy uniforms, who ostentatiously pays no attention to Hitler when attending a major speech, but instead surveys the audience through his lorgnon. These are things, however, which give little reason to hope.—

Much said about the Leipzig trial, which so far, according to our corpulent friend, is proceeding correctly. It is still in the preliminary stages. The discussion of what exactly took place is yet to come; they are still working on the character profiles of the principals. Our friend considers the presiding judge a decent German type, but credulous, insofar as he believes communism capable of every perfidy. They have not yet ruled out the customary legal procedures, but are relying on the "healthy" instincts of the judges. The position might be taken that the interests of the state have precedence over strict legality. Yet subjectively this position is not recognized; it simply reveals itself in practice.

Our young lawyer himself denies that any pressure has been put on him; he adheres stoutly to the standards of justice and truth, but there are inner pressures, not only outer ones, that prevent him from realizing these standards. The naively committed person, however honorable and intelligent he may be, will find freedom converging with necessity, so that he can retain his good conscience and sense of integrity even when he is responding to obvious necessity.

—They will probably forgo the "public hanging" of Van der Lubbe. In announcing it they were merely whipping up the revolution.—

—Hitler is considered to be soft, prone to compromise, and easily manipulated. The tremendous weight of responsibility sits heavily upon this noble man, this representative of the resentment-ridden lower middle class. Undoubtedly his mind is taken up with domestic politics; foreign policy scarcely interests him, and he is far from desiring actual war, which is however being prepared, meanwhile, with might and main. The situation is undoubtedly very different from what it was nineteen years ago, but Wilhelm was by nature far less disposed toward war than these people are, whose philosophy of "heroism" can easily collapse upon them.—In any case we concluded that the Leipzig trial will deepen the rift between Germany and the other nations.—

—It evidently did both men good to be able to speak their minds. This means that as an emigré one must always take into account the sensitivities of those still inside Germany. The latter are touchily aware that the emigré thinks he knows more than they, while they who (despite all repression) are actually living through it feel that *they* know more, and tend to despise the emigré's situation and his readily distorted, though understandable resentment, finding his role a tragicomic one.—

Commissioned Bumann to look into the possibility of rescuing the phonograph and the books stored at Feist's.

. . . .

Wednesday, October 4

. . . .

Yesterday we had only a light snack for supper, then dressed, and at around ten o'clock drove to the Reiffs', where they were having a post-concert party for Busch. In addition to the violinist and his wife we met the conductor Andreae with his family and a young Bulgarian pianist. A late supper, I sitting opposite Adolf Busch and Katia beside him. A singularly engaging man, strongly opposed to the Hitler nonsense; he has left Germany though he is considered to be *the* German violinist. Very gratifying, a kindred spirit. His scorn for Richard Strauss, whose music, which reflects his character, is superficial bilge. And Pfitzner?—Heaven help us! Sooner Strauss than him.—Spoke about Knappertsbusch's stupidity and the *Wagner* protest. Andreae: "Those people will regret it one day."—After supper we had a conversation with Busch about our situation and the German public, and about the general ruin the Hitler-Goering regime was bringing down on Germany. I spoke of the anomalous character of my position inside and outside the country and how discouraging that was. It may well be that those within Germany who have borne the brunt of the regime crave some display of character on the part of those to whom they turned in the past. But they would feel themselves betrayed anew if one cut oneself off completely from them. That I keep out of the country while at the same time making it possible for my books to appear there may represent a solution to the contradiction.

Katia's talk with Busch and Andreae had important consequences in connection with Bibi's musical training. The conductor wants to hear him play, and may recommend him as a pupil to the concertmaster of his orchestra. He will be enrolled at the conservatory while at the same time taking classes at a free preparatory school that Medi can also attend! The advantages of Zurich, which in fact were what drew us here, are coming to the fore.

The children, who had stayed for the second concert, were allowed to say good night to the distinguished violinist. I was gratified to see that the evening had a good effect on Katia, though she was repelled by her encounter with the Onegin-Penzoldt couple. (Busch: "Horrid people!")—The obsequiousness of our wealthy hosts, concerned only with preserving harmony for the celebrities in their hospice—"objective," "non-political," and embarrassed.

Naturally it was quite late when it ended, almost one o'clock when we drove home (I riding in the back), and two by the time I turned out my light.

Today cloudy and cool. The heat is on once more. Workmen from the telephone company in the house, one of them with a harelip.

I made revisions, went on with the titles, and drew up a table of contents for the eighteen completed chapters of the third volume.

Took the air for only a few minutes.

Erika and Frau Giehse to lunch. *The Peppermill* is a resounding success, the Zurich press unanimous in its praise and the public streaming in every night. That fills my heart with joy.

Erika told us how a young Communist was mistreated at a Storm Troop barracks. First they smashed his jaw with a revolver butt—for a beginning. As long as he could remain on his feet they made him recite verses in "praise" of Hitler. Finally, no longer recognizable, he was dragged off to the hospital. Later his father took away his passport, so that he would not be able to leave the country. If only he would toe the line nothing more would happen to him. But he obtained an excursion permit and was able to get out. He reported that as they did those filthy things to him the fellows were so drunk and stupified that he could hardly summon up any feeling of hatred during the whole episode. For their part, too, it was hardly a question of political hatred. It was merely an exercise in raw brutality, one they were obliged to carry out.

Unfortunate incident at S. Fischer's: the recently published book by H. Hauser contains a dedication, a "Heil!" or some such, to Captain Goering. That is a bit much. Here he is asking us emigrés to be exceptionally cautious; we are to keep absolutely mum lest trouble come to the firm. But this kind of abasement compromises us in the eyes of the world. One of the local booksellers has asked Erika whether it is true that my book will be published by Fischer.

—Read newspapers and rested.

The telephone is working. Spoke to Herzog about the licensed edition and in the evening we phoned the Franks in Lugano.

Wrote to Ida Herz, and took an hour's walk in the dusk before supper.

The freight shipment from Sanary arrived.

Clearer skies, crisp, cool air. Wrote further on the "Ten Years." At noon walked in the woods.

Good letter from Fiedler about Germany, bearing a Swiss postmark as always these days.

Ida Herz sent a telegram reporting the Jacob volume had arrived. I have sent copies to *Le Jour* and to the *New York Times* so that there will be no complications.

I see by the *Neue Freie Presse* that the charge of "intellectual treason" made against Schickele, Döblin, and myself by the Reich Agency for the Promotion of German Literature has been retracted. Idiots.—

Busy afternoon. While I was dictating a letter to Bermann about the truly humiliating matter of *Die Sammlung* and his behavior in connection with the Book Guild, a telegram was delivered from Schwarzschild; he must take a definite stand with regard to *Die Sammlung* and begs for private clarification. Had to dash off a letter to him immediately, one in part intended for publication; it was finished and mailed this evening after supper. In the midst of all this, a phone call from Herzog saying that Germany has withdrawn from the League of Nations and that the Disarmament Conference has collapsed; the evening edition of the *Neue Zürcher Zeitung* was supposed to have carried the story. We could find nothing about it there. I called an editor of the paper who confirmed the story, speaking in great excitement, and explained that they could get it into only part of the edition. Savage speech by Hitler on the radio: New Reichstag elections (?!), plebiscite, a mood of tragic exaltation. Wretched, isolated, demented people, misled by a wild, stupid band of adventurers whom they take for mythical heroes.

The most astonishing thing is that the most recent news from Geneva suggested that America, France, and England were coming round. Did they hope to gain advantages by bringing about a breach before a treaty could be signed? What happened to cause "Germany" to withdraw from negotiations, which she could have continued to use as a screen for her rearmament? The consequences cannot be foreseen. The Allied powers are obliged to put a stop to Germany's war preparations. Will they march in? Carve up the country? A Danube federation? One thing is sure: inside the country any consideration of outside opinion will now be cast aside. For one example, this will cost the defendents in the Leipzig trial their heads. But what a pestilence this farce of a trial is; after excluding foreign jurists from it, they will now probably exclude all foreign observers! So now this country once again wears the face of the enemy of mankind!

Klaus telephoned from Amsterdam, where they have also heard the news from Germany. He is prepared for Querido's counterdeclaration, which I quite understand.

Wrote all sorts of notes far into the night.

Very fresh, fair weather. Poor sleep as a result of yesterday's excitement, and I felt tired and worn out all day. Did some writing nevertheless, and took a walk with Katia at noon.

The Liefmanns from Frankfurt came to lunch, and we sat chatting in the living room until past four. Talked at length about German paranoia and how the times are testing people's character—with largely deplorable results. The moral superiority of the Jews.

Afternoon nap; quite exhausted.

After tea dictated the open letter to the participants of the Paris meetings.

Evening walk.

It seems that the German decision was not only intended to put pressure on the world. According to the special edition of the *Neue Zürcher Zeitung*, they maintain that they left the conference and announced their withdrawal from the League of Nations because what was being proposed was "offensive to the national honor." The Reichstag has been dissolved and new elections are scheduled—a laughable absurdity. To cap it all, they will conduct a plebiscite to determine if the people agree with the government's policy. According to a solemn declaration, that policy represents the highest desire for peace and for the unification of Europe, along with a determination to sooner suffer "hardship and despair" than dishonor. A pacifist declaration of war, the effect of which will be to drive the "heroic nation" to new heights of intoxication, but which will also arouse much hidden doubt and anxiety. After all, hardship and despair are not what was promised. Things seem to be moving along faster than we could have predicted.

Saturday, October 21

Brilliant, lovely fall day. Went on writing on the first five years. Toward noon the Alfred Neumanns came by in their car. We had a small late breakfast with red wine and went for a walk. Conversation in the living room about the usual subjects, the state of affairs in Germany, the so-called "Day of German Art," etc. They left at 3:30, taking along a copy of *The Tales of Jacob*.

After tea dictated letters, with which I am heavily burdened these days. Before supper went for another walk. Afterward wrote to Born about the Kokoschka matter, then read the *Tage-Buch* and the newspapers.

Received a letter from Vicco.

Had to take Phanodorm last night, since the hectic afternoon had robbed me of my ability to sleep. But in general things are much better in this respect. Neumann had the impression that I had come through victorious; and in fact I would willingly say that as far as my personal life goes I accept what has happened. I have already quoted these lines of Platen's in a letter:

> For banishment have many good men braved
> Who in their souls refused to conscience evil,
> While evil held the fatherland enslaved.
>
> Far better to accept such fate and travel
> Than carry on among a folk depraved
> And bear the hatred of its blinded rabble.

The Neumanns report that the nasty visages of the lower middle class that used to be scarcely visible now dominate the street scene as well as the national one, faces much uglier and racially inferior to those of the proletarians. This is the sociological layer that has risen to political power and now sets the cultural tone. The racial doctrine seems particularly ludicrous when espoused by such people, but in his semieducated fervor and vehemence Hitler deliberately represents them. In one of his recent speeches he kept coming back to the term "discrimination." Each time he stumbled over it and came out with "discrimation" instead. In an attempt to sound well-bred he pronounces "st" and "sp" as "s-t" and "s-p", following them with some blurred dark vowel or other that sounds vaguely Slavic.—Goering's mania for uniforms. He appeared in one city in white silk, a summer uniform complete with white general's stripes on the trousers—also in silk.

In the *Neue Zürcher Zeitung* there is a piece by Rychner from Cologne, in which he speaks of the isolation of Germany and her painful preoccupation with herself. For an analysis of this aspect of Germany, always out for different things from what the world needs, see Nietzsche.—

The furniture from Badenweiler is due any time. Also the books from Basel.

· ·

Monday, October 23

· ·

Felt ill all day yesterday. After working feebly for a while, attacked by a nervous weakness that was soon overcome but left me totally spent. At noon took a short walk with Katia. Erika came for lunch, along with young Landshoff from Querido Verlag. At tea, after my nap, we had little Herr Tennenbaum, who raved about *Death in Venice*, and to whom I gave a copy of the *Jacob*. Toward evening I wrote to Fischer and added a postscript to the letter already dictated to Bermann, taking him to task for his poor behavior with regard to the documentary material relating to *Die Sammlung* that he has been handing around abroad out of spite and jealousy. In the evening glanced through Claire Goll's novel *Arsenik* with interest, and with even more appreciation looked at J. Rabener's quite talented attempt at a prose epic, *Condemned to Live*, which has a contemporary, uninhibited quality and a kind of youthful exuberance.

Slept well; that at least is all right.

Misty, rather autumnal day, the sun breaking through around noon.

Host of business letters, since many foreign publishers are interested in the *Jacob*.

Looked several more times into Weigand's book on *The Magic Mountain*, which is an amazingly penetrating piece of work. I am particularly pleased by the connections with *Wilhelm Meister* that he reveals, especially with regard to *irony*. (Schlegel on Goethe.) Here is a genuine case of imitation in the mythical sense, and of discipleship. I can say of myself, more rightfully than Stifter could in truth, that I belong "to Goethe's family."—

Continued working on the five years. Took my walk alone. To tea Herr and Frau Kaula from Munich. The usual conversation. Their sincere envy of us for being outside Germany. When they go back they will have to report that things are going well for us. They admired the house.

After they left we drove with Golo to the Stadelhoferstrasse office of Attorney Rosenbaum, where Dr. Grigoroff, speaking in French, briefed a gathering of journalists and lawyers on the Leipzig trial. His talk did not tell us much that we did not already know, but meeting someone who had actually taken part in the crazy proceedings was interesting.

New reports in the newspapers about the declarations of experts who baldly state that Van der Lubbe could not have started the fire by himself, that it is certain others made the preparations for him. Dimitroff remarked sarcastically that he too had come to that conclusion. . . .

Sent off the two volumes of my novellas to Frau Marchesani in Sanary and a copy of *Jacob* to Dr. Heins in Munich.

Wednesday, November 1

Stormy weather, rain, dark skies.—Wrote a bit further.—More familiar objects from Poschingerstrasse have turned up: Kaulbach's portrait of Katia as a girl, the Venetian lion, the cobra candlestick, the old Joseph pictures, the Chinese ashtray, etc. I am again wearing one of my older winter suits, also part of the shipment, along with coats and furs. It feels very strange, and I am still struck by it. Many books, already unpacked, are piled up in the downstairs hall. They come mostly from my Munich study, and were not removed for safekeeping by Feist, although there are quite a number of them that I treasure. To be sure none of the really valuable ones are among them.—Some of the books are being carried up to my room.—

The Vienna *Arbeiter-Zeitung* has sent the proofs of my letter, which they are publishing *in extenso* along with their somewhat muted response.—Review of the *Jacob* in *Politiken*: "En dunkel og klog Roman."—Good letters from Kiefer in Basel and O. Basler in Burg.—

At noon the Fiat dealer picked up Katia and me to take us to his showroom. We mean to buy our car there, since the first car we owned was a Fiat and I have confidence in that make. We are wavering between a comfortable sedan and a sporty-looking convertible. Asked the dealer for the exact credit terms. Had not imagined that we would be making a purchase like this so soon in the style of our former existence.—

Crazy lies presented to the Leipzig court in the case against Torgler, who looks increasingly smaller and more woebegone. The arrest of the sole witness for the defense, who perjured himself out of fear, cries out to heaven in the face of all the other wildly implausible testimony admitted by this wretched court in order to bring in the verdict demanded by a criminal regime.—

Wrote to R. Kayser.

Fischer has forwarded the review from the *Literarische Welt* with its "obligatory rejection" of the book. Incredible bosh according to Katia and Golo, for I have not read it. The *Völkischer Beobachter* reports that certain Jewish ladies were seduced by Einstein. The same stuff over and over.

Chief Justice Buenger criticized by the *Beobachter* because he let Dimitroff get away with saying that the ring of incriminating evidence had come full circle from the National Socialist deputy to the condemned thief. The judge hastily took his cue and once more expelled the impertinent man from the courtroom.

Did not go out again. Rain and wind.

Phone call from Prof. Rheinstrom, who is staying at Dr. Fleischmann's; the latter has invited us for tomorrow.

Yesterday evening we had a light snack with red wine at 7:30, then the five of us (Katia, the children, young Hässig, and I) drove in the Fiat to the Polytechnic Institute, where I briefly collected myself in a conference room. Then made my entrance into the packed amphitheater, where I was greeted with loud and sustained applause. I read my statement of thanks to Switzerland, which was also warmly received, then remained on my feet for the hour-and-a-quarter reading of the "Coat of Many Colours" and the subsequent episodes with the brothers. It seemed to have an extraordinary effect, and the heavy, unanimous, and prolonged applause did my heart good.

Faesi, Korrodi, the Hanharts, the Hässigs, and others came into the anteroom. We drove to a restaurant, Zum Pfauen—the children having driven home—where we were served food and drink at a long table on the second floor. I had to sit with the young people, and listen to Faesi's stepson hold forth on theoretical physics, especially Planck's Quantum Theory. Later the talk turned to politics, the Versailles Treaty, Nicolson, Clemenceau, Grey, etc. We left at 11:30, taking Faesi home on our way.

Before falling asleep I read some more in *Don Quixote*, and was delighted by the droll, peasant humor of Sancho Panza's reply to the barber: "Nobody has made me pregnant."—

Slept until nine this morning. Letter from W. Born in Vienna thanking me for the letter about Kokoschka and describing its beneficial effect on the artist. In Germany they have placed his paintings in their "Chamber of Horrors" exhibitions. Kokoschka is suffering financial difficulties, and the death of his dealer, P. Cassirer, evidently left him completely helpless. He has repeatedly scrapped the drawings for the *Jacob* and done new ones. He is paralyzed by uncertainty. According to Born he is painting over excellent pictures, totally spoiling them.

Gray and damp. At 11:00 we drove to the Zurich railway station, where we parked the Fiat and took the train to Basel to visit Erika for her birthday. She met us at the Basel station and took us in her Ford to a pleasant restaurant, where the three of us had lunch. From there to the Hotel Drei Könige, which brought back strangely vivid memories, thanks to the position of Erika's room looking out onto the Rhine, of the spring days preceding our departure for France. We had coffee and liqueurs and I smoked. We chatted until 4:30, then Erika walked us back to the station. By 7:00 we were back home on Schiedhaldenstrasse.

In the evening edition of the *Neue Zürcher Zeitung* Korrodi's account of yesterday's reading was cordial, but said nothing special. We were to have had him here as a guest this evening, but he declined because of a cold. We are waiting for Faesi and Frau Guyer.

Yesterday at 5:30 I took the bus into town to attend Prof. Köhler's lecture on King David to which I had been invited. Walked from the Bellevue to the Aula of the University and again nearly arrived late. The lecture not earthshaking, but the material interesting. Large audience. Met Wölfflin afterward, who introduced me to the university's rector, Fleiner, and the lecturer. In the rector's car to his handsome house on the Zürichberg, where we had dinner. In addition to the Köhlers (he is an Old

Testament specialist) and Rector Fleiner (a historian), a man and wife, friends of the Fleiners, were there, also a cousin of the family and the poet H. Burte, a very loquacious and humorous fellow who strongly sympathizes with nazism by the way. Animated conversation, chiefly about politics. Rode home with Wölfflin and had to borrow two francs from him for the rector's chauffeur.—Found Katia still awake.—In the supplement to the *New York Herald Tribune* a review of *Past Masters* with a picture of me. The Wagner essay was dismissed. It seems to have been very badly translated.

Rain today. On instructions from Berne the furniture from Badenweiler, the desk, etc., has been released as household goods; I have only to go to customs with the papers and claim it in person.

In company yesterday I allowed myself to take a somewhat light and optimistic tone regarding future developments in Germany; especially in conversing with Burte, who was convinced, he said, that they would very soon be "fetching me back," in analogy to the decision of military doctors to call in a real doctor when faced with a genuine emergency.

Grotesque reports in yesterday's and today's papers about Van der Lubbe's sudden burst of rhetoric, his protests about the length of the trial and its "symbolism," his remarks about the "stupid fuss," which apparently makes no sense to him. Dimitroff's suspicion, challenged by the lawyer, that Van der Lubbe had been unwittingly used as a tool by the enemies of communism, of course makes more sense. It seems to me, furthermore, that in the final analysis the origin of the fire may itself remain as mysterious and elusive as the intellectual and subjective line dividing National Socialism from communism. As I see it, the unconscious meaning of the trial lies in its exposure of the closeness, the kinship, yes, even the identity of National Socialism and communism. Its "fruit" will be to push to absurdity the hatred between the two camps and their idiotic determination to annihilate each other, when in fact there is no need for such enmity. They are kindred though divergent manifestations of one and the same historical situation, the same political world, and are even less separable than capitalism and Marxism. Symbolic outbreaks like the Reichstag's going up in flames are, we sense, even if we cannot prove it, their joint work.—

It was ten o'clock before I woke up this morning, having taken Phanodorm at half past two. Reisiger came early. We chatted and took a brief stroll out in the rain, which turned into white snow flurries as we walked. After lunch, sat together in my room. Katia drove us into town after 3:00. When we had parted from Reisiger we picked up Tennenbaum's assistant and went with him to the customs warehouse to take care of the furniture matter. There were no difficulties, the permit for duty-free entry having come from Berne—to the astonishment of the official in charge—and all we had to do was sign a few papers. By eight tomorrow morning the things will be delivered to Schiedhaldenstrasse: my desk and desk chair, the reading chair with footstool, the Empire cabinets, the candelabras, and the radio-phonograph. I was handed the key to the desk drawer, which I suppose still contains various small objects, the Egyptian funerary figurine, the ivory paper knife, etc. How curious! How remote these entries are from the first diary notes of this period, written eight months and ten days ago in Arosa.

We were back home by five and had tea. I then spent the time before supper writing a long letter to R. Schickele in reply to his about the *Jacob* and the probable course of events in Germany.

In the evening read newspapers and the *Tage-Buch*.

The strange day has come; the Munich furniture is being delivered. I was up at eight, bathed, greeted Katia, had breakfast, and still had ample time before the celebration began. It is now 9:15 and sleet is falling. The truck is here and men are unloading it and carrying things in. My temporary writing desk has been pushed to one side, the now unnecessary chaise longue has been removed, while my own chairs, the easy chair from Hamburg and the one with the footstool, are being placed in my study. It is like being in a dream to see them again.

I wanted to go into town to withdraw money from the bank, but Katia, whom I would not allow to drive, sent Bibi to take care of it.—

The arranging and clearing away, the unpacking of little useful things and bibelots from the desk drawers, took up almost the entire morning. These are the first lines I have written at my own handsome desk, sitting in the chair that goes with it. After lunch I sat in the Empire armchair to read the newspapers. The collection of little plaques, all the familiar items, have been arranged in their old order on the desk. The day-by-day calendar was thick with pages, for it still read February 11. With mixed emotions I tore out the whole pack of days up until today. In the living room the handsome Empire cabinets that belonged to our family, the candelabras, and the radio-phonograph are already in place. On Monday we will have carpenters and other workmen in to do more. The arrival of the furniture has affected me strongly, so that I am left with a headache and great fatigue. Some pictures came as well: the one by L. von Hofmann, the little Lenbach, and the childhood portrait of Medi.

Tea at Katia's bedside. Afterward dictated letters.

Another change in our lives is impending; Katia's parents are due to arrive here this evening for a stay of some two weeks.

—Constantly outraged by the intellectual shamelessness of the German powers that be. According to *Le Temps*, the *Völkischer Beobachter* countered revelations from *Le Petit Parisien* by accusing that paper of whipping up war fever on behalf of the "armament industry." It was the armament manufacturers who for the sake of their filthy profits wanted to see the soil of Europe drenched with the blood of its young men. Anyone who made such statements in the past was branded as anti-German, called a peace-mongering hyena, a pacifist and traitor, a downright Republican, and is now forced to chant while sitting in a concentration camp, "I was a communist pig." The impudence with which they appropriate suppressed ideas is nothing new, but it never ceases to astound. Evidently they enjoy doing this. No one dares to point out their idiotic lack of principle.—

I went out in the damp, fresh air for another walk, and felt better.

At nine o'clock the old folks arrived, brought in Reiffs' car. The six of us had a late supper, then sat around the table in the living room, which is far more comfortable now that the Munich furniture has been installed.

Later I read a few more passages in Bachofen and found them highly stimulating. Joseph's lunar nature (the most material of heavenly bodies, most spiritual of earthly ones) is interesting. Telluric and spiritual "benediction." The realm of the artist.

Title page from the first edition of The Tales of Jacob, *the first of the novels of the tetralogy* Joseph and His Brothers.

Before the old folks came down I breakfasted with Bibi and worked with great delight at the handsome desk, whose newly polished surface has something noble about it. At noon went out with Katia and Medi. Now that the foehn has vented itself in precipitation the air is brisker. Katia turned back, while Medi and I made the circuit by way of Itschnach.

A proper Sunday dinner for six.

Clipping from the *Nouvelles Littéraires* sent by Peter Pringsheim from Brussels; an excellent review of *Jacob*, which all the best critical minds in France (in contrast to the grudging wretches in Germany) are taking notice of. A good exposition of the many-leveled character of the book and of its "singulière originalité." Their verdict: "un des sommets de la littérature européene moderne." I was very pleased.

In the afternoon read further in the Czech's Wallenstein novel, a decidedly powerful piece of work. Last night I read the part dealing with the battle of Lützen, marveling at the way it was handled; today read one of the closing chapters.

Wrote to Bermann and to Walter Bauer.

The children spent the greater part of the afternoon bringing phonograph records from the crates in the garage to the upstairs living room. After dinner, while the rest of us sat around the table piled high with albums, the two of them busied themselves for hours looking through the vast number of records and putting them in order. They lie scattered in albums and sleeves on chairs and all over the floor. A problem how to stow them away. We really ought to have the cabinet from Munich, otherwise another will have to be made.

In the evening went on reading Durych's novel.

Spent the morning writing an introductory section for the French lecture to be given in Lausanne on the 6th.

Went walking with Reisiger who stayed to lunch, after which the two of us looked over the cuts that had been made in his review of *Jacob* in the *Rundschau*.

In the afternoon worked some more on the introduction to the speech. In the evening we drove to the Reiffs' for dinner. Fritz Busch and his wife.

Quantity of evening mail at home when we got back. Bermann sends the latest sales figures for *Jacob* and reports that the revenue office has lifted its embargo, so that royalties can now be paid. Evidently the house is about to be released too. Bermann enclosed a review of *Jacob* from the *Vossische Zeitung* and a very good one by L. Weltmann from the *Bayrische Israelitische Gemeinde-Zeitung*.

The prize piece of mail, forwarded by Frau Kurz, is a communication from the Berlin Foreign Office instructing me to announce my resignation from the cultural commission of the League of Nations, and to do so, moreover, without expressing either personal regret or gratitude. A demand of almost unbelievable impudence. Rejecting it, as I must, may have interesting consequences. We shall see.

Low temperatures with heavy mist and haze. Went for a long walk after work. Dr. Hellmund to tea. Then into evening dress and with Katia to the Hotel Baur au Lac, where the PEN Club was giving a party in our honor. Sat between Frau Fleiner and Fräulein Meyer, the daughter of Conrad Ferdinand. Faesi gave the welcoming speech; I responded with a tribute to Switzerland and the developing humanism, then read "The Ishmaelites." Then dinner, in the course of which Korrodi gave an address. Sprightly conversation, numerous introductions, among others to Hans Henny Jahnn, who believes there will be a war within six months, and Prof. Griesebach, who instead believes in a holy German war to be fought with pitchforks. Wickihalder reported that the *Berliner Tageblatt* frequently mentions me, has for example published a comprehensive defense of *Joseph* from the theological viewpoint. Jahnn commented on the remarkable freedom of speech in Germany.—Drove home in the dark with the Faesis and their stepson. Reisiger, who was at the party, spoke of an urgent phone call from Bermann Fischer that he missed; he assumes it had something to do with me. Word from Katia's mother that everything has changed on Poschingerstrasse. Heins reports that "another obstacle has arisen." Ominous. Nevertheless calmed and strengthened by the fact that Jahnn and the Swiss agreed that it would be wrong to cut oneself off from Germany and the German public. They are sure that Blunck will act discreetly and obligingly in my case.

Friday, December 15

Woke very late. For a few hours heavy snow has been piling up and the cold continues. Nothing done. Toward noon with Katia to the architect Schneider, with whom we drove out to Zollikon to look at pieces of property, a somewhat pointless enterprise seeing that our prospects are so vague. It was dangerous driving in the snow and I shivered violently. Schneider stayed to lunch with us.

Telephone call from Dr. Brock, who wants to do a lengthy study on *Jacob*.

After tea dictated letters.—

We learned from reading the *Neue Zürcher Zeitung* in the theater yesterday that the prosecutor is demanding the death penalty for Torgler. What will that wretch Buenger and his henchmen do? Presumably it will not come to that, despite the base and bloodthirsty intimidation by that hangman of a "Prime Minister" who had eleven Communist youths beheaded in return for the shooting of a Storm Trooper in a political brawl.

The Italian edition has arrived, *Le Storie di Giacobbe*; a handsome volume. Also a letter in English from New York about the "Descent into Hell."

Various German publications—each time one looks into them one feels horror and disgust. Their historical jabs at me: "Th. Mann was only the top-ranking writer of his time, not the top-ranking poet" (*Der Bücherwurm*). Binding "advances the argument" that "no one incapable of writing verse is a true writer." Someone suggests my name to him—how wearisome, how unimaginative—and, "seemingly driven into a corner, . . . he ventures, after a few moments' reflection, the *at that time daring conclusion*" that I am therefore no true writer. "It was more than a *bon mot* or a brilliant evasion." Can one believe such twaddle possible? I ask myself that, thinking not only of Jean Paul, Dickens, Dostoevsky, Tolstoy, Balzac, Proust, Maupassant, et al.

Woke at 9:30 and did some work. At noon walked with Reisiger to Zollikon; light frost. Katia caught up with us and we drove to the Hotel Baur au Lac to have lunch with the Wassermanns. Wassermann is back from his Dutch tour; he looks quite unwell and has to have three insulin injections a day. His prospects are bleak. He gives the impression of being a finished man.

Coffee in the lobby. Bought cigarettes afterward, and rested after coming home.

Young Keilpflug came to tea, bringing greetings from W. Süskind, who has been assigned to correspondent work in the Third Reich.

Wassermann's story about Max Planck, who had requested a personal interview with Hitler regarding anti-Semitic dismissals of professors, and who was subjected to a three-quarter-hour harangue, after which he returned home completely crushed. He said it was like listening to an old peasant woman gabbling on about mathematics, the man's low-level, ill-educated reliance on obsessive ideas; more hopeless than anything the illustrious scientist and thinker had ever heard in his entire life. Two worlds coming together as the result of the one's rise to power: a man from the world of knowledge, erudition, and disciplined thought is forced to listen to the arrogant, dogmatic expectorations of a revolting dilettante, after which he can only bow and take his leave.

The owner of a chemical firm told Wassermann that "if things come to a head" some sixteen million people would be killed within six hours—roughly the number of casualties from four years of war in six hours.

Wrote some letters and then went out. After supper read newspapers. The morass of the Leipzig trial again concerns and oppresses me. Hard to imagine that Torgler will be convicted, no matter how grave his acquittal would be for Goering. But again I decided that if Torgler were to be convicted it would be a signal for me to come out openly and decisively against the regime.

Accomplished little work, as is usual these days. Walked with Katia. Could not get any rest in the afternoon. Tired through and through. Dr. Bloch and Herzog to tea, then Erika. We expect Reisiger for dinner, and for the occasion will open a bottle of champagne we have been hoarding.

As this year draws to a close the state of my nerves, my disposition, is not too hopeful. It is a state of weariness, spiritual weakness, and ennui, which, if viewed objectively, might well be cause for worry.—

Dinner with Erika and Reisiger. My appetite was good and I drank two glasses of champagne. Afterward the candles on the Christmas tree were lighted once more and we drank punch. Much laughter over an imbecilic letter from my cousin Anne Marie to Katia. After Erika and Reisiger had gone I listened to a Mozart violin concerto with Menuhin as soloist.

It is eleven-thirty. Bells are ringing. I have installed the new calendar pages, always a significant ritual for me, and am pleased to see that this time the Sundays and holidays are printed in red.

Letters came today from Born, from Ida Herz, and from Kiefer. I am going to bed. What a year it has been since last February. But my homesickness for our old life is slight. I am almost more homesick for Sanary, which in retrospect seems like the "happiest" period of the past ten months, and for my little stone terrace where I could sit in my wicker chair in the evening and look at the stars.

1934

Took Phanodorm last night and then slept well.

Spent the morning writing a letter to A. M. Frey and dedications in copies of *Jacob* for Vossler, Croce, Du Bos, Jeremias, et al.

Long walk in the snow with Katia. Young Podbielski from Cernowitz with us for lunch.

To tea Dr. Hanhart and his wife, who stayed late.

At 7:45 with Katia and the older sons to the reopening of *The Peppermill*. The room was packed with many acquaintances. Rich program, some of it excellent, a resounding success with the well-disposed audience. Outstanding numbers: the "Folksongs," Therese Giehse as a Tyrolian woman, "The Nurse," "Stupidity." Erika, though less successful as mistress of ceremonies, was quite moving in the final song about the "Cold." She and the rest of the cast were wildly applauded, and the enterprise seemed assured of continuing success.

It grew quite late. The drive home was pleasant after the stuffy air of the cabaret. Had a snack at home. The children have returned from their skiing trip to Flums.

Our decision to extend our lease on the house for three more months, despite an increase in the rent to 700 francs, has had a calming effect on me. This means we are settled until the end of June and have gained time in which to make further decisions.

Tuesday, January 2

Slept late and wrote only a few lines, utterly inadequate. Where will this lead?

At noon I walked along the road to Zollikon so as to meet the car with Katia, the boys, and Reisiger, who were driving back from town. The car passed by without their seeing me. Since I still had time for a proper walk I took one of the roads leading up into the woods and turned back toward Küsnacht by way of the high roads. On the way, partly because of the strain of the uphill climb and the strange and solitary surroundings, I was overcome by that familiar state of anxiety and panic, a nervous failure that effected my muscles and my heart and left me faint. It passed once I was back on familiar ground. Erika and Reisiger met me in the entry hall, and Reisiger informed me that Jakob Wassermann died yesterday. We were correct in our impression that he was close to the end. Still it is a great shock. His widow sent us a telegram in the afternoon from Alt Aussee. We replied.—Dictated letters after tea.—Klaus and Golo are leaving tomorrow. Moni will be doing so shortly. Reisiger, too, is eager to get home. It will be very lonely here by contrast, only the two of us again with the two youngest children.—No need to note the fact that the death of this good friend and contemporary raises with particular vividness the question of how much longer I myself will live.

Friday, January 5

Spent the morning and part of the afternoon in bed. Very weak and shaky. Ate only sparingly.

Proofs of *Young Joseph* yesterday, for which I need to make the division into chapters.

Am collecting documents relating to the coming of fascism to Europe. Schlumberger on "Threatened Intellectual Freedom." Sorrow and bitterness about the treatment of Wassermann's death in the hysterical German press: "One of the most highly regarded writers of November Germany. He had almost nothing to do with real German literature."—Is that my obituary too? Where is the "literature that runs counter to the heart of even the most well-meaning reader" that Germany, according to Schlumberger, has divested itself of?—

. . . .
Monday, January 29; Neuchâtel, Hotel Terminus
. . . .

(*Afternoon.*) Arrived here at three o'clock. Got up in Küsnacht at eight, bathed, had breakfast with Katia and Reisiger. The mail came while we were at table: newspapers and a few letters, including one from Schickele, whose situation is not a particularly happy one. He is moving to Nice. His wife is suffering from an inflammation of the nerves in her arm. She is nonetheless making the trip to Badenweiler in order to rent out the house.

I then packed, read the newspapers (the Chautemps cabinet has resigned; Herriot is expected to succeed him), and at eleven o'clock we drove with Reisiger to the Zurich train station. We had time to have something hot to drink in the restaurant. The ground was covered with a thick layer of very wet snow.

At about noon the train left. We are halfway decided that Katia will meet me in Berne, Reisiger too perhaps, though it is quite probable that he will go to Seefeld tomorrow. There was someone sitting across from me as far as Olten, but I shrewdly avoided conversation by studying my French lecture for this evening. Once he had gone I devoured my lunch of hard-boiled eggs with oranges to take care of my thirst. Changed to the Paris train in Berne at two o'clock.

Met by young Borel, Attinger, and their friends, who accompanied me to the hotel opposite the train station. The room, with three windows, has a foyer and a large bathroom. The view looks across a terrace of dense trees and the city itself toward the lake. Shortly after I left Zurich the weather cleared somewhat.

I unpacked a bit and lay on the bed, for I was nervous and strained. Now, at five o'clock, I have drunk some tea and am writing this while wearing the light gray silk dressing gown that I often used to wear when working in the mornings in Sanary.—

After I left, Katia took the files to Dr. Bumann at his hotel, charging him to convey our thanks and best wishes to Heins. Katia was reading some of them to me yesterday evening while lying in bed. I am preoccupied by them; they reflect a kind of ministerial conference between Esser, Frick, and Goebbels in Berlin, one in which my expatriation was rejected as being totally insupportable in terms of foreign opinion. The hateful demands for it on the part of certain Munich officials, who refuse to negotiate with any representative "of the likes of a Thomas Mann." At the same time I dread the possibility that the plan to forfeit my citizenship may become public and "unleash an unprecedented press campaign." Chief Inspector Meisinger of the Party police, having been won over by a skillful, warm letter from Heins, assures us that everything will be released five minutes after the application is denied in Berlin. But there seems to be a reluctance even to let this denial take place.—

—(*11:00* P.M.) I dressed, and was picked up by the young people. At my suggestion we went on foot, speaking French and German, to a restaurant in the inner city, where a German professor from the university hosted a dinner for the group. At half past eight we drove to the lecture building, so late that the lecture began almost immediately. A large, well-built [hall] with splendid acoustics, completely filled with an extraordinarily appreciative audience that greeted me with enthusiasm, listened with rapt attention, and applauded me at the end for a very long time. The organizers appeared to be delighted. We then drove to the Students' Club, where there was a reception complete with Neuchâtel wine and sandwiches. I conversed next to the fireplace with the German professor, some young ladies, and various students. At 10:30 I begged off, saying that I had a heavy schedule, a veritable Calvary ahead of me. Someone drove me to my hotel in his car. This initial appearance was successful and well received. I was given the first honorarium, 260 francs. Am to spend tomorrow here in Neuchâtel. Invited to Rector Niedermann's for breakfast.

Thursday, February 8; Olten, Hotel Aarhof

Was overtired and disturbed by noise in the room next to mine last night. Again took Phanodorm and had a good sleep.

Rang after 8:30 for breakfast and had it in my room, still in my dressing gown. Eating relieved mild pains caused by gas. The heating is scandalous; only the very top of the radiator warms up. I will be happy to be away from here.

Am glad to note the date. The eighth already; tomorrow the tour will be completed, the time got through.

I packed again and took a walk through the unnattractive town to buy tobacco. The weather has worsened, it is misty, windy, with snow in the air.—

Aarau, Hotel Aarauerhof, the same day. I checked out, went to the station before noon, where the kind Dr. Burckhardt turned up to say goodbye. Cold, quite chilled. Made the short trip here in an empty second-class compartment. The hotel bellman brought my bags from the station. On arrival, Dr. Günther, the chairman, was on hand to greet me. I was given a pleasant room with a telephone; several cuts above Olten, and cheering. Unpacked and had a good midday meal in the restaurant, including coffee. Afterward, while I smoked my cigar, I phoned the chairman in Baden, and, once we had arranged that I would arrive there tomorrow evening and leave for Zurich directly after the reading, I called Katia so that she could meet me at the station with the car.

She was upset about the developments in Paris, which I had read about in the Olten paper, sent me at the hotel by the editor-in-chief because it contained an article about me. Apparently the political landslide is continuing in France, set in motion by corruption scandals. In France there is also general disgust with the feeble and fruitless rigamarole of the parliamentary parties, the *république des camarades*. There have been bloody disturbances, which appear to have emanated more from the communist side than the fascist one however. Daladier's cabinet has resigned. Former president Doumergue has taken over the government, apparently with the acquiescence of both Tardieu and Herriot, and it looks as though the Chamber of Deputies will be dissolved and a directorate set up. I do not doubt that the necessary adjustments to the times will be accomplished with relative good sense and without all sorts of mystical filth. But some form of cooperation with Germany is plainly in the offing that could provide a boost for the "Third Reich."

February 11 falls on a Sunday and therefore appears as a red page on my calendar. It is not only our wedding anniversary, but also the anniversary of our unsuspecting departure from Munich on the *Wagner* lecture tour. There followed visits to the Hague and Amsterdam, Brussels and Paris, the sleeping car to Chur and Arosa, the news of the Reichstag fire, the "German Revolution," the barricades set up against our returning home. . . . Then Lenzerheide, Lugano-Montagnola, the trip to the border for the meeting with Heins, then Basel, Le Lavandou, Bandol, and Sanary, the summer there, then Zurich and this house—all of it a single journey without return, a year's cycle that has aged Katia and me by more than twelve months and has marked us more deeply than one would admit to the stupid and brutish forces whose doing all this is. I have written many letters during this time and attempted to write the epilogue to the Wagner essay, but it had to be laid aside along with other efforts to answer those forces that—and this is in no way to their honor—proved beyond me. (I also class the letters to Bertram among these efforts.) I have made what progress I could on the third volume of the *Joseph*, have put together the volume of essays, have supervised the French edition of the *Wagner*, and have seen *The Tales of Jacob* appear in a number of languages since I read the proofs in Sanary. Now established in this house, I am once again reading proofs, and as in the past summer I have to give thought to the queries marked in red on the page proofs of the second volume and make decisions.

These diary notes, resumed in Arosa during days of illness brought on by inner turmoil and the loss of our accustomed structured life, have been a comfort and support up to now, and I will surely continue with them. I love this process by which each passing day is captured, not only its impressions, but also, at least by suggestion, its intellectual direction and content as well, less for the purpose of rereading and remembering than for taking stock, reviewing, maintaining awareness, achieving perspective. . . .

The recovery of certain pieces of furniture, the books, the radio-phonograph, and my wardrobe also marked an epoch in this year of adventures. In this ever-onward journey, though often tremulous, I have in the end stood up like a man.

After the music yesterday evening, of which the closing scene from *Die Götterdämmerung* was the most moving, I had a spell of feverish overexhaustion. I read some *Don Quixote* in bed and then slept, with terrible and sensual dreams, awoke again feeling as if I had a cold and fever, took Phanodorm, then slept with the light on until morning. Am not ill as I had thought.

Reisiger was already at work; I had breakfast with Katia and Bibi, who is now practicing downstairs. While writing this I smoked another of my small cigars.

A stupid "address" by H. Johst preys on my mind these days, one that he gave for the German national chapter of the PEN Club, directing his remarks at Stickelberger, the Swiss. He stoutly defended the official German literature that now "speaks for Germany" against the "Feuchtwangers and various others" whose departure by no means suggests that the country has been stripped of all good talent, even though the "German" writers do not have access to the means of propaganda that these do, and therefore do not enjoy their international acclaim. Having to put up with such brutal and self-pitying distortions and disgusting lies—every utterance of official Germany now bears this tone—has been the greatest strain upon my nerves this year. This National Socialist literary lackey speaks of propaganda for he knows nothing else;

success, influence, world renown are to him only products of propaganda. It is to such clever propaganda that I am supposed to owe my own successes. Letters like the one from the young man in Princeton are only products of it! But these established, well-paid, and pampered mediocrities of the German Academy are aggrieved because the world refuses to love and honor them. Only because they lack skill at propaganda. What pitiful rubbish! But no one answers back, no one denounces such stupid distortions of the situation. Why not? Because in the first place it is impossible, and in the second it is not worth the trouble. Truly not? But it is upon such lying rot that these low beasts have built their reign of terror.—

Fine, bright weather again.

Worked through the page proofs. At noon walked with Katia and Reisiger through the village and down to the lake, lingering there enjoying the sun, whose brilliance already has a southerly quality to it.

After lunch, chatted and read. Had tea in my room and afterward dictated a host of letters. Took an evening walk in the chilly air.

After supper felt rather ill and very tired. Nevertheless drank a cup of the punch in celebration of our wedding anniversary and the other one. On the radio we heard carnival revelry from Berlin, songs jeering at the "German Republic" and at those who "struck the discordant note" in it. Talked with Reisiger about the inner reservations that prevent our coming to literary terms with the German crimes; horror and disgust play a large part in them. Already I can hardly bring myself to speak the name of that boogeyman whom success has elevated into a "historical" figure. And how come to terms with the upright stone tombs in the concentration camp at Oranienburg that Seger describes in his book? (An excerpt from it is in the *Tage-Buch*.) Were it not for the novel and my desire for artistic freedom, for detachment, for time! And finally also my feeling that a man of my years is perhaps not called upon to pass judgment on the world but might well let it go its own way.

During my evening walk I thought again about the Faust novella, and also spoke about it to Reisiger. An abstract symbol of this sort for the character and fate of Europe might perhaps be not only more promising but also more accurate and more suitable than a literal accounting.

Very tired and in need of sleep.

Tuesday, February 13

Yesterday evening read proofs of *Young Joseph* until midnight and frequently laughed out loud.

Before going to sleep read the lion chapter in *Don Quixote* with admiration.

Foehn today, dull light. Stomach not so good.

Prof. de Boor from Berne sent a treatise on Germanic versus Christian religious feeling.

A review of *Past Masters* from the *New York Times* arrived. The Wagner essay is not mentioned. It appears to have been very badly translated.

Continued a bit with the "Huia and Tuia" section. Went walking with Reisiger in the foehn wind. After lunch read *Die Sammlung*.

We had Herr Hennig to tea, who took the new manuscript for the third volume for copying, and Herr Gubler, former editor at both the *Frankfurter Zeitung* and the *Vossische*. Political conversation.

Telephoned to make an appointment with the dentist, Dr. Asper, and another with the German consul general.—

The editor told a shattering story about the abject condition of a man who was released from a concentration camp. Mute, frozen, a film over his eyes, unable to communicate; endlessly, crazily apologizing. People who have been to visit the pacifist Ossietzky claim he is insensible to anything said to him or asked of him, but simply marches in goose step around the room, saluting and shouting "Yes, sir!"—The world knows what is going on, but in its moral obtuseness and helplessness it suppresses any indignation and would cooly refuse to be moved by any appeal.

Press conference at "General" Goering's. Dressed with the greatest elegance, in the English style in shades of gray, with pearl studs, he walked up to the table and, toying with a long pencil, began to speak about the theater. After a time he slipped his hand into his pocket, causing his silk-lined jacket to gape open and reveal a golden dagger. His hair is artificially waved.—

Took care of letters. Sent Ida Herz the Swedish edition of the *Wagner*, along with press clippings from the lecture tour.

Invitation to Zofingen.

Talked with Reisiger about new reports of German horrors. In Vienna the battles continue. The workers putting up a valiant fight. But the Socialist party is already banned, its leaders have been arrested. Dollfuss wants to crush Marxism "in order to leave his hands free to combat National Socialism." The bourgeois press hails the victory of state authority, which is being imposed with all-out military methods. It seems madness that an anti-Nazi government should set about destroying its natural ally, and the attitude of the bourgeoisie is just as idiotic as it was in Germany. But if this saves Austria from being absorbed, even this Catholic form of fascism would represent some hope for Germany.

We listened to Tchaikovsky's Fifth Symphony.

· ·

Wednesday, February 21; St. Gall, Hotel Hecht

· ·

Went out for a bit yesterday evening, bought cigarettes, and ran into Dr. Hartmann from the museum, whom I had arranged to see in the evening. Had dinner in the hotel restaurant and chatted with the waiter. Was picked up around eight by Hartmann, who is a lawyer and who knows V. Heins, is in fact related to him.

Walked to the lecture hall, the auditorium of the Vocational College. The waiting room decorated with Swiss posters. The hall was pleasant, with some three hundred in the audience, including many young people. A friendly welcome, greatly attentive. Read the "Coat of Many Colours" and *A Man and His Dog*. Heavy and prolonged applause at the end.

Letter from the widow of Fechenbach, whom the Nazis murdered. She would have liked a complimentary ticket. Letter received too late.

After the reading walked back to the hotel, where the board of directors was assembled in the restaurant. Conversation over tea, sandwiches, and beer; I spoke animatedly. My precursor here was Sieburg, who spoke on Germany and explained that the Germans require metaphysical validation for leadership; claimed Hitler feels he has been appointed by God.

Went upstairs after 11:00 and slept tolerably well.

Today up at eight. The maid brought coffee instead of tea. I did not put up a fuss, but immediately had to contend with the shakes and overexcitement.—Took the train at about ten.—

Back home in Küsnacht, noon.

In St. Gall I paid my bill, then walked to the station, to which the bellman had brought my valise, and found a quiet seat on the train. Read newspapers: German-Italian relations could not be worse, extreme hostility from both sides. It amuses me as a sample of a "United Fascist Europe."

Katia at the station, the Fiat just washed and very handsome. In my absence a letter arrived from Heins, informing us of "tremendous progress" with the Berlin ministries. A new application has to be submitted, and in a few weeks a decision will be reached. . . .

Drove home. Vermouth and éclairs with Katia. Changed clothes and put things in order.

A variety of mail, including numerous Danish press clippings about *The Tales of Jacob* sent by Pio. In addition a well-meant and somewhat foolish letter from Dr. Herzfeld, Medi's godfather.

Fayard sent the welcome sum of 4,000 francs for *Buddenbrooks*.

Reisiger finally set out for Celerina this morning. He telephoned from there, quite beside himself, about his Mary Stuart novel, and because of the presumptuous demands he made of Katia in this matter she became quite impatient with him.

Ate with a good appetite at lunchtime. Later rested in bed and dozed.

Pinkus from Berlin to tea. Descriptions of the general air of stagnation and the demise of all cultural life. Convinced that the regime is bound to go under from its own shameless dishonesty. May it be so!

Letter from Bermann Fischer: 5,000 advance orders for *Young Joseph*, which is scheduled to appear on March 15. Walser's drawing for the dust jacket supposed to be even better than the one on the first volume.—New assurances that the Heins business is on the verge of a favorable outcome.

Wrote several notes and postcards.

The *Times* sharply critical of Germany for the continued imprisonment of Dimitroff. The *Neue Zürcher Zeitung* also minces no words in an editorial on "enforced conformity," which can only mean toughening up for war.

We listened to Tchaikovsky's Quartet. Chamber works like these contain as much as a full symphony.

New reading begun: something by Leskov that I had not read before and the essays of Fritz Ernst, given me by Tschudi in Glarus.

Sunday, February 25

Very fine, sunny, pre-spring day, the morning's dull foehn light changing to misty freshness and mildness. Last night I again took Phanodorm with my tea and evidently I slept more deeply, for I felt in a good and serene working mood this morning and for the whole day enjoyed a feeling of happiness and hope that probably also owes something to the air and light in this season of renewal.

Wrote further on the new chapter and studied up on the sex of trees. The mystical motif of bisexuality, thought of as divine, reminded me of Platen's mysterious and profound ghazel:

I am as wife to man, as man to wife to you.
I am as body to spirit, as spirit to body to you.
Whom else might you love, when from your lips
My eternal kisses have driven death away?

The spiritual fervor of these lines is enormous, and their mythical roots are far deeper than I had previously realized.—Considered expanding my Platen essay for the book version. That is the most beautiful of his poems, with the exception of the one with the superscription "Tristan." How his spiritualized passion, beyond eroticism, entered into my blood when I was in love!—

Dr. Brauer recently told me, as we were driving back from the university, how a German, a certain Herr von D., overflowing with the new spirit, had remarked to him about me: "Oh, no, he doesn't belong to us! Just look at the unhealthy eroticism of *The Magic Mountain*. We recently had a visit from Hans Pfitzner—now there's another man entirely!" Ah, yes.—

Katia and I walked by way of Johannisburg. It was so warm that I took off my coat.

After dinner read on with pleasure in the Ernst essays, on Hamann, Moritz, Goethe.—Before lying down I came upon some new material for *Joseph*: some things on gardening, the care of palm trees, and the mystical connection between Ishtar and Ischallanu. The crucial conversation between Joseph and Potiphar became clearer to me.

After tea we listened to a radio broadcast of fifteenth-century folk songs sung by Olten schoolchildren.

Frau Kurz is greatly delighted with the house. Apparently she had imagined us living in far more reduced circumstances, befitting exiles, and doubtless that is the picture that generally prevails in Germany.—

Resolved last night to take the past year's diaries with me to Arosa tomorrow so that I can mark the anniversary by rereading them.

Took care of a few letters and then went out for a while before supper.

After supper we listened to music. I then continued reading the Ernst essays.

· ·
February 28; Arosa
· ·

Last night a feverish head [. . .]. Took Phanodorm at one o'clock, then slept better.

Again a snowy day. Sometime after eight I made use of the handsome and comfortable new bath and ate breakfast with relish. I am smoking Ariston-Muratti cigarettes.

Last February. . . . We are now actually entering the month in which we were cut off from our former way of life. My efforts have been concentrated on restoring as much of it as possible. Here, in the externals, it is absolutely as it was; no one could see any difference. In Zurich it is to a great extent recaptured. A peaceful disengagement from Germany, the return of my property, and the transfer of the contents of the Munich house to Zurich would do wonders for my peace of mind. Katia cannot believe these things might happen, and she tries to prepare me to resign myself. But Theodor Wolff's experience runs counter to her pessimistic view. Supporting her is the shamelessness with which they continue to keep the three Bulgarians in prison, even though Dimitroff is not only a Russian citizen but also an honorary colonel in a

Soviet regiment, and the Soviet government has made repeated diplomatic attempts to intercede in his behalf. They do not respond and they take international censure in stride.

At tea yesterday we discussed the Nazi government's medical legislation, which I was inclined to find rather clever. Katia perceived more clearly the contradictory and deceptive nature of it. What is the point of creating a category of second-class doctors? For whom? There ought to be agreement about what is essential to the medical profession. If medical studies have taken five years heretofore, how can two or three years suddenly be considered sufficient? One is left with the conclusion that what they have done is something negative, something not at all welcome: they are eliminating the free proliferation of pseudomedical practice, of "quackery," and co-opting and regulating it by means of a state-approved course of study. Furthermore there is the "ethical" problem, namely that political convictions will play the decisive role, just as they do in determining which high-school graduates are admitted to university; only National Socialists will be allowed to become approved, nonacademic physicians. Seen in the clear light of day, this is again fraud and pretense like all the rest, a cheap semblance of democracy comparable to the charade of the "high-up" leadership's going out onto the streets to take up a collection for the Winter Aid campaign. Fake charity, a brilliant display of lying and clever advertising, in short propaganda for its own sake like everything else these counterfeits and bunglers dream up.

The "gigantic" mass swearing of unconditional obedience to Hitler by the "leaders" (a million "leaders"!) is in no way different. The *Völkischer Beobachter* calls it an event of "world-historic magnitude." How long will these people tolerate being stuffed with such bombastic fake history? The cheap cliché of heroism for mass consumption. The pseudorevolutionary fervor, born of emotional and intellectual inferiority, that can produce *nothing* that is truly progressive or conducive to human happiness. How is it possible that thinking people, people somehow of a better sort, people who write, feel, and see, can take seriously the "ideology," the "world view" of these inferiors and help to cultivate it, their concept of the Nation, of Race, etc.—when all it is, they even half admit it themselves, is at best a technique for manipulating the masses that has become necessary in the governing of people, its methods beyond or beneath the reach of moral and intellectual consideration, for the development of which the "right" individuals had to be found, hysterical charlatans and "hotheads" drawn from the revolutionary rabble. . . .

Wrote a few more picture postcards. Then went walking under skies that had cleared somewhat. The tame squirrels on the path named after them are charming. At my coaxing one came close and scrabbled at my glove. Met Katia, who was returning from the ski slope, and continued to walk with her. One quite uneven path made me a bit nervous.

Very good late breakfast, which I ate with a real appetite. Afterward on the balcony. We consecrated the handsome silver liqueur glasses we bought yesterday. I read newspapers. In a surprise move the three Bulgarians have been flown to Russia, significantly enough on the very anniversary of the Reichstag fire. Goering had to give in. They were welcomed with great fanfare in Moscow.—In a speech in Munich, Hitler announced that there will be an annual plebiscite. If the results suggest dissatisfaction with the government there will be a prompt response—a new propaganda campaign.

I rested outside in the sun. At around 4:30 we went by my byways to the Old India for tea, and afterward did a little shopping.

Back at the hotel dictated a few letters.

The weather seems colder and shows signs of trying to improve. The light on the high peaks as we walked home was lovely. White clouds halfway up the mountains. We walked in their gentle dampness.—

In the same Munich speech, Hitler also said that the first task was to win over the masses, and that now it was necessary to win over every last German to an acknowledgment of the power of this state. So the "elections" did not prove that they had already been won over?—

At dinner we met Ferdinand Lion, who had just arrived, and we chatted with him while we ate. He takes a very reserved stance regarding German developments, explaining that it is not yet time to take them on. Said that the intelligentsia has broken down in the face of the new political imperatives. Claimed that slogans like Alfred Weber's "nonegalitarian democracy" will not succeed in winning over the masses.— Ah, well.

I read some Leskov in the writing lounge and the ladies' salon. We then had a look at the newly redecorated downstairs rooms, a lounge, a game room, and the radio room.

....
Wednesday, March 14; Arosa
....

We have decided to leave the day after tomorrow at noon. The weather continues warmish and overcast. The wet snow has stopped falling.

The unfavorable weather may have contributed a great deal in making this stay that began with such high expectations increasingly disappointing. My mood has become gloomy, my nerves have proven unequal to the influences of the mountain air combined with my efforts to get some work done. The tendency toward panic, fear, and fits of nervous despair has returned. That the predictions from Berlin received during our first enthusiastic days here have failed to work out in fact (Heins recently wrote again in a decidedly dejected, negative tone) and also the brusque and hostile response from Munich have contributed to the lowering of my spirits.

Yesterday evening I had a talk in the salon with Lion, whose intelligent, although somewhat feeble sympathy I appreciate. We discussed my situation and came back to the same words in describing the falseness of it that had come to me at the beginning, a year ago now. The inner rejection of martyrdom, the feeling that it is not appropriate for me continues to be strong. Just now it has been reawakened, and was confirmed and reinforced when Lion quoted a remark made by Gottfried Benn a long time ago: "Do you know Thomas Mann's house in Munich? There is truly something Goethean about it."—The fact that I was driven away from that existence is a serious flaw in the destined pattern of my life, one with which I am attempting—in vain, it appears— to come to terms, and the impossibility of setting it right and reestablishing that existence impresses itself upon me again and again, no matter how I look at it, and it gnaws at my heart.

By the way, I gave Lion the proofs of *Young Joseph* to read. I frankly fear that the volume will not be a success, and I look forward to some encouragement from this astute and to a certain degree reliable critic.—

I awoke before dawn and several times thereafter, so that I did not get enough sleep.—

Our thoughts are much with Erika, whose friend and principal artistic partner, Frau Giehse, is to be operated on tomorrow for a very large tumor—a serious business.

Yesterday evening's newspaper reported that Stickelberger suffered a serious accident in the theater in Basel; at his première he fell into the orchestra and broke several ribs. I must reckon with the possibility that this incident may affect the scheduling of my own Basel evening.

A new novel by Fallada is reviewed in the *Neue Zürcher Zeitung*. Its subject is the fate of a convict, seemingly from a viewpoint of altruistic social concern. The author adds a note, however, in which he says that his portrayal of the administering of punishment no longer corresponds to current conditions in Germany, and he mocks and rejects as grotesque and comical the humanitarianism with which the preceding era attempted to regulate penal conditions. Why this cowardly blow against something that has already been defeated and forgotten? The book comes out in favor of decent treatment for the corrigible criminal after he has served his sentence. The novel itself thus takes a humane stand. But apparently it had to be reconciled with a regime whose expressed attitude is that anyone who has once been in prison cannot hope to live a normal life or be accepted again by society.—For a book to be published in Germany it must contain a foreward disavowing its humane sentiments and trampling them into the ground.

—Ida Herz wrote a card, coded so as to pass the censors, alluding to increasing anti-Semitism—particularly vicious in Nuremberg—and indicating that her planned trip to Switzerland is in jeopardy.

Letter from Reisiger.

A book from Bertram, his *Griecheneiland*, with an autograph dedication and a quote from Carossa, mottoes from Goethe, Hölderlin, and Stefan George; heroic philology, lofty stuff.—

Went down to the village in the morning to have my hair cut, as I had at the beginning of our sojourn here. Then stopped to see Katia at the practice slope and walked on by myself to Maran, where I sat for a while over a vermouth. Strong sun, springlike warmth that makes it seem a return to winter is no longer possible.

C. G. Jung's self-justifying article in the *Neue Zürcher Zeitung* is most unpleasant and disingenuous, even badly written and witless; strikes the wrong pose. He ought to declare his "affiliation" openly.

The "Aryan paragraph" is being applied stringently to the Reichswehr. For the near future compulsory military conscription has in effect been reinstituted (450,000 recruits a year) with the exclusion of "guest races," i.e. Jews and other non-Aryans. Even a half-Jewish grandmother makes a man a member of a "guest race" and shuts him out of the German racial community.—

In the afternoon on the loggia I finished reading the piece on Wagner and Nietzsche, which I find quite callow.

Walked with Katia to the Old India by roundabout ways, again quite a strain for me—after a half an hour here my nerves are always at the breaking point.—Clear sky, a touch of frost, and lovely light on the peaks. Further precipitation is thus predicted.

Packed up the proofs of *Young Joseph* for Melantrich and Athenaeum.

Wrote some lines of thanks to Prof. Frei in Zurich, who sent me an essay on "Men and Animals." "In an era when those who torture human beings feel obliged to pay lip service to humanitarianism by making rigid anti-vivisection laws, your courage in the cause of men and animals is particularly heartening."—

After dinner with Lion in the salon. He has already read as far as the "Coat of Many Colours" in *Young Joseph*. The opening chapters, including the chapter on God, left him cold. The latter he finds brilliant, but overly intellectual and unmotivated.

On the other hand, he is charmed by "The Grove of Adonis," by the echoes of great religious motifs and of the motif of the sacred ritual in the chatter between the two boys. I was worried about this chapter. It now appears I had more reason to worry about the dream of Heaven, which Lion has doubts about. He agrees with my wish to make a single whole out of the first and second volumes.

Later on Katia and I listened to some contemporary Italian music on the radio. Eclectic and powerful. The broadcast was from Hamburg. Over the same station we heard that the chancellor declared on leaving an exhibition that the manufacture of an automobile for the masses is a burning necessity.

. . . .

Tuesday, March 20

. . . .

Continued working on the conversation between Joseph and Potiphar.

Warm misty day. Went walking and thought alternately about *Joseph* and the letter to the Reich Ministry of the Interior.

Medi with us for lunch. Afterward a storm blew up and it began to rain.

Letter from Hermann Hesse; against Wagner. If it were up to him, "France would march across the Rhine now, and cause Germany to lose a war that in a few years it might possibly win."

The *Neue Zürcher Zeitung* carries one of Rychner's pro-Nazi articles, this one about the mood of confidence and hope in Germany, whose isolation is after all the common fate of all countries in the grip of a revolution. In league with the future, etc. It sounds like a paid advertisement, and Rychner may already be an agent of the Propaganda Ministry, as Sieburg admittedly is.

What is one to think of the mental capacity of intellectuals to resist? Ponten wrote Lion: "Hitler is to Stein as Luther was to Hus." In general, Hitler's similarity to Luther is much remarked upon. His kinship with Wagner, which he himself stresses, is much greater however. Gottfried Keller called Wagner "a hairdresser and a charlatan." The *repugnant traits* of Wagner, but only these to be sure, are precisely mirrored in Hitler.

Jacob Burckhardt as prophet: "How many things that cultivated people have held dear will they have to cast overboard as spiritual 'luxuries'! And how strangely different from ourselves the new generation will be! Perhaps we will strike them in much the same way as did the French emigrés, accustomed to living in the very grandest manner, who so puzzled the people among whom they had taken refuge."

True, and well said! I already find myself (or at least a part of me does) in just such a relationship vis-à-vis the new age. The Joseph book is a late work not only in terms of my career, it is in every sense a late work, already outdated, and must seem over-elaborate and oversophisticated, a piece of Alexandrianism, the more so thanks to its self-consciousness. One is prepared for every historical viewpoint. But if only one could be spared the infuriating and wretched Byzantinism with which the others deny and castigate that which is past. For instance the foreword to Fallada's new prison novel: "The *so-called* humane administration of justice, whose comical, grotesque, and deplorable effects are presented in these pages, is no longer in effect." So-called? For the sensibility that influenced penal conditions under the Republic there is no other word than "humane." Yet this sensibility nowadays deserves the epithets "comical, grotesque, and deplorable." Fallada himself calls for "humanity." He advocates employment for ex-convicts, which was what the Republic tried to provide. He calls for "understanding rather than grim, professional treatment." But it is precisely understanding that is *not* to be accorded the criminal any longer, and professional treatment can only be called grim if one is in a hurry to approve the abolition of it and in general to kowtow to the new system.

Could this be simply some sort of German code language that pretends to sneer at the humane viewpoint in order to make a secret plea for it? For even after an anti-humane revolution it is still ultimately the task and the natural calling of the writer to seek what is humane.—

Today is the publication date for *Young Joseph.* I really should have had a chance to see the book and the Walser drawing a bit before the rest of the world.—

Took an evening walk in pleasant spring air freshened by rain. Ate too much at dinner, and therefore did not feel very well during the lovely and interesting concert of old Italian music broadcast from Berne.

Alfred Weber from Heidelberg is here on publishing business and he telephoned. Since he is staying only two days we will not be able to see him, unfortunately, because of our trip tomorrow. It would have been interesting to talk with him, so it is a great pity.

An article by A. Suarès about the Prince murder in the 1934 issue of the Paris *Magasin.* "The crime bears the mark of Moscow and Berlin." But Moscow must surely be ruled out.

The financing behind the week-long strike by cabdrivers in Paris, one that caused untold upset and confusion, is a secret that also seems to bear the same "mark." It is probably from "Germany," which could spare many millions for such a thing while at the same time having Schacht explain in London that it cannot pay its debts. And just now Goering declares to a reporter from *Le Jour* that nothing stands between France and "Germany" but a "psychological misunderstanding" that is not worth going to war over. But there can be no misunderstanding of the criminal mentality of this "hope-filled" Germany with its uniform blood plasma.—

Finished reading Kerényi's *Griechischer Roman* and found it vaguely and provocatively stirring.

Wednesday, March 21

Once again setting out on a journey, and the advantages of traveling privately by car are soothing on the nerves. Packing can be more casual and one does not have to count the minutes.

The morning is pleasant, with a milky fog and no wind; the day may well turn sunny. We breakfasted at around nine, after which I shaved and dressed and readied my small amount of luggage. My literary equipment consists of the Wagner lecture, *Don Quixote,* and a volume of Leskov.—

Basel, Hotel Drei Könige, the same day. We left Küsnacht at 10:30 and soon ran into rain. Passed through Baden and Stein am Rhein, where we made a short stop. By 1:00 we were in Basel, where we took the same room here at the hotel that we had on our way to France. The familiarity of its view of the Rhine is amazing, evidence of the heightened intensity of our experiences back then.

Erika came to greet us, having just left the Women's Hospital, where everything is going well. Had lunch with her in the hotel dining room and coffee afterward in the salon, exchanging stories about the Fischers and others. Later rested. Dr. Schwabe of the PEN Club, Fräulein Waldstetter, and young Stickelberger appeared for tea. Then changed into evening clothes and made my first plunge into the crowd beginning to assemble downstairs. Looked over the auditorium and had the podium and lectern repositioned. In the course of this I managed a brief visit with Erika in the dining room, where she was having supper with her albino pianist. More and more people arrived, a whole procession of automobiles; a larger crowd than for Weingartner, Eri claimed. The small auditorium was packed. Dr. Kleiber of the *National-Zeitung* made the introductory remarks. Then the lecture, which I read with vigor, and which they listened to with great interest and rewarded with prolonged applause.

In the adjacent room places had been set for 127 people. Ate my supper sitting between Ruth Waldstetter and Frau Dr. Schulthess, with the Nietzsche expert Podach across from me. Amazingly awkward toast by the Germanist Prof. Hoffmann. I responded after the second course, criticizing the Germans' withdrawal from PEN. Everyone was talking too loud, and it was difficult to attend to one's own conversation.

Later the company withdrew to the outer salons. Coffee and beer. Erika also returned when her show was over after eleven. It turned out that once again the Wagner lecture was a remarkable success. Of the various comments the one that pleased me most was that of the English specialist at the university; he praised the lecture as such, and remarked that hearing it confirmed something he had always felt about my prose, which he has known since childhood, namely that it is first and foremost shapely, ideal for speaking aloud.

The evening wore on with more or less interesting exchanges with many people. The rest I got in Arosa and my improved, more tranquil inner state stood me in good stead. Erika accompanied us up to our room, and while chatting with her I finished my cigar.

. . . .

Sunday, March 25

. . . .

Dedicated the morning to correspondence. I dictated a host of letters to Katia: to Dr. Heins, Bermann Fischer, Bab, Platzer, Reclam, et al., and then myself wrote to Kerényi, to whom I also sent a signed copy of *Young Joseph*.

At noon walked with Ida Herz, who told us among other things that in Nuremberg 120 girls had been denied confirmation because they were found to be pregnant, their condition dating from the national Party celebration at which Hitler made his speech on culture.

Began reading Otto's book on the Greek gods.

Golo arrived for the Easter holidays.

Hermann Broch to tea.

In the evening went with Katia, Ida Herz, and the children to the cathedral, where the Busch Quartet played Haydn's *Seven Last Words of Christ*. Powerful and delicate harmony. Much naive ornamentation, but also much that is interesting and daring. Busch's cantilenas solemn and noble.

After driving home in the newly washed car, supper with tea.

Ida Herz, as always something of a burden to have around, so enjoys being out of the country and having a spiritual vacation from her frightful Nuremberg, one of the worst places in Germany, that she is frequently on the verge of tears.

Her vivid stories of the hideous cries of a Polish Jew being beaten by Storm Troopers on the street while many people watched from their windows. Of their search of her house, and how the brown-shirted rowdies lined up in a double column outside her front door so that when the housemaid opened it she was confronted with seven revolvers.

Monday, April 9

Rainy, turning beastly by afternoon.

I began to write the planned letter to the ministry in Berlin. Delayed by sartorial problems, so took only a very short walk.

Nervous. Too much music in the house, some of it unnecessary.

Read the newspapers. Massive propaganda. Prison officials and Storm Troopers to be punished for mistreatment of prisoners. This will make the intended favorable impression in England.—The tension between the Catholic church and Berlin is increasing, specifically because of the youth organizations. Also the Protestants, having begun to recognize the danger to their very existence, are now in permanent opposition.

Various letters. Notification from the publisher of another printing of 5,000 copies of *Young Joseph.*

Käthe Rosenberg spoke with evident intense feeling at tea of the book's uniqueness and excellence, it being something that defies the usual critical standards. That is basically my feeling too, so that I find reviews like Diebold's and others' incongruous and ridiculous, whether they praise or blame.

Wrote cards and letters. Dedicated a copy of *Young Joseph* to Käthe R.

After dinner Dr. Katzenstein and his wife. With them and the family in the living room. Tea, sandwiches, and sweets. Read aloud the incredible National Socialist directives for teachers at a German commercial school, smuggled out by one of the staff. The pitiful, raving, half-educated quality of these minds; their pseudomystical twaddle would be merely comical were it not so ghastly and recklessly threatening. What will become of them? Katzenstein believes in an inevitable development toward bolshevism, with retention of the nationalistic, petty-bourgeois, sentimental elements. He rules out a war, predicting an imminent halt in the armament program because of a lack of funds and because Schacht has been so successful with his anti-inflation policies. A rapidly increasing economic depression is inevitable, but the regime will manage to survive by dint of a strong social welfare program for the masses. We discussed the possibility of a Catholic rebellion in the South, and its affiliation with Austria in opposition to Prussian and Saxon bolshevism. However improbable such a development would seem, I have long felt that the break-up of the Reich would be the most fortunate outcome for the Germans themselves and for the world at large. This "Reich" has become an aberration and a sorrow—first for the Germans themselves, but also for Europe—so much I have been thinking and saying for a long time.

Raised the question whether Lutheran Christianity might not find its way back to Catholicism by abandoning differences in dogma. There is said to have been correspondence on this issue between Protestant German theologians and the Vatican. I objected, pointing out the cultural consequences of Protestantism, from which idealistic philosophy, Goethe, Nietzsche—in short the German intellectual tradition derives, which is by no means Catholic. But in any case this entire intellectual sphere is doomed, and the decline of culture might in fact make it easier for the opposing faiths to unite and thereby rescue Christianity.

Great amusement over the "Weiland Granite" letter that I received a year ago. I read it aloud once more as a finale to all the National Socialist balderdash.

Before we left for the concert yesterday Dr. Heins phoned to say how delighted he was with my letter to the ministry. He will have copies made and will use the text himself in various quarters, especially at the Foreign Ministry in Berlin.

Woke late. Katia had already fetched the manuscript of the lecture from the typist. The pages too large and the type too small.

Went over the lecture in the morning, making cuts and underlining passages to be emphasized.

Went down to the village to have my hair cut and returned by various byways.

The letter has been sent to the ministry.

Katia went to the American consulate, which has proved most accommodating in regard to the passport.

Tired all day long from yesterday's overexertion. Heart palpitations. In spite of this I shall carry out my evening's assignment satisfactorily. Moreover I intend to see Dr. Gigon while in Basel and consult him about my health. He comes strongly recommended by Annette Kolb and others.—

I finished my letter to Frank and put on evening clothes. At 7:30 we had a bite to eat and then drove to the theater, where Hans Rascher met me. I seem to have made a conquest there, or so Katia thinks. Since it was raining he escorted me under his umbrella to the lobby, where Hirschfeld was waiting, through whom I was able to reward the young fellow by giving him a complimentary ticket. The house was not very full; one could hardly expect it to be otherwise so late in the season and in view of this being my fourth appearance in Zurich. Virtually only the two-franc and one-franc seats had been sold. In spite of this I was in a good mood and read in a lively fashion for an hour and twenty minutes without tiring. I came out twice for curtain calls.

Smoked a cigarette in the greenroom with Hirschfeld, who seemed greatly moved by what I had read, particularly the communistic ending. I was also, happily, given my honorarium of 400 francs. Little Rascher appeared again and we agreed to go to his house for an impromptu party. We drove there with Frau Rascher, the young folks going on foot. Spent an hour together over tea, beer, sandwiches, and cake. The elder Rascher had news from Rome and Naples. Hans gave me a volume of Mussolini's writings and some lovely postcards with Hodler reproductions. His final preparatory school exams are coming up, but he is somewhat behind in his studying for them because he reads at night, especially my works. His delicately modeled face is disfigured by scars, the result of severe burns he sustained as a child when a cotton wool beard he was wearing caught fire. But his eyes are still beautiful, or rather gentle. He speaks a comical, half-incomprehensible Swiss German.

Today I had my bath at 6:45, drank a cup of tea, and drove into town with Katia to

Dr. Asper's (who had attended my reading) for an hour-and-a-half session during which he worked on the upper left roots under the crowns and the gum. [?] The difficult and tedious procedure was done under anesthesia. Afterward there was some acute pain in the gum and root area, but it soon subsided. At around ten o'clock Katia drove me home, where I had breakfast and spent the morning hours on correspondence (Pinkus, Rabener, Ida Herz, etc.).

The weather is cool, with frequent sunny intervals. At noon I took a walk by myself by way of Johannisburg. Passing the plant nursery I was pleasurably smitten by the sight of a young fellow working there, a brown-haired type with a small cap on his head, very handsome, and bare to the waist. The rapture I felt at the sight of such common, everyday, and natural "beauty," the contours of his chest, the swell of his biceps, made me reflect afterward on the unreal, illusionary, and aesthetic nature of such an inclination, the goal of which, it would appear, is realized in gazing and "admiring." Although erotic, it requires no fulfillment at all, neither intellectually nor physically. This is likely thanks to the influence of the reality principle on the imagination; it allows the rapture, but limits it to just looking.

—Ilse Dernburg left at noon with repeated expressions of obviously heartfelt thanks. After lunch I read newspapers and some of Schwarzschild's book.

Young Perl called up to inform me that a copy of Hofmannsthal's *Turm* with an autograph dedication to me had turned up for sale; it had been bought from Frau Litzmann back in December by the Munich antiquarian book dealer Wolff. Apparently I had lent it to her. Not bad.

Wrote a letter of congratulation to Max Brod for inclusion in the almanac being issued in honor of his fiftieth birthday.

In the evening we took the children to the Schauspielhaus for a performance of *Alpenkönig und Menschenfeind*, a delightful and original popular play whose good-natured elegance permits one to see how inferior and debased modern taste really is.

Tuesday, May 1; Küsnacht

After a good night's sleep we breakfasted and packed, and checked out of the Hotel Drei Könige at around ten. The weather was, and remains, clear and warm. Pleasant, happy drive through soothing landscape. We made a stop in Baden, where we walked about a bit and drank a vermouth on the terrace of a small hotel. The impressions of our trip came back to us in the course of the drive; we had the pleasant sensation of returning home *rebus bene gestis*, for all the stops and events of the enterprise, from the evening we attended *The Peppermill* to my own performance, turned out so well that we had every reason to be gratified. We recalled the alertness and intelligence of the Basel audience and its delight at the humorous passages in my talk. The image of the enchantingly delicate features of young Burckhardt in his white cap is also something for me to cherish in private.

By half past twelve we were here at home, where we found a lot of mail even though letters had reached us in Basel. Bermann Fischer expressed his approval of the forthcoming American trip, which might also have a positive effect on the state of my affairs in Munich. A discreet letter from Fiedler taking a critical and deeply pessimistic view of the economic situation in Germany, where the battle of culture is in full cry by the way.

Cable from Knopf: on the nineteenth of this very month we are to board a ship of the Holland-America Line, a vessel of 15,000 tons that takes nine days to reach

New York. However for the return on June 8 we are to take a ship of the same line with twice the tonnage that makes the crossing in only six or seven days. Questions of cost must surely have played a part in their choice, but after making a call to the Holland-America Line we decided not to make a fuss and to accept the present arrangements. First class is supposed to be excellent even on the smaller ship.—

We found the children well and contented in their accustomed routine. They are thrilled that we were with Busch and Serkin, and delighted by the latter's invitation to them.

Golo related a story told him by a girl he knows: Prof. A. Scharff, the Egyptologist, asked the writer Rudolf Stratz whether I had been "exiled" or was returning. Stratz answered, "The Propaganda Ministry would like him to come back, but we (writers) will manage to prevent it."—What an idiot!—

After lunch I looked through the newspapers, rested, and unpacked. Katia went to the Baur au Lac with the car to fetch the senior Fischers, who arrived today from Rapallo. I went down to the garage to greet them. Old Fischer very deaf. We sat together on the terrace for a while, then the children performed some music. After supper we discussed politics in the living room and made arrangements to see them tomorrow.

The Holland-America Line has sent brochures that bolster our confidence. Our plan is to disembark in Rotterdam on the return trip and visit the children.

. . . .
Wednesday, May 2
. . . .

Another warm day with wonderful spring flowers. I was tired, and spent the morning on correspondence, writing to Budzislawski regarding Ossietzky and to Lion. Readied the brief "Enoch" chapter for the printers; though dropped from the novel, the *Morgen* wishes to publish it.

We set out early for town, since we were due at the Baur au Lac at half past twelve to lunch with the Fischers. Our party also included former secretary of state Meier and his wife, quite agreeable people. We sat in high style on the large veranda, and the food was good. After lunch we lingered in the garden. Old Fischer quite remarkable and touching in his near-senility compounded with deafness, so that he often comes out with totally incomprehensible and irrelevant remarks. He still retains a certain sense of humor, and basically has a sharp awareness of the second-rate quality of those who are taking over from him. Yesterday he said that he does not really believe Suhrkamp is trustworthy when it comes to people. Claimed that Suhrkamp is not a "European," and does not understand anything about the larger human issues. There a generation was speaking that was greater and better than the present one. Fundamentally he has the same mistrust of his own Bermann. He suddenly asked me how I had got on with the latter. "It is good that you laid the groundwork for him," I replied. Today he remarked that all his authors ought to leave Germany. But then of course they would all have to.—This interspersed with much confusion and many lapses of memory.—I said good-bye to him with the feeling that this was possibly or probably the last time I would do so. As I was walking away I waved to him one last time and he nodded back in the friendliest manner; I felt a stab of grief, and I still feel it now.—

His wife said he had been unable to read *Young Joseph* for want of "concentration."

He specifically avoided saying anything to me about the book. However, Hauptmann
is supposed to have read aloud to him repeatedly from *The Tales of Jacob*.

Katia had some errands to attend to on the way home. Once we were back I lay down to rest and had tea with Katia and Bibi.

Another dental appointment.

Long letter from Kerényi about the "hermetic elements" in *Young Joseph*, with which he seems greatly impressed.

Ida Herz sent a "ritual murder" issue of the Nuremberg *Stürmer* that represents the extreme of criminal imbecility. How healthy is a country in which a thing like this is possible? Probably one should more accurately question the *times* that allow it. People would have laughed in disbelief at anyone in the nineteenth century who predicted such a relapse.

Toward dusk walked with Katia down to the village and mailed letters.

Began Hesse's new story in the *Rundschau* yesterday evening, and intend to continue with it.

Kerényi confirms my observations about the affinities between *Don Quixote* and the Greek novel, specifically *The Golden Ass*.

On the radio we listened to a bit of the Stadttheater's production of *Salomé* which we were supposed to have attended, sitting in the Reiffs' box with Strauss. I got a strong sense of the superficiality, the outdatedness, and the ridiculous coldness of this showpiece. It is distinctly prewar in its middle-class aesthetics. Has not Richard Strauss, this naive product of the imperial era, become far more old-fashioned than I? As an artist should he not be far more "impossible" in the Third Reich than I? He is stupid and wretched enough to place his fame at its disposal, and the Reich makes equally stupid and wretched use of it. It was the Jew Hofmannsthal who provided him with librettos. Now he is working with a libretto by the Jewish Stefan Zweig.

Sunday, May 6

Rain seemed to be threatening, but by afternoon the sky cleared and we had almost June-like spring weather; the sunlight over the lake and the densely built-up far shore is clear and delicate, and the pink and white blossoms of the shrubs and fruit trees are once more enjoying its warmth.

Slept badly because the root of the lower left tooth that is to be treated next is infected. Toward morning I painted the gum with iodine.

In the morning I began writing the dinner speech for New York. Went for a walk with Katia through the woods, the ground still damp and thickly carpeted everywhere with some bright green clover-like plant.

After lunch, began reading the manuscript of young Ehrenfeld's novel and was so weary that I almost fell asleep in my chair. Lay down, and with the toothache in abeyance had some decent sleep.

I have been reading Hesse's novella *The Rainmaker* in the *Rundschau* the last few evenings. It is a part of that larger context of themes that he has already touched on a number of times. The story is well made and offers a compassionate picture of primitivism without glorifying it.

Wanting to go on with the speech in the afternoon, I began looking in my old notebooks for some verses by Elizabeth Barrett Browning, and became engrossed in notes I made at the time of my relationship with Paul Ehrenberg in connection with my projected novella *Die Geliebten*. The passion and the melancholy psychologizing of that long-lost time came flooding back, familiar and deeply saddening. Thirty years and more have passed since then. Ah well, I have lived and loved, have in my own fashion "paid" for being human. I have been happy, even back then I was, but twenty years later I was even more so, and I have been permitted to clasp in my arms that which I desired.—I had secretly thought to find the passionate notes of that time in connection with the passion of Mut-em-enet, thinking I could make use of them in describing his hopelessly stricken condition. I also chanced upon the first notations for the project that is to follow the *Joseph*, namely the Faust novella.

The K. H. experience was more mature, more controlled, happier. But the over-powering intensity that is contained in certain utterances among the notes of the P. E. period, this "I love you. My God, I love you!"—an ecstasy such as is suggested in the fragmentary poem "But listen, Music! A shiver of sound wafts rapturous about my ears"—has happened only once in my life, which is doubtless as it should be. The early A. M. and W. T. experiences belonged still to my childhood and do not compare at all with this, and the one with K. H. was a late surprise, with a quality of benign fulfillment about it but already lacking the youthful intensity of feeling, the wild surges of exultation and deep despair of that central emotional experience at twenty-five. This is doubtless the normal course of human affections, and owing to this normality I can feel more strongly that my life conforms to the scheme of things than I do by virtue of marriage and children.—

Toothache. Must again use iodine and Veramon.

We listened to the Basel broadcast of *Oberon*. The "Ocean" aria is lovely.

. . . .
Tuesday, May 22; R.M.S. "Volendam"
. . . .

Its engines never resting, the ship plows onward day and night, moving westward steadily through the moderately choppy sea. We are not heading directly into the setting sun, but somewhat more toward the south. The weather cleared up yesterday afternoon, the sun shone, and sea and sky turned blue. Now, however, the cloudy conditions under which the voyage began are once more with us.

Yesterday at eleven we had to report to our boat stations for a lifeboat drill. The jovial head steward showed us where we were to go with our labels and life-jackets. The boat would then be lowered from the boat deck and he, the jolly one, would get us "home safe."—

Passed the day in the usual fashion, sleeping, going to meals, feeling dazed and oppressed and always half nauseated, which condition does not preclude a sense of hunger however. Short walks on the decks, tiring for the mind—benumbed, drugged. For tea and again after dinner in the red salon, where music was being played. I finished *Don Quixote*, reading the last pages before falling asleep. What a unique monument! Its taste conditioned by its time, for its sentiments are often wholly sub-missive and proper, yet in terms of literary sensibility it transcends its time by virtue of its free and critical spirit. Humor as an essential element of the epic mode. The human complexity of the two main characters, a virtue the author is keenly aware of in comparison to the detested, inferior continuation. Here Don Quixote is an utter fool, Sancho a mere glutton. The author's disdainful and zealous protest against such simplification. The indefinable moral and spiritual dignity of the grotesque hero, and Sancho's sincere admiration and fealty. The epic conceit of developing the adventures of the second part from the *literary* renown of *Don Quixote*, the book about him, and even at the end including a figure out of the false sequel and causing that figure to convince himself of the perfidy of the false Don Quixote. Limitations and orthodoxies: the devout Christian Catholicism, the subservience to the great Philip III and his edicts of expulsion. The close of the book is rather flat, not gripping enough; I mean to do better with Jacob. The death of a character who has become so familiar and important would have been deserving of more sympathetic development. As it stands, his death functions chiefly to save the character from further unauthorized literary exploitation. Also the deathbed conversion from foolishness and books of chivalry is scarcely edifying. A book whose poetic idea is to show the charm and dignity of idealistic folly, despite all kinds of humiliation, belittles itself by declaring its aim to be the reconciliation of the tales of chivalry. Would not the death of a Don Quixote converted from his folly be a death of despair?

Today another bath in the warm, sticky, faintly fetid-smelling seawater. Afterward on deck. Porridge with cream for breakfast. Rather nauseated afterward. Smoking Egyptian cigarettes bought on shipboard. The air has become warmer. The ship pitching less. Bouillon and crackers were served at eleven.

I began reading *Agathon* once again as I did once years ago. I expect it to be stimulating, despite a certain weakness in the narration.

The midday meal was excellent. Went up on deck afterward, then to bed again for a sound nap.

Tea in the salon at 4:30. Then walked on the upper deck and had a stab at a deck game that involves pushing a wooden disk into numbered squares. The weather cleared, blue skies. The sea smoother, although the ship's rocking is by no means over. Still it is easier to walk. A young Dutchman, apparently the only person on board who knows who I am, introduced himself and played shuffleboard with us.

Today our course is more directly toward the setting sun than yesterday. We stood in the forward section of the upper deck for a long time and contemplated our progress westward through the ocean's vastness.

Tuesday, May 29; New York, Hotel Savoy-Plaza

Yesterday evening the lights of Long Island appeared, stretching out in a long line. Early to bed. The ship at anchor. Up at 5:30, the ship moving once more, though slowly. Breakfast and final gratuities. Up on deck. Entry into the harbor. The Statue of Liberty, its face imperturbable, and skyscrapers silhouetted in the mist. Suddenly Alfred Knopf and a flock of reporters, who had come out by launch. Greetings and an interview on deck, to the amazement of Morazzi and Mrs. King, who were visibly impressed as they said good-bye. The passport examination amidst the great hubbub went easily, without delay. Debarkation and customs, the inspector looking through my *Joseph* manuscript since they are on the lookout for seditious writings.

The manager of the hotel. Drove with Knopf in his car through New Jersey and clusters of suburban houses into green countryside. We did not connect with the motorcycle policeman whom the mayor had assigned to escort us and only met up with him at the hotel.

Arrival there, elegant rooms on the twenty-fourth floor reached by a swift elevator. Pressure in one's ears as the car descends. Unpacked a bit. Then Knopf and one of his editors, who speaks some German and who brought the English translation of my speech (difficult), and a fair number of reporters. Strenuous question and answer session.

Lunched at 1:30 with Knopf and his wife in the dining room downstairs, which seemed much like that of a large steamship. One party exclusively ladies. Music. Ice water, hard on the stomach.

Then upstairs again, with reporters until 4:30. Lay down to rest. Tea. Dressed hurriedly. With Knopf in his Ford to dinner at a rooftop French restaurant. The lights of the city. Mencken. The editor of the *Saturday Review*. The famous woman writer to my left, Mrs. [?]. Intimate party. Superior food and wine. Later to the Knopfs' handsome apartment. Overtired, exhausted, nervous. Back home in the publisher's car. Fantastic view from our windows of the cyclopean buildings bathed in a rosy mist, glowing from electric signs.

. . . .

Tuesday, June 12; R.M.S. "Rotterdam"

. . . .

On the 8th, near midnight, after a last interview with the correspondent of the *New York Times* and a last dinner with the Knopfs in one of the elegant restaurants to which they kept taking us, we embarked on this ship, found our luxurious suite— unfortunately an inside one—which was full of flowers and presents, cherries, books, cigars. I marvel gratefully at Knopf's sense of organization, the splendid way he arranged our visit, his generosity and devotion. Think with pleasure of the recording of the Sibelius symphony he gave me on the sixth.

It was utterly impossible to keep diary notes. Since our departure I have written a few letters, notably to Ida Herz and Reisiger, in which I sketched in broad outline the ten days and their impressions: our handsome rooms on the twenty-fourth floor of the Savoy-Plaza, the bouquets and letters, the club receptions (PEN, Authors', Dutch Treat, with the pianist Egon Petri). The weekend at the Knopfs' (Warburgs, Pforzheim-like grounds), the naval parade, the big banquet at the Plaza Hotel on the sixth with the mayor attending, the cake with fifty-nine candles for me to blow out, the speeches, the pleasure, approbation, and sense of festivity radiated by the 250 guests, the radio speech. I recite it all as though enchanted. Silly of me. Well and good; it was an adventure, an accomplishment. What remains is a bitter or vaguely stale taste of regret and embarrassment, as from all of life. I carried it off. I stood up to it as best I could, often shamefully handicapped by the foreign language, and in fact Knopf expressed genuine satisfaction with the way the visit had gone. A number of days, including the one of the testimonial dinner, were tropically hot and humid.

Today is marvelously fresh after a few days of Gulf Stream sultriness. By now used to the motion. Our life at sea was barely interrupted, the westward trip is not yet "forgotten." No trace of seasickness.

Katia and I spent yesterday afternoon in our little salon looking over the New York newspapers and letters. What pleased me most was the portrait and article in *Time*. In the evening we dined with the Dutch-Americans whom we met through young De Reede. Afterward a ball in the social hall with hovering balloons. Not feeling well today, upset stomach. We got up very late, as we have every day on the return trip.

In the course of the day we exchanged a few words with Stokowski, who is a fellow passenger. Polo and shuffleboard with Katia. After dinner a second round of motion pictures, but they bored me. Thirsty, I had a glass of beer with Katia, then went walking on deck while she stayed to watch.

A lady employed by the line to act as chaperone to a group of Yale and Vassar students traveling to Europe asked me to speak with the young people on Thursday in tourist class.

Dictated to Katia a few essential letters to go back to America, to Sinclair Lewis, who sent a telegram on my birthday, and whose wife, Dorothy Thompson, wrote a very nice article about me and *The Tales of Jacob.*

Wednesday, June 20; Küsnacht

Day before yesterday in Rotterdam we had chocolate coupe with Klaus, then some coffee, and took a walk through the picturesque streets, which sometimes reminded me of Lübeck. Rather enervatingly sultry. We then returned to the hotel and checked out, together with Klaus, who was planning to return to Amsterdam and then go to the seaside. We went to the wrong railway station, then, having found the right one, from which our train was to take us to Belgium, Luxembourg, Alsace, Basel, we checked our luggage and the three of us had dinner in the station restaurant. After that we said good-bye to Klaus, who showed himself to be a friendly chap, as always, though his state of mind is not so good at the moment as he is still shaken by the death of his friend W. Hellmert, who killed himself with morphine. A sleeping car through to Basel. We were assigned a compartment, but sat up until we reached Brussels around midnight, where Peter Pringsheim, notified in advance by a telegram from Katia, was waiting for us. Drank a light Perle beer with him at the station restaurant and conversed about general and family matters.

After saying goodbye to him we lay down in our berths and slept so long that we missed breakfast in the dining car yesterday morning. At around eleven we were in Basel. There were difficulties again at the passport control. We did not have a re-entry visa. I was taken to a higher official and only after I had produced my French certificate of recommendation and the League of Nations one was the situation resolved in my favor. The case was dubbed an "exception" and I was required to pay a five-franc fee.

The luggage examination went smoothly. The phonograph records and cigars were allowed through. We had breakfast at a restaurant and traveled the familiar stretch to Zurich. At the station we were met by the children and Erika, who had meanwhile arrived from Strasbourg. Joyful reunion, flowers. She had to give up the scheduled appearances in Strasbourg because of the tense conditions there. Shooting in the streets, riots. Warlike situation in the Saar region. Street fighting in Toulouse between Nationalists and Socialists. Europe in a worrisome state.

I rode back to Schiedhaldenstrasse with Erika, who met with great success in Holland. Welcomed by Frau Kurz and the housemaids. Katia and Medi drove up simultaneously in Doll's car with the luggage. Delighted at the summery appearance of the house. Lunch without Bibi, who had stayed in town. Coffee at the new outdoor table on the terrace.

Looked through the many letters and books that had piled up here. Lay down for a while. Erika brought Therese Giehse to tea, who is living in Küsnacht. Later we played the recording Knopf had given us of the Paris comedian Bétove, and laughed greatly at his German imitation.

Unpacked. Put things away and organized the mail until dinner, which Frau Giehse had with us. Afterward more music and conversation. At 11:00 to bed.—

Up today at 8:45 and had my bath. Katia had already left to take Frau Kurz to the station for her return to Poschingerstrasse. Had breakfast by myself.

No news from Heins. Yesterday evening we discussed the danger of our being trapped in Switzerland in the event of a European explosion, a subject we had already taken up with Klaus in Rotterdam. Switzerland is a mousetrap. The south of France would be much safer, near Spain and the sea. Again considered moving to Nice after Medi has passed her preparatory school finals. Erika gave us a lovely photograph of herself in the white Pierrot costume, which I have put behind glass and take great pleasure in.

All the rest of the proofs of *Leiden und Grösse der Meister* have come. Erika advised against including the piece on Hauptmann. I justified it by pointing out the historical and documentary nature of the anthology.

Yesterday's mugginess relieved by afternoon thanks to rainstorm with thunder. Still raining heavily.

Bibi, with whom we are all very pleased, used our absence to catalogue and arrange all the phonograph records, a task requiring enormous patience.

Intelligent review of *Joseph* by W. Haas in the Jewish *Selbstwehr.*

Copies of the Secker edition of *The Tales of Jacob.*

Frau Giehse with us for dinner. Afterward took care of the proofs, letters, and newspapers. An impudent, not to say courageous speech by Papen. Hindenburg telegraphed approval. Hitler declares himself in agreement with the speech, but nonetheless banned it. Many other signs of disintegration and crisis.

Bruno Walter and his wife to tea. He had much to say about *Joseph.* Talked about Bibi and about conditions in Germany. Very friendly. Arranged to see each other again.

A sign of the mindless nervousness in Germany: Annemarie Schwarzenbach was there and visited Frau Thyssen. The latter was subsequently arrested and subjected to hours of grilling on the assumption that her guest had been sent in by Erika to act as a spy. What petty phobias and stupidity!

· ·
Wednesday, June 27
· ·

Lovely summer day freshened by yesterday's thunderstorms. Went on with my writing. While Katia took her parents for a ride I took my walk through the woods so as to get some exercise at last.

The mail brought a volume of Gide's *Journal,* a letter from Prof. Weigand of Yale, who was greatly moved by *Joseph,* a somewhat belated birthday greeting from Gottfried Kölwel, a book called *Dämmerung*—about Germany—by an unknown author. Knopf sent the books that had been left behind, among them the imposing one-volume edition of *The Magic Mountain,* which has won enormous attention and admiration in America.

Newspaper report of the death of Max Pallenberg in a plane accident. The end of a grotesque, complex genius, a brilliant phenomenon; we shall miss him. Telegraphed the Franks in Sanary.

Dictated letters in the afternoon.

Letters from Schickele and from Dr. Gigon in Basel.

Bermann informs me that he told Hauptmann about the inclusion in the book of my birthday speech in his honor, and that Hauptmann was very glad. This strengthens me in my decision to postpone publication of the volume, and Bermann agrees.

Bermann also speaks of "attacks" on me in German newspapers for my statement in New York, namely my letter to the Jewish Rescue League. He sent along clippings, the sewer-like stench of which made me feel quite "at home" again. Humiliating enough that I must account for my actions, to Bermann at least, for there is no chance for me to reply publicly.

We drove to the Reiffs', who were giving a small dinner party in their garden, which was decorated with paper lanterns. Else Heims evoked memories of the first Reinhardt productions at the Munich Künstler-Theater.

Wednesday, July 4

We are having a series of lovely summer days that dawn fresh and clear even though there has been no precipitation. Since early spring the weather has been unusually fine this year—at least from the standpoint of the nonfarmer.

Yesterday evening Golo arrived, his vacation ahead of him. Katia fetched him from Zurich with the car at eleven and we talked until midnight, sitting in the dining room with the old folks out of the way. We were in total agreement over the loathsomeness of the latest developments in Germany, and in our judgment as to their sinister meaning.

I then read a few pages of *Tristram Shandy* and was up today at my normal hour. Had breakfast outdoors and went on with the new chapter that tells of Joseph's advancement in the service of Potiphar.

In the afternoon the five of us took a walk, moving at a frightfully slow pace. At first the sunlight seemed pleasant, but in time it became oppressive, and the whole business took an hour and a quarter.

The old folks irritate me and try my nerves, especially Katia's mother's silly and pointless delight in contradicting, maintaining an objectivity that is supposed to represent intellectual superiority, but is in fact nothing but ignorance and unconscious self-protection. I have to control myself, and I dread an extension of their stay born of worry over their return. Naturally it is not pleasant for them to have to admit that they are living in a den of thieves, but to brush things off and "not believe" them because they are only in the newspaper, after all, is vexing to someone who suffers from them with his whole heart and soul.—I am also irritated by the eighty-year-old codger's fooling around with the pretty housemaid in a senile and by now quite shameless manner.

The "conspiracy" against the German state that had to be suppressed so bloodily is increasingly revealing itself to have been a criminal swindle on the order of the Reichstag fire and of last year's communist threat. It was well known that there was dissatisfaction among the Storm Troops, but the course of the investigation has produced little that would indicate that the commanding officers really meant to do what is ascribed to them. Nor does their refusal to testify against themselves prove anything, any more than do the shouts of "Heil Hitler" with which several are said to have died. The whole thing is a monstrous bit of "statesmanship" in the style of these demented minds, a preventive bloodbath on the Left and Right, the one providing the alibi for the other and vice versa, all of it presented as a great purge so as to revive morale, which had sunk to a terrible low. Possibly, and apparently, the petty bourgeois masses have once more fallen for the story, the obscene psychology of which was made to order for them, and they once more see Hitler as their savior. But will this renewed faith survive another fourteen months in the face of an ever-worsening economy and political isolation?

It is unclear how many were killed. But the number is surely very large. E. Jung was shot—Bertram was a great admirer of his book *Die Herrschaft des Minderwertigen*, and wanted me to read it. What must he think about the man's murder? General von Bredow, the Catholic Klausener, and ten or twelve other conservative patriots were murdered. *Le Temps* carried a more detailed account of the shooting of General von Schleicher and his wife. The Deutscher Klub, surely nationalistic and reactionary enough, was dissolved, and Gleichen and others have fled the country. I feel no sympathy for these people who paved the way for this misery any more than I do for those thugs Heines and Röhm, and yet their blood will also be on the "head" of this revolting swindler and murderous charlatan one day, a hero of history such as the world has never seen before, beside whom Robespierre seems downright honorable.—

Yesterday I dictated numerous letters and began writing a long one to Schickele. Finished the latter today.

Spent the evening in the company of the old folks in the living room. Listened to Brahms and Tchaikovsky.

. . . .
Monday, July 9
. . . .

Difficult, restless night; I managed to sleep until seven only with the help of Phanodorm and Veramon. Then got up. Radiantly clear, fresh day. After a cup of tea into town to see Asper, in whose waiting room we ran into Hichens. The doctor saw me almost immediately, the tooth was opened and some of the pus was drained. The swelling persists, but I can sense some relief. When I eat there is a danger that food could block the canal.

A variety of mail came while I was having breakfast in the garden. Moni is staying in Florence until August. Prof. Reinhardt in Frankfurt sent his book on Sophocles. Letter from the French translator in connection with the English edition. Frau Kurz sent the treasured book of Perrault fairy tales with Doré illustrations and various picture postcards. Communication from the League of Nations regarding Venice. The Italian government wants to see a summary of what is to be said on the subject of "art and the state," which makes me increasingly doubtful whether I will make the journey.

The press conflict between Germany and Switzerland is intensifying. Germany has banned Swiss newspapers for six months, allegedly because they have been publishing senseless falsehoods. That this regime, after all that has happened, should make a fuss over rumors or minor inaccuracies in dispatches is as idiotic as everything else about it. Hitler, in need of a rest, has been ordered by his doctors to take an ocean voyage. It seems that Treviranus was not among those murdered after all. The regime is laughing about reports that he had been. On the other hand I have information that the national hero Hermann Ehrhardt ("with the swastika on his helmet") was gunned down. For high treason. According to the *Prager Presse* the murder squad was on its way to Papen, and only the intervention of the Reichswehr kept it from carrying out its orders. If this is not true, it is nonetheless so probable that it cannot be laughed

Monika, Golo, Klaus, and Erika behind the Manns' summer house in Bad Tölz.   B1

B2   *Grillwork over the entry of the Bad Tölz house.*

Ernst Bertram, author of Nietzsche *and godfather of Elisabeth.*   B3

2

The first page of the diaries, containing the entry for September 11, 1918.

zu werden drohte. Verzicht auf das Abenteuer der Hoffnung der „Betrachtungen". Gebieten und letzter Hinweis in der Ge- wartung von allem Möglichen. Froh, daß für den Winter keine Reisen bevorstehen und wir überhaupt auf absehbare Zeit das Herzogparkhaus nicht verlassen werden. Ist es erst wieder in Ordnung, so wird es sich widerstandsfähig darin leben und ich bin auf alles gefaßt, habe zu viel Ausge- rag u. Vorhergesehenes, als daß mir eigentlich noch viel zu- geschehen wäre. Froh, für „Herr und Hund" brauchen, dann, ohne für die 100. Auflage von Buddenbrooks ein Vor- wort schreiben zu müssen, zur Beschäftigung mit dem Zau- berberg übergehen.

Fürchterlich meine bis zur Erschöpfung gehende Ab- spannung gestern Abend mit den Kindern: das „Frühstück" auf Urlaub, Rückkehr auf Spaziergängen, ich allein mit dem Gepäck-Wagen, das nass und bloß war, u. dem ich die frisch-kalten Stücke abnahm, aber nicht recht zu helfen wusste, u. das erschreckende Schreien, schauerlich unter dem Ein- druck meiner Hilflosigkeit. Fürchterlich, ein Unterkommen zu er- bitten. Nachher noch Aussprache mit der [illegible] Köchin. Zittern, Müdigkeit, Verstimmung. Heute besser.

<u>Donnerstag den 12. Sept.</u> Im [illegible] der Kinder an „Herr und Hund" geschrieben. Brief an [illegible] [illegible]

Top: *Erika, Klaus, Golo, Monika, and Elisabeth with their nurse. The dog is Bauschan.*

B6   Bottom: *Thomas Mann with his publisher, S. Fischer, and Hans Reisiger about 1920.*

Top: *Katia Mann with Michael (left) and Elisabeth in 1925.*

Bottom: *Katia's parents at the Mann summer house at Nidden, on the Baltic Sea.*

Tea on the porch at Nidden. From left to right: Thomas Mann, Hans Reisiger, Katia,
B8   *Michael and a friend, and Elisabeth.*

Thomas with Elisabeth in Nidden.

Erika and Klaus in 1927.

Katia Mann in 1930.

B13

B14

B16   *Thomas Mann, Erika, Lotte Lehmann, and Bruno Walter in Vienna, 1936.*

away. The government claims that the number of "condemned traitors" was well below fifty. Thus it assures us that it is ridiculous to speak of "fantastic numbers."

Wrote further ("Joseph is Reader"). At noon walked with Katia in the woods, where we sat on a bench beside the brook near the hut. Tired.

After lunch newspapers.

Very warm. The pain somewhat abated, but the swelling causes pressure.

The material on Venice indicates that the discussions will be devoted solely to painting and architecture—nothing to be said about the real problems. Of course it could not be otherwise on Italian soil. No sense making the trip.

I am concerned about Fiedler since I have not heard from him. Also I worry about that poor creature Ida Herz, who has been thrown into prison for speaking too boldly. Since she is not permitted to write she will probably not be allowed to receive letters. Should harm come to her I am more or less responsible, for she made too much of her "friendship" with me and found herself in over her head. No doubt she could not hold her tongue precisely because of her pride in this "friendship."—

Wrote several letters, notably one to Mayor Seitz who is in prison in Vienna.

At 7:30 we drove with Golo to Faesi's, where we had dinner in the garden. In addition to the host's sons, the party included a Zurich professor and his wife and Karl Wolfskehl. Wolfskehl complimented me profusely on the Wagner essay, which he was prompted to read because of the Munich protest. The conversation most pleasant. As dusk fell we sat around the table on the terrace overlooking the lake and had coffee and beer. Naturally the talk was largely about Germany, about the intellectuals who, like Bertram, see Hitler as the "savior" that Stefan George spoke of, etc. Wolfskehl said that disenchantment was bound to come, but that the illusion would last a long while yet, and that it was precisely the intellectuals who would put up the greatest resistance against recognizing their own folly. He also spoke of Spengler, with whom he corresponds and whose attitude he values. He stands alone and scorned in Germany. He forgets that he himself contributed to this philosophic brutalization.

Wednesday, July 11

Oppressively hot day.—Up at seven, and before breakfast went to Asper, who treated the infected root some more, then inserted an antiseptic packing that it just barely seems to tolerate, and put on a temporary cap.

After coming home and having breakfast I went on with the "Joseph is Reader" chapter, and because of the heat took only the shortest stroll at noon. No school today for Medi. Some young boys, doubtless also enjoying a day of no school, were walking up the Schiedhaldensteig as I was. One of them asked where I was going.—For a walk, I said.—"Can you see that I'm sweating?"—"Yes, you do look hot, a bit red in the face."—"But there are also drops of sweat on my face, great drops!" I affirmed that there were, and he seemed quite seriously and reflectively impressed by his own drops of sweat.

After lunch again listened to the first movement of the Tchaikovsky Violin Concerto, then read some in my Wagner essay, editing it here and there. It might be straight out of *The Magic Mountain*. All good things are distinguished by their *richness*.

Could not nap on account of the heat. Light thunder, light rain, which brought a nice smell but little cooling.

The *Manchester Guardian* confirms the theory that among the Leftists killed in

Germany there were many who were privy to the secret of the Reichstag fire. In general this secret knowledge had always played a greater role within the Party than was suspected.

In the *Prager Presse* the gripping report of an Englishman's account of a talk with Schleicher after his fall, which Papen had perfidiously engineered. Schleicher's "Marxism," that is to say his good and hopeful ideas for a socialist Reich after a brief military dictatorship. It is likely that at the end of June he thought the time had come to come back to these ideas that would have reconciled Germany with Europe: a civilized socialism. But they murdered him. For the sake of better ideas? Were Hitler, Goering, and Goebbels, those three villains chained together by their own crimes, justified in their bloody acts in a higher sense above morality? Were they acting in the name of an ideal that justified the people's being locked out and kept in ignorance, so that even now they only know that Schleicher and several leaders of the Storm Troops were killed? No, politics consists for them of total cynicism with regard to ideals. They have jettisoned the socialist program of "National Socialism." They have waded in blood in order to keep on top, in the high seats erected by their own lies and crimes. They were permitted the murders on the Right so long as they put an end, above all, to bolshevism among the Storm Troops. Does that constitute standing for an ideal? Is that historic heroism? It is swindle, and nothing more.

I asked Wolfskehl what the twentieth century had to show for itself in contrast to the underrated nineteenth century. His response was the existence of new and all-important work in theoretical physics, its new image of the world in the cosmos, thanks to which revised concept man emerges with a strange new sovereignty. One can learn only from young physicists what is actually happening. I at once understood that this has to be seen in conjunction with the new anthropology, with the entire new science of man, for taken together these would provide the foundation of the new humanism that is coming into being in the best minds in spite of all the barbarism. Wolfskehl heartily agreed, responding out of his own conviction. Only he considers the chance of "all being lost," as Ortega suggests in his book, to be very great.—

Short drive and refreshing afternoon walk with Katia, Golo, and Medi.

Music in the evening: Tchaikovsky and Sibelius.—A good essay of Heinrich's on the subject of propaganda in the *Europäische Hefte*.

. . . .
Friday, July 20
. . . .

The American General Johnson is a fine man. He explained to the workers in San Francisco that the right to strike was inalienable and might not be revoked by any government. But a general strike could lead to civil war, and therefore should be rejected as a tactic. Schleicher could have said the same. It seems that the "intelligent soldier" is the right man for these times.

Johnson let it be known that the events of June 30 in Germany had so affected him that he had to take to his bed, sick with disgust. He refused to retract that statement. But what does a German Protestant bishop by the name of Dietrich have to say? "On the 30th of June God gave us an overwhelming revelation of the greatness of our Führer."—Insanity does not send people to their beds as does that overwhelming disgust that testifies to moral and spiritual health.—

Wonderful summer day. Up at 7:30. Have once more begun doing a few morning calisthenics in the nude.

Received an identity card from Berne that is valid for a year. We are once more
provided with a valid passport, a pleasant and reassuring sensation.

—Did some writing and preparatory work. Walked with Katia after a short drive.
Erika was still with us for lunch, but left shortly afterward.

Read the *Tage-Buch*. Napped in the afternoon. After tea finished my letter to Pulver
and began writing to Lion in Flims, thanking him for his rather illegible comments
on the chapter he has read, which came this morning.

Prof. Löwenstein of Yale came to supper. We took a walk with him before eating.
Ate in the garden and remained outdoors talking of political and philosophic matters
(with Golo) until we accompanied our guest to the bus at 10:30.

Finished the letter to Lion and edited letters already dictated.

Sunday, July 29; Küsnacht

Yesterday morning we were still on the Lido beach, where I wrote several cards,
including one to Bertram, seated at the table in our beach cabaña. At midday we ate
at the beach restaurant. I then went up to our hotel room to rest, and at 3:30 packed
my suitcase. While shaving I clumsily nicked my nose, so that it bled for more than
half an hour. We had tea on the hotel terrace, which is very pleasant in the afternoon,
and after I had autographed a book for the hotel manager, Sigslowac, who hails from
Trieste, we took the hotel bus at 6:30 to the Excelsior. From there the motor launch
took us once more across the lagoon and past San Marco again on its way to the
railway station. A roomette in a Bulgarian car through to Milan. Dinner in the dining
car. Changed trains there to a first-class car on a Swiss train, where we settled in for
the night. Even before Chiasso and again at the border they came through *nine* times
to check passports, luggage, tickets. Absurd. We had a few hours' sleep on our rented
pillows, with our bathrobes serving as blankets. Arrived in Zurich at around seven.
Golo there with the car. Drove home, talking about developments in Austria, which
all in all, considering the way things stand in that country, represent a giant step
toward the liquidation of nazism.

Reunion with the children. The weather clear and blue, but very cool compared
to Venice, so that after breakfast, which we all had together in the garden, I hastened
to change into warmer clothing.

Accumulation of books and letters. American reviews of *Young Joseph*, one by
Lewisohn. Bertram sent his *Deutsche Gestalten*, the dedication of which implies that
his friend Glöckner died in June.

Before lunch read the Swiss newspapers and the *Tage-Buch*, which contains a dramatic and believable account of the events of June 30 by a foreign diplomat stationed
in Berlin.

After lunch a visit from a sister of Ida Herz, Frau Loeb from Kempten, who came
for coffee and gave us news of the poor, foolish unfortunate. Katia will write her in
care of Frau Loeb. We gave her photos.

Erika arrived in the afternoon. Greeted her at tea, after a short rest, then the four
of us, including Katia and Golo, had one of those long talks repeatedly forced on us
by these times about the situation, the shape of things in Germany, hopes for a
collapse, and even for a hopeless collapse. Considered the possibility of a *finis Ger-
maniae*, the country's possible political bankruptcy and dismemberment. Would this
be spiritually bearable, perhaps even a deliverance? After the history of German

unification? After what Germany was under Bismarck? "Dissolved like mist. . . ." But would a return to unreality, to being an intellectual people be possible? Will not the return from the historic intoxication of 1933 result in a worse hangover than the one from the intoxication of 1914? Germanism rejected the Republic because its ideological content, involving integration into civilization, seemed too watered down for its taste. The specifically German element, the Protestant element, the eternal racial uniqueness of the country, was enlisted in the cause of a new and ambitious historic creation— but enlisted as something debased and deformed, with the help of lies, brutality, and coarse, hysterical drunkenness—and that historic creation is about to reveal itself to be the most miserable failure ever perpetrated by a great people. What a bankruptcy! How will the Germans live, when they can only continue to exist as a second-rate people, a status to which they saw themselves quite unjustly consigned after the war, and which they might well have been spared under more fortunate circumstances. Perhaps history has in fact intended for them the role of the Jews, one which even Goethe thought befitted them: to be one day scattered throughout the world and to view their existence with an intellectually proud self-irony.

The honor of the language, of thought, of literature has been disgraced. Thought itself becomes disgusting thanks to those who think aloud today and have the power to act accordingly.

I glanced through Zweig's book on Erasmus. The historical allusion and parallels are unacceptable because they tender too much feeble virtue to the present. "Luther, the revolutionary, the demonic man driven by inchoate German racial forces." Who can fail to recognize Hitler? But that is just the point—that the disgusting travesty, the abject, hysterical mimicry is taken to be mythical recapitulation.

Frau Giehse with us for dinner.

The première of Richard Strauss's new opera in Germany is running into serious difficulties because in the first place the text is by Zweig, and in the second Strauss has a Jewish daughter-in-law.

Erika read us some delightful chansons from her new program in the living room after dinner.

. . . .
Saturday, August 4
. . . .

Low-hanging clouds. Rain and wind all day long.

Once more worked on the political notes, but probably will be unable to continue, feeling the uselessness of the undertaking and deeply depressed by the wretched and senseless developments, by Hitler's successful coup d'état and the obvious impression his triumphs make. It is all too ludicrous and disgusting and I do wrong to let it affect me so. One has only to remember that Rossbach, Heydebreck, and Ehrhardt, the war heroes and darlings of the people, men who had novels and songs named after them, have either been shot or forced to flee the country—only then can one appreciate what a betrayal the whole stupid thing has been. What remains of the whole concept of "National Socialism," this supposed product of glorious, dark forces of the people? The martyrdom of pacifists and pardoned criminals and a few inconsequential governmental reforms. The "Führer" sets the Party aside and goes over to the Reich, to the army, the generals, and industrialists. Many see danger in the ruthless enforcement of National Socialist ideals that may now take place. But no, the dog can enforce nothing, as he does not know how. But he and his system will keep going and the "power" will remain in his hands; power for its own sake, empty of content or purpose. In the way they accept their treatment, the rejected and trampled Storm Troops reveal that they consisted merely of an accumulation of rabble.

At noon took a long walk with Katia in the downpour, with coats and umbrellas, in order to have at least some exercise. By the way, I have recently begun doing calisthenics in the morning again.

After lunch the newspapers—I should be more distrustful of them, even when they print things that are encouraging. There is no integrity of feeling behind what they publish; they could be saying something else as well, and tomorrow they may well do so.

Was unable to rest in the afternoon. Extremely depressed all day.

A long letter from Reisiger concerning his decision not to join the Berlin writers' organization, which will mean that he will not write any further on his Mary Stuart book. Poor fellow. But am I any better off? I am not making any progress either, and my faith and courage are weak.—

Letters from Dr. Pulver and a Dr. Martha Wertheimer, who introduces herself as a long-standing follower of mine.

Continued to read Zweig's Erasmus book, and because of its subject have now practically finished the whole thing after all.

Therese Giehse and Annemarie Schwarzenbach to dinner. Lingered a while with the family and guests.

Golo back from Flims.

Penetrating cold, caused by the endless rain.

Repositioned my writing desk so that the light comes onto it from the left. To be sure it does not look so attractive in the new position.

Sunday, August 5

Erika brought a clipping from the *Berliner Tageblatt* containing Hauptmann's "eulogy" of Hindenburg. A strangely stupid, confused, and feeble thing. It should be kept for later reference. *Par nobile fratrum.* Exploded myths, tottering pillars of Germanism.

The German desire for legend and for myth, which runs counter to truth and counter to intellectual honesty, is surfacing ever more noticeably again these days. Although Hauptmann would be a good candidate for such legend-making he has been more or less passed by. It is because Hauptmann was a supporter of the Republic and of Ebert, thereby offending the spirit of Germanism, that he is now given short shrift despite his efforts to be restored to grace. Hindenburg was also involved in the Republic, but in a manifestly different sense, one that did no harm to his Germanic monumentality and his suitability as a mythic figure. There is not a word of truth to the legend about him. He was not the strategist of Tannenberg (where now he is to be buried with all the disturbing solemnity befitting a hero). A certain General Hoffmann showed him the plans and he merely approved them. As for the orderly retreat of the million-man army, the chief credit should go to the Workers' and Soldiers' Councils. His own claim to honor comes down to the fact that he did not turn and run. (Thanks to his popularity he had no need to.) He never thought along heroic lines. He advised the Kaiser against returning to Germany with the units that were still intact and crushing the revolution. It was certainly problematical that later, as President, he then assumed the position of the Kaiser. Out of class solidarity he continued the scandalous subsidies to the Prussian landowners, sacrificed Schleicher, and handed Germany over to the Hitler misery. But he is and will remain the Loyal Eckehart high on a pedestal and full of monumental loyalty. Einstein has called him "an old scoundrel." The Jews are always more acute where truth is concerned; their brains are not all befogged with myth.

The entire National Socialist "movement," including its instigator, is a prime example of the German spirit's wallowing in the manure of myth. With its fraudulent, timeworn pretension to be a "return," this movement offers a real feast to the Germans' hatred of truth, their lust for everything misty and vaporous.—

Zweig's book on Erasmus did provide me with a good deal after all. The Council of Augsburg, which Karl V hoped would bring about a reconciliation between the Protestants and the Church, and which offered good chances for preserving peace and humanely averting the terrible misery that followed, functioned in the manner that— owing to a deepest desire of mankind—such attempts always exhibit. The "recapitulation" can be acknowledged as such to the degree that National Socialism, being anti-rational, antihumane, and obsessed with blood and tragedy, its desire for peace being as phony as its denial of one of its essential elements, homosexuality, will once more play the tumultuous and bloody role that Lutheranism did. "When you come to see terrible chaos unleashed in the world, remember that Erasmus predicted it." The terrible chaos had to come because, with his unshakable convictions and his powerful imagery, the Brute of Wittenberg desired it, and at bottom mankind desires it as well, for mankind has no use for rational, decent order or tolerance, no yearning for "happiness" at all, but prefers recurrent tragedy and untrammeled, destructive adventure. *Habeat.* A cynical egotism, a selfish limitation of concern to one's personal welfare and one's reasonable survival in the face of the headstrong and voluptuous madness of "history" is amply justified. One is a fool to take politics seriously, to care about it, to sacrifice one's moral and intellectual strength to it. All one can do is survive, and preserve one's personal freedom and dignity.—

After making these notes I tried to make some headway on the manuscript, but was virtually prevented from doing so by my disinclination. In order to proceed I would have to have made the firm decision once more to devote myself to it wholly, and I have not done so, or not yet at least. I find this situation a painful one.

Venice was exhausting, and I feel the trip was a mistake psychologically, since the course of events did nothing for my self-esteem. The experience of "failure," even in the most insignificant form, is psychologically a most difficult and dangerous thing for me. The disappointments of the past few days contributed to my depression, and being blocked in my work pushes it to the extreme.

I took an hour-long walk with Katia, and spoke with her about this latter problem. She firmly rejects my own suspicion that by turning to a work that is political and confessional in nature I am in fact deserting an artistic undertaking that had come to bore me or that I found too difficult, and she denies with equal force that that undertaking is either useless or idle. She herself would like to see me issue a statement against the German horrors, one that would liberate me from the ambiguity of my position, my dependency on the country, and put an end at last to the undignified spectacle of my being led around by the nose with regard to my property. She is essentially correct, also in her fear that I may have reason to regret my outward passivity when the day of collapse finally comes. At the moment I am too weary and plagued by doubt and lack of faith to think anything but that such a day is very far off, even unlikely. Nevertheless I feel compelled to write such a statement for a number of reasons, even though I would thereby fall impossibly behind with the novel, which is lagging in any case. But it would be difficult even to find the right form for the piece; approaching it more or less as a segment of my autobiography would be easiest for me.

The weather has cleared. This afternoon it is warmer outside than in the house. In the living room after lunch I expressed myself badly in speaking to the grown-up children about the hopelessness and contemptibleness of "living historically," and I regret it.

Read several good things in the new issue of *Die Sammlung*.

Tuesday, August 21

Very warm day. Organized my material for the political piece. With Katia into town to see the optician. We then picked up Lion, who had lunch at our house. Good conversation with him before we went to table, which reminded me of conversations with Bertram during the *Betrachtungen* period. This time my interlocutor must be a Jew. He contended that a moment was coming when it would be pointless to pursue this or that cultural study, since culture itself hangs in the balance.

The foreign press not exactly overwhelmed by the results of the plebiscite. Amazement expressed at the audacity with which the Goebbels newspapers pretend that the outside world is deeply impressed.

At five we drove into town again to have tea at the Baur au Lac with the film magnate Carl Laemmle and his staff of German-American assistants. Photos taken in the garden. Interview on the American film, free pass to the Kapitol Theater, discussion of the *Joseph* movie, which would cost a million dollars to produce, according to Laemmle.

The story of Gründgens's appointment as general intendant on orders from on high. The decision made at 4 A.M. during a party at Hitler's. Director B. protested, but there was nothing to be done, and he allowed himself to be sent off on a trip with a salary of 40,000 marks, while Gründgens is getting 60,000. Hitler's partiality for him is interpreted as erotic. More offensive is the sheer waste.—

Before dinner took a half-hour walk in the twilight.

Golo's St. Cloud pupil from Strasbourg was here for dinner. Afterward we listened to some music, and then I read Taine.

Winifred Wagner as a propagandist for the elections: "The Republic heaped hatred and infamy on Richard Wagner. His miraculous reascendancy is thanks to Adolf Hitler." Outrageous.—Minister Neurath: "The world has ranged itself against Germany as in 1914.—Vote for Hitler!" A bitter choice; between one evil, so to speak.

Wednesday, October 3; Lugano, Villa Castagnola

Yesterday morning, getting a rather slow start, we left Küsnacht around nine, saying farewell to everyone at home. Moni and Golo will not be there when we get back. The animals, Monstre and Mouche, watched our departure with their usual keen excitement.

The lovely foehn weather continues. We drove along the familiar stretch through the Sihl Valley, passed the Zugersee, which looked very lovely through the mist, and on to the Lake of Lucerne, where once more I was struck by the situation and loveliness of the health resort of Brunnen, as has happened each time I have seen it. The famous Axenstrasse, with its tunnels, stone galleries, and views of the lake, impressed us greatly. At noon we reached the northern entrance of the St. Gotthard Tunnel, where we left the car to be loaded on a flatcar and ourselves boarded an earlier train to Airolo. I had been quite nervous and chilled the entire morning, and although Katia was not opposed to driving over the pass I preferred to take the train, as did another driver from Holland. In Airolo we had a quite decent midday meal in the garden of the Hotel des Alpes. After taking possession of the car again we discovered that the radiator was defective (needed flushing out, rusted and leaking as the result of some anti-freeze) and had to be soldered in a garage. Lost some time at this. Then drove on down the two large serpentine descents to [?], where we stopped at around five and had tea. They spoke French at the hotel. From there the drive across the plain was very pleasant, the familiar last stretch across the valley of Lago Maggiore. Arrived at the familiar garden driveway of this hotel at around seven, darkness having already fallen. Greeted by the hotelkeeper, checked into our rooms, which are near those we had last year, mine larger than before. Unpacked and changed clothes. At eight a belated dinner downstairs. The hotel fairly crowded because of a tennis tournament. Ate heavily. Afterward read in the *Italian Journey* in the lobby, smoking and drinking a glass of beer. Early to bed.

Up today at eight after a good night's sleep. Rain. Had breakfast with Katia at 8:30.

How different this sojourn is from that of the spring of 1933. We are set back into the landscape that became so familiar in the course of those six weeks, but the landscape and the familiar faces are perceived quite differently, much more calmly. Back then, still reeling from shock, we had come from the excessive turmoil of Arosa and the makeshift eight days in Lenzerheide into this gentle environment, and the visit to Montagnola heightened my grateful delight at being here. Here, close to the Franks, the Hesses, et al., was a good place to bide our time. Then came the bad days in Rohrschach and Basel, the weeks in Le Lavandou and Bandol; but from the moment when we began keeping a house of our own at La Tranquille, and even more since establishing ourselves in Küsnacht, where we have found a kind of life so similar to that in Munich and in many respects even preferable to it, my inner state has changed considerably, and my reaction to this refuge of that time is less a matter of sheer gratitude.

Still I am glad to be back again, and expect to profit from the fine shopping available. The refreshing change is good for both of us, especially for Katia, who needs to get away from household concerns.—

Went with Katia into town by car this morning, which was something new. I had my hair tended to while Katia made some purchases, and afterward I bought a pair of those narrow silk suspenders like the ones I found here last year.

Good appetite at lunch; but afterward felt ill and had an attack of nerves, which then passed. I napped for a while, and at four we drove in very bad weather up to Montagnola to the Hesses', where we were cordially received. A Swiss lady, a house guest of theirs, joined us for tea. Hesse increasingly gives the impression of an old Swabian peasant, contented, simple, and kind. He is having great trouble with his eyes. We arranged to see them again on Friday and drove back through pouring rain.

Read after dinner with a cigar, then had camomile tea in the main lounge.

Went on a bit with the novel, though little disposed to it. Depressed and worried all day about the damnable similarity between the course of events in Switzerland and the way things went in Germany. The "fanatical" rows caused by the Front under the banner of patriotism, extremely dangerous and confusing to the middle class. Nevertheless the balance of forces is different here, and Zurich should not be equated with the rest of Switzerland. The intellectual advantages of the modern city, formerly of a moderate and socialist temper, have been completely blasted by the evils stemming from the wretched state of mind of the modern masses. The Näf murder trial highlights the moral abyss and the rottenness of today's urban middle class. Zurich is worse than Basel and Berne because it is more modern, more "up to date."

Walked with Katia and Reisiger.

Erika had a sellout house yesterday as well, a Monday. They are considering extending the run.

Correspondence in the afternoon; a second letter to Ida Herz, since it is now certain that the first one went astray, probably purloined for political purposes. Let them have it!

Reisiger went into town in the evening. I read Eduard Meyer's book on the Jews. On Reisiger's return we talked together in my room.

Erika is again staying with us and comes home by bus, the Küsnacht policeman meeting her at the bus stop and escorting her here.

Wednesday, December 5

Breakfast with Katia, then work. ("Beknechons," politics; oblique and difficult.)

Long walk with Katia in the woods. The mild cloudy weather persists. Spells of miserable rain between flashes of sun.

The first day without Reisiger's company and with fewer people in the house, as it will be for several weeks. It is somewhat boring, but has the virtue that I will do more reading.

Professor Corrodi, from Küsnacht, wrote and sent his book on Schoeck.

News that Wilhelm Furtwängler has been relieved of all his posts—very significant, since it demonstrates that no person of any superiority can work with these people. The hatred for the educated keeps mounting, and the other countries are learning a new lesson. That is good. At the same time, however, the Saar matter seems about to resolve itself in a peaceful manner. Rearmament is being accepted, and once it is complete there will be a return to Geneva and doubtless a "bold" bid for peace, with the aim of securing economic aid and shoring up the regime. Hesse feels, surely correctly, that the system is "rotten through and through." Hiller wrote hopefully of our "return." Yet oddly enough, though I have a strong sense of how impossible these people are, I do not believe they will come to grief—my mistrust of these times in which, as I see it, the impossible is now possible. There may be further feuds, perhaps bloody ones, within the regime, and, with the collaboration of the Reichswehr, a new "purge" and felling of rebellious elements and those "out of tune" with the present. But I fear they will not permit themselves to be cheated out of their "new day"; they will save themselves by granting "grandiose" and "bold" concessions to the world, and

Hitler will remain in power. Above all, the masses must be spared the shock of losing their dream of the Führer.

In Sweden Branting has just published the notes of the Storm Troop Gruppenführer Karl Ernst, who, together with others who were likewise executed, was supposedly in charge of setting the Reichstag fire on orders from Goebbels and Goering.

Rascher sent a veritable mountain of new publications from his firm.

Rabener in Berlin writes good things about *Voyage with Don Quixote* and *Tristan*, and also announces his own new book.

Wrote to Dr. Veit in Berlin.

Beginning to worry that the December issue of the *Neue Rundschau* should be so late in arriving.

Sunday, December 30

Some work (departure of the Pharaoh).

Walked with Katia, Reisiger, and our dog Bill, who was permitted to run free and is beginning to get used to us.

Books and letters, A *vita* of Erasmus in Latin and German. Galleys of the *Voyage*. Long letter from Frank in London: the plans for filming *Royal Highness* have had to be shelved for the moment. Things are going better for him.

Very warm springlike weather with intervals of sun. We had our coffee in the garden after lunch.

At tea spoke with Reisiger about the decline of Europe, the phenomenon of the debasement of once authentic spiritual and historical phenomena, as illustrated by the relationship of Spengler to Nietzsche and Schopenhauer, or National Socialism to the Reformation. It would seem that we no longer have real history, but only mock semblances and degenerate epilogues, counterfeit history. As I see it, what we did not have before and what is no imitation is the conscious rejection of human achievement and return to previous conditions, moral setback out of hatred (especially in Germany) for common sense and progress. Nowhere in history, to my knowledge, is there a parallel to the scene in the Sportpalast in Berlin when Goebbels announced the abolition of human rights while tens of thousands cheered.

Reisiger suggested that the key trend of this epoch is the slow withdrawal from the churches, which are basically already dead, and gradual creation of a nonstructured religiosity.—

Wrote letters by hand. Evening walk. Dinner with Katia, Reisiger, and Golo. Afterward listened with interest to the *Meistersinger* records. The Prelude to Act III is very distinguished music. Later on talked with Reisiger about the mysterious power that National Socialist "doctrines" have over ordinary people. Perhaps it is because these are bringing such people into contact with thought of any kind for the first time, forcing some rudimentary use of their minds.—We also spoke of future prospects of the Catholic church, for which I have more esteem than he. It has a popular monopoly, after all, on "spirituality" as the principle of universal moral conduct, both as consolation for the lowly and humiliation of the proud.

The last day of our second year away from Germany—strange. My mind was lethargic while I worked and very perturbed afterward. All sorts of mail, including an old edition of Freiligrath's poems sent by Schickele as a New Year's greeting.

Went at noon to the Oprechts', where we had all been invited for lunch—including Reisiger and Dr. Landshoff, who had just arrived from Davos. Handsome old house, warm hospitality.

Afterward there were errands to do. I was exhausted, and rested for an hour. Dr. Landshoff to tea in addition to our usual circle.

Katia very optimistic regarding the political situation, in view of the news from the Saar (via Herzog) and from Germany, where decline and imminent overthrow cannot be disguised. God willing. Even I do not doubt the increasing loss of control of the Party, but I do have my doubts about whether the "movement" is really done for—outside Germany as well—and whether it will be abandoned.

Am ailing. Intestinal trouble, deep depression. Did not go out again, since on top of all this it was raining. Read in my chair; looked at the Herta Brauer book, but cannot bring myself to read it, out of a resistance to all things that are forced upon me. Schickele made a good choice in sending the Freiligrath volume:

> Must I take up my staff again
> And push on to another place?
> For even here in Tell's domain
> I feel the fury of their chase.

1935

Came down yesterday to a festive dinner table. In addition to Reisiger and the three oldest children we also had Landshoff and Annemarie Schwarzenbach with us. Feeling very weak, I ate little, and as soon as the meal was over I withdrew from the rest of the New Year's Eve festivities, which continued with punch and games. Went to bed at ten and read Gogol. My whole body ached. Stayed awake until the beginning of the year, marked by the pealing of bells, and waited for Katia, who made me camomile tea. Took half a pill along with it and then slept soundly with the little lamp on. Bathed at nine and had only tea and zwieback for breakfast. Feel better physically, but my nerves are still bad.

I changed the calendar, and so begins the year of my sixtieth birthday.

Wrote nothing but a few notes and postcards. At noon took a short stroll with Katia, Reisiger, and Bill, which tired me. Lunch with the older children, Reisiger, Landshoff, who had stayed overnight with us, and Therese Giehse. Dozed afterward. After tea Klaus and Landshoff departed, Golo driving them to the station.

I asked Reisiger to read me his work. Stretched out in my chair I listened to several fine episodes from his Mary Stuart novel, and we spoke of the differences between our present projects, the particular constraints that a specific work imposes. In *Joseph* the governing principle is the sense of humanity, which brings with it an element of exclusion and selectivity no matter how I strive for individuation and a semblance of reality. Art, the given work of art, that is, is the furthest thing from freedom.

Only four of us at dinner. Afterward [we] listened to part of a Bellini opera broadcast from Rome.—Still weak and lacking energy as a result of the restricted diet. But I improved by evening and could feel a degree of animation. Going to bed early.

Wednesday, January 2

Feeling better, but still frail. Drank tea in bed, wrote a bit, and at eleven had a cup of soup. Then drove to town with Katia to the Austrian and Czech consulates. Comically enthusiastic private reception at the Czech consul's.

Ate sparingly at lunchtime. Very tired. Lay down immediately to rest, then before five drove to town again with Katia and Golo to see the very appealing film *Der junge Baron Neuhaus.*

Letter from a young Czech, gratifying. Also one from Vossler, critical of my remarks about *Don Quixote.* A New Year's greeting from Heins, resigned and chagrined. My conviction grows increasingly stronger that I will not get my property back, and that the regime will not collapse in the foreseeable future.

After supper we listened to all kinds of music. The close of *Die Götterdämmerung* once more thrilled me.

Saturday, January 19 (sleeping car to Vienna)

Rose before eight this morning in Küsnacht and worked on the novel until I reached the point I had set for myself. Used the time normally reserved for my walk for packing and getting ready for the trip. After lunch had some coffee and continued packing. We left at 3:30 for the station (in Doll's taxi) after saying goodbye to the children and the housemaids, and settled ourselves in the sleeping car, which goes straight through. The lighting is inadequate, unfortunately. Passed the time with newspapers. At five o'clock went to the dining car for tea. The officer who checked our papers at the Austrian border town of Buchs proved to be a reader of mine and asked for my autograph.—Schlamm, writing in the *Europäische Hefte*, is correct in his analysis of the Saar plebiscite; he says the time is past when one had faith that the masses could be lifted up to the point of recognizing what is rational and in their own interest. Such belief is now hollow. But does that not really mean the end of Marxism? Is it not slowly dying everywhere from lack of faith in itself? In an age of tanks and radio, of massive propaganda campaigns with idealistic trimmings, is socialism, in the nineteenth-century sense, still possible? How caring it was even in its pessimism! An age of the masses is dawning, one which is at the same time an age of contempt for the masses and for mankind.

Sunday, January 20; on the train from Vienna to Prague

We ate à la carte in the dining car yesterday evening at 8:30, a ham omelet and a piece of cheese. The lighting situation grew worse and worse; the dynamo had frozen, and ultimately we had to undress in complete darkness, reading being totally out of the question. It was ten o'clock when we went to bed, each of us having taken a Phanodorm tablet. A whole one is quite a lot for me, and I slept so soundly that I was disturbed neither by the cold, which had bothered me during the evening, nor the repeated turning on and off of the lights.

Got up at eight, did the best I could to wash and dress, and had breakfast in the dining car, where Katia later joined me. It is a clear, cold winter day. Our arrival in Vienna was delayed, but we managed to get very quickly by taxi from the Westbahnhof to the Ostbahnhof, where we were on our way again by 10:15.

In the *Prager Tagblatt* there is a positive review of the première of *The Peppermill*, in which it is called a "resounding success." Their only reservations have to do with its excessive delicacy and melancholy.

The lead article in the same paper raises some things worth considering with regard to what can be learned from the referendum in the Saar, suggesting that populations as such are idealistic when it comes to larger issues, and do not vote from the point of view of economics. Although Germany is said to be suffering an economic crisis at this very moment, the Saar opted to join it anyway.—But was this the only "although"? Were there not other things, and more idealistic ones, that might have kept the Saarlanders from making this choice? Would it not have been perhaps more idealistic of them to vote otherwise? It ultimately comes down to a ranking of one's ideals. Furthermore one cannot overrate the mechanistic conquest of the people of the Saar by means of propaganda from the Reich, glorifying the Reich and its masses.

2:00 P.M. Much misfortune. On the heels of last night's disaster with the lighting in the sleeping car, a leak developed in the water reservoir of our new car and it flooded. After the pass control and baggage inspection, which were conducted in a friendly enough manner, the passengers were forced to change to another car that had been added on. The flooded one was German, by the way, and according to the Czech official the same thing happens every year.—Our new accommodations were ice cold at the beginning. Also it developed that we had no dining car, since the train that was to have brought it was excessively delayed. A few impossibly fat sausages were a poor substitute. In Brno we bought some ham sandwiches that tasted delicious.

The compartment filled up in Brno. The winter sun is shining in warmly and I have taken off my fur coat. Am reading Silone's *Fascism*.

Prague, Hotel Esplanade. We arrived at five o'clock, met by Frankl, his daughter, and some men from the radio station. Flowers for Katia. Came on foot to the hotel, where Stroh was also waiting for us. After checking into our room, which with its sitting room appears to be identical to the one three years ago, we had tea in the hotel café with the above-named and Erika. Slender from exhaustion and overwork, she had come directly from her sellout matinee performance. Talked about the tragedy in the Saar. Interview with the editor Manfred Georg.

Later back in our room, where Erika quickly ate some supper before her evening show. Telephone interview with Vienna, the *Sonn- und Montagszeitung*. Went through my greeting to Prague with Frankl, making corrections to bring it into line with opinion here. Frankl accompanied us to a restaurant on the Graben where we ate well and inexpensively. Came back to the hotel in a raw wind and unpacked.

Thursday, January 31; in the sleeping car, Vienna-Zurich

Left from the Westbahnhof yesterday evening at eight. Dinner in the dining car with Frau Rieser. Rather early to bed with half a pill. Finished Pushkin's *Dubrovsky*. Slept until 5:30, then managed no more real sleep. The compartment was cold and the daylight shone in disturbingly. Out of bed at around 8:30. Katia's voice returning somewhat. Her condition does not seem overly serious, thank God.

Breakfast in the dining car, where Katia later joined me. Began reading Pushkin's *The Captain's Daughter*.

The border checks went easily. The Austrian official beamed when he read my passport. No questions asked about the luggage.

At the border we bought Swiss newspapers, which proved rather uninteresting. Stupid, boastful speech by Hitler on the anniversary of the "Seizure of Power." Whatever one hears and reads from these people, their every utterance is on a pitifully low level. Bernhard Rust forbidden to take part in a memorial service for Fritz Haber. (The order was not obeyed, and Max Planck also gave a dignified address.) The property of sixty-year-old Fritz Kreisler is to be confiscated because he refuses to perform in Germany. One would not have thought possible the callow absurdity, the subaltern illogic that lies behind such a step.—

This form of travel, with one's sleeping compartment converted by day into a private roomette, is extremely pleasant.

High in the Vorarlberg region it was quite cold and wintry. Now, at 11:30, the terrain is mountainous still but less rugged. In about an hour we will be in Zurich. And so ends a journey perhaps richer in pleasant impressions and experiences than any previous one. My very person assumed a bright aura, proving it to be more radiant and dearer to people than those of the likes of Kolbenheyer and Ponten.

By the way, there is no question but that in addition to the annual rings of one's personal growth there is relative growth thanks to the general decline of these times. Against this spreading mediocrity people like me assume a kind of towering moral and cultural stature, and I do not deny that many of the honors I received on this trip may be understood as simple human respect in the presence of a survivor from a nobler era.

Back in Küsnacht.

Arrived in Zurich right on time. Surprised to find Reisiger at the station. Snow and ice. Driven home by Doll. The children. Mountains of mail. The corrected proofs of the essay volume.

Busied myself with these things after lunch.

Rested. The doctor in to see Katia. Her bronchi not congested. Prescriptions.

Tea at Katia's bedside. Then unpacked and dressed, for at 7:30 the Bermanns came with Reisiger. Dinner with them. Discussion of pending matters: the essay volume, Lion's Joseph book, Frau M. Wassermann's book on her late husband, and various business matters.

Finished the evening by reading aloud the conversation in the palm grove.

· ·

Friday, March 8

· ·

Up at around nine. Snow and bitter cold east wind.

Made an energetic start on the speech for Nice.

Lion sent the first section of his manuscript *Von Buddenbrooks bis zum Zauberberg.*

To my delight the Reclam books arrived, a handy and varied collection that promises more than merely renewed acquaintance with familiar things and stimulating conquest of new ones.

Drove with Katia into town to see Baumann, who treated both of us. I then went on foot toward Zollikon, where Katia picked me up with the car. Earlier I greeted the owner of the tobacco shop at Bellevue Platz, whom I know from Davos.

After lunch read the newspapers, from which it can be gathered that Hitler's ploy has been a success in spite of all. England's political idealism, her intelligentsia that feels the Treaty of Versailles represented a moral abdication on England's part, is in opposition to the government, which will have to defend itself in the House of Commons. This English decency, above all English socialism, which is evidently unmoved by the fate of its German colleagues, is something that the wretched fellow is trying to mobilize to his own advantage and to make use of in his "game." A painful farce. One cannot even condemn these lovers of peace and decency for feeling that as far as they are concerned domestic issues are more important than foreign ones, that the shirt is closer to the skin than the coat, and that their own morale is of greater urgency than someone else's.—

Then read Lion's manuscript, which is, thanks to his acuity, somewhat exciting reading.

Had my tea brought upstairs and cleaned off the table opposite my desk, transferring the books from it to the large pile, destroying many unnecessary papers, and lining up the new Reclam series on it.

Went on a bit with the writing.

Evening walk in cold and wind.

Spent the evening reading Lion's manuscript and the *Tage-Buch,* which contains several good pieces, among them a magnificently ironical essay by Schwarzschild on the new cult of blood.—Nietzsche quote: "If Germany does not fulfill her moral duty and fails to renounce her national egotism, if she does not disavow the doctrine of

234

Might makes Right and refuses to believe that Right makes Might—if she does not strive with all her strength and honesty for freedom and truth, then her fate is already sealed." (From a letter to Gast.)

Saturday, March 16

Last night, after smoking my cigar and reading journals in my chair, I went to bed at about one o'clock and read with interest in *Aladin*, which constitutes my bedtime reading these days. With half a tablet I managed to have several hours of good sleep, but was awakened too early by activity in the house, since the children were leaving on a school skiing expedition. Got up at 8:30, bathed, and had breakfast. Katia is typing up the letters I dictated yesterday, the subject of which, the American trip coming up in June, is much on our minds. If it can be paid for we certainly ought to undertake it, for the honor from Harvard would unquestionably be good and important vis-à-vis Germany, both friends and foes.

The clear pre-spring weather continues.

An article by W. Schlamm in the *Europäische Hefte* that I read yesterday has stayed with me. Titled "Der Einzelgänger," it says much that is perceptive and apt regarding the psychological situation of the world and the future of socialism, for which it is no longer the manifestly downtrodden masses that are decisive, but the cultivated individual in his moral autonomy.—Very important article.

Another one about psychoanalysis in Germany and the revolting conduct of Jung has caused me to reflect on the ambiguousness of human and intellectual phenomena. If a highly intelligent man like Jung takes the wrong stand, there will naturally be traces of truth in his position that will strike a sympathetic note even in his opponents. Jung is correct when he insists that only a kind of "soulless rationality" could overlook the fact that there is something positive about neurosis, that it is a precious part of the soul, and that the patient should not have to learn how to get rid of it, but how to live with it. "For he is the illness himself. . . . To lose a neurosis means virtually to lose the ground one stands on. . . ." That is entirely true, and it would be mean to respond by saying that it would be a fine doctor indeed who would refuse to cure a tubercular patient on the grounds that the tuberculosis was "precious" to him. For it might indeed be so. His scorn for "soulless rationalism" has a negative effect only because it implies a total rejection of rationalism, when the moment has long since come for us to fight for rationality with every ounce of strength we have. Jung's thought and his utterances tend to glorify nazism and its "neurosis." He is an example of the irresistible tendency of people's thinking to bend itself to the times—a high-class example. He is *not* a loner in the sense of the Schlamm article, is not one of those who remain true to the eternal laws of good sense and morality and thereby find themselves to be rebels in their time. He swims with the current. He is intelligent, but not admirable. Anyone nowadays who wallows in the "soul" is backward, both intellectually and morally. The time is past when one might justifiably take issue with reason and with the mind.—

—Sent off the letters to America. The Nice speech to Čapek. Inscribed a copy of *Jacob* to the singer Fred Destal.—

—Note anew how taking time out for a critical piece like the speech on literary freedom can throw one *off stride*.—

Once more trying to concentrate on the novel.

Went for an hour's walk in the sun, and felt with gratitude how the year is advancing toward the best of months, June, the time of my birth.—

Fritz Strich here for lunch; he went pale with shock upon hearing that I had doubts and hesitations about accepting the high honor offered me by Harvard. He gave us to understand that this was the most distinguished university in America and one of the foremost in the world, and he induced us to send a telegram of thanks in which I again expressed my confident hope that I can be present on Commencement Day. Uppermost in my mind is the effect in Germany. For this is the university that declined the grant from Hanfstängl, etc. That this honor is being awarded to me in particular has undoubted political significance as well.—

Read the speech for Nice to Strich, who was much impressed. The extent of the problems its translation will pose again became obvious. They are virtually insurmountable, yet to present it in German would make no sense.—

In the evening Katia and I went to the Raschers', having dinner with them *en famille* with only water to drink at table. The conversation afterward over tea was rather low-keyed. I looked at a handsome edition of Thiers's *History of the French Revolution* with magnificent copperplates. Also Burckhardt's biography of Richelieu. The old grandmother, who is over eighty, was also present. I flirted a bit with the older boy, Hans, who is an admirer of mine and has lovely eyes.—We left shortly after ten and had a glass of red wine when we got home.

Sunday, March 17

Somewhat cloudy, mild spring day. Up at 8:30. Used my working hours preparing to "embark" on the new chapter. Walked down to the village with Katia, Bibi, and the dogs, and then back uphill.

Fritz Busch's daughter with us for lunch; very German.

After lunch continued reading the page proofs of Kahler's book. The chapter on the essences of Germanism and Judaism is superlative. The intellectual approach is a compound of Jewishness and the Stefan George brand of Germanic thinking. It is a happy mixture, and may be the only way to get to the heart of things these days. But the Germanic element, which is usually insufferable when it speaks on its own behalf, is treated here with too much deference, at least in view of its present-day behavior.

Quite exhausted and tired in the afternoon. Napped a while. After tea dictated a long succession of overdue letters to all sorts of people.—

Heard reports—first from Tennenbaum, then over the radio—of the official and ceremonious reintroduction of compulsory military service in Germany. Hitler's return from Bavaria to Berlin. Speeches. Proclamation to the German people. Agitated reaction on the part of the European press. Sharp and bitter response in France. The British cabinet is meeting to discuss the projected trip of Simon and Eden, which will probably be cancelled. It is a brazen challenge. But it is too late; too much has been allowed to happen. The British government is to a degree justified vis-à-vis the Labour opposition because of its White Book; it is now clear that the provocation in Berlin and Hitler's taking ill were all tricks with which to pave the way for this stroke. Is the catastrophe growing closer?

Along with this, some ominous domestic developments. Arrest of the leaders of the Confessional Church movement, including Niemöller. This is also doubtless necessary to prepare the country for war. One sees how the arrogance of those in power has increased since the plebiscite. May that arrogance precipitate their downfall, but at not too great a cost to the rest of the world!

Saturday, March 23

Up at eight. Half rainy, half sunny April weather, with some strong wind. Worked energetically. Walked by myself.

Some days back, Julius Bab sent me the notice sent to all the "non-Aryan" members of the so-called Reich Literature Chamber, barring them henceforth from any literary activity in Germany. Today Käthe Rosenberg forwarded the same notice, which she had received as a translator. The mendacity and baseness of it cry out to heaven, particularly in the case of the translator, for whom the "ideological" justification is miserably invalid. The whole thing is put forward expressly "at the wish of the Führer and Reich Chancellor." My revulsion is so great that my desire finally to cut all ties with this country becomes ever more urgent. It is to be hoped and expected that Bermann will soon be shown the door, and that the essay volume will not appear there.—

After tea Katia and I drove into town and saw the Anglo-Indian film *Lives of a Bengal Lancer*, dubbed in German, one of the strongest things I have seen in this medium, with distinct patriotic overtones but with marvelous acting. Magnificently filmed battle scenes, and the intimate episodes equally well done. A curious feeling of shame in the face of this virility. Early poets, like the Scandinavian skalds and such, kept their own shame at bay by glorifying the hero in song. But taken though I was with the brave young men shown in the film—and true to life they certainly were, for these are a new breed of actors who do not merely pretend, but actually live their parts—the sentimentalizing of primitive masculinity by the admixture of patriotism ("England, England, all for England!") is unpleasant to me, for it is specious, and basically takes away from the pure manliness.—

Had supper alone with Katia.

Alexander Moissi has died in Vienna.

Sent the notice to the *National-Zeitung*.

Germany in a frenzy of enthusiasm over its rearmament, and actually over the possibility of war. The ani-aircraft tests in Berlin, realistic in all details, are unambiguous. These people have no other thought but war. It will only come about on their initiative, and they alone seem to have no distaste for it.

In the *Neue Zürcher Zeitung* an article by Faesi on Rilke as a critic, with interesting comments on the poet's review of *Buddenbrooks*. Also an insightful critical evaluation of Wassermann.

In the evening got back to my Goethe–Lotte Kestner project, and after some peripheral reading came across the story in Felix Theilhaber's book of their slightly grotesque encounter late in life in Weimar. Stirred.

Monday, April 1

Spring weather has returned. Worked with difficulty. Walked only around the pond, where a boy played an April Fool's joke on me: "You there! You have a hole in your sock!"—Letter from Forbes, in London, enclosing a maple leaf from our garden in Munich. Katia's brother Peter gave a belated account of Bertram's visit to Maximiliansplatz, and the unbelievable tactlessness with which he went on about "Germany's greatness," and how everyone, even though they might disagree about details, must work together. His was once a sensitive mind.—

In the afternoon a surprise telephone call from R. G. Binding, who then came to the house at 6:30. We talked until 7:45, during which time I did not conceal my opinion of Germany and met with little objection from him. He admitted to the country's total disorientation, its cultural destruction and hopelessness. He believes war will not come, because Germany lacks many of the resources it would need to wage it. I spoke about myself with pride, and mentioned the ways in which the world is making up for Germany's mistreatment of me. In this connection he spoke of his envy of me as a German, and repeatedly asked about my sixtieth birthday and what form I expected the occasion to take. I explained that it was not up to me. What he obviously wished to know was whether I wished to be back—and I let him know that such a possibility was a nightmare for me. That seemed to satisfy him more or less.

Inscribed a number of copies of *Leiden und Grosse der Meister.*

. . . .
Wednesday, April 10
. . . .

Suddenly at last another bright, warm, springlike day. My state of health improved, but still on a restricted diet. A heating pad in my reading chair. Rhubarb wine.

Worked more energetically, and at noon took a walk in the woods with Katia and the dogs.

Napped in the afternoon. To tea Dr. Sulzbach and Frau Joachim, the journalist, who stayed late. Showed them my study.

Letters from Heinrich and from old Privy Councillor Weiss from Budapest, who sent a highly favorable review of the *Meister* from the *Pester Lloyd.*

The ambiguous deaths of the two German emigré women in London were pronounced suicides by the English coroner. It is no wonder that German murderers are being credited with it nonetheless.

The wedding of Goering to Emmy Sonnemann is typical in every respect, not only for the gluttony and ostentation of these little people suddenly raised "so high, so *unimaginably* high"—the very people who, while subjecting the overthrown leaders of the Republic to foolish corruption trials, actually despise them for their lack of audacity, for not knowing how to really live it up at Germany's expense as they do. He gave his bride a piece of diamond jewelry worth 70,000 marks, while she gave him a luxury yacht, but one boasting a "people's cabin" that can be had for only 1,600 marks. Socialism! Lufthansa made him a present of a private plane upholstered in morocco leather and worth 100,000 marks. Meanwhile, almost as a sidelight to the wedding celebration with its gala opera (Strauss's *Die Ägyptische Helena!*) and reception in the foyer, their banquet for 300 people in the Kaiserhof, and their pompous exchange of vows in the presence of the "Reich Bishop," another victim was sacrificed to the Horst Wessel myth: a young Communist, who was at that time involved—probably indirectly—in the killing of the lad, was executed. A show of the power and pomp of this rabble would be incomplete without the taste of blood.

MacDonald, Simon, Flandin, and Mussolini are on the way to Stresa with their entire staffs. A European conference without Germany and nonetheless about Germany, even though England regards the exclusion of Germany as increasing the threat of war. Mussolini will testify that in dealing with these curs the one thing that is dangerous is the weakness and indecisiveness of Europe. Ever since he managed to *see* Hitler, he has known what he is up against.

Monday, April 15

Up shortly after eight. Breakfasted with Katia and Ida Herz at 8:30. Worked (the dream of Mut). After shaving, walked by way of Johannisburg with Katia and Ida Herz. Sun, then another downpour. After lunch read newspapers on the Stresa conference. They have finally arrived at as firm a stand as can be achieved in the present state of the world. The French note to the League of Nations is first rate—and approved by the others. The concessions made to Germany on her eastern borders, sponsored by England, are regarded on the one hand as a retreat and on the other as nothing to take too seriously. How can declarations by this regime be taken seriously or have any semblance of morality? Its profound falseness excites disgust, and makes any form of trust impossible. When Goebbels declares that a war will weigh heavily on the workers, that any defeat will be their defeat—that too is the purest dialectic, diversion, demagoguery, and falsehood. When these people talk in "European" terms they do so for tactical purposes, hypocritically aping the vocabulary of a world totally alien to them and in which they have not a trace of belief. They think that the others are also lying when they speak in such terms, and they pride themselves on their own cleverness in being able to speak the same lingo. But it does not go unnoticed.— Probably Rome will now insist that they give written assurances on Austria. Basically they are in a wretched position.—

Gratifying to hear how well the *Joseph* books are selling in Hungary. Letters from German readers about *Joseph*, *A Man and His Dog*, and the *Meister* have been forwarded by Bermann. He informs us, by the way, that he will be here at the end of the week, and speaks of Hesse, who will likewise be in Zurich then, in terms that almost suggest the firm is facing the major changes we have long anticipated.

To tea a friend of Ida Herz's, a Frau Spaet.

In the evening we picked up the Kahlers at the station and brought them here. They had dinner with us, together with Bernhard von Brentano. The conversation after dinner was lively, though as punishment for my good nature Ida Herz was something of a burden.

Friday, April 19 (Good Friday)

Took half a pill late last night and slept marvelously well until nine. Last breakfast with Ida Herz. But instead of the brief good-bye in the presence of the others that I had counted on, it developed that she would not be leaving until one o'clock with Katia, and thus was able to join me on my walk—without Katia.

Went on with the new section in the manner now required. Elements of the other version of the spells used to snare the young man must now be incorporated.

Went out at 12:15. Glorious weather. Summer coat that I later shed. The dogs ran along with us. I had the woman on my hands as far as Itschnach. Lamentable and embarrassing importunities of the hysterical old spinster. The stiffness and coolness with which I responded made me think of Mama, who used to treat unwelcome demonstrations of love in the very same way. Nevertheless I ended by expressing general goodwill and encouragement, although inwardly I resolved never to let this happen again. After I was free of her I set off in the sunshine with the dogs, following the Zumikon road past Johannisburg, rejoicing in my heart at being free of the burdensome creature and clarifying certain problems associated with my work in my mind.

For several days, in addition to my thinking about the novel, I have been toying with the idea of a new political project, an open letter or memorandum to the German people letting them know how the world feels about them and warning them against the fate of being branded *inimicus generis humani*—all this in a warm, sincere tone. Once more it would be an attempt to save their souls, politically, one for which I am constantly searching for the proper and suitable approach—also for the right opportunity and occasion, which may well have been provided again thanks to Stresa, Geneva, and the Jacob case. . . .

Unusually good appetite at lunch.

Afterward skimmed through Olden's *Hindenburg*, overcome by the gruesomeness of German history.

The heating pad once more helped me fall asleep in the afternoon.

Some handwritten notes and finishing of letters.

The Bermanns came to dinner, arriving somewhat early as they had just attended a matinee performance of the Bach B-minor Mass. They are on an automobile tour through Southern Germany and Switzerland. We sat in the living room after dinner and listened to some Bach, broadcast from Berne. The essay volume is going into a new printing and, along with Hesse's book of stories, is one of the firm's best sellers.

· ·
Thursday, May 16; Nice, Hotel d'Angleterre
· ·

The day before yesterday we left Küsnacht by car at nine. The weather was fresh and lovely, and we had a very pleasant day's drive to Geneva by way of Bremgarten, Biel, Solothurn, and Neuchâtel. Stopped in Ouchy, outside Lausanne, where we looked up Lion in the Hotel du Parc and had tea with him. Talked about his book and the plans for publishing sections from it; also about my third volume. He made me feel better about the long time the book is taking.—After saying good-bye to him we drove along Lake Geneva, where it was as clear and lovely as it had been along Lake Neuchâtel. Felt well throughout the whole trip, though to be sure I was quite tired by the time we reached Geneva. There we checked our luggage, had the car garaged, took a walk down to the lake, then turned back, and at eight were on our way again in a sleeping car, where the conductor recognized us. We had provided ourselves with edibles, and had a little supper once the train had started. Went to bed early. We were the only passengers in the car. Empty compartments where we could sit. Soon fell asleep and slept soundly.

Yesterday morning the train was already running along the sea, passing its coastal resorts that lay under gray, overcast skies in semirainy weather, cool. Arrived at 8:45. Heinrich at the station without his goatee and with a white moustache, looking odd and distinguished. He accompanied us to the hotel, where we talked for a long time in our room with its view of the sea and the jetty. After he had gone, Klaus came, and we likewise chatted with him at length. He has grown a little thinner, and I hear that he takes morphine, though in moderation.

Lunch at one at the hotel. Klaus and his handsome friend Katzenellenbogen turned up just as we were finishing our meal, and we sat with them at a sidewalk café along the promenade.—Afternoon rest. At five by taxi to Fabron to call on the Schickeles. Rain. Difficulty finding the place. Attractive house. Tea, like the days in Sanary. Schalom Asch joined us. Steady rain. Finally Hans Schickele, who drove us back to Nice and then to Heinrich's in the Rue du Congrès. We brought roses for Nelly Kröger. With Heinrich and Nelly to the Régence for dinner. The zest Heinrich brings to eating and drinking. On edge because of Nelly's stupid vulgarity. They ultimately walked us back to the hotel in the rain. The restaurant awakened memories of Paris, as does the city, which in parts has a very elegant and metropolitan quality. Read a bit in Bunin's short stories and soon fell asleep.

Today a continuation of the chilly, gray, damp weather. Out of sorts, half unwell, and irritable. After my bath and breakfast I made these notes.

Klaus came to see us and we went out with him to make various purchases in the department store, a perfume shop, and the tobacconist's. I am once more smoking Gitanes and the Diplomates cigars; memories of Sanary. The weather cleared. Wind, smelling of the sea. Energy returning. Drank a vermouth in front of the café we patronized yesterday on the promenade, listening to its unusual female orchestra and leafing through a few Paris newspapers. Laval in Moscow. Verdict in the Berne trial: mild sentences, trashy literature, appeal.—Had lunch at the hotel. Felt unwell after my cigarette. Rested for two hours, listening to band music from the jetty while Katia was off at Klaus's working over a translation with him.—Got up at four, wrote the lines I had formulated to the *Komsomolskaya Pravda* and a card to Reisiger.—Mail: they will not let Reisiger speak on the Zurich radio program, for a Swiss must do it. Very well then, Faesi. Forgot to mention my telephone conversation with him yesterday: the Zurich celebration is set for the twenty-sixth. An afternoon affair with parts of the third act of *Fiorenza*, music, Faesi's speech, and I must also say something.

At five Heinrich came to fetch us. We had tea in a pavilion restaurant on the sea, then took a walk to the lovely lake where the Hotel de Suisse is situated and on down to the harbor. Then by bus through the old part of town to the Rue de Congrès, where Klaus had arrived before us. Dr. Levy also there, a congenial person. Extremely well prepared and agreeable dinner in the living room. Red wine, coffee, and conversation until about eleven. Our hostess for the most part bustling about happily. We also spoke of Heinrich's congratulatory statement in *Die Sammlung*, a remarkably moving, pithy, and well-turned piece. He saw us back to the hotel. I read on in Bunin's stories for a while.

Sunday, June 16; M.S. "Lafayette"

The greater part of the ocean journey is behind us. Already it has been warmer for the past two days, milder on account of the Gulf Stream. I have a tendency to feel feverish in my head; on Friday it was so acute that I was convinced I had a temperature, since the fever was accompanied by an upset stomach and nerves. We did not go to dinner, but ate lightly in our cabin and went to bed early.—Little sun and much wind. Each day immediately after lunch we lie down to rest, and from three o'clock on we work in the writing room, where I am now making these notes, composing thank-you letters, which by now amount to an imposing pile. At five, after tea, we regularly betake ourselves to the cinema in the lounge.—Croce's *History of Europe in the Nineteenth Century*, with which I am now occupied, is nothing very exciting. I am more interested in *Der missbrauchte Mensch* by P. A. Robert, whose chapter on Nietzsche is especially gripping.—Yesterday and the day before I spent the mornings after breakfast writing a long letter to Bertram in a friendly and ironic vein.—I am still not at all familiar with the English version of the Goethe lecture.—Yesterday morning we received an invitation to dine at the captain's table. A diverse little group assembled in the smoking lounge, and at eight we went into the dining salon: an ambassador from Santo Domingo with his daughter, an Americanized West Swiss, an American widow, another American woman, quite attractive, who lives in Paris and speaks excellent French, the Belgian diplomat, and another Frenchman. We ate well, with caviar and champagne, and afterward sat in the main lounge where people were dancing. We excused ourselves at 10:30. The sea was very rough, the ship rolled, creaked, groaned, and pitched most unpleasantly. The captain, a congenial man who knows Bremen, had predicted bad weather as there were low-pressure areas all over the map; if this were winter we would really be in for a shaking. For a long while we could not relax in our beds, and thus have not had enough sleep. But we awoke at 7:30 as usual and I had a walk on the open deck. I want to write a note of thanks to Curtius.—This being Sunday, gentle morning music is playing in the salon. That is where a daily Mass is celebrated.—My stomach somewhat upset again.—

Was pleased with the way my note to Curtius in Bonn turned out.

Radio-telegram from Erika in London to say that her marriage to the writer Auden has taken place. "All love from Mrs. Auden!"

In the afternoon a boxing match in the salon between the youngest sailors and the waiters, the boys boxing in blindman's bluff fashion.

Finished another batch of thank-you letters. Then cinema as usual after tea, today's film being somewhat more appealing than yesterday's because American. I do not much care for Frenchmen on the screen.

Took a few turns on the promenade deck, played a little golf. The weather persistently foggy and windy, with only seldom a glimpse of sunlight.

· ·

Friday, June 21

· ·

We are on the train from Cambridge (Mass.) to Stamford, whence we are to go to Riverside to visit the Van Loons, who kindly invited us to stay with them, as did Sinclair Lewis.

Wednesday evening we arrived in Boston at eight and were taken by car (Conant's secretary) to Cambridge. Dinner in the president's elegant house with his wife and Mr. and Mrs. Norman Davis. To bed early.

Yesterday, the twentieth, the academic ceremonies, starting with music, to which we were taken by Prof. Walz at 9:30, after bath and a good breakfast. On the platform under a canopy. Six thousand people. Awarding of the honorary degrees with tremendous acclamation for Einstein and me. Pictures taken of us in academic regalia.

Cold lunch served outdoors. Seated next to a pleasant man, [?], a friend of Hemingway's. There followed another ceremony chaired by the president of the Alumni Association. Speeched by the governor and Henry Wallace.

Tea at the Conants'. Rested in my room. Good-sized dinner party at the president's. Retired early, exhausted.

Today up at 7:30, and after breakfast we went off with the professor who had yesterday volunteered to be our guide to see various buildings and institutes of the university, the excellent library, etc.—Drove in his car.

Back at the Conants', a telephone call from Dorothy Thompson. Settled that we would be going next to the Van Loons'.

Left at noon, direct train to Stamford (Pullman car). Great turmoil because Katia's main suitcase was mysteriously left behind. Annoying and disturbing.—Lunch of fish, coffee, and ice cream in the dining car. Then rested in our seats.

Friday, June 28; New York, Algonquin Hotel

Slept until nine, bathed, and breakfasted in the parlor. Telegraphed to Washington that we plan on a 6:30 arrival.

Once more cloudless skies. Very hot.

Katia spent the morning shopping. I stayed in our suite, prepared my suitcase for the flight, washed my hair, and shaved. Read in the New York *Staats-Zeitung* about the tension between England and France as a result of the naval treaty concluded between England and Germany, concerning which Naval Minister Piétri made a sharp speech, and about Mussolini's questionable intentions in Abyssinia, which have been denounced by the British press while the British government takes an ambiguous stand. Europe seems hopelessly demoralized and stupid.

Light lunch at the hotel. Katia bought herself a pretty summer dress.

Washington, Hotel Mayflower

At 3:30 we went by cab with the hotel's manager, Nägel, to the office of the Eastern Air Company, then continued by bus to the airport. Had to wait there, and read the *New York Times*. The big plane took off at five, the first time I was ever in such a thing. Hot. Secretly very nervous at take-off. The air, piped in through ducts, refreshing once aloft. A significant adventure, but not exactly pleasant. Rattling and shuddering. Jerky ascent. Pressure in the ears. Attacks of mild nausea. Looking down left me cold. Read newspapers. Adjusted.

Expected landings in Philadelphia and Baltimore, but there were none. We therefore reached Washington at 6:20 our time (5:20 theirs). We missed Mr. Muto. By taxi to the hotel. Handsome suite with a particularly fine parlor for eight dollars. Fans. Great heat and humidity. The hottest day of the year. There is a heat wave everywhere, by the way, almost catastrophic. Terrible storms in Germany.

Had tea. Then Mr. Muto, whom we had telephoned. He drove us to his little house. Met his wife and his young nephew. The little garden, the furniture. The Mutos drove us about. We saw the remarkably beautiful and dignified city, whose vistas are reminiscent of Paris classicism. We stopped at the Lincoln Memorial and read the solemn inscriptions. The Capitol. The government office buildings. The White House. Had dinner at an elegant hotel with an illuminated terrace. Dance floor, swimming pool, floor show. We stayed until close to midnight. Good pistachio-lemon ice-cream. The Mutos brought us back to the Mayflower. Extremely friendly and helpful.—Flowers from the hotel management. Fantastically hot.

Saturday, June 29; Washington, Hotel Mayflower

Up at eight. Cold shower after my bath, very refreshing. We went out after breakfast, I bought a white linen suit, and we had our hair done. Colored bootblacks.—Muto called for us at the hotel and took us to Congress. Introduced to the old liberal woman representative and to the Speaker. Excited session, liberalism versus dictatorship. Lunch in the House restaurant. Back to the hotel for some rest. Journalist from the *Washington Star.*—Taken by Muto on a drive to Alexandria and then on to the home of George Washington, which we viewed along with its garden. Magnificent site.—Tea at the Mutos', his mother present. Back to the hotel to dress. Then brought by the Mutos to the White House. Black boys and butlers. We waited in a drawing room. Mrs. Roosevelt. In the dining room the President in a wheelchair. Rather ordinary food. Quiet conversation in English. Besides us only a few ladies and a lad in a white dinner jacket. The President, intelligent face, in light-colored trousers and velvet dinner jacket. His conversation marked by energy and self-satisfaction. Scant respect for degenerating democracy and undisciplined overthrow of governments. "Prime Minister *and* President, they can't get me out!" American laughter. Pessimism about Italy. Afterward coffee, then upstairs for a too-long movie. Cigarettes, the incident with the match. Afterward saw his study with marine paintings. Mrs. Roosevelt gave the signal to disband. "Auf Wiedersehen." A tour of the rooms and apartments with the lady of the house.—We later walked to a café, where we drank a beer with great enjoyment.—Tropical heat all day.—Impressed at the beauty of Washington, quite the most imposing capital in the world.

Wednesday, July 10; M.S. "Berengaria"

Yesterday the ship rolled badly. I was affected by it, tired and irritable all day long. Yet it was lovely on the boat deck in the sun, where we had our chairs placed, and the sight of the blue and green waves was splendid.—In the afternoon we went to the cinema and afterward played some shuffleboard. After dinner the gentleman who had sent notes yesterday came to see us in the palm court; I was exhausted. Afterward we drank whiskey and soda with the Jewish businessman we found at the chief steward's.—Annoyed with Katia's vanity when it comes to English conversation. Took half a pill, felt nauseous, and fell asleep promptly without reading.

Much motion during the night. Today sunny and much smoother. Nerves restored by a good night's sleep.

According to the ship's newspaper Mussolini seems bent on war in Abyssinia, and he has broken off negotiations. Doubtless he will strike in the autumn. But it is generally held that he urgently needs these months to be sure of success—insofar as success can be insured. Let us keep in mind that it is a bankrupt nation that is hurling itself into this adventure. Mussolini's fiasco could spell the beginning of the end of the fascist era. But I am sure that Hitler will be all the more "prudent."—In the morning wrote a long letter to Bermann. Then in the tourist-class lounge with our acquaintances from yesterday evening, the group joined by a young half-Japanese and his American wife.

After lunch on the boat deck. Very fine, bright, warmer day. The sea calmer and wonderfully blue in the sun. The ship rolling slowly and only sideways, therefore not bothersome.—Read "The Foolish Pilgrimess."

At teatime a visit from young Broulingham, grandson of the old gentleman we met at Harvard, a most charming young chap who may visit us in Küsnacht.

Monday, July 15

[. . .] Phanodorm, slept late. Another brilliant day. Morning and afternoon devoted to letters. In the evening I excused myself and read through the packet of material Bermann had sent. Strange feeling. Much about the "exemplary" quality of my life that has given pleasure to so many, influenced them, and helped them. Others before me have no doubt had the same response: How they would truly marvel at this life if they only knew it from within!

Lion with us for lunch.

From Katia's mother I learned of the death of Otto Grautoff, my schoolboy chum and confidant during my passion for W. T., later elevated into Pribislav Hippe. For a long time I had given no thought to this pompous man who had come to bore me. But now the death of one who shared those youthful years so rich in sorrow and laughter is chilling and sad. Nevertheless, all I can feel is that he was an adjunct to my life and then wished to be something on his own, boorishly.

Golo arrived late in the evening.

Wednesday, September 4

Thunder and rain. Worked on the Ptach chapter. At 11:30 Dr. Heins arrived, on his way from the Dolomites. Conferred with him about shipping our possessions and the possible sale of the house. Both he and Frau Walter for lunch. Afterward out on the terrace. Tea at 4:30, then the five of us, including Medi, to the Urban Cinema, where we were delighted by some nicely made American films. Back at home, before dinner, a dramatically unexpected phone call from Heins's partner Bumann: on orders from Berlin my property is once more to be confiscated; the application for expatriation is once more under review. Heins very cast down at the news, which accords with my own suppositions and the sense of the situation I had been forming in recent weeks. But I am also disappointed, for the recovery of my possessions would have made me happy. This has now become unlikely (the confiscation may well be carried out by the Bavarian authorities without settlement of the expatriation question), and my greatest wish is that Bermann finally get out of the country so that I can have my independence—though restricted, it is true, as long as my books are permitted into Germany.

Just as Heins and his lady friend were saying good-bye, Eissi left too, bound for Vienna and thence perhaps to Persia.—

Katia rather relieved by the change in the Munich situation, since the arrival of an entire household of furniture and other effects would have been something of an affliction and a minor calamity for her.

Foehn, unseasonably warm. After work I took a walk by myself in the oppressive sunlight. At lunch Dr. Landshoff and Frau M. Wassermann. Discussed her Wassermann biography with her.—Used the afternoon for letters. A young writer from Santiago, Chile, writing in French, tells of my influence on current Chilean literature.—Skimmed through a book by a young German, Waterboer, a fascinating account of medical experiences in the tropics.—The Raschers to dinner with their son Albert. Accepted some of their firm's new publications, a book of selections from Nietzsche and one by Driesch. Very boring evening. Afterward the children compared young Albert Rascher to Klaus Heuser, and decided that the latter had been incomparably more handsome. Thought back on that time and its passion, the last variation of a love that probably will not flare up again. Strange, the happy and fulfilled man of fifty—and then *finis*. Goethe's erotic life continued into his seventies—"always girls." But in my case the inhibitions are probably stronger and so one wearies sooner, apart from the differences in vitality.

After breakfast a conference in my study with Bermann and Katia, with Reisiger sitting in, about the contracts with S. Fischer and the new publishing firm. Afterward some work at my desk. Interrupted by a visit from Klaus Heuser, who had passed through Zurich expressly in order to see me for ten minutes. Unchanged, or little changed; slim, still boyish at twenty-four, the eyes the same. Kept looking into his face and saying "My God!" Curious that I had been thinking of him only a short time ago in this diary with the gratitude for that time that I again felt in his presence. He expected me to kiss him, but I did not do so; I did manage to say something loving to him before he left, however. It was all over in a moment as he had to leave almost at once. I took a walk with Reisiger in the woods. Ida Herz to lunch, unfortunately. Reisiger agreed to come here with me for the weekend. At 3:30 Golo drove with me into town to the Huguenin. Meeting with Dr. Steiner. Then to the Bermanns'. In their car via the Sihl Valley and Zug to Küsnacht and on here. Very warm, clear foehn day. Lovely drive, the Axenstrasse. Tea at the Vitznau Park Hotel. Dinner with the Bermanns and Reisiger here at the Hotel Cerf, jolly, and an evening stroll.— Today Katia attended Medi's official graduation from her preparatory school.

Woke late. Began writing the preface for the Wassermann book. To lunch Privy Councillor Colmers with his Indian-looking son. He is in Zurich for negotiations with refugee placement agencies. The possibility of Baghdad. His wife, without a passport, could not come to Zurich to see her son. This man of my own age looks very drawn. His stories of the terrible pressures to which the Jews in Germany are subjected. Many suicides and strokes, which are hushed up. The systematic throttling and extirpation concealed from the outside world. When will the League of Nations begin to deal with this absurd criminality? But then Paragraph Sixteen could not be applied against rearmament, because its criterion is that rearmament must be "in preparation for war." These quiet atrocities are far more horrible than Mussolini's campaign, which was perhaps forced upon him by necessity. But meddling with the "internal affairs" of a sovereign state is impermissible. We see here the same obtuseness as in the penal code, which sets the highest penalties for acts of murder and homicide, but has nothing to say, contains no paragraph, about crimes against the soul, all the wretched and subtle forms of crime against a human being.

The Ossietzky letter, nicely typed, went off by airmail to Oslo.—Walks.—Katia to the opera with her father.

Sunday, November 3

Misty, fresh. Wrote on, somewhat wearily. Went walking with Katia by way of Johannisburg. Lunch with the five children and Therese Giehse. Drank a cup of coffee topped with whipped cream, which I particularly love. Read Gumpert's new book of physicians' biographies. After tea, at which we had Ida Herz and the rare-book dealer Wolff from Munich, I wrote to Prof. Scharff to ask what the word for seduction would have been in Egyptian, and began a letter to Fiedler. After dinner we listened to some contemporary Swiss music on the radio, some of it dreary stuff, some of it appealing, showing French influences, also Wagnerian ones.—Erika brought us photographs of the Joseph sculpture Elsie Attenhofer has completed; she is continuing to explore the theme, having tried her hand at another statuette as well as a portrait of Rachel.—Read the second half of the "Husband and Wife" chapter to Katia, Therese, Erika, and Medi, with great effect. Overcoming my reluctance, I calculated that the third volume already comprises 594 manuscript pages. I had not realized it, although in three years it could scarcely have come to less. We must now face up to the technical question of publication. Obviously there is so much more to come that *Joseph in Egypt* will have to be in two volumes, and in fact it is clear that the first part ought to end with the love story. I wonder whether we ought finally to accept the idea that successive publication may again be appropriate. It can be argued that the 650 pages before the catastrophe with Mut contain sufficient substance for a single volume that could come out in the spring of 1936 as the first title for Bermann's new publishing house.—A new and exciting prospect.—The photographs please me. The hermaphroditic figure, with its phallus, its one female breast, and a fantastic Oriental physiognomy, has considerable charm.

Saturday, November 9

Erika's thirtieth birthday. Brilliant fall weather. Worked, then went downstairs for the congratulations and gift-giving. At noon went for a walk in the woods with Katia and the birthday child. I was her age when she came into the world in those terrible thirty-six hours. Since then ten years have three times rolled around, years that have constituted "life." But this, our first child, I love with my whole heart, and in my heart I defend her with indignant fury against the stupid hatred she faces back home.— Newspapers after lunch. Letters with troublesome requests (Musil in Switzerland). Abegg has received a noncommittal answer from the Berne legation.—Annemarie Schwarzenbach to tea. Handwritten letters. Tired from yesterday.—Short stroll.—At dinner, along with the five children and Therese Giehse, Annemarie (wearing slacks) and little Sibylle Schloss. Champagne. Toasts to Erika. Afterward music and talk. Tired.

Up before eight. Lovely weather. After work I walked the forest path in the other direction with Katia and the dogs. Lunch with Annemarie Schwarzenbach and also Ida Herz, who brought roses and to whom I gave a copy of the Swedish edition of *Joseph* and the Dutch school anthology. Friends of Erika's to tea. Inscribed books for the bookseller couple in Winterthur, wrote a letter to Platzer, and spent the time until dinner dictating—responding, among other things, to the offer of Czech citizenship. Declined invitations to go to Brussels and to write an introduction for a book of Musil's. After dinner listened to some Saint-Saëns on the radio. This was the last meal with Golo for a time since he is leaving for Rennes. He stocked up on various books of mine on art and literary history.—Read in Eckstein's book, the chapter about Hugo Wolf.—Condolences to Mme. Goll.—Angered over the Germanic blood humbug of the writer Burte, who pleads for understanding for Germany's "Renaissance." It is too idiotic. Name me anything in or about Germany that a writer might rightfully experience and refer to as a "Renaissance."

The day began warm and misty, then turned bright. Worked more sluggishly. Followed the long woodsy road alone with Toby, and in the mild air sat on the bench from which one has a view of Itschnach and the (mist-shrouded) lake.—Coffee after lunch. A nice letter from a young Rumanian, a student in Munich, who is indebted to my books for the "best and most profound hours" of his life.—Report from Hartung about depositions from Einstein and Medicus backing up my efforts in Oslo.—Letter from Reisiger.—Thanks from Winterthur.—Read a bit in Hofmannsthal's letters.—After tea with Katia to the Bellevue Cinema, an overlong and dreary program of short subjects, during which I felt ill and sensed the onset of a feverish cold. I felt better once the feature started, a very good American thriller called *The Mummy*.—Picked up Erika and took her home. She had some interesting news from the *National-Zeitung*. According to their report Bermann has indeed sold out to the Bibliographical Institute for 800,000 marks, and has transferred himself *and* the firm, including the works of several of its principal authors (Hesse, myself, Annette Kolb, et al.) to Vienna—as have two other publishing houses, Piper and Hegner. Such a turn of events would be welcome for me.—The London correspondent of the *Völkischer Beobachter* has been expelled because of an attack on Churchill. Good.—There is other news, but what I dread more than the Saar plebiscite, or anything else that has served the purposes of Nazi propaganda so far, are the Olympic Games, the winter portion of which is to begin in January in Garmisch and threatens to become a vast advertisement of the Third Reich. If only their wretched and cynical lie of bringing peace and friendship to the world could be exposed! I often give thought to an article for the world press that would reply to the shameless Zurich speech by Lewald.—After dinner listened to a Serkin broadcast from Berne: the Schumann Concerto and a Beethoven sonata.

Up at eight. Cold. Worked. Walked in the sun by way of Johannisburg with Katia. Ida Herz with us at lunch; she needs a letter in support of her application for a visitor's and working permit.—Newspapers, the *Tage-Buch*. Dictated countless letters after tea, especially one to Heinrich, who is coming to Geneva on the twenty-sixth, countering his wish that I might meet him there with an invitation to him to come here instead.— Went down to the station with Katia to post letters.—Klaus unwell, morphine reaction. Dr. Stahel saw him, but naturally he could only deal with the deprivation symptoms by giving him a shot. Klaus believes he is capable of maintaining control over the drug, achieving a balance between voluntary withdrawal and occasional use. His fit of crying may well have caused him to see his mistake. Nevertheless he does not have a desire to stop using it altogether, as evidenced by his intention to have a consultation with Dr. Katzenstein.—Annemarie Schwarzenbach confesses that for a long time she has not had the slightest enjoyment from the drug, but only feels impossibly bad if she does *not* take it. This stage apparently reached quite quickly.

1936

Woke late, but since Golo and Reisiger came down even later I breakfasted alone with Katia. Installed the new calendar. The year that now begins has a 29th of February. Not that anyone expects anything better from it; Basler, for instance, in the note accompanying his gift of cigars and cigarettes, predicted that in the year 1940 I will be "standing at the Zurich train station, and in a tremulous voice simply begging for a ticket back to Munich."—Meager amount of work. Walked with Katia and Reisiger in the woods, enjoying the freshness of the air.—After lunch I read in the living room New Year's greetings from various people, including Pinkus and Wittkowski.—Upset at reading an amorous card to Klaus from Paris that I opened by mistake. Still overly sensitive about such things.—Reisiger's admiration for what I read yesterday very great. All during the walk he kept speaking of it with enthusiasm. I will be satisfied if this year brings the third *Joseph* volume and the Goethe novella to an end.—Handwritten correspondence, thank-you notes. Short stroll in the evening. Dr. Feist to dinner. Music afterward.

Up betimes. Dark and damp, perceptible foehn, unproductive efforts at work. Walked with Reisiger. To tea Dr. Feist and his lady friend, the armaments industrialist. Afterward handwritten correspondence. Letter to Annette Kolb. After dinner the *Tannhäuser* recordings. Then I read from the love story to Katia, Reisiger, and the children. Merriment, in which I joined, over Dûdu. My reading interrupted by a phone call from Erika, who was passing through on her way to Berne and waiting in the Tessin Room of the Carlton Elite in Zurich. All five of us drove there to see her and found her recovered. Talk and refreshments. Katia took Erika to the station to catch her train shortly before midnight, while we waited in the bar.—Today the mail brought the first sixty pages of the corrected galleys of *Joseph in Egypt*, identified on the sheets only as "the new work."

Woke late. A dark day. But worked with inspiration. Walked in the raw air and mist with Katia and Reisiger. After lunch newspapers. Things not looking bad on the political front: Ramsay MacDonald's protest against the German nonsense, Roosevelt's pronouncement against the dictatorships, and the open collaboration of England and France are gratifying developments.—In the afternoon dictated letters; one to Feist with a carbon of my letter of two years ago to Frick so as to give him the needed information for his forthcoming efforts.—More proofs.—At 7:30 a snack, then with Katia and Moni to the Bellevue Cinema, where we met Reisiger. Anglo-American women's film, largely *dégoûtant* although the photography was excellent. The only sensible character a young Indian.—Back home, supper with champagne to mark Reisiger's departure.

Woke late. Damp and icy, cold-catching weather. Katia and Medi down with sniffles. Worked on the "Chastity" chapter. At noon to Dr. Asper; replaced a crown and treated a sensitive molar. Walked to the Café Odeon, where Reisiger was waiting. Vermouth. Then joined by Katia, who drove us back home. Last lunch with Reisiger, with whom I then sat in the living room discussing various personal and political topics: the question whether the situation in Germany has reached a point where one could hasten developments by appealing to decent people to take concerted action. . . . Later traded ideas and insights for a Nietzsche essay. Reisiger left at 3:30, Katia driving him into Zurich. Sadness at losing this pleasant house companion, although at the time I was annoyed at his coming. But once again it is clear that he makes me more cheerful, more expansive, personally more productive and affable.—Rested. After tea wrote to Heinrich, Wittkowski, and Basler. Evening walk. Later in the evening in my study read the *Neue Rundschau* and a new volume of Gide. He writes during the war: "While the best intellects in France, all the intellects in France, work and struggle along with France—the best intellects in Germany rise up against those Prussian elements that push Germany into war." It will always be that way; for all their totalitarian measures, the Nazis cannot change that. That *I* tried, in my *Betrachtungen*, to throw my support behind Prussianism, will remain a strange misunderstanding, a paradox.

Up at 8:30. Overcast, mild, but toward noon the skies cleared and by evening it was colder. After bath and breakfast I worked on the manuscript: the motifs of the Syrian costume and Atum-Rê have to be woven into "The Second Year."—Toward noon to the ski slopes. With Katia to Maran, where we drank our customary vermouth.— Approving telegram from Annette Kolb.—After lunch, read proofs on the loggia and rested. Am not dissatisfied as I read it.—Afternoon walk and tea at the Old India.— Nice review of the Basel evening in the *Basler Nachrichten.*—To Fischer's production department: they should wait with the page proofs until the text has been divided into sections or books. Communicated my decision to call this volume (on Lion's advice) *Joseph in Egypt.* Have already established that the fourth volume will be *Joseph the Provider.*—Read proofs; also again after dinner in the salon, where Lion came to sit with me and began reading too. Was less satisfied today. The section between Menfe and the arrival at Peteprê's is probably the least comic one of the volume.— Remarkable article in the *Neue Zürcher Zeitung* on Sorel's study on violence. Interesting that he should have anticipated many elements of fascism, for instance the idea of the "mythos," the political fiction that captivates the masses though flying in the face of truth and common sense: Vittorio Veneto, Schlageter, Horst Wessel, *The Elders of Zion.*—A revolting article from the *Berliner Tageblatt* that Lion showed me maintains that the "Nietzschean Manes" are by no means in exile today, but have remained in Germany. It goes on to say that there are only surface differences between Nietzsche and National Socialism—the latter can lay rightful claim to him.—This should rather be said about Sorel. But Nietzsche, who stood for utmost "intellectual rectitude," for the Dionysian will to know, who smiled at *Faust* for being a "tragedy of knowledge" because he knew better, who was ready to endure every suffering caused by the truth and for the sake of truth—this man they want to claim in connection with myths of action of a mass appeal roughly of the level of the most degenerate popular dirty songs. What filth.—Bergson, Sorel, Péguy are the real spiritual forerunners of fascism. It was they who distorted socialism into nationalism. What, then, is "German" about it?

Monday, January 27; Küsnacht (evening)

This morning we got up in Arosa at 8:30, and, after a breakfast that tasted delicious, evidently because yesterday's champagne had strengthened my vital spirits, I wrote further on the new chapter. Then packed. Took a short stroll with Katia. The weather had turned lovely, clear, and warm as spring. Had lunch in the usual room off the main dining room. Tipped the waiters and chatted with the Kahlers and Brentanos in the lobby. Said good-bye to the latter, also to Dr. Richter, Wolfgang Born, etc. Walked in the considerable heat to the station, where the Kahlers joined us. He gave me the Brockhaus illustrated dictionary. They stayed until the train left. Coffee in Chur. Then continued the journey in gray, damp air and rain. Read a bit of Gwinner's *Schopenhauer.* Arrived in Zurich after six. Medi at the station. Doll drove us home. The household poorer by one member: Mouche, very sick, infected, enfeebled with age (toward the end she could not even keep down egg and cognac), her little face quite shrunken and equine, was put to sleep, Bibi in attendance, and fetched in a little wagon.—Toby gave us a hearty welcome.—Medi confused because of the conflict with Erika, whom she greatly fears and respects.—I plan an open letter to Korrodi; Katia sketched out a rough draft for it this morning.—Tea on arrival.—Finished unpacking by dinner time. Afterward made order in my study, arranging books, manuscripts, letters, etc. Some music once again and news broadcasts. So life can again proceed normally. Hoping and striving for the mood and inspiration needed to see me through the final part of the book.

Monday, February 3

In the morning went on with Section VII. At noon went out with the dog to meet Katia on the road, and we walked as far as Itschnach in the crisper weather that later turned rainy and snowy.—After lunch, newspapers (great diplomatic flurry, much putting together of heads out of concern over the Third Reich).—Read proofs: the "Mont-kaw" chapter is the finest in the book.—After tea dictated letters. In the interval the evening paper, which already carries my letter.

More dictation of letters, especially one to Knopf in connection with the collected stories, for which I am suggesting the title "A Life in Stories." Must write an introduction for it. Asked his advice on the possibility of acquiring American citizenship.— To Dr. Meng concerning the Freud committee.—Some stir resulting from the article, which the editors provided with a superfluous prefatory comment. Telephone calls from Dr. Wahl in Berlin, Beidler, the Fleiners. While I was out taking the air a call came from Behrens, the editor from the Basel *National-Zeitung*: much excitement there, this is the most important thing in a long time.—The sense that I have struck a body blow against the wretched regime fills me with satisfaction. It will try to take whatever revenge it can. Let it.

Freezing. Continued with Section VII, not feeling very well and doing without my cigar.—A new heap of respectful letters from acquaintances and strangers, also an ugly anonymous one in the tones of the National Front, expressing the vile depths to which the world will perhaps descend and from which only communism can save it.—With Katia into town to Dr. Ulrich, who treated my eczema and also had something to say about my letter. The Swiss seem mostly gratified by the way I took care of Korrodi.—Bought a good woolen vest and gloves at London House. Picked up Frau Hallgarten at Hirzel's villa and brought her to our house for lunch. Coffee with her in the living room.—After tea dictated the greater part of the introduction for the American collected stories. Meanwhile another batch of congratulatory letters came in, including one from Bruno Frank, not very well framed, and another from Hesse, who basically regrets my having taken this step because he foresees himself being published alone now in Germany, and also because he thinks I was blackmailed into doing it by the emigrés.—Klaus wrote a nice letter. Among the letters were long testimonials of gratitude from victims, largely, of course, from Jews.—In the evening with Katia and Medi to the small concert hall at the Tonhalle for a piano recital by Dorothea Braus: Schumann, Mozart, Beethoven, Liszt. Well done but dry. With her in the greenroom. Numerous acquaintances, among them Moellendorf, Schuh, Kahler, Braunfels, Goetz, Diebold.—Supper at home.

Freezing night, clear wintry day. Slept badly under the stress of politics. Wrote further on the love scene. After shaving I walked for an hour and a quarter, then had lunch with the children. Had coffee with whipped cream. Looked through the corrected proofs and read in Brentano's novel, which I think well of. After tea wrote letters to Emil Ludwig and Max Mohr. Took an evening walk from 7:30 to 8:30 and waited for the ladies, whose train was so late that they did not get in until after 9:00, bringing newspapers that utterly absorbed me. All my agitation over the brazen coup came flooding back. Gathering of the French Ministry heads with the chief of the general staff present. Rejection of the "memorandum" as unacceptable. Appeal to the League of Nations. Troop movements along the border in response to the long-prepared march of German troops into the cities in the demilitarized zone. Outrage on the part of the hoodwinked François-Poncet, who seems to want to leave Berlin. But England remains silent, and Italy, of which one felt so sure, backs Germany, so that France appears to stand alone and indeed contemplates no single-handed action. No question now but that the German troops will remain in the Rhineland, or that the plebiscite, under the slogan of "equal rights" and peace, will spell a victory for the regime. The *Neue Zürcher Zeitung* quite hostile toward Germany and her practice of politics by fait accompli.—Headache, extremely tired. Reading *Anthony and Cleopatra* before falling asleep.

Very fine, clear, pre-spring day. Erika and Therese Giehse left this morning while I was working, driving to Metz, where it is hoped they will not run into military difficulties. Katia and I took an hour-and-a-half walk through the gorge with Toby, who had a wonderful time. The Newfoundland Tilly also tagged along.—The political news for the moment favorable, especially word from Italy that it is ceasing hostilities in Africa and has issued statements backing France. At five drove with Katia to the Urban Cinema, where we saw a moderately good *Anna Karenina* with Greta Garbo. Perturbed and in acute suspense regarding political developments. If only the governments of the West and the South could just this once pull themselves together and stand fast against this hysterical brutality that plays so brazenly on the world's desire for peace, and wants to be taken back into the community of nations after a cynical breach of treaty! If only they would just once let it come to a showdown and allow things to move to the brink of war! There would be no war; instead the regime would fall. That is my devout prayer.—But there have been denials of the news from Italy, and samples from the English press manifest an apathy that is truly wretched after all the commotion over Abyssinia. It is hopeless. The wretch will again carry off his coup, and we may just as well bury our hopes.—Listened to the news broadcast. Eden's statement to the House of Commons very "reassuring" and moderate. Should a confrontation between France and Germany really take place, England would support France in line with the terms of the broken pact. In general every effort must be made to promote peace, making use of every possibility, and one must act not as a judge but as a statesman. This was not how he spoke in the case of Italy. Italy declares moreover that it has little interest in the pact, but great interest in proposals to reform the League of Nations.—What can France do in such a fix? What assurances will she be given? Sarraut and Flandin have pronounced the "memorandum" unacceptable, remilitarization intolerable. Troops are being massed along the northern and eastern borders; Alsace is said to look already as though the war had broken out. But if France is left in the lurch it can do nothing. Sanctions? But these cannot reverse the breach of the treaty. "The German people would endure any suffering, make any sacrifice . . . rather than lose its honor." What can poor France do against this sort of heroic blustering? Will she put up with Germany's being readmitted into the League of Nations even though it broke the pact? That is what England is pressing for.—Great pain and depression. Too wrought up to read, but I do manage to think about the novel.

Worked on the final part of the chapter; the dwarfs, philological studies. Walked with Katia by way of Johannisburg. Cold, overcast.—The political tension continues. Read the newspapers with great intensity. Haunted by the idea of sending a letter to the London *Times*. But shall not write one. The world does not want to take instructions from "spiteful emigrés." Why burn one's fingers over this? In recent days I answered many an inquiry in this vein.—Dictated numerous letters in the afternoon. Portions of the novel sent to *Litterära Magasin*. *A Sketch of My Life* to Prague as a suggestion for a proposed deluxe edition. The birthday greeting to Heinrich for the *Neue Weltbühne.*—To dinner Frau von Kahler and Tennenbaum. Brentano sent his novel, for which I thanked him by telephone.

⋯⋯⋯⋯⋯⋯⋯⋯⋯⋯⋯⋯⋯
Monday, March 16
⋯⋯⋯⋯⋯⋯⋯⋯⋯⋯⋯⋯⋯

Snow flurries in the morning. Did more on the little dwarf postlude. Forty-five-minute walk; cold.—The *Historical Survey of German Literature* by Sol Liptzin came. In the chapter on the "most representative novelist of twentieth-century Germany" it is *The Magic Mountain,* as always in America, that is stressed above all else: "a satire of human society of such devastating character that it may best be compared to Swift's satire on man."

In the afternoon wrote a page for Oprecht about Brentano's book.—Heinrich informs me that Querido cannot publish his book of essays because he would be risking imprisonment. We should try Oprecht. Heinrich sent the galleys and I read some in them. Some pieces of remarkable brilliance in the collection, which will one day no doubt be historic, but side by side with embarrassingly inferior stuff. The invective at times so blunt and crude that Oprecht will probably have to reject it as well.—At 7:30 with Katia to the Zurich station to meet the old folks, who appear to be fresh and spry enough, though with no notion of what has been happening and scarcely ruffled by events. A late supper. Afterward in the living room. Listened to news from Vienna: in London the German response is being interpreted as tantamount to a refusal, and they have replied in this spirit. Thus there will not be a German representative in attendance. What else can the League do but endorse France's motion for sanctions? But I envision a solemn appeal addressed by the League of Nations to Germany and to the world, one that not even the Germans could ignore, in which things would be called by their proper names, responsibility firmly assigned, and the social conscience awakened.

⋯⋯⋯⋯⋯⋯⋯⋯⋯⋯⋯⋯⋯
Thursday, April 9 (Maundy Thursday)
⋯⋯⋯⋯⋯⋯⋯⋯⋯⋯⋯⋯⋯

Bermann with us for breakfast. He had very favorable things to say about Vienna. In view of the remarkable cordiality shown by the chancellor, it would seem almost impossibly awkward for him to back away from the plan to move there.—Any day now we can expect that my books will be formally banned in Germany.—The merger with Heinemann is off, apparently for political reasons.

Distracted and depressed, unable to work; began a letter about Leonhard Frank's *Dream Mates.*—A short walk with Katia in milder weather.—The French memorandum strongest at the beginning, where they refute the German accusations. They are again taking up Briand's organizational suggestions, a propagandistic device, since that is the only way now.—Franz Werfel and his wife to tea, along with Prof. Hollnsteiner. They are by no means as alert to the question of Austrian security as Bermann thought. Much discussion of Hitler, Vienna, and Schuschnigg. We sent off a card to the latter. Chatted in the living room, out on the terrace, and in my study. Explained that we were postponing our decision because of present conditions here.—In the evening with Katia, Golo, and the children to hear the *Missa Solemnis.* Wore my new, comfortable evening clothes for the first time. Great beauty of the Sanctus; the rest inaccessible.

The tenor part sung by Julius Patzak of Munich.—Supper at home. Letter and copy of the *Meister* to Antonio Aita in Buenos Aires.

Friday, May 1

Worked on the lecture, approaching the end. Bredel wants it for the Moscow *Wort.*— Oprecht passed along something he had been told by a Jew who had served as a Nazi agent: the Nazis are hoping to disrupt or even to totally prevent my reading in Budapest.—Knopf and Brandt report that the Book-of-the-Month Club has taken 60,000 copies of *Stories of Three Decades*, which will yield me three thousand dollars.— Bermann came shortly before one o'clock, and we withdrew to my study to talk about the situation, without arriving at any new business arrangements. It seems that my books are still being permitted in Germany after all, so long as publicity for them remains discreet.—Typescript of the first half of the lecture delivered by Frau Lind; a good job. Read it through in the afternoon and did some more writing on it. Early supper, in the course of which Katia and I had some sharp words because I had not backed her up sufficiently during our discussion with Bermann.—With Katia to the Corso; many outstanding acts: the Hungarian acrobats, the amazing trained seal, an uncanny sword and flame-swallower, and above all the highly original American harmonica player, a sensitive musician and good comedian.—Listless, slack, sick at heart. Katia's charge that I treat her disrespectfully pains me.

Wednesday, May 13

I am writing this in the morning on the train from Prague to Vienna, after breakfast in the dining car.

The whole week too hectic for making notes. It started with the morning arrival in Vienna. Greeted by the Bermanns. The Hotel Imperial. A gathering at noon at Trebitsch's. Spent the evening of Thursday, the 7th, with the Walters; the opera *Der Corregidor*, afterward in a café. On Friday, the 8th, a luncheon affair at Alma Mahler-Werfel's, with the Walters, Hollnsteiner, et al. In the afternoon an audience with Schuschnigg. In the evening the tumultuous success of the Freud lecture in the packed hall of the Konzerthaus. That morning a visit to Freud's apartment, bringing him the portfolio and the manuscript; deeply moving impressions. After the lecture a banquet at the Imperial, I seated between Freud's son and daughter. On Saturday, the 9th, to Brno. Uncomfortable quarters in the provincial Grand Hotel. Gave the lecture to an audience of 800 speaking with a microphone. This followed by a reception attended by Thomas Theodor Heine, Oskar Maria Graf, Arne Novak, and his nephew, the chief rabbi. Sunday, the 10th, on to Prague. Met at the station. Hotel Esplanade. Luncheon at the Frankls'. Spoke on the radio in the afternoon. In the evening heard *Boccaccio* with pleasure at the Deutsches Theater. Monday, the 11th, the two of us to luncheon at the Hradschin with President Beneš and his wife. We talked in his office until 3:30. In the evening the lecture in the film room of the Urania, to a full house. Afterward a party in the Deutsches Haus. Speeches. Yesterday, Tuesday, the 12th, made a morning visit to the exhibition of paintings by the girl prodigy from Innsbruck.

Luncheon with Mimi Mann. Had guests to tea at the hotel: Czech-German theater people, Milka Pringsheim, Dr. Seidl, Emil Faktor. In the evening a repeat of the lecture in the small hall, once more filled to capacity. The writer Kurt Hiller's fainting spell. Afterward a reception at Dr. Eisner's (Čapek, the abbot, et al.). This morning we left after eight, with farewells at the station from the Frankls, Frau Eisner, Fucik. All these sojourns marked by numerous conversations, visits, the usual interviews.

In the meantime Oswald Spengler has died—mourned by the German press with ten lines on page seven. In Vienna negotiations between Schuschnigg and the Starhemberg people. We had a look at apartments and houses. There was one on Kobenzlstrasse in Grinzing that attracted us greatly. We were urged to settle in Prague also, where the political atmosphere is naturally more to our liking. The result of our vacillation is that we will remain in Switzerland—probably a sensible decision.—Beneš spoke optimistically, not only of English policy toward Germany (which we were glad to hear, for it made sense) but also of the Sudeten Germans, whose "loyalty" tactics he appears to accept. According to him, the agitation for an Anschluss was not coming from outside. He assured us there was no love lost between the Konrad Henlein people and the Sudeten representative in the Reichstag. All this is not very credible, and shows little understanding of the spirit of nazism. I remarked that the Nazis knew only two principles: lies and terror. He replied that he had been under the impression they had no principles at all, which is also nice to hear.—

Have crossed the border, our papers and luggage have been checked. Read in the *Neue Rundschau* a piece by Norbert Jacques on his travels in the Sudan.

· ·

Tuesday, July 21

· ·

Raining. We postponed the trip to the Engadin. Preparations for the final chapter. With Katia into town for pedicure and a visit with the Beidlers, where we had a look at the young white tomcat intended for us. Received a book, *Der hörende Mensch*, by Hans Kayser.—Golo had lunch with the two of us. Afterward newspapers and Turel's book.—The Budapest graphic artist Julius Conrad, who had written to me on my sixtieth birthday, sent two handsome plates in reply to my belated thanks, scenes from Hungarian folk life. This afternoon Katia brought Octave Aubry's *Napoleon on St. Helena* from town, as I have wanted to read it.—After tea wrote to Broch, Conrad, Amann, et al. After supper listened to the news: it would seem, both from the radio bulletins and the newspapers, that the Spanish Republican forces are on the point of quashing the uprising of the reactionaries—much to the disappointment of such organs of the bourgeois world press as the *Neue Zürcher Zeitung*, which would rather see the triumph of blackest reaction than the success of any Popular Front. The rebel generals describe their movement as "purely national, directed against Marxism, freemasonry, and everything international." All too clear! Nevertheless we must not underestimate the allure such a noble program will have in the world.—Read "The Bitch" to Katia and Golo, and the conversation afterward made me eager to go on to the tales of the fourth volume. This third one is indubitably rich in curious things and sophisticated humor. Criticism of it will not mean much, since the final volume is still needed to complete the picture. The only weak point in the third volume is the "Talk by Night," but I did not know how to improve on it and can only hope that it will "slip by."—Thoughts on holding art up to mockery, breaking out of it, dissolving it—all the while remaining absolutely and ruthlessly devoted to it. Nietzsche's comment may well be pertinent here: "Changed already have I seen the poets, and their glance turned against themselves. Penitents of the spirit I saw come, the issue of poets." (*Zarathustra*)

Saturday, August 1

Damp. Rainy. Cold. A beastly summer. Up at eight. Felt better than yesterday and worked better. Went for a walk through the woods with Katia, then picked up by car. After lunch newspapers. Napped. After tea dictated the letter to Koltzow about Erich Mühsam's widow, and some others. Before supper with Katia to the station to mail them. In the evening read an article in the *Neue Rundschau* on Spengler, who pursued the philosophy of history *sub specie mortis*. Long ago I called him a hyena of history, and truly his animal equivalent is more the hyena than the lion. The topsy-turvy romanticism (no less foolish for being topsy-turvy) of his beast of prey anthropology. What made him so hateful to me (after first being dazzled by his *chef d'oeuvre*) was precisely the certain kinship between our origins and spiritual inclinations. He too had drawn his concept of "decline" principally from Nietzsche—what concerned him most was the decline of his cultural organism—and I vividly recall how frequently his *Decline of the West* was linked with *Buddenbrooks* when it first came out. What this critic has to say about his wrong-headed contempt for human freedom I also said in my essay "On the Teachings of Spengler." He died young, in bitterness and sorrow I should think. But he did terrible things toward paving the way for what was to come, and early sounded the notes that deafen us today.

Swiss national holiday. Cannonades, rockets, fireworks.

Thursday, August 13

Overcast and rather warm, no rain. Worked on the next-to-last section until noon. Went walking with Katia past the villas and back through the woods. After having lunch and looking through the newspapers, turned to the novel by Sinclair Lewis, which I began yesterday and find quite amusing. Napped in the afternoon, and after tea worked again on the chapter, bringing on a headache. Went out with Katia for another short stroll. At dinner discussed with the boys the fact that basically all the higher and better minds the world over find fascism abhorrent, and that no revolution or world movement thus condemned by the intellect can be genuine or historically meaningful. Or has the world changed in this regard, so that there is now some dynamic force other than the mind, over which the mind and its critical intelligence have not the slightest influence? Is it obsolete idealism to hold that this cannot be so?—The two half-grown kittens we have just acquired, named Pizzi and Cato, are extremely comical with each other. Relations between the white one and Toby still very tense, a racial problem.—The position of the *Neue Zürcher Zeitung* with regard to Spain and France is absolutely monstrous; the hatred of this segment of the press for the Popular Front is so stupid and revolting that one is astounded at such baseness. The arrival of German bombers in Spain for use by the rebels is reported with perfect composure. A protest against this by the French Leftists is called "dangerous intervention." The Spanish people are fighting for their freedom themselves, while the so-called Nationalists have brought in Moorish battalions from Morocco and Foreign Legionnaires. Foreign planes bomb the Republican strongholds, but no indignation is felt at such a crime so long as the interests of world capitalism are safeguarded. What a swindle everything that calls itself patriotism now is. The Fascists within every nation are prepared at any moment to denounce their government, if it is leftist, in favor of their foreign ideological partners, and to stab it in the back. They operate as they please, thanks to political freedom. Once the power is in their hands they will take care that the same thing does not happen to them. So what other choice is there but a dictatorship of the Left? Democracy can function only if everyone is a democrat, otherwise it is soon destroyed. Back in Budapest I hit on the right formulation when I referred to a "militant humanism"—I was surprised at the thunderous applause.—It is evident that freedom of the press is no longer possible. Liberalism as a political principle is truly dead—we did not even need to have the Fascists to teach us that much. As early as the beginning of the twenties I wrote that the best form of government would be an enlightened dictatorship.—Listened to some music in the evening, and continued reading the Sinclair Lewis novel.

. . . .
Friday, August 14
. . . .

Fair weather, still crisp. Up early, and pushed ahead with the next-to-last section. At noon into town to see Prof. Ulrich, who is leaving on vacation for Norway. Then drove with Katia to the Uetliberg, where we climbed a short way up the extremely well-maintained steep footpath. Afterward we had a vermouth in the restaurant below. Then to the Paradeplatz to meet Wolfgang Hallgarten. With him to pick up his mother at the Hirzels'. The whole family came outside with her. Complimented the singer on "his" *Parsifal.* Luncheon with the Hallgartens, with coffee out on the terrace. Later the newspapers and the *Weltbühne*, which carries a good article by Budzislawski and one by Heinrich on the Nazis' "correctional system," written in his usual over-wrought manner. After tea handwritten letters to Ida Herz in Geneva in connection with the Comité pour le Placement etc. and a progress report to which I am to append a few words. Also to a Jewish gentleman in Zurich who sent me a clipping from the *Jüdische Rundschau*, reprinting an item from the *Essener Nationalzeitung* concerning the stupidities in Bucharest. The level of the Nazi press remains unchanged. "Prime Minister" Goering's newspaper offers up these brazen lies without a trace of embarrassment. And how the curs back each other up throughout Europe, representing one and the same international spirit: a Rumanian Fascist rag first prints the filth; a Czech Henlein-paper picks it up; the German Party press cannot wait to lay hands on it. And then the Zionists come along—perhaps only to expose the perfidy, perhaps also to curry favor. Personal experiences such as this are an object lesson on how fascism is undermining Europe.

At seven went out for a while with Katia. After supper tried unsuccessfully to hear the broadcast of the Salzburg production of *Die Meistersinger* under Toscanini, which was to be relayed from Warsaw.

Yesterday I was too tired by evening to open this notebook, since I had gone on working in the afternoon, and then Erich von Kahler was with us for dinner as well as Erika and Therese Giehse, who just arrived from Salzburg.

This morning I *finished "Joseph in Egypt"*—a momentous date when I consider that this project has been with me for three whole years and nearly six months, ever since we left Munich. I resumed work on it in Bandol, which I shall probably revisit on the upcoming trip. *Voyage with Don Quixote* and the essay on Freud have been the two principal side projects since then. There has been no dearth of distractions and long interruptions, foremost among them the two trips to America and the abandoned attempt at a political clarification. Provided I enjoy decent health, the fourth and last volume, in length more on the order of the second, should go more rapidly.—

Fair weather. At noon a walk with Katia and Erika. After lunch, coffee on the terrace. Then continued to read the Sinclair Lewis, which is only too horribly true to life and therefore very powerful.—Letter from Heer about the reading in Ermatingen.

Festive dinner with champagne and a torte, at which Medi lovably recited a comical poem of Erika's. Afterward a solemn reading of the end of the "Empty House" section, my audience consisting of Katia, Erika, Therese Giehse, Golo, and the two youngest. The ending and the figure of Potiphar especially effective. Enjoyable conversation over punch and torte until after midnight.

Thursday, November 19

Pleasant weather, mild, probably foreshadowing foehn. Tired. Made little progress. At noon Lion, who came along on my walk. I told him about the novella, the idea of which he applauded. He stayed to luncheon. Coffee afterward. Then with Katia and the youngest children to the Czech consulate, where I was formally naturalized as a Czech citizen. Strange event.—To tea the Rhenish literary historian from Berne who intends to write a book about me. Talked with him in my study, gave some directives.—Very tired. In the evening finished Giraudoux's *Tiger at the Gates*. Many well-said things and bon mots.

Thursday, December 3

Very dark and damp. Worked by electric light. Finished the first chapter of the novella. Spoke by telephone in the meantime with Bermann, who now agrees to my publicizing my Czech citizenship. Took a solitary walk in the gloom. A message of thanks from the American secretary of state, sent through the local consulate. After lunch read Goethe's *Urfaust*. Called the secretary of the Czech consulate about the press release. Wrote a short letter to the Reich Ministry of the Interior, in which I placed responsibility for the [step] "in the eyes of contemporary society and posterity" squarely on the present German government.—After tea a letter to Ida Herz. Began a letter to Klaus about his *Mephisto*. In the evening with Katia and Medi (the latter driving) to the Schauspielhaus. Gorky's *Lower Depths*, a good production, fine play, full of the lofty humanitarianism of Naturalism. My own native element, my own era. It was greater and better, of that there can be no question.—During the intermission we were with the Oprechts in the theater restaurant, where Kahler joined us. Supper at home.

Friday, December 25, First Day of Christmas

Up at 8:30. Below freezing, partly bright, partly misty day. Stollen for breakfast with Katia and Reisiger. Worked on the novella. Walked in the woods with Katia, Medi, and Reisiger. Lion with us for lunch. Coffee in the sitting room. Discussion of the Kafkaesque elements in Green. The crisis of the novel, illustrated by *The Counterfeiters, Ulysses,* and *The Magic Mountain.*—Poster from Kugel for the reading on January 14, the first printed appearance of the novella's title.—I almost forgot: a communication from the faculty of Bonn University, withdrawing my honorary doctorate in view of my loss of citizenship. Considering how I might answer.—After tea dictated letters and wrote cards relating to the trip. In the evening listened to recordings of the first act of *Die Walküre.* Astounding economy, tightly structured, intense. Along with this, atrociously German elements that live on in the "sacred destiny" of today.

Wednesday, December 30

Spent the morning writing to the dean of Bonn University. At noon an hour's walk with Reisiger in very warm sunlight. After lunch, read aloud a long letter from Hermann Broch, typical of the situation, dealing with a plan for reconstituting the League of Nations.—Letter from Dr. Walter Berendsohn in Lyngby concerning a Paris conference of intellectuals in exile.—Letter from Rabener.—Package of books and a long letter from Dr. Friedrich Muckle, a one-time believer in National Socialism now living in Switzerland, who is in despair and wishes to visit me. . . . His book on Goethe is lying on my table, and next to it is an issue of the Russian *Internationale Literatur* with a long essay about me. Symbolic.—After coffee I finished my letter to the dean in pencil. After tea I dictated the introduction to the catalogue for a Viennese exhibition of Max Liebermann, basing it on the piece in *Die Forderung des Tages.*

Handwritten letters.—Kahler and Hirschfeld came to dinner. After coffee we withdrew to my study, where Kahler read for an hour and a half from the Prussian section of his fine book, one of a high level. I then read my letter to the dean, which aroused great emotion. They strongly approved the idea of having it published as a pamphlet by Oprecht. Lively discussion.

Thursday, December 31

Up at 8:30. Mild weather. Resumed work on the novella. At noon with Katia into town to the studio of the sculptor Magg, where we met Reisiger. Fine work. Expressive large piece, *Jacob Wrestling with the Angel,* only blocked out.—With Reisiger walked to the Zürichhorn, where we had a vermouth at Bettini's. Katia came to fetch us.—Golo copied the letter to the dean.—Much mail, long letters: from Kerényi, Korrodi, Prof. Marck, Fleischmann, et al. Ida Herz wrote some interesting things about the growing anti-German feeling in the British press.—Called Dr. Oprecht to

arrange a meeting. After tea to his office on Rämistrasse. Read aloud the exchange
of letters, with Katia and Frau Oprecht present. The Oprechts very deeply stirred.
Discussed its publication, including the financial aspects. The publisher visibly gratified
at this opportunity.—Drove home with Katia. Revisions in the copy for the dean.—
Schweizer Monatshefte with a review of the third volume of *Joseph.*—Dinner with
Reisiger. Afterward punch and crêpes by the candlelit tree. Music. An emotional and
merry evening until midnight. Pealing of bells. The children went out again, as did
the maids and their boyfriends.

1937

In spite of having gotten to sleep late I awoke at eight. Dark, foggy, chilly morning. Breakfasted alone, joined somewhat later by Katia, who agreed that this Christmas and New Year's Eve were the happiest we have spent in years. My spirits are truly higher; my New Year's statement, made possible by the once so dreaded "expatriation," is an important and liberating step, a document from which I expect great inner rewards.—When I installed the new calendar yesterday I likewise felt a certain joyousness and eagerness for what the New Year might bring.—A new volume in the series of Silver Books with fine reproductions of Michelangelo came from the publisher, Woldemar Klein in Berlin, sent to a cover address in Zurich.—The Russians again sent 1,100 francs in royalties, which takes care of Christmas expenses. Today at breakfast there came a ceremonious New Year's greeting by telegram from Moscow, signed Annenkova.—Some work on the novella.—At noon a New Year's visit from Dr. Hanhart. Then Lion came. Walked with him, Katia, and Reisiger in dense fog. Lion stayed to lunch. To tea Leonhard Frank with his lady friend. Received them upstairs. After they left attended to some brief correspondence.—The invitation to give five readings at 500 dollars apiece at the New School for Social Research in New York is being much discussed. Löwenstein is very strongly in favor of it because of the "Academy."— Unusual quantity of mail. In the evening, music on the radio. Then read the periodicals.

Saturday, January 2

Rain. The introduction to the catalogue for the Liebermann exhibition in Vienna. Into town to have my hair cut at Bachmann's. New Year's greetings from his staff. Charming dark-haired young man who attended me.—Much mail, as has lately been the case. Enthusiastic letters about *Joseph* from Prof. Marck and Dr. Born.—Belated telegram to New York. In the afternoon took care of a variety of mail. Short stroll with Reisiger. Telephone call from the agent in Budapest; I finally agreed to come on the thirteenth after losing my temper over the ten-percent fee the agency wanted to deduct for itself, which he readily gave way on. With Reisiger in the living room. Schubert recordings. Head full of travel plans. Worried about the disruption of my work.—Fritz von Unruh sent his Basel "Europa" lecture, for which I thanked him. Letter about the links between *The Magic Mountain* and Novalis and Romanticism.

Sunday, January 3

Up before eight. Dark, the street lights still on in the village. Foehn. Worked on the novella. Walked with Katia and Reisiger by way of Johannisburg. At lunch Joseph Breitbach from Paris, a truly silly fellow. Conversed about the large gift from Frau von Mayrisch and the creation of a magazine, possibly with Lion as editor. Need to consult Schlumberger.—Said good-bye to Reisiger, who is going back to Seefeld. Am heavy-hearted, for he has perhaps the best effect on me of anyone.—After tea dictated numerous letters. Then went outdoors for a bit. Frau Hallgarten and her son with us for dinner. Some of *Die Walküre.* Very tired.

Monday, January 4

At eight o'clock the waning moon was visible in the clear sky, but then fog settled in and stayed all day.—Worked on the novella.—Somewhat lonely without Reisiger. Walked alone by way of Johannisburg in the mist.—Among the letters was one from Straussmann about the idiotic plagiarism business, which is evidently being played up in the Rumanian press. I cannot but feel a shudder at this underworld that threatens to take over. It also makes me furious that these curs should think of me as fair game. Considering writing to Georges Oprescu.—Brushes between the German and Spanish navies.—Handwritten correspondence in the afternoon. Walked before supper. Afterward read in Pierre Bertaux's *Hölderlin*. New instances of the debasement of honorable German concepts under National Socialism, as for example in such phrases as "categorical turning-point of time" and "patriotic reversal."—Said good-bye to Golo, who goes to Seefeld for a few days and is then meeting us in Prague.

Tuesday, January 5

Up at eight. Katia took Golo to the station. Bibi left for Paris yesterday. Since Medi is also off on an outing I am alone with Katia.—Worked on the novella. At noon with Katia into town, where as the guests of Breitbach we had a very elegant lunch upstairs at Huguenin's. Then went to Stäheli's bookshop to inscribe some books as a gift for Breitbach. Ordered the Diederichs edition of Tolstoy, an important acquisition. Later went to the shoemaker's in Küsnacht. Spoke with the proprietor's son, who had sent me as a favored customer a book on the Bata shoe manufacturing firm. He revealed some rather one-sided political views.—Tired, rested. Dictated many letters after tea, including one to Oprescu in Bucharest. Then read a long essay of Heinrich's in *Internationale Literatur* about the history of the German worker, a gripping piece of writing. Dinner alone with Katia. She is typing the first chapter of *The Beloved Returns*.—Oprecht informs me that he intends to issue the *Exchange of Letters* as early as the fifteenth. Great suspense over its impact. By the time we are back from Vienna it will have been published.

Thursday, January 7

Up before eight. Gray foehn light, later rain and wind. Completed the second chapter of the novella. Cut my walk short because of the bad weather. Read the *Annals*, underlining a good deal. After tea wrote a variety of letters and thank-you notes, and stayed indoors. Supper alone with Katia, both daughters having gone to the opera.— Our schedule for the forthcoming journey: invitation to tea with President Beneš, lecture at the Urania. From Prague (Proseč) by night train to Budapest. Staying with the Hatvanys. Gala evening at the Hungarian National Theater. From Vienna a letter from Prof. Hollnsteiner, not put out by my acquisition of Czech citizenship. Skeptical remarks about conciliation with Nazi Germany.—Letter from Jan Kožak (Prague) who thinks it possible that they will release my property. The publication of the *Exchange of Letters* will likely make any such possibility vanish. Inwardly I veer between feeling glad and feeling oppressed by its publication. One was not born for this, but for living in freedom and tranquility. And yet it is doubtless necessary and right, as was Jakob

Grimm's pamphlet of protest that served me as a model for publication in this matter—
if it is not completely false.—But that is scarcely possible. The Bonn affair, the forthcoming trip, the American plan, the political tension and uncertainty, the scandal and
agony in Spain—all these combine to produce a profound inner unrest. One hears
that after a decisive victory by Franco, that is to say by the Italians and Germans,
Hitler will make a new "peace offer" based on his earlier "constructive" suggestions.
Will they hand Europe over to this wretched individual?—Goethe's poems.—

Sunday, January 10; Prague, Hotel Esplanade

The trip here normal, with changing fellow passengers. Lunch in the dining car. Rested
afterward and read Frankenberger's book on *Faust I* that I had brought along. Tea
before we arrived. Into Prague at five. At the station (barrier) only Golo and Goschi
(misunderstanding). By cab to the hotel. The usual suite. Many letters, people announcing their intention to call on me, all of which had to be coordinated. Telephone
calls. Unpacked and shaved. With Golo to Mimi Mann's, where we spent the evening
en famille, tired. Back to the hotel early. Read in *Wilhelm Meister's Apprenticeship*.

Up at 8:30 today and had a bath. Foggy and cold. Unfortunately have already
caught cold. Telephoned Kožak. Will see him tomorrow. The people at the Deutsches
Theater very courteous, a box for this evening.—Visits from Hans Natonek (interview
to appear in the *Prager Tagblatt*) and the former public prosecutor, Dr. Goldschmidt
of the Jewish Emigrants' Aid. Documented report, donation.—Wrote to Bruno
Frank.—Walked to the Urania with Golo, where we had lunch with the Frankls.
During coffee, interview with a better sort of journalist from the *Montagsblatt*.—
Rested a little back at the hotel. Then by cab to Mimi's for a large afternoon gathering.
Kožak and his wife, the very tall rector of the Czech university (a medical man), a
minister, Budzislawski, Čapek, who again broached the question of the radio direc-
torship. Back to the hotel at seven. Then off to the Deutsches Theater and our box,
comfortable. Excellent [production] of *Der Rosenkavalier*; in spite of being very tired,
I was quite moved by the fine playing of the orchestra and the sensitive writing. Mimi
Mann joined us with her daughter, Golo, and Milka Pringsheim. After the opera in
the Café Elektra, overtired.

Monday, January 11; Prague

Spent the morning receiving callers. Then to Jan Kožak's and from there to the Foreign
Ministry, where I was received by a consul instead of by Krofta himself, who had
fallen ill. From there to the Interior Ministry, where we had to wait, since Černý,
the minister, was not yet in. The porter acted as though he did not know who I
was.—Had lunch with Golo on the Graben. Then rested at the hotel. At four o'clock
by taxi to the Hradschin for tea with the president of the Republic. Was alone with
him for two and a half hours talking politics.—Back to the hotel, into evening dress,
then to the Urania, waiting in the office. Then the reading: a packed hall, much
applause, introduction, the first chapter of *The Beloved Returns*, and after the intermission "The Ladies' Party" from *Joseph in Egypt*. It went off splendidly. Dear Golo
highly pleased. Ludwig Hardt in the greenroom, also the German minister and others.
Reception at the Frankls'. Leo Kestenberg, František Langer, Czech's children. The
evening a great success.

271

The morning taken up with callers, Friedrich Burschell. With him to Dr. Bacher's, an opulent house, for a meeting of the committee of the Thomas Mann Fund.—At 12:30 the Foreign Ministry's car called for us at the hotel to take us to Proseč. Fleischmann, Golo, two motion-picture cameramen. A drive of some three hours, during which I at first felt unwell, but then improved after a snack. Coffee at the postmaster's. Then a meeting of the town council, with speeches by the mayor and the postmaster. My speech of thanks. Letters from the citizens. A crowd of townsfolk outside the town hall. In front of Fleischmann's house a salute in three languages offered by the Communists. At Fleischmann's endless books to be autographed. A copious meal with only water to drink. Later more guests for coffee. The old manufacturer with pipes for me and Golo. Gift of embroidered table napkins for Katia. At around 8:30 taken by car to the railway station, a nervous chauffeur, problems with the engine and the lights. Nonetheless reached the station with ample time. Said goodbye to Golo. Tea in the restaurant. Sleeping car.

In Budapest yesterday morning more visitors, Dr. Robert Klopstock and Johann Mohr. At about 10:30 we left in the car driven by the Hatvanys' chauffeur Petér, after a warm farewell from his employers, who mean to come to Arosa.—Pleasant, clear cold weather. A good drive, stopping for a snack and then a moderate lunch an hour from the border, which we crossed with few formalities. In Vienna by four, and soon afterward arrived at the Hotel Imperial. Said good-bye to the likable Petér. Handsome suite on an upper floor, flowers, bonbonnière, all the trimmings. The telephone began ringing immediately. Unpacked, had tea and a few minutes' rest, then dressed. Brüll, Born, and Oppenheimer came to fetch us. To the Konzerthaus. The impresario Georg Kugel. The usual bustle. Began at 7:45. The hall well filled. Heavy applause after *The Beloved Returns*, especially when I came out again, and at the end persistent clapping and cheering. "The Ladies' Party" for the second half of the program. Responsive laughter. The greenroom thronged. My 500 schillings. Frau Walter, Ernst Benedikt, and others. Dinner at Hartmann's with the Bermanns, Oppenheimer, Brüll, Born, Dr. Amann, Frau Meier-Graefe. Hungry and thirsty. Palatschinken. Pilsner beer. Coffee. Left after midnight.

Slept well with the help of half a Phanodorm tablet. Up about 8:30 this morning. After breakfast spoke on the telephone with Beer-Hoffmann and Robert Musil. Many other calls.

Luncheon at the hotel as guests of Brüll.

Tea reception at Trebitsch's, with Auernheimer, Schönherr, Frau Mahler-Werfel, the Bermanns, etc.

Dinner at the Bermanns' with Frau Walter and Frau Mahler-Werfel, the Zuckerkandls, Prof. Hollnsteiner. Read them the Bonn exchange, copies of which had come this morning, with profound effect.

Slept quite well. Up at 7:30. Clear, cold. The beauty of the mountains. Finished dressing. Coffee and rolls for breakfast. Worked on the second chapter of the novella until eleven. Into the village to shop. To the barber's. Sent out a number of copies of the pamphlet. Sat on the loggia after lunch reading Frankenberger on Goethe's "Walpurgis Night." At four o'clock with Katia to the Old India for tea. Then various errands. Somewhat fatigued, upset by the altitude. Dictated letters to Schlumberger, Breitbach, Madame Mayrisch, and others, and wrote several more by hand.—A good deal of mail. Letters from Heinrich (about the pamphlet and *Joseph*) and Reisiger about the leaflet (pointing out annoying misprints, perhaps spelling errors of my own). Letters from Sweden, where the Bonn exchange appeared in the *Dagens Nyheter*. Letter from Otto Strasser. Offer from a lawyer in Temesvar to take on my case without a fee. He writes that Rumanian judges are capable of anything.—After dinner sat in the small salon talking with Lion. More about the magazine.

Sunday, January 31; Arosa

Up at eight. Fine day, later the sun was obscured and foehn moved in. Worked on the third chapter out on the loggia for a while. Vermouth with Katia in Maran. Medi off skiing with Kahler. Lunch with the Hatvanys. Then read *Goethe und die Seinen* out on the loggia. Rested there. Met Medi and Kahler in the café at teatime. Back at the hotel, did no more work except to write something in Hatvany's album.—Fine letter in French about the Bonn exchange from the secretary of the Dutch PEN Club, De Meyier: "This answer struck me to the heart, and I am still greatly moved." Remarkable: ". . . the writer whose masterworks are on a par with those of Goethe . . . (for your style has qualities that always remind me of that great genius Goethe, of whom I am a loyal and ardent disciple) . . . ."

Moving letter from a German lady in Zurich, whose first act upon arriving there was to read the Bonn exchange, which overwhelmed her.

Six of us at dinner. Lingered a while afterward in the salon to listen to music, applauding the young violinist who played Boccherini and Kreisler very prettily. Then into the small lounge. Discussed the magazine with Kahler and Lion. Lion presented his outline for five issues. Oprecht the only publisher under consideration.—Lion described Hitler's speech of yesterday, which he had listened to. Filthy nonsense.— Tried to extend our stay by several days but were prevented from doing so by a shortage of rooms.

Sunday, February 14

Brilliantly clear day with deep snow. Worked on the Riemer scene with a weary head. At noon Breitbach was here briefly to discuss the magazine and its patroness. Went walking in the strong sunlight. Lion to lunch. Discussed the program of *Mass und Wert* over coffee. At 4:15 with Katia and Lion to the Oprechts'. Tea with them, Frau Mayrisch, Lion, Schlumberger, and Breitbach. Conference on financial and literary aspects. Bi-monthly or monthly. Consensus of opinion for the latter. Suggested advisory board, in addition to me: Prof. Muschg, Strich, Karl Barth, Otokar Fischer, and an Austrian.—Walked part of the way home in the clear, cold evening.—After supper listened to a broadcast from Vienna of a fine Johann Strauss concert conducted by Weingartner.—Sent the *Exchange of Letters* to Karl Barth.

· ·

Friday, March 5

· ·

Up before eight. Somewhat springlike weather after all the wintriness. Added a bit to the Riemer chapter and went on with the writing. Morning and afternoon mail unusually heavy. Short walk with Katia. At lunch an American friend of Klaus's, a good-humored girl, heavily made up. Read letters and newspapers. Three large crates arrived, containing the hundred-volume Goethe set from Munich. Unpacked two of the crates after tea and dinner. Some volumes in poor condition and needing repair. But a magnificent possession nonetheless. Discussed where to shelve them.—Two telegrams from Alvin Johnson, New York. "Vitally important" that I come. To whom? Katia is strongly for the trip, and in fact there are a number of arguments in its favor, except that I do not feel enterprising, which is only the obverse of some inner resistance. Tired, out of sorts. Disquieted and troubled.—Lion and Breitbach sent an issue of the *Echo de Paris* with a lead article by Academy member Louis Gillet titled "Excommunicated." He writes: "Everyone knows that Monsieur Thomas Mann is the most imposing literary personage in Europe today. Excepting Paul Claudel or Gabriele d'Annunzio, and perhaps H. G. Wells and Bernard Shaw, the present-day world holds no artist figure of higher or more majestic stature."—Words of this sort please me, for they bolster the mythic game that the world seems so eager to play.

· ·

Sunday, March 21

· ·

Lost myself yesterday evening in my diary from 1927, the period of my passion for the boy Klaus H. Deeply stirred—and aware of how I have grown inwardly and outwardly in the intervening ten years.—This morning was cold and rainy, turning springlike at midday. Worked further on the Riemer conversation up to the point where Lotte's confessions begin. Went walking by way of Johannisburg with Katia. Therese Giehse with us for lunch. Coffee in the living room. Finally looked over the fragment of the second book of *Felix Krull* and prepared it for publication. After tea dictated a series of letters, some difficult: a statement to the Paris committee for the Popular Front, a note of thanks to the French poet René Etiemble, and others. Read in Schneider's biography of Schopenhauer. Dinner with Katia and Medi. Sore throat. Looked over manuscripts in preparation for dictating my dinner speech for New York, which I hope will not get in the way of my work on *The Beloved Returns*. Decided yesterday to shorten the trip by leaving out Holland and possibly London as well; a calming simplification.—Schickele's novel, which I am now [reading] at bedtime, is unfortunately tedious.

We were driven to the station yesterday evening by Medi and Bibi. The Beidlers and Klaus were there to say goodbye. Sleeping car. Evening newspaper with English and French rumors of a rapprochement between Germany and Russia. Amusing.—Short and restless night, which I began by reading Čapek's novel. Nicely done, well-informed satire.—Up this morning at 6:45. Paris. To the Gare Saint-Lazare. Fit of anger with a man who tried to commandeer a taxi we had already hailed. Had breakfast at a table in the passage outside a café in the station, egg and café au lait. Then boarded the boat train to Le Havre, a three-hour trip. Americans in our compartment. Read Čapek. Much checking of our papers. At Le Havre we boarded this huge ship. Cabin opening onto a private deck. Lunch and coffee in the cathedral-like dining salon. Then looked over the public rooms. Rested on the good bed. Pulled away from the dock after three. It was raining heavily, but has since cleared. Moderate pitching. Tea at 5:30 in the large salon. After that in the cinema for a while. Then unpacked my large suitcase. Dinner at eight, assigned to table 39. Good. Afterward in the salon. Read. Linden-blossom tea. Another movie. To bed at eleven.

Friday, April 9; S.S. "Normandie"

Slept quite well. Toward morning started to feel pain, but was able to find a position that allowed me to fall asleep again. The toothache subsided during the night. Woke up around eight, the clock having been turned back. Saltwater bath and cold shower. Breakfast with two eggs. Then went over the English version of the Goethe lecture with Katia. Visited by the ship's reception officer. On deck. With Dr. Bollack to the sheltered chairs on the tennis deck. Strong westerly wind, but the ocean calm and the enormous ship sailing smoothly. On the topmost deck the rolling is plainly visible however.—Visited the Huxleys in tourist class. Soon after lunch to the cinema; *Romeo and Juliet,* tedious. Then napped for a while. Tea in our cabin. The rocking is worse. Read Gide's *Return from the U.S.S.R.* and finished it in the salon after dinner. Curious sensation. Talked a bit with the Sterns.—In the afternoon rather seasick. Early to bed, very tired.

Saturday, April 10; S.S. "Normandie"

Toward morning a heavy siege of pain. Fell asleep again afterward. In the morning a bad pain again in my leg. Warm, humid, the Gulf Stream, cloudy. Bathed and showered. Breakfast in bed. Practiced the lecture in English. The reception officer came with an invitation to dine with the captain, unavoidable.—Read in English with Katia.—Customs forms already, radio messages.—On the upper deck in a raging storm. Read the essays of Rolland out on our little deck. Lunch followed by coffee, very good and bracing. Afterward continued my reading on our deck. Napped a bit. Tea in the salon with the Huxleys. Handicapped by the language. With them for a while in the cinema. To the baggage master's. Looked at the swimming pool. Fog. The air cooler again. Much pain in my leg and also my tooth. If only I were at home.—Excused ourselves from the captain's dinner. The evening spent as usual. Early to bed.

Have been on this ship for four days, after eleven days in New York filled with strain and achievement that also opened new vistas for our lives (invitation to Hollywood). The lectures at The New School, the dinners and meetings, interviews, hordes of visitors, flowers, books, mountains of letters. The pleasant Bedford Hotel, the devoted Herr Nägel. Being with Erika and working with her. Her relationship with Gumpert. Her friends Maurice Wertheim and "the murderer." Theater. Beatrice Lillie. The young dancer who was so dazzling in the role of Casanova. Private soirées with champagne and readings from *The Beloved Returns*. Curt Riess. Erika's fish poisoning. The almost constant pain in my leg, neuritis, sciatica. Dr. Gumpert. Dr. Bucky, the Colmers. Codeine. Pain worse again on the ship, mornings almost unbearable.—The Knopfs' restaurant parties. Miss Willa Cather. Dorothy Thompson and her sensational article. Dictated talks and addresses. Erika serving as translator. At noon on the twenty-fourth we boarded the ship, taking affectionate farewell from the dear child, who may be expecting.—Our neighbor on the ship the tenor Josef Schmidt. Also the Kammer-sänger Emanuel List. The friendly young businessmen from New York with *Young Joseph* and *The Magic Mountain*.—Living the life of luxury but nonetheless in pain. Fine weather yesterday with the ocean violet-colored. Today gray, damp, and mild. Veramon toward morning when the pains begin.—Dictated letters to Katia: Fiedler and various Americans. Wrote by hand to Reisiger.—The ship the most agreeable one so far.—Reading Thomas Wolfe's *Look Homeward, Angel*. Good, powerful. Before that, much Tolstoy, with my old and ever-new admiration.—Looming chores to be done in Zurich: introduction for the magazine, the preface for Schickele. Bringing *The Beloved Returns* to a close I do not know when—after that I can begin growing rich in Hollywood at 3,000 dollars a week. (?)

The desired movie scripts of *The Magic Mountain* and *Royal Highness*.—

Back here since Sunday morning. Docked in Le Havre on the afternoon of the thirtieth. Elaborate customs formalities. A two-and-a-half hour journey to Paris in a Pullman car, in which we had dinner. The two New York Jews, one a perfume dealer and the other a dealer in costume jewelry, had once more managed to seat themselves near us. Arrived in Paris in the evening. Gare Saint-Lazare. Bibi. Hotel Westminster, rue de la Paix. Exhausted, in pain. On the first (a national holiday) with Katia and Bibi to a champagne brunch at Annette Kolb's, rue Casimir-Perier. Breitbach. In the afternoon took another long nap. Dinner with Bibi upstairs at the Café de la Paix. Then to the Landsbergs' townhouse. Good-looking wife from the Rhineland. Drove us in their D.K.W. to the Gare de l'Est after the heavy luggage had been taken care of. Little Joseph Schmidt and his manager. Sleeping car. In the morning unbearable pain. Arrived at eight in the morning on the second at the Enge Station. Bracing coffee in the restaurant while we waited for Medi, who had gone to the Central Station. Drove home. Spring, blue skies, charming views of the city and the lake. Green, everything in bloom, joy in spite of severe pain. The newly-clipped Toby. Breakfast. Impossible mountain of mail. The big trunks. Unpacked, looked through things, put them into order; fatigued.—The little bronze head of Medi brought to us from Munich by the cellist Feuermann.—Therese Giehse here.

Yesterday, the third, spent the morning making essential excerpts from the Berne Goethe books, which were then returned. Lovely warm weather. At noon a walk with Katia. After lunch, coffee on the terrace. Then to Dr. Katzenstein at the Psychiatric Clinic. Consultation about my sciatica, which he hopes to get rid of. Prescribed Pyramidon, electric pad, and tonic. Rest. Canceled the planned trip to Paris to receive honors. In the afternoon napped with the heating pad. In the evening with Katia and Medi to the theater: *Nathan der Weise* with Bassermann and the Viennese troupe. On the verge of tears. The parable of the ring a great success. Still a faulty play.

Today awakened early by the pain. In torment, hot. Nevertheless the pain seemed to lessen somewhat after I got up. For breakfast dry cereal, orange juice, Pyramidon, and the tonic.—Last night I managed to skim through a manuscript received from Hollnsteiner, an apology for the Catholic church, badly written. The magazine a burden, an embarrassment, a worry. The foolish carryings-on of Brentano and Glaeser. Strong temptation to toss the whole thing aside.—Yesterday a letter from Paris addressed to "Monsieur Thomas Mann, Exchange of Letters, Zurich."—

Tuesday, May 4; Küsnacht

Wrote to Kerényi and Freud in the morning. Took care of other chores. Overcast, mild, raining. Walked by way of Johannisburg with Katia, my leg often excruciatingly painful. Newspapers after lunch, read all manner of things; painful to sit. Napped thanks to the heating pad. After tea sorted letters and dictated to Katia. Tired. Kahler here for dinner. The Kahler-Brentano correspondence. Glaeser's letter. Hopeless misery. My physical condition can barely take it. I'd like to be free of the magazine.

Saturday, May 22

Clearer weather. As always lately I awoke too early. Up by 7:30. Finished the introduction to my relative satisfaction. Twenty-two pages.—Heat treatment. Then with Katia to the zoo, though we did not see much on account of my painful leg. Impressive aquarium, a chimpanzee that uses a chamber pot, mating scene.—Vermouth on the terrace of the restaurant. Drove back home through the green woods.—After lunch, newspapers on the terrace. In the afternoon an ill-fated visit to the movies: shocking film of the Zeppelin disaster, with screams of the burning victims. Afterward a stupid Viennese society film, though with Paula Wessely in the cast. I had wanted to see the coronation ceremonies.—Stopped in the Küsnacht woods, the pain too bad.— Back home, wrote to Lion and sent him various materials.—Stirring letter from the journalist Koestler writing from Gibraltar. Sentenced to death and only saved at the last moment, he claims he was able to endure the ordeal with the help of my writings, specifically the Schopenhauer chapter in *Buddenbrooks*. When his letter arrived I was reading that very chapter in Schopenhauer, "Concerning Death," which I had not looked at for thirty-five years. Life's strange games. "In the past I would not have believed that art could have so strong an influence on life." Nor would I have, in the past.

Bad night, Katia watching over me for a part of it. Toward morning Veramon let me get some sleep.—Worked, *quand même*.—After the heat treatment we went to the Chevrolet dealer's, where we bought the car shown us yesterday after lunch, a sedan, dark red, very nice, for 5,000 francs (against which we were allowed 3,000 for the old Fiat). An important transaction.—Letter from Hirschfeld about the introduction. (The question of the signature and of "socialism.")—Extremely interesting essay on *Faust II* by Max Kommerell in the *Corona*.—After tea wrote some thank-you letters. Had tea late, and later the five of us went to the opera house for the première of Alban Berg's *Lulu*. A box with Kahler. *Tout* Zurich. Superlative production of the fragmentary and difficult work. Wedekind's icy and overwrought dialogue is softened by the music, which is at its loveliest in the interludes. Often there were *Tristan*-like effects, proving that Wagner was at his most modern and most influential in that work.—Oprecht came over to us in the intermission. His wife is in Bad Gastein, having been turned back at the Italian border.—Supper at home with the ladies toward midnight.—Wrote the Lachesis lines from *Faust II* in Oprecht's guest book.

My sixty-second birthday. Terribly distressing, wakeful night. Terrible pain in the morning. Warm, overcast day. Had breakfast on the terrace with Katia, who was very loving. The pain grew somewhat milder. Then received some fine presents: a chair for my bedroom, a soft bathrobe, a chest of tea, china, some fine phonograph records, etc. Handsome flask from Erika. Worked for a few hours on the article for Bruno Frank. Afterward, at my suggestion, drove to the Luft restaurant with Katia, the daughters, and Toby; snack of vermouth and Emmenthaler. The car open. Sat a while in the restaurant garden and read letters received from Heinrich, Schickele, and others. The four of us had lunch, with excellent nut torte baked by Frau Späth. Napped in the afternoon. Wrote cards of thanks. The now customary toilsome walk in the woods with the folding stool. Dinner for the four of us with champagne. Then listened to music in the living room, playing my new records: the *Leonore* Overture, Hugo Wolf songs, the *Siegfried Idyll*. Family chat. The wine made me very tired, but I was able to sit with almost no pain.—Klaus phoned Erika from Budapest. Worried about him. Decided to call Dr. Klopstock.—Magnificent bouquet, sent anonymously, was delivered by a chauffeur.

Thunder and rain all through the night and most of the day.—In the morning *finished the Riemer chapter*, more than a hundred pages long. Went out in the rain with Katia, sitting on the folding stool in the rain.—Erika having difficulty because certain papers required by the American consulate have not arrived from her official husband, Wystan. Her presence, sadly soon to be withdrawn again, is always enlivening and cheering.—Dictated letters in the afternoon. (Dr. Klepper, Paris; wretched case of a Jewish-Aryan couple in Syria; others.)—Another walk with Katia. Pain. In the evening celebrated Katia's birthday a bit early with the five children and Therese Giehse. After dinner listened attentively to the *Leonore* Overture. Then all came to my study, where I read aloud the entire second half of the Riemer chapter. Champagne punch with peaches in the intermission and afterward. Heartening response. It was agreed that in such a grim situation what is most important is to be amusing, and that this I have achieved. Riemer's dialectical exposition on All and Nothing is true to that time, since Hegel's *Logic* begins with such a theme.—Talked until nearly one o'clock.—Today the mantel clock came back from the repairman's.

Saturday, July 17

Last night finished reading Silone's *Fontamara*, a fine book, more to my taste than most. In all of the dictatorships the same murderous, lying, torture-loving spirit—a phenomenon of the times not limited to single nationalities, uniform and deliberate. For the first time I did not get up in the night and did without tea and a painkiller. Pains toward morning. Up at eight. Breakfast with Katia. Made revisions to the Riemer chapter and studied material. At noon drove with Katia toward Zumikon and walked a little. Sat on the campstool surrounded by meadows. Tired. Lunch with the five children. Lay down for a long while in the afternoon. After tea wrote a reply to Hermann Kesten. Looked in on Erika while she packed. Went out with Katia and walked as far as the yellow house. Skies clearing, the foehn abating. Dinner with the children, Therese Giehse, and Annemarie. Afterward, while Erika finished getting her many pieces of luggage ready, listened to music: Sibelius and Mahler. Erika and Klaus leaving for Paris, then she goes on to New York. Farewells. Melancholy. Pain. I thought of the death of Grautoff, the causes of which I do not know. A gloomy warning. I often feel that I will not recover from my present condition, and that it is the beginning of the end.—Stayed home alone while Katia, Medi, Golo, Therese, and Annemarie accompanied the travelers into Zurich.

Monday, August 2

Clear day, sunny after yesterday's rain, steamy.—Katia ailing and in bed. Obvious consequence of having been overburdened. Worried.—The early morning hours unpleasant. Worked on the Adele chapter. Stahel came to give me my injection. With him to see Katia.—Took my walk alone with the campstool, taking the path through the lower woods with almost no trouble. Am improving almost daily as far as walking goes. Sat down a few times in the shade to enjoy the dewy, sunlit scenes.—Long letter from Heinrich full of praise for Golo, with whom I shared it. About Russia, the "Club of the Clean-handed," Klaus, Bernhard, etc. One-sided, naive, and unjust in his sense of his own importance as always.—Newspapers: rebellion on the part of Moorish and Spanish troops against the Italians. Mass executions in the Alhambra. Italian-English "agreement" on the Mediterranean? Four-power alliance of England, France, Germany, Italy?—Napped.—Began a letter to Heinrich but discarded it. Less urgent correspondence. Went out again, the weather having cleared after an afternoon thunder shower.—Editorial letter from Lion, which I carefully deciphered with Golo. The situation impossible. Essential to have Lion settled here.

Sultry, some sun, finally more rain.—Wrote about Masaryk and the manuscript affair. Walked in the woods with Reisiger. Broke out in a sweat. Sniffles. After lunch worked further on the Masaryk piece in my reclining chair. Finished after tea and did some revising on the clean copy. Kahler came to dinner. With him in the living room afterward. Showed him the piece. Then gave a long reading for him, Reisiger, and Golo from the beginning and later portions of the Riemer chapter. They were highly moved, and discussed the exciting things about the chapter. The pulsing of life in it and its wealth of interpretive insights. A high point in my work.—Medi, back from *Das Cornichon*, drove Kahler home. Sat a while longer alone with Reisiger. Talked about Hesse, my courting of him and his resistance, his preferring not to hear anything about me, out of uneasiness, possibly envy.—Late to bed. Read for a while in *Dichtung und Wahrheit*, having finished *Père Goriot* yesterday.

Chilly, no rain. Up around eight, breakfasted by myself and got to work. Into town with Katia and Reisiger. Bought Reisiger a fountain pen at Scholl's. Writing paper. Appointment with Dr. Asper. Diagnosis: all my upper teeth must come out and a complete plate made. Something of a shock. Made a date for Friday. Discussed the procedure for this first, most gruelling session.—Copies of the new *Confidence Man* edition arrived from Querido. Handsome. Therese Giehse with us for lunch. Coffee. Afterward read letters and periodicals. Dictated many letters after tea. In the evening read Goethe's "The Man of Fifty" to the end.—Broadcast date set for November 15.—Preparing the New York dinner speech for Bermann's almanac and marking the things that were originally in German for the translator of the Gide foreword.

Clear, cool, fine day. Coming toward the end of the "tale." With Katia and Reisiger into town. Saw Katzenstein at the institute. Discussed the forthcoming dental business. Prescription of Optalidon and Neurostabil. Collected Reisiger from a nearby café, where he was deep in conversation. Walked with him part of the way home. Coffee on the terrace after lunch. Then drove to Lucerne with Golo, Katia, and Reisiger, Medi doing the driving. Visited Tribschen. Toured the rooms. Curious impression. Dreadful oil paintings, utterly Hitler. One absolutely revolting gigolo of a Siegfried. Nietzsche's *The Case of Wagner* placed next to a copy of *The Birth of Tragedy* under glass, a stupid touch. Interesting photographic group portraits of Wagner's family and friends. A bust of Chamberlain. Magnificence of the view through the windows. Furnishings in better taste than that of the tenants. One upholstered chair he added himself, Bayreuth style. Siegfried in a variety of guises, looking for all the world like a Jew in a more youthful picture. The poem to Cosima that accompanied the *Siegfried Idyll*—one can only say "hmmm." Elements of a frighteningly Hitleresque quality plainly discernible, even though only latent and anticipatory, ranging from the over-blown kitsch to the Germanic fondness for boys.—Walked in the garden by the lake where Nietzsche and he used to stroll. Hot chocolate in the café of the Kunst-Haus.

Walked across the old bridge. The exquisite beauty of the mountains. Drove back and were home by seven.—Looked through the mail. Reisiger staying until Sunday. After dinner listened to records of *Die Walküre* with admiration.

. . . .

Thursday, October 21
. . . .

Fog, through which the sun could not break this time. Continued working on Chapter Six. At noon to Asper, who took the final plaster impression. Some extremely unpleasant moments, followed by a feeling of relief and the comforting sense that the present unsatisfactory state will soon be over.—Fetched Blanche Knopf from the Hotel Baur au Lac. Bought some sweets with her. Then to the house for lunch, at which in her usual irritating way she declined to eat anything, accepting only coffee. With her in my study discussing my travel schedule and the publication of *Joseph in Egypt* in February. Discussed the publication of the expanded *Krull*.—In the afternoon dictated letters, most of them having to do with the American trip: acceptances to the American Committee for Christian German Refugees, to Yale, to Weekend College, etc. In the evening with Mrs. Knopf to the Schauspielhaus: première of a mostly successful Viennese play, a vehicle for Therese Giehse. Talked with Brentano during the intermission. Then went to the bar at the Baur au Lac with Blanche, whose red claws irritated me. Had tea, coddled eggs, and ice cream. Talked about problems in America, the many strikes in which a number of people have been killed, England's lamentable policies, and the weakness of France. Also about the cooperative line the Italians are taking in the Non-Intervention Committee, which seems to mean they are sure Franco will win. Pessimistic article by Robert Dell in the *National-Zeitung* about Sir Robert Vansittart and his pro-German policy, with its ruinous consequences for France.—Said goodbye to Blanche. Tired. Essential to get down to work on the talks for America.

. . . .

Monday, October 25
. . . .

Return of bright autumnal weather.—Still on the sixth chapter. To Asper with Katia to discuss the denture and have something done about the pressure toward the back. After our return home, went walking with Katia for a while. Ate alone upstairs. Then talked with Golo in the living room about letters from Lion and about the magazine. In the afternoon wrote in a humorous, melancholy vein to Reisiger about the denture experience. In truth the thought that I will be wearing this thing to the end of my days often makes me very gloomy.—Evening walk with Katia. In the evening, read in *Internationale Literatur* selections from Heinrich's *Henry, King of France* and an article by Georg Lukács on Heine as a political figure. Then returned to *Tasso*.—Drank cocoa in the morning.—Remarkable letter from "a citizen of the German Reich," posted in Salzburg and unsigned out of fear; a cry of anguish.

. . . .

Tuesday, October 26
. . . .

Foggy, mild. Cocoa for breakfast. Had begun sketching out the *Democracy* when Oprecht phoned to pass along a request from the Stadttheater that I give a talk in mid-November as an introduction to their entire *Ring* cycle. I had some doubts, but for the sake of Germany, for the sake of Zurich, and also because of the topic, the invitation, which was apparently unanimous, strikes me as interesting and important, and I may well accept. Another change of plan—to be sure a more appealing one.—Walked out to meet Katia and went around the pond with her. Had lunch by myself again. Then read what Wagner wrote concerning the *Ring*. The personal aspects repellent. His insistence on being "loved" as a man.—A cold coming on; cough, hot forehead. After tea took care of handwritten correspondence. In the evening went with Katia and Golo to the Tonhalle: Brahms's Fourth Symphony, Beethoven concerto (played by Adolf Busch), and the Prelude to *Die Meistersinger*. Talked in the intermission with Wölfflin, who told me that Fritz Fleiner died today. Moved.—Felt unwell and feverish. Busch played superlatively. Andreae gave a good and powerful rendition of the Prelude. Katia with the children to the Reiffs' to have supper with the musicians. I was driven home in the Reiffs' new Mercedes, where I found Medi, who had also caught cold. Had an egg, farina, and a baked apple.

Saturday, November 13

Up at eight. Lovely weather. Finished, God be praised, the lecture *Richard Wagner and the Ring.*—Shocked by the publicity given in the *National-Zeitung* to my letter to the Paris Committee for Freedom and Justice in Germany, in which I expressed myself in the strongest terms. Worry about troublesome consequences.—Drove to the golf course with Katia and Toby, and walked in the good air up there. To tea a young American of Danish origin by the name of Jensen, extremely likable. Spoke in English about the danger of fascism in America and ways to avert it.—Handwritten letters. At dinner discussed with Katia and Golo the possible historical role of fascism, the world's inexorable trend in that direction, the senseless sacrifice one makes—for whom, one does not know—poisoning one's own blood in trying to fight it. No more offers of help! No statements and answers! Why arouse hatred? Freedom and serenity. One ought to claim one's right to them at last.

Tuesday, November 16

Clear sunny weather, hoarfrost in the morning. Shaved at once. Took care of some handwritten letters, then picked up by Katia and taken to the rehearsal at the Tonhalle, where Ansermet from Geneva was conducting Debussy and then Milstein played the Tchaikovsky. With Beidler in the greenroom. Milstein, a young Russian Jew, a virtuoso to the fingertips, provides the great delight of watching absolute technical mastery. Ran into him and the conductor out on the street. Walked along the lake, then rode home in the car with Medi and the little Moser girl. With Katia to the golf course for a walk in the sun. Newspapers after lunch. Wrote several cards in the afternoon. Evening dress. After seven a snack with caviar and red wine. Then with Katia, Golo, and Medi to the university (first going to the Institute of Technology by mistake). The auditorium sold out, in spite of the other events happening at the same time. In the anteroom with the Oprechts and members of the Stadttheater guild. Hearty welcome by the audience. Comfortable podium, and I was in good spirits. The audience very attentive, and showed great appreciation at the end. At a dramatic spot near the end there was a bad moment with the denture, but managed to surmount it. In the greenroom afterward expressions of thanks and congratulations. Party upstairs at the Peacock: the intendant of the Stadttheater and his wife, members of the guild, the Beidlers, the Oprechts, the Leisingers, Therese Giehse, and others. Omelet and mulled wine. Mood of satisfaction. Not unduly tired. Back home, had another snack with caviar and tea in the company of Katia and the children. One o'clock.

Thursday, November 25

Worked on the lecture in the morning, sketching it out and writing further. Just a short walk by myself. To lunch the piano virtuoso Horowitz and his wife, a daughter of Toscanini. Also Therese Giehse. Much talk about the dictatorships and Russia.—More new books coming in.—After tea dictated letters. In the evening with Katia to the Schauspielhaus: *Wallenstein's Camp* and *The Piccolomini* in an impressive production. Followed the action with the liveliest pleasure and appreciation. What brilliant historical sense!—Drove home with Brentano and had supper with Katia. Read proofs of *Mass und Wert*.

Friday, November 26

Clear, cold night; brisk, cloudless day. Worked on the lecture, making only slow progress. Walked toward Johannisburg, met by Katia along the way and brought home in the car. Toby bitten by a watchdog. After lunch looked at the mail: letter from Schickele (concerning the Riemer chapter) and much else. Newspapers and periodicals. The eerie insolence of a press without opposition; the *Völkischer Beobachter* on the Russian elections! Total contempt for the people—and from what a source!—The curtain that was supposed to keep out light from the bedroom has passed the test and will be kept.—Dictated letters: to Lion, Burschell, et al. Took another hour's walk in the cold. Supper with Katia and Golo.—In the evening read Joseph von Bradish (New York University), "Dichtung und Wahrheit über Schillers Hingang." Also a German writer, Schoeps, on Nietzsche and Kafka.

Saturday, November 27

Cold, clear day. Spent the morning on the speech for America. Democratic idealism. Do I believe in it? Am I only adopting it as an intellectual role? In any case, it is well to remember this world.—Took only a short walk with Katia. After lunch the newspapers. After tea wrote to Schickele about the Platonic dialogue as an art form—which as such can be exploded (Riemer on Goethe's prose, Chapter III of *The Beloved Returns*).—Soirée at Dr. Kaufmann's, an elegant villa on the shore of the lake. With Horowitz, Denzler, et al. Champagne supper. The little daughter who looks like Nico was sick in bed. Horowitz, with whom I talked after supper, stayed a long time with the child while the others played bowls. Toward the end of the evening the intendant of the Stadttheater and his wife arrived. Left rather late. Kaufmann and his brother-in-law, Hans Ernst (a cousin of the essayist), saw us out to the car.—Warmer air, thaw.

Cold, hoarfrost, light snow. Worked on the lecture. Walked by way of Johannisburg with Katia. Therese Giehse to lunch. After coffee read Jean Cocteau's King Arthur play. Charming. Hermann Hesse and his wife to tea. Cordiality overlaid with egotism. Afterward finished my letter to Schickele, and in the evening wrote a letter to Brock after we had listened to some French music on the radio.—Sent copies of translations to Angell. *Krull* and the *Avertissement* to Schickele.

Wednesday, December 1

Foggy, warmer. Worked on the American lecture. Short walk with Katia. The newspapers on the British-French conference of ministers, the plan for allotting some colonial mandates to Germany. But can the regime adhere to the predictable conditions? Can it bring itself to participate in a universal solution? Has England any notion of the overweening national egotism of the Germans? The British are living on another planet, in other *times*.—Much said about Schacht's resignation and the victory of the war economy.—After tea some handwritten letters.—Reichner Verlag in Vienna is launching a new translation of Shakespeare.—Read the manuscript by a professor in Uppsala who opposes international law, even law in general, evidence of the incredible barbarization of people's minds.—Evening clothes, snack. Reading at the Merchants' Hall: the first part of *The Beloved Returns* and "The Ladies' Party." Large audience of lower-echelon employees, extremely attentive and responsive. Strenuous, tired. At supper afterward talked with Golo about the League of Nations and the spiteful satisfaction people take in the failure of things—while at the same time the more or less conscious desires of mankind are nonetheless fulfilled in due course.

Wednesday, December 15

Freezing, light scattering of snow. Up early, dark. Coffee for breakfast. Dr. Katzenstein was already here looking at Bibi, who is well on the way to recovery however. Gave Bibi some pocket scissors.—Worked on the speech for Yale. Walked with Katia at noon. After lunch glanced at new books, which have been arriving in great quantities. Kesten's *I, the King* masterly but cold, lacking all that I would have given it.—After tea prepared for the reading of the "Mont-kaw" chapter of *Joseph in Egypt* in the evening at the Volkshaus, sponsored by the Education Committee of the Social Democratic Party. Fine chapter. Greetings afterward in the corridor. Brought little Tennenbaum home afterward. The adhesive powder for the denture works well.—Supper with Katia and the children. Golo entrusted with the typescript of the American speech.—Handwritten letters. Broadcast of *Tonio Kröger* with music from Prague.

Up at eight. Coffee and an egg after my bath. Poor appetite. Drafted some of the *Schopenhauer* with enthusiasm. In the sunny cold I walked the forest loop alone. After lunch read in *The World as Will and Idea*. At tea letters from Fiedler, J. Lesser, and the editor of *Internationale Literatur* regarding *The Beloved Returns* and the *Confidence Man*.—Informed by the Writers' League in Prague that it has awarded me its "Herder Prize."—Handwritten letters to Frey (Salzburg) and others.—The table clock is back from the repairman's.—Schopenhauer.

Thawing, wet. Up shortly after eight. At breakfast wanted only yogurt. Unpleasant taste in my mouth. Read and made notes for *The Beloved*, invigorating. At noon welcomed Lion and discussed questions of the magazine with him. A short walk together. He had lunch with us.—Newspapers and the *Tage-Buch*. The *Weltbühne* carries a good article on Brüning in New York.—The deluxe edition of *Krull* arrived from Querido.—Bibi again worse since yesterday. Severe pain in his eyes and sensitivity to light. Dr. Bollag in for a consultation this afternoon. Infection of the iris, a disease resulting from the meningitis. The doctors stayed a long time. Katia greatly downcast. The condition lasts at least four weeks, and the treatment is very demanding. Distressing development, which means that Katia will not be able to go to Arosa. A dismal Christmas.—The gift-giving postponed until quite late. The patient had his own little tree and presents in his room (Erika's). Therese Giehse the only guest. The candles lit once more. Katia had provided delightful gifts for everyone. Among mine the silver candelabrum is most noteworthy. Records of Verdi's Requiem. A light supper, very late, with pâté and champagne. Afterward some music and talk in the living room. Constantly bothered and disgusted from the salty bad taste produced by saliva trapped under the denture.

Reading *Swann's Way* the past several nights. Woke late, having felt unwell in the evening and only very late taken a Phanodorm in order to get to sleep. Worked in the morning on the August chapter. Enormous amount of mail, with many New Year's greetings, especially from America. Letter from Käte Hamburger in Sweden about my most recent publications. Prof. Sommerfeld, Northampton, sent a book on Goethe, together with a long letter. Other letters from Fiedler, Annette Kolb, and so on. Card from Heinrich. Letter from Mrs. Eugene Meyer, Washington.—At noon a short walk by myself. After lunch sorted the mail and read the *Weltbühne*, containing Heinrich's strong article on the German regime.—The Bermanns came to tea at half past five, then stayed on through the evening. Beforehand I wrote to Lion, exerting my authority in the matter of Annette Kolb's contribution.—Dinner with the Bermanns by the light of the new candelabrum. Their present of records: the Brahms *Variations on a Theme by Haydn* and *Siegfried's Rhine Journey*, both conducted by Toscanini, hence quite accurate but somewhat dry.—Punch and crêpes. The guests left before midnight. I went on listening to music by myself, gave my New Year's greetings to Bibi, who was having crêpes in the company of Katia; he can already see well again out of the affected eye. Then I installed the new calendar.—The coming year promises to be quite strenuous. I mean to write the Schopenhauer essay in Arosa. Then comes a three-month jaunt in America. In May or June there will be a trip to Prague or Vienna. Let us hope that the summer, during which a trip to the seashore is planned, or at the latest the autumn, brings with it the completion of *The Beloved Returns*. This "bringing" is really all I can believe in and hope for, not my own energy and industry. Time brings all things. If only I am given time!

1938

Up at 8:30. Freezing, with light snow. Had coffee and wrote further on the August chapter, but not happy with it; the indirect dialogue no longer seems tenable; the "play" is making its own claims.—Around noon the Bermanns came. Talked business with him in Katia's room. Then the three of us took a walk. Discussed the proposed volume of essays. I decided to postpone a purely political volume until later and to publish the Wagner and Schopenhauer pieces in Bermann's essay series.—Bermanns to lunch. The Beidlers came for coffee.—Today's mail also heavy. The actor Wolfgang Langhoff much taken with *Krull*. Letter of thanks from Willem de Boer. New Year's greetings.—After tea wrote Heinrich and took care of other letters. Evening walk in the snow. During supper with Katia and Medi, listened to music of Rimsky-Korsakov on the radio. Telephone conversation with Brentano about his drama. Peaceful evening.

Tuesday, January 11; Arosa, Waldhotel

Yesterday in Küsnacht worked on the dialogue between Charlotte and August until eleven. Then packed. We lunched at 12:45. The weather mild and bright. Left soon after lunch, Golo driving the Chevrolet. Beidler at the station to see us off. Busied myself on the way to Chur (foreigners in the compartment) with reading letters and newspapers, resting a bit. Had coffee in Chur. Had the compartment to ourselves on the way up here. The whole trip quite comfortable. After having the luggage loaded onto the sleigh, we walked through town to the hotel. "Continuity"; reentering the accustomed milieu directly, quite as though one had never been away. The hotel as always. Greeted by the concierge and his staff. Dr. Richter, who saw us up to the usual suite on the fourth floor, which we had "just" left and where we are now settling in again in recapitulation (one that will be varied somewhat, have different substance). Comfort, space, practical well-being. Moved at my own pleasure in resuming this pattern of life. Unpacked. Put up the dark curtain and lined up my books on the chest of drawers. Shaved and put on dark suit. To dinner at 7:30. Our present table in the corner next to last year's. The "Son-in-Law." The roast veal too rare. But ate with the appetite that comes from a change of air. After dinner, Lion. With him in the back lounge. Discussed the magazine, the matter of Ter Braak and that of Chiaromonte, the emigré, in anticipation of seeing Oprecht. Drank beer. Tired. Upstairs at 9:30 and made camomile tea. In bed continued reading *Swann's Way*.

Disturbed in the late hours by noisy guests returning from a costume ball. Helped to sleep by half a Phanodorm tablet, then slept well until 8:15. Had a bath. Breakfast with tea, very bothersome because of the denture. Must still commend the hotel's excellent graham rolls with honey, which I could not eat without the upper teeth.— Arranged my writing table.—Dark, snowing. Opened the package of books and organized the reading I had sent ahead (Schopenhauer material).—Tinkered with the August dialogue, uncertainly. Perhaps I would do better to turn to the Schopenhauer essay and let *The Beloved* rest for the present.—Fur rug under the desk.—At noon with Katia into the village to shop. Walking stick. Read the political manuscript from Döblin in our room after lunch, finding it dubious at best. Rested, depressed. To tea with Katia at the Old India. Back home, dictated letters: to W. Türk (Oslo), Bonnier (Stockholm), Ter Braak (The Hague), and others.—After supper sat in the little salon with Lion. Upstairs, camomile tea.

· ·
Saturday, January 15
· ·

Up at eight. Foehn, warm, snowing heavily.—Tired. The work on *Schopenhauer* toilsome. Washed my hair. Walked along the road to Maran. After lunch sat on the loggia while snow fell heavily. Letters and periodicals. Klaus writes from Hollywood, is giving a lecture on me in California. Ida Herz reports that Peat was in London and informed the press that my fifteen lectures in the States are completely sold out.—Walked around the lake through the snowstorm to tea. Newspaper: governmental crisis in France. Purchases in the village. Display for *Mass und Wert* in the window of the bookshop. Back home, dictated a host of letters: to Mendel (New York), Hollnsteiner (Vienna), and others. After dinner sat in the small salon talking to young Kilpper from Stuttgart. Fatuous, musical young German.

· ·
Friday, January 21
· ·

Up at eight. Bathed. Worked energetically for a long time. Beautiful day. Clear, glistening snowdrifts, mountains deeply covered. Walked with Katia from the ski slope toward Maran. Oprecht joined the three of us at lunch. Read proofs of De Broglie's lecture on physics (indeterminism) out on the loggia. Then a piece, "Kallistos," submitted by a Yugoslav scholar, Rebal. Eros as god of light (Pharus), love, and consciousness. Noted it for Joseph's talk with Amenhotep.—Walked past the sanatoriums. Marvelous panoramas. Quantities of American mail: Angell, Weigand, Mrs. Meyer of the *Washington Post*. The *Joseph* manuscript to be sent to Yale, along with other material for display; difficult. Mrs. Meyer writes about the Yale talk and her own essay on *Joseph*, which will be published in a number of places in connection with my arrival. The trip threatens or rather promises to assume a highly ceremonial character. Excitement and fatigue. Weigand on the Riemer chapter. Other mail.—Four of us at dinner, including Oprecht. Afterward with him in the salon. Read in proofs Koestler's excellently written book on his adventures and imprisonment in Spain. Made cuts in Chiaromonte's article that make it publishable.—In the *Tage-Buch* a good essay by H. Kesten on *Krull*. How dully and indifferently the book was once received in Germany. Absolutely true that German literature needs the Jews!—Read Dostoevsky's "An Unpleasant Predicament" last night. Masterful, the height of painfulness, hardly bearable, but penetratingly true and human.

· ·
Thursday, January 27
· ·

Slept fitfully. [. . .] Up at 8:30. Worked on *Schopenhauer*. Dark skies, snow flurries, deep drifts. With Katia into the village to shop: liqueur and cigarettes. Walking difficult. After lunch sat on the loggia reading proofs of the magazine. Cold. Rested in our room. Katia on a ski tour to Lizi-Rüti. We met at Orelli's, where we had our tea. Back home, finished my letter to Kesten and took care of other handwritten correspondence. Dinner with Katia, Medi, and the engaged couple. Musicians at our table needed tipping. In the back sitting room with Lion. Read what I have so far done on the *Schopenhauer* to him, Katia, and the children. Sat up late editing the foreword for Schickele and writing to him.

Monday, January 31; back in Küsnacht

The last night in Arosa very restless, upset by the evening's talk and my many thoughts and worries. Moreover coughing. Sleepless until well after three. A whole Phanodorm, slow to take effect. Spent some time sitting by Katia's bed. Walked up and down the room. Toward morning a few hours of rest. Got up there at 8:30. After breakfast worked until eleven on *Schopenhauer*. Katia has a very bad cold, very hoarse, truly miserable. From eleven to one packed books and suitcases. Lunch with Brentano. I spoke of my youthful impressions of middle-class life, Travemünde. Left in the sleigh at around two o'clock, after saying goodbye to Richter and the staff. The weather, which seemed disposed to clear after yesterday's storm, darkened again. Great drifts of snow. Sleighride to the railway station, where Christa Hatvany and Lion were waiting for us. Medi stayed until the four o'clock train. Katia very sick and visibly uncomfortable. Coffee in Chur. In the Zurich train we were missing one piece of hand luggage, which then turned up among some other people's bags. Read Dostoevsky's *The Double* on the trip. Arrived at six. Golo there with the car. Drove home. Katia straight to bed. Had tea and unpacked. Then looked through the mail until dinner with Golo and Bibi. Afterward inspected the new arrangement of the record collection that Bibi has devised. The new cabinet complete with curtain. With Katia, who has a temperature. Talked to Golo about Schopenhauer, his beleaguered position viv-à-vis professional philosophers, his being essentially a European man of letters, his friends Jewish, his character only half German, his rigidity, always expanding and buttressing the single notion without a trace of development.—The monthly of the "German Freedom party." Skeptical.

Wednesday, February 9

Late to bed but slept well with the aid of half a Phanodorm, and feel better than yesterday. Worked on the *Schopenhauer*. At noon to Mrs. Hottinger's to practice the Yale talk with her. Walked back toward the Zürichhorn, then was met by the car. Frau Wassermann had already been picked up and we rode home together, where she lunched with us and with Dr. Lányi. Occupied with the essay in the afternoon but did not write any further. In the evening read in *La Flèche* the speech by Gaston Bergery against the Chautemps cabinet. Against the banks and against Moscow, calling for the country to unite in opposition to these two forces, ergo against the Union Nationale, which makes it a sort of fascism without racism, dictatorship, or a fascist foreign policy.—Letter from Kesten, enthusiastic over the Riemer dialogue.—Wolfgang Paulsen, Reading, England, sent an article on Kafka.

This journey being undertaken under the woeful shadow of the Austrian catastrophe.— Were with Annette yesterday in Paris. The ladies left me sitting by the fireplace fire for an hour, then we had lunch with her, old and ailing, a meal prepared with touching care and accompanied by champagne. Bibi joined us. Then coffee in the parlor and our rapid departure with the many pieces of hand luggage. Gare Saint-Lazare. Train to Cherbourg. Crowded compartment. Closed my eyes. Then went on with Koestler's book on Spain, not exactly cheering reading. A four-and-a-half-hour journey. Tea in the dining car on the way. Arrived at seven. Telegram from the *New Republic* requiring a response. Stood in line. Depression and pervasive sense of the meaninglessness of the whole thing. Boarded the tender. Sat with Katia on a sofa in a small ladies' compartment. Long wait. Then transferred to the *Queen Mary*, Bibi astounded at its gigantic size. Found our cabin, a quite tasteful one that made a happy impression on us. The wardrobe trunks. Sense of comforting refuge. To dinner in the serenely elegant dining salon. Caviar, soup, tournedos, and ice cream. Chablis and coffee. Then with Bibi inspected the shops and lounges.—Troubles in the cabin: the one bottle of medicine had been smashed and the cross-braces in my wardrobe trunk broken. The suitcase containing manuscripts missing. Took this latter rather casually. Overtired. Continued reading *The Eternal Husband* in my (excellent) bed.

Smooth sailing all night. Slept very well. Up before eight new time, unintentionally in fact. Breakfast of grapefruit, tea, egg, and honey. The missing bag delivered—it would have been disastrous for the trip if it had been lost. The ship's newspaper on the tragedy in Austria. Appalling. Schuschnigg forced to welcome the murderers of Dollfuss and his own would-be assassins. The Nazi minister of the interior off to Berlin. Goering expected in Vienna. Austrian patriots disheartened, Catholics and Jews in a panic. Hostility toward anything "anti-German," of course, and ban on periodicals (*Mass und Wert*!).—Cold and cowardly statements by Eden in the House of Commons. Horrible. The consequences for Prague? The effect on Switzerland? Where to go? Paris? London? America?—Stayed in bed until after ten, then shaved and bathed. The sea so calm that the ship merely glides along. Walked with Katia and Bibi on the various decks. Then read Koestler's book in the main lounge. At 12:30 lunch with coffee. Then lay down and napped a while. After four to tea in the main lounge, where at 4:45 a movie was shown, a feeble American film based on a Molnár play. Katia in the swimming pool. I walked several times around the main deck and am now about to dress for the evening.—Austria's situation constantly on my mind; worried and depressed, wondering what the consequences will be.

Heavy pitching during the night. Only managed to fall asleep with Phanodorm, but am not well rested. Tired all day long. After breakfast went through the Goethe lecture in English. Spent the day much as yesterday. Smoother voyage. The fog colder. Upset stomach. Napped in the afternoon. Lovely opera film. Katia having trouble with her eye; worried.—At table we established that we had been married thirty-three years. Shock and dizziness at this realization: I said I shouldn't like to repeat this life in which painfulness has predominated. Afraid that I hurt Katia by saying this. Senseless to pass such judgments on life, one's own life, which is after all identical with one's self (for I am my life).—

Sunday, March 20; on the train (drawing room) to Denver, morning

Arrived in Kansas City yesterday evening after dinner in the dining car. Beer in the station bar. Erika bought liquor as a hedge against Prohibition. My nerves strained. Back onto the train. Discovered over our chicken that the trip to Salt Lake City is much longer than we had thought, that we will get there not tonight but rather tomorrow morning. Newspapers on the train. They are already starting in on Czechoslovakia, demanding that she abrogate the treaty with Russia and tighten bonds with "Germany." It was bound to turn out this way. Numbskulls who did not see that once Austria was surrendered there was no further stopping the process. The Greater German Reich of a hundred million is being formed by violent means. What a triumph for the majesty of force! What consequences for European thought! But once more what a role the Germans will play in the world and before its moral consciousness! No heart, no intelligence, no will in opposition, no one even capable of making a strong and decent statement. Total demoralization by Germany. Terrible bombardment of Barcelona by German and Italian planes, with the horrible effect of the new German high-explosive bombs.—After Lithuania's acceptance of the Polish ultimatum there was a pogrom against the Jews in Warsaw, launched by the disappointed mob.— Anguish and worry thinking of my writing, wondering if there is anyone interested in reading it.—

Slept not too badly after reading in *The Idiot*. Assailed again in the morning by worry and anxiety. Up at 8:30. Shaved in the roomette for the first time. Tea and eggs for breakfast in the dining car with Katia, later joined by Erika. Have been crossing the plains now for hours. Sun, heat. Grazing cattle.—Gave some thought to our itinerary (San Francisco-Los Angeles).

Layover in Denver for several hours in the afternoon. Nice modern hotel room. Lunched at two in the hotel restaurant, tasty. Then went to bed and finally got some rest. Cup of tea at five. Then resumed the trip in a drawing room to Salt Lake City. Read in the newspaper of Jewish "labor battalions" in Vienna. Warlike build-up of German troops in Austria. Obviously poised against Czechoslovakia. The English cabinet ministers out of town for the weekend. It is relatively clear that they are letting the man manage things exactly as he pleases. Someone has to take control. Whether war comes or not it seems increasingly inadvisable for us to return to Switzerland. If things continue as they are the monster will soon stop at nothing. Plan that Erika return to Europe alone, dissolve the household, arrange the children's situation, and see to the shipment of our possessions. Still we must wait and see how things develop during the next few weeks.—In spite of its strenuousness this trip could be a happy one, mainly thanks to Erika, were it not for the horrifying political background. Presumably we were again fortunate in being away. I must trust that the characteristically fortunate quality of my life will see me through. Also the preservation of German intellectual life of my stamp will be possible one way or another, possibly by

Knopf's establishing a German-language publishing house.—Anti-Hitler demonstrations in New York and Denver. "Stop the killers!" (For the English public they have gone "too far" with Austria.)

. . . .
Tuesday, March 22; on the Streamliner between Salt Lake City and California
. . . .

The stay in Salt Lake City yesterday and today was remarkable: mountains, 5,000-foot elevation, stimulating air. Continental breakfast in the Hotel Utah. Press conference. Visit with the president of the Mormon church, eighty-two years old. Organ recital in the Tabernacle. Lunch at the hotel with the president of the university, George Thomas, and professors. In the afternoon a drive up into the mountains. In the evening the lecture at the university. Two thousand people. Introduced by the president. Attentive audience, frequently interrupting with applause, even at the "socialist" passages (students). Spell of weakness during the second half, so that I merely "read" several pages. Recovered by the end. Great impression. Very tired. (The altitude.) Supper for the three of us in our hotel sitting room; very hungry, ate scrambled eggs and ham, smoked a cigar.

Got up in Salt Lake City this morning at 7:30, since we were planning to leave at ten. Bathed, breakfasted with coffee, and packed. Then discovered that the train time had been changed, that we could not leave until almost evening on the Streamliner, which will nonetheless get us into Los Angeles earlier than we had planned.—Sat in the lobby with Miss Knight, the agent for Peat. The railway office greatly upset (according to Mr. Thomas); they were impressed by the telegrams from Los Angeles.—Drove in the mountains with Miss Knight. Lunched with her. Rested on my bed. Had tea at 4:30 with Katia and Erika. Excellent cinnamon buns. Left sometime afterward, Mr. Thomas at the station to see us off. Amazing rocket-shaped train with an average speed of eighty miles an hour.

Shaken all day long by the political news, which we have only gotten in skeleton form thanks to the inadequacy of the newspapers. Vienna—terrible. Freud. Friedell throwing himself out of a window. Mass arrests among the higher aristocracy with mistreatment of prisoners, the basest, most cowardly sadism as usual. Bruno Walter's daughter arrested. Moreover the agreement made between England and Hitler is becoming quite obvious: Poland and Lithuania are to keep Russia from coming to the aid of Czechoslovakia. England frankly sacrificing Czechoslovakia in exchange for Germany's relinquishing its colonies, which are no longer required "with her enlarged territory." Greater Germany as a mighty political and economic power. And this is how it had to come into being.

Quantities of mail. Telegram from Bermann in Zurich. Mrs. Meyer about Princeton; positive.

. . . .
Friday, April 1; Beverly Hills Bungalow Hotel
. . . .

Yesterday, ended pleasantly what has been a pleasant trip. Arrived in Los Angeles at six. Colin at the station. Half-hour drive here. Took possession of the handsomely illuminated house in a park. Sherry from the Franks. Visit from them. Quickly unpacked and shaved. Evening clothes. Picked up and taken to a party given by Warner, the wealthy producer. Hundred-dollar-a-plate benefit dinner for the refugees. Stars. Showy house and grounds. Beautiful library; votive lights on the tables in the dining room. After-dinner speeches in German. More speeches later in the library, Frank and I. Questions. Enormous sums collected. Very tired. Back home, sherry with Colin.

Not up today until ten. (A whole Phanodorm.) Continental breakfast on the veranda. Unpacked. Switched bedrooms. Installed myself in the study. The Franks. Looked at a rental car, a four-passenger Ford convertible, and took it. Warm, brilliantly clear day. Urgently need a lighter-weight suit.—New offer from Peat for lectures next year.—Cardinal Newman Award, Detroit, accepted.—The three of us had lunch on the hotel terrace. Autographed books. Radio and workmen.—Utterly charming place. Ready to get to work. Read parts of *Schopenhauer.* Thought yesterday about the conclusion of *The Beloved Returns.*—Intend to have summer clothes sent here from Küsnacht.—Had a late nap, then shaved. Snack of a sandwich and tea at 6:30. Evening clothes. With Colin in Hammerstein's car to Los Angeles. Waited behind the stage of the colossal amphitheater while it filled with an audience of roughly six thousand. Reinhardt, the Franks, and others. Long row of speakers and guests of honor on the stage. Introductions. Delivered my lecture well, frequently interrupted by applause, and with great effect. More speeches afterward: Frank, warm and good. Awards. Sinclair Lewis, humorous. Erika gave the touching appeal for Austrian refugees that she had been working on all afternoon. Collection taken, then the closing ceremony. Everyone quite satisfied. Photographers. To Hollywood and the Franks', hungry. Beer, meat loaf, and eggs. Elizabeth Meyer, whose mother is smoothing the way for our citizenship with Cordell Hull in Washington. Sent a telegram to Hull requesting that he expedite through diplomatic channels the fifteen hundred dollars to the Thomas Mann Funds in Prague and Zurich. Cheerful atmosphere at the Franks'. Nearly two before we got to bed.

Thursday, April 14; Beverly Hills

Got to sleep late, Phanodorm. Drank coffee. Wrote a page and was stimulated. Outing to the beach with the Huxleys, the weather clearing rapidly and becoming warmer, where we got out and took a rather long walk along the glistening blue-and-white ocean at ebb tide. Many condoms on the beach. I did not see them, but Mrs. Huxley pointed them out to Katia.—Lunch in Palos Verdes Estate. Lovely view of the wide bay from the terrace. Soup, roast chicken (tough), ice-cream cake, and coffee. Spoke more English than usual. Came back at around three. Had tea at home after four. Colin brought a new report on negotiations with Goldwyn. Did better at expressing my gratitude to him. Rested a while. Went to the office of a woman notary concerning the extension of our visitors' visa. Signatures. While we were out Erika arranged for our return trip via Chicago, Cleveland, and Toronto with the assistant at the agency.—Tea with the ladies.—Dinner at home. Then with Edwin Knopf's assistant to the MGM studios for a private screening of *Night Must Fall,* an excellent film with Robert Montgomery, who represents a good psychological type and has distinctly Joseph-like moments. Quite interested.—At home with Colin, who leaves tomorrow, pleased with what has been accomplished. Said good-bye to him until New York.

Wrote a page in the morning. The three of us lunched with Liesl Frank in front of the Miramar. Before that on the beach. At home read the *Tage-Buch*. Horrifying reports in letters from Vienna. About Friedell's death.—Dictated a second detailed letter to Bermann in the afternoon. Evening clothes. Party at Edwin Knopf's. Felt uncomfortable for a while, but got better. Afterward the Franks came to our place for tea and cake.—English-language Bible given me by the Knopfs.

Trip to Champaign on Friday. Drawing room. Prepared my talk, rested, and drank tea. Arrived in the late afternoon, met by Father O'Brien and a German professor. Most uncomfortable lodgings. Shown around the campus. Student music contest, concerto rehearsal. Evening clothes. Had dinner without appetite with the other father, served by the housekeeper. A mistake; it would have been better to eat with the others. Picked up before the lecture. A large crowd, mood of great anticipation. Testimonials and pinning on of the medal. Read my piece, after which O'Brien spoke. Then chatted with a number of people. Afterward beer and tea at our lodgings.

Slept Friday night in the improvised beds, with wretchedly small lavatory. Katia, Erika, and I given breakfast by the housekeeper. Discussion with Father O'Brien about communism. Out of sorts. Walked on the university grounds. Greenhouses. Pleasure in the spring green. Departed with the help of the Italian student, with whom we had lunch at the station: sandwich, ice cream, coffee. Left for Chicago, a bad train. Dozed a bit and read in Balzac's *Lily of the Valley*. Arrived at 4:30. Erika took charge of the luggage. Checked into the Drake Hotel. Had tea. Sat in the lobby feeling unwell from being whirled around of late. Letter mail. Upset digestion, result of upset meals. Tired and apparently unable to eat. Dinner around seven in the French restaurant we had visited before. The food again excellent, and this time it was crowded. Then went to a gigantic, packed cinema, dancing and singing, then a comedy starring Beatrice Lillie, whom we had seen in New York. From there to the station, since the sleeping car was available from ten o'clock on. A short wait, then went to bed very tired, and after reading some in Balzac slept quite well.

Today it is fair, sunny, and fresh. Left the already stationary sleeping car at eight. Peat there to meet us. Came with him to the Hotel Cleveland, which is adjacent to the station. Fine suite. The three of us had breakfast, talking with Peat, autographing books. Then retired to the bath, relishing the comforts unavailable at the last place. Digestion restored. After dressing walked with Katia to the lake, no promenade. The couple that was to take us to lunch at Rabbi Silver's was waiting for us at the hotel. English garden, handsome situation of the house by the lake. Some ten guests, the table conversation in English. Left soon after coffee. At three a press conference in our sitting room. Photographs taken and the usual questions asked, answered in English by Erika. Rested from four to five. Pleased that Katia slept, for she has had some bad nights and is worrying about her parents because of the new confiscation law.—Drank tea at five. Then organized the regular lecture again.—In yesterday's mail there were also letters from Europe: one from Lion, who is concerned about my future, and himself advises against Switzerland, recommending London instead. Editorial letter from Golo. The fifth number of the periodical has appeared.

Friday, May 6; New York, Bedford Hotel

Slept soundly after looking through the fifth number of *Mass und Wert* (with the third part of *The Beloved Returns*). A gripping article on Austria.—Up at around nine. After breakfast wrote to Lion, then worked on the foreword for Erika. Lunch in the bar with Gumpert and with a Princeton professor here to discuss Commencement Day. Afterward received some ladies regarding an affidavit for Hermann Broch in Vienna. Long letter from Klaus about his meeting with Dr. Osborn concerning Reisiger, who is in Berlin and has a passport, but is confused, frightened, and in a state of extreme indecision. Worried about him.—Rested. After tea dictated a host of letters to Katia, especially to Consul Laška in Zurich, informing him of my cable to President Beneš and amplifying on the text of it.—Lectured in the evening at Carnegie Hall. Large crowd. Warmest possible welcome and the talk a success. Standing ovation at the end. Many visitors in the greenroom. Afterward at the Plaza Hotel with Gumpert, Katzenellenbogen, Colin, and the Knopfs.—The newspapers carry appalling accounts of Hitler's behavior in Rome. Glassy-eyed, morose, and apathetic after his talk with Mussolini, which evidently took a negative turn.

Tuesday, May 24; Jamestown, Rhode Island, the home of Miss Caroline Newton

Departed from Grand Central Station at noon on Sunday, after saying good-bye to Colin and Landshoff. Comfortable trip to Kingston with Bibi, four hours, Pullman and dining cars. Met by Miss Newton, driven to the ferry that brought us across to this island. House reasonably comfortable, sea air, picturesque natural spot. Enjoying the quiet and the unspoiled surroundings. At first we were somewhat cramped due to the presence of our hostess and the Ulmann girl from Munich. Have gotten to know the nearby village, also Newport yesterday afternoon, which can be reached by ferry.— Shopped, made the initial arrangements for a rental car. Am promised the Propyläen edition of Goethe; some Goethe items in Reclam editions here in the house.—The weather is mild, foggy, and windy, with rain today toward evening.—At noon the welcome departure of the strangers, and we had our first lunch with just the three of us, lamb chops we had bought ourselves, prepared and served by Lucy, the Negro cook.—Took possession of the room designated as my workroom, arranged my things and set up a writing table.—The letter from Princeton arrived today: impressive and flattering offer of six thousand dollars a year for being a member of the faculty and giving four lectures, three of them having to do with either Goethe or Schopenhauer. The fourth about *Faust*. The compass is pointing in that direction. Dictated a letter to Mrs. Meyer. Another to Oprecht concerning the publication of the lecture, the German manuscript of which Erika took with her. Took care of other correspondence yesterday and today.—The *New York Times* daily from the village. Relaxation of the

European situation, obviously thanks to the impressive stance of the Czechs.—One feature of this place is the nearly perpetual sound of the foghorn.—Uncertain whether we will stay past the beginning of July, when the owner is expecting to return. Living together with her almost inconceivable. The next weeks are taken care of, though to be interrupted by trips to New York and Yale for degree ceremonies on the 31st and the 20th.—Determined to get to bed early here.—In the mornings I have café au lait out of the Chinese cup that Miss Newton gave me.—Bibi is practicing in the garage, very pleased with the place.—Lowering skies, fog, the sound of the wind and the foghorn. Frequent spells of anxiety. Hope to recuperate.—

Saturday, June 11; Jamestown

Thick fog and rain the entire day. Impossible to go out.—Another feature of this island is a kind of small but strong, tough-bodied bug that bores its head into your skin. Hard to dislodge them, and once fully implanted, as recently happened to me, they can only be cut off with scissors. Have killed great numbers of them. Revolting.— Up before eight. Worked better on the August chapter. Read in the *Times* after lunch about the Czech defensive measures, the looting of Austria, and the refusal to make reparation payments.—A statement from Bielsko, Poland, about ways and means to liberate Austrian intellectuals; fairly hopeless, but well written, possibly by Brüll. Good characterization of that band of thieves.—News of the music festival in Lucerne with Toscanini, Walter, and Strauss is interesting and reassuring.—Read the notes and sketches for *Dichtung und Wahrheit*, much useful material.—Once more experiencing the sensually stimulating and arousing effect of island air. Aphrodisiacal, especially in wet weather.

Spoke with Colin on the telephone in the morning, inviting him to keep me company while Katia is in Princeton. He accepted gladly.—Gave Katia the manuscript of *Schopenhauer* in the afternoon.—Did not go out. Heavy fog. Took care of handwritten correspondence after tea: to Frank, to Ida Herz, thank-you letters, and to Fiedler.

Thursday, June 23; New York, Bedford Hotel

On Tuesday a nice drive in our little car from Jamestown to New Haven, with a stop for lunch at an eighteenth-century inn. No beer. Arrived at the master's house of Prof. French in New Haven at around four. Rested briefly. Tea at the home of the former president's widow, who was herself away at a game. Dinner at French's in the evening (Weigand).—Yesterday, the 22nd, had breakfast with our hosts and other guests. Then the commencement exercises began: got into robe, academic procession, the hall, entrance, orchestra (*Die Meistersinger*), ceremonious proceedings. Walt Disney and I received the strongest applause. Another degree. Very hot day. Other recipients: the governor general of Canada, the conductor Koussevitzky, whom I got to know afterward over refreshments and at the lunch that followed in the large hall. Speeches. Close of the festivities at 2:30. Back to French's, packed, and said good-bye. Train at 4:15 to New York, Pullman. Rested somewhat. New doubts about whether we shouldn't sail earlier on the *Statendam*. No.—To the hotel. Different rooms on the fourteenth floor. Visits from Riess, Colin, Gumpert. Our luggage from Jamestown and the boxes of books from Küsnacht brought to our room. Riess and Colin off to the sensational boxing match between Max Schmeling and the Negro champion. We left with Gumpert in his car to have dinner at the rooftop restaurant of the St. Moritz. A cool breeze up there after the appallingly muggy heat that greeted us on our arrival and in our rooms. Afterward drove with Gumpert in Central Park and to Harlem. At the news that their man had KO'd Schmeling in the first round, the Negroes broke out in a frenzy of joy, with kissing, dancing, honking of horns, cannonades, racing cars. Mounted police. (Schmeling had received a telegram from the "Führer" congratulating him before the fight.)—To bed at around midnight, read Brecht with increasing distaste.

Had difficulty falling asleep. Extremely hot. Got up this morning at 8:30. Showered. Waited a long time for breakfast. Unpacked. Opened the book cartons. Washed my hair, shaved. Katia went out shopping with Colin. Call from Heinrich Koppel. Toilsome business of unpacking the boxes that were sent for too soon, the contents of which I will miss in Switzerland despite the notes I have made. At the office with the Knopfs. Saw Koshland, autographed books. In Alfred's office discussed the prospects for a *Joseph* film, the translations, etc. They have sold 16,000 copies of *Joseph in Egypt.*— With the Knopfs to the nearby luncheon club with its mirrors and its starry ceiling. Writers, publishers, and motion picture people. Ate with a good appetite. Introduced to Fadiman.—Back at the hotel, went on with the work of unpacking books, assisted by Katia. Then had a rest. Tea alone.—At six a visit from the ship's agent. Colin informs me that come winter I will receive the Gold Medal from the Jewish Center, along with a cash prize.—Dinner with Riess in his little French restaurant. Walked afterward in the hurly-burly of Broadway to a cinema there, the newsreel of the Schmeling-Louis fight. Late to bed; read some in Tolstoy's *The Cossacks.*

Monday, June 27; Mount Kisco, Seven Springs Farm

Yesterday morning at around 10:30, after a bout of packing and organizing, we left to come here in the Meyers' car. Markedly cooler. Spacious grounds, quiet, wealth, and comfort. Countless number of people for lunch, aperitifs on the terrace beforehand. Very lovely garden house. Thunder, persistent rain. Very cool, short underwear, sniffles. More company at tea. Afterward took care of some urgent letters with Katia. Dinner *en famille* at eight, my stomach overstuffed. Conversation in the library. Upstairs at a reasonable hour, but great difficulty falling asleep. Phanodorm and Evipan. Sat up in the chair in my dressing gown. Slept adequately at last.

Up today at nine. Have caught cold, upset stomach. Rain. Breakfast brought up to us. Then shaved and dressed. Called the real-estate agent, arranged for the trip to Princeton with our hostess. Disclosures about the basis of my appointment at Princeton: the six thousand dollars are chiefly from the Rockefeller Foundation, whose trustees are "all friends of mine" (Mrs. Meyer). My obligation to the university not too strict; extension available if I so wish. The long and short of it is that I scarcely have any financial problems in America.—

Drove with Mrs. Meyer into the city at eleven, where she had to attend a meeting on economic policy. Philipps, the hard-of-hearing chauffeur, drove us on to Princeton.

Lunch there at the Peacock Inn, no appetite. From there with the woman agent to the Library Place house, 65 Stockton Street. Mr. and Mrs. Mitford, readers of mine, are returning to England, would like to give my lecture to the prime minister to read. Shown through the elegant and practical house, discussed the arrangements, agreed that half of the books in the studio would be removed. Fine bedrooms, one of which, together with an adjacent room and bath, would make an excellent suite for me. We rented the house for one year at two hundred fifty dollars a month. The owners hope that they might sell the house more easily with us living there—or that we might buy it ourselves. A significant day for having brought such a decision. Compared to Küsnacht the house represents a definite step upward in our standard of living. They will leave a good car in the two-car garage, where we can also park the Jamestown Chevrolet. Tasteful sitting rooms. The study not large, and somewhat dark, but comfortable and detached, with the requisite sofa. Might ultimately serve as an apartment for Golo.

Continuous rain. Drove back to New York, picked up Mrs. Meyer at the Plaza Hotel, and returned with her to Mount Kisco. Had tea there. Have caught cold, sore throat. At 7:30 a family dinner without the master of the house. Not feeling well. In the evening we all went to the theater, the performance of a prizewinning play, the author's first, about college life; quite trivial, though well acted. No attractive faces among the young people. Young American men not particularly appealing.—Home in pouring rain.

. . . .
Thursday, July 7; Küsnacht
. . . .

Arrived back in Zurich this morning after an absence of nearly four months.—Yesterday morning I spent in a deck chair on the S.S. *Washington*, also some time after lunch. Interrupted for picture-taking and farewells. Docked in Le Havre at 4:30. Passport inspection, debarkation, customs formalities. Sent a telegram to Annette Kolb, who had waited for us for lunch in vain, and another to the children. Train to Paris, Pullman. Dinner served at around seven. Read the *Atlantic Monthly*, which contained a fine review of *Joseph*. In Paris at nine. Drove to the Gare de l'Est with our eleven pieces of hand luggage. Had been given the wrong arrival time for Zurich. Sent another telegram to the children. Unsuccessful attempt to reach Annette by telephone. Sleeping car. Whole Phanodorm. Slept well. Café au lait this morning in Basel. Splendid blue summer morning. Lovely landscape. Medi and Golo at the station. The older children in Spain. The Chevrolet. Drove home. Everything as in a dream. Greeted the maids, the dog. Breakfast table out on the terrace bright with flowers. Joy and sense of well-being. Much discussion of the times and the situation. Unpacked. Prodigious amount of mail, both letters and parcels, even though some had been forwarded to the S.S. *Statendam*. Katia's worries somewhat relieved upon hearing from her parents that their letters might have been held up. Letter from Valentin Heins in Munich with exorbitant demands for payment, which he is unable to collect from the state despite its own legislation.—Short stroll with Katia before lunch. The novelty of reading Swiss papers, the *Weltbühne*.—Fine summer day, not too warm. Still have the cold I caught in Mt. Kisco; severe attacks of coughing.—After tea looked up some things in the big Goethe edition.—Filled up the gaps in the library shelves with other books.—Telephone conversations with Kahler and with Therese Giehse (in Sils). Annemarie Schwarzenbach in serious condition because of morphine addiction.—News that old Herr Reiff died three weeks ago.—Kahler to dinner. Read aloud in my study the "Pages from a Journal" from Beverly Hills. Impression of only partial success; the subject matter to blame. The point of it, namely Hitler as artist or anti-artist, even anti-Christ, would have to be treated separately.—Much talk of America and Europe. The burden of Austria. The remarkably short-lived reaction to that tragedy. The necessity of carrying on in spite of it.—I will finish the volume of Tolstoy that I last was reading in America before I fall asleep tonight. One o'clock.—In the mail a letter from Bermann from Stockholm: about the continuation of the firm in Vienna by the Nazis, the shipment of my books abroad! About a new edition of my books, the volume of novellas in a series of cheap editions.

Sunday, July 17; Küsnacht

Got to sleep late last night, but no need for a sleeping pill. Up at 8:30. Mild, overcast, pleasant day. Worked on the August chapter (Arnim). At noon drove with Katia to the woods near Heslibach, where we used to walk with the campstool during the sciatica period. Looked at building lots for a European *pied-à-terre*, excited at the notion. Decided to acquire a lot with the help of a businessman.—To lunch Frau M. Wassermann, who is endlessly difficult. Promised to help her in her endeavor to get to America.—Dictated letters in the afternoon: South American publishing prospects, an answer to Werner Türk and intervention on his behalf with Mrs. Meyer, *Washington Post*. Others.—Before dinner walked with Katia around the pond, which with its reeds and waterlilies presented a picture of surpassingly colorful beauty. Gazed at it with intense pleasure.—In the evening listened to parts of *Tannhäuser* and *Tristan*. Read several Goethe poems. Afterward read again for a long time in Fiedler's autobiographical manuscript. A curious document, charming yet disturbing, a mixture of religious earnestness and self-complacency. He wants a chance to discuss it with me.

Monday, August 15; Sils Baseglia

Slept well, got up at 8:15. Continuing sense of satisfaction at the success of my reading aloud. Weather somewhat improved. Bathed. Had breakfast alone, tea.—Began writing the *Faust* lecture, interrupted by a visit from John Knittel. Sunny. Walked with Katia over the Chasté to the Nietzsche plaque. Lunch at one, then, in the garden, read the Helena book, the *Neue Zürcher Zeitung* on German military preparations. After I had gone, there was a scene between Katia and a German Jew who had spoken insultingly of me and my family to a well-meaning Swiss lady.—Rested, heart palpitations. Rendezvous with the Walters at 4:30 in the Suvretta House for tea, eventually joined by the children. Friendly exchange. Afterward into St. Moritz to do shopping. Cable about the dramatization of *Mario and the Magician*.—Chilly. Winter suit in the evening. At the children's with Dr. Klopstock from Budapest.

Changeable weather, warm, windy. Worked on the lecture. At noon with the ladies in the small garden, then drove with Katia to Fexthal, where we walked. After lunch in the garden, much mail from America, including a letter from Caroline Newton, also one from Bermann about the *Schopenhauer*. Finished an excellent article by Annemarie Schwarzenbach-Clarac on the American South that I had begun last night. At four picked up by Bill Hutchinson, who took us to his delightful peasant house in Fexthal. Tea there with a Swiss-German couple. Shown through the house, the massive roof beams, magnificently primitive. Massing clouds, rain and wind. After dinner over to Erika's. Dr. Klopstock there. Coffee and kirsch. Erika read a chapter of her book on emigrés, nicely done. Much talk of the threat or promise of war. England seems more and more forced in that direction. The incomprehensible inability of political organs to do what is necessary at the right time, and the utterly bizarre phenomenon that they are willing to pay in the familiar currency of war a hundred times what it would cost if they had the courage to adopt less orthodox measures.

Hold fast to time! Use it! Be conscious of each day, each hour! They slip away unnoticed all too easily and swiftly.—A new month. The month in which we will re-cross the ocean, resettle. Today the major moving day. The packers failed to come in the morning. After breakfast I went on writing the *Faust* lecture, still using my desk. At noon the "elevator" van arrived. Drove with Katia and Heinrich to the lovely Zumikon forest, where we took our walk. After lunch the furniture and crates were carried out. I had stowed many small items, including the funerary servant figurine (wrapped in cotton wool), in the drawers of my desk, which I then removed on instructions from the packer. Waited alongside the van for the desk to appear, so that I could personally lock the drawers again. Sat on the stone ledge of the garden terrace, watching the pieces of furniture carried out, the Empire armchair in which I wrote the last part of my letter to Bonn. Katia and Eri came and joined me. In the end I delegated responsibility for the drawers to Katia, so that I might lie down for a bit.— Busy at teatime making the place tolerably livable again. Am again writing at the table I used five years ago, before the furniture from Munich arrived. The living room looks bare without the cabinets and the radio-phonograph.—The first proofs of *Schopenhauer* came.—Evening clothes. With Katia, Klaus, Moni, and Medi to the Schauspielhaus for the opening night of *Troilus and Cressida*. Box. Amazing play, nihilistically bitter, problematic in both structure and plot. Coffee during the intermission with Oprecht and the Falkes. In addition greeted many other people: the Faesis, Frau Rothbart, Lavinia Mazzucchetti, the Kaufmanns, Kahler.—The play's spirit at the furthest remove from Homer's Thersites. Shakespeare, the modern writer.—Declined to take part in the banquet afterward. Drove home. Starry sky. The house neat and bare. Supper with the family. We are expecting numerous guests in these next days.

Up at 8:30. Fine weather. Worked on the article for Fadiman, tired and bored. At noon took the long walk through the woods alone with the dog. After lunch finished the proofs of the essay volume. Some handwritten letters after tea: Amann's manuscript (via Hesse) to Jakob Welti. The Falkes. With them into town. Dinner at a restaurant (very good). After having been depressed and grumpy all day, my state of mind improved. To the Schauspielhaus after dinner, a box with the Falkes, Golo, and Medi. Good production of a dramatization of *Crime and Punishment*. Coffee during the intermission with the Falkes, Hirschfeld, Freund. After the play I sought out Dr. Wälterlin in his box. Took the Falkes home with us, Golo driving them to Feldbach afterward.—Bleak news from Czechoslovakia. Disastrous article in the London *Times*, officially disclaimed, urging the Czechs to cede the Sudeten territories to Germany. England's treachery becomes increasingly plain. The country is to be sacrificed in cold blood. There will be no war—which is not to say that war will not some day become necessary, and under the most disadvantageous conditions conceivable.

Awoke quite early. Overcast, brisk, sea slightly choppy. Up at 7:45, dressed immediately, and had breakfast by myself in the dining room. Afterward up to the promenade deck. Kerényi's article on the Greek novel. Before that worked in pencil on the *Faust* lecture until the lady in the next chair began looking over my shoulder. Clearer weather, pitching. The three of us took several turns around the upper deck. Cup of coffee after lunch. Then again in the deck chair. Reread sections of *Faust*. The ship's newspaper. The situation as bad as it could be. Daladier and Chamberlain agreed that only a plebiscite can save the peace. Both putting pressure on Beneš. Secession of the "purely German regions" and self-determination in the mixed ones. Then international guarantees for the new borders of Czechoslovakia. Doubtless meaning neutralization and dependence on Germany. New statement by Hodža to the effect that the Republic refuses to hold such a plebiscite. What will happen if it holds to this position?—Will France openly break her treaty?—It is incomprehensible madness. No one wants war— and it could be averted if only they stood up to Hitler. He couldn't wage one; it would mean the end of him. Therefore it must be that no one wants him out of the way at any price. Why not? Because they are afraid of bolshevism. And according to them bolshevism would be the result of any war. So neither war nor the fall of Hitler, in that they keep him from going to war. Instead they give him the Republic of Czechoslovakia without war, just as he wanted them to. They willingly let him carry out his simple, openly proclaimed program step by step. The world has never seen a more abject and stupid misery.—Tea on the handsome covered deck overlooking the ocean. Walked on the upper deck. Rather heavy forward pitching. Waves breaking over the foredeck. Rainbow.—Katia went back to the cabin right after dinner, feeling somewhat seasick. I sat with Medi in the lounge reading letters from the young Hofmannsthal to George in the *Corona*. Glanced through other articles. The magazine's dignified intellectual tone, its magnificent impartiality that I used to find unpleasant. Then went with Medi to see an uncommonly stupid film, its central character a female ice-skating champion.—Ship rolling badly.

Heavy rolling during the night, fitful sleep. Up at 7:45, showered and had breakfast in the dining room. The morning dark and blustery, then periods of clearing. On deck tried to do some writing until inhibited again by the people in the chairs on either side of me. A lady I cannot place introduced a Herr Lippschütz from Antwerp. Heard the most lamentable news from him: Prague has had to capitulate in the face of terrible pressure. It first tried to resist, relying on its pact with Russia and France, but just before 1:00 A.M. it had to accept the partitioning and the plebiscite, the replacement of its alliances by an "international guarantee." The implications and the terrible consequences need not be spelled out. I share Katia's deep depression, even though, as always, I try to feel hopeful and remind myself that this is by no means the end of the world. Nonetheless it is surprising that Beneš and his people defend the capitulation.—Sore upper jaw since yesterday, evidently caused by the new denture, which I must have adjusted in New York. Am wearing the old one.—Katia to bed after lunch. I stayed on deck reading Goethe's *Annals*, but soon felt hemmed in again by the people beside me. Read up on the sorrowful news in the *Ocean Post*. The British Cabinet divided and at odds, but the betrayal seen as necessary. The *News Chronicle* comments that it is to be feared that the terrible sacrifice will have been in vain. That may well be so. Russia announced that it would offer no help except for planes and matériel if France did not march in. The Czechs found themselves standing alone so had to give in. After the first shock there was such outrage in Prague that Englishmen and Frenchmen could not show themselves in the streets. It is unquestionably one of the greatest disgraces in history. The Czech state was created by the victors of 1918. They themselves have acknowledged step by step that their victory is untenable and mistaken, and they have relinquished it. Very probably fascism will stretch out its tentacles to America. But it is also still possible that the war will have to be fought in any case, whether over Strasbourg or Switzerland. But this strikes me as unlikely, since the breakthrough to the east will cure the German economy and consolidate the Hitler regime.—Detachment, detachment! One must restrict oneself to his own immediate concerns and the life of the mind. I require serenity and the consciousness of my favored existence. Impotent hatred must not consume me.—Tea in the lounge with live music; plenty of room, since many people are seasick. Afterward a few times around the open deck in the wind. Showered with spray from a high wave.—Yesterday radioed to Erika in Paris: "Publication impossible." Glad to be free of the appeal, which did not originate with me in any case.—Will Bermann dare to bring out the essay after that wretch's triumph? It is more apropos than ever.—Katia is typing the article for Fadiman.—Wrote further on the *Faust* lecture sitting in the armchair next to my bed. After dinner, in the lounge with Attorney Löwenfeld. Drank beer. With him to the cinema, a film of Remarque's *Three Comrades*, very mediocre.

Congratulate myself a little for working yesterday afternoon, being able to fall asleep easily last night without a pill, and having a good night's sleep. Composure, mental calm, imperturbability, and steadfastness. Who knows what is in store? I can live and hold my own come what may.—Got up at 7:30, shaved and showered, wore my cashmere sweater to breakfast in the dining room: grapefruit, green tea, coddled eggs, brioche, dark bread, and honey. Then out on the deck revising the "short philosophical statement" for Fadiman.—Gloomy weather. Temperature rose during the night (Gulf Stream). Sailing more smoothly.—Worked a good while in the deck chair on the *Faust* essay, drank bouillon at eleven, went walking with Katia on the upper deck in a gentler wind. The news appalling. The Czechs calling desperately for their cause to be submitted to the court of arbitration promised them in their treaties, declaring that giving in to Hitler's demands will mean the dissolution of their state. And in fact those demands are now being extended to include the Polish and Hungarian portions of the country. England and France declare that Czechoslovakia's response to the German ultimatum is "unsatisfactory," and insist on total capitulation if invasion is to be avoided. Frightening and most brutal situation for a small, industrious people that was proud of its country, and with good reason. The news very scanty, telling nothing about the mood in the democracies or the atmosphere in Prague. Will the populace demand a war of desperation? Such a demand would be ill-advised and humanly impossible. But it would be a great contribution to morale and would more or less save the honor of Europe if these people did not submit without a fight. Must not England be regarded as disgraced? And after this France is no longer a country whose alliances mean anything. It is the total defeat of democracy and of all justice. The dissolution of a vital state that was valuable to civilization in response to the blackmail demands of a power scornful of civilization is without precedent. I can think of people who will take their own lives after this experience.—Machine-gun skirmishes on the Czech-German border. The ultimatum runs out this evening. Submission is virtually certain.—After lunch read Horváth's *A Child of Our Time* in my deck chair. Rested on my bed and brooded. Tea on the fine deck veranda. Afterward in the cinema for a while, where every seat was taken.—Walked on the upper deck, with Lippschütz at the last. Calm, swift sailing.—Radiogram from Mrs. Meyer insisting that we stay with her until the Princeton house is ready.—Dinner. Afterward with Medi's friends, the Zurich actress and the Indian. Read the Horváth, which loses steam but remains a fine book. I had mistakenly anticipated a Wagner concert. Went once more to the cinema instead. Kept checking the ship's bulletin board, but learned nothing new. Early to bed thanks to having set back the clock.

Sunday, September 25; New York

Slept quite well, but am tired, and after my coffee felt terrible. Nonetheless finished the speech in English for this afternoon and read it to Katia and to Klaus, who had just arrived on the S.S. *Champlain*. Corrections. Had it typed.—Fine, warm day.—No word from the children in Paris.—*New York Times*: optimism on the part of the German press. Either Czechoslovakia will accept the terms or the war will remain localized.—At noon with Katia and Colin for a stroll on Park Avenue. Lunch with Dr. Klopstock and Klaus at the hotel. Rested briefly. Then taken to Madison Square Garden. Introductions in the anteroom. Gigantic auditorium filled with 18,000 people; another 10,000 waiting outside. Czech peasant girls, the national anthem. Speeches. Dorothy Thompson. Fantastic demonstration upon my appearance at 4:30. Another at my words, "Hitler must fall!"—An impressive event. Spoke with the Czech speaker. They will fight. It is expected that the Germans will invade from the Austrian side.— At 5:30 back to the hotel. Tea with Klopstock and Klaus. Cable from Erika, who is sending the two boys but seems to be staying behind herself, as we had thought.— Great and profound suspense. Will Hitler hurl himself into his destruction? Any surprise is possible. The war might be a short one, but might also precipitate the most drastic changes. If only it could accomplish, possibly without really breaking out, the demystification of the worldwide fascist nonsense and show up those cowards who grovel before its would-be millennial grandeur.—Sent a cable authorizing the Paris appeal.—With Katia and Medi to dinner at Dr. Gumpert's. His pretty little daughter. Presented with his Dunant book in English. After dinner Curt Riess with news: the Czechs have rejected the ultimatum, making counterproposals which will most certainly be rejected. Troops from all of Germany moved to the Czech border. A speech by Hitler is announced for the Sportpalast. He will again pull out all his infamous stops in order to place the Western powers in check and throw the world into confusion. The Germans are afraid enough of going to war in an alliance with the Italians and Poles. But it is to be feared that the others will also go to war, motivated by their guilty conscience with regard to the Treaty of Versailles, of which Czechoslovakia is a part.—What if it began with the toppling of Mussolini? Hitler would soon follow. If a wider war breaks out, the others will be paying for their countless mistakes since Versailles.

Monday, September 26; New York

Up at 7:30. The weather continues fair. Worked on the *Faust* essay. Pictures taken. Dr. Koppel on bookdealers' business. Klaus. Prospects and conjectures. Went out with Katia and Medi. Necessary shopping, Optimo cigars. At noon taken by Koppel to his apartment with its fine view of park and city. Cold lunch. Over coffee and cigar listened to the broadcast of Hitler's speech at the Sportpalast. Railing against Beneš and falling back on the Berchtesgaden compromise. No war for certain, and a way for the dictatorship to save face. No invasion before October 1. The possibility that Prague will be held to carrying out the concessions already agreed to. Promise that this is "the last territorial demand" he will make (but of course one that leaves him so powerful that there can be no refusing his next ones). A serious setback brought about with a deftness tuned with hysteria. Depressed and at the same time indifferent, conscious of the advantages of not having war. Something has happened nevertheless.— At 4:30 to Dr. Brodsky's to have the denture adjusted. Walked back to the hotel. The photographer; bought several pictures.—Discussed the situation with Riess, who sees it less pessimistically. Visit from Oprecht's agent, the bookdealer Krause, and his wife. Profound absentmindedness. Taken to dinner by Alfred Knopf. News on the car radio that France and England will guarantee the carrying out of the Berchtesgaden demands. Probably a false rumor. Newspapers with headlines about a Russian-English-French alliance to defend Czechoslovakia. Excellent dinner with Knopf in a French restaurant. Blanche joined us. Katia very depressed and without appetite. My attitude calmer. It is quite possible that Hitler will not attain his real goal even if the territory is ceded to him, because the independence of Czechoslovakia will be preserved.—

After coffee to the Knopfs'; some music. Charmed by pieces by Rossini and Chopin. Back at the hotel, telephone conversation with Klaus. The morning papers are not reporting any change in the situation. The speech is seen as intransigent, war closer. The French completing their mobilization rapidly.—During dinner Knopf said that I was Hitler's most formidable enemy.—A new printing of *Buddenbrooks* is in the works.— Article by Mrs. Roosevelt on *The Coming Victory of Democracy.*—

Tuesday, September 27; New York

Overstimulated. Slept with the help of Phanodorm. [Up] at 8:30. Overcast, sultry. Quickly wrote a bit after coffee. German-American journalist, columnist, political discussion. Declined a further meeting. Once more packed our luggage. Went out a bit with Medi. Crowds on Fifth Avenue. Lunch alone with Katia. Then read in our room while Katia listened to Chamberlain's speech: a very human voice, deeply stirred, grave, little hope for peace. Better to fight than to live in a world where force reigns supreme.—The luggage picked up on instructions from Caroline Newton. Rested for an hour. Around 4:30 by taxi to Dr. Brodsky. In his living room with his wife and a Prof. Bernstein. Discussed the situation, its political and intellectual aspects. Adjustment to the denture satisfactory. Rain, thunder. Back by taxi. Katia read newspapers: war seems unavoidable. Mussolini states that Italy is preparing to fight on Germany's side. Troubled about Switzerland. No question but that Germany would inflict terrible things; still the blindness of these people is monstrous.—Five and a half years since I began keeping these diary records in Arosa after the loss of my German existence.— Visit from Mr. Ritchie, agreed to the Chicago dinner on the first of December. Visit from Peat about lectures in March that will bring in lots of money.—Peat told us that Churchill foretold this very course of events to him several months ago. He and Eden will be taking over the government. The duel between fascism and democracy was probably inevitable. From the start, Germany and Italy have been bent on war, the whole thing senseless without the expectation of war. Only through war can their "world view" prove itself. The thesis to be demonstrated is that nations so constituted are invincible.—Dinner with Colin in a kosher restaurant on Broadway, excellent food. Then a very funny Marx brothers film. People enjoying themselves on the brightly lighted street. Beautiful views. The illuminated headlines atop the *Times* building. Mobilization of the British navy. In France it is still hoped that pressure from the democratic powers will avert war. At this moment I too cannot believe that Hitler will run headlong to his destruction. His entire plan is wrecked. Did England want war just now? Have they gone through all this in order to make the empire ripe for war? Has Hitler walked into a trap?—The Italians rejoicing over Chamberlain's last hopes for peace. Unquestionably war at the side of Germany is highly unpopular. Perhaps the first surprises will come from that quarter.—Review of *The Coming Victory* by Stampfer in the *Volkszeitung.* Attack in the *Staats-Zeitung*: "One must not speak out against one's own country." (Did I do that?)

Tuesday, October 4; Princeton

Up at 8:15. Clear and cool. In the morning finished the observations on *Faust,* which come to forty-two pages.—Colin sent the Dorothy Thompson article on the political situation, which calls things by their right names. "A fascist coup d'état." Very true, and it will leave its mark on Europe for decades. At least I see no other possible outcome and cannot fathom what these reverses and alterations would be that many people seem to expect in the near future. The whole thing has unfolded in too sequential and consistent a manner and is rooted too deeply in the half-unconscious collective will of the European bourgeoisie.—The betrayal of the peoples.—The role played by Daladier in Munich. Goering, who slaps him on the back and urges him to stay for the Oktoberfest.

At noon in the barber shop, oil massage, etc. Then went on a short walk with Katia.—Again deeply depressed all day long. As Senator Beneš could not appear at the meeting, a substitute was found, someone of no account, so that I decided not to participate and my preparations were in vain.—Mrs. Conner came with the typescript.—After lunch with letters and newspapers on the terrace. Klaus arrived at teatime. No word from Erika. She is supposed to have gone to Prague. Klaus surprised by the elegance of the house, in which I take no pleasure at all.—Dictated a pile of overdue letters to Katia, replies to letters from California dating back to February and March. Long letter from Ida Herz on the war scare, which was engineered in order to frighten the peoples of Europe.—Four of us at the dinner table, including Klaus.— My next assignment must be writing a foreword to the volume of essays, another pretext for putting off *The Beloved Returns.*

Wednesday, October 19; Princeton

Once more back to *The Beloved.* Long handwritten letters to Lion and Kahler. After lunch received a woman reporter interviewing me for the *New York Times* on the sun porch. Dean Gauss and his wife to tea. In the evening listened to *Die Götterdämmerung* with intense enjoyment. Read Huizinga's *Der Mensch und die Kultur.* Good and sensible.—Bibi sick. Local doctor. Jaundice or food-poisoning.

Monday, October 24; Princeton

Rainy, very dark. Prepared the manuscript of *This Peace* for Knopf. Worked on Chapter VII. Forty-five-minute walk. In the afternoon dictated endless letters. Verdi's Requiem in the evening.—Tender with Medi. Erika's tales of the misery in Prague, the collapse—actually the murder—of a faith. The mistreated Czech couple driven out of their little town because its population was predominately German. The entire thing will always remain an irresponsible crime.—The *Prager Presse* carries an appeal by the Czech intellectuals to the educated world with portions excised by the censors, heart-rending.—Read much about Helena and the exchanges with Boisserée.

Went by car to New York on Tuesday afternoon in oppressively warm, humid weather. Tedious drive. The Bedford. Rooms on the twelfth floor. With the Stevens family to *Hamlet* at the St. James Theater. Interesting evening. During the long intermission, dinner at the Astoria. Afterward at Erika's.—Wednesday: Erika back from Ellis Island in the morning, having succeeded in getting Gret Moser released. At noon the *Herald Tribune* luncheon at the Astoria, 1,100 people. Cocktails beforehand. Speeches by Dorothy Thompson and two people from the press. Then my speech, nervous and emotional. Many people greeted me.—Koppel and Landshoff to tea at the hotel to discuss the publishing venture. The problem of Bermann, who in a flash of vengefulness is taking it upon himself to publish the book and the brochure, the latter in an edition of 10,000 copies.—In the evening a birthday party in our living room for Erika. Guests were Gumpert, Riess, Katzenellenbogen, Gret, Medi, Bibi. Champagne, soup, pâté, pheasant, Baumkuchen. Left around eleven with Medi driving. Unpleasantnesses with a highway patrolman. Arrived home after midnight.

Slept well until 8:30. Telephone: *Faust* lecture moved up to the end of November.— Corrected the *Faust* lecture for Helen Lowe-Porter. Took it to her. Fine, cool, clear weather. Walked. Prof. Simons with us for lunch. Coffee in the garden. Looked through the mail. Slept. After tea dictated letters. Numerous things attended to. Evening dress, early dinner. Chamber music at Flexner's in honor of his birthday. Great many guests, enjoyed the music, which was well performed. Back home marked quotations for Lowe-Porter.

Saturday, November 12; Princeton

The fine weather continues; warm, the sun once more too hot. Worked somewhat more energetically. Cable from Bermann about dropping "This Man is My Brother" in light of the pogroms and possible personal consequences. At first wanted to leave it up to him, then definitely decided against publication and suggested holding back the book. Piles of mail. Reply from Messersmith, detailed and absolutely negative. The immigration problems of the children—endless difficulties. In addition, constant pleas for assistance for others coming in (Marck).—Levy of a billion marks on the German Jews, which means radical expropriation. Great indignation in England.— From early in the day again very drained and depressed because of gloomy reflections and overwork. Letters from Lion about the magazine. Sent him manuscripts of the *Faust* lecture and the August chapter. Telephoned Erika regarding the problem of Golo; further attempts to resolve it must be made in New York. Much time spent reading and arranging letters. After dinner we went to a nearby movie house to see a film out of Nazi Germany. Aside from the commentary, it tended to show the country in a favorable light. The two youngest went back with Gret Moser. Missed hearing Bibi's radio concert.—Letters full of disturbing descriptions of the perilous situation even in America.—Princeton full of people today; football game; streets clogged with cars.

Overcast, cool, later rain. The English and American press declare that events in Germany no longer conform to Western European norms, but must be compared to what took place during the Russian Revolution. (This after six years!) Gloomy speeches by English Conservatives: England will have to fight for its very existence.—Did some work. At 12:30 Eugene Meyer and his wife from Washington. Drank sherry with them. All took a short stroll. Lunch and coffee with them. With Mrs. Meyer in my study discussing her work and the intellectual substance of *The Magic Mountain* and *Joseph*. The individual and the collective. Balance—wisdom—goodness. Democracy a balance between the individual and the collective as opposed to fascism and bolshevism.—The billion-mark levy on the German Jews is not total expropriation, since Jewish assets are said to total four billion. They are being obliged to repair the damages of the pogrom out of their estates before expropriation. Insurance monies to go to the state!—After tea wrote to Lion in connection with the manuscripts. Then worked on letters with Katia until dinner time. In the evening read for a long time in *Goethe als Persönlichkeit*, neglecting the contest manuscripts.

Bitter cold, heavy snowfall. Spent the morning going over the lecture, then worked a bit on Chapter VII. Walked with Katia. Medi back with us, *rebus bene gestis*. After lunch the lecture again. Dr. Meisel. Much mail, newspapers and periodicals from Europe. Finished letters after tea. Then dressed. With Katia and Medi to dinner at Dean Gauss's. Then to Alexander Hall. Introduced by Gauss. The lecture, "Goethe's *Faust*," manfully delivered to enthusiastic applause. Afterward a group of professors at the club, beer and sandwiches. Home by taxi, where Katia and Medi greeted me.—Letter from Brüll. Letter from Golo, still in Zurich. Worried about his getting safely out of Prague.

Fine day. Worked on Chapter VII. Went to have my hair cut. Afterward walked with Katia on the Pine estate. To lunch Hans Meisel and his wife with the conductor Maier. Growing resistance to reading and the masses of letters; sense of satiety and rebellion. Self-communion, personal choice, procrastination.—To tea Mr. M., the real-estate man and insurance agent, who reveals a streak of bigotry in his conversation; signed documents. Afterward with Meisel, dictating a letter to Borchardt, delegating others, attempting to help Oppenheimer's brother in Vienna via Stockholm. Wrote Christmas inscriptions in copies of *This Peace* and *Schopenhauer* for a number of admirers. After dinner read in Hermann Rauschning's book.—Very tired, nerves strained.

Slept without pills. Up at eight, as I was yesterday. Extremely vivid nostalgia for my rooms in Küsnacht.—Katia to New York after breakfast. Struggled with the article for *Survey Graphic.* Began too broadly. The usual suffering at being kept away from my principal work. Enervated and tired. At noon Dr. Meisel; discussed letters with him. Walked down Springdale Road with Medi in the cold, clear air. Lunch alone with Medi. After coffee read in *The Social and Economic History of the Roman Empire* by Rostovtzeff, the decline of the culture of antiquity. Central phenomenon: gradual absorption of the educated classes into the masses, "simplification" of all functions of political, social, economic, and *intellectual* life: barbarization.—Tea with Medi. Holiday greetings and various testimonials.—Wrote to Korrodi in Zurich about being elected to the Academy and the auction of the manuscripts.—Katia back, met by Medi and me. Presents from the Knopfs (wine) and the Meyers (handbag, jade ashtray, embroidered handerkerchiefs for Medi). Interesting articles in the *Zeitschrift für freie deutsche Forschung.*

1939

Cold, sunny, windy day. Worked more energetically on Chapter VII. At noon took an hour's walk with Katia in the intense cold. After lunch read various things, Swiss papers, *Das neue Deutschland*, Karl Barth on the Church and politics. Not much done with Meisel. Einstein visited, bringing his citation for the medal; I then wrote my reply. Dinner at 7:30. Afterward with Katia to a concert by the young violin virtuoso Margolies. Gifted young man, but with a small tone. Tea back at home.

Monday, January 23; New York, Bedford Hotel

Up at 9:30. Clear. Breakfast after my bath. In Germany the "revolution" seems to be taking a pronounced turn to the left. Return to '34 and Röhm. Strengthening of the Storm Troops. The officer class being deposed. Many will be impressed; at the moment it appears to be the best way to raise morale, which by all accounts has reached a new low.—Studied the lecture.—With Katia on Fifth Avenue to buy Bibi a dressing gown, which I am now wearing here.—Lunch at the hotel with Colin, Klopstock, Klaus, and Golo.—To tea Mrs. Brodsky in connection with her *Twice a Year* project. Then a meeting with a representative of Ambassador Dodd to discuss educational and propaganda matters. Long taxi ride to Union Theological Seminary. Prof. Niebuhr's apartment. Paul Tillich and his wife. Dinner. Then through the tunnel; first to the lecture hall, thence, because of the overflow crowd, to the chapel. First reading of the freedom lecture. Good. Prolonged applause. Afterward amplifying statements from Tillich and Niebuhr. Questions from the audience. Back to Niebuhr's apartment. Discussion of the World's Fair matter. Protest by the Italians and the necessity of executing the plan outside the regular framework. Left at 11:30. Intense cold.

Thursday, January 26; Princeton

Medi spent the night in our sitting room at the Bedford yesterday. Woke there this morning at nine. Afterward Erika came, having just met W. H. Auden, also Riess, at the boat. Talked with her about Spain, the impending fall of Barcelona, the massacres that will follow, the English loans to Franco that will enable him to pay off Italy and Germany—scandalous all of this. The betrayal of Spain may be even worse than that of Czechoslovakia. Must try not to brood too much on it. Partial mobilization again in Italy and Germany. France is quite done for, its government having banned a film showing the plight of Chinese and Spanish refugees. The defense of national honor, sacrificed by capitalist interests, is everywhere being relegated to the Left, where it runs afoul of the pacifist tradition. Only the Communists are militant.—In the morning an interviewer from the Associated Press in connection with the article in *Survey Graphic*. Also Peat: the new lecture, the itinerary, and the question of Erika's participation.—Left in the car around noon, Medi doing the driving. Extraordinarily cold. The heater. Bibi and his bride-to-be with us. Arrived here at 1:45. Discussed political matters with Golo. After lunch read *Goethe als Erbe seiner Ahnen* by Joseph Bradish. Went to bed, where I warmed up and napped for a while. Meisel reported in after tea. Typescript of the Freud lecture. Unpacked. Occupied myself before and after dinner with the Freud lecture. Bradish's study.—Early to bed.

Pouring rain, the snow melting. Worked on Chapter VII, things looking up. Erika and Klaus arrived with W. H. Auden and Liesl Frank. Erika reported on her trip to Washington and tea at the White House. Roosevelt thinks well of the Freedom pavilion idea.—Out for a while with Katia. The streets like running brooks. Seven for lunch. Little Liesl Frank spoke of her husband's desolate state. Over coffee listened to Hitler's Reichstag speech on the radio, which dragged on for two and a half hours. Listing his triumphs and making threatening demands for economic aid. Discussed letters with Meisel after tea, then with Katia wrote a letter to Oprecht asking him to furnish me with the balance sheets.—Present from Auden: *The Oxford Book of Light Verse*, with a clever introduction by him. Read the *Tage-Buch, Weltbühne, Zukunft.*—Arranged with Liesl Frank, who returned to New York in the evening, a lecture date in Holly-wood to benefit the pavilion and the magazine.

Moderately cold, clear. Breakfast with the English guests. Worked on Chapter VII, changing associations and rewriting.—Ludwig Hardt and his wife. Took a brief walk with them. Lunch with them. Over coffee discussed an evening of readings at our house. Talked about Heine's *Börne* and read some from it. How Heine knew his Germans, and how little things have changed, essentially, since his day.—After tea, with Meisel. Handwritten letter to Mrs. Meyer, who has written encouragingly about the funding of *Mass und Wert.*—In the evening to the Kahlers'. Dinner with the old lady. Later Klaus and Medi; Kahler read us his essay "Die moralische Einheit der Welt," intended for an American periodical, good, apt, and useful.—New, vigorous speech by Roosevelt in reply to charges in the German press that America is the center of "warmongering."

Up at 8:30. Clear, cold. Worked on Chapter VII (the kiss). Walked with Katia along Mercer Street. To lunch Prince Löwenstein and his wife, also Bermann-Höllriegel. More contest manuscripts. Contributed the manuscript of *This Peace* to the auction. Copies of *Achtung Europa!* as presents to the guests. Took care of letters and signatures with Meisel. Autographed books.—Rested in my chair. To tea the Ladenburgs with their daughter. Discussed the painful business with President Roosevelt, his disavowal of his own speech. The American press is publishing scurrilous comments on him from the Italian and German papers. Impossible situation. Hitler also hand in glove with the Roosevelt opposition. Never against a nation as a whole, but always dividing it, pitting one group against another, subverting it, calling his partisans "the American people" while branding all the others as Jews, Marxists, and warmongers.—Worked over some matters with Katia. Looked at Martha Dodd's book on Hitler Germany. Glanced through the *Tage-Buch.*—Sore throat. Constantly dissatisfied with the level of energy I bring to my work.

Up at 8:30. Clear, windy, mild day. Some accomplished on Chapter VII. At noon drove out with Katia and Medi and walked a bit. Seven of us at table, with the three sons, Medi, and Gret. After coffee the lecture and German periodicals. Found the introduction to Erika's book on education in the *Weltbühne*. Meisel here for tea; did letters with him afterward. Evening dress. Dinner at 7:15. To Alexander Hall with the children: Freud lecture. Very large audience and a good performance in spite of some nervousness. Extremely attentive and highly appreciative. Gauss there (in spite of a faculty dinner), and he told me in the anteroom that it was "the most interesting lecture in my experience." Back home, rolls, tea, and beer with the family and Kahler. At first quite exhausted, but then grew calmer and better. Lively discussion of the lecture, the political picture, Schiller's ballads, German poetry in the world. The Princeton astronomer denounced nazism in a recent speech with clenched fists. Contented and relieved, *rebus bene gestis*. Return engagement likely.

Tuesday, February 14; Princeton

Tired. No writing. Drove out at noon to the "New Sihl Valley." To bed in the afternoon. Mrs. Shenstone to tea. Worked with Meisel. Dictated to Katia (Van Loon, Karl Löwenstein). Handwritten letter to Hans Rastede. Kahler came after dinner. Klaus gave a reading from his emigré novel. Aesthetic and political discussion. The impossibility of a satirical novel (*Dead Souls*). The phenomenon of National Socialism's being undeserving of the artist's skill. Failure or despair or renunciation of the word, the feebleness of denunciation. Have reality and art ever before been so utterly incompatible? Art not applicable to "life." The deadliness of nazism, the paralysis it spreads.

Monday, February 20; Princeton

Abnormally warm, the sun baking hot. Worked on the seventh chapter, which has gained interest and attraction for me since I read aloud from it. Washed my hair, shaved, and took an hour's walk with Katia. Much mail, many books, among them Heinrich's *Henry, King of France*, Kesten's *Children of Guernica*, J. M. Cain's *Serenade*. Looked through them after lunch. Georges Duhamel sent his *White War of 1938*. Worked with Meisel during tea on letters relating to the forthcoming trip. Signed letters, drafted some in English, wrote to Knopf with Katia.—At dinner talked to Golo about the tameness of the Holy Alliance compared to the present-day counterrevolution. The incomparably stronger conviction of the latter and its ability to sweep along its opponents. Its extreme brutality. (Guernica.)—Periodicals: *Zukunft, Tage-Buch, Weltbühne*. Budzislawski thinks that Spain spells the end of the class conflict, that imperialist interests are now emerging in full force. I doubt it. Class conflict is not the right term, for we are dealing with a generalized counterrevolutionary movement, I fear, that is in its ascendancy.—*Serenade* is attractive.

Tuesday, February 28; Princeton

Rain, huge puddles. Progressed in Chapter VII. Pains. Walked only a little at noon because of the wet. New stationery from Alliance. Erika to tea (letter to Spiecker). New issue of *Mass und Wert* with the August chapter and a rhapsodic review by Kesten of *Henry, King of France*. Hardt came at 6:30. Felt unwell while conversing with him. Talked in my bedroom with Gumpert and Klopstock, who were among the forty or so guests arriving from Princeton and New York. Went downstairs just as people were being seated. A too long and overly dramatic performance by Hardt. Hamsun's "The Fly" delightful. My "School Sickness." Kafka, Heine, and Goethe. Cold buffet. Talked with Mrs. Gauss and Lowe-Porter. Einstein. The New Yorkers left early, Erika among them. Stayed up talking with Katia, the children, and Kahler.— On our walk Katia informed me about the relationship between Medi and Borgese, who wishes to marry her.

Saturday, March 4; Princeton

Rainy. Slept quite well. Worked a bit on Chapter VII. At noon a walk with Katia. To lunch Prof. Broneer and Miss Stevens. Napped. In the afternoon severe pain, evidently from going without medication. Much mail to discuss with Meisel and Katia. Personal letters from Heinrich, Agnes Meyer, Oprecht, Bermann. Copies of "This Man is My Brother" to Schwarzschild to be distributed. To tea Herr Laubruch and his wife, who brought a gift of records. Wrote to Mrs. Meyer. After dinner, Medi with the news that the young couple mean to have a church ceremony on Monday. Our departure set for Tuesday evening.—Persistent, wearing pain.

Tuesday, March 7; Princeton

The night somewhat better, though still restless. Weather clear and windy. Hardly wrote, tired and distracted. Packed my two suitcases and shaved before lunch. Did not have my hair cut, since my scalp is too tender. After lunch the German periodicals. Political events: a sort of coup d'état in Spain, a military government that wants a "Spanish Peace" and excludes the anarchists.—Rested and packed. Did some work with Meisel. The little dog Jimmy with us at tea.—Am taking Chapter VII along on the trip. At 7:30 we leave for Princeton Junction, are stopping over at the Bedford briefly, and going on to Boston this evening with Erika.

The trip.

Spent the night of the seventh in a sleeping car to Boston. There the Ritz Carlton Hotel. Interviews at noon, including Katia and Erika. Before that a visit of the man from the Forum. Blue skies and extreme cold. Walked with Katia in the Public Gardens. An attractive city with a European air. Lunched at the hotel restaurant. Rested in bed. Erika's publisher to tea. Shaved and changed clothes. German professor and his wife in the bar for an aperitif, then dinner in the club across the way with him, a colleague of his, and two Americans, while Erika and Katia ate with the ladies. Afterward to the lecture in the Ford Hall Forum series. The usual turmoil. Packed hall, Erika and Katia on the platform with me. Introduced by the German professor. Delivered the *Freedom* forcefully. Prolonged applause. Questions with Erika. The

320

Marxist newspaper vendor. Very tired. Afterward, in response to desperate urging, to Harvard to join the German Club in its tower room: caps, beer, German songs, toasts. Made an honorary member. Little speeches at the beginning and the end. Back at the hotel, hastily packed, had tea and sandwiches, left at midnight. Read in *Brothers Karamazov* and slept tolerably for a few hours. Throat and back of my head very sensitive, but seem to be improving.—

Sunday, March 12; Detroit, Book-Cadillac Hotel

Lunched Friday noon with the Knopfs at the St. Regis. Packed in the afternoon, the children and various Bedford friends stopping by. Left at 6:30. Dinner on the train, club car. Sleeping car to Detroit, where we arrived yesterday morning. Book-Cadillac Hotel, elegant. Nice suite. Breakfast. Then press conference with the rabbi and Eckstein [?] of the *Free Press*. Tedious, picture-taking. Washed hair and shaved. Lunch at noon with the rabbi in a Russian restaurant. Cabbage soup, pirozhki, and roast mutton. Longish nap back at the hotel. After tea worked with Erika on shortening the first part of the lecture, writing a new opening. Evening clothes. Fetched early by the rabbi. By cab to the gigantic opera house. Nervous and tired. Began at around 8:30. Enormous auditorium seating 5,000. Heavy applause. Introduced by the rabbi, fresh applause at the beginning and several outbursts during the speech. Was weak at first, but then became steadier and better. Numerous expressions of gratitude. Long question period handled by Erika. Written questions. Went satisfactorily. With the rabbi to the café in our hotel, jam omelets and tea. After he left, sat with Erika in the sitting room, where she told us about the venturesome Keiler and his proposal.

Slept amply. Up at 9:30, bathed, had café au lait for breakfast. After dressing, dictated some words on Kesten's *Guernica* for the Alliance Book Corporation.—Rainy, foggy, cold weather like yesterday's. Did not go out, spent the morning reading in our suite. Lunched at the coffee shop, hearty appetite. Then smoked in the lounge. Rested, and drank a cup of tea at five. Then packed the suitcases again. Erika bought a portable radio. The three of us to the large movie house; variety show and film based on a novel by James M. Cain about the marriage of a singer, charmingly acted. Well entertained. Spent two hours there, then had dinner at the coffee shop of the Statler; ordered Burgundy, which did not agree with me. Felt ill during our departure in two taxis with fourteen pieces of luggage. Forgot our coats. Boarded the train around eleven. Left at midnight.

Monday, March 13; Cincinnati, at the Kühns'

Arrived here at 7:30. Fair weather. Both Christian and Jewish representatives on hand to greet us. Photographers. Mrs. Kühn's car. We are staying at her house, well situated on a hill outside the city. Three rooms on the second floor. Breakfast with oatmeal and coffee. Press conference. Erika off to her hotel. Shaved. Taken for a drive, and walked in the hills. Lunch at the University Club with Rabbi Heller, Mr. Goldman, and General. . . . Talked about Max Brod. Home again for a nap. Tea with Mrs. Kühn. Dressed. Dinner. Driven into town for the reading. Chairman, photographers. Made my entrance with Erika. Applause, introduction. The second half of the lecture again proved effective. Prolonged, grateful applause. Questions with Erika, innocuous. Opponents present, both Catholics and Nazis, but the police there to supervise; cordial and friendly spirit. Introductions, signed autographs in the lobby. Later a reception at the home of Mrs. Kühn's son-in-law; a great number of people, buffet, coffee. Went on past midnight. *Brothers Karamazov.*

. . . .
Tuesday, March 14; on the train to Chicago
. . . .

Warm, clear weather. Got up at 8:30 in Cincinnati. Had breakfast in our rooms. Then packed the luggage. Some young people showed us designs for their new magazine. Rabbi Heller came to fetch us and took us to the Hebrew University. Spinoza collection, Torah collection. Brief speech to the students in the chapel. Many autographs. Then with Mrs. Kühn to the Taft Museum: Gainsborough, Turner, a fine portrait of a man by Frans Hals, two Ingres portraits of women.—With our hostess to lunch, along with Mr. Fletcher. Heller joined us and told us that Brod's appointment had been approved.—Heller played us part of his oratorio. Departed at three. Erika met us at the train. Said farewells at the train to our hostess, an admirable woman engaged in worthwhile social activities (people's housing projects, which we saw).— Private compartment. The day overshadowed by the political news of new German incursions in the East. Ultimatum on the dissolution of Czechoslovakia. The army "dispassionate." The shattering effect of predictable things, their impact always worse than anticipated. The threat to Switzerland also increased. Throws doubt on the possibility of our visiting there.—Tea in the dining car. Tired and nervous. Hoping that tomorrow in Chicago I will be able to do something on Chapter VII. Bothered by my hair being too long, but cannot have it cut because of the rash.—

Chicago, Drake Hotel. Had dinner in the dining car. Arrived here at 8:30. Met by members of the committee, interviewed with photographers. To the hotel; very pleasant, comfortable suite. Beer in the sitting room, the latest newspapers: Hitler completely successful in the East. Occupation of Prague, the steel-making region. Rumania and Hungary will follow. Clear to the Black Sea. Oil and grain. Fantastic increase in strength. England and France not lifting a finger. Russia—a sphinx.—Invited to see Beneš tomorrow at 10:30.

. . . .
Wednesday, March 15; Chicago, Drake Hotel
. . . .

Icy gale, snow. Up at 8:30, after having fallen asleep with difficulty. Bathed and had breakfast with coffee. Shaved. Taken to the Windermere Hotel for the meeting with Beneš. His nephew, also Dr. Jan Masaryk, then the President and later his wife. Discussed political matters for nearly two hours. Deep feeling of sympathy, in spite of my sense that with somewhat more vigor and boldness on his part events might have been made to take a different turn.—Afterward annoyed and disappointed to learn that the meeting had been arranged as a journalistic coup.—Lunch for the three of us at the hotel. Then a telephone interview and picture-taking. Afterward worked over the first third of the lecture with Erika to bring it up to date. Rested. Tea. Evening clothes. Erika translated and typed. To dinner at Mr. and Mrs. M.'s of the Temple Society, along with the rabbi and his wife. Excellent food. To the temple for the lecture. The hall filled. Spoke well. Question period with Erika. Reception afterward in the anteroom. Back to the hotel. Telephone conversation with Beneš and

Masaryk. Beer and sandwich. Spoke on the telephone with Klaus in Princeton.—The
Germans in Prague. Czechs given German passports.

Thursday, March 16; Chicago, Drake Hotel

Troubled sleep. Up at 8:30. Clear, cold, windy. Had coffee for breakfast, then had
the barber come up to give me a haircut, my first since the shingles began; successful
operation. The rash continues to itch—a sign it is healing.—Took up Chapter VII.
Wrote a few lines and managed to keep the thread between the phone's ringing and
Erika's relaying the latest newspaper reports. Chamberlain's regrets. No one could
have foreseen these developments! Dissolution of the amputated Czech state from
within. At the same time the British newspapers are publicizing the statement by the
Czech minister, revealing that Hitler had vowed to destroy Prague if he were not
asked to march in. The booty is very considerable. The country's gold holdings were
three times those of Germany.—At noon walked a bit along the lake with Katia in
wind and cold. The three of us to lunch at the French restaurant Jacques, with the
aviary. Then visitors: the man from the teachers' union, a journalist, and others whom
I did not see. Rested on the bed. Tea. Erika left for a lecture in the vicinity, came
back at night.—Went to the movies with Katia: *Pygmalion*, based on the Shaw play,
a nicely made film. Tired afterwards. Dinner at a restaurant on the same street as the
movie house. Back at the hotel, newspapers; shameful, agonizing reading. Manhunt
and wave of suicides in Prague. Romantic tripe about the "Holy German Empire."
Hitler's legislation! Speeches in the House of Commons nonetheless. Lady Atholl
shouted down. Their so-called "autonomy" consists in the Czechs' being totally excluded from the administration of the country. Pained and disgusted.

Monday, March 20; St. Louis

Overstimulated. Heavy dose of pills. After four before I got to sleep. Today very
warm, as was yesterday as well. Silk underdrawers. Got up at ten. Coffee for breakfast.—Yesterday reports of Hitler's triumphal return to Berlin. He looked "weary and
grim." American boycott. Military preparedness and diplomatic cooperation between
England, France, Russia, and the United States. Report today of the Russian note to
Germany, excellent.—Autographed books.—With Rabbi Isserman to the admirable
zoo. Lunch at the hotel. Then packed. Left around four. The Texas Express. Officials
of the rail line at the station. Coca-Cola in our compartment, since I was very thirsty.
Radio. German newspapers. Dinner at 7:30 in the dining car. Cigar in the club car.
Early to bed.

Thursday, March 23; on the train to Kansas City

Fell asleep after reading some, but took another Phanodorm at 1:30 and then slept
soundly until 8:30, when I awoke. Shared the washroom with a young man who was
shaving. Breakfast with Katia in the dining car, café au lait and eggs. Warm, clear day.
Perfectly pleasant, fertile countryside. Farms.—Political developments proceeding in
the face of increasing world opposition, though so far Hitler is not being prevented

from carrying out his program by force. Ultimatum to Lithuania. By warship to Memel. Mussolini declares that Versailles made a general war inevitable. State of emergency in France, mobilization along the Maginot Line. Yet this "crisis" will doubtless blow over once again without war. But I remain convinced that these German attempts to shape history will prove to be nonsense. A good article by Dorothy Thompson on the "Fourth Reich," instructive and useful.

Kansas City. Arrived here at two in the afternoon. Lunch in the coffee shop of the Hotel Muehlebach. Today a day of rest. Napped after lunch. Tea at six. At seven the three of us went to the nearby cinema: pleasant film with Charles Boyer in delightful interplay with his American leading lady. Nice Disney movie. Pictures of the papal coronation. Pictures of Mexico, whose socialist government is selling oil to the Nazis. The capitalist world is closing ranks swiftly enough against those countries attempting socialism.—Dinner at the coffee shop. Then settled down by ourselves in our red leather sitting room with the radio. Beer. To bed around midnight.

Friday, March 24; Kansas City

Slept well. Weather cooler than yesterday. Bathed and had coffee for breakfast. Am writing at the small red desk in the sitting room. The German-Rumanian "economic agreement" is nothing but submission to the ultimatum—which aroused so much bogus fuss and so much bogus resistance. There was never any question but that the countries to the east would be handed over; all gestures to the contrary are a fraud, and once Czechoslovakia had been abandoned any resistance would have made no sense. The "war threat" was as much of a fraud as before Munich. Possibly the day will come when it will become a reality, when Hitler, after annexing southern Denmark, will turn against the West. In the meantime Switzerland and Holland are protected by military treaties, and the Western rearmament is formidable. Before the year is out there may very well be fighting. But it is perfectly possible that the nazification of the West will proceed as "peacefully" as it did in the East, and, if this occurs without actual aggression but out of simple momentum, there will be little chance to stop it. Hitler, speaking in Memel, declared that the "inequities" were now almost eliminated. The whole wretched world is puzzling over what that man of might may mean by that "almost."—Letter to an accusatory Communist from Bratislava. Cards to Kahler and Meisel.

Omaha, Nebraska. Spent the whole morning in Kansas City working on Chapter VII. Packed. Felt out of sorts and had no appetite. Had only vegetable soup in the coffee shop. Left at around two. Luggage problems. Club car. Rested in my seat. Tired and chilled. Tea in the dining car. Arrived here about 6:30. Representatives from the lecture bureau. With them to the outlying hotel. Sherry with them. Asked to be allowed to rest. A journalist, Erika handling the interview. Dinner in our room, hungry. Letters from Prague before its fall: Max Brod, Ludwig Winder. Letters from Klaus and Golo.

Tuesday, March 28; on the train between Portland and Seattle

On the train to Portland slept well until six. Clear, cool morning. Were called at seven. Changed trains in Portland. Breakfast in the station restaurant, once more with the ski contestants, French, Swiss, and Americans from the forty Mayflower families. Oatmeal and coffee. Boarded again at ten. Compartment. Pleasant countryside, canals, meadows, fruit trees. The newspaper: the surrender of Madrid. The Loyalist soldiers emerging from the trenches with white flags. So ends the agony of a nation that was ignorant of the fascist Satanism of Europe and still believed in progress, in national pride and freedom. A misunderstanding, behind the times.—At odds with Bonnet, Daladier has insisted that the Italians spell out their proposals, and has declared himself capable of defending his rights. The chief of the English general staff is in Paris. Goebbels in Hungary, which is putting pressure on Bratislava. Lithuania in an uproar against the surrender of Memel and the minister responsible for it, who has had to resign.—Thought about the perfidy of England and her connivance in this restructuring of the economic zones of Central Europe—the purpose of which is self-sufficiency in case of war—a senseless idea, since this "Reich" could only have been patched together in the absence of war, and could not be held if war really came. But fascism is seen as a bulwark against social revolution, and that does it. Yet only social revolution could bring about a federated Europe.—

Wednesday, March 29; Seattle

Lunch on the train yesterday. Arrived here at around 2:30. No one to meet us, no publicity, no hotel reservations, although mail was waiting. The hotel manager pleasant and polite enough, but mistrustful. Inquiries and confirmation.—Rested. After tea the three of us went to the movies: a gangster film and a society comedy, nice. Very weary. Dinner in the hotel's elegant dining room. Good food. Cigar in the sitting room. Early to bed.

Was awakened too early this morning by the daylight. Up at nine. Bathed. Oatmeal and tea for breakfast. At 10:30 a crowded press conference. At noon all three of us went out. Bought a coat for Katia. Lunch at one at the hotel with the Danish-American professor Sophus Winter and his German-born colleague Groth from the German Department as our guests. The latter so agitated that he ate nothing.—Rested. To tea, Instructor Schertel of the German Department, a Nazi who did his doctoral thesis on me and has "complete understanding" for my position.—Erika with the newspaper. Gratifying speech by Daladier, rejecting what Mussolini had to say and characterizing the world situation; virtually a first "peep"—and after six years.—The signs seem to point to war, though all will probably back away from it again, only to succumb in the end. The capitalist world will find itself forced into war by its pampered child, fascism.—Dressed. Taken to the lecture by Prof. Winter. Sold-out house, about 3,000 people. Introduced by Winter. Spoke well. Great success. Questions with Erika. Afterward the usual crowd and autographs. Reception at a private house. Whiskey and buffet. Tired, and made a quick escape.

Easter Monday, April 10; Chicago, Congress Hotel

Slept quite well. Bathed. Tea and egg for breakfast. Have a bit of a cold and my body aches. Bleak weather, dark, cold, rainy. Adapting the Hollywood speech for the American Committee for Christian German Refugees. Haircut in our room. Washed hair and shaved. Telephoned the Committee. Letter from Erika, written on the train, concerning her visit to Borgese and the marriage idea. Poignant and strange. Their tentative summer plans. (Erika already in New York.) Telegrams to the Franks and to Mrs. Meyer.—The political picture terrible. Threats against Poland and Greece, Albania already done for, Yugoslavia turning to the Axis, so that the Balkans are more or less lost to the democratic powers. The warlike mood thoroughly fraudulent.— Lunched at the Blackstone with Mr. Mack and his party, his wife and son, taken out of school for the occasion, Rabbi X. and his wife. The complete trust these people have in me, their gratitude and their simple-hearted exploitation. The everlasting question period. Exhausted and felt wretched. Back at the Drake there was mail waiting: European printed matter, the *Tage-Buch* containing "This Man is My Brother."—Rested. The weather ghastly, rain changing to snow. Worked on the speech. Statement for the *Chicago Daily News* on the question of a world peace conference. Riess phoned. Around eight taken to the lecture: meeting of the American Committee for Christian German Refugees. The large hall filled with an audience of some 2,500. Waited in an overheated corridor. Met the bishop and others. Entrance, applause, organ, religious talk by the bishop, I introduced by the chairman, my speech, which went well and was punctuated by applause that became very strong at the end, repeated expressions of thanks. Afterward Frau Kayser, gracious and pleasant, and an American. Good and profitable evening. The organizers pleased. Autographed books and talked with people on the stage, including a nice blond young man with questions about what I considered my best book and about politics. Brought back to the hotel by the Committee's representative. Supper in the tavern waiting for Riess, who failed to appear. Afterward, in our suite, smoked a cigar and read the German periodicals. Late to bed.

· ·
Saturday, April 15; Washington
· ·

Before going to bed read in *Faust II*. Slept well. Up at nine. Talked with the hostess about "myself." Very open and cooperative.—Warm, overcast. Lovely drive with mother and daughter to the Washington house and grounds. Wonderful spring sights, lilac blossoms, young yellow-green foliage.—Lunch at home with Mr. Meyer. Short rest. Tea reception at four at the Meyers'. The talk of the hour concerned President Roosevelt's message to Hitler. A memorable document, but two-edged. A calculated move for reasons of domestic politics? Is it not plain that Hitler could not be a member of a peaceful world?—The Russian, Czech, and Rumanian attachés on hand. Staff of the *Washington Post*. Lemonade, thirsty. Left the gathering at five. Started using the two new desk pens, which seem to function well.—Tails. After seven taken by car, accompanied by the Meyers' young daughter, to the large press dinner where the president was expected. Looked for Meyer in the crush of male guests. Introductions, cocktails. Everyone gradually congregated in the immense dining room. Roar of voices, music. Seated at the head table between Meyer and Senator X. Long, drawn-out meal, constantly interrupted by humorous skits. Formal presentations. Measured applause for the various diplomats. Joint introduction for the Albanian and the Czech, acclamation. China. The biggest ovation for Finland (because its war debts paid up). Spotlight on each person named. Friendly demonstration for me. Very tired off and on. Then improved. Drank much wine with water. Champagne. Deeply moved by the sight of the genuinely admired president, who gave a brief address at around midnight; gracious and most appealing. His standing up energetically but with effort. His hobbling out, supported by the chief of the Secret Service, passing right beside us.— Much said about the message, which is said to have been as good as rejected already. Strong applause for Hull, who has a fine Anglo-Saxon head.—Driven home alone.

Friday, April 28; Princeton

Up at 8:30. Very cool and dark with fog. Shaved, bathed, and dressed for the day. Worked some on Chapter VII after breakfast. Then went with Katia (John driving) to New Brunswick. Home of the president of Rutgers University. Welcomed there, then escorted to the gymnasium where there was a dense crowd of thousands of young people. Introduced to various people and helped into my gown in the dressing room. Once on the platform there first was singing, a benediction, introduction, then my forty-two minute speech, which was given an exceptionally warm reception. Then awarded the honorary doctorate, the hood, the citation. An imposing ceremony. Lunch at the president's house. Much talk about Hitler's "answer," which to be sure was relatively moderate but totally negative, and showed a thickheaded lack of comprehension of the situation. Farewells. Left early. Already back home by three. Finished letters in English. Rested in my chair. Discussed matters with Meisel over tea. Talked to Erika about a plan to smuggle the work of emigré writers into Germany. Increasingly desirous of influencing the people. Simon considers it a foregone conclusion and unavoidable that I would have to be president after Hitler's fall. . . . Churchill on the radio discussing Hitler's speech, weak.—Must prepare talks for the Spanish dinner, the PEN Club, the booksellers, and also the *Magic Mountain* lecture.

Monday, May 15; Princeton

Up at eight. Bright and cool. Went out before breakfast. Afterward wrote further on Chapter VII. Walked at noon with Katia. Lunch with all six children. Then went on with the writing in order to reach the point after the second dictation. Then out into the garden in the sun. Discussed "Moral Aid" with Erika. German periodicals. Prof. Weil and his wife to tea. Drove to the Junction at six with Katia to meet Annette Kolb, who will be spending several days here with us. Selected some passages about Freud for Knopf. Prepared recommendations for various books. Had dinner at the long table with Annette and the children. Afterward read next to the fire in the library the twenty-five new pages of Chapter VII. The tragicomic side of politics in the scene with John. Kahler, who had come for the reading with his wife: "Preserving the mythic, universal element despite the ironic, critical approach." A more audacious counterpart to the *Joseph*. Discussion.

Yesterday's peace speech by Mussolini: "None of the problems of Europe is worth a war." Sour grapes. But how will they survive peace? Essential portions of the speech were kept from the Germans. Temptation in Washington to come back to the idea of a conference.

Got up this morning in New York at nine (having had difficulty falling asleep). Have been reading stories by Mérimée the past few nights. Bathed and dressed. Oatmeal and coffee for breakfast. Visit from Prof. Hans Staudinger, whom I do not like. Afterward an interview about the Russian pavilion. Just before leaving, looked in on Erika, who was unwell and in bed. Dr. Gumpert. Settled that we will leave for Europe on the *Ile de France* with Erika on June 6. Took the 11:30 train. Studied the doctoral address in the Pullman car. Met by John at the Junction. Fine, warmer weather. Lunched with Annette. After coffee read the *Tage-Buch*, with important articles by Rauschning and Schwarzschild on Hitler's predicament. News from Staudinger, too, about the increasingly pathological cast of Hitler's mind. The situation dangerous and hopeful.—Rested a while. Picked up in President Dodds's car at four. Tea with a small group on the lovely terrace of the president's house. Then to the Faculty Club. Donned academic gowns in the president's office. Procession into the very dignified hall, a good-sized audience, Katia up front with the two sons and Medi. Speech by the dean, some Latin words from the president, presented with my hood. Speech by Dodds praising my academic activity and expressing his wish that I continue it. Then my speech. Spoke well. Congratulations in the office. Photographs in the auditorium. Made our departure. Saw something very lovely and moving outside as we were driving away. Worked a bit with Meisel back home. Talked with Golo about adjustments to the speech for the new honorary degree on the 29th.—Manuscript on the subject of pederasty and homosexuality from Bruno Kreitner in Barranquilla, Columbia. His psychological explanation of the mystery debatable but not without insight.

Got up early in order to do something on the chapter. Drove at 10:30 with Flexner to the Negro college—a forty-five-minute trip to the other side of Trenton—whose financial benefactor is Mr. Bard of Philadelphia. The guests (Einsteins, Panofskys, Swarzenskis, etc.) assembled outside the building. The procession of the men and women students in the auditorium. Spirituals, beautifully sung. The awards and the words of thanks from the guests. The recessional also a lovely sight. Introductions. Conversed with a charming young Negro. Lunch with Einstein and the officers of the college. Drove home with Flexner in a gathering thunderstorm that broke once I was back, but at a distance. Very tired. Rested in my chair. To tea a learned lady from Washington, a political economist. Katia off to a tea party. I with the stranger and Annette. The latter left this evening after warm farewells. Wrote a long letter to Mrs. Meyer, pressing her for the two thousand dollars for *Mass und Wert*. Again only three of us at table, including Golo. Read some in Freud's *Moses*.

Steamy and hot, intermittent thunderstorms. Up at eight. Worked on the chapter until almost noon. Then went to the ceremony of the cornerstone laying for the Institute for Advanced Studies. Speeches. Lunch at the Princeton Inn: Flexner, Miss Bamberger, address by Einstein.—Worked on correspondence in the afternoon with

Mann

Zuname: . . . . **Mann**

Vorname: . . . . **Thomas**

Geboren am: **6. 6. 1875**

in: . . . . **Lübeck**

Beruf: . . . . **Schriftsteller**

Letzter inländ. Wohnsitz: **München**

Der deutschen Staatsangehörigkeit für verlustig erklärt durch Bekanntmachung vom 2.12.1936, veröffentlicht in der Nr.282 des Deutschen Reichsanzeigers und Preußischen Staatsanzeigers vom 3.12.1936.

Top: *Thomas Mann's Czech passport, 1936.*

Bottom: *The announcement of the Nazis' revocation of German citizenship.*

C1

C2

Above: *Katia and Thomas on their second crossing to America, in 1935.*

Opposite page, top: *The newlyweds W. H. Auden and Erika Mann in 1935.*

Opposite page, bottom: *The writer and longtime friend of the Manns', Annette Kolb, 1937.*   C3

C4

Above: *Thomas Mann writing in his diary in Princeton.*

Opposite page, top: *With Albert Einstein in Princeton, 1939.*

Opposite page, bottom: *The house rented by the Manns in Princeton from 1938 to 1941.*   C5

C6

Top: *Playing boccie after giving a lecture in Fort Worth, Texas, in March 1939.*

Bottom: *Thomas Mann with two of his publishers, Gottfried Bermann Fischer and Emil Oprecht, in Noordwijk, Holland, July 1939.*

Opposite page, top: *With Carl Laemmle, Max Reinhardt, and Ernst Lubitsch, Hollywood, 1938.*

Opposite page, bottom: *Heinrich and Nelly Mann in California.*

C8   *Thomas Mann in Saltsjöbaden, Sweden, 1939.*

Meisel and Katia; dictated a letter to Lewisohn about his novel. Letter from the
Liefmanns, who have unexpectedly arrived in New York. After dinner Dr. Wertham
phoned with the terrible news that Ernst Toller hanged himself in his bathroom.
Requested that I speak at the funeral, highly depressing and scarcely possible. In the
Tage-Buch an article by Koestler on the senseless death of the poet Attila József.—
Zukunft carries a good article on the relationship of the German opposition and a
Germany of the future with the Soviet Union.—Damaged one of the new fountain
pens, to my great chagrin.

Monday, May 29

After a not very restful night in our roomette (read *Anna Karenina*, took a whole
Phanodorm), we arrived in Geneva in the morning and were met by President Eddy
and his wife. Taken to our rooms and a family breakfast in their columned house on
the lakeshore promenade. Changed and went off to the commencement exercises on
the campus. Donned academic gown and was introduced to people. Procession to the
canopied dais in front of the audience. My speech scheduled close to the start. Then
came the honorary degrees, I last in line after the bishop, the Marine Corps general,
Orchard, the producer of "The March of Time," etc. After the ceremony, rested back
at the house for a while. Then to the large luncheon, the place of honor between
Eddy and the former president, with whom I was able to talk about music. Speeches
of the degree recipients at the end, English-German remarks in defense of German
culture. Conducted by Mrs. Eddy across the vast lawn to the house. Napped. A tea
reception downstairs at 4:30 and burdensome question period. Afterward walked along
the lake with Katia, where a friendly couple invited us in to look at their house and
garden. Back at the president's house, packed and shaved. Dinner at seven *en famille*.
Phonograph music during coffee. Took our bags with us to the cinema, where as nearly
always we were well entertained. Then to the station. Mr. Thomas Orchard a fellow
passenger. Compliments on my "two" speeches up to the last moment. Farewell from
our hosts. Single beds. Washroom. Beer in the club car with Mr. Orchard.—Read
Tolstoy until half past twelve.

Monday, June 5; Princeton

Up at 8:30. Fine, warm day. Bathed, walked in the lane, had tea, and worked with
more concentration than I have recently. Then physical work; rinsing out the pens,
packing up my materials, filling the big trunk in the bedroom.—Katia off in Newark
and New York from morning until teatime seeing the attorney in connection with our
papers, much harassed.—Lunch alone with Medi. Looked through the *Tage-Buch* and
other periodicals and papers. To tea Dr. and Mrs. Meisel, who will be occupying the
house in our absence. Katia back. Expect a discussion of our uncertain situation. Since
there are likely to be severe crises in the early autumn, we may possibly not get to
Switzerland at all. Sweden would be the best place, from the point of view of work
as well. To be hoped that I am soon in the mood to write the forewords so that some
definite progress on *The Beloved Returns* can be made in the course of the summer.—
Speeches by Hitler and Daladier on the encirclement. Führer Hitler draws parallels
with 1914, the abysmal stupidity of which are on a par with the Nazis' refusal to

allow the "old folks" to leave Germany should we get to Switzerland. All in the same spirit—one that hopes to rule the world.—Farewell to the Meisels. Got on with the packing.—Golo back at dinnertime. He reported on the writers' meeting at which Klaus spoke. They elected me honorary president of the association!—Malted milk for dessert.—Manuscript of Chapter IV of *The Beloved* coming along on the trip. The bags filled to bursting.

· ·
Tuesday, June 6
· ·

My sixty-fourth birthday. Departure day. Wakened by Katia at 6:30 with congratulations. Finished packing and had breakfast. Left in two cars at 7:45 with all the luggage (the three blacks in their new sedan), Medi driving us, heading for New York, an hour-and-a-half drive to the dock and the *Ile de France*. Unloaded. Caroline Newton. Boarded the familiar ship. A-deck, cabin 295, Erika's right next door. Klaus, Golo, Medi, Klopstock, Gumpert, the painter X., journalists wanting interviews, Landshoff who is convalescing and traveling with us, other guests. Flowers, gifts, candy, and cigars. Pleased with an elegant pencil from Caroline Newton. A fountain pen from the teacher. Sorry for Medi, who was sharply scolded by Erika for her forgetfulness and was already shaken and confused, in tears. Tried to soothe her. Klaus staying back for want of papers. Golo's plans uncertain.—Tumultuous farewells. Music and noise as the visitors left. With Erika and Landshoff in our cabin. Sailed sometime after eleven. Champagne and cookies. Letters and telegrams. Arranged the flowers in vases. Lunch at one o'clock at a temporary table. Afterward in my deck chair. Still warm. Read in the lovely first edition of Heine's *The Romantic School*, a birthday present from Mrs. Shenstone. Dozed a while. Tea at 4:30 with Katia and Erika in the lounge. Further discussion of where to stay. Inclined toward a seaside resort in Holland while waiting out our time before Switzerland.—In the cinema a jazz musical, tedious.— Walked on deck. Did some unpacking in our stateroom. Shaved. Dinner at eight at our own table. Champagne. Afterward read Heine during the concert hour. Later in Erika's cabin with Landshoff. Phonograph. Good cigar from Knopf. Gradual change of time. To bed very tired at around eleven.—I began this notebook on the ship that was taking us to America. The record of more than eight months' worth of days is bracketed between that voyage and this one.

· ·
Friday, June 16; Noordwijk, Huis ter Duin
· ·

Yesterday, Thursday, in Paris. Had breakfast alone and took care of packing and dressing until Katia returned from the Belgian consulate, *rebus bene gestis*. Left the Astoria at around 10:30 with Erika in two taxis. Problems with the excess baggage at the station, and delay owing to telephone calls to the consulate. Pullman, good accommodations. Lunch at 12:30. From the very start and all along the trip a succession of French, Belgian, and Dutch inspections and much stamping of passports. All went well with our special credentials, however, and instructions had been received at the border. Our passports accepted without trouble, and we were exempted from all baggage inspection. The conductor looked astonished. Tea at around five. Read the *Tage-Buch*. Gazed out the window as we crossed into Holland. Very warm. Spoke at length with Erika about England's and Russia's responsibility for the delay in the pact.

. . . .

Title page from the first edition of Lotte in Weimar (The Beloved Returns).   331
. . . .

Lack of goodwill on both sides. The fifteen or sixteen capitalist arch-villains in the world who call the tune.—The Hague at 5:30. Again in two cars, drove along pleasant wooded roads to this spot. The gentleman at the reception desk. Rooms on the fourth floor, quite elegant but at reasonable pension rates. Unpacked eagerly. Late dinner at 8:30 in the empty, glassed-in dining room. Swiss waitresses. Coffee afterward in the lounge near the dance band. Fell asleep only after taking two pills. Perturbed and depressed about the lost key to my desk in Princeton, the unavailability of my Zurich doctors (ears, teeth, pedicure?), and all the rest. Slept after the red capsule.

Tired today. Up late. Fine, gentle weather. Out on the beach a while after breakfast. After lunch to the little bathing resort, where we had coffee at a table outside a German café. The coffee too expensive, as was yesterday evening's. We were also exploited when we exchanged our dollars at the hotel. Bought cigars and cigarettes. Wrote a card to Bermann and dictated a letter to Ida Herz concerning *A Sketch of My Life*, which I need for the German version of the *Magic Mountain* lecture that is to serve as the introduction to a new German edition.—Long telephone calls from Landshoff to Erika, his psychiatric counsellor. The death of the alcoholic Joseph Roth is said to have occurred as a direct reaction to Toller's suicide.—Napped on the bed for a while. Afterward the three of us had tea on the large terrace overlooking the ocean. Walked along the beach with Katia. Then sat a while in a chair in the sun. Letter to Mrs. Shenstone. Dinner at around eight. Then all of us in the sitting room, each reading a copy of the new issue of *Mass und Wert* with Rauschning's essay on "passive resistance." Camomile tea, good.

· ·
Sunday, June 18; Noordwijk
· ·

Wrought up last night, mournful, and in tears. Finally fell asleep with the help of a red capsule. Got up earlier, fine weather. Worked on the foreword to *Royal Highness*, writing in pencil and sitting comfortably in a wicker beach shelter. Mild cigar. Afterward walked on the beach for a while. Coffee out on the terrace after lunch. Great many Sunday visitors, German manufacturers among them. Read the issue of *Mass und Wert* out on the balcony, critical remarks about Brecht and other articles. Satisfied with the journal. Letter from Oprecht about Golo's visa difficulties and the problem of the editorship. Haunted by what Landshoff told us, namely that the seventy-five-year-old Richard Strauss had lunch with Hitler the day after the gala opening of his latest opera in Vienna, which Hitler had also attended.

Tea downstairs, and afterward dictated letters to Oprecht, Rauschning, Mme. Servicen regarding Flinker, etc. Walked on the beach. Evening clothes for dinner. Spent the evening in the hotel lounge, where I began reading Georg Kaiser's novel in manuscript with the jazz music in the background. Battle of Tannenberg.—Tired and out of sorts, the climate to blame.

· ·
Friday, June 30; Noordwijk
· ·

Up at around 8:30. Letters from Lion (my Chapter VII being used in Vol. 3, No. 1) and Bermann (in praise of the introduction to *The Magic Mountain*). Added to my letter to Mrs. Meyer. Helped load Erika's things between ten-thirty and eleven, then drove with her to Amsterdam. Located the Rijksmuseum, which Katia and I visited while Erika was getting her room at the Amstel Hotel. The Van Gogh collection, an impressive survey. The somber tones of the earlier pictures, the breakthrough of light. His *Self-Portrait*, quite demented, something vicious in the eyes. A passionate picture, the wheat field with a dark blue sky and crows. The famous *Yellow Room* leaves me cold.—The four of us, including Landshoff, had lunch in the restaurant at the Hotel Europa. From there to Erika's room, where we lay down on her beds. Tea at five with her on the hotel terrace above the river, reminiscent of Basel. The *Daily Telegraph* with a remarkably direct and pointed speech by Lord Halifax on Germany's self-isolation. Increased tension in Danzig, where they are insolently making military preparations. Discussed returning to America in view of the imminent peril of war. Erika would join us.—After six to the car (with the copies of the first part of Chapter VII). The keys to the Ford handed over to Katia. Landshoff there. Parting from Erika, pain and grief. Pressed her hand to my cheek and kissed it.—Left with Katia. Very nervous and shaken by the leave-taking and the difficulty of finding our way out of the city amid the swarms of bicycles. Highway to the road between Leiden and Noordwijk. Erika's room already made up again. The wind subsided. Dressed and went down to dinner at eight, during which Erika phoned, having been given the misinformation several times that we were not yet back. Told us about an article in the *Tage-Buch* by Rauschning in which he relays details from Germany about Hitler's psychological state.

Wednesday, July 5; Noordwijk

Phone call from Erika yesterday evening: according to someone in touch with a high Nazi official, war is set for the beginning of August with the assent of the general staff. Skeptical, but decided in any case that we will reserve ship passage to America for the beginning of August.—Summery weather today. Up at eight, and worked all morning in the beach hut on the Tolstoy preface. At noon went from the bathhouse into the water for my first brief swim, the water very cold. To lunch Emanuel Querido from Amsterdam, along with his woman colleague and Landshoff. Erika unexpectedly came with them and I discussed the situation with her. Out on the terrace after our meal. More manuscript of Chapter VII to Landshoff. Another parting from Erika, who leaves this evening for Paris. Letter from Oprecht, saying that Golo has finally announced his arrival for the end of the month. The problem of Lion. Bothered about the advisability and possible consequences of Golo's coming over. Preoccupied with the situation.—Had tea in the village and walked a bit. Dictated letters and wrote cards. Dutch papers carry interviews with me.—Sitting outdoors now after dinner. Drinking beer as a nightcap.

Wednesday, July 19; Noordwijk

Sultry, stormy. Up at eight, and worked on the beach until eleven. Then drove to The Hague, where Ter Braak was waiting for us at the Mauritshuis. Went through the gallery. Mysterious flowering and decline of Dutch painting. The Rembrandts. Most strongly impressed by the portrait of his father. The so-called Homer, the rabbi, the *Sorrow of Our Lord*, Jacob. The early painting of a presentation in the temple. *Saul and David*, the unveiled eye. The Jewish boy.—Lunch with Ter Braak at the hotel. Then across the street to a café to meet Dr. Falk, discussing his German-Jewish studies, Biblical subjects, Hebrew writing, Nibelungen verses, quite remarkable.— Drove back after 3:30 in a thunderstorm. Rested until 5:30. Tea in a wicker chair on the terrace. More rain. Read the masquerade scene in *Faust*. Walked on the beach. Read the *National-Zeitung* at dinner. Danzig will be annexed peacefully, while Poland's strength is being built up so that they can avert a fate like that of Czechoslovakia.— Telegram from Mrs. Meyer in London relates that she is flying to Hamburg, Lübeck, and Munich. Amusing.

. . . .
Wednesday, August 9; Zurich
. . . .

Up at eight. Weather improved. Along with our coffee, had some of the good cake the Beidlers baked for us. Worked until 11:30. Took the Dolderbahn into town. Looked at the magnificent window displays on Bahnhofstrasse, then ran into Katia, who took me to a nearby street to show me the handsome little Peugeot she had just rented for only eighteen francs per day. Bought a pair of gray trousers that I needed. Went to the Bellevue Pharmacy; joy of the staff on seeing me. With the car to the hotel. Lunch here, then looked over the poetry of Karl Kraus out on the veranda. Rested on the bed. After tea drove with Katia out to Küsnacht, the familiar route through an even more familiar landscape, the woods where I took a thousand walks, Johannisburg. Stopped at the Studer-Guyers', where we found only the sister at home. Then to Schiedhaldenstrasse. We drove the car into the open garage and went up the overgrown steps. The stone wall where I sat as the furniture was carried down to the van. The terrace outside the dining room, robbed of its hedge. A glimpse into the living room with some of its familiar pieces of furniture, into the dining room. Looked up at my study, where the third volume of *Joseph*, the letter to the dean, the larger part of *The Beloved Returns* originated. Deeply moved, shaken with memories of that life, sadness and pain. . . . Drove back through the woods to the Zürichberg and the hotel.—Dictated letter to Mme. Mayrisch. Wrote to Signora Mazzucchetti about Jollos. Dinner in the dining room. At nine the Beidlers and Golo. Sat with them in Katia's room over beer, cigars, and coffee. Shared Mrs. Meyer's letter about Germany. Friendly conversation, subdued because of people in the next room, evoking memories of evenings in my study on Schiedhaldenstrasse.

. . . .
Tuesday, August 22; London
. . . .

Gloomy day. Big headlines in the *Telegraph*: Ribbentrop flying to Moscow to sign a nonaggression pact. A "complete surprise" for the British. Meeting of the full cabinet today. Frau Olden telephoned to say her husband would not be going to Stockholm. He would like to speak with me.—Along with the miserable political news, the private misery on learning that Grete Walter was shot in Berne by her husband, who then killed himself. Composed a telegram expressing our dismay. Did not work. In the morning with Lányi to the British Museum, where Prof. Saxl undertook to be our guide. Assyria, Ur, Egypt. Lunch afterward with Lányi in a little restaurant. Back to the hotel by bus. Rested—without getting any rest. Went by bus to Ida Herz's for tea, then picked up by Moni and her husband. People from the Warburg Institute, with Prof. Saxl. Back at the hotel, visit from Rudolf Olden and his wife. Discussed the situation and the Stockholm Congress. Dinner with them at the Speranza. Evening paper with reactions to the Russo-German pact. Japan troubled. *L'Oeuvre*: "Russia joins the Anti-Comintern Pact." Disbelief that the treaty will stick. Poland maintaining firm stance for the present. Here a meeting of Parliament is called for Thursday. No question but that the threat of war is magnified. Sense of the cynical frivolity of this step, which could only have issued from Hitler's raging impatience to take revenge on Poland. With Prague he made a mockery of nationalist ideas, and now he makes a mockery of his own anti-bolshevist principles. Mindless capitulation.—Erika and Golo attending the funeral in Zurich.

Wednesday, August 23; London

Did a little work on Chapter VIII in the morning. Went with Katia to the Swedish consulate after eleven, bus trips each way. To lunch with the Lányis at the Speranza. At the hotel, tedious packing of the hand luggage. While resting afterward had some ideas regarding the final chapter. A farewell tea with the "aunties," who accompanied us down to the cab and stood watching us go with gratitude and sadness.

Rode to St. Pancras Station. The Lányis and Ida Herz on hand, the latter with marzipan. Plenty of time. Farewells to the young people; in case of war I must make certain they enjoy the protection of Murray and Nicolson. Moni's delicate and wasting appearance gives rise to tender concern.

Pullman trip to Tilbury, reading newspapers about the German-Russian coup, the effects of which are doubtless disillusioning in Germany.—Very tedious passport inspection. Many Swedes returning home.

On board the "Suecia." Sailed down the Thames. Rather small but well-appointed ship. Cramped cabin. Sat on the deck. Dinner at eight in the dining room. A strange old man at our table, a Parsee from Bombay, Padisha by name, who guessed who I was in the course of our conversation. Later joined by two American girls, one of them extremely pretty. Coffee afterward in the lounge on the top deck. People gathered around to listen to news on the radio. The broadcast offered nothing significantly new. The firm British statement not being reported inside Germany. They are insisting on the Germans' right to seek their own best interest. The "diplomatic defeat," perceived as such in America and in Switzerland, is being taken quite calmly by England and France. How far-reaching is it? It is likely that the pact contains the clause forbidding attack on a third party. Reply to the Japanese ambassador in Berlin: the agreement does not affect the anti-Comintern alliance, since it was not reached on any ideological basis. Boundless lack of principle, as always.—Henderson in Berchtesgaden to deliver the message from the cabinet.—I continue to doubt that it will come to war. Even given the neutrality of Russia, war would still be a wild gamble for the Nazis, one that they would not risk lightly. Moreover Stalin is surely not in favor of the partition of Poland. But Hitler has managed to throw the moral fronts into chaos, has prevented a union of socialism and democracy into a free world that is not only conservative. The world of the future—or so it seems—and the world of the past are now confronting each other.—The decision to make a pact with bolshevism probably originated with Goebbels.

Early to bed last night, took the red powder, and after reading for a time slept peacefully until six. Got the luggage ready. Breakfast (coffee and porridge) with the Parsee. Afterward the necessarily nerve-wracking entry formalities in uncomfortable heat. Baggage checked and stowed away on the train to the station. After we had bought tickets to Stockholm free passes arrived. The train cars models of elegance and cleanliness. Lakes, cliffs, summery countryside.—My mind continually preoccupied with the situation. Germany, cut off from the "West" perhaps for good, has gone over to the side of the East. England's position could be most critical in case the Balkans and Turkey (where Papen is currently visiting) adhere to the dictatorships. Nevertheless there seems to be disappointment in Germany and particularly in Italy at England's uncompromising stance. Evidently they had fervently hoped that the Russian shock would save "the peace." Such a hope has now been explicitly rejected. If one understands correctly, the Poles have "encircled" Danzig, where the Gauleiter Forster has taken control. Council of war in Berlin. Feverish war preparations everywhere. Still possible that things will be smoothed over and peace prevail, but I do not conceal from myself that I want the war, precisely *because* its effects are unpredictable and would lead away from the present state of affairs, probably in Germany as well. Above all it would be so revolting to see Hitler march in once more without meeting any resistance that anything is preferable. The manifestos by Roosevelt and the small neutral nations are probably quite without significance.—Good lunch with many cold appetizers. Smoked a cigar and read afterward. Reached Stockholm at three. The Bermanns at the station. With them in Frau Fischer's Mercedes to:

Saltsjöbaden, Grand Hotel. Rooms with a loggia in a charming and attractive setting. Much mail. The proofs of *The Magic Mountain, Buddenbrooks, The Beloved Returns*, publicity for *The Beloved*, etc., all prepared by Bermann. Tea for the four of us on the loggia. Much talk about the grotesque turn things have taken in Germany and Russia, suffused with *faux pas*. While Katia unpacked (the Zurich bags having been delivered here without a hitch) I read letters: a long one from Mrs. Meyer about Lübeck and her impressions of Germany; from Random House highly appreciative of the Tolstoy introduction, etc. Phoned Erika in Zurich. She is off to Paris this evening and returning immediately to America, having had to settle for a slow ship and a poor cabin. She had wanted to come to Sweden as we hoped she would, but heard of the run on ships bound for New York. We have firm reservations for September 19. But the return voyage cannot be assured in case of war, which America would very likely enter swiftly.—Visit from Frau Fischer and her daughter Hilla. Many years since I had seen her. Could not get rid of one journalist and his photographer, though we had sent others away. Dinner with the Fischers in the dining room. Afterward in the garden with them under the colored lanterns. Phone conversation with Bermann, who had no definite news. Henderson again visited Hitler at the latter's request, then returned to London. They are firmly convinced in Germany that it will not come to war, that another Munich is in store. May they prove to be mistaken! Still no sign of Poland's refusal. The Japanese deeply insulted, absenting themselves from the Party rally.

Up at 7:30. Very warm, mild. Wrote a letter of sympathy and condolence to Bruno Walter in Lugano, which took up my morning. Short walk with Katia. Lunch (smorgasbord) with Frau Fischer, Hilla, and the Bermanns. Afterward read them the first chapter of *The Beloved Returns* out on the loggia. Rested on the chaise longue, very tired. Evening clothes. Fetched at six by the Bonniers' car. To their house, about an hour's drive through Stockholm and out into the country. Garden reception. Floral borders. The house dates from 1750, with later additions. Ceiling frescos of Jacob and Joseph at the well, the planets, and signs of the zodiac. The old Bonniers, the young hostess, Swedish writers, the president of the PEN Club, and academicians. Dinner in a handsome tentlike room. Speech by Tor Bonnier. I spoke also, paying tribute to Bermann Fischer and his family. Tour of the house after dinner. Spent a good part of the evening with the older Bonnier. Swedish radio news. While during the afternoon it looked like another appeasement, in the evening there was again the sense that war is inevitable. The English cabinet meeting today and tomorrow. Message to Hitler, also one to Daladier. Complete war footing in Germany. Airspace closed off, etc. By means of the pact with Russia Hitler has created a favorable position, at least for the beginning. Nevertheless, the people will tremble at the prospect of fighting the Western world. What war might bring is unpredictable, for the world, for the destinies of all of us.—

Drove back through the night with the Fischers. Telegram from Bibi that he is bound for England. Disturbing phone call from poor Erika in Amsterdam. All of her valuable luggage stolen, including manuscripts, on the trip through Belgium to Rotterdam—where, moreover, she learned that her ship had already sailed, her train being three hours late. We both spoke to the poor child, who was crushed and weeping, though without being able to offer any real comfort. She alerted the police—not very promising in the midst of the rumblings of war. The train's cashbox also stolen. The dreadful situation is aggravated for those who were robbed in that tomorrow is a Sunday. The fruits of her whole summer's work, heirloom jewelry, the new wardrobe that she had bought with her own earnings and in which she took such pleasure. Terribly sorry for her, which kept us awake for a long time. The poor dear child, always so brave, was quite shattered by this. And yet worse things might have happened. She is considering coming to Sweden if it is possible. This same "if it is possible" applies to our return. . . .

Up at eight after only a few hours of sleep. Very warm weather. Coffee and porridge for breakfast on the loggia. Overcome with pity for Erika and worry over what lies ahead. Although a catastrophe has always represented the morally desirable outcome after all that has happened, the fear of it breaks through in the form of sheer physical dread, such that one could almost prefer to see the triumph of what one finds detestable.—Did some work on the eighth chapter in the morning. Read it over. At noon a short walk with Katia. To lunch with the Fischers. Afterward went over the proofs of the novel on the loggia. Took a brief nap. At four picked up by Dr. Philipson, the owner of a fine motorboat, and his friend X. With them and the Fischers on an hour's cruise along the cliffs to Dalarö, where the Bermanns and the children were waiting for us at the landing. High tea in their garden. Miniature croquet game with the children. Much talk about the apparently inevitable crisis. Depressed over Erika's misfortune. Did not start back until nearly nine o'clock. The dinner we ordered brought up to our suite took more than an hour. Read proofs of the third chapter. Happy telegram from Erika reporting that her luggage turned up. Great relief. Renewed skepticism about the war. It will not come. To be sure, the possibility of an agreement that would really free us from the present predicament is not in sight, but it is again as good as certain that the war will not take place. Mussolini is the most ardent advocate of peace. He has his reasons. But his "millions of lives should not be sacrificed" still means: You must give us everything we ask for. In the face of such thinking, such people, there is no hope of doing what is actually necessary. Therefore?—

. . . .
Wednesday, August 30; Saltsjöbaden
. . . .

Erika arrived this morning as I was dressing. Received her lovingly. Leisurely breakfast on the loggia and discussion of the ridiculous and puzzling political situation. The general tendency is unquestionably toward peace, since Hitler, as I always knew, neither wants nor is able to wage war. The befuddled populace is behaving desperately, now that they finally grasp the danger of the situation—far behind the Italians, whose inability to act has become perfectly evident. In Japan, a pro-English government. England has a free hand in the Mediterranean. Obvious retreat by the dictatorships, whose weakness is being fully exposed. The controlled German press has changed its line, is now courting England after all this time berating her so crudely. Delayed ratification of the Russian pact, which has completely misfired and only done harm to the Nazis. The policy of blackmail seems to have played itself out. What else will they try?

Managed to do some work. Took a walk around the little bathing island. Lunch with Erika and the Fischers. Read proofs. After tea a walk with Katia and Erika. After dinner we listened to some beautiful records in Erika's room: Schubert lieder sung by Karl Erb with extraordinary artistry. Soothing to the spirit.—I miss newspapers. In the evening a news broadcast in German from London.

. . . .
Thursday, August 31; Saltsjöbaden
. . . .

The warm weather continues, unusual for Sweden at this time of year. Breakfast with Katia and Erika on the loggia. At noon with Erika to the bathing island to fetch Katia. Read proofs after lunch. At five o'clock a large press conference in the lounge. Had to talk a good deal. Afterward a repeat of the same. The journalists said to have been very well satisfied. Relaxed by strolling in the garden. The Bermanns stayed to dinner. Afterward read the eighth chapter, almost as far as I have gotten, to the Fischers, the Bermanns, Katia, and Erika. Katia worried about Bibi in London, which is being evacuated. Telephone connections proved to have been broken. Evening news from London. The suspense is reaching a fever pitch. War council in Germany, headed by Goering, who is empowered to issue directives without Hitler's signature. Difficult to see how war can still be averted. The pact with Russia finally ratified. There too they are calling up. Full mobilization everywhere. Have they finally resolved not to let the man wriggle out again and to end the unbearable situation at any cost?

Bombardment of Warsaw and other Polish cities. Hitler's troops marched into Poland. Bombardment of Danzig, its annexation proclaimed. Full mobilization of the Western powers. Chamberlain: "If Mr. Hitler's declaration means that Germany has declared war on Poland. . . ." Statement by Molotov, quite enlightening. Hitler declared Italy's nonparticipation.

Did some writing after breakfast, distracted as I thought I would have to give a speech at the Town Hall. Lunch there after a tour led by the mayor. Fetched and brought back by an official car. Bert Brecht and his wife among the guests. In the Ratskeller, personal toasts wishing that all will turn out well. On the way back we picked up a radio, over which Katia and Erika unfortunately heard Hitler's "address" to the Reichstag. Protest from a couple in the room above ours about the Hun's voice.—Questionable whether we shall be able to leave here. Yesterday's interview in all the papers. The date of our departure imprudently mentioned. Very tired and irritable.—Read proofs.

Saturday, September 2; Saltsjöbaden

Up at 7:30. Cool, rainy, then better. Battles, bombardments in Poland. Breakfast with Erika. Wrote some on the eighth chapter. At noon Fräulein Dr. Hamburger from Göteborg, with whom I walked on the island and who stayed for lunch. Coffee with her in the sitting room. After tea, took a walk with the Frenchman who had come to Sweden to buy precision instruments and is now cut off from Paris; he has three sons in the army. After dinner read proofs. Then listened to the broadcast from London. England's ultimatum. The determination to put an end to the National Socialist regime. Declarations of loyalty from the dominions. A comment by a university German teacher, simple and effective, summarizing world press opinion. Now they are speaking our language, calling Hitler a madman. Late, very late! Halifax even inquired after Schuschnigg. . . . All the same, the shock is great. I often think of the letter to Bonn and its prophecies. We sat together talking for a long time. If the wretched man had a spark of that "love for Germany" that allegedly started him on the course of his crimes, he would put a bullet through his head and leave orders that they pull out of Poland.—H. G. Wells, arrived in Göteborg, declared that he had come because of me.

Sunday, September 3; Saltsjöbaden

Again more summery weather. I wrote my page as usual, awaiting events. At noon took a walk along the cliffs of the bathing island, and while sitting on a bench was spoken to by a Swedish teacher, with whom I conversed for some time. The English ultimatum ran out at noon. Since that moment England and France have been at war with Germany. The German radio is playing marches, which is their response to the English demand (their usual obstinate mendacity), and Hitler's announcement to the troops in the East that he is on his way to inspect them. Fate now taking its course. They plan to bring Poland to her knees within two weeks and turn away the enemy from the West Wall. There are comments about months "and years" to come. Will the people of Germany be willing to wait out those years? Elsewhere in the world no one thinks they can.—The S.S. *Kungsholm* sailed for New York with an overload of passengers. The assumption is that we will be able to leave from Bergen on the twelfth.—Address by the king of England. Speeches in the House of Commons. In Germany all radios capable of receiving transmissions from abroad are being confiscated.—Chamberlain's message to the German people.

. . . .
Friday, September 8; Saltsjöbaden
. . . .

Slept well until early morning. Up at 7:30. Fine weather. Had coffee and finished the pariah addition to the seventh chapter. Erika in the city. No word from her until noon. A state of uncertainty that prevents us from packing yet. Phoned Bermann about the manuscript. Telegram from Mrs. Meyer informing us that the State Department has intervened with the ambassador.—Rumor that Hitler has flown back to Bavaria from Poland as a result of messages from Mussolini. So they are thinking of calling off what is not yet recognized as a world war.—While we were having lunch, news from Erika that we had our plane reservations.—Entrusted the new supplementary manuscript to Bermann's courier.—Packed. Waited for Erika.—She arrived. Tea. At 6:30 the Bonniers' car called for Katia and me. Dinner at the elder Bonniers' in the beamed hall, some thirty guests, including Prince Vilhelm, H. G. Wells, etc. After-dinner speech. Left with the Bermanns at 8:30. Erika at the station, having taken care of the luggage. Sleeping car to Malmö. Farewells to the Bermanns.

. . . .
Saturday, September 9; on the plane to Amsterdam
. . . .

Woke up quite early in our sleeping car. Up by 6:45. Our washbasin not functioning, did my washing up in the lavatory. Luggage trouble in Malmö. By bus to the airport. A beautiful morning. As might have been expected, we were forced to leave the greater part of our luggage behind, so that Erika was once again parted from her manuscripts. The bags will go back to Bermann for forwarding.—Short flight to Copenhagen. Hot coffee and a few puffs from a cigarette. The plane flew low over Denmark, ascending to over 6,500 feet over the North Sea. Bright sun, smooth flight. Pleasant stewardess. In an hour we are supposed to be in Amsterdam.—

On the train from London to Southampton. Landed in Amsterdam. Landshoff with Rini, very cordial. Controls very strict. Vermouth in the restaurant. Farewells and another takeoff. Very warm. English plane. A skillful landing at around three o'clock on the long, narrow airstrip. As expected, a very extensive and rigorous inspection of our baggage, especially the printed and written materials, although they knew who I was. Hour-and-a-half ride on a bus through the summery countryside with its many trees. Weekend atmosphere. From the airline office a taxi to Waterloo Station. Tea and hot buttered toast there. Departed at 6:30.—Our "escape" thus far a success. Word has it that during the past few days German planes have been swooping down above the wings of Dutch aircraft, the Germans peering in at their passengers.— English newspapers. Revolting blather about peace from Goering. Flatly rejected. The regime has been sentenced; let us hope that the verdict holds. These speeches are the whinings of a criminal regime that feels its days are numbered. The world has risen up irrevocably against it—or one must at least believe it has.—Advance by the French.

Saarbrücken seems not easily taken. Fighting, it appears, on the outskirts of Warsaw.— English planes flying in close to Berlin, dropping millions of leaflets, no bombs, no losses. The West seems to hope to crush the enemy with a minimum of bloodshed.

Tuesday, September 19; Princeton

Six most remarkable, endless days on the S.S. *Washington*, difficult to get through thanks to the crowded conditions on board, though the weather was calm and even quite lovely toward the end of the voyage. The worst and most difficult day, gloomy, sultry, dark, and wet, was the one on which Russia's intervention in Poland became apparent and word came that Russia had declared war on England and France—which proved false to be sure. I suffered a great deal, but with good meals and sleep aided by pills I maintained my composure and trust in my own destiny—with the growing perception that the end of this process cannot be foreseen, either its duration or its results, and that I cannot be certain of experiencing the end of it.—Woke early (6:30) and had ten minutes to myself in the bath one flight down from the dormitory. After breakfast (coffee and oatmeal), sat in the deck chair and worked in pencil on the eighth chapter, stubbornly. At one o'clock vermouth in the crowded bar. Lunch at 2:30, dinner at 8:30. Afterward usually played casino with Katia and Eri, whose presence was very comforting and helpful. By hook or crook managed to get through the various speeches and meetings expected of me. The lazy boy. The pro-Russian brother of Knopf's friend Smith. Tea with the captain, along with the Kreislers. Robert Montgomery. Almost finished the novel by Hutchinson, a most interesting work.

Yesterday we arrived; we made it. Still wrote some in the morning. The luggage had alrady been attended to. Welcoming cable from Caroline Newton. After having only the one Canadian plane flying above us en route searching the water for submarines, there were now all manner of large and small airplanes in the brilliant fall sky. We docked between four and five o'clock. Mobs. Got separated from Katia and Erika, since after lunch I had retired to the washroom below. The passport inspection went without difficulties. Journalists and photographers on deck. Disembarked. There to greet us: Meisel, Gumpert, Hans Rastede, then Caroline Newton. Long wait for the baggage. Customs. John with the car. Erika taken to the Bedford. Drove with Katia and the happily chattering Negro to Princeton. There purchased vermouth and brandy. Homecoming—of a sort. America my fated berth and refuge, perhaps for the rest of my life; there is much talk of the "war" lasting ten years. Vansittart, bitter that his warnings went unheeded for six years, predicts as much and foresees the end of civilization.—Back in the house after three and a half months. Wound the Swiss clock. Unpacked. Dinner alone with Katia. Mrs. Shenstone. We will be alone a good deal. Very tired. Alone in my big bedroom, the wide bed with my down comforter.

Today got up at 7:30 and took the familiar morning walk down the lane. Breakfast with Katia. Fireplace fire in the still summery, shaded library. Filled the desk pens in preparation for work.—Telephone conversation with Knopf.

Russia and Germany dividing Poland between them, leaving only a tiny buffer state. Now that the forces of peace have made order in this fashion they are asking what in the world the forces of disorder can hope to achieve by war. They would like to perpetuate the previous "peace" for purposes of order.

Sent cables yesterday evening to Bibi and Golo; very much wish they were here.

Telephone conversation with Mrs. Meyer, who invites us to visit in Mt. Kisco along with Erika.

Medi arrived at eleven, though Katia missed her at the station. With her in the library. The three of us had sherry in the living room.—Newspapers with pictures and articles about our voyage.—

Borgese very pessimistic. Italian submarines. An attack on Tunis expected.—What I anticipate and hope for is that Germany might become the battleground for the struggle between Russia and the Western powers, with a communist revolution and the overthrow of Hitler. The downfall of the regime and severe punishment of the guilty country is basically all that I could wish for.—

After shaving at noon took a walk with Katia and Medi. Hot sun. Before lunch listened on the radio to Hitler's speech in Danzig; the expected peace offensive, the web of lies, frequent invocation of God. Utterly repulsive.—Good lunch. Coffee out in the garden. Busy with books that had come in. Very tired. Rested. Meisel to tea, with whom I later discussed letters for a long time.—In the evening read Nikolai Berdyaev's *Origin of Russian Communism.*

. . . .

Thursday, October 26; Princeton

. . . .

Up yesterday at 8:30. Had coffee and eggs for breakfast and went on with the ninth chapter, approaching the end. At noon took a short walk around the neighborhood with Katia. After lunch, went on sketching the end in pencil.—Ribbentrop's speech in Danzig disgustingly stupid and brazen.—I lay down in the afternoon without sleeping, and after tea worked again until nearly 7:30, bringing *The Beloved Returns* to its conclusion, ending it on a note of reconciliation as it will now stand. This too has been accomplished. I looked up my entries in these notebooks made in Küsnacht in September 1936, announcing the beginning of this project. Thirty-seven months. When one considers how quickly a month goes by, filled with its minor and major incidents and occurrences, it is not so very long. Many fairly considerable things have intervened: *Schopenhauer,* the *Faust* lecture, *Richard Wagner and the Ring,* also the contents of *Achtung Europa!,* the American lectures, *The Coming Victory of Democracy,* and *The Problem of Freedom.* The last hundred pages of the novel were produced with relative speed.—Hard to judge the final product. As a book it is certainly original, a rich fabric of references, much of which is compilation and appropriation, exploiting sources. The Goethe portrait is intimate, lively, new, not without intimate knowledge of greatness, offset by a certain democratic irony.—May it find its niche—in my oeuvre and in the world of letters.—Announced its completion to Katia, at 552 pages. The Kahlers here for dinner, a very good one: roast chicken and champagne. Coffee afterward. Later, in the library, read a section of the dinner and the final chapter to the Kahlers, Katia, and Medi, and was sincerely praised. Though very tired and feverish, I read well and was able to take an objective view of the text along with my listeners. Went to bed late and still read some Leskov.

Woke up today at around 8:30. Mild, overcast weather, the trees still brilliant. Breakfast with Katia and Medi. Embargo bill passed by the Senate. The German press calling for air attacks on England, while the French are being urged through loudspeakers to lay down their arms. Flattering words for America, but on the other hand they have sunk an American commercial vessel.—Cable from Bermann regarding the forwarding and addressing of the final chapter, also asking me to send another copy of Chapter VIII, which has evidently failed to reach him.—Cleared away the material for *The Beloved.* The last pages taken by Katia to Meisel for typing.—

Up today at 8:30. As warm as summer. Spent the morning writing a piece in English for the pavilion ceremony. At noon drove out with Katia into the woods and walked on the wet fallen leaves. After lunch practiced reading the English of the *Magic Mountain* lecture and worked on the Wagner-Hitler problem for *Common Sense.* After tea the opening words in English. Picked up at seven by Hans Rastede and his friends. Drove to the tavern from last year, where we had dinner. Back home early. Went over the copy of the final pages and transcribed changes. Put the complete manuscript of the novel in order and set it aside.—Copies of the Swedish edition of *The Problem of Freedom* from Bonnier.

Tuesday, November 7; Princeton

Got up at 8:30. Outside with Nico. Eggs and tea. Wrote on the Wagner letter. Walked with Katia and the poodle. Mr. and Mrs. Lowe-Porter to lunch. With Meisel in the afternoon. Went out with the poodle. In the evening read in the European journals from Paris, issues of the *Tage-Buch.* A good statement by Broch to the Guild. Extracts from the English press in German.—Joint offer to mediate a peace by Belgium and Holland. Prompt rejection by Halifax. The step an expression of understandable fear, especially on the part of Holland, which appears to be threatened by imminent German invasion. The rights of war and preparedness for flood. It would doubtless be an act of desperation on the part of the wretch, and proof that he is quite afraid of a winter of war.

Monday, November 16; Princeton

Up at 8:30. After breakfast some work on the essay. At eleven to the Junction to catch the train for New York, where we said good-bye to Klaus. Visited the Walters at the [?] Hotel. Emotional reunion. Lunch with them in the dining room. Afterward in their sitting room. Rested in Lotte's bedroom. Tea with the Walters. About his plan for a Mozart festival in 1941. Left with the suitcase containing some things of Grete's that they had saved for Eri. Not feeling well as a result of drinking coffee for lunch. Our car at the Junction. Medi there to meet us, with Broch and the poodle. Back home, vermouth and a rest. Medi with us for dinner. Lobster and a whipped concoction prepared by means of a very practical mechanical mixer. Afterward went over the *Werther* lecture. Listened to Swing's commentary and took Nico out. Almost sick ever since morning thanks to an interview with Papen in which he declared that Germany's war aim was to create a European confederation. Commonwealth! A Nazi commonwealth! Every time one would have thought such brazen stupidity, such stupid brashness impossible.—But Reynaud is in London holding discussions on total cooperation between the French and the British. This would be the first step toward a federated Europe.

Friday, November 24; Princeton

Yesterday evening the wedding dinner with Roger Sessions, the Shenstones, Frau von Kahler, Gumpert, and Auden, who left early. Medi very touching in her white wedding dress. Words with Borgese. Sessions played. Retired at 10:30.—The newlyweds left this morning after breakfast. Long accounts in the newspapers.—Worked on the essay, bowing to God's will. At noon in fine wintry weather (below freezing during the night) took a cross-country walk with Katia and the poodle to the lake. Spent the afternoon working with Meisel. Section of the Freud essay for the Writers' League. Translation of my letter to the League. Interesting issue of the *Zukunft*: article on "extraterritorial influence" as the latest form of capitalist imperialism.—Alarming signs of Germany's capabilities in the counter-blockade war, the German mining technique. Another British battleship damaged by them.

Friday, December 15; Princeton

Late to bed, late getting up. Worked on the essay. At noon to the Knopfs at the Princeton Inn, where we met the Lowes. They took us to the Institute and showed us through the rooms, especially Prof. Lowe's office. Lunch with Klaus and Curtiss, whom the Knopfs took back to New York in their car. Amusing letter from Golo with Korrodi's quotation-studded paean to *The Beloved Returns* from the *Neue Zürcher Zeitung*. Nevertheless a stimulating and gratifying document. Dear and enthusiastic letter from Annette Kolb on the same subject.—Mrs. Lowe to tea. Discussed the translation with her. Special problems in the seventh chapter. The English title.—Began on a letter to Mrs. Meyer, but broke off, not in the mood.—British victories at sea. Letter from an American Communist pleading the cause of peace-loving Russia, attacked by the Western powers through the puppet state Finland.—Appeal from the Paris *Tageblatt*, which needs 25,000 francs immediately. Letter from Jules Romains on the situation of the interned exiles.

Tuesday, December 26; Princeton (Second Day of Christmas)

Clear and cold. Up at 8:15. With Katia and the poodle down the lane. Pointed Christmas speech by Daladier directed against Germany, which this time will have to suffer what it has inflicted on others.—Spent the morning sketching out the novella *The Transposed Heads*. At noon took a drive with Katia, Medi, and the poodle to the lake. Much mail. The Wagner letter in *Common Sense*.—Much unrest these days. Mr. and Mrs. Sessions to tea, along with the elder Mrs. S. Wrote to Fiedler. The Borgeses to dinner at the Kahlers'. Discussion of the pope's message on the radio. Seconded by Mussolini's peace proposal, calling for the reestablishment of Poland and Czechoslovakia. An idle wish, since Hitler could not accept it and would not be able to be a partner in peace if he wanted to. His only hope the revolution in France—as described by Rauschning on the spot.

Socialist statement by Kurt Hiller, little inclined.

Up at 8:30. Extremely cold. Morning walk in the lane, then studied up for the new novella. At noon W. Hallgarten, with whom we went for a walk and had lunch. Read up on India. After tea, short handwritten letters to Klopstock (Boston) and Caroline Newton (Philadelphia), from whom a very warm telegram regarding *The Beloved* came this morning.—Alone with Katia. Listened to all kinds of things on the radio and read more on India.—Bitter cold.—More on Hitler's New Year's message: it will be essential to dismantle the sovereign states, and England's long-standing threat to the world must come to an end. (Appropriation and rejection.) "The new world, socialistic." The wretch, the wretch.—Word from Germany of the increasing proletarianization of life.—

The second close of a year in this country. Installed the new calendar. With what suspense one regards the year ahead! One's work more and more assumes the character of a pastime. May it be an honorable one!

Notes on the Text

1918

September 11 1. *Tegernsee.* The Mann family spent the summer of 1918 in the rented Villa Defregger in Abwinkl on the Tegernsee south of Munich. TM had sold their vacation house nearby in Bad Tölz in the autumn of 1917.

2. *"Betrachtungen."* TM's book of political and philosophical ruminations, *Betrachtungen eines Unpolitischen* ("Reflections of a Nonpolitical Man"), begun in October 1915, completed in mid-March 1918, and published in late October 1918. The work has not been published in English.

3. *Bauschan.* The Mann family dog, lovingly described by TM in the idyll *A Man and His Dog.* Both during the writing of this novella and after its publication TM frequently referred to the work itself simply as "Bauschan."

4. *Katia.* TM's wife, Katharina, née Pringsheim.

5. *Bertram's Nietzsche book.* Ernst Bertram's *Friedrich Nietzsche. Versuch einer Mythologie.* Conceived and written at the same time as TM's *Betrachtungen,* Bertram's book was also published in the same month, October 1918.

6. *Arcisstrasse.* Katia Mann's parents, Alfred and Hedwig Pringsheim, lived in the house that Professor Pringsheim had built at No. 12 Arcisstrasse in Munich. They were forced out of it in the autumn of 1933, when the building was torn down by Nazi officials to make room for a Party headquarters.

7. *Golo.* TM's second son.

8. *The little one.* TM's third daughter, Elisabeth Mann-Borgese.

9. *The Herzogpark house.* TM had built the house at No. 1 Poschingerstrasse in the Herzogpark section of Munich in 1914.

10. *"A Man and His Dog."* TM began writing this novella in mid-March 1918, immediately after completing the *Betrachtungen.* It occupied him until mid-October (see entry for October 14, 1918).

11. *"Buddenbrooks."* TM's first novel, begun in Rome in 1897, completed in Munich in 1900, and first published in 1901. A special issue was designed and illustrated by Emil Preetorius to mark the 100th edition of the novel. Of the 1,000 copies printed in this edition, 210 were numbered and signed by TM, of which 200 were for the trade.

12. *"The Magic Mountain."* TM had interrupted work on this novel, originally conceived as a novella, in the autumn of 1915, so as to be able to devote himself fully to his political book, the *Betrachtungen.* He did nothing further with it until the spring of 1919 (see the entry for April 20, 1919).

September 12 1. *The Kaiser's speech.* Kaiser Wilhelm II visited the steelworks in Essen on September 9, 1918, where he addressed an assembly of thousands of workers. He explained that his peace offer of December 1916 had been met by the enemy with "an unqualified desire for [Germany's] destruction."

2. *The field marshal.* Paul von Hindenburg.

3. *Mama.* Julia Mann.

September 14 1. *The hexameter poem.* See note 1 for November 2, 1918

2. *"The Confidence Man."* TM's novel *The Confessions of Felix Krull, Confidence Man,* originally planned as a novella. Work on it was suspended in the summer of 1911 in favor of a new conception, *Death in Venice.* A first section of the work was published in 1911, and further fragments appeared through the years in bibliophile editions and elsewhere. It was not until April 1953 that TM again devoted himself to the material, completing the novel as it is now known in February 1954.

September 15 1. *"Bauschan."* See note 3 for September 11, 1918.

2. *"Sprüche" — "Scherz, List und Rache."* Goethe's rhymed proverbs and his early satyr-play are marked by broad language and humor.

3. *Heinrich.* TM's older brother, Luiz Heinrich Mann.

September 16   1. *Burian note.* Without the knowledge of the German government, Austria's foreign minister, Count Burian, proposed peace talks to the combatants in September 1918, a proposal unanimously rejected.

September 18   1. *Privy Councillor Pringsheim.* Katia Mann's father, Alfred Pringsheim. In Wilhelminian Germany the honorific "privy councillor" (Geheimrat) was very liberally bestowed on distinguished scholars and professional men, and it does not indicate any genuine governmental function on the part of the bearer. It therefore could have been omitted from this translation altogether with little loss of sense. TM's use of it does however reveal something of the Germans' fondness for indications of status, and in this present case something of the formality of the relationship between the novelist and his father-in-law.

September 19   1. *Lula.* TM's sister Julia Löhr.
2. *[. . .]* This and subsequent bracketed elipses are taken over from the German edition. They indicate the omission of brief passages considered all too private by the original editor.

September 20   1. *Eissi.* TM's oldest son, Klaus Mann.

September 22   1. *"Indian Summer."* Novel (1857) by Adalbert Stifter.
2. *Asking for copies.* On behalf of the Writers' League, Kurt Martens had arranged to publish TM's *A Man and His Dog* in advance of the regular publication in a bibliophile edition with illustrations by Emil Preetorius, the proceeds of its sale to go to needy writers. For this purpose several copies of the manuscript were required.

September 26   1. *Her two sisters.* Erika and Monika.
2. *Erika.* TM's oldest daughter, Erika Julia Hedwig Mann-Auden.
3. *"Ivan Ilyich."* Leo Tolstoy's novel *The Death of Ivan Ilyich* (1886).
4. *"Palestrina."* Opera (1917) by Hans Pfitzner.
5. *Hülsen's Platen novel.* Hans von Hülsen's *Den alten Göttern* (1918), a novel based on the life of the poet and dramatist Count August von Platen Hallermund.

September 28   1. *Book on German music.* Hermann Ludwig von der Pfordten's *Deutsche Musik* (1917).
2. *Carlyle's "Frederick the Great."* A complete German translation of Thomas Carlyle's *History of Friedrich II of Prussia, called Frederick the Great* (1865) appeared during the First World War. TM reviewed it for the *Frankfurter Zeitung* on February 24, 1916, long before these final volumes of the edition were published.
2. *The "Unliterary Country" chapter.* Chapter II of TM's *Betrachtungen.*
3. *The two Ivans' argument.* In Nikolai Gogol's story "The Tale of How Ivan Ivanóvich Quarreled with Ivan Nikiforovich."
4. *Lisa.* Early nickname for TM's third daughter, Elisabeth, later called "Medi."

September 30   1. *Zarek's volume of stories.* *Die Flucht* (1918) by Otto Zarek.
2. *"Vorwärts."* The central organ of the German Social Democratic party, founded by Wilhelm Liebknecht in 1876. *Vorwärts* was banned by the Nazi regime in 1933.

October 4   1. *The article.* The obituary "Zum Tode Eduard Keyserlings," published in the *Frankfurter Zeitung* on October 15, 1918.
2. *Vicco.* TM's younger brother, Viktor Mann.
3. *Meyer's letters.* The correspondence, published in 1918, between Conrad Ferdinand Meyer and Julius Rodenberg.

October 12   1. *Bavarian war minister.* Baron Philipp von Hellingrath.
2. *"Die Schweizerfamilie."* Opera (1809) by Franz Weigl.

October 13 1. *The Russian essays. Russlands politische Seele* (1918), a collection of "Russian confessions" edited by Elias Hurwicz.

October 14 1. *Fiedler and Herzfeld.* Pastor Kuno Fiedler officiated at the baptism of Elisabeth Mann-Borgese; Günther Herzfeld-Wüsthoff and Ernst Bertram were appointed her godfathers.
2. *"Die moderne Welt."* An illustrated journal edited by Ludwig Hirschfeld that appeared from October 1918 to September 1939.
3. *Katia's mother.* Hedwig Pringsheim.
4. *Deutsche Gesellschaft 1914.* A Berlin organization of some influence during the First World War, composed of politicians, journalists, industrialists, bankers, writers, and artists.

October 18 1. *"Madame Legros."* Play (1913) by Heinrich Mann.
2. *"Hermann and Dorothea."* Verse epic (1796–97) by Goethe.
3. *In Gräf.* Goethe's comments on his own works were collected in the nine-volume *Goethe über seine Dichtungen* (1901–14) by Hans Gerhard Gräf.

October 30 1. *Answer to the Kammerspiele.* The Munich theater had sent a questionnaire regarding performances of Russian drama.

November 2 1. *"To My Youngest Child."* This long hexameter poem was ultimately titled *Gesang vom Kindchen*, and it occupied TM until the end of March 1919. It was first published in book form together with *A Man and His Dog* by TM's regular publisher, S. Fischer, in 1919. The work has not been published in English.
2. *"Luise."* Verse epic (1795) by Johann Heinrich Voss, subtitled "A Pastoral Poem in Three Idylls."

November 7 1. *"Die Zukunft."* This leading literary and political journal founded by Maximilian Harden had been repeatedly forbidden to publish by the censors during the First World War.
2. *The composer of "Prinzessin Brambilla."* Walter Braunfels. His opera *Prinzessin Brambilla* was first performed in 1908.

November 8 1. *". . . the spirits I called forth."* A quotation from Goethe's "The Sorcerer's Apprentice."
2. *The king.* Ludwig III of Bavaria.
3. *The "Council."* The Political Council of Intellectual Workers.
4. *Kept by a movie star.* Wilhelm Herzog married the screen actress Erna Morena.

November 10 1. *The "Norddeutsche Allgemeine."* A moderate, liberal Berlin daily in existence since 1862.

November 12 1. *Galleys for Leipzig.* For the 100th edition of *Buddenbrooks* (see note 11 for September 11, 1918).

November 29 1. *"The Patrioteer."* This novel by Heinrich Mann (in German *Der Untertan*, in England *The Man of Straw*) was completed before the outbreak of the First World War. Its serialization in a Munich journal was broken off by the censors, however, and the author then withheld the book until the war was over. His publisher Kurt Wolff brought out the novel in an edition of 100,000 copies in November 1918, and the book became an overnight sensation.

December 1 1. *Munich Political Society 1918.* Nothing further is known about this fledgling organization.

December 8 1. *A magazine "for Order and Justice."* The belligerently nationalist journal *Auf gut deutsch.*

December 20 1. *Sitting with Schwegerle.* The sculptor Hans Schwegerle did busts of both TM and his daughter Elisabeth.

2. *Little Feodora.* The grand duchess was an ardent admirer of *Buddenbrooks.*

3. *The Club.* The Herrenklub in the Palais Preysing, composed mainly of doctors, lawyers, professors, writers, and artists.

. . . .

December 29 1. *Prize established by Consul Lassen.* In 1918 the Swedish consul in Hamburg established a Nietzsche Prize to be awarded by the Nietzsche Archive in Weimar. When consulted about it, TM proposed as its first recipients Oswald Spengler and Rudolf Pannwitz. It was however awarded to TM himself for his *Betrachtungen,* Ernst Bertram for his *Friedrich Nietzsche. Versuch einer Mythologie,* and Gerhard von Mutius, Germany's ambassador in Copenhagen, for his *Die drei Reiche.*

1919

. . . .

January 16 1. *Their theatrical performance.* The older Mann children had recently formed an acting club with their friend Ricki Hallgarten. This performance of Theodor Körner's *Die Gouvernante* in the Mann home was the first of several productions. The group soon grew to include the daughters of Bruno Walter and other Herzogpark children. Klaus Mann relates the history of this "Mimik-Bund" in his autobiographical *Kind dieser Zeit.*

2. *Wassermann's novel.* The World's Illusion (*Christian Wahnschaffe*) by Jakob Wassermann (1919).

. . . .

January 20 1. *The Berlin "Heimatdienst."* The journal of the semi-official Reich Central Office for National Service, dedicated to "general enlightenment of the populace" and propaganda in the electoral districts. TM had been requested to provide a statement, as had other notables, to the effect that the revolution in no way spelled the collapse of Germany.

2. *"The Prince of Homburg."* Patriotic drama (published 1821) by Heinrich von Kleist.

3. *"The Maid of Orleans."* Drama (1801) based on the life of Joan of Arc by Friedrich Schiller.

. . . .

February 17 1. *The two younger children.* Golo and Monika.

2. *My prisoners-of-war letter.* The *Frankfurter Zeitung* had published an ironic and sarcastic piece by TM, "Unsere Kriegsgefangene," on February 4, 1919. By many it was taken at face value and hence misinterpreted.

3. *"Zuspruch."* In order to clarify his position regarding prisoners of war (see preceding note) TM submitted a more obviously patriotic piece ("Exhortation"). It was printed in the *Frankfurter Zeitung* on February 14.

. . . .

February 18 1. *Reich Central Office.* See note 1 for January 20, 1919.

2. *"The World's Illusion."* See note 2 for January 16, 1919.

. . . .

February 22 1. *A Center deputy.* Customs Inspector Heinrich Osel.

2. *The archbishop.* Michael von Faulhaber. The rumor that he had been murdered proved false.

. . . .

February 24 1. *Verse.* The lines from Goethe's *Achilleis,* beginning with line 576, read:

Dieses redest du bieder und wohl, ein verständiger Jüngling.

. . .

Damals war beschlossen der unvermeidliche Jammer

. . .

Lass dies alles uns nun beseitigen! Jegliche Rede,
Wie sie auch weise sei, der erdegeborenen Menschen
Löset die Rätsel nicht der undurchdringlichen Zukunft.

February 26 1. *"Dichtung und Wahrheit."* Goethe's autobiography, *Aus meinem Leben. Dichtung und Wahrheit.*

March 1 1. *Goethe's "Conversations."* These were edited and published in five volumes (1909–11) by Baron Flodard von Biedermann.

March 2 1. *"The Beaver Coat."* Drama (1893) by Gerhart Hauptmann.

March 24 1. *The "Death in Venice" edition.* The Phantasus-Verlag in Munich, a bibliophile publishing firm founded by TM's friend Georg Martin Richter, was planning to bring out a deluxe edition of this novella, but nothing came of it. Two works by TM were produced by the firm, however, *Little Herr Friedemann* (1920) and *Blood of the Walsungs* (1921).
2. *Werkbund.* An association of artists, architects, and craftsmen dedicated to improved standards in design.

March 25 1. *"Herr und Hund."* A Man and His Dog.
2. *World freemasonry.* The book studied by TM has not been identified.

March 31 1. *The "Museum."* TM was to read from *A Man and His Dog* on April 2 in the hall of the Museum Society in Munich.

April 1 1. *Professor Anfrommel.* Unidentified. Likely this was a slip of TM's hand, and it was Otto Frommel to whom he wrote.

April 5 1. *Kurt Wolff-Verlag.* Originally founded in Leipzig in 1909 by Kurt Wolff and Ernst Rowohlt, and until 1912 bearing only the latter's name, this noted publishing house continued to be based in Leipzig until 1919, when (as noted by TM) it purchased the firm of the late Georg Hirth in Munich, publisher of the influential magazine *Die Jugend.* The Kurt Wolff publishing operation was moved to Munich in the fall.

April 7 1. *The 100th edition.* See note 11 for September 11, 1918.
2. *A scholarly work on Hölderlin.* Adolf von Grolman, *Friedrich Hölderlins "Hyperion." Stilkritische Untersuchungen* (1919).
3. *The business with Amann.* Paul Amann had published an extremely negative essay, "Politik und Moral in Thomas Manns *Betrachtungen eines Unpolitischen,*" in the February/March 1919 number of the *Münchner Blätter für Dichtung und Graphik.*
4. *The whereabouts of my debtor.* A former sergeant by the name of Roth had written to TM in November 1918, requesting a loan of 300 marks to cover doctor bills and delinquent taxes. Frau Roth visited TM on November 30 to press for the money, and after Roth himself called by appointment on December 2 TM gave it to him, noting in his diary that he seemed "an honorable man." On December 17 the diary records that Roth had written to ask for an additional 100 marks: "Will probably say yes, but sternly." On January 7 there is the terse comment, "The good sergeant has not been heard from." On the 10th: "Sent a reproachful registered letter to my debtor, the municipal employee Roth." The present sardonic reference is the last we hear of the man.

April 9 1. *Ludwig.* Gustav Ludwig.
2. *Fee for the "Gesang vom Kindchen."* The poem appeared before publication in the April and May issues of the *Neue Merkur.*

April 13 1. *"Peter Schlemihl."* The Romantic tale *The Wonderful History of Peter Schlemihl* (1814) by Adelbert von Chamisso.

April 17	1.	*"Mittelalterliche Weltanschauung."* Friedrich Eicken, *Geschichte und System der mittelalterlichen Weltanschauung* (1887).

April 18	1.	*"The Ass's Skin."* Fairy tale by Charles Perrault.
	2.	*Ludwigs.* Alois Ludwig and his wife.

April 19	1.	*"Royal Highness."* Novel (1909) by TM.

April 20	1.	*"Master and Man."* Novella (1895) by Leo Tolstoy.

April 21	1.	*A healthy boy.* Michael Thomas ("Mischa," "Bibi") Mann.
	2.	*Katia's twin brother.* Klaus Pringsheim.
	3.	*The maid Josefa.* Josefa Kleinsgütl.

April 22	1.	*Klaus's friend Marcks.* Otto Marcks.
	2.	*Sologub's story.* "In the Crowd."

April 27	1.	*The Carolinum.* A private clinic in Munich.

April 30	1.	*Meredith's novel.* George Meredith's *Lord Ormont and His Aminta*.

May 5	1.	*"Black Flags."* Novel by August Strindberg.

May 13	1.	*"Virgin Soil."* Novel (1876) by Turgenev.

May 25	1.	*Papa.* Thomas Johann Heinrich Mann.

June 3	1.	*Speech for the Pfitzner celebration.* A dinner speech, "Tischrede auf Pfitzner," given by TM on the occasion of the composer's fiftieth birthday and first published in the *Süddeutsche Monatshefte*, October 1919.
	2.	*Study on Greek landscape.* Josef Ponten, *Griechische Landschaften* (1915).
	3.	*Dehmel's war diary.* Richard Dehmel, *Zwischen Volk und Menschheit. Ein Kriegstagebuch* (1919).

June 7	1.	*Moni.* TM's second daughter, Monika Mann-Lányi.
	2.	*Hatzfeld's poems.* Adolf von Hatzfeld, *An Gott* (1919).

June 15	1.	*"Birotteau."* Balzac's novel *The Rise and Fall of César Birotteau* (1837).
	2.	*"Der arme Heinrich."* Opera (1895) by Hans Pfitzner.

July 2	1.	*The "Decline."* Oswald Spengler's *Decline of the West*, of which the first volume appeared in 1918.
	2.	*"The World as Will and Idea."* Arthur Schopenhauer's magnum opus deeply influenced TM while he was writing *Buddenbrooks*.
	3.	*A Berlin neurologist.* Dr. Gustav Blume.
	4.	*"Martin Salander."* Novel (1886) by Gottfried Keller.

July 4	1.	*Toller's play.* Ernst Toller's first play, *Die Wandlung* (1918).

July 5	1.	*Something about Keller for Zurich.* Eduard Korrodi had requested a contribution by TM for the *Neue Zürcher Zeitung* on the occasion of the 100th birthday of Gottfried Keller on July 19, 1919. TM complied with the piece "Meine Liebe zu Gottfried Keller."

July 9   1. *"Der grüne Heinrich."* Novel (1854–55) by Gottfried Keller.
       2. *A book I intend to order.* Viktor Bibl's *Der Tod des Don Carlos* (1918).

July 24   1. *Tutti.* Brigitte Fischer.
       2. *Their little girl.* Hilde Fischer.

July 31   1. *Continuing to read Keyserling.* Count Hermann Keyserling's *Travel Diary of a Philosopher* (1919).

August 15   1. *The Pribislav episode.* The fifth section of Chapter Four of *The Magic Mountain*, in which Hans Castorp recalls his schoolboy worship of Pribislav Hippe.

September 13   1. *"Jane" Mann.* Baroness von Heister.

September 17   1. *The Pfitzner speech.* See note 1 for June 3, 1919.

September 21   1. *"St. Petersburg."* Novel (1913) by Andrei Biely.

October 21   1. *Clemen's book.* Paul Clemen, *Kunstschutz im Kriege* (1919).
       2. *The "Palestrina" essay.* A chapter in TM's *Betrachtungen* was given over to a discussion of Hans Pfitzner's opera *Palestrina*. S. Fischer published the piece separately in the autumn of 1919 under the title *Pfitzner's "Palestrina."*
       3. *The "School Sickness."* This episode from the unfinished *Confessions of Felix Krull, Confidence Man* was published in the 1919 edition of the *Kestnerbuch*, an annual put out by the Kestner Society in Hannover, a cultural organization named after the diplomat and art collector Georg August Kestner (1777–1853).
       4. *The Fontane essay.* TM's 1910 study *The Old Fontane* appeared in slightly altered form in *Das Fontanebuch. Beiträge zu seiner Charakteristik*, published by S. Fischer in the autumn of 1919.
       5. *"Mercurius."* "The Thermometer," the tenth and last section of Chapter Four of *The Magic Mountain*.
       6. *The Kestner Society.* See note 3 above.

November 6   1. *Dr. Freytag's premiere.* Georg Kaiser's drama *Gas* was first performed on November 7, 1919, at the Munich Schauspielhaus.
       2. *The hated Feldafing-Richter matter.* In March 1919 TM agreed to assist his friend Georg Martin Richter in the purchase of a vacation house in Feldafing, with the understanding that a room in it would be kept available to him at all times for use as a retreat. The previous month Richter had drawn TM into a bit of speculation in art objects; TM had bought a Dutch painting and a French marble relief with the understanding that the art dealer Karl Bachstitz would quickly find buyers for them at attractively higher prices.
       3. *"Little Herr Friedemann."* The title story of TM's first collection of novellas (1898). Concerning the deluxe edition, see note 1 for March 24, 1919.

November 23   1. *The Society for Artistic Culture.* This group organized literary readings and lectures in Munich, but nothing further is known about it.
       2. *The invitation to Vienna.* TM had been asked to give a reading in Vienna early in December in connection with the planned performances of his *Fiorenza*. After some vacillation he accepted (see entries for December 4–12, 1919).

November 25   1. *The Fontane book.* Conrad Wandrey's *Theodor Fontane* (1919).
       2. *"Effi Briest."* Novel (1895) by Theodor Fontane.

3. *"Frau ohne Schatten."* TM was reading the original Hofmannsthal tale (1919), not the libretto for the Richard Strauss opera based on it.

December 4   1. *Trebitsch's new book.* Presumably Siegfried Trebitsch's *Die Frau ohne Dienstag.*
2. *Her own and Eri's recovery.* Both Katia and Erika were suffering severe bronchial catarrh when TM left Munich on the evening of December 1.
3. *The dress rehearsal.* TM's 1905 drama, *Fiorenza*, was being performed on December 6–8 at the Akademie-Theater in Vienna, with a cast drawn from the Volkstheater and the Burg-theater and directed by Friedrich Rosenthal.

December 6   1. *Concordia.* An association of Viennese writers and journalists.

December 8   1. *"Tristan."* Title story from a collection of novellas (1903) by TM.

December 9   1. *The magazine.* Hugo von Hofmannsthal was at this time hoping to establish a journal to be called *Figura*, and had enlisted TM as a potential contributor.
2. *The Urania Society.* The Urania is a public adult education institute in Vienna.

December 10   1. *Müller's Galileo Drama.* Hans Müller's *Die Sterne.*

December 12   1. *Three one-acts by Salten.* The collective title of Felix Salten's three plays was *Kinder der Freude.*

December 15   1. *Fischer's Fontane book.* See note 4 for October 21, 1919.
2. *Deluxe edition of "Gesang vom Kindchen."* The Rupprechts-Presse, Munich, issued a limited edition of 200 copies of the poem, with designs by F. H. Ehmcke, in 1920.

December 17   1. *The article.* "Zum 100. Geburtstag Theodor Fontanes," TM's review of Conrad Wandrey's *Theodor Fontane*, was published in the *Berliner Tageblatt* on December 25, 1919.
2. *Grossmann's magazine.* Stefan Grossmann and Ernst Rowohlt founded the liberal cultural and political journal *Das Tage-Buch*, which began publication in Berlin in January 1920 and over the years counted TM among its occasional contributors. Leopold Schwarzschild became a co-publisher in 1922, and once the magazine had been banned by the Nazis in 1933 Schwarzschild continued to publish it in exile in Paris as *Das Neue Tage-Buch.* For the next seven years it was the most influential of the German exile journals. TM's open letter to Count Hermann Keyserling appeared in Vol. I, No. 11/12 of *Das Tage-Buch* in 1920.

December 19   1. *The Progress office.* A stenographic and duplicating service in Munich where TM frequently dictated his manuscripts to a typist. A typewriter came into the Mann household only much later, when Katia took over much of the necessary copying. TM himself never used a type-writer.
2. *Russian love stories.* *Russische Liebesnovellen*, translated and edited by Alexander Eliasberg.

December 21   1. *"Minna von Barnhelm."* Comedy (1767) by Gotthold Ephraim Lessing. Concerning this performance, see note 1 for January 16, 1919.

December 25   1. *The Fontane article.* See note 1 for December 17, 1919.
2. *Vicco's wife.* Magdalena ("Nelly") Mann, née Kilian.

December 31   1. *The article.* The open letter to Count Keyserling.
2. *Emma Bonn's novellas.* *Die Verirrten* (1919).

1920

. . . .

January 8   1. *The Saltykov.*   *The Messieurs Golovlev* (1881) by N. Shchedrin (pseudonym of Mikhail Saltykov).

   2. *Hauptmann's latest verse play.*   The dramatic poem *Indipohdi* by Gerhart Hauptmann.

. . . .

January 20   1. *Pfitzner's polemic.*   Hans Pfitzner, *Die Neue Ästhetik der musikalischen Impotenz* (1920).

   2. *Her brother's ashes.*   The remains of Katia Mann's oldest brother, Erik Pringsheim.

   3. *The open letter to Elchinger.*   Richard Elchinger, features editor of the *Münchner Neueste Nachrichten*, had invited responses to an article about the National Theater. TM's reply was printed in that paper on January 27, 1920, under the title "Was dünkt Euch um unser bayerisches Staatstheater?"

. . . .

February 10   1. *A new theme for "The Magic Mountain."*   Developed in the "Fullness of Harmony" section in Chapter Seven.

   2. *Settembrini's visit with Hans.*   In the "Soup-Everlasting" and "Sudden Enlightenment" sections of Chapter Five.

   3. *Heinrich's wife.*   Heinrich Mann was at this time married to his first wife, Maria ("Mimi") Kanova. TM had little use for either of his sisters-in-law.

   4. *"The Hungry."*   Story (1903) by TM. Stefan Zweig was an avid collecter of manuscripts.

   5. *"The Blood of the Walsungs."*   Novella (1906) by TM. Concerning Richter's deluxe edition, see note 1 for March 24, 1919.

   6. *The facsimile edition.*   TM's manuscript of the novella *Tristan* was reproduced in 1920 as the first in a series of facsimiles from modern German writers by the Verlags-Buchhandlung Lehmann, Dresden.

   7. *The journal proposition.*   Johannes von Guenther wished to publish a cultural magazine to be called *Odeon*, with TM as its editor. It never materialized.

   8. *My "Old Fontane."*   See note 4 for October 21, 1919.

. . . .

February 20   1. *The baptism.*   At the baptism of the infant Michael Mann on February 26, 1920, Pastor Georg Merz officiated. Georg Martin Richter and Joseph Löhr were named as godfathers.

   2. *Read further in Pannwitz.*   TM had recently received from the publisher two new books by Rudolf Pannwitz, *Die deutsche Lehre* and *Baldurs Tod. Ein Maifestspiel.*

. . . .

February 24   1. *Keynes's book on Versailles.*   *The Economic Consequences of the Peace* (1920) by John Maynard Keynes.

. . . .

February 29   1. *"The Idiot."*   Novel (1868–69) by Dostoevsky.

   2. *The Erzberger trial.*   The Reich finance minister Matthias Erzberger had been attacked in a pamphlet by a political opponent, Karl Helferich. Erzberger brought a libel suit against him and the case was tried between January and March 1920.

. . . .

March 3   1. *"Ulenspiegel."*   Charles de Coster's *The Legend of Ulenspiegel and Lamme Goedzak* (1868).

. . . .

March 14   1. *His little girl.*   Heinrich Mann's only child, Leonie ("Goschi") Mann.

   2. *The new government in Berlin.*   The Kapp-Lüttwitz regime.

. . . .

March 15   1. *Hellerau.*   Paul Claudel's German publisher, Jakob Hegner-Verlag, was located in Hellerau, near Dresden.

. . . .

March 22   1. *The Zurich currency matter.*   Eduard Korrodi had requested a section from *The Magic Mountain* for publication in the Easter number of the *Neue Zürcher Zeitung*, thus providing

TM with an opportunity to receive some welcome Swiss francs (see entry for April 19, 1920).

2. *Babr's essay.* Hermann Bahr, *Adalbert Stifter. Eine Entdeckung* (1919).

3. *Bertram's.* Ernst Bertram, *Adalbert Stifter, Wesen und Welt* (1919).

March 26 1. *Read some Péladan.* TM was then reading Joséphin Péladan's *La rondache.*

April 8 1. *"Don Gil of the Green Trousers."* Comedy (1635) by Tirso de Molina.

April 11 1. *J. S. Bach.* In his "Anekdote" Heinrich von Kleist ascribes this retort to Bach, but in fact the story was first told about the composer Georg Benda (1722–1795).

April 29 1. *The October morning meeting.* In the "Sudden Enlightenment" section from Chapter Five of *The Magic Mountain.*

2. *Small pieces by Jammes.* A collection of stories by Francis Jammes translated by E. A. Rheinhardt as *Das Paradies.*

May 5 1. *My edition of Baudelaire.* TM owned the four-volume edition of the works of Charles Baudelaire edited by Max Bruns and published by the J. C. C. Bruns-Verlag (1902–07).

2. *Hatzfeld's manuscript.* Presumably the manuscript of Adolf von Hatzfeld's novel *Die Lemminge* (1923).

May 21 1. *The Pniower affair.* The literary historian Otto Pniower had claimed in an article in the *Vossische Zeitung* on May 5 that the editor of Theodor Fontane's literary remains, Josef Ettlinger, had misprinted a line in one of Fontane's poems. TM disagreed strongly—and apparently incorrectly—and responded with an article of his own that was published, after some delay, on June 8.

2. *The Altenberg publication.* *Das Peter Altenberg-Buch* (1922), edited by Egon Friedell.

May 25 1. *Grete.* The younger of Bruno Walter's two daughters.

May 26 1. *"Der Corregidor."* Opera by Hugo Wolf.

May 27 1. *Flake's journal.* Otto Flake attempted to produce a journal in Munich in 1920, doing most all of the writing himself. Called *Die fünf Hefte,* it did not survive its first year.

June 6 1. *The Marckses' niece.* Elisabeth Deneke (b. 1896).

July 11 1. *The letter about German style.* TM's "Erziehung zur Sprache," in the form of a letter to a teacher of writing, appeared in the *Vossische Zeitung* on August 1, 1920.

2. *Lion's chapter on Venice.* TM was reading the manuscript (never published) of Ferdinand Lion's *Venezianische Philosophie.*

3. *Eissi's story.* Golo Mann recalls that the "impossible" story submitted to *Simplicissimus* by his brother Klaus was called "Monika Nachtigall," and dealt with "an old and once moderately successful opera singer" living "in melancholy retirement" who makes one disastrous return to the stage.

4. *"Lost Illusions."* Novel (1836–43) by Balzac.

July 14 1. *The majolica.* Professor Pringsheim owned an extremely valuable collection of Renaissance pottery, silverwork, and bronzes. Clearly it had been packed away or placed in storage during the unsettled times just past. The Nazis forced him to sell the collection at auction in London in 1939. It fetched but a fraction of its true value, and seventy-five percent of the proceeds of the sale were paid to the Third Reich as a precondition of Pringsheim's emigration with his wife to Switzerland.

. . . . . .

. . . .

July 25   1. *Kerner's "Totengräber."*   *Der Totengräber von Feldberg* (1811), a drama by Justinus Kerner. 1920

             2. *Emelianuschka.*   The down-at-heel old drunkard in Dostoevsky's novella *An Honorable* 1921
Thief. From the Notes of an Unknown Man.

. . . . . .

. . . .

July 28   1. *Zweig's "Dostoevsky."*   The essay appearing in Stefan Zweig's *Drei Meister. Balzac, Dickens,*
Dostojewski (1920).

. . . .

October 17   1. *Meyers.*   Presumably Georg Heinrich Meyer and his wife.

. . . .

October 31   1. *"Don Carlos."*   See note 2 for July 9, 1919.

             2. *The Viennese countess.*   Unidentified.

. . . .

December 29   1. *Meetings on orthographic reform.*   At the urging of school authorities, the Ministry of the
Interior had established a committee to modernize German orthography. Composed of teachers, publishers, editors, and journalists, the committee first convened in January 1920. TM
was invited to represent the writing profession at its December meetings. The resultant proposals toward the simplification of style and spelling were published the following April.

             2. *My "Wardrobe."*   Short story (1899) by TM.

             3. *Article on the Editiones Insulae.*   TM's article on this series of masterworks of world
literature published by the Insel-Verlag appeared in the *Münchner Neueste Nachrichten* on
December 24/25, 1920.

             4. *"Children's Games."*   The most revealing testament relating to TM's childhood we have,
this autobiographical sketch was written in 1904. It was not published in its complete form,
however, until its inclusion in the Christmas edition of the *Vossische Zeitung* in 1920.

             5. *Introductory piece for the Russian issue.* "Zum Geleit," a preface to the February 1921 issue
of the *Süddeutsche Monatshefte,* which was dedicated to "Masterworks of Russian Narrative."

1921

. . . .

February 6   1. *The Hottingen Club.*   A literary society founded in Zurich in 1882.

. . . .

February 23   1. *The Hohenlohe-Langenburg family.*   Prince Ernst zu Hohenlohe-Langenburg, his wife, Princess Alexandra of Saxe-Coburg and Gotha, and their daughters.

             2. *The prince.*   Heinrich XXV, Crown Price Reuss.

             3. *"A Weary Hour."*   Story (1905) by TM.

             4. *Glorious mural by Hodler.*   Ferdinand Hodler's *Exodus of the Students of Jena in 1813* (1908).

             5. *Peter and Klaus.* Peter and Klaus Pringsheim. Klaus was married to Klara ("Lala") Koszler.

             6. *"The Railway Accident."*   Novella (1909) by TM.

             7. *The essay volume.*   TM's *Rede und Antwort* (1922).

             8. *"Gewissen."*   A conservative Berlin journal published by Baron Heinrich von Gleichen-Russwurm.

             9. *Heinz Pringsheim's wife.*   Olga Markowa Meerson.

             10. *The Georg Kaiser trial.*   The dramatist Georg Kaiser had been accused of embezzlement,
was tried, and was sentenced to a term in prison. The trial attracted considerable attention
because it publicized the miserably poor financial situation of even quite well-known writers.

             11. *Jaeger's "Kranke Liebe."*   A translation (1920) of Hans Henrik Jaeger's trilogy, *Syk kjaerlihet,*
Bekjendelser, and *Faengsel og fortvilelse.*

. . . .

March 1   1. *Heine.*   The bibliophile edition of *The Blood of the Walsungs* was illustrated with lithographs
by Thomas Theodor Heine.

| March 4 | 1. *Künstlerdank.* A foundation for the aid of wounded artists established during the First World War. Hanns Martin Elster transformed it into a peacetime organization that sponsored readings, lectures, and exhibits. |

| April 4 | 1. *Monocle-wearing writer.* Unidentified. |
| | 2. *His dissertation.* Carl Helbling's work was actually titled *Die Gestalt des Künstlers in der neueren Dichtung. Eine Studie über Thomas Mann.* |

| May 13 | 1. *My statement.* The J. G. Cotta publishing firm had asked TM for support for its publication of Bismarck's *Gedanken und Erinnerungen,* about which a copyright battle was being waged concerning letters from the Kaiser that were included among the chancellor's memoirs. TM's testimony appeared under the title "Um Bismarcks dritten Band" in the *Berliner Tageblatt* on June 6, 1921. |

| May 19 | 1. *The article on Ungar.* "Knaben und Mörder," TM's review of the novel of the same title by Hermann Unger, published in the *Vossische Zeitung* on May 29, 1921. |
| | 2. *Uriel Birnbaum's poems.* Doubtless his *In Gottes Krieg* (1921). |

| May 22 | 1. *"Colonel Chabert."* Novel (1832) by Balzac. |
| | 2. *Owner of Philharmonic Hall.* Peter Landecker. |

May 24	1. *A new book of Freud's.* *Beyond the Pleasure Principle.*
	2. *Angry telegram to Fischer.* TM was displeased with progress in the preparation of his essay volume *Rede und Antwort.*
	3. *"Frederick the Great and the Grand Coalition."* First published in 1915, TM's essay had gone through a number of printings as a separate booklet. Since he was now including it in *Rede und Antwort* TM saw no reason to keep it in print separately.

May 31	1. *Reisiger's translations.* Hans Reisiger was translating a major selection of Walt Whitman's poems for publication by S. Fischer.
	2. *The lecture.* *Goethe and Tolstoy,* which TM was writing for delivery in Lübeck in September 1921. The lecture developed into a major essay, of which the Lübeck address was a highly abridged version.
	3. *The Tolstoy biography.* Pavel I. Biryukov's three-volume *Leo N. Tolstoy. A Biography.*
	4. *Bielschowsky.* Albert Bielschowsky's *Goethe. Sein Leben und seine Werke* (1896).
	5. *Mahrholz's book.* Werner Mahrholz, *Deutsche Selbstbekenntnisse. Zur Geschichte der Selbstbiographie von der Mystik bis zum Pietismus* (1919).
	6. *Nordic Week.* The festival held in Lübeck, September 2–8, 1921, to which TM had been invited.

| June 3 | 1. *Negotiations with Rikola-Verlag.* The Viennese publishing firm established by the financier Richard Kola had purchased the noted Musarion-Verlag, Munich. It was extremely eager to be able to count TM among its authors and was prepared to pay handsome royalties. A deluxe edition of the 1911 fragment of *The Confessions of Felix Krull, Confidence Man* was published by Rikola in 1922. |

| June 6 | 1. *"Little Lizzy."* Novella (1900) by TM. The story was published in the April 1921 issue of *The Dial,* New York, under the title "Loulou," in a translation by Kenneth Burke. |

| June 26 | 1. *Blüher's book on Christ.* Hans Blüher, *Die Aristie des Jesus von Nazareth* (1921). |
| | 2. *Pavlova.* This was not the famed Russian dancer Anna Pavlova, but a certain Claudia Pavlova, about whom little more is known. |

3. *Carl Ehrenberg's opera.* Presumably his *Annaliese* (1922), based on a text of Hans Christian Andersen.

4. *Wilhelm Meister's Travels.* Novel (1829) by Goethe, the sequel to his *Wilhelm Meister's Apprenticeship* .

August 1   1. *"Norm und Entartung."* Kurt Hildebrandt, *Norm und Entartung des Menschen* (1920).

September 17   1. *The Mengstrasse and Beckergrube houses.* The house at No. 4 Mengstrasse in Lübeck had belonged to TM's grandmother, and was sold after her death in 1890, having been in the Mann family for precisely fifty years. It is the so-called Buddenbrooks House. The house at No. 52 Beckergrube was built by TM's father in 1881–82, and the author lived there from age eight until it too was sold after the death of his father in 1891. Both are described in *Buddenbrooks*. The Mengstrasse house is preserved; the Beckergrube house was destroyed during the Second World War.

2. *"Purgatory."* A small alleyway near Lübeck cathedral.

3. *Katia's cousins.* The sisters Käthe Rosenberg and Ilse Dernburg.

4. *The Burghaus.* An apartment in the old city gate in Lübeck placed at the disposal of Ida Boy-Ed by the city for as long as she lived. TM was her houseguest there on several occasions.

5. *The bust in the Behn house.* One of the copies of Hans Schwegerle's bust of TM (see note 1 for December 20, 1918) was displayed in this old patrician house, then a Lübeck municipal museum.

6. *"The Dance of Death."* A medieval mystery play.

7. *"The Weavers."* Drama (1892) by Gerhart Hauptmann.

8. *Matthäikirchstrasse.* The home of Else Rosenberg.

9. *"Herod and Mariamne."* Drama (1847–48) by Friedrich Hebbel.

10. *Klaus.* Klaus Pringsheim.

11. *"Kean."* Drama by Kasimir Edschmid.

September 22   1. *Letter to Frisch.* Efraim Frisch had requested a contribution from TM to a special number of the *Neue Merkur* devoted to the Jewish question. TM complied with his "Zur jüdischen Frage" (see entry for October 28, 1921), but withdrew the piece before publication.

2. *"Sárarany."* Novel (1910) by Zsigmond Móricz, published in German in 1921 as *Gold im Kote*.

October 28   1. *Martens's autobiography.* Kurt Martens, *Schonungslose Lebenschronik* (1921–24).

November 6–13   1. *C. F. Meyer's daughter.* Camilla Elisabeth Meyer.

2. *"Liebestrank."* Frank Wedekind's comedy *Der Liebestrank*.

3. *"Strom."* The drama *Der Strom* by Max Halbe.

4. *Article on Martens's autobiography.* TM's "Ein Schriftstellerleben," published in the *Neue Zürcher Zeitung* on November 30, 1921.

November 20   1. *Answer to "Politiken."* This has not been located.

2. *"Der Schwierige."* Comedy by Hugo von Hofmannsthal.

December 1   1. *"The Miser."* Comedy by Molière.

2. *Two-act play by Turgenev.* The Family Charge (*Nahlebnik*), 1848.

3. *A summation.* Ernst Robert Curtius had published an essay, "Deutsch-französische Kulturprobleme," in the June 1921 number of the *Neue Merkur*. André Gide replied to it in a very positive way in his "Les rapports intellectuels entre la France et l'Allemagne" in the November issue of the *Nouvelle Revue Française*. TM referred to both articles in his own "Das Problem der deutsch-französischen Beziehungen" in the January 1922 issue of the *Neue Merkur*, using them as a pretext for dealing at length with French criticism of his *Betrachtungen* and

redefining his own position: "That book was a revolt against the 'enslavement of intellect' by politics—nothing more."

4. *Little piece for the "Prager Presse."* TM's review of Knut Hamsun's *The Women at the Pump* appeared in the *Prager Presse* on January 29, 1922.

1933

. . . .

The record that TM intended to preserve begins with the first entry included here, one for the Ides of March, 1933. Five weeks earlier, on February 10, TM read his lecture *Sufferings and Greatness of Richard Wagner* in Munich in commemoration of the fiftieth anniversary of the composer's death. The following day TM and his wife set out on a tour to Amsterdam, Brussels, and Paris, where further readings of the lecture were scheduled. They then proceeded to Arosa for a planned holiday before returning home to Munich. The political situation in Germany had changed considerably in their absence however. Though Hitler had become chancellor on January 30 it was by no means clear—especially in Bavaria—what was to come. Then on February 27 the Reichstag was burned in Berlin, the following day Hitler was granted dictatorial powers, and on March 12 the Nazis forced the resignation of the minister president of Bavaria. During his absence TM received repeated warnings that he might be in danger if he returned to Germany because of what the Nazis called his "pacifist excesses" and "intellectual treason." It was only on March 12 however, alerted by his children Erika and Klaus of the most recent developments, that TM was finally convinced to remain abroad, and his long exile began.

. . . .

March 15   1. *The Wagner essay. Sufferings and Greatness of Richard Wagner,* written in early 1933 and first given in abbreviated form as a lecture at the University of Munich on February 10. It was first published in full in the April 1933 issue of the *Neue Rundschau.*

2. *The Writers' League.* TM belonged to the executive committee of the Munich branch of this organization, the Schutzverband deutscher Schriftsteller, founded in 1909 to promote the interests of writers. The League was "conformed" in 1933 and ultimately absorbed into the Nazi Reich Literature Chamber.

3. *Medi.* Elisabeth Mann-Borgese.

4. *"Mario."* TM's novella *Mario and the Magician* (1930), in which he was outspokenly critical of the Italian Fascist regime.

5. *"Corona."* A literary bi-monthly founded and published in Zurich and Munich by Martin Bodmer and Herbert Steiner. The journal appeared from 1930 to 1943, and TM was a frequent contributor.

6. *My Goethe lecture.* "Goethe's Career as a Man of Letters" appeared in Vol. 3, No. 3 (February 1933) of *Corona.*

7. *The third "Joseph" volume.* TM began writing a novel based on the Biblical Joseph, "a kind of mythical confidence man," in December 1926. By 1933 he was well into what would have to be a third volume of the work, but only portions of it had been published in literary journals. With acute foresight Erika immediately brought her father from Munich the manuscript on which he was then working together with the appropriate files of sketches and notes, making it possible for him to continue its composition in exile. The book publication of the work was as follows: *The Tales of Jacob,* S. Fischer, Berlin (1933); *Young Joseph,* S. Fischer, Berlin (1934); *Joseph in Egypt,* Bermann-Fischer, Vienna (1936); and *Joseph the Provider,* Bermann-Fischer, Stockholm (1943).

8. *Bertram's poems. Wartburg. Spruchgedichte* (1933).

. . . .

362   March 16   1. *Gyldendal Forlag and Jespersen and Pio.* TM's two most important Danish publishers.

March 17   1.   *"Die Weltbühne."*   A left-leaning Berlin cultural and political weekly founded by Siegfried
Jacobsohn in 1905. Carl von Ossietzky took it over in 1927, and once the magazine was banned
by the Nazis it continued to appear in exile in Prague as *Die Neue Weltbühne.* During the
Prague period Heinrich Mann was one of its chief contributors.

March 18   1.   *The declaration.*   Members of the literary section of the Prussian Academy of Arts had
been sent a questionnaire by Max von Schillings, president of the Academy. Drafted by
Gottfried Benn, it read: "Are you willing to continue to be identified with the Prussian
Academy of Arts in light of the changed historical situation? A positive response to this question
will prohibit you from any public activity against the government and commit you to loyal
collaboration in the national cultural tasks—recognizing the changed historical situation—falling
by statute to the Academy." A distinct yes or no was required.
2.   *Call from Döblin.*   Alfred Döblin was the only member present at the February 15 meeting
of the Prussian Academy to strongly protest the removal of Heinrich Mann from his office of
president of the literary section.
3.   *Hauptmanns.*   Gerhart Hauptmann and his wife were accustomed to spending a few weeks
each spring in Lugano with S. Fischer and other friends. Hauptmann and TM were superficially
on cordial terms, but at this time TM did not yet know that Hauptmann would respond
affirmatively to the Academy poll and make his peace with the Hitler regime.

March 19   1.   *German Academy.*   TM had belonged to the German Academy for the Cultivation of
Germanism Abroad since its founding in Munich in 1925.
2.   *PEN Club.*   An international writers' society founded in London in 1921. The initials stand
for "poets, essayists, and novelists."
3.   *The League of Nations committee.*   The Comité permanent des Lettres et des Arts.
4.   *Old diaries and papers.*   TM kept his diaries and other personal papers in the so-called "safe
cupboard" upstairs in the Munich house, the key to which he had with him in Switzerland.

March 20   1.   *The Madrid meeting.*   The annual conference of the League of Nations' Comité permanent
des Lettres et des Arts was scheduled for Madrid in May 1933.
2.   *The Horst Wessel song.*   Hitler decreed that "Die Fahne hoch!," written by the student
martyr Horst Wessel, be sung as a national anthem as well as *Deutschland, Deutschland über
alles.*

March 21   1.   *Strauss.*   Bruno Walter had been forced to decline an engagement with the Berlin Philharmonic in the middle of March and Richard Strauss substituted for him.

March 27   1.   *Fayard.*   The Paris publishing firm of Arthème Fayard brought out the French edition of
TM's *Sufferings and Greatness of Richard Wagner.*
2.   *The Reichstag fire.*   The burning of the Berlin Reichstag building on the night of February
27, 1933, has never been fully explained. It was used by the Nazi regime as an excuse and
signal for the brutal persecution of the political Left. The Dutchman Marinus Van der Lubbe,
the Communist Reichstag deputy Ernst Torgler, and three Bulgarians residing in Berlin—
Dimitroff, Popoff, and Taneff—were accused of arson and tried before the Supreme Court in
Leipzig. Van der Lubbe was found guilty and executed, the three Bulgarians were released to
the Soviet Union, and Torgler was imprisoned until the end of 1936. Though it was widely
suspected that the National Socialists themselves had set the blaze, it could not be proved.
Immediately after the fire a series of carefully prepared emergency measures was proclaimed,
whereby constitutionally guaranteed freedoms were withdrawn and Hitler achieved absolute
power.

March 29   1.   *Her Swiss cabaret project.*   Erika Mann was attempting to revive in Switzerland the cabaret
The Peppermill, which she and Therese Giehse had opened in Munich on January 1, 1933.

....

March 30   1. *Deutscher Klub.* A conservative, monarchist organization founded by Baron Heinrich von Gleichen-Russwurm in Berlin in 1924.
2. *Bibi.* Michael Mann.
3. *Hans.* Hans Holzner.
4. *The "Coopération."* The Commission Internationale de Coopération Intellectuelle of the League of Nations.
5. *My "message."* The allusion is unclear.
6. *The Foyer.* TM had given his Wagner lecture at the Foyer de l'Europe in Paris.

....

March 31   1. *"Past Masters."* The 1933 American collection of essays by TM, *Past Masters and Other Papers*, which included the Wagner essay.
2. *The "Völkischer Beobachter."* The Nazi party newspaper.
3. *Their collection.* See note 1 for July 14, 1920.

....

April 1   1. *"The Coat of Many Colours."* The first chapter of Section IV in *Young Joseph.*

....

April 3   1. *The Faust story.* This is the first indication that TM thought to turn to the Faust theme, one suggested in his notebooks as early as 1904, after completing his *Joseph.* He finally did so in 1943–47 in the novel *Doctor Faustus.*
2. *Nansen passport.* The so-called Nansen passport was an internationally valid personal pass created by the League of Nations at the urging of the Norwegian explorer Fridtjof Nansen (1861–1930), one available to political refugees, exiles, and stateless persons.

....

April 6   1. *The children's book.* Presumably Erika Mann's *Muck, der Zauberonkel* (1934).

....

April 7   1. *Wassermann's problems.* Jakob Wassermann was drawn into endless legal battles during the last years of his life by his first wife, Julie Wassermann-Speyer. They ruined him financially and undermined his health.
2. *Jünger's book.* Ernst Jünger, *Der Arbeiter. Herrschaft und Gestalt* (1932).

....

April 8   1. *"Sketch of My Life."* An autobiographical essay by TM published in the *Neue Rundschau* in June 1930.
2. *The Käte Hamburger matter.* In the autumn of 1932 Käte Hamburger sent TM her study *Thomas Mann und die Romantik*, which led to an extensive correspondence. TM was attempting to locate a teaching position in the United States for her.

....

April 9   1. *Croce's most recent book.* Benedetto Croce, *History of Europe in the Nineteenth Century* (1932), the German edition of which was dedicated to TM.

....

April 13   1. *Ludwig.* Emil Ludwig.
2. *The Veterans Association.* The "Stahlhelm," a nationalistic, paramilitary society of former front-line soldiers founded in 1918.
3. *Furtwängler's letter.* In an essay on German cultural life the conductor Wilhelm Furt-wängler had argued for continued employment in Germany for Jewish artists such as Bruno Walter, Otto Klemperer, and Max Reinhardt, whereupon Propaganda Minister Goebbels remarked, "There isn't a single filthy Jew left in Germany that Herr Furtwängler hasn't stood up for."
4. *"Gneisenau."* The highly successful drama, *Neidhart von Gneisenau* (1926), by Wolfgang Goetz.

....

April 17   1. *That radio broadcast.* See following note.

April 19   1. *"Protest by Munich, the Wagner City."* A group objection to TM's Wagner lecture, in which TM discusses less admirable traits of the composer, appeared in the *Münchner Neueste Nachrichten* on April 16, 1933. The document was signed by numerous close acquaintances of TM's, among them Richard Strauss and Hans Pfitzner. The protest was simultaneously broadcast.

2. *My reply.* "Erwiderung auf den 'Protest der Wagner-Stadt München.'" The piece was published in the four journals mentioned.

May 3   1. *"Critica."* A journal begun in 1903 by Benedetto Croce and for the most part written by him.

2. *Katia's brother.* Peter Pringsheim.

May 8   1. *The "accident" of young Mendelssohn.* The Berlin writer Felix Manuel Mendelssohn had fled to Switzerland. While visiting Erich Maria Remarque in Ascona he was killed in the dark on Remarque's property, seemingly in an accident, but more likely by political agents.

May 9   1. *Ricarda Huch.* In fact Ricarda Huch resigned from the Prussian Academy at the end of March 1933.

May 17   1. *The suitcase.* The valise containing TM's diaries, the object of so much anguish for the writer, was delivered safely into his hands on May 19.

June 8   1. *Pelzer's.* A luxury restaurant in Berlin.

June 11   1. *Maria.* Maria Ferber.

June 17   1. *Arranging the text.* TM was preparing *The Tales of Jacob* for publication. As written, the manuscript was only divided into main sections. TM divided these further into sub-sections or chapters with appropriate headings at this time. He had followed the same procedure with *The Magic Mountain,* the arrangement of which is similar to that of the Joseph novels.

July 3   1. *Pfitzner.* See note 1 for April 19, 1933.

July 20   1. *Heinrich's lady friend.* Nelly Kröger, later Heinrich's wife.

2. *"The Great Hoaxing."* The fourth chapter of Section IV of *The Tales of Jacob.*

3. *"Scenes of Nazi Life."* Portions of Heinrich Mann's *Der Hass. Deutsche Zeitgeschichte* (1933).

4. *The reply to Pfitzner's article.* TM's "Antwort an Hans Pfitzner" remained unpublished, for Peter Suhrkamp felt he could not print it in the *Neue Rundschau* and TM did not want to place it merely in one of the exile journals.

5. *90 Bülowstrasse.* The offices of S. Fischer, publisher of the *Neue Rundschau,* in Berlin.

6. *Querido.* In the summer of 1933 Fritz Landshoff set up a German division within the Dutch publishing firm of Emanuel Querido, and this was to become the most important of the German emigré publishing houses for the remainder of the decade, bringing out countless works of German exiles in their original language.

7. *"Witiko."* Novel (1865–67) by Adalbert Stifter.

September 3   1. *Barth's pamphlet.* *Theologische Existenz heute.*

September 6   1. *"Die Sammlung."* A literary and political monthly published by Querido Verlag in Amsterdam from September 1933 to August 1935. Its advisory board was made up of André Gide, Heinrich Mann, and Aldous Huxley; its editor was Klaus Mann. The first issue contained essays by Heinrich Mann, Jakob Wassermann, and Alfred Döblin, a short story by Hermann Kesten, and a novel fragment by Joseph Roth. A preview of forthcoming issues in that number mentioned contributions by Stefan Zweig, René Schickele, and Thomas Mann, among others. TM had given his permission for such use of his name, but under pressure from S. Fischer Verlag he was forced to retract it.

September 7   1. *"Europäische Revue."* Prince Rohan's journal was founded in Leipzig in 1924. It was purportedly dedicated to European understanding, but even during the last years of the Republic it had begun to sound a rather nationalist tone. It was "conformed" in 1933 and ceased publication in 1944.
2. *Klaus's trick.* TM and René Schickele were led to believe that *Die Sammlung* would be a purely literary journal, but the Heinrich Mann essay included in the first number gave it from the start an unmistakably political, polemical tone.

October 1   Four days earlier the Manns had moved into the house at No. 33 Schiedhaldenstrasse in Küsnacht, near Zurich.
1. *The long "Arrival" section.* Section III of *Joseph in Egypt.*
2. *The concordat.* The Hitler regime and Pope Pius XI had reached a diplomatic agreement on July 22, 1933, the so-called "Reichskonkordat."
3. *The Leipzig trial.* See note 2 for March 27, 1933.

October 4   1. *Knappertsbusch.* The conductor Hans Knappertsbusch was one of the initiators of the Munich protest against TM's Wagner lecture.
2. *The Onegin-Penzoldt couple.* Sigrid Onegin and her husband, Fritz Penzoldt.
3. *"The Peppermill."* See note 1 for March 29, 1933.
4. *Book by H. Hauser.* Heinrich Hauser's *Ein Mann lernt fliegen* (1933).

October 14   1. *"Ten Years."* This was TM's working title for the first chapter of the fourth section of *Joseph in Egypt,* ultimately called "How Long Joseph Stayed with Potiphar."
2. *Charge of "intellectual treason."* The Reich Agency for the Promotion of German Literature, directed by Alfred Rosenberg, published a massive attack on *Die Sammlung* and its contributors in the October 10, 1933, issue of the *Börsenblatt für den deutschen Buchhandel,* closing with the sentence: "It will be obvious to the German bookseller that he handle no books by authors engaging in intellectual warmongering against Germany abroad." Bermann Fischer promptly submitted for publication in the same journal declarations by TM, René Schickele, and Alfred Döblin, in which they distanced themselves from *Die Sammlung,* and these were published on October 14. The Reich agency withdrew its accusation.
3. *The Book Guild.* The large Swiss book club Büchergilde Gutenberg, the German branch of which was "conformed" by the Nazi regime.

October 15   1. *Open letter.* Unidentified.

October 21   1. *The Kokoschka matter.* Oskar Kokoschka made several drawings inspired by TM's *Joseph,* two of which were published in the *Wiener Kunstwanderer* in November 1933 together with an essay, "Joseph und seine Brüder," by Wolfgang Born.
2. *Lines of Platen's.* The close of a sonnet by Count August von Platen Hallermund. In the original they read:

> Denn wer aus ganzer Seele hasst das Schlechte,
> Auch aus der Heimat wird es ihn verjagen,
> Wenn dort verehrt es wird vom Volk der Knechte.
>
> Weit besser ist's, dem Vaterland entsagen,
> Als unter einem kindischen Geschlechte
> Die Wut des blinden Pöbelhasses tragen.

November 1 1. *Kaulbach's portrait of Katia.* Apparently TM refers to the portrait of Katia as a girl not by Kaulbach, but by Franz von Lenbach.
2. *The Vienna "Arbeiter-Zeitung."* On the heels of the *Sammlung* controversy (see note 2 for October 14, 1933) the *Arbeiter-Zeitung* published a sharp attack on TM's position, to which he responded with an open letter printed in that paper on October 25.

November 9 1. *Frau Guyer.* Lux Studer-Guyer.

November 24 1. *The Egyptian funerary figurine.* A painted wooden statuette of a striding man in wig and loincloth, a burial figure from roughly 1900 B.C. It is now in the Thomas Mann Archive in Zurich.

November 26 1. *The Czech's Wallenstein novel. Bloudeni*, a trilogy about Wallenstein by Jaroslav Durych, appeared in German translation in 1933 as *Friedland*.

December 1 1. *The French lecture.* The French translation of the *Sufferings and Greatness of Richard Wagner.*

December 31 1. *My cousin Anne Marie.* Anne Marie Schneider.

1934

January 1 1. *Our lease on the house.* In fact the Manns continued to lease the house in Küsnacht until they moved to Princeton in the autumn of 1938.

January 29 1. *My French lecture.* The French translation of *Sufferings and Greatness of Richard Wagner.*

February 11 1. *The volume of essays.* TM's *Leiden und Grösse der Meister*, published in March 1935.
2. *The German national chapter of the PEN Club.* At the 1933 International PEN Congress in Dubrovnik the German delegation walked out after having been sharply attacked for its National Socialist position. A German national PEN Club was founded, and at one of its meetings Emanuel Stickelberger was a guest participant.
3. *Seger's book.* Gerhart Seger, *Oranienburg. Erster authentischer Bericht eines aus dem Konzentrationslager Geflüchteten* (1934).

February 21 1. *His Mary Stuart novel.* Hans Reisiger's work in progress, *Ein Kind befreit die Königin* (1939).

February 25 1. *Platen's ghazel.* Number 40 of a series of lyrics based on this Arabic form by Count August von Platen Hallermund. TM has transposed the first two lines. The original reads:
Ich bin wie Leib dem Geist, wie Geist dem Leibe Dir.
Ich bin wie Weib dem Mann, wie Mann dem Weibe Dir.
Wen darfst Du lieben sonst, da von der Lippe weg
Mit ewigen Küssen ich den Tod vertreibe Dir?

March 14 1. *New novel by Fallada.* Hans Fallada's *Wer einmal aus dem Blechnapf frisst* (1934).

March 20 1. *The Prince murder.* A French Conseiller, Prince, had been placed unconscious on a railway track by unknown criminals attempting to feign his suicide. He was struck by a train and killed, and the case was given enormous attention in Paris.
2. *Kerényi's "Griechischer Roman."* Karl Kerényi, *Die griechisch-orientalische Romanliteratur in religionsgeschichtlicher Beleuchtung.*

1. *Otto's book.* Walter F. Otto, *The Gods of Greece.*

April 9 1. *The "Weiland Granite" letter.* This allusion is unclear. Doubtless it has to do with one of the countless hate letters sent by Nazis to TM.

April 23 1. *The lecture.* TM delivered his 1932 lecture *Goethe as Representative of the Bourgeois Age* on this occasion, standing in for his brother Heinrich who was unable to make a scheduled appearance.

April 25 1. *Schwarzschild's book.* Leopold Schwarzschild, *Das Ende der Illusionen* (1934).
2. *"Alpenkönig und Menschenfeind."* A play by Ferdinand Raimund.

May 2 1. *The "Enoch" chapter.* "Der Knabe Henoch," originally written as part of the third section of *Young Joseph* but omitted because TM felt it had a "dragging effect."
2. *"Der Morgen."* A Berlin Jewish monthly.
3. *The Nuremberg "Stürmer."* The rabidly anti-Semitic sheet published in Nuremberg by Julius Streicher, the Franconian Gauleiter condemned to death at the Nuremberg trials and executed.
4. *Hesse's new story.* Hermann Hesse, "The Rainmaker."
5. *"The Golden Ass."* Novel by Lucius Apuleius.
6. *"Salomé."* Richard Strauss's 1905 opera based on a text by Oscar Wilde.

May 6 1. *The dinner speech.* The "American Address" written for the gala banquet given at the Plaza Hotel in New York by Alfred Knopf in honor of TM's fifty-ninth birthday.
2. *Ehrenfeld's novel.* Unidentified.
3. *"Die Geliebten."* TM began making many notes for a novella with this title in 1902, but it was never written.
4. *K. H.* Klaus Heuser.
5. *A. M.* Armin Martens.
6. *W. T.* Willri Timpe.

May 22 1. *Finished "Don Quixote."* In September 1934 TM developed his thoughts on reading Cervantes and his impressions of his first Atlantic crossing in *Voyage with Don Quixote*, first published in serial form in the *Neue Zürcher Zeitung*, November 5–15, 1934.
2. *"Agathon."* Novel (1766) by Christoph Martin Wieland.

May 29 1. *The mayor.* Fiorello La Guardia.

June 12 1. *The big banquet.* See note 1 for May 6, 1934.
2. *Dorothy Thompson's article.* "The Most Eminent Living Man," in the *New York Herald Tribune* for June 10, 1934.

June 20 1. *The piece on Hauptmann.* TM's address "An Gerhart Hauptmann," delivered on the occasion of the playwright's seventieth birthday on December 11, 1932, in Munich. Having revised his opinion of Hauptmann thanks to the latter's acceptance of the Nazi regime, TM did decide to omit this eulogy from his new collection, substituting his newly-written *Voyage with Don Quixote.*

June 27 1. *Gide's "Journal."* André Gide's *Journal 1889–1939* was not published until 1939. Presumably TM here refers to his *Pages de Journal 1929–1932*, published in 1934.
2. *The Jewish Rescue League.* While in New York TM was asked to lend his support to this organization and he responded with a positive letter, distorted versions of which, together with statements made during an interview given in New York, were published by the Berlin *Acht-*

Ubr-Abendblatt and the *Deutsche Wochenschau* on June 15 and 16 respectively. TM promptly sent the full text of the letter to Bermann Fischer and to his attorney, Valentin Heins, requesting that they set things straight with the German authorities.

July 4   1. *"Tristram Shandy."* Novel (1760) by Laurence Sterne, in full *The Life and Opinions of Tristram Shandy.*
2. *The new chapter.* "Joseph is Reader and Body-Servant," the first chapter of the fifth section of *Joseph in Egypt.*
3. *The "conspiracy."* TM is here reacting to news of the Blood Purge of June 30, 1934, in which Hitler summarily dealt with supposed "radicalism" in the Sturmabteilung by having its leaders slaughtered.

July 9   1. *The French translator.* The Joseph novels were translated into French by Luise Servicen.
2. *Perrault fairy tales.* This deluxe edition of Perrault had been among TM's books as a child in Lübeck.
3. *Venice.* An international art congress was to be held in Venice at the end of July 1934, and in spite of his hesitation TM attended.

July 11   1. *Ortega.* José Ortega y Gasset, in his *Revolt of the Masses* (1930).

July 29   1. *"Dissolved like mist . . . ."* Quoted from Wagner's *Die Meistersinger.*
2. *Strauss's new opera.* Richard Strauss's *Die schweigsame Frau* was finally premiered in Dresden in 1935, but after a second performance it was dropped from the repertory on orders from on high.

August 4 1. *The political notes.* Since the beginning of his exile TM had kept detailed notes on current events in Germany, and he now made extracts from them, adding commentary and expanding on them. These were to form the substance of a political polemic he intended to write, to which he repeatedly referred as his "Politicum." The notes were first published privately in Los Angeles in 1946 as *Leiden an Deutschland. Tagebuchblätter 1933–1934.*
2. *The Berlin writers' organization.* The newly-formed Reich Literature Chamber. Membership in this "academy" was obligatory if one wished to be published in Germany.

August 5 1. *Hauptmann's "eulogy."* President Hindenburg died on his estate Neudeck in West Prussia on August 2, 1934. Hauptmann wrote of him: "A mighty rock supporting the castle on the mountain summit, immovable, and imbued with all the strength of Nature, has rolled into the abyss. God was in this man. In this vessel eternal forces concocted Germany's destiny."

August 21 1. *Taine.* Presumably Hippolyte Taine's *Les origines de la France contemporaine* (1871–94).

October 3 1. *Monstre.* An ill-tempered tomcat picked up by Golo Mann in Sanary the year before.
2. *Mouche.* A Maltese dog.
3. *The "Italian Journey."* Goethe's journal of his sojourn in Italy in 1816–17.

November 27 1. *Eduard Meyer's book on the Jews. Die Israeliten und ihre Nachbarstämme* (1906).

December 5 1. *"Beknechons."* The fourth chapter of Section V in *Joseph in Egypt.*
2. *Corrodi's book on Schoeck.* Hans Corrodi, *Othmar Schoeck. Eine Monographie* (1931).
3. *"Voyage with Don Quixote."* See note 1 for May 22, 1934.

December 31 1. *Freiligrath's poems.* Ferdinand Freiligrath's collection *Ça ira!* (1846).
2. *The Herta Brauer book. Flucht aus dem Zwielicht* (1934).

3. *The verse.* The lines are from Freiligrath's poem "Springer."

> Mir is, als müsst' ich auch von hier
> Den Stab noch in die Weite setzen;
> Als würden auch aus Tells Revier
> Die Launen dieses Spiels mich hetzen!

1935

January 19   1. *The trip.* TM had scheduled a lecture trip in late January to Prague, Brno, Vienna, and Budapest, on which he would give readings from *Joseph in Egypt* and his lecture *Sufferings and Greatness of Richard Wagner.*

January 31   1. *The essay volume.* Leiden und Grösse der Meister.
2. *Frau M. Wassermann's book.* Marta Karlweis, *Jakob Wassermann. Bild, Kampf und Werk* (1935).

March 8   1. *The speech for Nice.* TM's address to the conference of the League of Nations' Commission Internationale de Coopération Intellectuelle in Nice in April 1935 was published (in French) among the papers of the meeting and also in the original under the title "Achtung Europa!" ("Europe, Beware!") in the *Neues Wiener Journal* on February 15 and 22, 1936.
2. *Lion's manuscript.* Ferdinand Lion's book on TM was first published in 1935 under the title *Thomas Mann in seiner Zeit.*

March 17   1. *Fritz Busch's daughter.* Eta Busch, the second of the conductor's three daughters.
2. *Kahler's book.* Erich von Kahler's *Israel unter den Völkern* (1936).

March 23   1. *Sent the notice to the "National-Zeitung."* Presumably the note received from the Reich Literature Chamber by Julius Bab and Käthe Rosenberg.
2. *Rilke as a critic.* Rainer Maria Rilke's long and perceptive review of *Buddenbrooks* appeared in the *Bremer Tageblatt* on April 16, 1902.
3. *My Goethe–Lotte Kestner project.* TM had begun making notes for a projected novella based on the reunion in old age of Goethe and a love of his youth, Charlotte Kestner, née Buff. Out of these beginnings grew the novel *The Beloved Returns* (1939).
4. *Theilhaber's book.* Felix A. Theilhaber, *Goethe, Sexus and Eros* (1929).

April 1   1. *Maximiliansplatz.* Katia Mann's parents, Alfred and Hedwig Pringsheim, had taken a flat at No. 7 Maximiliansplatz in Munich (see note 6 for September 11, 1918).

April 10   1. *The two German emigré women.* Mathilde Wurm and Dora Fabian were discovered dead in their London flat. Though suicides, the press suspected the deaths were somehow connected to the abduction of Berthold Jacob (see note 2 for April 19, 1935).

April 19   1. *A new political project.* TM was again considering the political essay he had envisioned in 1934 (see note 1 for August 4, 1934).
2. *The Jacob case.* Berthold Jacob, living in exile in France, was particularly hated by the Nazis because of his early revelations concerning the so-called "Black Reichswehr." In 1935 he was lured across into Switzerland by a Nazi agent and taken from there by the Gestapo to Germany. Thanks to intervention by the Swiss government he was released and returned to Switzerland.
3. *Hesse's book of stories.* Hermann Hesse, *Das Fabulierbuch* (1935).

May 16   1. *Bunin's short stories.*   Presumably Ivan Bunin's *The Man from San Francisco*, published in a German translation by Käthe Rosenberg in 1922.

June 16   1. *The Goethe lecture.*   It is not clear which of TM's two Goethe lectures from the Goethe centenary year of 1932 is meant here, *Goethe as Representative of the Bourgeois Age* or *Goethe's Career as a Man of Letters.* TM had had one of these translated into English so as to have something at hand if asked to give a lecture while in America. As it happened he delivered no lectures on this trip.

2. *Mrs. Auden.*   Erika Mann's German citizenship was revoked by the Nazi regime on June 16, 1935. In anticipation of such a move, her brother Klaus had asked a friend, the already well-known English poet W. H. Auden, if he would enter into a pro forma marriage with her, thereby providing her with British citizenship and a valid passport. Though he had not met Erika, Auden telegraphed Klaus that he would be "delighted," and accordingly Erika went to England and was married on June 15, the day before her expatriation. Originally the match was considered to be a pure formality, but in fact there developed a warm relationship between Auden and the whole Mann family, especially during their later years in the United States, and Erika Mann-Auden retained her British citizenship to the end of her life. Christopher Isherwood, who likewise belonged to the circle of Klaus Mann's English friends and was an intimate associate of Auden's, relates in his memoirs that Klaus first asked him to marry Erika, but that he recoiled at the idea because his mother would not have approved.

July 10   1. *"The Foolish Pilgrimess."*   A novella contained in Goethe's *Wilhelm Meister's Travels.*

July 15   1. *The death of Otto Grautoff.*   This information proved to be erroneous. It was Otto's brother Ferdinand who had died.

2. *W. T.*   Willri Timpe.

September 14   1. *A book by Waterboer.*   Heinz Waterboer's *Das Tagebuch des Dr. Sarraut* (1935).

2. *One by Driesch.*   Possibly Hans Driesch's *Parapsychologie* (1932).

October 15   1. *The preface for the Wassermann book.*   "Zum Geleit" (see note 2 for January 31, 1935).

2. *The Ossietzky letter.*   TM's recommendation of Carl von Ossietzky for the Nobel Peace Prize, "An das Nobel-Friedenspreis-Comité, Oslo."

November 3   1. *Gumpert's new book.*   Martin Gumpert, *Das Leben der Idee. Neun Forscherschicksale* (1935).

November 10   1. *Eckstein's book.*   Friedrich Eckstein, *Alte unnennbare Tage* (1936).

1936

January 1   1. *The Goethe novella.*   In fact TM did not begin *The Beloved Returns* (see note 3 for March 23, 1935) until October 1936, completing it only three years later, in late October 1939.

January 7   1. *New volume of Gide.*   Volume IX of André Gide's *Oeuvres complètes* was published in 1935. It contains the essay "Réflexions sur l'Allemagne," from which TM's citation is taken.

January 16   1. *The Basel evening.*   TM had given a benefit reading of the "Mont-kaw" chapter from *Joseph in Egypt* on January 10, proceeds from it going to the Geneva-based Comité International pour le Placement des Intellectuels Refugiés.

2. *Vittorio Veneto.*   World War I battlefield.

3. *The Elders of Zion.* An 1865 French satire on Napoleon III by Maurice Joly titled *A Conversation in Hell between Machiavelli and Montesquieu* was soon transformed in Russia by the tsarist secret police (Ochrana) into a supposed plan for a worldwide Jewish conspiracy, and issued as *The Protocols of the Elders of Zion.* Though repeatedly revealed to be a fraud, the tract was circulated by the millions in Europe and America.

....

January 27   1. *Open letter to Korrodi.* "An Eduard Korrodi," an article cast in the form of an open letter to the *Neue Zürcher Zeitung* appeared in that paper on February 2, 1936. In it TM decisively challenged Korrodi's "Deutsche Literatur im Emigrantenspiegel" from January 26, which characterized exile German literature as Jewish and "unrepresentative." "What has been transferred abroad?" Korrodi had written, ". . . We cannot think of a single real poet. Chiefly what has emigrated is the novel industry. . . ." TM's response, openly declaring his solidarity with the German exiles, was his first public renunciation of Nazi Germany, and given the brevity of its text he spent much care and thought on its composition, requiring four days, as the diary reveals, to complete it. The day Korrodi's piece appeared, Klaus Mann and Fritz Landshoff had telegraphed TM from Amsterdam: "Earnestly beg you respond to Korrodi's fateful article however and wherever stop this time it is really a matter of life and death for all of us." A letter from Klaus written on February 5 congratulates his father "for the beautiful answer to the evil Korrodi," assuring him that "especially thanks to the bold conclusion it unquestionably takes on the importance of a decisive document."

....

February 3   1. *The collected stories.* The American volume appeared as *Stories of Three Decades.* TM's preface to this 1936 collection is dated February 1936.
2. *Superfluous prefatory comment.* The "Editors' Comment" preceding TM's open letter to Korrodi (see note 1 for January 27, 1936) read as follows: "We hasten to give space to this frank and resolute document by Thomas Mann that concludes with a declaration whose consequences the writer is fully prepared to bear. Let us avoid one misunderstanding, however. When we spoke of the novel industry in the article 'Deutsche Literatur im Emigrantenspiegel' we by no means intended to suggest a writer of the stature of Thomas Mann. . . . *Eds.*"

....

March 8   1. *Brentano's novel.* Bernard von Brentano, *Theodor Chindler. Roman einer deutschen Familie* (1936).
2. *The brazen coup.* On March 7 German troops marched across the Rhine bridges and occupied the demilitarized zone of the Rhineland, thereby abrogating the Treaty of Locarno.

....

March 14   1. *The birthday greeting.* "Dem Fünfundsechzigjährigen," a congratulatory article on Heinrich Mann, published in the *Neue Weltbühne* on March 26, 1936.

....

March 16   1. *Heinrich's book of essays.* *Es kommt der Tag. Ein deutsches Lesebuch,* Europa-Verlag (Oprecht), 1936.

....

April 9   1. *The chancellor.* Kurt von Schuschnigg.

....

May 1   1. *The lecture.* *Freud and the Future,* written for delivery in Vienna on the occasion of Sigmund Freud's eightieth birthday, May 8, 1936, and first published in *Imago,* Vol. XXII (1936).
2. *The Moscow "Wort."* The German exile literary journal *Das Wort* appeared in Moscow from July 1936 to March 1939. Its publishers were Bertolt Brecht, Lion Feuchtwanger, and Willi Bredel; its editor was Fritz Erpenbeck.
3. *My reading in Budapest.* TM attended the conference of the Commission Internationale de Coopération Intellectuelle in Budapest on June 8–12, 1936, delivering on June 9 the address *Humaniora und Humanismus,* portions of which were published under the title "Der Humanismus und Europa" in the *Pester Lloyd* on June 11, 1936.

May 13 1. *Freud.* TM first met Freud in March 1932, while in Vienna to deliver his lecture *Goethe as Representative of the Bourgeois Age.* Previously, in Munich in 1929, he had given the lecture *Freud's Position in the History of Modern Thought.*

2. *Freud's son and daughter.* Anna Freud and Ernst L. Freud. Their father was prevented from attending the gala by illness.

3. *"Boccaccio."* Operetta (1879) by Franz von Suppé.

4. *Urania.* Adult education institute in Prague.

5. *The girl prodigy from Innsbruck.* Roswitha Bitterlich (b. 1920), daughter of the Innsbruck painter Hannes Bitterlich. Her precocious paintings and graphics were first exhibited in 1932.

July 21 1. *Turel's book.* It is unclear which of Adrien Turel's numerous publications this might have been.

August 1 1. *"On the Teachings of Spengler."* A portion of TM's first "German Letter" for *The Dial*, New York, 1922. First published in German in the *Allgemeine Zeitung*, Munich, March 9, 1924, and included in TM's 1925 essay collection *Bemühungen.*

August 13 1. *Novel by Sinclair Lewis.* *It Can't Happen Here* (1935).

2. *Back in Budapest.* See note 3 for May 1, 1936. At one of the meetings TM was moved to make an improvised statement in which he developed this concept.

August 14 1. *Comité pour le Placement, etc.* In full, Comité pour le Placement des Intellectuels Refugiés, Geneva.

August 23 1. *The reading in Ermatingen.* TM had read three of the final chapters of *Joseph in Egypt* in Ermatingen on August 17.

November 19 1. *The novella.* See note 1 for January 1, 1936.

December 25 1. *The reading on January 14.* TM was scheduled to give a reading from *The Beloved Returns* in Vienna in the course of a lecture tour to Prague, Vienna, and Budapest.

2. *Withdrawing my honorary doctorate.* The "communication" read:

Philosophical Faculty
of the Rhenish
Friedrich-Wilhelms University
J.-Nr. 58

Bonn, December 19, 1936

Herr Thomas Mann, writer!

In agreement with the rector of Bonn University I must inform you that the philosophical faculty has seen fit, as a result of your expatriation, to strike you from the list of its honorary doctors. Your right to use this title, in accordance with Article VIII of our Rules for Promotion, is revoked.

(Illegible)
Dean

December 30 1. *His book on Goethe.* *Goethe's Frömmigkeit* (1932), the first volume of Friedrich Muckle's *Die Rettung des Abendlandes durch den Geist der Goethezeit.*

2. *My letter to the dean.* TM's reply to the dean of the philosophical faculty of Bonn University appeared under the title "An Exchange of Letters" in the *Neue Zürcher Zeitung* on January 4, 1937, and shortly afterward as a brochure with the same title published by Oprecht-Verlag, Zurich. The first printing consisted of 8,000 copies, but within only a few weeks some 20,000 had been distributed. Translations of the documents quickly appeared in virtually all

of the major languages and in Germany the correspondence passed from hand to hand in countless reproductions.

3. *Introduction to the catalogue.* "Gedenken an Liebermann" was written for the catalogue of an exhibition at the Otto Kallir gallery in Vienna. It was based on TM's earlier "Max Liebermann zum achtzigsten Geburtstag" (1927).

4. *"Die Forderung des Tages."* Essays (1927) by TM.

5. *Kahler's book.* Erich von Kahler, *Der deutsche Charakter in der Geschichte Europas* (1937).

1937

January 1   1. *My New Year's statement.* TM's reply to the dean of the philosophical faculty in Bonn.

2. *Expatriation.* TM's German citizenship was revoked on December 2, 1936. His wife and four younger children were included in the document. The move was lacking in legal significance inasmuch as TM and his family had been granted Czech citizenship two weeks earlier, and he had renounced his ties to the German Reich.

3. *The Russians.* Between 1934 and 1938 the Gospolitizdat publishing house in Leningrad produced a six-volume edition of TM's collected works in Russian. Shortly before this payment they had issued a two-volume edition of *The Magic Mountain*, and in 1938 they brought out a volume of collected essays.

4. *Annenkova.* The telegram, in German, was sent from the *Deutsche Zentral-Zeitung* in Moscow.

5. *His lady friend.* Baroness Ester von Pidoll.

6. *The New School for Social Research.* Alvin Johnson, the director of the New School, worked tirelessly for the cause of emigré intellectuals and opened that institution to them.

7. *The "Academy."* In 1935, Prince Hubertus zu Löwenstein had founded the American Guild for German Cultural Freedom in New York, enlisting the support of noted personalities from American cultural life. This organization then called on all German intellectuals living in freedom to unite in a "German Academy" in New York for the purpose of "working toward the reconstruction and defense of German cultural monuments and administering funds raised by the 'American Guild for Cultural Freedom,' expending them in the most fruitful ways possible." Löwenstein was able to enlist TM, Heinrich Mann, Bruno Frank, Alfred Neumann, Lion Feuchtwanger, René Schickele, and countless others in the service of the Academy. TM was a member of its governing board and sat on various committees of the American Guild.

January 2   1. *"Joseph."* *Joseph in Egypt*, the third volume of the Joseph tetralogy, was published in October 1936.

2. *Fritz von Unruh.* Unruh's lecture, "Europa erwache!," had been delivered at a rally of the Europa Union in Basel in May 1936.

January 3   1. *The creation of a magazine.* Thanks to a generous donation by Aline Mayrisch de Saint-Hubert, TM was able to establish in 1937 the bi-monthly *Mass und Wert*, a major emigré journal. The magazine was produced by the Oprecht-Verlag, Zurich, with Konrad Falke as co-publisher. Ferdinand Lion served as the journal's first editor, a function later assumed by Golo Mann. TM was himself extremely active in the solicitation and selection of contributions. The first number was issued in August and dated September/October 1937.

January 4   1. *The plagiarism business.* In May 1936 a certain Sietcu Petru had accused TM of plagiarism in the Rumanian Nazi journal *Porounca Vremii*. He charged that TM was fashioning his Joseph tetralogy from a verse drama in thirty acts titled *Visul Faraonitor* ("The Dream of Pharaoh") by a Rumanian writer, Aurelian Pacurariu. He claimed that the Rumanian dramatist had contracted with an editor of the *Pesti Hirlap* in Budapest to have his work translated into

German, and that this "Jidan" (Jew) had sold the work through a middleman, Dezsö Straussmann, to the "Jidan" and "bandit" TM, who then reworked it and published it under his own
name. TM denounced the whole story as a grotesque farce in a letter to the newspaper
Adeverul in July 1936, insisting that he had never read the work *Visul Faraonitor*, never heard
the names Pacurariu or Straussmann, and moreover that the Egyptian section of his tetralogy
had not even been published yet. Pacurariu initiated legal proceedings nonetheless, and TM
was obliged to appoint a defense lawyer (see entry for January 21, 1937). The case was
repeatedly postponed and finally dropped.

January 7 1. *The "Annals."* Goethe's *Tag- und Jahreshefte* (1830).
2. *Jakob Grimm's pamphlet.* The eminent philologist was dismissed from his teaching post in
Göttingen because of a political protest in 1838. He immediately published in Basel a pamphlet
about the action, *Über meine Entlassung.*

January 10 1. *Frankenberger's book.* Julius Frankenberger, *Walpurgis. Zur Kunstgestalt von Goethes Faust*
(1926).
2. *Golo in Prague.* Golo Mann, now a Czech citizen, had gone to Prague in hope of securing
a teaching position.
3. *Goschi.* Leonie Mann.

January 11 1. *The German minister.* Ludwig Czech.
2. *Czech's children.* See preceding note.

January 12 1. *Thomas Mann Fund.* A foundation established in Prague to aid needy emigré writers.
2. *Proseč.* At the instigation of Rudolf Fleischmann, merchant and town official, this small
workers' community in Central Bohemia had extended the right of domicile to TM and his
family on August 18, 1936, thereby satisfying a precondition of their attainment of Czech
citizenship the following November.

January 15 1. *Hartmann's.* Luxury restaurant in Vienna.

January 21 1. *"Dagens Nyheter."* Swedish daily published by the firm of Albert Bonnier.
2. *Lawyer in Temesvar.* József Kende (see note 1 for January 4, 1937).

January 31 1. *"Goethe und die Seinen."* A book (1908) of documentary sources relating to Goethe and
his family by Ludwig Geiger.

February 14 1. *The Riemer scene.* The third chapter of *The Beloved Returns*, in which Lotte Kestner
converses with Goethe's former secretary, Friedrich Wilhelm Riemer.

March 5 1. *The hundred-volume Goethe.* The so-called "Sophien-Ausgabe" of Goethe's *Werke*, published
under the patronage of Grand Duchess Sophie of Saxony between 1887 and 1919. The edition
comprises 133 volumes.

March 21 1. *My diary from 1927.* Destroyed by TM along with other diaries from the period preceding
1933.
2. *Klaus H.* Klaus Heuser.
3. *Fragment of "Felix Krull."* At this point the novel *The Confessions of Felix Krull, Confidence
Man* consisted of the first book, which had appeared in various editions, and a fragmentary
second book extending as far as the fifth chapter (the recruiting scene) as yet unpublished. Fritz
Landshoff suggested a new edition that would reprint the first book together with the unpublished fragment, and it was this text that was issued by Querido Verlag in the autumn of 1937.
Of this printing there was also a deluxe edition of 100 numbered and signed copies, of which

375

each of the first ten included a page from the original manuscript and was bound in parchment and stamped in gold. Forty copies were bound in morocco. The proceeds from these deluxe copies went to the Thomas Mann Society, Prague. (See also the entries for October 9 and December 24, 1937.)

4. *Statement to the Paris committee.* An organizing committee of the German Popular Front was conferring under the chairmanship of Heinrich Mann in Paris.

5. *Dinner speech for New York.* "The Living Spirit," given at a gala banquet at the New School for Social Research on April 15, 1937.

6. *Schickele's novel.* René Schickele, *Die Flaschenpost* (1937).

April 7   1. *Čapek's novel.* *War with the Newts* (1936) by Karel Čapek.

April 9   1. *The Goethe lecture.* *Goethe's Career as a Man of Letters* (1932).

2. *"Romeo and Juliet."* The 1936 Metro-Goldwyn-Mayer version starring Norma Shearer and Leslie Howard.

April 10   1. *The essays of Rolland.* A collection of essays by Romain Rolland was published in German in 1937 under the title *Gefährten meines Weges.*

April 28   1. *The "murderer."* Unidentified.

2. *Dorothy Thompson's article.* "To Thomas Mann," in the *New York Herald Tribune* for April 14, 1937.

3. *Introduction for the magazine.* TM's foreword to the first issue of *Mass und Wert.*

4. *The preface for Schickele.* "Zur französischen Ausgabe von René Schickeles Witwe Bosca," published (in French) in *La Veuve Bosca,* Paris, 1939.

May 4   The diaries contain two successive entries with this date. Presumably the first of them was written in the morning as a recapitulation of the previous few days, the second in the evening, dealing with the events of that single day.

1. *The bronze head of Medi.* See note 1 for December 20, 1918.

2. *"Nathan der Weise."* Drama (1779) by Gotthold Ephraim Lessing.

3. *Manuscript from Hollnsteiner.* Unidentified.

4. *The magazine.* *Mass und Wert.*

May 22   1. *The coronation ceremonies.* George VI had been crowned king of England in Westminster Abbey on May 12.

2. *"Concerning Death."* From the second part of Schopenhauer's *The World as Will and Idea.*

June 2   1. *The introduction.* See note 3 for April 28, 1937.

2. *"Lulu."* Alban Berg's opera based on two plays by Frank Wedekind was incomplete at the composer's death, lacking the instrumentation of the third and final act. The two finished acts were premiered at the Zurich Stadttheater on this date.

June 6   1. *The article for Bruno Frank.* "Bruno Frank zum 50. Geburtstag," published in the *National-Zeitung,* Basel, on June 13, 1937.

July 17   1. *Annemarie.* Annemarie Schwarzenbach-Clarac.

2. *The death of Grautoff.* Otto Grautoff had died in Paris on April 27.

August 2   1. *The Adele chapter.* The fourth chapter of *The Beloved Returns,* describing the visit to Lotte Kestner of Adele Schopenhauer, sister of the philosopher.

2. *"Club of the Clean-handed."* Leopold Schwarzschild and Konrad Heiden established an association of exiled German writers and publicists called the Free Press and Literature League

in Paris in June 1937. Impressed by the Moscow trials, they advocated a "clean" political and moral stance, specifically disassociation from all popular front movements or communist groups.

September 15 1. *Wrote about Masaryk.* Tomáš Masaryk died on September 12. TM's eulogy "In Memory of Masaryk" was published in *Das Neue Tage-Buch*, Paris, on September 25, in the *Prager Presse* on September 26, and (in a translation by Helen Lowe-Porter) in the *Nation* on October 9.

2. *The manuscript affair.* Two medieval Czech manuscripts containing epics and lyrics from the heroic age and "discovered" in 1917 had contributed considerably to the strengthening of a Czech national consciousness. In truth they were nineteenth-century forgeries, and Masaryk, then a professor in Prague, had published in his journal *Athenäum* an article by the linguist Jan Gebauer exposing the whole fraud. Ardent Czech nationalists felt that the debunking of this "necessary falsehood" was unpatriotic, and could not forgive Masaryk for his part in it.

3. *"Das Cornichon."* A Swiss literary and political cabaret founded in the wake of Erika Mann's *Peppermill* in Zurich. In it Elsie Attenhofer made her first appearance as an actress to great acclaim.

4. *"Père Goriot."* Novel (1834) by Balzac.

October 9 1. *The new "Confidence Man."* See note 3 for March 21, 1937.

2. *"The Man of Fifty."* A novella contained in Goethe's *Wilhelm Meister's Travels.*

3. *The Gide foreword.* André Gide had provided a foreword for TM's *Avertissement à l'Europe*, a collection of recent essays. The Gide piece was considered for inclusion in *Mass und Wert*, but appeared instead (translated by Ferdinand Hardekopf) in *Das Neue Tage-Buch*, Paris.

October 13 1. *Tribschen.* The house near Lucerne where Richard Wagner lived from 1865 to 1872.

2. *Siegfried.* The first reference is to the Siegfried of the *Ring*; the second to Siegfried Wagner, son of the composer.

October 25 1. *"Tasso."* Goethe's verse drama *Torquato Tasso* (1790).

October 26 1. *The "Democracy."* The lecture *The Coming Victory of Democracy*, written for TM's lecture tour to the United States in early 1938 and published separately by Knopf in June of that year.

2. *A talk in mid-November.* TM delivered the lecture *Richard Wagner and the Ring* on November 16 in Zurich. The text then appeared in the January/February 1938 issue of *Mass und Wert*.

November 16 1. *The intendant of the Stadttheater.* Karl Schmid-Bloss.

November 25 1. *The lecture.* See note 1 for October 26, 1937.

2. *"Wallenstein's Camp" and "The Piccolomini."* The first two sections of Friedrich Schiller's dramatic trilogy *Wallenstein* (1799).

November 26 1. *Schoeps.* Hans-Joachim Schoeps's *Gestalten an der Zeitwende. Burckhardt, Nietzsche, Kafka* (1936).

November 27 1. *The little daughter.* Susi Kaufmann

2. *Nico.* Nico Kaufmann.

3. *The essayist.* Fritz Ernst.

November 28 1. *Cocteau's King Arthur play.* *Les Chevaliers de la Table Ronde* (1937).

2. *The "Avertissement."* See note 3 for October 9, 1937.

December 1   1. *New translation of Shakespeare.* By the Austrian dramatist, essayist, and Shakespeare scholar Richard Flatter (1891–1960).
2. *Professor in Uppsala.* Unidentified.

December 15   1. *The speech for Yale.* TM read the speech "Zur Gründung einer Dokumentensammlung in Yale University" at the ceremony opening the Thomas Mann Collection on February 25, 1938.
2. *Kesten's "I, the King."* An historical novel (1938) by Hermann Kesten based on Philip II, a subject to which TM had long been attracted himself.
3. *The "Mont-kaw" chapter.* The last chapter of Section V of *Joseph in Egypt*, called "Account of Mont-kaw's Simple Passing."

December 20   1. *The "Schopenhauer."* Longmans, Green & Co. in New York had asked TM for a foreword to a selection from Schopenhauer's *The World as Will and Idea* they were publishing. Predictably, the foreword grew into an essay so long that it had to be shortened for the American publication. The complete essay, *Schopenhauer*, was published by Bermann-Fischer Verlag, Stockholm, in 1938. The abridged version appeared in *The Living Thoughts of Schopenhauer, Presented by Thomas Mann* (1939).

December 24   1. *Article on Brüning.* Klaus Mann, "Brüning in New York," in *Die Neue Weltbühne*, December 23, 1937.
2. *Deluxe edition of "Krull."* See note 3 for March 21, 1937.

December 31   1. *"Swann's Way."* The first novel (1913) of Marcel Proust's *Remembrance of Things Past*.
2. *The August chapter.* Chapter VI of *The Beloved Returns*, in which Goethe's son August calls on Lotte Kestner.
3. *A book on Goethe.* Martin Sommerfeld's *Goethe in Umwelt und Folgezeit* (1935).
4. *Annette Kolb's contribution.* Ferdinand Lion wished to decline an article on the late Count Harry Kessler submitted to *Mass und Wert* by Annette Kolb, and intended on sending her a "charming" letter of rejection. TM felt that such a rejection would result in her never sending them anything again and insisted that the essay be published. In his letter to Lion TM wrote: "Annette Kolb absolutely counts among those writers who answer *themselves* for what they write and bear all responsibility for it; in such a case an editor can simply wash his hands." The article appeared in the March/April number in 1938.

1938

January 1   1. *Proposed volume of essays.* The collection of TM's recent political essays that was published by Bermann Fischer late in the year 1938 under the title *Achtung Europa!*
2. *Bermann's essay series.* The series called "Ausblicke" was begun by Bermann Fischer in Vienna and continued in Stockholm. TM's *Freud and the Future* was the first volume in this format, and his *Schopenhauer* appeared in it as well, but not the Wagner essay. Other authors represented in the series were Claudel, Musil, Valéry, Huizinga, Werfel, Zuckmayer, Huxley, Nicolson, Schnitzler, and Borgese.

January 11   1. *Manuscript from Döblin.* Unidentified.

January 21   1. *De Broglie's lecture.* In the March/April 1938 number of *Mass und Wert*.
2. *Her own essay on "Joseph."* Agnes E. Meyer's "A New Novel by Thomas Mann: *Joseph in Egypt*" in the *Washington Post*, February 27, 1938.
3. *Koestler's book.* Arthur Koestler, *Spanish Testament* (1937).

378

4. *Chiaromonte's article.* Nicola Chiaromonte reviewed G. A. Borgese's *Goliath. The March of Fascism* in the May/June 1938 issue of *Mass und Wert*.

5. *Essay by H. Kesten.* "Hochstapler Krull," in *Das Neue Tage-Buch*, January 22, 1938.

January 27 1. *The engaged couple.* Michael Mann and Gret Moser.

2. *The foreword for Schickele.* See note 4 for April 28, 1937.

January 31 1. *The monthly of the "German Freedom party."* *Das wahre Deutschland*, edited by Karl Spiecker and Hans Albert Kluthe, and published in London (though appearing to come out of Berlin). The German Freedom party, a loose association of liberal and conservative emigrés, was formed in late 1936 to promote cooperation among opponents of Hitler of all political and ideological persuasions (excepting Communists).

February 17 1. *The Eternal Husband.*" Novel (1869) by Dostoevsky.

February 19 1. *The Goethe lecture.* TM brought along the English text of his lecture *Goethe as Representative of the Bourgeois Age* in case he were pressed into giving a literary lecture while in America.

March 20 1. *"The Idiot."* Novel (1868–69) by Dostoevsky.

March 22 1. *President of the Mormon Church.* Heber J. Grant (1856–1944).

2. *The lecture.* *The Coming Victory of Democracy.*

3. *Bruno Walter's daughter arrested.* Bruno Walter, since 1935 director of the Vienna State Opera, was fulfilling an engagement in Amsterdam at the time of the German invasion of Austria. He telegraphed his resignation and did not return to Vienna. His older daughter, Lotte, was arrested by the Gestapo and placed in jail. After her father had resorted to every possible bit of influence available to him she was released on March 28, and in April received a permit to emigrate to Switzerland.

4. *Mrs. Meyer about Princeton.* Agnes E. Meyer had gone to some effort to secure for TM a guest professorship or similar position at Princeton so that he would be able to remain in the United States.

April 1 1. *Cardinal Newman Award.* The Cardinal Newman Award of the University of Illinois at Urbana was presented to TM on April 29, 1938 (see entry for May 1). The mention of Detroit here is presumably the result of a misunderstanding.

April 14 1. *"Night Must Fall."* A film based on the play of the same name by Emlyn Williams.

May 1 1. *The medal.* See note 1 for April 1, 1938.

2. *The regular lecture.* *The Coming Victory of Democracy* was TM's standard lecture through the whole of this tour.

May 6 1. *The foreword for Erika.* TM provided a preface to Erika Mann's *School for Barbarians* (1938). A portion of his essay was published under the title "Deutsche Erziehung" in *Die Neue Weltbühne* on February 2, 1939.

2. *Affidavit for Hermann Broch.* TM attempted to find a sponsor or some kind of guaranteed income for Hermann Broch, so that he might emigrate from occupied Austria to the United States.

3. *Long letter from Klaus.* From this acquaintance of Hans Reisiger's whom Klaus had met in a Zurich café he had learned that Reisiger's indecision at that time was "almost clinical," that the writer feared above all that Nazi authorities would discover TM's letters to him. Reisiger supposedly felt it was essential that those letters be placed in safekeeping at once, and that his own to TM be burned.

4. *My cable to President Beneš.*   In his communications to Beneš and Consul Laška, TM denied the rumor that he was about to forsake his Czech citizenship and become a naturalized American.

. . . .

May 24 1. *Lucy.* Lucy Long.
2. *The lecture.* *The Coming Victory of Democracy.*
3. *Degree ceremonies.* TM was to receive honorary doctorates in the next weeks from Columbia University and Yale University.

. . . .

June 23 1. *Governor general of Canada.* John Buchan, Lord Tweedsmuir (1875–1940).
2. *The Negro champion.* Joe Louis (b. 1914).

. . . .

June 27 1. *The prime minister.* Neville Chamberlain.

. . . .

July 7 1. *Review of "Joseph."* Wilson Follett, "Time and Thomas Mann," in the June 1938 issue of *Atlantic Monthly.*
2. *"Pages from a Journal."* The central portion of this work originally commissioned by *Cosmopolitan* was ultimately published under the title "This Man is My Brother" in *Esquire*, March 1939, and as "Bruder Hitler" in *Das Neue Tage-Buch*, Paris, March 25, 1939.

. . . .

July 17 1. *Arnim.* A meeting between Goethe's son August and the poet Achim von Arnim is described in Chapter VI of *The Beloved Returns.*
2. *Fiedler's autobiographical manuscript.* Kuno Fiedler's *Die Flucht* (unpublished).

. . . .

August 15 1. *The "Faust" lecture.* "Goethe's *Faust*," written for delivery at Princeton University (see entry for November 28, 1938).
2. *The Helena book.* Karl August Meissinger, *Helena.*

. . . .

August 20 1. *Her book on emigrés.* Erika Mann (with Klaus Mann), *Escape to Life* (1939).

. . . .

September 8 1. *The article for Fadiman.* "The Coming Humanism," TM's contribution to Clifton Fadiman's book *I Believe. The Personal Philosophies of Certain Eminent Men and Women of Our Time* (1939).
2. *The essay volume.* TM's *Schopenhauer.*
3. *Amann's manuscript.* Paul Amann, *Kristall meiner Zeit* (1956).
4. *Disastrous article.* On September 7, 1938, the London *Times*, whose editor-in-chief was Geoffrey Dawson, an intimate of Chamberlain's, published a lead article suggesting to the Czech government that it consider if it were not better to make a single homogeneous state out of the Czech Republic by giving up "the border territories containing foreign populations." On the same day an official disclaimer was issued, insisting that the suggestion by the *Times* "by no means represents the thinking of His Majesty's government." Yet this was precisely the solution agreed to in Munich only weeks later.

. . . .

September 19 1. *Kerényi's article.* Karl Kerényi, "Die Papyri und das Problem des griechischen Romans," published in the papers of the Congrès International de Papyrologie, 1938.

. . . .

September 20 1. *The appeal.* A circular drafted by TM in support of Hugo Simon's attempt to establish an opposition organization in Paris, the "Bund Neues Deutschland," for which financial backing had been promised from England.
2. *The essay.* "This Man is My Brother."

September 25 1. *The speech in English.* The brief address for the Czechoslovakia rally in Madison Square Garden.

September 26 1. *Article by Mrs. Roosevelt.* Unidentified.

October 4 1. *Senator Beneš.* Vojta Beneš, brother of Eduard Beneš.
2. *Foreword to the essay volume.* "Die Höhe des Augenblicks," TM's preface to the collection of his political essays *Achtung Europa!* (1938). Its text is virtually identical to that of the separately published essay *This Peace* (1938).

October 24 1. *"This Peace."* See preceding note.
2. *Exchanges with Boisserée.* Goethe's correspondence with Sulpiz Boisserée was published in 1862.

November 10 1. *The Stevens family.* The family of George Stevens.
2. *"Hamlet."* The uncut Maurice Evans production.
3. *My speech.* A brief address on freedom of speech written especially for this Book and Author Luncheon sponsored by the *New York Herald Tribune.*
4. *The book and the brochure.* See note 2 for October 4, 1938.

November 13 1. *"Goethe als Persönlichkeit."* The three-volume supplement to the Propyläen edition of Goethe's works (1908–22), containing contemporary testimony regarding the poet's character.
2. *The contest manuscripts.* TM was to read and judge novel manuscripts submitted for a prize from the American Guild for German Cultural Freedom.

December 14 1. *Oppenheimer's brother.* Friedrich Oppenheimer.
2. *Hermann Rauschning's book.* *The Revolution of Nihilism* (1938).

December 20 1. *The article for "Survey Graphic."* TM's "Culture and Politics" appeared in *Survey Graphic,* New York, on January 28, 1939. The original German text was published under the title "Zwang zur Politik" in *Das Neue Tage-Buch,* Paris, on July 22, 1939, and as "Kultur und Politik" in the *National-Zeitung,* Basel, on July 23, 1939.
2. *Elected to the Academy.* On December 17, 1938, TM was named an honorary member of the American Academy of Arts and Letters in New York.
3. *The auction of the manuscripts.* A fund-raising event of the American Guild for German Cultural Freedom.

1939

January 20 1. *Citation for the medal.* On the occasion of its eightieth anniversary, the American journal *Jewish Forum* established the Einstein Medal, an award to be given annually to someone chosen by Einstein himself for his outstanding humanitarian service. Previous winners were James Grover McDonald and Franz Werfel. The organizers planned a banquet in honor of TM, but he did not wish it. Accordingly the medal was presented to him by Einstein at a small private ceremony at TM's house in Princeton on January 28, 1939.

January 23 1. *The lecture.* *The Problem of Freedom,* written in late December 1938 and early January 1939 as the regular lecture for his scheduled speaking tour in March and April.
2. *Her "Twice a Year" project.* This entry apparently reveals a misunderstanding on TM's part. The lady in question, Mrs. Ralph Brodsky, never had anything to do with the semi-annual almanac *Twice a Year.*

3. *The World's Fair matter.* It was proposed that a Freedom pavilion be erected at the 1939 World's Fair in New York to publicize the anti-Fascist cause.

. . . .

January 26 1. *The Freud lecture.* The English translation of *Freud and the Future,* which TM was to read at Princeton on February 13.

. . . .

January 30 1. *"Zukunft."* A German-language weekly published by Willi Münzenberg in Paris from October 1938 to May 1940. Its first editor was Arthur Koestler. Erika, Klaus, Heinrich, and Thomas Mann were all contributors.

. . . .

February 1 1. *The English guests.* W. H. Auden and Christopher Isherwood. The latter had arrived in Princeton on January 31, and a *Time* photographer had spent two hours that afternoon photographing the two English writers with the Mann family. Auden and Isherwood had landed in America on January 26.

2. *The old lady.* Antoinette von Kahler, mother of Erich von Kahler.

. . . .

February 4 1. *Martha Dodd's book. Through Embassy Eyes* (1939).

. . . .

February 13 1. *The introduction to Erika's book.* See note 1 for May 6, 1938.

2. *The Princeton astronomer.* Henry Norris Russell.

. . . .

February 14 1. *"New Sihl Valley."* A spot near Princeton where TM liked to walk, so named by him because it reminded him of a pleasant valley near Zurich.

2. *Klaus's emigré novel. Der Vulkan. Roman unter Emigranten* (1939).

3. *"Dead Souls."* Novel (1842) by Nikolai Gogol.

. . . .

February 28 1. *Alliance.* Alliance Book Corporation in New York, affiliated with Bermann-Fischer Verlag, Stockholm.

. . . .

March 7 1. *Erika's publisher.* Ferris Greenslet, director of Houghton-Mifflin Co., Boston.

. . . .

March 12 1. *The rabbi.* Unidentified.

2. *Keiler.* Unidentified; allusion unclear.

3. *Film. Wife, Husband and Friend,* based on the James M. Cain story "Career in C-major."

. . . .

March 13 1. *Talked about Max Brod.* TM had had correspondence with Robert Goldman concerning the possible appointment of Max Brod to the faculty of Hebrew University in Cincinnati.

. . . .

March 14 1. *Brod's appointment.* Though TM's efforts in Max Brod's behalf (see preceding note) met with success, Brod chose to emigrate to Palestine instead. He remained extremely grateful to TM, however, for this "act of noblesse."

2. *Beneš.* Czech president Beneš had come to Chicago as a professor of sociology at the University of Chicago.

. . . .

March 15 1. *His nephew.* Bohuš Beneš.

. . . .

March 16 1. *"Pygmalion."* The 1938 British film with Leslie Howard and Wendy Hiller.

. . . .

March 28 1. *The minister responsible.* Lithuanian prime minister Vladas Mironas.

. . . .

April 10 1. *The Hollywood speech.* The previous winter Dorothy Thompson had urged TM to draft a personal manifesto against force and injustice that would then be signed by a number of leading personalities and widely circulated abroad. The piece was ultimately not used for this purpose after all, and TM adapted it as an address, "To the Civilized World," for a Hollywood meeting of the American Committee for Christian German Refugees on April 5. He repeated it at a Chicago meeting of the same organization.

April 15   1. *The hostess.*   Agnes E. Meyer. Mrs. Meyer was planning a book on TM.

2. *Roosevelt's message.*   Following the Italian invasion of Albania on April 7, 1939, Roosevelt sent a message to both Hitler and Mussolini asking for their guarantee that they would not attack a list of thirty countries.

April 28   1. *John.*   John Long.

2. *President of Rutgers University.*   Robert C. Clothier (1885–1970).

3. *My forty-two minute speech.*   The Problem of Freedom.

4. *The Spanish dinner.*   A banquet honoring former Spanish foreign minister Julio Alvarez del Vayo in New York on May 4.

5. *The PEN Club.*   TM was to address the International PEN Congress in Stockholm in early September. Because of the worsened political situation the meeting was canceled at the last minute.

6. *The booksellers.*   TM had been invited to speak at a banquet of the American Bookdealers Association on May 17.

7. *The "Magic Mountain" lecture.*   "The Making of *The Magic Mountain,*" written for delivery at Princeton on May 10.

May 15   1. *The second dictation.*   In Chapter VII of *The Beloved Returns,* Goethe dictates to his secretary John.

2. *"Moral Aid."*   TM's epithet for the Committee to Defend America by Aiding the Allies.

May 18   1. *The doctoral address.*   TM's speech of thanks on receiving an honorary doctorate from Princeton University. The manuscript of the German text is in the Firestone Library at Princeton.

2. *New degree on the 29th.*   Hobart and William Smith College in Geneva, New York, conferred its honorary doctorate on TM on May 29 (see entry for that date).

3. *Bruno Kreitner's manuscript.*   Nothing further known.

May 20   1. *The Negro college.*   Cheyney State College in Cheyney, Pennsylvania.

2. *A learned lady.*   Unidentified.

3. *Freud's "Moses."*   Moses and Monotheism (1939).

May 22   1. *Lewisohn's novel.*   Ludwig Lewisohn, *Forever Wilt Thou Love* (1939).

May 29   1. *Arrived in Geneva.*   Geneva, New York (see note 2 for May 18, 1939).

2. *The bishop.*   Henry St. George Tucker (1874–1959), bishop of the Episcopalian Church in America.

3. *The Marine Corps general.*   Major General Thomas Holcomb (1879–1965), commander of the U.S. Marine Corps.

4. *The former president.*   William H. Cowley (1899–1978), at that time president of Hamilton College, Clinton, New York.

June 5   1. *The forewords.*   One for the new (third) edition of *Royal Highness* being issued by Knopf, and another for the M. H. Welsh translation of Tolstoy's *Anna Karenina* published by Random House in 1940.

2. *The "old folks."*   TM's parents-in-law were awaiting their emigration visa to Switzerland.

They had cabled to TM that he had best not visit Switzerland until they were safely out of Germany or their visa might be refused.

3. *The writers' meeting.* The congress of the League of American Writers, in New York.

. . . .

June 6 1. *Klaus staying back.* Klaus Mann was in the United States on a visitor's visa and did not have the first papers required for immigration, without which he could not obtain a reentry permit. With nothing but his Czech passport he could not risk leaving the country.

. . . .

June 18 1. *Critical remarks about Brecht.* The July/August 1939 number of *Mass und Wert* included a scene from Brecht's *Private Life of the Master Race* and two unsigned pieces about Brecht's dramaturgy, one by Walter Benjamin, the other presumably by Ferdinand Lion. The latter is apparently the one to which TM refers.

2. *Richard Strauss's lunch with Hitler.* Hitler did indeed attend the Austrian première of Strauss's *Friedenstag* on June 10, 1939, but there is no record that the two lunched together on this occasion. It is likely that Strauss had breakfast the following morning (his seventy-fifth birthday) with Goebbels, however, and the story of such a meeting may well have become garbled in transmission.

3. *Georg Kaiser's novel.* Presumably his *Villa Aurea* (1940).

. . . .

June 30 1. *Vol. 3, No. 1.* The November/December 1939 issue of *Mass und Wert.*

. . . .

July 5 1. *The Tolstoy preface.* See note 1 for June 5, 1939.

2. *His woman colleague.* Alice Nahys von Eugen, translator and co-director with Fritz Landshoff of the German Querido Verlag, Amsterdam.

. . . .

August 9 1. *Poetry of Karl Kraus.* Presumably the 1931 collection, *Zeitstrophen.*

. . . .

August 22 1. *Stockholm.* See note 5 for April 28, 1939.

2. *Grete Walter shot.* During a "last talk" in Zurich granted by Grete Walter to her estranged husband, the German film producer Robert Neppach, he first shot and killed her and then himself. TM's mention of Berne is erroneous.

3. *The Warburg Institute.* The distinguished art history research library established by Aby Warburg. The Institute was moved from Hamburg to London in 1934, and was later incorporated into the University of London.

. . . .

August 23 1. *The "aunties."* The sisters Käthe Rosenberg and Ilse Dernburg.

2. *The firm British statement.* A communiqué from the British cabinet following its meeting on August 22 categorically declared that the nonaggression pact between Germany and the Soviet Union "in no way lessens Great Britain's obligations to Poland, which have been repeatedly affirmed by the British government and which it is firmly committed to fulfill."

. . . .

August 26 1. *President of the PEN Club.* Gustaf Hellström, writer, and president of the Swedish branch of the writers' organization.

. . . .

September 8 1. *The pariah addition.* Only days before completing Chapter VII of *The Beloved Returns,* TM had chanced upon the Goethe poem "Paria," which provided him with new material that he inserted into Goethe's monologue at this time.

. . . .

September 9 1. *Rini.* Sara Catharina ("Rini") Otte.

. . . .

September 19 1. *The novel by Hutchinson.* Ray Coryton Hutchinson's *Testament* (1938).

October 26 1. *The embargo bill.* Legislation intended to ensure American neutrality by forbidding shipment of weapons and matériel to the combatants.

2. *The pavilion ceremony.* The opening of the Palestine pavilion at the New York World's Fair.

3. *The Wagner-Hitler problem.* TM's "In Defense of Wagner," a response to an article by Peter Viereck, appeared in the January 1940 issue of *Common Sense*.

November 7 1. *Nico.* A new poodle, the gift to TM of Caroline Newton.

2. *Statement by Broch.* On October 19 TM had written a letter of resignation to the American Guild for German Cultural Freedom, as he felt that for want of funding the organization was no longer accomplishing anything. On the 28th, in a "memo regarding the prize contest of the Guild," Hermann Broch, to whom TM had delegated the judging of prize manuscripts, informed the secretary of the Guild that TM was concerned to delay his withdrawal until the novel competition could be satisfactorily concluded.

November 16 1. *The essay.* TM's *This War* (1940) was originally intended for the Paris press agency Coopération, which placed articles by well-known writers in newspapers the world over. The piece outgrew this original intention, however, and took on the dimensions of a small book.

2. *The "Werther" lecture.* "Goethe's *Werther*," a talk given at Princeton on November 17, 1939.

November 24 1. *Section of the Freud essay.* An unexplained allusion.

2. *My letter to the League.* The November issue of the *Bulletin* of the League of American Writers carried an article by Elliot Paul titled "France Today," the strongly communist line of which TM regarded as an "act of Stalinist wartime sabotage, a political action against the democracies for the benefit of Hitler and Stalin." TM was the honorary president of the League, but in this letter he tendered his resignation.

December 15 1. *The English title.* Mrs. Lowe-Porter's translation of TM's new novel was published in America as *The Beloved Returns*, whereas the English edition bore the original German title, *Lotte in Weimar*.

2. *Appeal from the Paris "Tageblatt."* In fact the appeal was from the *Pariser Tageszeitung*, the successor to the *Pariser Tageblatt*. The exile daily was suffering severe financial difficulties, and ceased publication on February 18, 1940.

December 26 1. *"The Transposed Heads."* While reading an essay of Heinrich Zimmer's, "Die indische Weltmutter," in the *Eranos-Jahrbuch* for 1938, TM conceived of a novella on an Indian theme. This was on November 12, 1939. There is a brief mention of his development of the plan on December 9. It was on this present date, the day after Christmas, that he first began to work on the new story in earnest.

Biographical Notes

A

ABEGG, Wilhelm (1876–1951). One-time Prussian secretary of state; attorney in Zurich.

ADALBERT, Prince of Bavaria (1886–1970). Diplomat and historian.

AITA, Antonio. Argentinean literary critic and essayist.

ALBERTS, Wilhelm. Author of *Thomas Mann und sein Beruf,* one of the first monographs on TM.

ALTENBERG, Peter (pseudonym of Richard Engländer, 1859–1919). Viennese essayist.

AMANN, Paul (1884–1958). Austrian philologist, cultural historian, and translator; ardent pacifist and admirer of Romain Rolland. Though they had not met, TM and Amann corresponded frequently during the period 1915–18, when TM was writing the *Betrachtungen.* Relations between the two were severed as a result of Amann's critical article referred to in the diaries in 1919. On Amann's initiative they again began corresponding in 1935, and in 1937 they met for the first time in Vienna.

AMMANN, Dr. Munich physician.

ANDREAE. Real-estate broker in Basel.

ANDREAE, Volkmar (1879–1962). Swiss conductor and composer.

ANDREYEV, Leonid (1871–1919). Russian novelist and playwright.

ANGELL, Joseph Warner (b. 1908). American Anglicist and military historian. Founder of the Thomas Mann Collection at Yale University.

ANSERMET, Ernst (1883–1969). Swiss conductor.

ARCO AUF VALLEY, Count Anton von (1897–1945). Reserve lieutenant and member of the Bavarian Catholic student fraternity who shot and killed Kurt Eisner on a Munich street on February 21, 1919.

ARETIN, Baron Erwein von (1887–1952). Conservative, monarchist writer and columnist in Munich. Survivor of the concentration camp at Dachau.

ASCH, Schalom (1880–1957). Yiddish dramatist and writer.

ASPER, Dr. Hans. Zurich dentist.

ATHOLL, Katharine Marjorie, Duchess of (d. 1960). Scottish noblewoman and British MP, 1923–38. Opponent of Chamberlain's policy of appeasement, and champion of the Spanish Republic.

ATTENHOFER, Elsie. Swiss actress, originally a painter and sculptor. Wife of Prof. Karl Schmid, the literary historian and rector of the Eidgenössische Technische Hochschule in Zurich who was instrumental in establishing the Thomas Mann Archive at that institution.

ATTINGER. Unidentified student in Neuchâtel.

AUBRY, Octave (1881–1946). French historical writer.

AUDEN, W. H. (1907–1973). Anglo-American poet. Husband of Erika Mann.

AUER, Erhard (1874–1945). Social Democratic politician. Bavarian minister of the interior in the government of Kurt Eisner.

AUERNHEIMER, Raoul (1876–1948). Viennese dramatist and writer.

AXELROD, Tovia. Russian writer and one-time press chief for the Soviet government. Axelrod attached himself to Kurt Eisner in Munich and served as political commissar and deputy people's agent for finance in his government. He was sentenced to fifteen years' imprisonment in July 1919, but was claimed as a diplomat by the Russian government and released.

B

BAB, Julius (1880–1955). Berlin writer, critic, and dramatist.

BACHER, Dr. Franz. Editor of the German-language daily *Bohemia,* Prague.

BACHMANN. Zurich hairdresser.

BACHOFEN, Johann Jakob (1815–1887). Swiss jurist and social anthropologist.

BACHSTITZ, Karl. Munich architect and art dealer.

389

BAEUMLER, Alfred (1887–1968). Writer and professor of philosophy in Dresden. Director of the Berlin Institute for Political Pedagogy under the Nazis.

BAHR, Hermann (1863–1934). Austrian writer, dramatist, and essayist.

BALFOUR, Arthur James (1848–1930). Conservative British statesman. Foreign minister, 1916–19.

BALZAC, Honoré de (1799–1850). French novelist.

BAMBERGER, Caroline (d. 1944). Wife of Felix Fuld. Together with her brother Louis Bamberger, donated in 1930 the sum of five million dollars to establish the Institute for Advanced Study in Princeton.

BARD, Guy Kurtz (1895–1953). Wealthy American politician. Benefactor of Cheyney State College, Pennsylvania.

BARTH, Karl (1886–1968). Swiss Protestant theologian. Professor in Bonn until 1935, then in Basel.

BASLER, Otto (b. 1902). Essayist and teacher in Burg, Switzerland, who became acquainted with TM in 1930 and received some 150 letters from him over the next quarter-century.

BASSERMANN, Albert (1867–1952). Noted German actor. Emigrated to the U.S. in 1934.

BATA, Thomas (1876–1932). Czech shoe manufacturer who built up a worldwide fabricating and retailing concern.

BATTISTINI, Mattia (1857–1928). Italian baritone.

BAUER, Gustav (1870–1944). German politician. Ministry president, 1919–20; vice-chancellor, 1921–22.

BAUER, Walter (1904–1976). German workingman's poet and writer.

BAUMANN. Zurich hairdresser.

BAUMFELDT, Frau. Viennese art patroness, wife of the banker Richard Peter Baumfeldt.

BAUMFELDT, Dr. Richard Peter (b. 1881). Viennese banker and writer.

BAUMGARTEN, Franz Ferdinand (1880–1927). Hungarian essayist and literary critic.

BECHER. Attorney in Lugano.

BEER-HOFMANN, Richard (1866–1945). Austrian poet and playwright.

BEER-WALBRUNN, Ida. Wife of the composer Anton Beer-Walbrunn (1864–1929).

BEHR, Rudolf. Architect and designer living in Upper Bavaria.

BEHRENS, Eduard (1884–1944). Writer and journalist, political contributor to the *National-Zeitung*, Basel.

BEIDLER, Franz W. (b. 1901). Zurich writer, grandson of Richard Wagner.

BEKKER, Paul (1882–1937). Music historian, critic for the *Frankfurter Zeitung*, 1911–25. Emigrated to the United States in 1933.

BENEDIKT, Dr. Ernst (1882–1973). Publisher and editor-in-chief of the *Neue Freie Presse*, Vienna.

BENEŠ, Bohuš. Writer and journalist, nephew of Eduard Beneš.

BENEŠ, Eduard (1884–1948). Close colleague of T. G. Masaryk, and his successor as president of the Czechoslovak Republic in 1935. Beneš remained in office until the Munich Accord in 1938. Served briefly as guest professor at the University of Chicago, then as president of the Czech government in exile. Returned to Prague in 1945, and again held the office of president until the Communist coup in 1948.

BENN, Gottfried (1886–1956). Berlin physician and noted Expressionist poet; briefly somewhat attracted to National Socialism, 1933–34.

BERBER, Fritz (1871–1930). Munich violinist.

BERDYAEV, Nikolai (1874–1948). Russian philosopher.

BERENDSOHN, Walter A. (b. 1884). Lecturer in Scandinavian literature in Hamburg. Emigrated to Denmark in 1933, to Sweden in 1943, where he taught at the University of Stockholm. With his book *Die humanistische Front. Einführung in die Emigrantenliteratur* (1946) he gave a first stimulus to the study of German exile writing.

BERG, Alban (1885–1935). Austrian composer.

BERGERY, Gaston (b. 1892). French attorney and radical politician; one of the founders of the Popular Front against fascism and of the newspaper *La Flèche*.

BERGSON, Henri (1859–1941). French philosopher.

BERMANN FISCHER, Gottfried (b. 1897). Originally a surgeon, Gottfried Bermann married in 1926 Brigitte Fischer, daughter of the publisher S. Fischer. Bermann became the director of the firm in 1928, and at the wish of his father-in-law appended the Fischer name to his own. At the time of the Nazi takeover Bermann, thirty-five years old, was virtually solely responsible for the business. Early in 1935 he succeeded in making an arrangement with the Nazi Ministry of Propaganda whereby stocks of books by Fischer authors who were undesirable or banned in Germany, as well as various securities, were released under the condition that the Fischer family sell all remaining portions of the business and transfer it to "reliable" hands. A group of financial backers was found to buy the firm and it was continued in Germany under the direction of Peter Suhrkamp. Bermann Fischer wished to establish a new publishing house in Switzerland, but he failed to receive official permission to do so because of objections by Swiss publishers. He therefore founded the new Bermann-Fischer Verlag in Vienna, which began publishing in the early part of 1936. This business he then moved to Stockholm in 1938.

BERMANN, Richard A. (1883–1939). Austrian writer (under the pseudonym Arnold Höllriegel) of popular travel books and features for the *Berliner Tageblatt*. Emigrated to the United States in 1938.

BERNER. Bookseller in Freysing, near Munich.

BERNHARD, Georg (1875–1944). Berlin journalist. Editor-in-chief of the *Vossische Zeitung*, 1920–30; Democratic Reichstag deputy, 1928–33. Emigrated in 1933 to Paris, where he founded the *Pariser Tageblatt*, a German emigré daily.

BERNHART, Dr. Josef. Munich writer.

BERNHEIMER. Munich antiquarian.

BERNOULLI, Dr. Christoph. Attorney in Basel, long-time close acquaintance of TM's.

BERNSTEIN, Elsa (1866–1949). Wife of Max Bernstein. Together they fostered a cultivated literary and musical salon in their Munich home. It was there that TM was first introduced to his future wife, Katia Pringsheim.

BERNSTEIN, Eva. Violinist, daughter of Max and Elsa Bernstein. Married Klaus Hauptmann, the third son of the playwright Gerhart Hauptmann.

BERNSTEIN, Max (1854–1925). Prominent Munich attorney and defense counsel.

BERNSTEIN, Dr. Otto. Munich attorney.

BERNSTEIN, Prof. Unidentified.

BERRSCHE, Alexander (1883–1940). Munich writer on music.

BERTAUX, Félix (1881–1948). French Germanist and translator.

BERTAUX, Pierre (b. 1907). Germanist, Hölderlin scholar, writer, and politician; son of Félix Bertaux, friend of Golo Mann's.

DE BERTOL, Munich black marketeer.

BERTRAM, Ernst (1884–1957). Germanist, poet, and essayist associated with the Stefan George circle. Originally from Elberfeld, long a resident of Munich, later professor in Cologne. From 1910 Bertram was one of TM's very closest friends, and during the First World War he was TM's constant advisor during the writing of the *Betrachtungen*. His later open sympathy for National Socialism led to a complete estrangement, though Bertram sought to maintain contact with TM and tried to convince him to move back to Germany after the Second World War. The two met again in Cologne in 1954, and a superficial reconciliation was effected between them.

BETHMANN-HOLLWEG, Theobald von (1856–1921). German statesman. Chancellor, 1909–17.

BÉTOVE. Popular Parisian comedian and singer.

BIBL, Viktor. Viennese professor of history.

BIELSCHOWSKY, Albert (1847–1902). Goethe biographer.

BIELY, Andrei (pseudonym of Boris Bugaev, 1880–1934). Russian Symbolist writer.

BINDER, Sybille (1898–1962). Actress.

BINDING, Rudolf G[eorg] (1867–1938). Conservative German poet and writer.

BIRNBAUM, Uriel (1894–1956). Austrian poet, essayist, and graphic artist.

BISCHOFF, Ernst. Unidentified official in the Berlin Foreign Office.

BISMARCK, Prince Otto Eduard von (1815–1898). Prussian statesman. First chancellor of the German Empire.

BISSING, Elisabeth von. Wife of the Egyptologist Friedrich Wilhelm von Bissing (1873–1956).

BJÖRKMAN, Carl. Unidentified Lübeck acquaintance of TM's.

BJÖRNSON, Björn (1859–1942). Norwegian writer and actor, son of the poet Björnstjerne Björnson.

BLEI, Franz (1871–1942). Austrian writer, translator, and editor.

BLOCH, Ernst (1885–1977). Marxist philosopher. Emigrated to Prague in 1933, proceeded to the U.S. in 1938, and returned to Germany (East) in 1949.

BLOCH, Dr. Oscar Thorwald (1847–1926). Danish surgeon and writer.

BLÜHER, Hans (1888–1955). Writer and thinker, highly regarded by the German Youth Movement for his in part anti-Semitic, homoerotic studies of masculine organizations.

BLUME, Dr. Gustav (b. 1882). Berlin neurologist.

BLUNCK, Hans Friedrich (1888–1961). Regional writer, president of the Reich Literary Chamber during the Third Reich.

BODENSTEIN, Ernst and Johanna. Munich artlovers about whom nothing further is known.

BODMER, Hans (1891–1956). Zurich literary patron and philanthropist.

BOEHM, Dr. Gottfried (b. 1879). Munich radiologist.

BÖHM, Karl (1894–1981). Austrian conductor.

BOISSERÉE, Sulpiz (1783–1854). Wealthy merchant and art collector in Cologne.

BOLL, Franz (b. 1867). Heidelberg professor of classical philology.

BOLLACK (Pollack?), Dr. Unidentified fellow passenger from Prague on the S.S. *Normandie* in 1937.

BOLLAG, Dr. Harry. TM's Zurich ophthalmologist.

BONDI, Georg. Noted Berlin publisher of the works of Stefan George and his circle. Bondi's second wife was Eva Dohm, a sister of Katia Mann's mother's, Hedwig Pringsheim.

BONN, Emma (b. 1879). New York–born German writer living in Upper Bavaria.

BONN, Prof. Moritz Julius (1873–1965). Political economist in Munich and Berlin. Emigrated to England in 1933.

BONNET, Georges (1889–1973). French politician and diplomat. Minister of foreign affairs, 1938–39.

BONNET, Henri (b. 1888). French diplomat and historian. Member of the secretariat of the League of Nations, and chairman of its Comité permanent des Lettres et des Arts.

BONNIER, Karl Otto (1856–1941). Owner of the Stockholm publishing firm of Albert Bonnier, which produced, beginning in 1904, almost all the Swedish editions of TM's works.

BONNIER, Tor (1883–1976). Oldest son of Karl Otto Bonnier, and his successor in the publishing firm in 1941. The younger Bonnier became associated with Gottfried Bermann Fischer in 1938, and was of assistance in his rebuilding of the Bermann-Fischer Verlag, destroyed in Vienna.

BORCHARDT, Hermann H. Otherwise unidentified dramatist.

BOREL, Pierre. Student in Neuchâtel.

BORGESE, Giuseppe Antonio (1882–1952). Historian and literary scholar, professor of Italian literature at University of Chicago. Married Elisabeth Mann in 1939.

BORN, Wolfgang (1894–1949). Munich painter and graphic artist.

BORRMANN, Martin (b. 1889). Journalist and travel writer in correspondence with TM, 1915–25.

BOTHMER, Count Felix von (1852–1937). Bavarian general.

BOTHMER, Count Karl von. Munich writer and editor.

BOY-ED, Ida (1852–1928). Highly popular writer in Lübeck at the turn of the century, whom TM knew while he was still a preparatory school student. She championed him early in his career, later effected his reconciliation with his birthplace, and remained a fond acquaintance to the end of her life.

BRAAK, Menno ter (1902–1940). Dutch philologist, writer, and critic. Friend of Klaus Mann's, and contributor to his journal *Die Sammlung*.

BRADISH, Joseph von (1883–1970). Austrian-American Germanist.

BRANDENBURG, Hans (1885–1968). Munich writer and frequent walking companion of TM's.

BRANDES, Georg (1842–1927). Eminent Danish literary historian, whose six-volume history of nineteenth-century literature (1872–90) was of considerable influence on TM during the writing of *Buddenbrooks*.

BRANDT & BRANDT. TM's American literary agents in New York.

BRANTING. Unidentified Swedish publisher.

BRANTING, Hjalmar (1860–1925). Swedish statesman. Co-founder of the Swedish Social Democratic party in 1889, and soon thereafter its leader. Winner of the Nobel Peace Prize in 1921.

BRANTL, Maximilian (1881–1959). Munich attorney, Heinrich Mann's lawyer and friend, and acquaintance of TM's. During the long breach between the two Mann brothers, Brantl served as their sole personal tie.

BRAUER, Dr. Ernst. Archaeologist. Emigré from Silesia who served briefly as curator of the Egyptian collection at the University of Zurich.

BRAUER, Herta. German refugee writer.

BRAUN, Otto (1872–1955). Social Democratic politician. Prussian minister president, 1920–33.

BRAUNFELS, Walter (1882–1954). German pianist and composer.

BRECHER, Gustav (1874–1940). Conductor in Leipzig. Emigrated to Belgium, where he took his own life at the time of the German invasion.

BRECHT, Bertolt (1898–1956). The well-known German poet and playwright emigrated with his wife, the actress Helene Weigel, via Prague, Vienna, Switzerland, and Paris to Denmark in 1933. He proceeded to Sweden in 1939, where he encountered TM, thence in 1940 to Finland, and in 1941 via Moscow to the United States, where again he crossed paths with TM.

BREDEL, Willi (1901–1964). Communist writer, co-publisher with Bertolt Brecht and Lion Feuchtwanger of the German-language literary monthly *Das Wort*, Moscow.

BREDOW, General Kurt von. Friend of Kurt von Schleicher's, and secretary of state in his cabinet, 1932–33.

BREITBACH, Joseph (1903–1980). German-French writer and dramatist.

BREITSCHEID, Rudolf (1874–1944). German Socialist politician. Emigrated to France in 1933, was turned over to Germany by the Vichy government, and died in Buchenwald.

BRENTANO, Bernard von (1901–1964). Novelist and biographer. Editor of the *Frankfurter Zeitung*, 1925–30; emigrated to Switzerland, 1933.

BRENTANO, Lujo (1844–1931). Munich professor of political economy.

BRIAND, Aristide (1862–1932). French statesman. Four times prime minister, including the years 1921–22.

BROCH, Hermann (1886–1951). Austrian novelist and essayist. Emigrated via Scotland to the United States in 1938.

BROCK, Erich (1889–1976). Swiss Germanist.

BROCKDORFF-RANTZAU, Count Ulrich von (1869–1928). Leader of the German delegation at Versailles, later Germany's first ambassador to the Soviet Union.

BROD, Max (1884–1968). Prague writer; friend, biographer, and literary executor of Franz Kafka.

BRODSKY, Dr. New York dentist.

BRODSKY, Mrs. Ralph. Popular American writer under the name Ruth Nanda Anshen.

DE BROGLIE, Louis (b. 1892). French Nobel Prize–winning physicist.

BRONEER, Oscar Theodore (b. 1894). Swedish-born American archaeologist and Greek scholar.

BROULINGHAM. Unidentified fellow passenger on the M.S. *Berengaria* in 1935.

BRUCKMANN, Alfons Ritter von. Austrian consul general in Munich.

BRÜLL, Oswald. Textile manufacturer from Bielitz, Poland, resident in Vienna; a long-time admirer of TM's and writer of a number of articles on him.

BRÜNGER. Unidentified student in Munich.

BRÜNING, Heinrich (1885–1970). German statesman. Last chancellor of the Republic; lecturer at Harvard University, 1937–39.

BUCKY, Dr. Gustav (1880–1963). German-born American radiologist in New York.

BUDZISLAWSKI, Hermann (b. 1901). Publicist, editor of the *Neue Weltbühne*, Prague.

BÜHL, Reich Councillor von. Otherwise unidentified essayist.

BÜHLER-KOLLER, Colonel Eduard (1862–1932). Manufacturer in Winterthur, Switzerland.

BÜLAU, Dr. Unidentified.

BUENGER, Judge. President of the Superior Court in Leipzig before which the accused of the Reichstag fire were tried.

BULLER, Wilhelm and Hedwig. TM's hosts in Mühlheim in 1921; he a manufacturer, she the daughter of friends of TM's from Bad Tölz.

BUMANN, Walter. Munich attorney, partner of TM's attorney, Valentin Heins.

BUNIN, Ivan (1870–1953). Russian poet and novelist.

BURCKHARDT, Carl Jacob (1891–1974). Swiss diplomat and historian.

BURCKHARDT-SCHATZMANN, Helene. Mother of Carl Jacob Burckhardt.

BURCKHARDT, Jacob (1818–1897). Swiss historian of art and culture.

BURCKHARDT, Dr. Jakob (b. 1913). Swiss jurist and diplomat.

BURCKHARDT, Dr. Paul (b. 1892). Preparatory school teacher in Olten, Switzerland.

BURIAN, Count Stefan (1850–1941). Austro-Hungarian statesman. Foreign minister, 1915–16, and again from April to October 1918.

BURRI, Franz Xaver (1864–1941). Forest inspector in Lucerne.

BURRIAN, Karl (1870–1924). Heldentenor in Dresden and Vienna.

BURSCHELL, Friedrich (1889–1970). German writer. Emigrated to France and then Spain in 1933; lived in Prague, 1934–38, where he was instrumental in organizing the Thomas Mann Society in 1936.

BURTE, Hermann (1879–1960). Nationalist German poet, writer, and painter.

BUSCH, Adolf (1891–1952). Eminent German violinist. Moved to Basel in 1926, to the U.S. in 1940. Younger brother of Fritz Busch.

BUSCH, Fritz (1890–1951). Conductor. At the Dresden Opera, 1922–33; emigrated in 1933.

BUSCHING, Paul Rudolf (1877–1945). Munich theater and music critic.

BUXBAUM, Friedrich (1869–1948). Viennese cellist. Emigrated to England in 1938.

C

CAIN, James M. (b. 1892). American writer; noted for his writing for films.

ČAPEK, Karel (1890–1938). Czech dramatist and novelist. Member of the League of Nations' Comité permanent des Lettres et des Arts.

DON CARLOS (1545–1568). Son of Philip II of Austria.

CARLYLE, Thomas (1795–1881). Scottish historian.

CAROSSA, Hans (1878–1956). Bavarian physician and novelist.

CASSIRER, Bruno (1872–1941). Berlin publisher.

CASSIRER, Paul (1871–1926). Berlin art dealer and publisher.

CATHER, Willa (1873–1947). American novelist and short-story writer.

CECONI, Dr. Ermanno. Dentist born in Trieste and practicing in Munich; married to the writer Ricarda Huch.

ČERNÝ, Josef (1885–1971). Czech minister of the interior, 1932–38.

CHAMBERLAIN, Houston Stewart (1855–1927). English cultural philosopher. Married Richard Wagner's daughter Eva in 1908 and lived in Bayreuth. His controversial work *The Foun-*

dations of the Nineteenth Century (1899) was influential in the development of Nazi racist ideology.

CHAMBERLAIN, Neville (1869–1940). British statesman. Prime minister, 1937–40.

CHAMISSO, Adelbert von (1781–1838). German Romantic writer.

CHAUTEMPS, Camille (1885–1963). French Radical Socialist politician. Premier, 1930, 1933–34, and 1937–38.

CHIAROMONTE, Nicola (b. 1905). Italian anti-Fascist writer. Went into exile in Switzerland in 1934.

CHURCHILL, Sir Winston (1874–1965). British statesman.

CLAUDEL, Paul (1868–1955). French poet and dramatist.

CLEMEN, Paul (1866–1947). Professor of art history in Bonn.

CLEMENCEAU, Georges (1841–1929). French politician and statesman.

COCTEAU, Jean (1889–1963). French surrealist poet, painter, and film-maker.

COHEN. Unidentified Munich businessman.

COLIN, Saul C. (1909–1967). Rumanian-born impresario and theater and film agent who represented American film companies in Paris, 1928–33. Colin emigrated to the United States in 1935. Erika and Klaus Mann had known him in Paris and introduced him to their father. He went to great effort to promote a filming of the *Joseph* novels. TM portrayed him as the concert agent Saul Fitelberg in *Doctor Faustus*.

COLMERS, Franz. Chief physician at the hospital in Coburg.

CONANT, James Bryant (1893–1978). President of Harvard University, 1933–53.

CONNER, Mrs. Boudinot R. Princeton neighbor of TM's.

CONRAD, Julius (1877–1959). Hungarian artist.

CORRODI, Hans. Professor, neighbor of TM's in Küsnacht.

COSSMANN, Paul Nikolaus (1869–1942). Co-founder of the *Süddeutsche Monatshefte* and editor of that journal from 1904 to 1933. During the 1920s, simultaneously political editor of the *Münchner Neueste Nachrichten*.

COSTER, Charles de (1827–1879). Belgian writer.

COURVOISIER, Walter (1875–1931). Swiss composer and professor of music in Munich.

CROCE, Benedetto (1866–1952). Italian historian and cultural philosopher. Though a declared anti-Fascist, Croce was tolerated by Mussolini out of consideration for his fame and Italian public opinion.

CURTISS, Thomas Quinn ("Tomski") (b. 1907). American theater critic and journalist whom Klaus Mann met at the home of the Hatvanys in Budapest, and with whom he then maintained a close relationship for a number of years.

CURTIUS, Ernst Robert (1886–1956). German literary historian, professor of French in Bonn, Marburg, and Heidelberg.

CZECH, Ludwig (1870–1942). Sudeten German head of the German Social Democratic party in Czechoslovakia.

D

DALADIER, Edouard (1884–1970). French statesman and Radical Socialist politician. Premier in 1933, 1934, and 1938–40. Signed the Munich Accord; declared war on Germany on September 3, 1939, after Hitler refused to withdraw from Poland.

D'ANNUNZIO, Gabriele (1863–1938). Italian poet, writer, and soldier.

DAUTHENDEY, Max (1867–1918). German poet and dramatist.

DAVIS, Norman H. (1878–1944). American financier and diplomat.

DE BOER, Willem (1885–1962). Dutch violinist and teacher. Concertmaster of the Zurich Tonhalle orchestra and teacher of Michael Mann at the Zurich conservatory.

DE BOOR, Helmut (1891–1976). Swiss Germanist.

DEHMEL, Richard (1863–1920). German lyric poet and dramatist. Dehmel was greatly encouraging to TM in his early writing career.

DELBRÜCK, Hans (1848–1929). Berlin professor of history.

DELBRÜCK, Joachim von (b. 1886). German writer and critic.

DELL, Robert. Liberal British commentator and publicist.

DENZLER, Robert F. (1892–1972). Swiss conductor.

DE REEDE, Dirk. Unidentified fellow passenger on the R.M.S. *Rotterdam* in 1934.

DERNBURG, Ilse (1880–1964). Daughter of Else Rosenberg's, cousin of Katia Mann's.

DESTAL, Fred. Singer with the Zurich Opera.

DIBELIUS, Otto (1880–1967). Protestant bishop of Berlin and Brandenburg.

DIEBOLD, Bernhard (1886–1945). Swiss writer and theater critic for the *Frankfurter Zeitung*. Returned to Switzerland in 1933.

DIEDERICHS, Eugen (1867–1930). Prominent publisher in Jena, married to the poetess Lulu von Strauss und Torney.

DIETRICH, Bishop. Unidentified German Protestant clergyman.

DIETZ, Supreme Court Justice. Otherwise unidentified.

DIETZ, Frau. Unidentified.

DIMITROFF, Georgi. Bulgarian resident in Berlin who was among those accused of setting the Reichstag fire. Released to the Soviet Union in 1934.

DISCLEZ, Josef. Cellist.

DODD, Martha. Daughter of William E. Dodd.

DODD, William Edward (1869–1940). Historian; American ambassador to Berlin, 1933–37. Dodd was a decisive opponent of the Nazi regime and was detested by Hitler. His posthumously published *Ambassador Dodd's Diary 1933–1937* (1941) is an important sourcebook for the times.

DODDS, Harold W. (b. 1889). Political scientist; president of Princeton University, 1933–57.

DÖBLIN, Alfred (1878–1957). German physician, novelist, and dramatist. Emigrated in 1934.

DÖDERLEIN, Prof. Albert (1860–1941). Munich gynecologist.

DOHM, Hedwig (1835–1919). Berlin writer and champion of women's rights; maternal grandmother of Katia Mann.

DOLL. Chauffeur in Küsnacht.

DOLLFUSS, Dr. Engelbert (1892–1934). Austrian statesman. Chancellor, 1932–34; murdered during an attempted Nazi putsch.

DOUMERGUE, Gaston (1863–1937). French statesman. President, 1924–31; premier, 1934.

DRIESCH, Hans (1867–1941). German biologist, philosopher, and parapsychologist.

DU BOS, Charles (1882–1939). French literary historian and translator.

DUHAMEL, Georges (1884–1966). French physician and writer.

DÜNZL. Admirer of TM's from Lower Bavaria who occasionally supplied the family with dairy products in Munich; nicknamed by them "Butter Dünzl."

DURIEUX, Tilla (1880–1971). German actress.

DURYCH, Jaroslav (1886–1962). Czech novelist.

DYCK, Prof. Walter von (b. 1856). Munich mathematician.

DYSING, Walter. Munich actor.

E

EBERS, Hermann E. (1881–1955). Munich painter and illustrator.

EBERT, Friedrich (1871–1925). German Social Democratic politician. First president of the German Reich, 1919–25.

ECKART, Dietrich (1868–1923). Nationalist, anti-Semitic writer and editor; first editor-in-chief of the Nazi *Völkischer Beobachter.*

ECKSTEIN, Friedrich. Writer, friend of Hugo Wolf's.

EDDY, William Alfred (1896–1962). President of Hobart and William Smith College.

EDEN, Anthony (1897–1977). Conservative British statesman. Secretary of state for foreign affairs, 1935–38, 1940–45, and 1951–55; prime minister, 1955–57.

EDSCHMID, Kasimir (pseudonym of Eduard Schmid, 1890–1960). Leading German Expressionist writer and dramatist.

EGLOFFSTEIN, Baron. TM's reference is either to Baron Ludwig von und zu Egloffstein, a retired army captain, or to Baron Wilhelm, a retired major. Both were residents of Munich.

EHRENBERG, Carl (1878–1962). Composer and conductor. Brother of Paul Ehrenberg.

EHRENBERG, Paul (1876–1949). Munich painter. In TM's early years in Munich he enjoyed a close friendship with the brothers Carl and Paul Ehrenberg, one that continued until TM's marriage in 1905. A long homosexual attachment existed between Paul Ehrenburg and TM, one described in intimate detail in TM's notebooks of the period. Later the two maintained only a superficial acquaintance, Ehrenberg having married the painter Lily Teufel. The figure of Rudi Schwerdtfeger in *Doctor Faustus* is based on Paul Ehrenberg.

EHRENFELD, Ernst. Young Viennese novelist who visited TM several times in 1934. Otherwise unidentified.

EHRHARDT, Hermann (1881–1971). Naval officer, commander of an anti-Communist volunteer corps in Munich.

EINSTEIN, Albert (1879–1955). The Nobel Prize–winning physicist was a neighbor of TM's in Princeton, and the two were close acquaintances.

EISNER, Kurt (1867–1919). Journalist and Socialist politician. Organized the revolution that overthrew the Bavarian monarchy in 1918, and became the first minister president of the Bavarian Republic. Assassinated by Count Anton Arco auf Valley.

EISNER, Pavel (1889–1958). German-Czech journalist and critic, author of numerous articles on TM and translator of a number of his works into Czech.

ELCHINGER, Richard (1883–1955). Munich writer and critic. Features editor of the *Münchner Neueste Nachrichten.*

ELIASBERG, Alexander (1878–1924). Munich literary historian, editor, and translator of Russian literature.

ELSTER, Hanns Martin (b. 1888). Berlin writer and critic. Editor of the monthly *Die Horen,* 1924–31.

ELTZBACHER, Paul (1868–1928). Berlin social science professor.

ENDER, Franco. Otherwise unidentified engineer in Lugano.

ENDRES, Elisabeth, née von Heigel. Wife of Fritz Endres.

ENDRES, Major Franz Carl (1878–1954). Novelist. Founder, in November 1918, and secretary of the Council of Intellectual Workers in Munich.

ENDRES, Dr. Fritz (1886–1945). Munich historian and regular contributor to the *München-Augsburger Abendzeitung.* Close acquaintance of TM's and author of a monograph on him; later became a Nazi party member.

ENDRES, Theodor Carl (1887–1944). Public prosecutor in Munich, brother of Franz Carl and Fritz Endres.

ENGEL, Fritz (1867–1935). Berlin theater critic and features editor of the *Berliner Tageblatt.*

EPP, Franz Xaver von (1868–1946). German general, commander of the Bavarian rifle corps that overthrew the Bavarian Soviet Republic; Nazi governor of Bavaria, 1933–45.

ERB, Karl (1877–1958). Lyric tenor at the Munich Opera.

ERMATINGER, Emil (1873–1953). Zurich professor of literary history.

ERNST, Fritz (1898–1958). Swiss literary historian and essayist.

ERNST, Dr. Hans. Zurich attorney, cousin of Fritz Ernst.

ERNST, Karl. SA squad leader murdered in the Blood Purge of June 30, 1934.

ERZBERGER, Matthias (1875–1921). German statesman. Minister of finance, 1919–20.

ESSER, Hermann (b. 1900). Early adherent of Hitler's in Munich; Bavarian secretary of state.

ETIEMBLE, René (b. 1909). French writer, literary historian, and comparatist.

EULENBERG, Herbert (1876–1949). German essayist and dramatist.

EVERS, Pastor Johannes (1859–1945). Lübeck clergyman.

F

FABRICIUS, Ludwig (1875–1968). Professor of forest management, Munich neighbor of TM's.

FADIMAN, Clifton (b. 1904). American literary critic and editor.

FAESI, Robert (1883–1972). Zurich professor of German literature.

FAKTOR, Emil (1876–1941). Theater critic, editor-in-chief of the *Berliner Börsen-Courier* until 1933.

FALCKENBERG, Otto (1873–1947). Theater director at the Munich Kammerspiele.

FALK, Dr. Unidentified linguist whom TM met in The Hague.

FALKE, Konrad (pseudonym of Karl Frey, 1880–1942). Swiss writer, dramatist, and translator; co-publisher with TM of *Mass und Wert*.

FALLADA, Hans (pseudonym of Rudolf Ditzen, 1893–1947). German novelist.

FALTIN, Dr. Hermann. Munich gynecologist.

FAULHABER, Michael von (1869–1952). Archbishop of Munich and Freysing, became a cardinal in 1921.

FECHENBACH, Felix (1894–1933). Member of the Workers' and Soldiers' Council in Munich and secretary to Kurt Eisner; arrested and murdered by the Nazis in 1933.

FEHR, Prof. TM's reference is to either Henri Fehr, professor of mathematics in Geneva, or Max Fehr, music historian and Wagner scholar in Zurich.

FEIST, Dr. Hans (1887–1952). Originally a physician, later a noted translator; friend of the Mann family's in Munich.

FERBER, Maria. Housemaid of the Manns' in Munich and later in Küsnacht.

FEUCHTWANGER, Lion (1884–1958). Novelist and dramatist. Acquainted with TM in Munich, moved to Berlin in the 1920s. Feuchtwanger emigrated to France in 1933, and became co-publisher with Bertolt Brecht and Willi Bredel of the Moscow literary journal *Das Wort* beginning in 1937. In 1940 he fled to the United States, where he was a neighbor and once again a close friend of TM's in Pacific Palisades.

FEUCHTWANGER, Marta. Wife of Lion Feuchtwanger.

FEUERMANN, Emanuel (1902–1942). Austrian cellist.

FIEDLER, Kuno (1895–1973). Protestant pastor who began corresponding with TM in 1915 and who baptized Elisabeth Mann-Borgese. Deposed by the church because of his book *Luthertum oder Christentum*. Escaped Nazi arrest in 1936 and fled to Switzerland, where he spent the rest of his life.

FISCHER, Brigitte ("Tutti") (b. 1905). Older daughter of Samuel Fischer and wife of Gottfried Bermann Fischer.

FISCHER, Hedwig, née Landshoff (1871–1952). Wife of Samuel Fischer.

FISCHER, Hilde ("Hilla") (b. 1916). Younger daughter of Samuel Fischer.

FISCHER, Otokar (1883–1938). Literary historian and translator, professor at the Czech university in Prague.

FISCHER, Samuel (1859–1934). Founder of the publishing firm S. Fischer in Berlin, and distinguished publisher of Gerhart Hauptmann, Hermann Hesse, Henrik Ibsen, Thomas Mann, etc.

FLAKE, Otto (1880–1963). Munich essayist and writer.

FLAMMARION, Camille (1842–1925). French astronomer.

FLANDIN, Pierre Etienne (1889–1958). French politician. Premier, 1934–35.

FLASKAMP, Christoph (1880–1950). Political columnist in Munich.

FLAUBERT, Gustave (1821–1880). French novelist.

FLEINER, Fritz (1867–1937). Swiss historian and professor of constitutional law. Rector of the University of Zurich.

FLEISCHMANN, Dr. Carlo. Attorney, Rumanian consul in Zurich.

FLEISCHMANN, Rudolf (1904–1966). Merchant in Proseč, Czechoslovakia.

FLETCHER, Mr. Unidentified luncheon companion in Cincinnati.

FLEXNER, Abraham (1866–1959). American educator. Director of the Institute for Advanced Study in Princeton, 1930–39; instrumental in bringing TM to Princeton in 1938.

FLINKER, Martin (b. 1895). Austrian bookseller, writer, and publicist. Emigrated to France, 1938.

FOCH, General Ferdinand (1851–1929). French soldier. Supreme commander of Allied forces in 1918; marshal of France, 1918.

FOERSTER, Friedrich Wilhelm (1869–1966). Munich professor of philosophy and ardent pacifist.

FÖRSTER-NIETZSCHE, Elizabeth (1846–1935). Sister of the philosopher and guardian of his literary remains; founded the Nietzsche Archive in Weimar.

FONTANE, Theodor (1819–1898). German poet, novelist, and essayist.

FORBES, Vivian (1891–1937). English painter and illustrator.

FORSTER, Albert. Nazi Gauleiter in Danzig.

FRANCKE, Dr. Leo (1884–1943). Editor and publisher in Dresden.

FRANCKENSTEIN, Baron Clemens von (1875–1942). German composer and conductor.

FRANÇOIS-PONCET, André (b. 1887). French diplomat. Ambassador to Germany, 1931–38.

FRANK, Bruno (1887–1945). Novelist, poet, and dramatist. Frank and TM became friends in 1910. At first Frank lived in a small villa above Feldafing, where TM often visited, then in 1925 he and his wife moved into the house next door to TM's in Herzogpark in Munich. The Franks emigrated in 1933; first to Switzerland, then England, and ultimately to the United States, where once again they were neighbors of TM's in California.

FRANK, Elisabeth ("Liesl") (1903–1979). Wife of Bruno Frank, daughter of Fritzi Massary.

FRANK, Leonhard (1882–1961). German novelist. Emigrated in 1933 to Zurich, went on to Paris in 1937, and to the United States in 1940.

FRANKL, Oskar Benjamin. Director of the Urania in Prague, where TM lectured on various occasions.

FRED, W. A. (1879–1922). Viennese writer.

FREI, Walter (1882–1972). Professor of veterinary science in Zurich.

FREILIGRATH, Ferdinand (1810–1876). German lyric and political poet.

FRENCH, Robert Dudley (1888–1954). Yale professor of English literature.

FRENZEL, Thea. Governess in the Mann household in Munich.

FREUND, Dr. Robert. Partner in the publishing firm of R. Piper in Munich. Emigrated to Vienna, then to the United States.

FREY, Alexander Moritz (1881–1957). Munich novelist acquainted with TM from the turn of the century. Emigrated in 1933 to Salzburg, then Switzerland. Frey published numerous articles on TM and the two were in continual correspondence during the exile years.

FREYTAG, Eduard Erich. Director of matinee productions at the Munich Schauspielhaus.

FRICK, Wilhelm (1877–1946). Nazi minister of the interior, 1933–43.

FRIEDELL, Egon (1878–1938). Viennese theater critic, actor, essayist. Plunged to his death from a window to escape arrest by the Gestapo.

FRIEDENTHAL, Joachim (b. 1887). Munich correspondent for the *Berliner Tageblatt*.

FRIEDMANN, Judge. Otherwise unidentified.

FRIEDRICH, Hans (b. 1884). Munich writer, executive of the Writers' League.

FRIESS, Karl. Munich drama and art critic.

FRISCH, Efraim (1873–1942). Writer and translator. Publisher of *Der Neue Merkur*, 1914–16, and again from 1919 to 1925.

FROMMEL, Otto. Professor of theology in Heidelberg.

FUCIK, Bedřich. Director of the Melantrich-Verlag, Prague.

FULDA, Ludwig (1862–1939). German translator of Molière, Rostand, etc. Fulda was dismissed from the Prussian Academy as a Jew in 1933 and left the country. Driven by homesickness, he later returned, and committed suicide in Berlin.

FUNK, Dr. Philipp. Editor of the *München-Augsburger Abendzeitung*.

FURTWÄNGLER, Wilhelm (1886–1954). German conductor. At the Berlin Philharmonic, 1922–45; became director of the Berlin Staatsoper in 1933. Furtwängler was also president of the Reich Music Chamber, and in a dispute over the composer Paul Hindemith, whom Furtwängler championed, he resigned all his various posts in December 1934, only to resume them in April 1935.

G

GANGHOFER, Ludwig (1855–1920). German playwright and novelist.

GAST, Peter (pseudonym of Heinrich Köselitz, 1854–1918). Composer friend of Friedrich Nietzsche's.

GAUSS, Christian (1878–1951). American Romanicist, professor of modern languages and dean of the college at Princeton, 1925–45; influential in TM's appointment to Princeton in 1938.

GEFFCKEN, Walter (1872–1950). Bavarian painter.

GEORG, Manfred (1893–1965). Journalist in Berlin. Emigrated in 1933 to Prague, and in 1938 to the United States, where from 1939 to his death he served as publisher and editor-in-chief (as Manfred George) of the New York German weekly *Der Aufbau*.

GEORGE, Stefan (1868–1933). German poet and mentor to a distinguished circle of aesthetes, among them Friedrich Gundolf and Ernst Bertram.

GERHARD, Adele (1868–1956). Berlin novelist with whom TM was in correspondence for many years; emigrated to the United States in 1938.

GERLICH, Dr. Fritz (1883–1934). Catholic publicist in Munich and a fierce opponent of National Socialism. Arrested on March 9, 1933, in the editorial offices of the journal *Der gerade Weg*, founded by him, and taken to the concentration camp at Dachau. He was rumored to have died shortly afterward, but it was not until the following July that he was shot.

GIDE, André (1869–1951). French man of letters.

GIEHSE, Therese (1898–1975). Celebrated actress. Founder with Erika Mann of the cabaret *The Peppermill*. Fled from Munich in 1933 to the Tyrol, later taking up residence in Switzerland.

GIGON, Dr. Alfred (1883–1975). Physician in Basel.

GILLET, Louis (1876–1943). French art historian and critic.

GINZKEY, Franz Karl (1871–1963). Austrian poet and writer.

GIRAUDOUX, Jean (1882–1944). French novelist and playwright.

GISELA, Princess of Bavaria. Daughter of Emperor Franz Joseph of Austria.

GLAESER, Ernst (1902–1963). German novelist. Emigrated to Switzerland in 1933, but made his peace with the Nazi regime and returned in 1939.

GLEICHEN-RUSSWURM, Baron Heinrich von (1882–1959). Conservative political writer in Berlin and publisher of the journal *Das Gewissen*, 1919–20. Founder of the Deutscher Klub in Berlin in 1924.

GLÖCKNER, Ernst (1885–1934). Devoted disciple of Stefan George's and life's companion of Ernst Bertram. Glöckner disapproved of Bertram's friendship with TM because of George's disdain for him.

GODWIN, Katharina. Munich writer.

GÖHR, Fritz. Bookbinder in Munich.

GOETHE, Johann Wolfgang von (1749–1832). German man of letters.

GOETZ, Bruno (1885–1954). Baltic poet, writer, and essayist.

GOETZ, Curt (1888–1960). Actor and playwright.

GOETZ, Walter (1867–1958). Historian. Democratic Reichstag deputy, 1920–28.

GOETZ, Wolfgang (1885–1955). Writer and dramatist.

GOGOL, Nikolai (1809–1852). Russian writer.

GOLDENBERG, Dr. Theodor (b. 1880). Surgeon in Nuremberg.

GOLDMAN, Robert P. President of the Union of Hebrew Congregations and member of the board of Hebrew Union College in Cincinnati.

GOLDSCHMIDT, Dr. Siegfried (b. 1890). Public prosecutor in Breslau. Emigrated to Prague, later to the United States.

GOLDWYN, Samuel (1882–1974). Hollywood film producer.

GOLL, Claire (1901–1977). German-French poet and writer, wife of the writer Ivan Goll.

GOLL, Prof. and Mme. Unidentified acquaintances in Sanary.

GONCHAROV, Ivan (1812–1891). Russian novelist.

GORKY, Maxim (1868–1936). Russian writer and dramatist.

GOSCH, Dr. Wolfgang. Munich dentist.

GOTTHELF, Jeremias (pseudonym of Albert Bitzius, 1797–1854). Swiss novelist.

GRÄF, Hans Gerhard (1864–1942). Literary historian and Goethe scholar.

GRAF, Oskar Maria (1894–1967). Bavarian writer and friend of Kurt Eisner's. Emigrated in 1933 to Vienna and Brno, in 1938 to the United States.

GRAUTOFF, Otto (1876–1937). Art historian and translator, school friend of TM's in Lübeck and intimate acquaintance until after the turn of the century.

GREEN, Julien (b. 1900). French novelist.

GREINER, Leo (1876–1928). Director of the drama division at S. Fischer Verlag, Berlin.

GREY, Sir Edward (1862–1933). British Liberal statesman. Foreign minister, 1905–16.

GRIESEBACH, Eberhard (1880–1945). Philosophy professor in Zurich.

GRIGOROFF, Dr. Bulgarian observer at the Leipzig trials, 1933–34.

GRILLPARZER, Franz (1791–1872). Austrian writer and dramatist.

GRIMM, Jakob (1785–1863). German philologist and mythologist.

GROLMAN, Adolf von (1888–1973). Literary historian and musicologist.

GROSSMANN, Stefan (1875–1935). Viennese writer and editor.

GROTH, John Henry (b. 1893). German professor at the University of Washington, Seattle.

GRUBER, Dr. Munich physician.

GRÜNDGENS, Gustaf (1899–1963). Actor and director at the Deutsches Theater in Berlin, 1928–32; appointed intendant of the Berlin State Theater in 1934; director of the Düsseldorf Schauspielhaus after the Second World War; and general intendant of the Deutsches Schauspielhaus in Hamburg, 1955–63. Married to Erika Mann, 1925–28.

GUBLER, Friedrich T. Features editor of the *Frankfurter Zeitung*.

GÜNTHER, Dr. Carl (1890–1956). Chairman of the literary society in Aarau, Switzerland.

GUENTHER, Johannes von (1886–1969). Munich writer, translator, and publisher.

GULBRANSSON, Olaf (1873–1958). Munich artist and caricaturist.

GUMPERT, Martin (1897–1955). Berlin physician and writer. Emigrated to the United States in 1936, where he became a close friend of Erika and TM's.

GWINNER, Wilhelm (1825–1917). Jurist and philosopher, friend of Arthur Schopenhauer's.

H

HAAG, Henry (d. 1920). A cousin of TM's, son of his aunt Elizabeth, the prototype for Tony in *Buddenbrooks*.

HAAS, Willy (1891–1973). Writer and critic. Co-founder with Ernst Rowohlt of the weekly *Die Literarische Welt*, which he directed until 1933, and to which TM was a frequent contributor. Emigrated to Prague, India, and finally London.

HABER, Fritz, (1868–1934). German Nobel Prize–winning chemist.

HACKLÄNDER, Friedrich Wilhelm (1816–1877). German popular writer.

HAENISCH, Konrad (1876–1925). Prussian minister of culture, 1918–21.

HÄSSIG, Alfred. Zurich architect. Father of Hans-Alfred Hässig.

HÄSSIG, Hans-Alfred. Student at the Polytechnic Institute in Zurich who arranged to have TM give a reading there in 1933.

HÄUSER, Fräulein. Associated with the Musarion Verlag in Munich. Otherwise unidentified guest of Georg Martin Richter's in Feldafing.

HAGEMEISTER, August (1877–1923). Left-wing Socialist, member of the Central Council of the Bavarian Soviet Republic.

HALBE, Max (1865–1944). German playwright and novelist.

HALIFAX, Edward Frederick Lindley Wood, Earl of (1881–1959). English statesman. Foreign secretary, 1938–40.

HALLGARTEN, Constance (1881–1969). Wife of Robert Hallgarten and co-founder of the International Women's League for Peace and Freedom. Emigrated with her son Wolfgang in 1933.

HALLGARTEN, Richard ("Ricki") (1905–1932). Younger son of Robert Hallgarten and close friend of Erika and Klaus Mann's; committed suicide at age twenty-seven.

HALLGARTEN, Robert (1870–1924). Germanist in Munich. The Hallgartens lived near the Manns in Herzogpark and were close acquaintances. Their home was an intellectual and artistic center of the city, renowned especially for its excellent chamber music concerts.

HALLGARTEN, Wolfgang, later George W. (1901–1976). Political scientist, older son of Robert Hallgarten. Emigrated with his mother to France in 1933, staying for various periods in Switzerland, proceeding later to the United States.

HAMANN, Johann Georg (1730–1788). German writer and philosopher.

HAMBURGER, Käte (b. 1896). Germanist. Emigrated to Sweden in 1933, returning to Germany and a professorship in Stuttgart after the war.

HAMMERSTEIN, Oscar III (1895–1960). American playwright and librettist.

HAMSUN, Knut (1859–1952). Norwegian novelist, winner of the Nobel Prize in 1920.

HANFSTÄNGL, Erna. Daughter of the wealthy, American-born Munich widow of the same name who was one of the first respectable hostesses in Munich to open her doors to Hitler, and sister of Ernst ("Putzi") Hanfstängl. The younger woman was much admired by the future dictator. The family were neighbors of the Manns in Herzogpark.

HANFSTÄNGL, Ernst ("Putzi") (1887–1975). Brother of Erna Hanfstängl, Harvard graduate, and friend of Hitler's in Munich. It was in Hanfstängl's country home that Hitler took refuge after the Munich Putsch of 1923, and the piano-playing scion of a wealthy Munich family later became Hitler's foreign press chief. Hanfstängl offered a scholarship grant to Harvard University after he had been appointed to that post, but it was declined. After a falling out with Hitler in 1937 Hanfstängl fled to England, later to Canada.

HANHART, Dr. Ernst (1891–1973). Professor of medicine in Zurich.

HARDEN, Maximilian (1861–1927). Writer and commentator. In 1892 founded the political and literary weekly *Die Zukunft*. A long-time friend of Katia Mann's parents', he was to be found at their home on Arcisstrasse when in Munich.

HARDT, Ludwig (1886–1947). German monologist acquainted with TM in Munich. Emigrated to Prague, then in 1938 to the United States.

HARNACK, Adolf von (1851–1930). German Protestant theologian.

HARNISCH, Johannes W. (b. 1883). Berlin political publicist.

HARTMANN, Dr. Otherwise unidentified attorney in St. Gall.

HARTUNG, Gustav (1887–1946). Theater director in Darmstadt. Emigrated to Switzerland.

HASENCLEVER, Justice. Otherwise unidentified.

HATTINGBERG, Dr. Hans von. Munich psychotherapist.

HATVANY-WINSLOE, Christa. Writer and playwright, first wife of Lajos von Hatvany; friend of Erika and Klaus Mann's.

HATVANY, Jolan ("Loli") von. Third wife of Lajos von Hatvany.

HATVANY, Lajos von (1880–1961). Hungarian nobleman and writer (in German and Hungarian) long acquainted with TM and his wife.

HATZFELD, Adolf von (1892–1957). German Expressionist novelist and poet.

HAUPTMANN, Gerhart (1862–1946). German playwright and novelist. TM was always a great admirer of the writer Hauptmann, however strong his reservations about the man. The two met at S. Fischer's in 1903, but only became better acquainted after the First World War. During the 1920s they appeared together at a number of ceremonious occasions, and in 1922 TM celebrated the playwright as the "king of the Republic" in his speech *Von deutscher Republik*. TM's use of character traits of Hauptmann's in his creation of the figure of Mynheer Peeperkorn in *The Magic Mountain* led to a serious breach that was however healed by a candid letter of apology from TM in the spring of 1925. Hauptmann, a Nobel laureate himself, strongly championed TM for the Nobel Prize in 1929. TM strongly objected to Hauptmann's compromising stance vis-à-vis the Nazi regime, but the playwright's death moved him deeply, and he insisted on giving a memorial address in Frankfurt on the occasion of Hauptmann's ninetieth birthday in 1952.

HAUPTMANN, Klaus. Son of Gerhart Hauptmann.

HAUSENSTEIN, Wilhelm (1882–1957). Essayist and art historian. Co-editor with Efraim Frisch of the *Neue Merkur* after 1920, and later editor of the *Frankfurter Zeitung*.

HAUSER, Heinrich (1901–1955). German novelist of the "New Factuality."

HEBBEL, Friedrich (1813–1863). German playwright.

HEER, Gottlieb Heinrich (1903–1967). Swiss writer.

HEIGEL, Marie von. Widow of the historian Karl Theodor von Heigel and mother-in-law of Fritz Endres.

HEILBORN, Ernst (1867–1941). Berlin literary and theater critic, editor of *Das Literarische Echo*.

HEIMANN, Moritz (1868–1925). Dramatist, writer, and essayist; editor at S. Fischer Verlag from 1896 until his death.

HEIMS, Else (1878–1958). First wife of the theater director Max Reinhardt.

HEINE, Albert (1867–1949). German actor and director.

HEINE, Heinrich (1797–1856). German lyric poet and literary critic.

HEINE, Thomas Theodor (1867–1948). Graphic artist in Munich and co-founder of *Simplicissimus*.

HEINES, Eduard. SA officer killed in the Blood Purge of June 30, 1934.

HEINS, Valentin (1894–1971). Munich attorney retained by TM in 1933 to represent his interests vis-à-vis the Nazi regime.

HEISE, Carl Georg (1890–1979). Art historian, curator of the Lübeck municipal museum.

HEISTER, Baroness "Jane" von, née Mann. A Hamburg cousin of TM's.

HELBLING, Carl (1897–1966). Swiss literary historian.

HELD, Hans Ludwig (1885–1954). Munich librarian and writer.

HELD, Heinrich (1868–1938). Minister president of Bavaria, 1924–33; forced to resign by the Nazis in March 1933.

HELLER, Hermann (1891–1933). Sociologist and professor of constitutional law in Berlin and Frankfurt am Main.

HELLER, Hugo. Viennese bookseller, publisher, and lecture agent.

HELLER, Rabbi James Gutheim (1892–1971). American composer and musicologist.

HELLINGRATH, Baron Philipp von (1862–1939). Bavarian war minister, 1916–18.

HELLMERT, Wolfgang (1906–1934). Poet and writer; close friend of Klaus Mann's.

HELLMUND, Dr. Heinrich (1897–1937). German philosopher and writer.

HELLPACH, Willy (1877–1955). Heidelberg professor of psychology; executive in the German Democratic party.

HEMMER, Colonel von. Staff officer under Count Felix von Bothmer in the First World War; otherwise unidentified.

HENDERSON, Sir Nevile (1882–1942). British ambassador to Germany, 1937–39.

HENLEIN, Konrad (1898–1945). Sudeten German pro-Nazi agitator, later Sudeten Gauleiter.

HENNEBERGER, Johann. Munich shoemaker.

HENNIG, Herr. Otherwise unidentified emigré from Dresden who did typing for TM in Küsnacht in 1934.

HERMANN, Georg (1871–1943). Berlin novelist.

HERMANN, Lucian. Otherwise unidentified author.

HERMANNS, Dr. Leo. Munich physician.

HERMS, Frau. The Herms family lived near the Manns in Herzogpark, and the children Christine and Klaus Herms were schoolmates of the Mann children. Frau Herms was a daughter of the poet Paul Heyse.

HERRIOT, Édouard (1872–1957). French statesman. Leader of the Radical Socialist party; premier, 1924–25 and 1932.

HERRMANN, Eva (b. 1901). Artist, close friend of Erika and Klaus Mann's.

HERRMANN, Dr. Helene. Berlin Germanist.

HERTLING, Count Georg von (1843–1919). German statesman. Chancellor, 1917–18.

HERTWIG, Oskar (1849–1922). German anatomist and biologist.

HERZ, Ida (b. 1894). A bookseller in Nuremberg, Ida Herz became acquainted with TM in 1925, and was employed by him to put his Munich library in order. She became a passionate collector of every imaginable document and scrap of ephemera relating to TM, and in time he himself sent her countless clippings, periodical references, and manuscript copies, knowing that they would be best preserved in her collection. She managed to take this unique collection with her into exile in London, and later donated it, together with her extensive correspondence with TM, to the Thomas Mann Archive in Zurich.

HERZFELD-WÜSTHOFF, Dr. Günther (1893–1969). Book collector and antiquarian. Herzfeld was wounded as a young lieutenant in the First World War. He wrote to TM from his military hospital, and TM quoted from his letters in the *Betrachtungen*. He was named a godfather to Elisabeth Mann-Borgese.

HERZOG, Wilhelm (1884–1960). Writer, editor of the Munich pacifist journal *Das Forum* until the beginning of World War I, in which he strongly attacked TM for his chauvinism. Herzog was also a close friend of Heinrich Mann's, and by the end of the war TM felt nothing but loathing for him. Later however, after TM's political transformation and conversion to democracy, the two achieved a certain degree of friendly agreement, and during their years in exile they stood on good terms with each other.

HESSBERG, Dr. Richard. Ophthalmologist in Essen.

HESSE, Hermann (1877–1962). Writer and novelist, winner of the Nobel Prize in 1946. Though born in Swabia, Hesse's pacifist views rendered life in Germany impossible for him, and he settled in Switzerland in 1913, becoming a Swiss citizen in 1923. Hesse's novel *Demian. The Story of a Youth* was published by S. Fischer (under the pseudonym of Emil Sinclair) in 1919, and TM was highly appreciative of it. Henceforth the two writers maintained a relationship of mutual respect, corresponding regularly.

HESSE, Ninon (1895–1966). Third wife of Hermann Hesse.

HEUSER, Friedrich Wilhelm (1878–1961). Germanist at Columbia University, New York.

HEUSER, Klaus (b. 1910). Son of Prof. Werner Heuser, director of the art academy in Düsseldorf. TM met the seventeen-year-old Heuser while on holiday in Kampen on the island of Sylt in 1927, and developed a deep affection for him. He later invited the young man to visit him in Munich and devoted considerable time and attention to him, returning the visit himself in Düsseldorf.

HEYDEBRECK, Hans Peter von. SA squad leader murdered in the Blood Purge of June 30, 1934.

HEYKING, Elizabeth von (1861–1925). Popular German writer made famous by her successful novel *Briefe, die ihn nicht erreichten* (1903).

HICHENS, Robert (1864–1950). English popular writer.

HILDEBRANDT, Kurt (1881–1966). Psychiatrist and philosopher in Kiel.

HILLER, Kurt (1885–1972). Writer and political activist. Editor of the annual *Das Ziel*, 1916–24; emigrated in 1933 to Prague, in 1938 to London.

HINDENBURG, Paul von (1847–1934). German general and statesman. Named field marshal, 1914; elected second president of the Republic, 1925; forced to yield to Nazi power by appointing Hitler as chancellor, 1933.

HINTZE, Paul von (1864–1941). German naval officer and diplomat. Foreign secretary, 1918.

HIRSCH, Dr. Otherwise unidentified Munich visitor in Basel.

HIRSCHFELD, Georg (1873–1942). German novelist and playwright.

HIRSCHFELD, Kurt (1902–1964). Theatrical producer and director. Emigrated to Switzerland in 1933 and was long associated with the Zurich Schauspielhaus, becoming its director in 1961.

HIRZEL, Max (1888–1957). Celebrated heldentenor at the Zurich Opera.

HOCH, Frau. Unidentified guest in Munich.

HODLER, Ferdinand (1853–1918). Swiss painter.

HODŽA, Milan (1878–1944). Czech statesman. Prime minister, 1935–38.

HÖLDERLIN, Friedrich (1770–1843). German poet.

HÖNN, Richard. Munich bookbinder.

HOERSCHELMANN, Rolf von (1885–1947). Munich painter and draftsman.

HOFFMANN. Unidentified boyhood friend of Klaus Mann's.

HOFFMANN-KRAYER, Eduard (1864–?). Germanist and folklorist in Basel.

HOFFMANN, Elisabeth (b. 1891). Daughter of Arthur Hoffmann, delegate to the Swiss federal council from St. Gall, and wife (m. 1925) of Felix Berber.

HOFFMANN, Johannes (1867–1930). Social Democratic politician, Bavarian minister of culture in the Eisner government, member of the Central Council in the Bavarian Soviet Republic.

HOFFMANN, General Max. Head of the general staff of the German Eighth Army in the East, 1914.

HOFMANN, Ludwig von (1861–1945). Munich art nouveau painter. TM bought his painting *The Spring* in early 1914.

HOFMANNSTHAL, Christiane von (b. 1902). Daughter of Hugo von Hofmannsthal; married the Indologist Heinrich Zimmer (1890–1943).

HOFMANNSTHAL, Gerty von (1880–1960). Wife of Hugo von Hofmannsthal.

HOFMANNSTHAL, Hugo von (1874–1929). Austrian poet, playwright, and librettist.

HOFMILLER, Josef (1872–1933). Munich essayist and literary critic. Co-editor of the *Süddeutsche Monatshefte* from 1904, contributor to the *Münchner Neueste Nachrichten* from 1919.

HOLLNSTEINER, Johannes (b. 1895). Professor of ecclesiastical law in Vienna.

HOLM, Korfiz (1872–1942). School friend of TM's in Lübeck; born in Riga. Director of the Albert Langen-Verlag, Munich.

HOLZNER, Hans. For many years the Manns' trusted chauffeur in Munich; ultimately discovered to be an informer to the Brown House and the Munich Party police.

HONSELL. Munich barber.

HOROWITZ, Vladimir (b. 1904). Virtuoso pianist, son-in-law of Arturo Toscanini.

HOROWITZ, Wanda, née Toscanini. Wife of the pianist.

HORVÁTH, Ödön von (1901–1938). Dramatist and novelist. Emigrated to Vienna in 1934, and in 1938 via Czechoslovakia, Yugoslavia, Italy, and Switzerland to Holland. Died as the result of an accident while on a brief visit to Paris. *A Child of Our Time* was published posthumously with a foreword by Franz Werfel and memorial by Carl Zuckmayer.

HORWITZ, Fritz. Director of a Munich booking agency who arranged for numerous public readings by TM.

HOTTINGER-MACKIE, Mary (1893–1978). Writer, translator, and editor; lecturer in English literature at the University of Zurich. She translated several of TM's speeches into English and helped him prepare for them by coaching him in English pronunciation.

HUCH, Ricarda (1864–1947). German poet, writer, and literary historian.

HÜLSEN, Hans von (1890–1968). Prolific German novelist, became acquainted with TM in 1908.

HUIZINGA, Johan (1872–1945). Dutch historian.

HULL, Cordell (1871–1955). American statesman. Secretary of state, 1933–44.

HUS, Jan (1369?–1415). Bohemian religious reformer.

HUTCHINSON, Bill. Unidentified acquaintance of the Manns' in Switzerland.

HUTCHINSON, Ray Coryton (b. 1907). English writer.

HUXLEY, Aldous (1894–1963). English novelist and essayist.

HUXLEY, Maria. Wife of Aldous Huxley.

I

ILGENSTEIN, Dr. Otherwise unidentified Swiss attorney.

IMPEKOVEN, Niddy (b. 1904). German dancer; emigrated in 1933 to Switzerland.

ISELIN, Hans (1878–1953). Surgeon and professor in Basel.

ISSERMAN, Rabbi Ferdinand Myron (1898–1972). Chief rabbi of Temple Israel, St. Louis.

IVOGÜN, Maria (b. 1891). Soprano at the Munich Opera.

J

JACOB, Berthold (1898–1944). Berlin commentator; editor and military-political contributor to *Die Weltbühne* under Carl von Ossietzky. Emigrated to Strasbourg in 1934, where he published the bilingual *Unäbhangiger Zeitungsdienst*.

JACOBSOHN, Siegfried (1881–1926). Berlin critic and publicist, editor of *Die Weltbühne*. Jacobsohn owned a vacation house on the island of Sylt.

JACOBSON, Leopold (1878–1949). Viennese librettist.

JACQUES, Norbert (1880–1954). German writer and travel journalist.

JAEGER, Hans Henrik (1854–1910). Norwegian novelist.

JAFFÉ, Prof. Edgar (1866–1921). Munich economist. Bavarian minister of finance under Eisner and Segitz. Married to Elsa von Richthofen, sister of D. H. Lawrence's wife, Frieda.

JAFFE, Heinrich (1862–1922). Bookseller in Munich.

JAHNN, Hans Henny (1894–1959). German writer, dramatist, and organ builder.

JAMMES, Francis (1868–1938). French poet and essayist.

JEAN PAUL (pseudonym of Jean Paul Friedrich Richter, 1763–1825). German writer and novelist.

JEREMIAS, Alfred (1864–1935). Assyriologist and religion scholar in Leipzig.

JESSEN, Dr. Friedrich (1868–1935). Director and chief physician of the Waldsanatorium in Davos, where Katia Mann was treated for a lung ailment for six months in 1912. TM's visit with her there in May and June of that year provided him with the germ of his novel *The Magic Mountain*. Dr. Jessen appears in the novel as Hofrat Behrens.

JOACHIM-DANIEL, Anita (b. 1902). Popular German writer.

JOËL, Hedwig. Sister of Karl Joël.

JOËL, Karl (1864–1934). Professor of philosophy in Basel.

JOHNSON, Alvin (1873–1971). American economist. Editor of the *New Republic*, 1917–23; director of the New School for Social Research in New York, 1922–46. Johnson worked tirelessly to aid the exiled intellectuals of Germany.

JOHNSON, General Hugh (1882–1942). American attorney and commentator. Head of the American National Recovery Administration, 1933–34.

JOHST, Hanns (b. 1890). Expressionist dramatist and writer. Became an SS brigade leader and served as president of the Reich Literature Chamber, 1935–45.

JOLLOS, Waldemar (1886–1953). Swiss writer, husband of Lavinia Mazzucchetti.

JORDAN, Henry. Czech journalist.

JÓZSEF, Attila (1905–1937). Hungarian lyric poet. Committed suicide on December 3.

JUNGER, Ernst (b. 1895). German novelist and writer noted for his posture of "heroic nihilism."

JUNG, C. G. (1875–1961). Swiss psychologist and psychiatrist.

JUNG, Edgar J. (1894–1934). German nationalist essayist.

H, I, J,
K

K

KAFKA, Franz (1883–1924). Austrian writer and novelist. Though it is clear that TM had not heard of Kafka before 1921, the Prague writer had already published five volumes of novellas and sketches and had received the Fontane Prize in Berlin for the first two of these collections. To be sure his major novels, upon which his posthumous fame was based, were at that time still unknown.

KAHLER, Erich von (1885–1970). Sociologist and cultural historian. Though Kahler and TM became acquainted in Munich, it was not until their years as neighbors in Princeton that they became devoted friends. Kahler emigrated to Switzerland in 1933 and settled in Princeton in 1938. He wrote a number of essays on TM, including *The Orbit of Thomas Mann* (1969). The correspondence between the two writers was published in English in 1975 under the title *An Exceptional Friendship.*

KAHR, Dr. Gustav Ritter von (1862–1934). Bavarian statesman. President of Upper Bavaria, 1917–24; appointed general commissioner of state in 1923 and given executive power. Participated in, but then suppressed Hitler's Beer Hall Putsch in 1924. Murdered by the Nazis during the Blood Purge of June 30, 1934.

KAISER, Georg (1878–1945). German Expressionist playwright.

KALCKREUTH, Count Leopold von (1855–1928). German Impressionist painter.

KAPP, Wolfgang (1858–1922). German government official who organized the Monarchist putsch in 1920 and declared himself chancellor. After the failure of his revolt Kapp fled to Sweden. He returned to Germany in 1922 and died while awaiting trial for treason.

KARDORFF, Siegfried von (1873–1945). Peoples' party deputy to the Reichstag, 1920–33.

KARL I of Austria (1887–1922). Last emperor of Austria, 1916–18; abdicated in 1918 and was formally deposed by the Austrian parliament in 1919.

KARL V (1500–1558). Holy Roman emperor.

KÁROLYI, Count Mihály (1875–1955). Hungarian statesman. President of the Hungarian People's Republic from November 1918 until overthrown by Communists in March 1919.

KARPATH, Ludwig (1866–1936). Influential music critic in Vienna.

KASSNER, Rudolf (1873–1959). Austrian philosopher of culture.

KATZENELLENBOGEN, Konrad, later Konrad Kellen (b. 1913). Friend of Klaus Mann's who had emigrated to Paris in 1933 and went on to the United States in 1936. Kellen served as TM's secretary from 1941 to 1943, when he was drafted into the U.S. Army.

KATZENSTEIN, Dr. Erich (1893–1961). Zurich neurologist.

KAUFMANN, Alfred (Freddy). A friend of Bruno Frank's and Wilhelm Speyer's from their school days. Kaufmann ran The Jockey, an artists' bar in Berlin, until 1933, when he emigrated to Shanghai.

KAUFMANN, Dr. Felix (1895–1949). Philosopher of law and professor, first in Vienna, after 1938 in New York.

KAUFMANN, Nico. Pianist in Zurich; son of Willi Kaufmann and close acquaintance of the younger Mann children's.

KAUFMANN, Dr. Willi (1887–1942). Physician, president of the Zurich theatrical society.

KAULA, Friedrich. Commercial advisor and arbitrator, neighbor of the Manns' in Munich.

KAULBACH, Friedrich August von (1850–1920). Munich genre and portrait painter.

KAYSER, Frau. Unidentified Chicago acquaintance.

407

KAYSER, Hans (1891–1964). German musicologist and historian. Emigrated to Switzerland in 1933.

KAYSER, Rudolf (1889–1964). German essayist and critic. Editor of the monthly *Die Neue Rundschau*, 1922–33; emigrated to Holland in 1933, to the United States in 1935.

KEILER. Unidentified.

KEILPFLUG. Unidentified guest in Switzerland.

KELLER, Gottfried (1819–1890). Swiss novelist.

KEMMERICH, Max (1876–1932). Art and cultural critic in Munich.

KERÉNYI, Karl (1897–1973). Hungarian classical philologist and religion scholar. Kerényi initiated a correspondence with TM in 1934 that continued until the novelist's death, providing him with many ideas regarding myth and religion that found their way into TM's creative work. The letters between the two men were published in English in 1975 as *Mythology and Humanism*.

KERNER, Justinus (1786–1862). German poet and physician.

KERR, Alfred (1867–1948). Berlin writer and theater critic. Emigrated to France.

KESSLER, Count Harry (1868–1937). Writer, bibliophile, and diplomat.

KESTEN, Hermann (b. 1900). Writer and editor, one of the founders of the "New Factuality" in German fiction. Kesten was an editor in the Kiepenheuer Verlag in Berlin until 1933, when with Walter Landauer, a former director of that firm, he founded the second-largest German emigré publishing house as part of the Allert de Lange Verlag in Amsterdam, and served as its literary advisor. He was a close acquaintance of Klaus Mann's and Fritz Landshoff's, and he and Landshoff worked amicably together while representing the competing publishing firms of De Lange and Querido, in which the greater part of German exile literature was henceforth at home. Kesten was interned in France in 1940. Upon his release he managed to get to New York, where he worked energetically toward the rescue of German emigré writers remaining in France.

KESTENBERG, Leo (1882–1962). Pianist, music advisor to the Prussian Ministry of Education, 1918–32. Emigrated to Prague in 1933, to Palestine in 1938.

KESTNER, Charlotte, née Buff (1753–1828). Friend of Goethe's in 1772 in Wetzlar, the original of Lotte in his *Sorrows of Young Werther*.

KEYNES, John Maynard (1883–1946). British economist.

KEYSERLING, Count Eduard (1855–1918). Writer of novels of life on the Baltic seacoast.

KEYSERLING, Countess Goedela (b. 1896). Wife of Count Hermann Keyserling, daughter of Prince Herbert von Bismarck-Schönhausen.

KEYSERLING, Count Hermann (1880–1946). German writer and social philosopher.

KEYSSNER, Gustav (1867–1928). Stuttgart editor and critic.

KIEFER, Wilhelm. Political journalist and writer. Living in Switzerland, Kiefer was possibly a Nazi agent, managing to dupe TM and others. He was evicted from Switzerland because of his National Socialist activities in 1945.

KIEL, Hanna. Art historian, collaborator of Bernard Berenson's.

KIEVE, Rudolf. Otherwise unidentified friend of Monika Mann's.

KILPPER, Son of Gustav Kilpper, a Stuttgart publisher and owner of the Deutsche Verlagsanstalt.

KING, Mrs. Unidentified fellow passenger on the R.M.S. *Volendam* in 1934.

KIRSTEN family. Otherwise unidentified Hamburg shipbuilders.

KLAUSENER, Erich (1894–1934). Leader of the "Catholic Action" and strong critic of Hitler's racial and religious politics. Murdered in the Blood Purge of June 30, 1934.

KLEIBER, Otto (1883–1969). Features editor for the *National-Zeitung*, Basel.

KLEIN, Woldemar (1892–1962). Berlin art publisher.

KLEINSGÜTL, Josepha. A maid in the Mann household from 1905 to 1919. It was finally discovered that she had stolen from the family in the most sophisticated manner for years, and she had to be dismissed in extreme enmity. During the ensuing court case she managed to lie her way out of the charges and emerge victorious. Klaus Mann relates the highly dramatic criminal tale in his autobiography, *Kind dieser Zeit*.

KLEIST, Heinrich von (1777–1811). German writer and dramatist.

KLEPPER, Otto (1888–1957). Attorney and banking authority, Prussian minister of finance. Escaped to France in 1933.

KLITSCH, Wilhelm (1882–1941). Viennese actor.

KLÖPFER, Frau. Presumably a Munich acquaintance of the Manns' visiting in Lugano.

KLOPSTOCK, Dr. Robert (1899–1972). Physician, scholar, and man of letters in Budapest. Emigrated to the United States.

KLOSE, Friedrich (1862–1942). Munich composer.

KNAPPERTSBUSCH, Hans (1888–1965). German conductor. Director of the Bavarian State Opera, 1922–35.

KNEUSSL, Lieutenant General Paul Ritter von. Commander in the military overthrow of the Bavarian Soviet Republic.

KNIGHT, Miss. Assistant to TM's American lecture agent, Harold Peat.

KNITTEL, John (1891–1970). Travel writer and author of adventure novels.

KNOCHE, Dr. Erich. Munich dentist.

KNOPF, Alfred A. (b. 1892). TM's American publisher.

KNOPF, Blanche (1894–1966). Wife of Alfred Knopf.

KNOPF, Edwin. Film producer with Metro-Goldwyn-Mayer in Hollywood, brother of Alfred Knopf.

KNUCHEL, Eduard Fritz (1891–1966). Features editor for the *Basler Nachrichten*.

KOCH. Proprietor of a Munich music shop.

KÖCKENBERGER, Dr. Munich's most "elegant" midwife, who always rode in a taxi when visiting her patients, a distinct oddity in those days. Dr. Köckenberger is presumably the model for Doctor Gnadenbusch in *Royal Highness*.

KÖHLER, Ludwig (1880–1956). Zurich professor of Biblical studies.

KÖLWEL, Gottfried (1889–1958). Munich writer, poet, and dramatist.

KÖNIGSBERGER, Lieutenant. Commander-in-chief of the Bavarian army in Munich for one week in November 1918.

KÖSTER, Kai (1911–1976). Student friend of Golo Mann's.

KOESTLER, Arthur (b. 1905). Journalist and writer, in Spain as a correspondent for the London *News Chronicle* during the Spanish Civil War. Imprisoned at the time of the fall of Malaga and after four months condemned to death, but released thanks to intervention by the British.

KOKOSCHKA, Oskar (1886–1980). Austrian painter, designer, and dramatist.

KOLA, Richard. Viennese financier and publisher.

KOLB, Annette (1870–1967). German novelist and essayist of French descent, a childhood friend of Katia Mann's. Annette Kolb introduced TM to the work of Marcel Proust in 1920, at a time when he was completely unknown in Germany. Always a champion of Franco-German understanding, Annette Kolb left Germany to live in her native Paris in 1933 out of disgust for the chauvinism and anti-Semitism of the Nazi regime. In 1941 she fled to the United States, returning to Europe in 1945.

KOLBENHEYER, Erwin Guido (1878–1962). German poet and novelist.

KOLTZOW, Michail Jefimovich (1898–1942). Russian publicist. Features editor of *Pravda*, 1922–38.

KOMMERELL, Max (1902–1944). German literary historian, poet, and essayist.

KOPPEL, Heinrich Günther. Founder and director of the Alliance Book Corporation, New York.

KORRODI, Eduard (1885–1955). Swiss literary critic, features editor from 1914 for the *Neue Zürcher Zeitung*. Korrodi was long an admirer of TM's and published countless articles about him. Their relationship was severely strained in 1936 (see note 1 for January 27, 1936) but the two effected a superficial reconciliation after the end of the Second World War.

KOSHLAND, William A. Managing editor at Alfred A. Knopf, publishers, New York.

KOUSSEVITSKY, Serge (1874–1951). Conductor of the Boston Symphony Orchestra, 1924–49.

KOŽAK, Jan B. (b. 1888). Philosophy professor in Prague. President of the Thomas Mann Society there, which was established in 1936 to aid needy emigré German writers.

KRAUS, Karl (1874–1936). Viennese writer, commentator, and critic; famous for his epic drama *The Last Days of Mankind* and his outspoken periodical, *Die Fackel.*

KRAUSE, Friedrich. Owner of the American distributing firm for Bermann-Fischer Verlag, Stockholm, and New York agent for Oprecht Verlag, Zurich.

KRECKE, Dr. Albert (1863–1932). Munich surgeon.

KREISLER, Fritz (1875–1962). Virtuoso violinist and composer.

KREITNER, Bruno. Otherwise unidentified Columbian correspondent of TM's.

KRELL, Max (1887–1962). Writer, critic, and editor active in the Munich Writers' League; later moved to Berlin.

KRÖGER, Nelly. See Mann, Nelly, née Kröger.

KROFTA, Kamill (1876–1945). Czech historian and professor in Prague. Foreign minister, 1936–38.

KUCKHOFF, Adam (1887–1943). Writer, theatrical producer and director in Frankfurt am Main.

KÜHN (or KUHN?), Mrs. TM's Cincinnati hostess has not been identified.

KUGEL, Georg. Director of a concert and lecture agency in Vienna.

KURZ, Marie. The Manns' housekeeper in Munich.

KUTSCHER, Artur (1878–1960). Literature and theater historian, professor in Munich.

KYSER, Hans (1882–1940). German writer and dramatist.

L
. . . .

LADENBURG, Rudolf Walter (1882–1952). Physicist. University friend of Katia Mann's and her brother Klaus Pringsheim's in Munich, and godfather of Golo Mann. Professor at Princeton University, 1931–52.

LAEMMLE, Carl (1876–1939). Founder of Universal Studios, Hollywood.

LAGERLÖF, Selma (1858–1940). Swedish novelist.

LA GUARDIA, Fiorello (1882–1947). American politician; mayor of New York, 1934–45.

LANDAUER, Gustav (1870–1919). Philosopher, literary historian, and Socialist politician. His theoretical *Aufruf zum Sozialismus* (1911) was extremely influential. He was arrested in Munich on May 1, 1919, and shot without trial.

LANDECKER, Peter. Owner of Philharmonic Hall and the adjacent Beethoven Hall in Berlin.

LANDSBERG, Paul-Ludwig (1901–1944). German emigré philosopher.

LANDSHOFF, Fritz H. (b. 1901). Publisher. Director of Kiepenheuer Verlag in Berlin until 1933, when he established the German division of the Querido Verlag in Amsterdam, which became the most important of the publishing houses available to German emigré writers. An admirer of TM's even in his youth, and a particularly close acquaintance of Erika and Klaus Mann's, Landshoff repeatedly tried to win over TM for the Querido Verlag. At the time of the German invasion of the Netherlands, which reduced the Querido establishment to rubble, Landshoff was by chance in London. From there he went to New York, where with Gottfried Bermann Fischer he founded the L. B. Fischer Verlag. After the war he returned to Holland to again head the German division of Querido until its merger with the newly-established S. Fischer concern. He is today a director in the New York publishing firm of Harry N. Abrams, Inc.

LANDSHOFF, Ludwig (1874–1941). Music historian and conductor in Munich; emigrated in 1933 to Italy, later to Paris and New York.

LANG, Joseph Burkard (1874–1941). Pharmacist in Davos.

LANGER, František (1888–1965). Czech physician, writer, and dramatist.

LANGHAMMER. Otherwise unidentified colleague of Ernst Bertram's.

LANGHOFF, Wolfgang (1901–1966). German actor. Arrested in 1933 and interned in a concentration camp, he nonetheless managed to get to Switzerland in 1934, where he wrote of his experiences and worked, until 1945, at the Zurich Schauspielhaus.

LÁNYI, Jenö (1902–1940). Hungarian art historian and Donatello scholar, husband of Monika Mann. Drowned when the ship on which he and his wife were sailing to the United States, the *City of Benares,* was torpedoed off the coast of England.

LAŠKA, Jan. Czech consul in Zurich.

LASSEN, Christian. Swedish consul in Hamburg in 1918.

LAUBRUCH. Unidentified. Perhaps a misreading of TM's handwriting.

LAVAL, Pierre (1883–1945). French politician. Minister of foreign affairs, 1934–36.

LAWRENCE, D. H. (1885–1930). English novelist.

LEISINGER, Dr. Hermann. Dentist in Küsnacht.

LENBACH, Franz von (1836–1904). German portrait painter.

LEOPOLD, Prince of Bavaria (1846–1930). General and field marshal.

LEPPMANN, Franz (1877–1948). Berlin literary scholar and critic, author of one of the earliest monographs on TM.

LESKOV, Nikolai Semyonovich (1831–1895). Russian novelist.

LESSER, Jonas (1896–1968). Austrian philologist and writer.

LESSING, Gotthold Ephraim (1729–1781). German dramatist and critic.

LESSING, Theodor (1872–1933). German physician and cultural philosopher. Fled from the Nazi regime and was murdered in Marienbad. TM was engaged in a bitter controversy with Lessing in 1910 over the latter's attack on the critic Samuel Lublinski, who had called TM "the most important modern novelist."

LEVIEN, Max (b. 1885). Student and pretended Ph.D. born in Moscow, Levien worked as a Communist agitator in postwar Munich. Co-founder in 1919 of the Spartakist League and the German Communist party in Munich.

LEVINÉ, Eugen (1883–1919). Communist party leader in Munich. Editor of the *Münchner Rote Fahne* and chairman of the Central Council of the Soviet Republic from April 13 to 27, 1919. Accused of high treason and shot on June 5.

LEVY, Oskar Ludwig (1867–1946). Nietzsche scholar and friend of Heinrich Mann's.

LEWALD, Theodor (1860–1947). President of the German Olympic committee, 1936.

LEWANDOWSKI, Herbert. Dutch lecture agent.

LEWIS, Sinclair (1885–1951). Nobel Prize–winning American novelist.

LEWISOHN, Ludwig (1882–1955). American writer and translator, one of the first American admirers of TM.

LEYEN, Friedrich von der (1873–1966). Germanist in Munich, later in Cologne.

LIEBERMANN, Max (1847–1935). German Impressionist painter.

LIEBKNECHT, Karl (1871–1919). German Social Democratic politician. Leftist Reichstag deputy sentenced to a prison term for his opposition to the First World War. After being pardoned in 1918 Liebknecht joined Rosa Luxemburg at the head of the Spartakist League, proclaiming the "Free Socialist Republic" on November 9, 1918, and organizing the Spartakist uprising in Berlin in January 1919. Arrested and murdered while being transferred to prison.

LIEFMANN, Dr. Emil (1878–1955). Frankfurt physician, lover of art and literature, host to TM on various of his lecture tours. Emigrated to New York in 1939.

LILLIE, Beatrice (b. 1898). English music hall actress and comedienne.

LIND, Frau. Zurich typist who transcribed the manuscript of *Joseph in Egypt.*

LINDPAINTNER, Otto. Stepson of the painter Franz von Stuck.

LINK, Frau. Former singer and devoted admirer of Bruno Walter's in Munich.

LION, Ferdinand (1883–1965). German-speaking Alsatian essayist and critic. Served as first editor of the bi-monthly *Mass und Wert,* published in Zurich by TM and Konrad Falke.

LIPMANN, Heinz (1897–1932). Berlin theater historian.

LIPPSCHÜTZ, Herr. Unidentified fellow passenger on the *Nieuw Amsterdam* in 1938.

LIPTZIN, Sol. American literary historian.

LIST, Emanuel (1888–1967). Austrian bass at the Berlin Staatsoper, later the Metropolitan in New York.

LITZMANN, Berthold (1857–1926). Professor of literature in Bonn.

LITZMANN, Grete. Second wife of Berthold Litzmann and ardent admirer of TM's.

LLOYD GEORGE, David (1863–1945). British statesman. Prime minister, 1916–22.

LOEB, Dr. Albert (d. 1919). Munich internist, the original of the Jewish physician Dr. Sammet in TM's *Royal Highness*.

LÖHR, Eva-Marie. Oldest daughter of Julia Mann Löhr.

LÖHR, Josef ("Jof") (1862–1922). Munich banker, husband of TM's sister Julia Mann.

LÖHR, Julia ("Lula") Mann (1877–1927). The older of TM's two sisters, wife of Josef Löhr and mother of three daughters. The Löhr marriage was precarious, and several years after the death of her husband the melancholy woman took her own life. TM depicted her in the figure of Ines Institoris in his novel *Doctor Faustus*.

LÖWE. Presumably the Austrian conductor Ferdinand Löwe (1865–1925).

LÖWENFELD, Philipp (1887–1963). Munich defense counsel; emigrated to Zurich in 1933, to the United States in 1938.

LÖWENSTEIN, Prince Hubertus zu (b. 1906). Emigré political publicist. Founder of the American Guild for German Cultural Freedom.

LÖWENSTEIN, Karl (1891–1973). Munich attorney, later Yale professor of constitutional law.

LÖWY, Siegfried (1857–1931). Viennese writer and journalist, specialist in theater history and contributor to all the major Viennese journals. Secretary and organizational director of the Concordia Club.

LONG, John and Lucy. Black American couple first encountered in the service of Caroline Newton in Rhode Island. The Manns later employed them as chauffeur and cook in Princeton.

LOWE, Elias. American paleographer, professor at Oxford from 1914 to 1937. Returned to America in 1937 to accept a chair at the Institute for Advanced Study in Princeton. Husband of Helen Lowe-Porter.

LOWE-PORTER, Helen (1877–1963). Translator into English of nearly all of TM's works between 1924 and 1951. Wife of Elias Lowe.

LUBBE, Marinus van der (1910–1934). Dutch brick mason condemned and executed in Leipzig for alleged implication in the Reichstag fire on February 27, 1933.

LUDWIG III of Bavaria (1845–1921). Last reigning king of the house of Wittelsbach, 1913–18; abdicated.

LUDWIG, Alois (1872–1969). Munich architect who with his brother Gustav designed TM's house in Herzogpark.

LUDWIG, Emil (1881–1948). German writer and biographer.

LUDWIG, Gustav (1876–1952). Munich architect, brother of Alois Ludwig.

LÜTTWITZ, Baron Walter von (1859–1942). German general, commander-in-chief of the German army in 1919. Resigned after participating in the unsuccessful Kapp Putsch of 1920.

LUKÁCS, Georg (1885–1971). Hungarian writer and Marxist literary critic. Lukács lived in exile in Vienna during the 1920s, and it was there that TM became acquainted with him in 1922. From their single documented conversation at that time TM derived features and details which he then utilized in the creation of the figure of Naphta in *The Magic Mountain*. Lukács lived in Moscow from 1929 to 1945, when he returned to become a professor of philosophy in Budapest. He published numerous studies on TM.

LUXEMBURG, Rosa (1870–1919). German Socialist agitator. Leader with Karl Liebknecht of the Spartakist League, and involved in its insurrection in 1919. Arrested and shot on January 15, 1919.

M

MACDONALD, James Ramsay (1866–1937). British statesman. Prime minister, 1924 and 1929–35.

MACK, Mr. and Mrs. Unidentified luncheon companions in Chicago.

MAENNER, Emil (b. 1893). People's agent for finance in the Bavarian Soviet Republic, 1919.

MAGG, Alfons. Swiss sculptor.

MAHLER-WERFEL, Alma (1877–1964). Widow of Gustav Mahler, wife of Franz Werfel.

MAHLER, Gustav (1860–1911). Austrian composer.

MAHRHOLZ, Werner (1880–1930). Munich literary historian and critic, later editor of the *Vossische Zeitung* in Berlin.

MAIER. Unidentified conductor, guest in Princeton.

MAJER, Herr. Unidentified visitor of Dr. Loeb's in Munich.

MANN-BORGESE, Elisabeth Veronika ("Lisa," "Medi") (b. 1918). TM's third and youngest daughter. Married the Italian-American literary historian Giuseppe Antonio Borgese in 1939, at which time he was a professor at the University of Chicago. They had two daughters, and in 1950 returned to Italy. Mrs. Borgese taught for many years at the Center for the Study of Democratic Institutions in California and currently lives in Halifax, Nova Scotia, where she is a professor of political science at Dalhousie University. Her specialty is the law of the sea; she serves as a member of the Austrian delegation to the International Law of the Sea Conference, and herself founded and serves as chairman of the International Ocean Institute. A writer, in English, her works include: *To Whom it May Concern*, a collection of novellas (1960); the sociological study *Ascent of Woman* (1963); *The Drama of the Oceans* (1975); and *Seafarm* (1980).

MANN-AUDEN, Erika Julia Hedwig (1905–1969). TM's oldest daughter; originally an actress, later journalist and commentator in the fields of culture and politics. From 1925 to 1928 she was married to the actor Gustaf Gründgens, and in 1935 she married the poet W. H. Auden. During the last decade of her father's life she became his constant companion on his lecture tours and a trusted assistant in his work. She later administered his literary remains, editing a three-volume selection of his letters (1961–65). Her books include: *School for Barbarians* (1938); *The Lights Go Down* (1940): *The Last Year of Thomas Mann* (1958); in addition to seven children's books and the texts for her cabaret *The Peppermill*. In collaboration with her brother Klaus she also published *Escape to Life* (1939) and *The Other Germany* (1940).

MANN, Golo (Angelus Gottfried Thomas) (b. 1909). TM's second son. Received his doctorate in philosophy and history under Karl Jaspers in Heidelberg in 1932. He left Germany in the early summer of 1933, taught in St. Cloud and Rennes in France, and later served as co-editor of the periodical *Mass und Wert*, published by TM in Zurich. In May 1940 he left Switzerland to do volunteer work in France, was interned there, but managed to escape and reach the United States in the late autumn of that year. There he taught at Olivet College in Michigan and Claremont College in California. From 1960 to 1964 he was a professor of political science at the Technische Hochschule in Stuttgart. Since then he has lived in Kilchberg, near Zurich, as a free-lance writer. He is the editor of the new *Propyläen Weltgeschichte* and co-editor since 1963 of *Die Neue Rundschau*. His works include: *Friedrich von Gentz. Geschichte eines europäischen Staatsmannes* (1947); *Vom Geist Amerikas. Eine Einführung in amerikanisches Denken und Handeln im zwanzigsten Jahrhundert* (1954); the essay volumes *Geschichte und Geschichten* (1961) and *Zwölf Versuche* (1973); and the biography *Wallenstein* (1971).

MANN, Gret, née Moser (b. 1916). School friend of Elisabeth Mann-Borgese's in Zurich; married Michael Mann in 1939.

MANN, Luiz Heinrich (1871–1950). TM's older brother Heinrich was one of the most important German novelists and essayists of the first half of the century, famous for his novels *Die Göttinnen, The Little Town, The Blue Angel,* and *The Patrioteer.* A long-standing strain in the relationship between the two brothers widened until they found themselves, at the outbreak of the First World War, representing bitter differences of opinion in philosophy and politics. After Heinrich published an essay on Zola that TM interpreted as an attack on himself, and to which his protracted *Betrachtungen* were written as a response, a complete breach was accomplished. The two neither saw nor spoke to each other for the entire duration of the war, and TM was sensitive to even the mention of his brother's name—especially inasmuch as Heinrich, a long-time opponent of the Reich, Francophile republican and pacifist, came to enjoy considerable success and recognition once the war was over. Only when Heinrich lay critically ill in January 1922 was there a first attempt at a reconciliation; a complete resumption of ties had to wait until after 1933. From 1931 to 1933 Heinrich Mann served as president of the literary section of the Prussian Academy of Arts. He was dismissed from that office as soon as Hitler came to power, and he fled to France, where he lived until proceeding to the United States in 1940. His last years were spent in California. He was planning a return to Germany at the time of his death.

MANN, Julia, née da Silva-Bruhns (1851–1923). TM's mother. Born in Brazil, but raised in Lübeck, Julia married the prominent merchant and city consul Thomas Johann Heinrich Mann in 1869. They had five children: Heinrich, Thomas, Julia, Carla, and Viktor. After her husband's death the Frau Senator moved to Munich, and once the children were out on their own she lived in a succession of spots in the Munich environs. Her last years were spent in Polling in Upper Bavaria, where TM frequently visited her.

MANN, Katia (Katharina), née Pringsheim (1883–1980). TM's wife. Katia Pringsheim was the only daughter—there were four sons—of Professor Alfred Pringsheim and his wife, Hedwig, née Dohm. Their home in Munich was an affluent center of the city's artistic and cultural life, and the spirited and attractive Katia was pursuing university studies (under the noted physicist Roentgen, among others)—a highly irregular course for a young woman at the time—when TM persuaded her to marry him in 1905. Henceforth she devoted herself wholly to her husband and his career, bearing him six children, administering his household and business affairs, and assisting with his voluminous correspondence. A brief book of her reminiscences, *Unwritten Memories,* was published in 1975.

MANN, Klaus Heinrich Thomas ("Eissi") (1906–1949). TM's oldest son. In the late twenties and early thirties Klaus Mann produced a rapid succession of plays (*Anja und Esther*), novellas (*Vor dem Leben*), and novels (*Der fromme Tanz, Alexander, Treffpunkt im Unendlichen*), as well as essays and autobiographical writings. By the time of the Nazi seizure of power he was already at twenty-six a well-known writer under constant attack from the political Right. He left Germany with his sister Erika in March 1933. In the autumn of that year, in Amsterdam, he began publishing the important German emigré literary journal *Die Sammlung.* His novel based on the career of Gustaf Gründgens, *Mephisto,* appeared in 1936. He later emigrated to the United States, as had all the rest of the family, and in New York he edited the magazine *Decision.* By war's end he was serving as an American soldier in Europe. In despair over what seemed to him the hopeless situation of the intellectual in postwar Europe, he committed suicide in Cannes in 1949. His autobiography *The Turning Point* is a valuable and fascinating document of the times.

MANN, (Henriette Marie) Leonie ("Goschi") (b. 1916). Heinrich Mann's daughter from his first marriage, and his only child. Lived with her mother, Maria ("Mimi") Kanova, in Prague.

MANN, Magdalena ("Nelly"), née Kilian (1895–1962). Wife of Viktor Mann.

MANN, Maria ("Mimi"), née Kanova (1886–1946). First wife of Heinrich Mann, born in Prague, originally an actress. Returned to Prague after her separation from Heinrich in 1930, and after Heinrich's flight from Germany in 1933 she managed to rescue, with the help of the Czech government, the manuscripts, letters, and books he had left behind. She lived with her daughter, Leonie, in very modest circumstances in Prague. During the Nazi period she spent five years in the concentration camp at Theresianstadt.

MANN, Michael Thomas ("Mischa," "Bibi") (1919–1977). TM's third son and youngest child. Michael was still a schoolboy in Munich when TM was forced into exile. He joined his school class on a trip to Rome over the Easter holidays in 1933, and his parents kept him in Switzerland on the way back. He studied at the Zurich Conservatory, becoming a violin and viola soloist who specialized in the modern repertoire. He concertized in America (with Yaltah Menuhin), the Far East, and Europe. However he gave up his musical career and chose to study German literature at Harvard University, where he wrote a dissertation on Heinrich Heine's music criticism and received his doctorate in 1961. He then became a professor of German literature at the University of California at Berkeley.

MANN-LÁNYI, Monika (b. 1910). TM's second daughter. Monika left Germany in 1933 with her brother Golo to join her parents in the south of France. She later lived in Florence, where she studied music. In 1939 she married the art historian Jenö Lányi in London. She survived the sinking by German torpedoes of the ship that was to bring her and her husband to the United States, though Lányi drowned before her eyes, and was then brought to her family in America by her sister Erika. She now lives on Capri. She is the author of several books, including an autobiography, *Vergangenes und Gegenwärtiges.*

MANN, Nelly, née Kröger (1898–1944). Second wife of Heinrich Mann, originally from Lübeck. Heinrich Mann had met Nelly Kröger in Berlin, but when he left Germany in 1933 she stayed behind. He soon sent for her, and they were married in Nice in 1939. She emigrated with him to America in 1940, where in 1944 she took her own life.

MANN, Thomas Johann Heinrich (1840–1891). TM's father, one-time consul and later senator in Lübeck, the last of the Manns to manage the prominent grain and shipping business built up by the family in that city.

MANN, Viktor ("Vicco") (1890–1949). TM's younger brother, originally an agronomist, but later engaged in banking. Like his brothers he lived in Munich, but he remained in Germany through the Hitler years. After the war he wrote a chronicle of the family—not altogether reliable in its details—which was published posthumously as *Wir waren fünf. Bildnis der Familie Mann.*

MANNHEIMER, Dr. Viktor. Private scholar in Munich.

MARCHESANI, Lisa. A German woman, married to an Italian, long a resident of Sanary. Since she was addicted to morphine, the Manns often referred to her as "Frau Morphesani." Mother of the English writer Sybille Bedford.

MARCK, Siegfried (1889–1957). Professor of philosophy in Breslau, after 1933 in Dijon. Later in the United States.

MARCKS, Erich (1861–1938). Historian and professor in Munich, neighbor and close friend of the Manns' in Herzogpark.

MARCKS, Erich Jr. (1891–1944). Career army officer, division commander on the Eastern front and finally commanding general on the Channel coast.

MARCKS, Friederike. Wife of the historian Erich Marcks.

MARCKS, Gerta. Daughter of Erich and Friederike Marcks.

MARCKS, Otto (b. 1905). Son of Erich Marcks and childhood friend of Klaus Mann's.

MARGOLIES. Unidentified violinist.

MARIL, Dr. Konrad (b. 1889). Director of the drama division at S. Fischer Verlag.

MARILAUN, Karl. Viennese writer.

MARTENS, Armin (b. 1876). School friend of TM's at the Katharineum in Lübeck, last traced to Africa. Martens was TM's first love, and served as the model for Hans Hansen in TM's novella *Tonio Kröger.*

MARTENS, Kurt (1870–1945). Munich writer, features editor for the *Münchner Neueste Nachrichten.* TM first met Martens in 1899, and he became one of his closest friends during his early years in Munich. The friendship cooled during the 1920s, and later Martens moved to Dresden, where he took his own life shortly after the Allied bombing of that city.

MARTIN. Unidentified French economic advisor in Mainz.

MASARYK, Jan (1886–1948). Son of Tomáš Masaryk. Czech ambassador in London, 1925–39; close associate of Eduard Beneš in the Czech government in exile.

MASARYK, Tomáš Garrigue (1850–1937). Czechoslovak statesman and philosopher; first president of Czechoslovakia, 1918–35.

MASSARY, Fritzi (1882–1969). Operetta diva, mother of Liesl Frank.

MATUSCHKA, Count. Unidentified Moravian nobleman.

MAUPASSANT, Guy de (1850–1893). French novelist and short-story writer.

MAURACH, Johannes. Theater director in Essen. Later in Strasbourg, Freiburg, and Dortmund.

MAURY, Geneviève. Essayist and French translator of *Tonio Kröger* and other novellas of TM's.

MAX, Prince of Baden (1867–1929). Last chancellor under Wilhelm II. It was he who proposed abdication to the Kaiser and announced the step on November 9, 1918, when he surrendered the government to the Social Democrat Friedrich Ebert.

MAYNC, Harry (1874–1947). Critic and professor of literature in Bern, later in Marburg.

MAYRISCH DE SAINT-HUBERT, Aline. Widow of the Luxembourg steel magnate Emile Mayrisch. Mme. Mayrisch contributed generously to the financing of TM's journal *Mass und Wert.*

MAZZUCCHETTI, Lavinia (1889–1963). Italian Germanist, translator of many of TM's works into Italian.

MEDICUS, Fritz (1876–1956). Professor of philosophy in Zurich.

MEIER-GRAEFE, Anne Marie. Wife of Julius Meier-Graefe; later married Hermann Broch.

MEIER-GRAEFE, Julius (1867–1935). Art historian, proponent of the Impressionists and rediscoverer of El Greco.

MEIER, Oskar (1876–1961). German secretary of the interior. Emigrated in 1933 to Zurich; later at the University of California.

MEISEL, Hans (James) (b. 1900). German novelist, winner of the Kleist Prize in 1927. Emigrated to Italy in 1934, went on to Austria in 1936, and to the United States in 1938. Translated Sinclair Lewis's *It Can't Happen Here* into German for Querido Verlag. Worked as TM's secretary in Princeton, handling above all the tremendous correspondence with other emigrés who sought aid and advice from TM.

MEISSINGER, Karl August (1883–1950). German literary historian.

MELBA, Nellie (1861–1931). Australian soprano.

MENCKEN, H. L. (1880–1956). American critic and cultural philosopher.

MENDEL, Alfred O. Editor-in-chief at Longmans Green & Co., publishers, New York.

MENDELSSOHN-BARTOLDY, Albrecht (1874–1936). Professor of international law in Würzburg, Hamburg, and (from 1933) at Oxford University.

MENDELSSOHN, Felix Manuel. Berlin journalist (see note 1 for May 8, 1933).

MENDELSSOHN, Gerda von. Widow of the writer Erich von Mendelssohn (1887–1913.)

MENG, Dr. Heinrich (1887–1972). Psychoanalyst in Basel.

MENUHIN, Yehudi (b. 1916). Violinist.

MEREDITH, George (1828–1909). English novelist.

MEREZHKOVSKI, Dmitri (1865–1941). Russian essayist, novelist, and biographer.

MÉRIMÉE, Prosper (1803–1870). French man of letters.

MERREM-NIKISCH, Grete. Opera singer, wife of Arthur Philipp Nikisch.

MERZ, Pastor Georg (1892–1959). Munich clergyman and professor of religion.

MESSERSMITH, George S. (1883–1960). American diplomat. Assistant secretary of state, 1937–40.

MEYER, Agnes E. (1887–1970). American essayist, wife of Eugene Meyer. Mrs. Meyer was born in the United States of German emigré parents and studied at the Sorbonne in Paris, where she was acquainted with Rodin and Claudel. Active in politics and social causes, she was a frequent contributor to the *Washington Post,* the *New York Times Book Review, Atlantic Monthly,* and other journals. She came to know TM during his American sojourn in early 1937 and became very attached to him, making use of her connections to help secure his appointment to Princeton in 1938. Fluent in spoken and written German, she translated his

essay *The Coming Victory of Democracy* and the foreword, "Standards and Values," to the
first issue of *Mass und Wert.*

MEYER, Camilla Elisabeth (1879–1936). Daughter of Conrad Ferdinand Meyer.

MEYER, Conrad Ferdinand (1825–1898). Swiss poet and historical novelist.

MEYER, Elizabeth. Daughter of Agnes E. Meyer.

MEYER, Eugene (1875–1959). American financier, philanthropist, and owner and publisher of the *Washington Post.*

MEYER, Georg Heinrich (1869–1931). Director of the Kurt Wolff-Verlag from 1914.

MEYER, Lieutenant. Unidentified Berlin admirer of TM's.

DE MEYIER, Fenna. General secretary of the Dutch PEN Club, 1934–39.

MHE, Herbert. Hamburg sculptor.

MICHALSKI, Heinrich. Leftist writer and propagandist in Munich.

MILSTEIN, Nathan (b. 1904). American violin virtuoso, born in Odessa.

MITFORD, Rupert and Flora. Owners of the house in Princeton that the Manns rented in 1938.

MÖHL, Lieutenant General Arnold von (1867–1944). Bavarian army commander.

MOELLENDORF, Wilhelm von (1887–1944). Professor of medicine in Zurich.

MOHR, Johann. Presumably a friend of the Hatvanys in Budapest.

MOHR, Max (1891–1944). German physician and successful writer and dramatist. Emigrated to China in 1934.

MOISSI, Alexander (1880–1935). Austrian actor noted for his performances in Max Reinhardt productions in Berlin.

MOLOTOV, Vyacheslav Mikhailovich (b. 1890). Russian statesman, commissar of foreign affairs from 1939.

MOMBERT, Alfred (1872–1942). German poet and philosopher. Though ostracized as a Jew, Mombert did not want to leave Germany. He was placed in a concentration camp in France until, deathly ill, he was taken by friends to Switzerland, where he died.

MONTERNACH. Unidentified. Presumably an official of the League of Nations.

MONTGOMERY, Robert (b. 1904). American film actor.

MORAZZI, Mr. Unidentified fellow passenger on the R.M.S. *Volendam* in 1934.

MORGEN, Ruth von. Unidentified fellow houseguest in Switzerland.

MORGENSTERN, Christian (1871–1914). German poet and translator.

MÓRICZ, Zsigmond (1879–1942). Hungarian novelist and dramatist.

MORITZ, Karl Philipp (1756–1793). German novelist and thinker, friend of Goethe's.

MOSER, Gret. *See* Mann, Gret, née Moser.

MOTTA, Giuseppe (1871–1940). Swiss statesman. President in 1915, 1920, 1927, 1932, and 1937.

MOY, Count Max von. Army colonel, adjutant to the Bavarian court.

MUCKLE, Friedrich (b. 1883). German private scholar living in Basel.

MÜHLL, Hans von der. Architect in Basel.

MÜHLL, Theodora von der. Wife of Hans von der Mühll and sister of Carl Jacob Burckhardt.

MÜHSAM, Erich (1878–1934). Leftist Socialist, anarchist politician, and writer. As a member of the Revolutionary Workers' Council he helped to establish the Bavarian Soviet Republic in 1919; was sentenced to fifteen years' imprisonment but pardoned in 1924. Murdered by the Nazis in the concentration camp Oranienburg.

MÜHSAM, Kreszentia (d. 1962). Widow of Erich Mühsam.

MÜLLER, Dr. Adolph. German ambassador to Switzerland.

MÜLLER-HOFMANN, Wilhelm (1885–1948). Viennese painter, close friend of Hugo von Hofmannsthal's.

MÜLLER, Dr. Friedrich von (1858–1941). Munich internist.

MÜLLER, Hans (1882–1950). German playwright.

MÜLLER, Karl Eugen (1876–1951). Journalist and political commentator. Editor-in-chief of the *Münchner Neueste Nachrichten*, 1917–20; later lead political writer for the *Berliner Tageblatt.*

MUMMENHOFF family. Unidentified hosts of TM's in Bochum.

MUNCKER, Franz (1855–1926). Literary historian and professor in Munich.

MURET, Maurice. French essayist and literary critic, author of more than twenty articles and reviews on TM.

MURRAY, Gilbert (1866–1957). English classicist and translator. Fellow member of the Comité permanent des Lettres et des Arts; extremely helpful to German emigré intellectuals.

MUSCHG, Walter (1898–1965). Swiss literary historian, poet, and dramatist.

MUSIL, Robert (1880–1942). Austrian novelist and essayist.

MUTO, Anthony. Chairman of the association of White House press photographers in Washington.

N

NADOLECZNY, Dr. Max. Munich ear, nose, and throat specialist.

NÄF, Hans. Zurich dental technician accused of murdering his wife and perpetrating insurance fraud.

NÄGEL, Mr. Manager of the Algonquin Hotel, later of the Bedford Hotel, New York.

NATONEK, Hans (1892–1963). German writer. Features editor until 1933 of the *Neue Leipziger Zeitung;* prolific contributor to various German-language papers in Prague and the important emigré journals.

NAUMANN, Hans (1886–1951). Historian and Germanist, professor in Jena, Frankfurt am Main, and Bonn.

NEUMANN, Alfred (1895–1952). Writer and dramatist. Neighbor and friend of TM's in Herzog-park in Munich. During their exile years Neumann and his wife were again neighbors of the Manns' in California, and were among their most intimate friends.

NEUMANN, Johann Martin Andreas (1865–1928). Mayor of Lübeck.

NEURATH, Baron Konstantin von (1873–1956). German diplomat. Minister of foreign affairs, 1932–38; appointed Reich Protector for Bohemia and Moravia, 1939; sentenced to fifteen years' imprisonment in Nuremberg and released in 1954.

NEWTON, Caroline (1883–1975). American psychoanalyst. An early admirer of TM's, whom she first met in 1929. Miss Newton owned a large collection of early signed first editions, letters, manuscripts, and photographs of TM, most of which are now in the Firestone Library at Princeton. A quite wealthy woman, she was able to place her summer home in Rhode Island at the Manns' disposal in 1938, and provided much assistance toward getting them settled in the United States.

NICOLSON, Harold (1886–1968). British diplomat, politician, writer, and commentator.

NIDERLECHNER, Max. Bookseller in Frankfurt.

NIEBUHR, Reinhold (1892–1971). American Protestant theologian, professor at Union Theological Seminary, New York.

NIEDERMANN, Max (1874–1954). Classical philologist and comparative linguist in Neuchâtel.

NIEMÖLLER, Martin (b. 1892). Protestant theologian and pastor. A determined opponent of the National Socialist "German Christians," Niemöller was dismissed from his post in Berlin-Dahlem by the bishop of Prussia in 1934. He ignored the ban, continued to conduct his pastoral duties, and remained a leading member of the Confessional Church. He was arrested in 1937 and held in various concentration camps until the liberation. A president of the World Council of Churches, 1961–68.

NIETZSCHE, Friedrich Wilhelm (1844–1900). German philosopher.

NIKISCH, Arthur Philipp (1889–1968). Administrative attorney in Dresden, later professor of labor law at various German universities. Son of the conductor Arthur Nikisch, married to the opera singer Grete Merrem-Nikisch.

NOELLE. Unidentified manufacturer, host of TM's in Lüdenscheid.

NOLDE, Emil (1867–1956). German Expressionist painter.

NOSKE, Gustav (1868–1946). German statesman and politician. Commanded the troops that put down the Spartakist uprisings in 1919; first Reichsminister of defense; resigned after the Kapp Putsch.

NOVAK, Arne (1880–1939). Czech literary historian.

NOVALIS (Baron Friedrich von Hardenberg, 1772–1801). German Romantic poet.

O

O'BRIEN, Father John A. (1893–1980). Progressive American Catholic scholar and priest, director of the Newman Foundation at the University of Illinois at Urbana.

ÖHLER, Adalbert. Mayor of Weimar, member of the Nietzsche Prize committee.

ØSTERGAARD, Carl V. Danish translator.

OESTVIG, Karl Agaard (1889–1968). Norwegian tenor.

OLDENBOURG, Rudolf (1887–1921). Munich art historian.

OLDEN, Rudolf (1885–1940). Berlin attorney and columnist, political editor of the *Berliner Tageblatt*. Emigrated to England in 1933, where he was a co-founder of the German PEN Club in exile.

ONEGIN, Sigrid (1891–1943). Mezzo soprano, noted for her Wagnerian roles.

ONNO, Ferdinand (1881–1969). Viennese actor.

OPITZ, Walter (b. 1879). German writer, friend of TM's from his early Munich years.

OPPENHEIMER, Carl (1874–1941). Professor of biochemistry in Berlin.

OPPENHEIMER, Franz (1864–1943). Political economist in Frankfurt; brother of Carl Oppenheimer.

OPPENHEIMER, Friedrich (1886–1960). Austrian novelist (under the pseudonym Friedrich Heydenau). Brother of Max Oppenheimer.

OPPENHEIMER, Max ("Mopp") (1885–1954). Viennese painter. Lived in exile in Switzerland, later the United States.

OPRECHT, Emil (1895–1952). Swiss bookseller and publisher. His bookshop in Zurich was a meeting place for exiled German intellectuals, and the publishing firms founded and directed by him, Dr. Oprecht und Helbling and the Europa-Verlag, were the leading anti-Fascist publishers in Switzerland.

OPRECHT, Emmie. Wife of Emil Oprecht, and equally active in the assistance of German refugee intellectuals in Switzerland.

OPRESCU, Georges. Rumanian art historian and professor.

ORCHARD, Thomas (b. 1910). Chief producer of *The March of Time*, the newsreel weekly founded by Henry Luce.

ORTEGA Y GASSET, José (1883–1955). Spanish cultural philosopher.

OSBORN, Dr. Unidentified friend of Hans Reisiger's.

OSEL, Heinrich (1863–1919). Center deputy to the Bavarian Landtag, killed in the assassination attempt on Erhard Auer.

OSSIETZKY, Carl von (1889–1938). Leftist Democratic publicist. Editor-in-chief of the weekly *Die Weltbühne* from 1926 to 1933. Arrested by the Nazis in 1933 and placed in a concentration camp the following year; awarded the Nobel Peace Prize in 1936—thanks in part to the efforts of TM—but was not permitted to accept it; died under police guard in a Berlin clinic.

OTTE, Sara Catharina ("Rini") (b. 1917). Dutch actress, married in 1946 to Fritz Landshoff.

OTTO, Walter F. (1878–1941). German scholar of ancient history and papyrology.

P

· · · · · · · · · ·

PADISHA. Unidentified fellow passenger on the *Suecia* in 1939.

PALLENBERG, Max (1877–1934). Well-known German character actor, husband of Fritzi Massary.

PANNWITZ, Rudolf (1881–1969). German cultural philosopher and critic highly admired by TM. Strongly influenced by Nietzsche, Stefan George, and Edmund Husserl.

PANOFSKY, Erwin (1892–1968). Art historian and professor in Hamburg, later at the Institute for Advanced Study, Princeton.

PAPEN, Franz von (1879–1969). German diplomat, soldier and statesman. Chancellor from June to December 1932; after the fall of the Schleicher government, which he helped to bring about, he entered into Hitler's government as vice-chancellor.

PAQUET, Alfons (1881–1944). German essayist and travel journalist.

PATZAK, Julius (1898–1974). Austrian tenor.

PAULSEN, Wolfgang. Germanist in England.

PAYER, Friedrich von (1847–1931). Democratic parliamentarian leader. German vice-chancellor, 1917–18.

PEAT, Harold. TM's American lecture agent.

PÉGUY, Charles (1873–1914). French religious writer.

PÉLADAN, Joséphin (1859–1918). French mystical writer and novelist.

PENZOLDT, Dr. Fritz. German physician, husband of Sigrid Onégin.

PERL, Walter H. (1909–1975). Germanist, contributor to the *Neue Zürcher Zeitung*. Emigrated to the United States in 1938.

PERRAULT, Charles (1628–1703). French writer, famous for his *Contes de Ma Mère l'Oye*.

PETERSON, Prof. Presumably Houston Peterson (b. 1897), professor of philosophy at Rutgers University and author of several studies on TM.

PETRI, Egon (1881–1962). Virtuoso pianist and pedagogue.

PFAEHLER, Albert (1877–1941). Pharmacist in Solothurn.

PFITZNER, Hans (1869–1949). Munich composer. TM was a great admirer of Pfitzner's work, especially his opera *Palestrina*, and the two were cordial acquaintances in Munich. Differences of opinion in matters of culture and politics came between them, however, and in 1933 Pfitzner was among the signers of the Munich protest against TM's lecture on Richard Wagner.

PFITZNER, Maria ("Mimi"). Wife of Hans Pfitzner.

PFITZNER, Paul. Son of Hans Pfitzner.

PFORDTEN, Baron Hermann Ludwig von (1857–1933). Music historian, professor in Munich.

PHILIPPE, Charles-Louis (1874–1909). French novelist.

PHILIPSON, Dr. Ivar. Swedish attorney in the publishing firm of Albert Bonnier and legal advisor to Bermann-Fischer Verlag.

PICCAVER, Alfred (1884–1958). English tenor.

PIDOLL, Carl von. Composer, conductor, and novelist. Close friend of the Pringsheim family.

PIDOLL, Baroness Ester von. Once married to Carl von Pidoll; long-time friend of Leonhard Frank.

PIÉTRI, François (b. 1882). French naval minister.

PILAR, Princess of Bavaria (b. 1891). Painter.

PILOTY, Melanie von. Wife of Robert von Piloty (1863–1926), a Munich professor of constitutional law.

PINDER, Wilhelm (1878–1947). Professor of art history in Munich, later in Berlin.

PINKUS, Klaus. Life-long acquaintance of Heinrich Mann's. TM first met him in 1933 in Sanary.

PIOKARSKA, Frau. Housekeeper for Georg Martin Richter.

PIXIS, Dr. Presumably Erwin Pixis, director of the Munich Kunstverein.

PLANCK, Max (1858–1947). Nobel Prize–winning German physicist.

PLATEN HALLERMUND, Count August von (1796–1835). German poet.

PLATZER, Martin. Essayist, contributor to the *National-Zeitung*, Basel.

PNIOWER, Otto (1859–1932). Berlin literary historian.

PODACH, Erich F. (1894–1967). Nietzsche scholar in exile in Switzerland

PODBIELSKI. Unidentified luncheon guest in Küsnacht.

POINCARÉ, Raymond (1860–1934). French politician and statesman. President, 1913–20.

PONTEN, Josef (1883–1940). German writer and novelist.

PONTOPPIDAN, Henrik (1857–1943). Nobel Prize–winning Danish novelist.

PRANTL. Munich stationers.

PREETORIUS, Emil (1883–1973). Munich graphic artist, illustrator, and stage designer; among TM's closest friends in Munich from 1918. The figure of Kridwiss in *Doctor Faustus* is based in part on him.

PRINGSHEIM, Alfred (1850–1941). Katia Mann's father. Professor of mathematics at the University of Munich, ardent Wagnerite, and collector of Renaissance majolica, silver, and bronzes. Pringsheim and his wife emigrated to Switzerland in 1939.

PRINGSHEIM, Emilie ("Milke") (1912–1976). Actress, niece of Katia Mann's, daughter of Klaus Pringsheim.

PRINGSHEIM, Erik. Oldest brother of Katia Mann. Died before the First World War on his *estancia* in Argentina.

PRINGSHEIM, Hedwig, née Dohm (1855–1942). Katia Mann's mother.

PRINGSHEIM, Heinz (1882–1974). Brother of Katia Mann's, archaeologist and music critic.

PRINGSHEIM, Klara ("Lala"), née Koszler. Wife of Klaus Pringsheim.

PRINGSHEIM, Klaus (1883–1972). Twin brother of Katia Mann, composer, conductor, and music pedagogue. Student of Gustav Mahler's and musical director of the Reinhardt theaters in Berlin. From 1931 conductor and teacher at the Imperial Conservatory, Tokyo.

PRINGSHEIM, Olga, née Markowa Meerson (1880–1929). Russian painter and pupil of Matisse. Wife of Heinz Pringsheim.

PRINGSHEIM, Peter (1881–1963). Brother of Katia Mann's, physicist and professor. He was attending an international physics conference in Australia at the time the First World War broke out, and was interned there as an enemy alien. Emigrated to Brussels in 1933; went on to the United States in 1940, where he worked at the Argonne National Laboratory in Chicago.

PRINZ, Robert. Munich writer.

PRITTWITZ, Maria Luise von, née Countess Strachwitz. Wife of Friedrich Wilhelm von Prittwitz und Gaffron (1884–1955), German ambassador in Washington from 1927 to 1933.

PROUST, Marcel (1871–1922). French novelist.

PULVER, Max (1889–1952). Swiss graphologist.

PUSHKIN, Aleksander (1799–1837). Russian poet.

PUTZ, Arnold. Munich actor.

Q

QUERIDO, Emanuel (1871–1943). Dutch publisher.

QUIDDE, Ludwig (1858–1941). German historian and pacifist. Awarded the Nobel Peace Prize in 1927.

R

RABENER, Johann (b. 1909). German novelist.

RADEK, Karl (1885–1941?). Russian Communist journalist and politician active in the reorganization of the German Communist party in 1918–19.

RAFF, Helene (1865–1942). Munich writer and editor, neighbor of the Manns' in Herzogpark.

RAIMUND, Ferdinand (1790–1836). Austrian playwright.

RASCHER, Hans. Son of Max Rascher.

RASCHER, Max (1883–1962). Publisher in Zurich.

RASTEDE, Hans Gerhard (1898–1955). German teacher at the Lawrenceville School near Princeton; admirer of TM's.

RATHENAU, Walther (1867–1922). Industrialist, economist, writer, and politician. Became German foreign minister in 1922 and was assassinated by reactionaries.

RAUCH, Dora (1883–1972). Girlhood friend of Katia Mann's.

RAUSCHNING, Hermann (b. 1887). Onetime National Socialist politician. Became president of the senate in Danzig in 1933 and was held to enjoy Hitler's confidence; resigned in 1934 and fled via Poland to Switzerland, where he became an outspoken anti-Nazi writer. His books the *Revolution of Nihilism* and *Conversations with Hitler* were widely read at the beginning of the war.

REBAL, Amica Savic. Yugoslav essayist.

REIFF, Hermann (1856–1938). Zurich silk manufacturer, artlover, and philanthropist. TM portrayed the Reiff salon and its artistic offerings in Chapter XXXIX of *Doctor Faustus*.

REIFF-SERTORIUS, Lilly (1886–1958). Wife of Hermann Reiff, one-time pupil of Franz Liszt's.

REINACHER, Eduard (1892–1968). Alsatian writer and dramatist.

REINHARDT, Delia (1892–1974). Soprano at the Munich Opera, discovery and friend of Bruno Walter's.

REINHARDT, Karl (1886–1958). Classical philologist in Frankfurt am Main.

REINHARDT, Max (1873–1943). Austrian theater producer and director. In Hollywood from 1938.

REISIGER, Hans (1884–1968). Writer and translator. Became acquainted with TM in 1913, and remained one of his closest and dearest friends, beloved by the entire Mann family. TM portrayed him in *Doctor Faustus* in the figure of Rüdiger Schildknapp.

REMARQUE, Erich Maria (1898–1970). German novelist.

RENN, Ludwig (originally Arnold Vieth von Golssenau, b. 1889). German revolutionary writer.

RENNER, Paul (1878–1956). Munich illustrator and type designer.

REQUADT, Paul (b. 1902). Student in Munich in 1918, from 1947 a lecturer in literature at the University of Mainz. Wrote *Jugendstil im Frühwerk Thomas Manns* (1966).

REUSS, Crown Prince Heinrich XXV (1895–1945). Writer, artlover, and theater director in Gera.

REVENTLOW, Count Ernst von (1869–1943). Berlin political columnist.

REYNAUD, Paul (1878–1966). French politician. Minister of finance, 1938–40; premier, 1940.

RHEINHARDT, Emil Alphons (1889–1945). Austrian writer and translator living in the south of France before 1933. Served in the French Resistance, was denounced and arrested, and died in the concentration camp at Dachau.

RHEINHARDT, Gerty. Singer, wife of Emil Alphons Rheinhardt.

RHEINSTROM, Heinrich (b. 1884). Professor of finance and tax law in Munich, later in the United States.

RIBBENTROP, Joachim von (1893–1946). Hitler's chief foreign advisor. German ambassador to London, 1936–38; foreign minister, 1938–45. Condemned to death at Nuremberg as a chief war criminal and executed.

RICHTER, Dr. Owner of the Neues Waldhotel in Arosa.

RICHTER, Georg Martin (1875–1941). Munich art historian, art dealer, and bibliophile publisher. Close friend of TM's and godfather of Michael Mann's.

RIEDER, Prof. Hermann. Munich radiologist.

RIEMER, Friedrich Wilhelm (1774–1845). Scholar and literary historian. Tutor of Goethe's son and literary assistant to Goethe until 1812.

RIESER, Marianne. Wife of Ferdinand Rieser, the director of the Zurich Schauspielhaus, and sister of Franz Werfel.

RIESS, Curt (b. 1902). Berlin journalist, friend of Erika and Klaus Mann's. Emigrated via Prague and Vienna to Paris in 1933; worked as a New York correspondent for various European papers, 1934–43; military reporter for the U.S. Army, 1943–44.

RILKE, Rainer Maria (1875–1926). German poet.

RITCHIE, Frank. Representative of the American Committee for Christian German Refugees.

ROBERT, Paul Anton (pseudonym of Paul Roubiczek, 1898–1972). Czech writer and philosopher.

RODENBERG, Julius (1831–1914). German poet, writer, and editor.

RÖHM, Ernst (1887–1934). One of Hitler's earliest supporters and head of the SA. Murdered on Hitler's orders on June 30, 1934.

ROHAN, Prince Karl Anton. Publisher of the conservative *Europäische Revue* in Leipzig.

ROHRSCHEIDT, Dietrich von (1885–1965). Cousin of Katia Mann's, the son of her father's sister, Marta von Rohrscheidt.

ROHRSCHEIDT, Marta von (d. 1921). Sister of Alfred Pringsheim's.

ROLLAND, Romain (1866–1944). French writer, essayist, and musicologist. TM strongly objected to Rolland's pacifism and internationalism during the First World War.

ROMAINS, Jules (1885–1972). French novelist and dramatist. President of the International PEN Club, 1936–41.

ROSAR, Anni (1888–1963). Viennese actress.

ROSÉ, Alfred. Son of Arnold Rosé.

ROSÉ, Arnold (1863–1946). Austrian violinist.

ROSÉ, Justine, née Mahler. Wife of Arnold Rosé, sister of Gustav Mahler's.

ROSENBAUM. Unidentified Zurich attorney.

ROSENBERG, Else, née Dohm. Katia Mann's aunt in Berlin, who until the death of her husband, the banker Hermann Rosenberg, maintained an imposing house at No. 19 Tiergartenstrasse, then moved with her two daughters into a large flat on Matthäikirchstrasse. TM visited with her whenever in Berlin.

ROSENBERG, Hans. Astronomy professor in Tübingen. Cousin of Katia Mann's, son of Else Rosenberg.

ROSENBERG, Käthe (1883–1960). Noted translator from French, English, and Russian. Cousin of Katia Mann's, daughter of Else Rosenberg. Emigrated with her sister, Else Dernburg, to London.

ROSENTHAL, Friedrich (1885–1940). Viennese theater director and dramatist.

ROSSBACH, Gerhard (1893–1967). Founder and commander of a Baltic volunteer corps.

ROSSHAUPTER, Albert (1878–1949). Munich editor. Minister of defense in the Eisner government.

ROSTOVTZEFF, Michael Ivanovich (1870–1952). Russian-born American historian.

ROTH, Joseph (1894–1939). Successful Austrian novelist. Emigrated from Berlin to Paris in 1933. Already extremely ill and hopelessly alcoholic, Roth collapsed in a Paris café when he read the news of Ernst Toller's suicide, and died four days later in delirium tremens.

ROTHBART, Margaret. Representative of the Institut International de Coopération Intellectuelle, Paris.

RUFFO, Titta (1878–1953). Italian baritone.

RUSSELL, Henry Norris (1877–1957). Astrophysicist, Princeton professor of astronomy.

RUST, Bernhard (1883–1945). Reichsminister for science, education, and popular culture.

RYCHNER, Max (1897–1965). Swiss literary historian, essayist, and critic.

S

SAENGER, Samuel (1864–1944). Professor and political scientist, became political editor and co-publisher of the *Neue Rundschau* in 1908. Emigrated to France in 1939, worked briefly on the *Neue Tage-Buch* in Paris, then escaped to America.

SALISBURY, Robert Arthur Talbot Gascoyne-Cecil, Third Marquis of (1830–1903). British statesman. Prime minister and foreign secretary.

SALTEN, Felix (1869–1945). Viennese writer and dramatist.

SALZ, Prof. Arthur (b. 1881). Political economist and sociologist in Heidelberg and Munich. Emigrated to the United States in 1934.

SALZER, Dr. Fritz. Munich ophthalmologist.

SARRAUT, Albert (1872–1962). French politician. Premier from January to June 1936.

SATZ. Hotelkeeper in Glücksburg.

SAUBER, Fritz (b. 1884). Chairman from November 10, 1918, of the Bavarian Workers' and Soldiers' Council.

SAUERBRUCH, Prof. Ferdinand (1875–1951). Munich surgeon.

SAUNDERS, Arthur Percy (1869–1953). Professor at Hamilton College, New York.

SAXL, Fritz (1890–1948). Viennese art historian, director of the Warburg Institute in London.

SCHACHT, Hjalmar (1877–1970). German financier. Stabilized the German mark while commissioner of currency in 1923; twice president of the Reichsbank; acting minister of national economy, 1934–37. When Goering was appointed head of the Four-Year Plan and thereby essentially economic dictator, Schacht resigned. In 1944 he was interned in a concentration camp because of his opposition stance, and at the Nuremberg trials he was acquitted.

SCHARFF, Alexander (1892–1950). Egyptologist, curator of the state museums in Berlin.

SCHARNAGL, Karl (1881–1963). Mayor of Munich, 1925–33.

SCHEIDEMANN, Philipp (1865–1939). Social Democratic politician. As people's commissioner proclaimed the Republic on the abdication of the Kaiser, and was elected its first prime minister.

SCHELLONG, Retired naval officer.

SCHENK, Baron. Otherwise unidentified acquaintance in Glücksburg.

SCHERTEL, Max (1880–1961). German instructor, University of Washington, Seattle.

SCHICKELE, Hans. Son of René Schickele.

SCHICKELE, René (1883–1940). Alsatian writer. Moved to Sanary for reasons of health in 1932, and encouraged other writers to take refuge there after the Nazi takeover. During the First World War Schickele had attacked TM in his pacifist journal *Die Weissen Blätter*, but they later became good friends. TM was able to use Schickele's home in Badenweiler as a cover address in 1933, and as a French citizen Schickele was helpful in getting portions of TM's estate out of Germany.

SCHILDKRAUT, Rudolf (1862–1930). German actor, from 1926 in Hollywood.

SCHILLER, Friedrich (1759–1805). Poet and playwright.

SCHILLINGS, Max von (1868–1933). Composer. Became president of the Prussian Academy of Arts in 1932, forced the resignation of Heinrich Mann from his office as president of the literary section in February 1933, and proceeded to oversee the "conforming" of the Academy.

SCHIPPER, Zacharias Emil (1882–1957). Austrian baritone.

SCHLAGETER, Albert Leo. Nazi martyr. Saboteur executed by the French.

SCHLAMM, Willi, later William S. (b. 1904). Austrian Trotskyite columnist. Emigrated from Vienna to Prague in 1933, where with Hermann Budzislawski he published the *Neue Weltbühne*.

SCHLEGEL, Friedrich (1772–1829). German literary critic and philosopher of history.

SCHLEICHER, Kurt von (1882-1934). German soldier and statesman. Helped bring about the collapse of the Brüning government in May 1932; appointed Reichswehr minister in the succeeding Papen cabinet; served as chancellor from December 1932 to January 1933. Murdered by the SS on June 30, 1934.

SCHLOSS, Sibylle. Actress in the ensemble of Erika Mann's cabaret *The Peppermill.*

SCHLUMBERGER, Jean (1877–1968). French novelist and publicist; co-founder of the *Nouvelle Revue Française.*

SCHMALENBACH, Hermann (1885–1950). Professor of philosophy in Basel.

SCHMELING, Max (b. 1905). World heavyweight boxing champion, 1930–32.

SCHMID-BLOSS, Karl. General director of the Zurich Opera, 1932–47.

SCHMIDT, Joseph (1904–1942). Rumanian-born German tenor.

SCHNEIDER. Zurich architect.

SCHNEIDER-KAINER, Lene. Wife of the painter and stage designer Ludwig Kainer.

SCHNITZLER, Arthur (1862–1931). Austrian writer and dramatist.

SCHNITZLER, Heinrich (b. 1902). Actor and director, son of Arthur Schnitzler.

SCHNITZLER, Lili (1909–1928). Daughter of Arthur Schnitzler.

SCHNITZLER, Lily von (b. 1889). Wife of the jurist Georg von Schnitzler. Betweeen 1913 and 1920 the Schnitzler salon in Munich was a meeting place for lovers of art and literature.

SCHNITZLER, Olga (1882–1970). Wife of Arthur Schnitzler.

SCHOCH, Paula von. Wife of General Karl Georg von Schoch (b. 1858), a professor of history in Munich.

SCHÖLL, Dr. Else. Munich mathematician, student of Alfred Pringsheim's, and frequent visitor with her sister Hedwig to the Mann home.

SCHÖLL, Hedwig. Piano teacher in Schwabing and friend of the Mann family.

SCHÖNE. Unidentified writer in Magdeburg.

SCHÖNHERR, Karl (1867–1943). Austrian writer and dramatist.

SCHOEPS, Hans-Joachim (1909–1980). Professor of religion and intellectual history. In exile in Sweden, 1938–47.

SCHOLL. Stationers in Zurich.

SCHOPENHAUER, Arthur (1788–1860). German philosopher.

SCHOTT, Werner (b. 1891). Actor in Vienna, later in Berlin.

SCHREMPF, Claus (1895–1963). German essayist.

SCHRENCK, Edith von. Dancer.

SCHUH, Dr. Willi (b. 1900). Music critic for the *Neue Zürcher Zeitung.*

SCHULTHESS-REIMANN, Paula. Berlin actress.

SCHUSCHNIGG, Kurt von (b. 1897). Austrian statesman. Chancellor, 1934–38; arrested and imprisoned after the Nazi occupation and placed in a concentration camp.

SCHWABE, Rudolf (1883–1976). Publisher in Basel.

SCHWARZENBACH, Annemarie (1908–1942). Swiss writer, daughter of a wealthy industrial family. A close friend of Erika and Klaus Mann's who accompanied them on many of their travels.

SCHWARZSCHILD, Leopold (1891–1950). Political publicist. Editor of *Das Tage-Buch* in Berlin, 1922–33; moved the journal to Paris and continued publishing it there as *Das Neue Tage-Buch.*

SCHWEGERLE, Hans (1882–1950). Munich sculptor. In addition to the Schwegerle bust of TM and head of Elisabeth Mann-Borgese, TM owned a bust of Luther by the sculptor and a Hermes statue that stood in the garden of the Herzogpark house.

SEGER, Gerhart. Social Democratic Reichstag deputy who escaped a Nazi concentration camp and published in 1934 one of the first reports about them.

SEIDEL, Willy (1887–1934). Munich writer.

SEIDL, Walter (1905–1937). German writer. Emigrated to Prague and died in Naples.

SEIF, Dr. Leonard. Munich nerve specialist.

SEITZ, Karl (1869–1950). Social Democratic mayor of Vienna, 1923–34.

SERKIN, Rudolf (b. 1903). Piano virtuoso and pedagogue, son-in-law of Adolf Busch.

SERVICEN, Louise (1896–1975). French translator of nearly all of TM's works following *The Tales of Jacob* (1935).

SESSIONS, Roger (b. 1896). American composer and teacher. The libretto for Sessions's opera *Montezuma* was written by Giuseppe Antonio Borgese.

SEVERING, Karl (1875–1952). Social Democratic politician. Prussian minister of the interior, 1920–26 and 1930–33; German minister of the interior, 1928–30.

SHCHEDRIN, N. (pseudonym of Mikhail Saltykov, 1826–1889). Russian writer and novelist.

SHENSTONE, Molly (1897–1976). Wife of Princeton professor of physics Allen Shenstone. Assisted Katia Mann with TM's correspondence until 1941.

SIEBURG, Friedrich (1893–1964). Correspondent in Paris and London for the *Frankfurter Zeitung.*

SIEVEKING, Heinrich (1871–1945). Zurich professor of economic history.

SILONE, Ignazio (b. 1900). Italian anti-Fascist writer.

SILVER, Rabbi Abba Hillel (1893–1963). Noted American Jewish scholar.

SIMMEL, Georg (1858–1918). German sociologist and philosopher.

SIMON, Heinrich (Heinz) (1880–1941). Publisher and editor-in-chief of the *Frankfurter Zeitung* until 1934. Emigrated to the United States in 1938.

SIMON, Hugo (b. 1880). Berlin banker and friend of literature and the arts. Emigrated to Paris.

SIMON, Sir John (1873–1954). Conservative British politician. Foreign secretary, 1931–35; home secretary, 1935–37.

SIMONS, Hans (1893–1972). Teacher and writer. Director of the Institut für Politik, Berlin, 1925–29; professor at the New School for Social Research from 1935, president from 1950 to 1960.

SKUHRA, Alexander. Director of the Rikola-Verlag, Vienna.

SMITH, Bernard. Director in the firm of Alfred A. Knopf, publishers.

SOLOGUB, Fëdor (pseudonym of Fëdor Teternikov, 1863–1927). Russian Symbolist poet, novelist, essayist, and dramatist.

SOMMERFELD, Martin (b. 1894). Professor of German, Smith College.

SONNEMANN, Emmy. Actress, wife of Hermann Goering.

SOOMER, Walter (1878–1935). Wagnerian singer.

SOREL, Georges (1847–1922). French journalist and philosopher of revolutionary syndicalism.

SPAET, Frau. Otherwise unidentified friend of Ida Herz's.

SPÄTH, Frau. Unidentified cook in Zurich.

SPECHT, Richard (1870–1932). Viennese music historian.

SPENGLER, Oswald (1880–1936). German historian.

SPEYER, Wilhelm (1887–1952). German novelist. Boyhood friend of Bruno Frank's and longtime acquaintance of the Manns'. Emigrated to Austria in 1933, later to America.

SPIECKER, Dr. Karl (1888–1953). Catholic publicist. In exile in Paris, edited the monthly *Das wahre Deutschland.*

SPIEGLER, Albert. Viennese scholar, philanthropist, and friend of music. He and his wife Nina were close friends of Bruno Walter's, and it was they who first introduced him to Gustav Mahler.

STÄHELI, Kurt. Bookseller in Zurich.

STAHEL, Dr. Jakob (1872–1950). Mann family physician in Küsnacht.

STARHEMBERG, Prince Ernst Rüdiger (1899–1956). Austrian statesman. Vice-chancellor under Dollfuss and Schuschnigg, 1934–36; minister for security, 1935.

STAUDINGER, Hans (1889–1980). Prussian secretary of state until 1933. Emigrated to the United States and became professor at the New School for Social Research, New York.

STEEGEMANN, Paul (1895–1956). Avant-garde publisher in Hannover.

STEIN, Baron Friedrich vom und zum (1757–1831). Prussian statesman.

STEIN, Leo. Viennese newspaperman.

STEINBÖCK, Felix (1897–1974). Viennese actor.

STEINER. Presumably Dr. Herbert Steiner (1892–1966), co-publisher and editor of the bi-monthly *Corona*, Zurich and Munich.

STEINICKE, Georg. Munich bookseller.

STEINRÜCK, Albert (1872–1929). German actor in Berlin and Munich.

STENGEL, Baron Paul von. Adjutant to the Nazi "governer" Epp. Stengel warned TM against returning to Germany.

STERNS. Unidentified fellow passengers from Zurich on the *Normandie* in 1937.

STEVENS, George. Editor-in-chief of the *Saturday Review of Literature*, New York

STEVENS, Miss. Presumably Rachel Stevens, a Princeton neighbor.

STICKELBERGER, Emanuel (1884–1962). Swiss novelist.

STICKELBERGER, Rudolf Emanuel (1911–1975). Writer and pastor, son of Emanuel Stickelberger.

STIFTER, Adalbert (1805–1868). Austrian writer and novelist.

STOKOWSKI, Leopold (1882–1977). American conductor.

STRASSER, Otto (1897–1974). National Socialist politician. Brother of Gregor Strasser, who was murdered by Hitler on June 30, 1934. Belonging to the left wing of the Party, Strasser founded the "Black Front" of Revolutionary National Socialists after his break with Hitler in 1930.

STRASSER, Dr. Stefan (Istvan). Otherwise unidentified conductor and friend of the Pringsheim family.

STRATZ, Rudolf (1864–1936). German popular novelist.

STRAUSS, Richard (1864–1949). German conductor and composer.

STRAUSS, Dr. Richard. Viennese physician.

STRECKER, Karl (1862–1933). Berlin dramatist and critic.

STRICH, Fritz (1882–1963). Literary historian and professor, first in Munich, where TM was acquainted with him, and later in Berne.

STRINDBERG, August (1849–1912). Swedish playwright and novelist.

STROH, Heinz (1899–1952). Berlin essayist and critic. Emigrated to Prague in 1933, in 1939 to London.

STUCK, Franz von (1863–1928). German painter and sculptor.

STUDER-GUYER, Lux. Zurich architect. Builder and owner of the house at No. 33 Schiedhaldenstrasse in Küsnacht rented by the Manns.

SUARÈS, André (1868–1948). French biographer and essayist.

SÜSKIND, W[ilhelm] E[manuel] (1901–1970). Munich writer. A close friend of Erika and Klaus Mann's until 1933 who sought to convince them to return to Germany.

SUHRKAMP, Peter (actually Heinrich) (1891–1959). Successor to Rudolf Kayser as editor of the monthly *Die Neue Rundschau*, published by S. Fischer Verlag, in 1932. Suhrkamp took over what remained in Germany of the S. Fischer firm when Gottfried Bermann Fischer sold it in 1935.

SULZBACH, Ernst (1887–1954). Editor at Ullstein-Verlag, Berlin.

SUTRO-KATZENSTEIN, Dr. Nettie (1889–1967). Wife of the Zurich neurologist Erich Katzenstein and founder in 1933 of the Swiss Auxiliary for Emigré Children, which took care of nearly ten thousand homeless refugee children between 1933 and 1947.

SWARZENSKI, Georg (1876–1957). Art historian and museum director in Frankfurt am Main and later in Boston.

SWING, Raymond Gram (1887–1968). American journalist and radio commentator. Respected around the world for his well-informed coverage for the Mutual Broadcasting System of the Munich crisis and the progress of the war.

T

. . . .

TAGORE, Rabindranath (1861–1941). Indian poet and philosopher.

TAINE, Hippolyte (1828–1893). French historian and philosopher of history.

TARDIEU, André (1876–1945). French politician. Premier of France, 1929–30, and again in 1932.

TENNENBAUM, Richard. Zurich businessman recommended to TM by Liesl and Bruno Frank. Tennenbaum advised TM in financial matters and was helpful in securing part of the Mann estate from Munich.

TÉREY, Edith von (d. 1929). Hungarian writer and essayist.

THÄLMANN, Ernst (1886–1944). Communist politician and Reichstag deputy.

THEILHABER, Felix (1884–1956). German physician and writer. Emigrated to Palestine in 1935.

THIERS, Adolphe (1797–1877). French statesman and historian.

THIERSCH, Friedrich (1852–1921). Munich architect and painter.

THOMAS, Adrienne (b. 1897). Alsatian writer.

THOMAS, Otto. Secretary of the Munich Workers' Council.

THOMPSON, Dorothy (1894–1961). American journalist and political commentator. Foreign correspondent in Berlin from 1924 to 1934; expelled by Hitler because of her sharply anti-Nazi reporting. Wife of Sinclair Lewis.

THYSSEN, Fritz (1873–1951). German industrial magnate. Though one of the first industrialists to give financial support to the Nazi party, Thyssen fell out with the regime in 1935 because of its increasing persecution of Jews. He emigrated to Switzerland in 1939, was arrested in Occupied France in 1941, and was held in a concentration camp with his wife until 1945.

TILLICH, Paul (1886–1965). Theologian and philosopher of religion.

TIMM, Johannes (1866–1945). Bavarian minister of justice in the Eisner government.

TIMPE, Willri. Schoolmate of TM's in Lübeck, son of a professor with whom TM boarded after his family had moved to Munich.

TISZA, Count István (1861–1918). Minister president of Hungary, 1903–5 and 1913–17; murdered by mutinying soldiers in Budapest.

TÖRRING, Count. Unidentified.

TOLLER, Ernst (1893–1939). Expressionist poet and playwright. Toller, an army veteran from the First World War, was studying in Munich when he met TM in the summer of 1917. In 1918 he became associated with Kurt Eisner as a moderate Independent Socialist, and from April 7, 1919, he served as chairman of the provisional Central Council in the first Bavarian Soviet Republic. He was a clear opponent of the radical Communists Levien and Leviné, however, and as a commander of the Red troops near Dachau he strove for the suspension of hostilities. Neither in Toller's notes nor in TM's is there substantiation for the often-repeated claim that it was thanks to Toller's personal intervention that TM's house in Herzogpark was spared by plunderers. After the overthrow of the Soviet Republic, Toller was arrested and sentenced to five years' imprisonment. TM stood up for him with a testimonial during his trial. Toller wrote several of his first plays while in prison. He fled to England in 1933 and somewhat later proceeded to the United States, where he committed suicide in New York City.

TOLSTOY, Count Alexei Nikolaevich (1882–1945). Russian novelist and dramatist.

TOLSTOY, Count Leo (1828–1910). Russian novelist.

TORGLER, Ernst. Communist Reichstag deputy accused of setting the Reichstag fire.

TOSCANINI, Arturo (1867–1957). Italian conductor.

TRAGL. Unidentified Munich painter.

TREBITSCH, Siegfried (1869–1956). Viennese writer and dramatist. Trebitsch was the first translator of George Bernard Shaw into German, and helped to make him famous in Germany.

TREVIRANUS, Gottfried (1891–1971). German politician. Nationalist Reichstag deputy, 1924–32; emigrated in 1933.

TROG, Hans (1864–1928). Editor and art and theater critic of the *Neue Zürcher Zeitung.*

TRÜBNER, Wilhelm (1851–1917). German painter.

TRUMMLER. Unidentified student in Munich.

TSCHUDI, Dr. Director of a cultural society in Glarus.

TUCHOLSKY, Kurt (1890–1935). Essayist and political satirist, chief contributor to the *Weltbühne,* Berlin. Tucholsky had been living in Paris for some time when the Nazi takeover occurred in Germany. He later moved to Sweden, where he committed suicide.

TÜRK, Werner (b. 1901). German emigré writer.

TUREL, Adrien (1890–1957). Swiss sociologist, essayist, and poet.

TURGENEV, Ivan (1818–1883). Russian novelist and playwright.

U

UEXKÜLL, Baron Jakob Johann (1864–1944). German biologist and professor.

UHDE-BERNAYS, Hermann (1873–1965). Munich art and literary historian.

ULMANN, Fräulein. Presumably the daughter of Munich acquaintances of the Manns', Emil and Agnes Ulmann.

ULRICH, Dr. Konrad. Ear specialist in Zurich.

UNGAR, Hermann (1893–1929). Czech novelist and short-story writer.

UNRUH, Fritz von (1885–1970). German anti-militarist novelist, poet, and playwright.

UNTERLEITNER, Hans (b. 1890). Bavarian minister of social welfare.

V

VAIHINGER, Hans (1852–1933). German philosopher.

VALÉRY, Paul (1871–1945). French man of letters.

VAN AKEN. Unidentified attorney in Lugano.

VAN LOON, Hendrik Willem (1882–1944). Dutch writer living in America and writing in English, extremely hospitable and helpful to German emigré writers.

VANSITTART, Sir Robert (1881–1957). British diplomat. Permanent undersecretary of state for foreign affairs, 1930–38.

VEIT, Dr. Otto (b. 1898). National economist and publicist in Frankfurt am Main.

VERMEHREN, Julius (1855–1928). Lübeck senator.

VIERECK, George Sylvester (1884–1962). American writer and pro-German propagandist in both World Wars.

VILHELM, Prince of Sweden (1884–1965). Second son of King Gustavus V. Noted writer, poet, and dramatist; prominent member of the Swedish PEN Club.

VITZTHUM von ECKSTÄDT, Count Hermann (1876–1942). Boyhood friend of TM's in Lübeck.

VOLLMOELLER, Karl Gustav (1878–1948). German dramatist and poet, translator of Gabriele D'Annunzio. Lived in Basel, later in Hollywood.

VOSS, Johann Heinrich (1751–1826). German poet, translator, and classical philologist.

VOSSLER, Karl (1872–1949). Munich Romanicist.

W

. . . .

WÄLTERLIN, Oskar (1895–1961). Actor and director. Manager of the Zurich Schauspielhaus, 1938–61.

WAGNER, Cosima, née Liszt (1837–1930). Wife of Richard Wagner.

WAGNER, Erika. Viennese actress.

WAGNER, Siegfried (1869–1930). Son of Richard Wagner.

WAGNER, Winifred, née Williams (b. 1897). Widow of Siegfried Wagner. Became director of the Bayreuth Festival after her husband's death. An enthusiastic supporter of Hitler's.

WAHL, Rudolf (1894–1961). German manufacturer and historian.

WALDAU, Gustav (pseudonym of Baron Gustav von Rummel, 1871–1957). Munich actor.

WALDSTETTER, Ruth (pseudonym of Martha Geering, 1882–1952). Swiss writer.

WALLACE, Henry A. (1888–1965). American Democratic politician. Secretary of agriculture, 1933–40; vice-president, 1941–45.

WALSER, Karl (1877–1943). Painter and illustrator. Designer of the dust jackets for the first three volumes of TM's *Joseph* tetralogy.

WALSER, Robert (1878–1956). Swiss lyric poet and writer.

WALTER, Bruno (1876–1962). Conductor. Bruno Walter and his family were close neighbors of the Manns' in Herzogpark in Munich—Walter served as conductor at the Munich Opera from 1913 to 1923—and the two families were then, and remained, extremely close. The Walters were again neighbors of TM's in Beverly Hills.

WALTER, Elsa. Wife of Bruno Walter.

WALTER, Frau. Munich friend of the attorney Valentin Heins.

WALTER, Grete (1906–1939). Younger daughter of Bruno Walter.

WALTER, Lotte (1903–1970). Older daughter of Bruno Walter.

WALZ, John Albrecht (1871–1954). Harvard professor of German.

WANDREY, Conrad (1887–1944). German literary historian.

WARBURGS. It is unclear which New York members of this international banking family TM met while visiting Alfred Knopf in 1934.

WARNER, Jack L. (1892–1978). Vice-president and general production director at Warner Brothers Pictures in Hollywood.

WASSERMANN, Jakob (1873–1934). Novelist and essayist. TM met Wassermann before the turn of the century in Munich and the two writers remained good friends until the latter's death. TM maintained a certain ironic distance from Wassermann the man, but he respected him highly as a writer.

WASSERMANN-KARLWEIS, Marta. Widow of Jakob Wassermann.

WASSERMANN, Oskar (1869–1934). Director of the Deutsche Bank.

WASSMANN, Hans (b. 1873). Comic actor at the Reinhardt theaters in Berlin.

WATERBOER, Heinz (b. 1907). Novelist and travel writer specializing in Africa and the Far East.

WEBER, Alfred (1868–1958). Political economist and sociologist in Heidelberg, brother of Max Weber.

WEBER, Carl Maria (b. 1890). Munich poet and teacher.

WEBER, Hans von (1872–1924). Munich publisher.

WEBER, Max (1864–1920). German economist and sociologist, professor in Munich.

WEDEKIND, Frank (1864–1918). German poet and playwright.

WEESE, Arthur (1868–1934). Professor of art history in Berne.

WEGENER, Paul (1874–1948). German actor and director in Berlin.

WEIGAND, Hermann (b. 1892). American Germanist and professor at Yale University.

WEIGL, Joseph Franz (1766–1846). Austrian cellist and composer.

WEIL, Prof. and Mrs. Unidentified.

WEINGARTNER, Felix von (1863–1942). Swiss conductor.

WEISS, Julian (1858–1944). Essayist and publicist in Budapest.

WEITBRECHT, Günther (1900–1964). Student acquaintance in Munich.

WELLS, H. G. (1866–1946). English novelist, sociological essayist, and historian.

WELS, Otto (1873–1939). German Social Democratic politician.

WELTI, Jakob (1893–1964). Features editor and theater critic of the *Neue Zürcher Zeitung*.

WELTMANN, Lutz (1901–1967). Teacher and librarian in Berlin.

WERFEL, Franz (1890–1945). German novelist, poet, and playwright.

WERTHAM, Fredric (b. 1855). German-born American psychiatrist and neurologist.

WERTHEIM, Maurice. New York banker and friend of the theater.

WERTHEIMER, Dr. Martha. Unidentified.

WESSEL, Horst (1907–1930). Nazi student killed in a political brawl and revered as a martyr of the movement.

WESSELY, Paula (b. 1907). Viennese stage and screen actress.

WICKIHALDER, Hans (1896–1951). Theater director in Zurich.

WIEGAND, Heinrich (1895–1934). German music critic and essayist.

WIELAND, Christoph Martin (1733–1813). German poet, writer, and translator.

WILDGANS, Anton (1881–1932). Austrian poet and playwright.

WILHELM II. German Kaiser and king of Prussia (1859–1941). Abdicated on November 28, 1919, fled to Holland, and lived at a chateau in Doorn, near Utrecht.

WILLER, Luise. Munich singer.

WILLICH, Fräulein. Presumably Charlotte Willich, daughter of the Munich historical painter Willich.

WINDER, Ludwig (1889–1946). Writer in Prague. Escaped to London in 1939.

WINTER, Sophus Keith (b. 1893). Professor of English, University of Washington, Seattle.

WINTERFELDT, Joachim von (1865–1945). Reichstag deputy and state director of Brandenburg.

WINTERSTEIN. Unidentified Bavarian politician.

WITKOP, Philipp (1880–1942). Germanist and professor in Freiburg.

WITTGENSTEIN, Paul (1887–1961). Viennese pianist, brother of the philosopher Ludwig Wittgenstein. Though he lost his right arm early in the First World War, Wittgenstein continued his virtuoso career, and commissioned many piano works for the left hand alone.

WITTKOWSKI, Victor (1909–1960). German lyric poet living in exile in Geneva.

WÖLFFLIN, Heinrich (1864–1945). Historian of the art of the Renaissance.

WOLF, Hugo (1860–1903). Austrian composer.

WOLFE, Thomas (1900–1938). American novelist.

WOLFER, Dr. Rudolf Hans (b. 1879). Owner of a sanatorium in Davos.

WOLFF, Hans. Munich antiquarian book dealer.

WOLFF, Kurt (1887–1963). Publisher in Leipzig, later in Munich, who introduced a number of important Expressionist writers in his series *Der Jüngste Tag*. Heinrich Mann and Franz Kafka were among the authors he championed. Wolff liquidated his firm in 1930, and emigrated to southern France in 1933. He later moved to Italy, and finally in 1941 to the United States. In New York he founded Pantheon Books. He returned to Europe in 1959 and died from an accident in Marbach. TM always maintained cordial relations with Kurt Wolff.

WOLFF-METTERNICH, Count Paul (1853–1934). German diplomat. Ambassador to London, 1901–12; to Constantinople, 1915–16.

WOLFF, Theodor (1868–1943). Publicist, editor-in-chief of the *Berliner Tageblatt* from 1906 to 1933. Emigrated to France; arrested by Occupation authorities in 1943.

WOLFSKEHL, Karl (1869–1948). German poet, closely associated with Stefan George.

WÜTERICH, Dr. Physician in Lugano.

Z

ZAREK, Otto (1898–1958). German playwright and short-story writer.

ZECH, Countess Isa von, née Bethmann-Hollweg. Wife of Count Julius von Zech, daughter of chancellor Bethmann-Hollweg.

ZECH, Count Julius von (1885–1945). German diplomat. Ambassador to The Hague from 1927 to 1940.

ZECHBAUER, Max. Munich tobacconist.

ZEMLINSKY, Alexander von (1872–1942). Viennese composer.

ZILLMAN, Dr. Friedrich. German essayist and critic.

ZUCKERKANDL, Dr. Viktor (1896–1965). Conductor, music critic, and philosopher. Worked as an editor in the Bermann-Fischer Verlag, Vienna.

ZWEIG, Stefan (1881–1942). Austrian writer. TM began corresponding with Zweig in 1914 and the two writers were close acquaintances, though TM was never particularly admiring of the other's work.

Index of References to
Thomas Mann's Works

Page numbers in roman type refer to the text of the diaries; those in *italics* refer to the notes.

A

Achtung Europa! (1938), 291, 311, 318, 342; *378, 381*. French ed.: *Avertissement à l'Europe* (1937), 285; *377*
Address at Book and Author Luncheon, New York (1938), 311; *381*
Address at Czech rally, New York (1938), 307–8; *381*
Address on receipt of honorary doctorate, Princeton (1939), 328; *383*
Address to American Bookdealers Association, New York (1939), 327; *383*
"American Address" (1934), 209, 211–12; *368*
"An das Nobel-Friedenspreis-Comité, Oslo" (1935), 247; *371*
"An Eduard Korrodi" (1936), 255; *372*
"An Gerhart Hauptmann" (1932), 214; *368*
"Anna Karenina" (1940), 329, 333, 336; *383*
"Antwort an Hans Pfitzner" (1933), 165, 166; *365*
Arbeiter-Zeitung, reply to. *See* "Erwiderung"

B

"Bauschan." See *A Man and His Dog*
The Beloved Returns (1939), 237, 253, 284, 287, 291, 297, 329, 334; *370, 371, 385*. Writing of: Chapter I, 263. Chapter II, 264, 269, 270, 273. Chapter III, 273, 274, 278; *375*. Chapter IV, 279; *376*. Chapter V, 280. Chapter VI, 282, 286, 291, 300, 310; *378, 380*. Chapter VII, 312, 317, 320–28 *passim,* 340; *383, 384*. Chapter VIII, 335, 337, 339, 341. Chapter IX, 342. Readings from, 271, 272, 276, 279, 280, 285, 330, 337; *373*. Publication of, 286, 299, 311, 332, 333, 336, 338, 339, 342–43. Reception of, 344, 345. Ill., 331
Bemühungen (1925), *373*
Betrachtungen eines Unpolitischen (1918), 3,
5, 6, 9, 11, 12, 14, 22, 44, 50, 56, 66, 70, 223, 254; *349, 361–62, 389, 404, 414*. "Pfitzners *Palestrina*" chapter in, 67, 120; *355*. Publication of, 9, 10, 61, 118, 120, 122, 123. Reception of, 14, 15, 16, 17, 21, 24, 26, 33, 41, 42, 48, 51, 57, 60, 67, 74, 84, 87, 88, 91, 112, 114, 117; *352, 353*
Bismarck. *See* "Um Bismarcks dritten Band"
The Blood of the Walsungs (1906, 1921), 85, 104, 111, 114; *353, 357, 359*. Ill., 113
Bonn University. See *An Exchange of Letters*
"Brief an Hermann Grafen Keyserling" (1920), 76, 77, 79, 83, 85, 94; *356*
"Bruno Frank zum 50. Geburtstag" (1937), 228; *376*
Buddenbrooks (1901), 3, 7, 21, 23, 44, 77, 120, 123, 197, 237, 261, 277, 309, 336; *349, 351, 354, 361, 370, 393, 401*

C

Children's Games (1904, 1920), 105; *359*
Collected Works, 60, 111, 120, 123
"The Coming Humanism" (1939), 305, 306, 307; *380*
The Coming Victory of Democracy (1938), 282, 284, 285, 296, 298, 299, 309, 342; *377, 379*
Confessions of Felix Krull, Confidence Man (1911, 1937), 4, 6, 27, 37, 46, 58, 69, 88, 89, 285; *349*. Readings from, 33, 40, 74, 75, 115–16, 320. Publication of, 67, 68, 274, 280, 282, 286; *355, 360, 375–76*. Reviews of, 291, 292
Confidence Man. See *Confessions of Felix Krull, Confidence Man*
"Culture and Politics" (1939), 313, 317; *381*

D

Death in Venice (1912), 6, 11–12, 41, 72, 83, 98, 100, 101, 105, 123, 178; *349, 350, 353*

"Dem Fünfundsechzigjährigen" (1936), 258; *372*

"Deutsche Erziehung" (1938), 299, 319; *379*

Doctor Faustus (1947), 144, 146, 195, 210; *364, 395, 397, 412, 421, 422*

E

"Editiones Insulae" (1920), 105; *359*

Elchinger, Richard, open letter to. *See* "Was dünkt Euch um unser bayerisches Staatstheater?"

"Erwiderung" (1933), 179; *367*

"Erwiderung auf den 'Protest der Wagner-Stadt München' " (1933), 152; *365*

"Erziehung zur Sprache" (1920), 100, 101, 102; *358*

"Europe, Beware!" (1935), 234, 235, 236; *370*

An Exchange of Letters (1937), 264–65, 269, 274, 334, 339; *373–74*. Publication of, 265, 270–71, 273. Reception of, 272, 273, 277

F

Fadiman anthology. *See* "The Coming Humanism"

Felix Krull. See *Confessions of Felix Krull, Confidence Man*

Fiorenza (1905), 70, 71, 72–73, 74, 241; *355, 356*

Fontane, Theodor. See *The Old Fontane;* "Über einen Spruch Fontanes"; "Zum 100. Geburtstag Theodor Fontanes"

Die Forderung des Tages (1927), 264; *374*

Frank, Bruno. *See* "Bruno Frank zum 50. Geburtstag"

Frederick the Great and the Grand Coalition (1915), 115; *360*

Freedom speech. See *The Problem of Freedom*

French-German relations. *See* "Das Problem der deutsch-französischen Beziehungen"

Freud and the Future (1936), 259, 263, 317, 319; *372, 378, 382*

Freud's Position in the History of Modern Thought (1929), *373*

G

"Gedenken an Liebermann" (1936), 264, 269; *374*

Die Geliebten (projected novella), 210; *368*

"German Letter I" (1924), *373*

German style. *See* "Erziehung zur Sprache"

Gesang vom Kindchen (1919), 4, 5, 46, 50, 56, 58; *351*. Writing of, 16, 17, 24, 25, 26, 31–41 *passim*. Reworked, 67. Readings from, 73, 74. Publication of, 45, 59, 76, 100; *353, 356*. Reception of, 52, 59, 69, 83, 85, 86

Goethe and Tolstoy (1921), 116–20 *passim*, 122, 149; *360*

Goethe as Representative of the Bourgeois Age (1932), 206, 294; *368, 371, 373, 379*

Goethe's Career as a Man of Letters (1932), 128, 275; *362, 371, 376*

"Goethe's *Faust*" (1939), 303–8 *passim*, 310, 311, 312, 342; *380*

"Goethe's *Werther*" (1939), 343; *385*

"Gruss an Prag" (1935), 233

H

Hamsun, Knut. *See* "Die Weiber am Brunnen"

Hauptmann. *See* "An Gerhart Hauptmann"

"Die Höhe des Augenblicks." See *This Peace*

"Der Humanismus und Europa" (1936), 259; *372*

The Hungry (1903), 85; *357*

I

"In Defense of Wagner" (1940), 343, 344; *385*

"In Memory of Masaryk" (1937), 280; *377*

T

"This Man is My Brother" (1939), 303, 306, 311, 320, 326; *380*

This Peace (1938), 310, 311, 312, 318; *381*

This War (1940), 343, 344; *385*

"Tischrede auf Pfitzner" (1919), 57, 59, 66, 67; *354*

Tolstoy introduction. *See* "Anna Karenina"

Tonio Kröger (1903), 6, 63, 105, 151, 285; *350, 415*

"To the Civilized World" (1939), 325; *382–83*

The Transposed Heads (1940), 344; *385*

Tristan (1903), 72, 85, 90, 102, 226; *356, 357*

Two idylls. See *A Man and His Dog* and *Gesang vom Kindchen*

U

"Über einen Spruch Fontanes" (1920), 96, 97; *358*

"Um Bismarcks dritten Band" (1921), 114, 117; *360*

Ungar, Hermann. *See* "Knaben und Mörder"

"Unsere Kriegsgefangenen" (1919), 33, 39; *352. See also* "Zuspruch"

V

Von deutscher Republik (1922), *403*

Voyage with Don Quixote (1934), 226, 231, 263; *368*

W

Wagner essay. See *Sufferings and Greatness of Richard Wagner*

Wagner protest, reply to. *See* "Erwiderung auf den 'Protest der Wagner-Stadt München' "

The Wardrobe (1899), 104; *359*

"Was dünkt Euch um unser bayerisches Staatstheater?," 84; *357*

Wassermann biography. *See* "Zum Geleit" (1935)

A Weary Hour (1905), 110; *359*

"Die Weiber am Brunnen" (1922), 123; *362*

Y

Yale speech. *See* "Zur Gründung einer Dokumentensammlung in Yale University"

Z

"Zum Geleit" (1921), 105, 109, 110; *359*

"Zum Geleit" (1935), 246; *371*

"Zum 100. Geburtstag Theodor Fontanes" (1919), 76, 77, 78; *356*

"Zum Tode Eduard Keyserlings" (1918), 12; *350*

"Zur französischen Ausgabe von René Schickeles *Witwe Bosca*" (1938), 276, 293; *376*

"Zur Gründung einer Dokumentensammlung in Yale University" (1938), 285, 292, 293; *378*

"Zur jüdischen Frage" (1921), 120; *361*

"Zuspruch" (1919), 33; *352*

General Index

Page numbers in roman type refer to the text of the diaries; those in *italics* refer to the notes. Words containing an *ä, ö,* or *ü* are alphabetized as if the letter were followed by an *e*. Illustration references (always at the end of the entry) are to the three picture sections, labeled A, B, and C. Locations of alphabetical headings in the Biographical Notes are not included here.

A

Abegg, Wilhelm, 150, 247
Abendzeitung. See *München-Augsburger Abendzeitung*
Academy. *See* Prussian Academy of Arts
Acht-Uhr-Abendblatt (Berlin), *369*
Adalbert, prince of Bavaria, 104, 117
Adolf Friedrich VI, grand duke of Mecklenburg-Schwerin, 26
Agence Littéraire Internationale, 137, 148
d'Agoult, Countess, 168
Aita, Antonio, *259*
Alberts, Wilhelm, 62
Alexandra, princess of Saxe-Coburg and Gotha, 110; *359*
Allgemeine Zeitung (Munich), 96; *373*
Alliance Book Corporation, New York, 320, 321; *382*
Altenberg, Peter, 97; *358*
Alvarez del Vayo, Julio, *383*
Amann, Paul, 44, 260, 272, 305; *353, 380*
American Academy of Arts and Letters, 313; *381*
American Bookdealers Association, 327; *383*
American Committee for Christian German Refugees, 282, 325, 326; *383*
American Guild for German Cultural Freedom, 312, 313, 318, 343; *374, 381, 385*
Ammann, Dr., 42, 50, 51, 53
Andersen, Hans Christian, *361*
Andreae, 155
Andreae, Volkmar, 174, 175, 283
Andreyev, Leonid, 32
Angell, Joseph Warner, 285, 292
Annenkova, 269
Ansermet, Ernst, 283
Antonini (notary), 151
Apuleius.
    The Golden Ass, 209; *368*
Arbeiter-Zeitung (Vienna), 179; *367*
Arcisstrasse, Munich, *349.* Ills. A4–5

Arco auf Valley, Count Anton von, 34, 37, *55,* 84, 128
Aretin, Baron Erwein von, 133
Arnim, Achim von, 303; *380*
Arnold (haberdashers), 76
Asch, Schalom, 241
Asper, Dr. Hans, 196, 206–7, 216, 217, 254, 280, 282
Athenaeum, publishers, Budapest, 201
Atholl, Katharine Marjorie, duchess of, 323
Atlantic Monthly, 302; *380*
Attenhofer, Elsie, 247; *377*
Attinger, 192–93
Aubry, Octave.
    Napoleon on St. Helena, 260
Auden, W. H., 242, 278, 317, 318, 344; *371, 382.* (Ed.) *The Oxford Book of Light Verse,* 318. Ill. C2
Auer, Erhard, 34, 36, 37, 39
Auernheimer, Raoul, 71, 74, 272
Auf gut deutsch, 25; *351*
August Wilhelm, prince of Prussia, 15
Auslandspost (Munich), 87, 94, 96, 114, 116
Axelrod, Tovia, 53

B

Bab, Julius, 34, 204, 237; *370*
Bach, Johann Sebastian, 94, 135, 240.
    Mass in B-Minor, 240. *St. Matthew Passion,* 46, 76, 99
Bacher, Franz, 272
Bachmann, 269
Bachofen, Johann Jakob, 182
Bachstitz, Karl, 68; *355*
Bad Tölz house. Ills. B1, 2
Baeumler, Alfred.
    Metaphysik und Geschichte, 87, 88
Bahr, Hermann, 86.
    Adalbert Stifter, 92; *357*
Balfour, Arthur James, 6
Balzac, Honoré de, 59, 185.
    Adieu, 115. *Colonel Chabert,* 115; *360.*

Girl with the Golden Eyes, 95. *Lily of the Valley*, 298. *Lost Illusions*, 100; *358*. *Père Goriot*, 280; *377*. *The Rise and Fall of César Birotteau*, 59, 60, 61; *354*
Bamberger, Caroline, 328
Bard, Guy Kurtz, 328
Barth, Karl, 274, 317.
   Theologische Existenz heute, 168, 170; *365*
Basler, Otto, 179, 253, 254
Basler Nachrichten, 254
Bassermann, Albert, 94, 120, 277
Bata, Thomas, 270
Battistini, Mattia, 84, 97, 122
Baudelaire, Charles, 96
Bauer, Gustav, 91
Bauer, Colonel Max, 93
Bauer, Walter, 184
Baumann, 234
Baumfeldt, Frau, 70, 71, 73, *75*
Baumfeldt, Richard Peter, 71, 73
Baumgarten, Franz Ferdinand, 14, 20, 25, 41
Bavarian People's party, 137, 143, 144, 164
Bavarian Soviet Republic, 36, 37, 38, 39, 43–55 *passim*, 57
Bayerische Israelitische Gemeinde-Zeitung, 184
Bayerischer Kurier (Munich), 38
Becher, 151
Beer-Hofmann, Richard, 74, 272.
   Jacob's Dream, 74
Beer-Walbrunn, Ida, 33
Beethoven, Ludwig van, 26, 72, 76, 86, 93, 94, 248, 256. *Leonore* Overture, 278, 279. *Missa Solemnis*, 104, 258–59. Ninth Symphony, 90. Seventh Symphony, 42. Violin Concerto, 283
Behr, Rudolf, 67
Behrens, Eduard, *255*
Beidler, Franz W., 167, 168, *255*, 260, *275*, 283, 291, 334
Bekker, Paul, 84
Bellini, Vincenzo, 231
Benda, Georg, *358*
Benedikt, Ernst, 272
Beneš, Bohuš, 322
Beneš, Eduard, 259, 260, 270, 271, 299, 305, 306, 308, 322; *380, 382*
Beneš, Vojta, 310
Benjamin, Walter, *384*
Benn, Gottfried, 200; *363*
Beobachter. See *Völkischer Beobachter*

Berber, Fritz, 17
Berdyaev, Nikolai.
   Origin of Russian Communism, 342
Berendsohn, Walter, 264
Berenson, Bernard, *408*
Berg, Alban.
   Lulu, 278; *376*
Bergery, Gaston, 293
Bergson, Henri, *255*
Berliner Illustrierte, 138
Berliner Lokal-Anzeiger, 21
Berliner Tageblatt, 9, 24, 41, 77, 78, 117, 159, 163, 185, 221, 254; *356, 360*
Bermann, Richard A., 318
Bermann Fischer, Gottfried, 129, 131, 142, 149, 171, 185, 197, 204, 234, 244, 245, 272, 286, 291, 296, 298, 320, 332, 337–38. And S. Fischer Verlag, 144, 152, 160, 161, 163, 165–66, 176, 178, 184, 208, 214–15, 234, 246, 259; *366*. And TM's German interests, 159, 162, 168, 207, 263; *369*. Emigration of, 237, 239, 248. Ill. C7
Bermann-Fischer Verlag: Vienna, 246, 247, 248, 280, 291, 303; *362*. Stockholm, 303, 304, 306, 311, 336, 340, 342–43; *362, 378, 382, 392*
Berner, 4, 49
Bernhard, Georg, 164, 279
Bernhart, Josef, 38
Bernheimer, 158
Bernoulli, Christoph, 155
Bernstein, Elsa, 26
Bernstein, Eva, 26, 68
Bernstein, Max, 26
Bernstein, Otto, 134
Bernstein, Prof., 309
Berrsche, Alexander, 153
Bertaux, Félix, 132, 136, 137
Bertaux, Pierre, 154, 155, 156, 157, 158.
   Hölderlin, 270
de Bertol, 67
Bertram, Ernst, 3, 4, 8, 14, 18, 20, 21, 33, 47, 52, 54, 55–56, 57, 65, 66–67, 75, 100, 102, 104, 114, 119, 120. Bonn professorship, 13, 40. Literary advisor to TM, 40–41, 53, 95, 223. Godfather to Elisabeth, 52; *351*. TM's estrangement from, 143, 151, 194, 216, 217, 238, 242. *Adalbert Stifter*, 92; *357*. *Deutsche Gestalten*, 219. *Friedrich Nietzsche*, 3, 4, 5, 6, 13, 14, 44, 90;

349, 352. *Griecheneiland*, 201.
   Wartburg, 128; *362.* Ill. B3
Bethmann-Hollweg, Theobald von, 11
Bétove, 213
Bibl, Viktor.
   Der Tod des Don Carlos, 104; *355*
Bibliographisches Institut, Leipzig, 248
Biedermann, Baron Flodard von, *353*
Bielschowsky, Albert.
   Goethe, 116; *360*
Biely, Andrei.
   St. Petersburg, 67; *355*
Binder, Sybille, 94
Binding, Rudolf G., 161, 168, 185, 238
Birnbaum, Uriel, 114, 116; *360*
Biryukov, Pavel I.
   Leo N. Tolstoy, 116; *360*
Bischoff, Ernst, 62
Bismarck, Prince Otto von, 5, 20, 34, 67,
   170, 220; *360*
Bissing, Elisabeth von, 33
Bitterlich, Roswitha, 259; *373*
Bizet, Georges.
   Carmen, 97, 115, 117
Björkman, Carl, 117
Björnson, Björn, 117, 122
Blei, Franz, 76
Bloch, Ernst, 186
Bloch, Oscar Thorwald.
   Vom Tode, 86
Blood Purge (1934), 215–18, 219, 220
Blüher, Hans.
   Die Aristie des Jesus von Nazareth,
   117–18; *360. Die Rolle der Erotik in der*
   männlichen Gesellschaft, 66
Blume, Dr. Gustav, 61, 62
Blunck, Hans Friedrich, 185
Boccherini, Luigi, 273
Bodenstein, Ernst, 109
Bodmer, Hans, 135
Bodmer, Martin, 362
Boehm, Dr. Gottfried, 86
Böhm, Karl, 117
Börsenblatt für den deutschen Buchhandel,
   366
Boisserée, Sulpiz, 310; *381*
Boll, Franz, 69
Bollack, Dr., 275
Bollag, Dr. Harry, 286
Bondi, Eva, née Dohm, 120
Bondi, Georg, 120
Bonn, Emma, 16, 85, 120.
   Die Verirrten, 79; *356*

Bonn, Moritz Julius, 21, 26
Bonnet, Henri, 132, 137, 140, 325
Bonnier, Albert, publishers, Stockholm,
   343; *375*
Bonnier, Karl Otto, 146, 151, 154, 292,
   337, 340
Bonnier, Tor, 337
Bonn University, 64, 65, 264; *373–74*
Book-of-the-Month Club, 259
Borchardt, Hermann H., 312
Borel, Pierre, 192–93
Borgese, Giuseppe Antonio, 320, 326,
   342, 344; *378, 426. Goliath, 379.*
Born, Wolfgang, 87, 98, 102, 120, 177,
   180, 187, 255, 269, 272; *366*
Borrmann, Martin, 46
Bothmer, Count Karl von, 54, 88
Boy-Ed, Ida, 76, 115, 118, 119; *361*
Boyer, Charles, 324
Braak, Menno ter, 291, 292, 333
Bradish, Joseph von.
   "Dichtung und Wahrheit über Schillers
   Hingang," 284. *Goethe als Erbe seiner*
   Ahnen, 317
Brahms, Johannes, 17, 64, 99, 216.
   Fourth Symphony, 283. Horn Trio,
   72. *Variations on a Theme by Haydn,*
   286. Violin Concerto, 40
Brandenburg, Hans, 25, 48, 61
Brandes, Georg.
   The Romantic School in Germany, 100
Brandt & Brandt, 259
Branting, 582
Branting, Hjalmar, 23
Brantl, Maximilian, 25
Brauer, Ernst, 198
Brauer, Herta.
   Flucht aus dem Zwielicht, 227; *369*
Braun, Otto, 140
Braunfels, Walter, 17, 18, 46, 256.
   Prinzessin Brambilla, 17; *351*
Braus, Dorothea, 256
Brecher, Gustav, 149
Brecht, Bertolt, 140, 301, 332, 339; *372,*
   384, 398
Bredel, Willi, 259; *372, 398*
Bredow, Kurt von, 216
Breitbach, Joseph, 269, 270, 273, 274,
   276
Breitscheid, Rudolf, 65
Bremer Tageblatt, 370

Brentano, Bernhard von, 239, 255, 277, 282, 284, 291, 293. *Theodor Chindler*, 256, 258; *372*
Brentano, Lujo, 26
Briand, Aristide, 258
Broch, Hermann, 204, 260, 264, 299, 343; *379, 385, 416.* "Eine Leichte Enttäuschung," 146
Brock, Erich, 185, 285
Brockdorff-Rantzau, Count Ulrich von, 31, 33
Brod, Max, 207, 321, 322, 324; *382*
Brodsky, Dr., 308, 309
Brodsky, Mrs. Ralph, 317; *381*
de Broglie, Louis, 292; *378*
Broneer, Oscar Theodore, 320
Broulingham, 245
Browning, Elizabeth Barrett, 209
Bruckmann, Alfons Ritter von, 13, 69, 99
Brueghel, Pieter (the Elder), 73, 85
Brüll, Oswald, 71, 75, 83, 272, 300, 312
Brünger, 38
Brüning, Heinrich, 286; *378*
Bruns, Max, *358*
Buchan, John, Lord Tweedsmuir, 300; *380*
Bucky, Dr. Gustav, 276
"Buddenbrooks House," Lübeck, 119; *361*
Budzislawski, Hermann, 208, 262, 271, 319
Büchergilde Gutenberg, 176; *366*
Der Bücherwurm, 185
von Bühl, 88
Bühler-Kohler, Eduard, 109
Bülau, Dr., 38
Buenger, Judge, 173, 179, 185
Buller, Wilhelm, 104
Bumann, Walter, 171, 173, 174, 192, 245
Bunin, Ivan. *The Man from San Francisco*, 241; *371*
Burckhardt, Carl Jacob. *Richelieu*, 236
Burckhardt-Schatzmann, Helene, 155
Burckhardt, Jacob, 202
Burckhardt, Jakob, 207
Burckhardt, Paul, 193
Burian, Count Stefan, 5; *350*
Burke, Kenneth, *360*
Burri, Franz Xaver, 109
Burrian, Karl, 97

Burschell, Friedrich, 272, 284
Burte, Hermann, 181, 248
Busch, Adolf, 174, 175, 204, 208, 283
Busch, Eta, 236; *370*
Busch, Fritz, 184
Busching, Paul Rudolf, 99
Buxbaum, Friedrich, 73

C

Cain, James M. "Career in C-Major," 321; *382. Serenade*, 319
Calvin, John, 99
Čapek, Karel, 235, 260, 271. *War with the Newts*, 275; *376*
Don Carlos of Spain, 63
Carlyle, Thomas. *Frederick the Great*, 9, 10; *350*
Carossa, Hans, 201
Caruso, Enrico, 84
Cassirer, Bruno, Verlag, Berlin, 96
Cassirer, Paul, 180
Cather, Willa, 276
Ceconi, Dr. Ermanno, 20, 86
Center party, 91, 131, 134
Černý, Josef, 271
Cervantes, Miguel de, 210–11. *Don Quixote*, 170, 180, 194, 195, 203, 209, 210–11; *368*
Chamberlain, Houston Stewart, 280
Chamberlain, Neville, 302, 305, 309, 323, 339, 340; *380*
Chamisso, Adelbert von. *Peter Schlemihl*, 46; *353*
Chautemps, Camille, 192, 293
Chekhov, Anton, 53, 55. *The Bear*, 123
Cheyney State College, Pennsylvania, 328
Chiaromonte, Nicola, 291, 292; *379*
Chicago Daily News, 326
Chicago Tribune, 56
Chopin, Frédéric, 42, 118, 309
Churchill, Winston, 50, 248, 309, 327
Claudel, Paul, 90, 274; *357, 378*
Clemen, Paul, 67. *Kunstschutz im Kriege*, 67; *355*
Clemenceau, Georges, 6, 16, 18, 21, 23, 84, 131, 180
Clothier, Robert C., 327; *383*

Cocteau, Jean.
  Les Chevaliers de la Table Ronde, 285;
  377
Cohen, 31
Colin, Saul C., 296, 297, 299, 300, 301,
  307, 309, 310, 317
Colmers, Franz, 110, 246, 276
Comité Permanent des Lettres et des Arts,
  131, 132, 159; *363*
Comité pour le Placement des Intellectuels
  Refugiés, 262; *371*
Commission Internationale de
  Coopération Intellectuelle, 140, 184;
  364, 370, 372
Committee to Defend America by Aiding
  the Allies, 327
Common Sense (New York), 343, 344;
  385
Communist party, German (KPD), 36,
  39, 44, 45, 48, 54, 131, 132, 133
Conant, James Bryant, 242, 243
Conner, Mrs. Boudinot R., 310
Conrad, Julius, 260
Das Cornichon, 280; *377*
Corona (Munich and Zurich), 128, 130,
  278, 305; *362*
Corriere della Sera (Rome), 83
Corrodi, Hans.
  Othmar Schoeck, 225; *369*
Cosmopolitan (New York), *380*
Cossmann, Paul Nikolaus, 5, 8–9, 57, 66,
  87, 116
Coster, Charles de.
  *The Legend of Ulenspiegel and Lamme
  Goedzak*, 87; *357*. *The Wedding Trip*, 94
Cotta'sche, J. G., Verlagsbuchhandlung,
  Stuttgart, 114, 115; *360*
Courvoisier, Walter, 99.
  Die Krähen, 114. *Der Zaubergeiger*, 114
Cowley, William H., 329; *383*
Critica, 155; *365*
Croce, Benedetto, 155, 191; *365*.
  *History of Europe in the Nineteenth
  Century*, 149, 242; *364*
Curtiss, Thomas Quinn ("Tomski"), 344
Curtius, Ernst Robert, 105, 123, 242;
  361. *Die literarischen Wegbereiter des
  neuen Frankreich*, 105
Czech, Ludwig, 271

D

Dagens Nyheter (Stockholm), 273; *375*
The Daily Telegraph (London), 333, 334
Daladier, Édouard, 193, 305, 310, 325,
  329, 337, 344
d'Annunzio, Gabriele, 66, 274
Dauthenday, Max, 4
Davis, Norman, 242
Dawson, Geoffrey, *380*
de Boer, Willem, 175, 291
de Boor, Helmut, 195
Debussy, Claude, 117, 118, 283
Dehmel, Richard, 31, 62, 87.
  Zwischen Volk und Menschheit, 57; *354*
Delbrück, Hans, 58
Delbrück, Joachim von, 11
Dell, Robert, 282
Democratic party, German (DDP), 90, 91,
  98
Denecke, Elisabeth, 99; *358*
Denzler, Robert F., 284
Dépêche (Toulouse), 160
de Reede, Dirk, 212
Dernburg, Ilse, 119, 159, 160, 161, 162,
  164, 207, 335
Destal, Fred, 235
Detroit Free Press, 321
Deutsche Allgemeine Zeitung, 141, 152
Deutsche Gesellschaft 1914, 14; *351*
Deutscher Klub, Berlin, 140, 216; *364,
  400*
Deutsche Wochenschau (Berlin), *369*
Deutsche Zentral-Zeitung (Moscow), *374*
The Dial (New York), *360, 373*
Dibelius, Otto, 168
Dickens, Charles, 185
Diebold, Bernhard, 160, 205, 256
Diederichs, Eugen, 110, 111
Diederichs, Eugen, Verlag, Jena, 270
Diederichs, Frau, 110
Dietrich, Bishop, 218
Dietz, Frau, 75
Dietz, Justice, 91
Dimitroff, Georgi, 179, 181, 197, 198,
  199; *363*
Disclez, Josef, 86
Disney, Walt, 300, 324
Dodd, Martha.
  Through Embassy Eyes, 318; *382*

449

Dodd, William Edward, 317
Dodds, Harold, 328
Döblin, Alfred, 85, 130, 131, 176, 291;
    *363, 365, 366. Predigt und
    Judenverbrennung,* 87
Döderlein, Albert, *55*
Dohm, Hedwig, *57*
Doll, 213, 231, 234, *255*
Dollfuss, Dr. Engelbert, 164, 196, 294
Doré, Gustav, 216
Dostoevsky, Fëdor, 12, 84, 89, 103, 185.
    The Brothers Karamazov, 85, 321, 322.
    Crime and Punishment, 84, 85, 305 (as
    play). *The Double,* 293. *The Eternal
    Husband,* 294; *379. An Honorable Thief,*
    101; *359. The Idiot,* 87, 88, 89, 91, 92,
    295; *357.* "An Unpleasant
    Predicament," 292
Doumergue, Gaston, 193
Driesch, Hans, 246; *371*
Droucker, Sandra, 42
Du Bos, Charles, 191
Dünzl, 13
Duhamel, Georges.
    The White War of 1938, 319
Durieux, Tilla, *59*
Durych, Jaroslav.
    Bloudeni, 184; *367*
Dyck, Walter von, 40
Dysing, Walter, *59*

E

Ebers, Hermann E., 26, 112
Ebert, Friedrich, 20, 36, 91, 157, 171,
    221
Écho de Paris, 274
Eckart, Dietrich, 25
Eckstein, 321
Eckstein, Friedrich.
    Alte unnennbare Tage, 248; *371*
Eddy, William Alfred, 329
Eden, Anthony, 236, 257, 294
Edschmid, Kasimir.
    Kean, 120; *361*
Egloffstein, Baron, 120
Ehmcke, F. H., *356*
Ehrenberg, Carl, 118; *361*
Ehrenberg, Paul, 66, 109, 141, 150,
    209–10
Ehrenfeld, Ernst, 209

Ehrhardt, Hermann, 216, 220
Eicken, Friedrich.
    *Geschichte und System der mittelalterlichen
    Weltanschauung,* 48, 50, 51, 52, 53;
    354
Einstein, Albert, 87, 120, 144, 179, 222,
    242, 248, 317, 320, 328; *381.* Ill. C4
Eisner, Kurt, 18, 19, 21, 22, 23, 24, 25,
    33, 34, 36, 37, 38, 39, 41, 62
Eisner, Pavel, 260
Elchinger, Richard, 69, 84, 100
Eliasberg, Alexander, 33, 55, 66, 76, 85,
    94, 102, 103, 105, 110, 118.
    (Ed.) *Russische Liebesnovellen,* 76; *356*
Eliasberg, Frau, *55,* 102, 103
Elster, Hanns Martin, 85, 111, 112; *360*
Eltzbacher, Paul, 105
Ender, Franco, 142
Endres, Elisabeth, 62, 78, 83, 90, 109
Endres, Franz Carl, 3.
    Bosporuswellen, 3
Endres, Fritz, 9, 33, 34, 46, 55, 61, 69,
    78, 83, 89, 91, 103, 109, 111
Endres, Theodor Carl, 61, 69
Engel, Fritz, 41
Epp, Franz Xaver von, 47, 48, 56, 90,
    134, 143, 156, 157, 158, 159, 163
Eranos-Jahrbuch (Zurich), *385*
Erasmus, 39, 143, 220, 221, 222, 226
Erb, Karl, 104, 338
Ermatinger, Emil, 109
Ernst, Fritz, 284.
    Iphigeneia und andere Essays, 197, 198;
    367
Ernst, Hans, 284
Ernst, Karl, 226
Erpenbeck, Fritz, *372*
Er und Sie, 133
Erzberger, Matthias, 87, 89; *357*
Esquire (Chicago), *380*
Essener Nationalzeitung, 262
Esser, Hermann, 192
Etiemble, René, 274
Ettlinger, Josef, *358*
Eulenberg, Herbert, 38, 103
Europäische Hefte (Prague and Paris), 218,
    232, 235
Europäische Revue (Leipzig), 169–70; *366*
Europäische Zeitung (Munich), 24
Europa-Verlag, Zurich, *372*
Europe, 132
Evans, Maurice, *381*
Evers, Johannes, 112

F

Fabian, Dora, 238; *370*

Fabricius, Ludwig, 68

Fadiman, Clifton, 301, 305, 306, 307; *380*

Faesi, Robert, 109, 122, 180, 185, 217, 237, 241, 304

Faktor, Emil, 260

Falckenberg, Otto, 87, 94, 128, 129

Falk, Dr., 334

Falke, Konrad, 304, 305; *374*

Fallada, Hans.
Wer einmal aus dem Blechnapf frisst, 201, 202–3; *367*

Faltin, Hermann, 3, 6, 8, 11, 42

Faulhaber, Archbishop Michael von, 36, 37, 128; *352*

Fayard, Arthème, publishers, Paris, 136, 163, 197; *363*

Fechenbach, Felix, 196

Fehr, Prof., 105

Feist, Hans, 127, 129, 133, 134, 135, 154, 171, 174, 179, 253

Feodora, grand duchess of Mecklenburg-Schwerin, 26; *352*

Ferber, Maria, 162

Feuchtwanger, Lion, 101, 102, 160, 194; *372, 374. Josephus*, 139, 162

Feuermann, Emanuel, 276

Fiedler, Kuno, 14, 58, 101, 138, 161, 176, 207, 217, 247, 276, 286, 300, 344; *351, 380. Luthertum oder Christentum*, 101

Figura (proposed journal), 73, 85; *356*

Fischer, Brigitte ("Tutti"), 63, 64, 152, 161, 240, 259, 272, 286, 291, 336, 337–38, 340

Fischer, Hedwig, 63, 64, 104, 120, 130, 142, 146, 203, 208, 336, 337, 338

Fischer, Hilde ("Hilla"), 64, 336, 337, 338

Fischer, Otokar, 274

Fischer, S[amuel], 16, 44, 61, 62–64, 77, 104, 111, 123, 130, 139, 142, 203, 208; *363*. Ill. B6

Fischer, S., Verlag, 9, 10, 41, 56, 60, 66, 67, 74, 75, 85, 96, 115, 116, 123, 134, 139, 141, 144, 162, 165, 168, 170, 175, 178, 179, 246, 254; *351, 355, 360, 362, 365, 366, 391*

Flake, Otto, 64–65, 99; *358*

Flammarion, Camille, 87

Flandin, Pierre Étienne, 238, 257

Flaskamp, Christoph, 31

Flatter, Richard, *378*

Flaubert, Gustave, 8, 14

La Flèche (Paris), 293

Fleiner, Frau, 185, 255

Fleiner, Fritz, 180–81, 255, 283

Fleischmann, Carlo, 179

Fleischmann, Rudolf, 264, 272; *375*

Fletcher, 322

Flexner, Abraham, 311, 328

Flinker, Martin, 332

Flotow, Baron Friedrich von.
Martha, 97

Foch, Ferdinand, 6, 17

Förster-Nietzsche, Elisabeth, 26, 31, 110

Foerster, Friedrich Wilhelm, 24, 41

Follett, Wilson, *380*

Fontane, Theodor, *355, 358. Effi Briest*, 69, 84; *355*

Forbes, Vivian, 238

Ford Hall Forum, Boston, 320

Forster, Albert, 336

Francke, Leo, 111

Franckenstein, Baron Clemens von, 18

Franco, Francisco, 271, 282, 317

François-Poncet, André, 164, 256

Frank, Bruno, 14, 19, 22, 26, 39, 68, 85, 93, 101, 120, 128, 129, 130, 153, 158, 175, 224, 226, 278, 296, 297, 298, 318; *374, 376*. Editor of TM's French, 115, 116. Munich Rotary Club and, 146, 147, 149. Response to *Wagner* protest, 151, 152. Correspondence with, 64, 133, 134, 161, 206, 214, 256, 271, 300, 326

Frank, Elisabeth ("Liesl"), 128, 129, 130, 136, 142, 143, 147, 149, 151, 153, 175, 224, 296, 297, 298, 318

Frank, Leonhard, 269.
Dream Mates, 258

Frankenberger, Julius.
Walpurgis, 271, 273; *375*

Frankfurter Zeitung, 10, 21, 31, 32, 33, 34, 36, 38, 42, 56, 58, 63, 84, 150, 151, 152, 157, 164, 165, 195; *350, 352*

Frankl, Oskar Benjamin, 233, 259, 260, 271

Fred, W. A., 97
Frederick II (the Great), 5; *350*
Frei, Walter, 201
Freie Presse (Amsterdam), 166
Freiligrath, Ferdinand, 227; *369–70*
French, Robert Dudley, 300
Frenzel, Thea, 114
Freud, Anna, 259
Freud, Ernst, 259
Freud, Sigmund, 160, 259, 277, 296,
    327; *372, 373*. *Beyond the Pleasure
    Principle*, 115. *Moses and Monotheism*,
    328; *383*
Freund, Robert, 305
Frey, Alexander Moritz, 191, 286.
    Spuk des Alltags, 112
Freytag, Eduard Erich, 68
Frick, Wilhelm, 192, 253
Friedell, Egon, 41, 296, 298; *358*
Friedenthal, Joachim, 25, 57
Friedmann, Judge, 69
Friedrich, Hans, 133, 139
Friess, Karl, 83–84
Frisch, Efraim, 24, 26, 40, 45, 120, 123;
    361
Frommel, Otto, 42, 43; *353*
Fucik, Bedřich, 260
Fulda, Ludwig, 136, 137–38, 139, 140,
    141, 142, 144, 145, 147, 148, 149,
    150, 151
Funk, Philipp, 25
Furtwängler, Wilhelm, 134, 151, 225;
    364

G

Gainsborough, Thomas, 322
Ganghofer, Ludwig, 102
Garbo, Greta, 257
Die Gartenlaube, 77
Gast, Peter, 235
Gauss, Alice, 310, 320
Gauss, Christian, 310, 312, 319
Gazette de Lausanne, 39
Gebauer, Jan, 377
Geffcken, Walter, 61
Geiger, Ludwig.
    Goethe und die Seinen, 273; *375*
Georg, Manfred, 233
Georg, prince of Saxe-Meiningen, 110,
    111

George VI of England, 340; *376*
George, Stefan, 65, 112, 117, 119, 201,
    217, 236, 305; *391, 392, 431*
Gerhard, Adele, 3, 101, 111.
    Sprache der Erde, 3
Gerlich, Fritz, 128, 133
German Academy, New York, 269; *374*
German Academy for the Cultivation of
    Germanism Abroad, 131; *363*
German Freedom party, *379*
Das Gewissen (Berlin), 85, 111; *359*
Gide, André, 123; *361, 365*.
    The Counterfeiters, 264. *Oeuvres complètes*,
    Vol. IX, 254; *371*. *Pages de Journal
    1929–1932*, 214; *368*. "Préface à
    quelques écrits récents de Thomas
    Mann," 280; *377*. *Return from the
    U.S.S.R.*, 275
Giehse, Therese, 127, 128, 130, 139,
    140, 148, 149, 156, 157, 173, 257,
    284, 303. Pressured to return to
    Germany, 129, 141, 146. In *The
    Peppermill*, 175, 191; *363*. Illness of,
    200, 203. Guest at table in Küsnacht,
    213, 214, 220, 221, 231, 247, 248,
    263, 274, 276, 278, 279, 280, 285,
    286. At Zurich Schauspielhaus, 282.
Gigon, Dr. Alfred, 206, 214
Gillet, Louis, 274
Ginzkey, Franz Karl, 71
Giraudoux, Jean.
    Tiger at the Gates, 263
Gisela, princess of Bavaria, 104
Glaeser, Ernst, 277
Gleichen-Russwurm, Baron Heinrich von,
    25, 88–89, 90, 216; *359, 364*
Glöckner, Ernst, 65, 66–67, 95, 114, 219
Godwin, Katharina, 66, 133
Goebbels, Joseph Paul, 141, 143, 151,
    162, 192, 218, 223, 225, 226, 239,
    325, 335; *364, 384*
Göhr, Fritz, 76
Goering, Hermann, 132–33, 142, 150,
    161, 170, 174, 175, 203, 218, 262,
    294, 310, 338, 340. Extravagance of,
    161, 162, 238. Uniform mania of, 173,
    178, 196. Reichstag fire and, 186, 199,
    226
Goethe, August von, *378, 380*
Goethe, Johann Wolfgang von, 5, 15,
    112, 116, 201, 205, 220, 237, 246,
    320, 342. TM's identification with, 37,
    38, 178, 200, 264, 342. *Achilleis*, 37;

352. *Annals*, 270, 306; *375*. *Campaign in France*, 38. (Conversations) ed. Baron Flodard von Biedermann, 39; *353*. *Dichtung und Wahrheit*, 37, 280, 300; *353*. *Der ewige Jude* (fragment), 37. *Faust I*, 5, 254, 271, 299, 305, 334. *Faust II*, 278, 326. *Urfaust*, 263. *Hermann and Dorothea*, 15; *351*. *Italian Journey*, 224; *369*. Poems, 271, 303: "Paria," *384*. "The Sorcerer's Apprentice," 19; *351*. *Sämtliche Werke* (Propyläen edition, including *Goethe als Persönlichkeit*), 299; *381*. *Scherz, List und Rache*, 5; *349*. *The Sorrows of Young Werther*, 343; *408*. *Sprüche*, 5; *349*. *Das Tagebuch*, 86. *Torquato Tasso*, 282; *377*. *Werke* ("Sophien" edition), 274, 302; *375*. *Wilhelm Meister's Apprenticeship*, 178, 271. *Wilhelm Meister's Travels*, 118, 245, 280; *361, 371, 377*

Goetz, Bruno, 256
Goetz, Curt, 123
Goetz, Walter, 84
Goetz, Wolfgang, 151; *364*
Gogol, Nikolai, 9, 231.
    Cossack stories, 25. *Dead Souls*, 319; *382*. "The Tale of How Ivan Ivanovich Quarreled with Ivan Nikiforovich," 9; *350*
Goldenberg, Dr. Theodor, 69
Goldman, Robert P., 321; *382*
Goldschmidt, Siegfried, 271
Goldwyn, Samuel, 297
Goll, Claire, 248.
    Arsenik, 178
Goll, Prof., 168
Goncharov, Ivan.
    A Common Story, 53
Gorky, Maxim.
    The Lower Depths, 263–64
Gosch, Dr. Wolfgang, 31, 33, 36, 38, 39, 40, 41, 45, 56, 99, 114
Gospolitizdat, publishers, Moscow-Leningrad, *374*
Gotthelf, Jeremias.
    Barthli der Korber, 112
Gräf, Hans Gerhard.
    Goethe über seine Dichtungen, 15; *351*
Graf, Oskar Maria, 259
Grant, Heber J., 296; *379*
Grautoff, Ferdinand, *371*
Grautoff, Otto, 245, 279; *371, 376*
Green, Julien, 264

Greenslet, Ferris, 320; *382*
Greiner, Leo, 120
Grey, Sir Edward, 180
Griesebach, Eberhard, 185
Grigoroff, Dr., 178
Grillparzer, Franz.
    The Poor Fiddler, 8, 10
Grimm, Jakob.
    Über meine Entlassung, 270–71; *375*
Grolman, Adolf von, 44, 90; *353*
Grossmann, Stefan, 76, 87; *356*
Groth, John Henry, *325*
Gruber, Dr., 78
Gründgens, Gustaf, 223
Grünewald, Matthias, 25
Gubler, Friedrich, 195
Günther, Dr. Carl, 193
Guenther, Johannes von, 68, 85; *357*
Gulbransson, Olaf, 114
Gumpert, Martin, 276, 299, 301, 308, 311, 320, 328, 330, 341, 344. *Dunant. A Novel of the Red Cross*, 308. *Das Leben der Idee*, 247; *371*
Guyer, Frau. *See* Studer-Guyer, Lux
Gwinner, Wilhelm.
    Arthur Schopenhauer aus persönlichem Umgang dargestellt, 255
Gyldendal Forlag, Copenhagen, 129, 131; *362*

H

Haag, Henry, 98
Haas, Willy, 128, 214
Haber, Fritz, 233
Hackländer, Friedrich Wilhelm, 85
Haenisch, Konrad, 62
Hässig, Alfred, 180
Hässig, Hans-Alfred, 180
Häuser, Fräulein, 97
Hagemeister, August, 39
Halbe, Max, 49.
    Der Strom, 122; *361*
Halifax, Lord, 333, 339, 343
Hallgarten, Constance, 19, 37, 40, 46, 84, 92, 100, 104, 109, 114, 256, 262, 269
Hallgarten, Richard ("Ricki"), 46, 77, 101; *352*
Hallgarten, Robert, 17, 40, 41, 84, 99, 100, 104, 109, 114
Hallgarten, Wolfgang, 37, 262, 269, 345

Hals, Frans, 322
Hamann, Johann Georg, 198
Hamburger, Käte, 148, 152-53, 167, 286, 339; *364*
Hammerstein, Oscar III, 297
Hamsun, Knut, 43, 65. "The Fly," 320. *Growth of the Soil,* 16, 24, 25, 42-43, 45-46, 65. *The Women at the Pump,* 123; *362*
Handel, George Frideric, 135
Hanfstängl, Erna, 34
Hanfstängl, Ernst ("Putzi"), 236
Hanhart, Ernst, 122, 180, 191, 269
Hardekopf, Ferdinand, *377*
Harden, Maximilian, 12, 17, 57, 62; *351*
Hardt, Ludwig, 94, 95, 104, 118-19, 120, 271, 318, 320
Harnack, Adolf von, 120
Harnisch, Johannes W., 88
Hartmann, Dr., 196
Harvard University, 235, 236, 242-43, 321; *402*
Hasenclever, Justice, 119
Hattingberg, Dr. Hans von, 69
Hatvany-Winsloe, Christa, 293
Hatvany, Jolan ("Loli") von, 270, 272, 273
Hatvany, Lajos von, 270, 272, 273
Hatzfeld, Adolf von, 61, 68, 96; *358*. *An Gott,* 58; *354*
Hauptmann, Gerhart, 62, 63, 78, 120, 130, 143, 157, 209, 214-15, 221; *363, 368, 369. The Beaver Coat,* 40; *353. Indipohdi,* 83; *357. The Weavers,* 119; *361*
Hauptmann, Klaus, 68
Hausenstein, Wilhelm, 27
Hauser, Heinrich. *Ein Mann lernt fliegen,* 175; *366*
Haydn, Joseph, 17. *Seven Last Words of Christ,* 204
Hebbel, Friedrich, 56. *Herod and Mariamne,* 119-20; *361*
Hebrew University, Cincinnati, 321-22; *382*
Heer, Gottlieb Heinrich, 263
Hefele, Hermann. *Das Gesetz der Form,* 37, 38, 39
Hegel, Georg Wilhelm Friedrich, 279
Hegner Verlag, Leipzig, 248; *357*
Heiden, Konrad, *376-77*
Heigel, Marie von, 61
Heilborn, Ernst, 118, 120

Heimann, Moritz, 96
Der Heimatdienst (Berlin), 32
Heims, Else, 215
Heine, Albert, 71, 74
Heine, Heinrich, 94, 282, 320. *Ludwig Börne,* 318. *The Romantic School,* 330
Heine, Thomas Theodor, 111, 259; *359*
Heinemann, William, Ltd., publishers, London, 258
Heines, Eduard, 216
Heins, Valentin, 153, 154, 159, 162, 163, 171, 179, 185, 192, 194, 196, 197, 200, 204, 206, 214, 231, 245, 302; *369*
Heise, Carl Georg, 119, 161
Heister, Baroness "Jane" von, 66
Helbling, Carl, 112, 144-45, 154; *360*
Held, Hans Ludwig, 173
Held, Heinrich, 137, 144, 149
Helferich, Karl, *357*
Heller, Hedwig, 72
Heller, Hermann, 128
Heller, Hugo, 70, 71, 72, 73, 74, 75, 78
Heller, Rabbi James Gutheim, 321, 322
Hellingrath, Baron Philipp von, 13; *350*
Hellmert, Wolfgang, 213
Hellmund, Heinrich, 185
Hellpach, Willy, 36, 142
Hellström, Gustaf, 337; *384*
Hemingway, Ernest, 242
Hemmer, Colonel von, 88
Henderson, Nevile, 335, 336
Henlein, Konrad, 260, 262
Henneberger, Johann, 68, 77
Hennig, 195
Hermann, Georg, 66
Hermann, Lucian, 88
Hermanns, Dr. Leo, 66, 88, 90, 91, 92, 94, 102, 112
Herms, Frau, 60
Herms, Klaus, 60
Herrenklub, Munich, 26, 39; *352*
Herriot, Édouard, 192, 193
Herrmann, Eva, 167
Herrmann, Helene, 84
Hertling, Count Georg von, 11
Hertwig, Oskar. *Allgemeine Biologie,* 101, 102
Herz, Ida, 204-5, 217, 239, 246, 247, 249, 262, 264, 292, 334, 335. Sends out *Joseph* material, 135, 161. Reports from Nazi Germany, 148, 201, 209.

As TM's archivist, 196, 248, 332.
Correspondence with, 140, 142, 175,
176, 187, 207, 212, 225, 263, 300,
310
Herzfeld-Wüsthoff, Günther, 3, 8, 14, 57,
197; *351*
Herzog, Wilhelm, 19, 20, 21, 22, 85,
175, 176, 186, 227; *351*
Hessberg, Richard, 104
Hesse, Hermann, 67, 135, 136, 138, 140,
143, 145, 151, 160, 202, 224, 225,
239, 248, 256, 280, 285, 305. *Das
Fabulierbuch*, 240; *370.* "The
Rainmaker," 209. Ill. B12
Hesse, Ninon, 133, 135, 136, 138, 140,
144, 145, 146, 151, 224, 285
Heuser, Friedrich Wilhelm, 145
Heuser, Klaus, 210, 246, 274
Heydebreck, Hans Peter von, 220
Heyking, Elizabeth von, 110
Hichens, Robert, 216
Hildebrandt, Kurt.
Norm und Entartung des Menschen, 119;
361
Hiller, Kurt, 225, 260, 344
Hiller, Wendy, *382*
Hindemith, Paul, *400*
Hindenburg, Paul von, 3, 13, 23, 91,
134, 143, 214, 221–22; *369*
Hintze, Paul von, 11
Hirsch, Dr., 156
Hirschfeld, Georg, 50
Hirschfeld, Kurt, 206, 264, 278, 305
Hirschfeld, Ludwig, *351*
Hirth, G., publishers, Munich, 43; *353*
Hirzel, Max, 256, 262
Hitler, Adolf, 128, 143, 170, 186, 202,
214, 223, 234, 236, 237, 257, 271,
296, 301, 303, 305, 308, 309, 324,
326, 332, 336, 337, 338; *362, 363,
384.* Seen as savior, 145, 196, 216,
217, 226. Speeches of, 148, 176,
177–78, 199, 200, 204, 233, 273,
318, 327, 329, 342, 345. Mussolini
and, 149, 239, 244, 299, 340, 344.
Psychology of, 174, 328, 333. Blood
Purge and, 215–16, 218, 220–21; *369.*
Compared to Luther, 220, 222; to
Wagner, 280. Annexes Czechoslovakia,
305–7, 322, 323. Invades Poland, 335,
339, 342
Hobart and William Smith College,
Geneva, New York, 329; *383*

Hoch, Frau, *59*
Hodler, Ferdinand, 111, 206; *359*
Hodža, Milan, 305
Hölderlin, Friedrich, 44, 201, 270; *353*
Hönn, Richard, 88
Hoerschelmann, Rolf von, 33, 66, 75
Hoffmann, 46
Hoffmann-Krayer, Eduard, 204
Hoffmann, Elisabeth, 17
Hoffmann, Johannes, 37, 39, 46, 47
Hoffmann, General Max, 221
Hofmann, Ludwig von, 32, 182
Hofmannsthal, Christiane von, 71, 122,
123
Hofmannsthal, Gerty von, 71, 122, 123
Hofmannsthal, Hugo von, 71, 73, 85,
122, 123, 209, 305; *356. Die Frau ohne
Schatten*, 69–70, 76, 83; *356.* Letters
of, 248. *Der Schwierige*, 123; *361. Der
Turm*, 207
Hofmiller, Josef, 5, 14, 69
Hohenlohe-Langenburg, Crown Prince
Ernst zu, 110; *359*
Holcomb, General Thomas, 329; *383*
Hollnsteiner, Johannes, 258, 259, 270,
272, 277, 292; *376*
Holm, Korfiz, 25
Holzner, Hans, 140, 143, 158
Homer, 304
Honsell, 98
Horowitz, Vladimir, 284
Horowitz, Wanda, née Toscanini, 284
Horváth, Ödön von.
A Child of Our Time, 307; *405*
Horwitz, Fritz, 2, 94
Hotel Schatzalp, Davos. Ill. A6
Hottinger-Mackie, Mary, 293
Howard, Leslie, *376, 382*
Huch, Ricarda, 157; *365, 394*
Hülsen, Hans von, 11, 48, 120.
Den alten Göttern, 9; *350*
Huizinga, Johan, *378.*
Der Mensch und die Kultur, 310
Hull, Cordell, 297, 327
Hurwicz, Elias.
(Ed.) *Russlands politische Seele*, 13; *351*
Hus, Jan, 202
Hutchinson, Bill, 304
Hutchinson, Ray Coryton.
Testament, 341; *384*
Huxley, Aldous, 146, 167, 275, 297;
365, 378
Huxley, Maria, 167, 275, 297

I

Ilgenstein, Dr., 138, 139
Illustrierte Leipziger Zeitung, 16, 56
Imago (Vienna), *372*
Impekoven, Niddy, 109
Independent Social Democratic party
 (USPD), 36, 44, 91, 93
Ingres, Jean Auguste Dominique, 322
Insel-Verlag, Leipzig, 51, 105, 140; *359*
Institute for Advanced Studies, Princeton,
 328, 344; *390, 399*
Internationale Literatur (Moscow), 264,
 270, 282, 286
Iselin, Hans, 109
Isherwood, Christopher, 318; *371, 382*
Isserman, Rabbi Ferdinand Myron, 323
Ivogün, Maria, 90

J

Jacob, Berthold, 240; *370*
Jacobsohn, Siegfried, 119; *363*
Jacobson, Leopold, 71, 75
Jacques, Norbert, 260
Jaeger, Hans Henrik, 111; *359*
Jaffé, Edgar, 49
Jaffe, Heinrich, 16, 66, 67, 69, 91
Jahnn, Hans Henny, 185
Jammes, Francis.
 Das Paradies, 95; *358*
Jean Paul, 112, 185.
 Der Titan, 95
Jensen, 283
Jeremias, Alfred, 191
Jespersen and Pio, publishers, Copen-
 hagen, 129, 133, 134, 197; *362*
Jessen, Dr. Friedrich, 109
The Jewish Forum (New York), *381*
Jewish Rescue League, 215; *368–69*
Joachim-Daniel, Anita, 238
Joël, Hedwig, 146, 150, 155
Joël, Karl, 109, 146, 150
Johnson, Alvin, 274; *374*
Johnson, Hugh, 218
Johst, Hanns, 58, 194.
 Der Kreuzweg, 122
Jollos, Waldemar, 334

Joly, Maurice, *372*
Jordan, Henry, 165
Le Jour (Paris), 176, 203
Joyce, James.
 Ulysses, 264
József, Attila, 329
Jüdische Rundschau (Berlin), 262
Jünger, Ernst, 148.
 Der Arbeiter, 146; *364*
Die Jugend (Munich), *353*
Jung, C. G., 201, 235
Jung, Edgar, 216.
 Die Herrschaft des Minderwertigen, 216
Der junge Baron Neubaus (film), 231

K

Kafka, Franz, 119, 120, 284, 293, 320
Kahler, Antoinette von, 318
Kahler, Erich von, 47, 239, 255, 256,
 263, 264, 273, 277, 278, 280, 303,
 304, 310, 318, 319, 320, 324, 327,
 342, 344. *Der Beruf der Wissenschaft*,
 103. *Der deutsche Charakter in der
 Geschichte Europas*, 264; *374*. *Israel unter
 den Völkern*, 236; *370*. "Die moralische
 Einheit der Welt," 318
Kahler, Josefine von, 239, 255, 258, 318,
 327, 342, 344
Kahr, Gustav Ritter von, 91
Kainer, Lene, 120
Kaiser, Georg, 96, 111; *359*.
 Gas, 68; *355*. *Villa Aurea*, 332; *384*
Kalckreuth, Count Leopold von, 32
Kapp, Wolfgang, 89, 90, 91, 92, 93
Kardorff, Siegfried von, 137
Karl I, emperor of Austria, 23
Karl V, Holy Roman emperor, 104, 222
Karl Eduard, duke of Saxe-Coburg and
 Gotha, 110
Károlyi, Count Mihály, 41
Karpath, Ludwig, 71, 72
Kassner, Rudolf, 25, 26.
 Zahl und Gesicht, 69, 79
Katzenellenbogen, Konrad, 241, 299, 311
Katzenstein, Dr. Erich, 205, 249, 277,
 280, 285
Kaufmann, Alfred, 93
Kaufmann, Felix, 74
Kaufmann, Lily, 304
Kaufmann, Nico, 284

Kaufmann, Susi, 284
Kaufmann, Dr. Willi, 284, 304
Kaula, Friedrich, 178
Kaulbach, Friedrich August von, 179; *367*
Kayser, Frau, 326
Kayser, Hans.
  Der hörende Mensch, 260
Kayser, Rudolf, 120, 179
Keiler, 321; *382*
Keilpflug, 186
Keller, Gottfried, 62, 202; *354.*
  Der grüne Heinrich, 63; *355. Martin
  Salander*, 61, 63, 65; *354. Zurich
  Novellas*, 98
Kemmerich, Max, 103
Kende, József, 273; *375*
Kerényi, Karl, 204, 209, 264, 277, 305;
  *380. Die griechisch-orientalische
  Romanliteratur*, 203; *367*
Kerner, Justinus.
  Der Totengräber von Feldberg, 101; *359*
Kerr, Alfred, 62, 76, 143, 150
Kessler, Count Harry, 104, 128; *378*
Kesten, Hermann, 168, 279, 292, 293,
  320; *365, 379. Children of Guernica*,
  319, 321. *I, the King*, 285; *378*
Kestenberg, Leo, 271
Kestner, Charlotte ("Lotte"), 237; *370,
  375, 376*
Kestner, Georg August, *355*
Kestner Society, Hannover, 68; *355*
Keynes, John Maynard.
  The Economic Consequences of the Peace,
  87; *357*
Keyserling, Count Eduard, 10
Keyserling, Countess Goedela, 67
Keyserling, Count Hermann, 67, 83, 85,
  152. *Travel Diary of a Philosopher*, 42,
  64, 65; *355. Was uns not tut*, 76, 77
Keyssner, Gustav, 36, 41
Kiefer, Wilhelm, 139, 141, 146, 156,
  167, 179, 187
Kiel, Hanna, 128, 130, 132–35 *passim*
Kieve, 132
Kilpper, 292
King, Mrs., 211
Kirsten family, 63, 64
Klausener, Erich, 216
Kleiber, Otto, 204
Klein, Woldemar, 269
Kleinsgütl, Josepha, 52, 109
Kleist, Heinrich von, 37, 94.
  The Prince of Homburg, 32; *352*

Klemperer, Otto, *364*
Klepper, Otto, 278
Klitsch, Wilhelm, 71, 72, 73, 112
Klöpfer, Frau, 151
Klopstock, Robert, 272, 278, 303, 304,
  307, 308, 317, 320, 330, 345
Klose, Friedrich, 41
Kluthe, Hans Albert, *379*
Knappertsbusch, Hans, 174; *366*
Kneussl, Paul Ritter von, 53
Knight, Miss, 296
Knittel, John, 303
Knoche, Dr. Erich, 145, 148
Knopf, Alfred A., 159, 161, 207,
  211–12, 213, 214, 276, 296, 299,
  301, 308–9, 313, 321, 330, 341, 344;
  368
Knopf, Alfred A., publishers, 141, 146,
  162, 255, 259, 319, 327; *377, 383*
Knopf, Blanche, 212, 276, 282, 299, 301,
  308–9, 313, 321, 344
Knopf, Edwin, 297, 298
Knuchel, Eduard Fritz, 109
Koch, 154, 158, 172
Köckenberger, Dr., 42, 50, 51
Köhler, Ludwig, 180–81
Kölwel, Gottfried, 214
Königsberger, Lieutenant, 20, 22
Körner, Theodor.
  Die Gouvernante, *352*
Köster, Kai, 133
Koestler, Arthur, 277, 329; *382.
  Spanish Testament*, 292, 294; *378*
Kokoschka, Oskar, 177, 180; *366*
Kola, Richard, 120; *360*
Kolb, Annette, 102, 140, 151, 155, 156,
  170, 206, 248, 253, 254, 276, 286,
  294, 302, 327, 328, 344; *378*. Ill. C2
Kolbenheyer, Erwin Guido, 233
Koltzow, Michail Jefimovich, 261
Kommerell, Max, 278
Komsomolskaya Pravda (Moscow), 241
Koppel, Heinrich, 301, 308, 311
Korrodi, Eduard, 21, 92, 95, 96, 109,
  122, 146, 150, 152, 180, 185, 255,
  256, 264, 313, 344; *354, 357, 372*
Koshland, William A., 301
Koussevitzky, Serge, 300
Kožak, Jan, 270, 271
Kraus, Karl, 334; *384*
Krause, Friedrich, 308
Krecke, Dr. Albert, 32
Kreisler, Fritz, 233, 273, 341

457

Kreitner, Bruno, 328; *383*
Krell, Max, 10, 11, 15, 16, 19, 21, 22, 23, 32, 39, 46, 49, 52, 54, 55, 57
Krofta, Kamill, 271
Kuckhoff, Adam, 48
Kühn, 321–22
Künstlerdank, Berlin, 112
Küsnacht house. Ill. B14
Kugel, Georg, 264, 272
Kurz, Marie, 129, 138, 145, 153, 159, 184, 198, 213, 214, 216
Kutscher, Artur, 61
Kyser, Hans, 119

L

Ladenburg, Rudolf Walter, 318
Laemmle, Carl, 223. Ill. C6
Lagerlöf, Selma.
  "A Fallen King," 52
La Guardia, Fiorello, 211, 212
Landauer, Gustav, 38.
  Aufruf zum Sozialismus, 36
Landecker, Peter, 115
Landsberg, Paul-Ludwig, 276
Landshoff, Fritz H., 178, 227, 231, 246, 299, 311, 330, 332, 333, 340; *365, 372, 375, 384, 408, 419*
Landshoff, Ludwig, 47
Lang, Josef Burkard, 109
Langer, František, 271
Langhammer, 104
Langhoff, Wolfgang, 291
Lányi, Jenö, 293, 334, 335
Laška, Jan, 299; *380*
Lassen, Christian, 26, 32, 44, 56, 57, 100; *352*
Laubruch, 320
Laval, Pierre, 241
Lawrence, D. H., 146
Lawrence, Frieda, *406*
League of American Writers, New York, 330; *384, 385*
League of Nations, 14, 15, 16, 33, 51, 54, 135, 136, 176, 177, 216, 239, 246, 256, 257, 258, 264, 285; *363, 364*
Lehmann, Lotte. Ill. B16
Leipzig trial, 173–74, 176, 178–79, 181, 185, 186, 198–99
Leisinger, Dr. Hermann, 284

Lenbach, Franz von, 182; *367*
Lenin, Nikolai, 45, 90
Leopold, prince of Bavaria, 36
Leppmann, Franz, 11, 21.
  Thomas Mann, 11
Leskov, Nikolai Semyonovich, 130, 197, 200, 203, 342
Lesser, Jonas, 286
Lessing, Gotthold Ephraim.
  Minna von Barnhelm, 77; *356. Nathan der Weise,* 277; *376*
Lessing, Theodor, 168
Levien, Max, 34, 36, 39
Leviné, Eugen, 53, 57, 59
Levy, Oskar Ludwig, 241
Lewald, Theodor, 248
Lewandowski, Herbert, 170
Lewis, Sinclair, 213, 242, 297.
  It Can't Happen Here, 261, 262, 263; *373, 416*
Lewisohn, Ludwig, 147, 150, 219.
  Forever Wilt Thou Love, 329; *383*
Leyen, Friedrich von der, 69
Liebermann, Max, 32; *374*
Liebknecht, Karl, 31, 32
Liefmann, Dr. Emil, 176, 329
Lillie, Beatrice, 276, 298
Lind, Frau, 259
Lindpaintner, Otto, 55
Link, Frau, 13
Lion, Ferdinand, 87, 100, 200, 201, 202, 223, 245, 254, 263, 264, 273, 274, 292, 293; *358, 384.* As editor of *Mass und Wert,* 269, 273, 277, 279, 282, 284, 286, 291, 299, 311, 312, 332, 333; *374, 378.* Other correspondence with, 208, 219, 299, 310. *Thomas Mann in seiner Zeit,* 234, 240; *370*
Lipmann, Heinz, 83
Lippschütz, 306, 307
Liptzin, Sol.
  Historical Survey of German Literature, 258
List, Emanuel, 276
Liszt, Franz, 168, 256
Das literarische Echo (Berlin), 118
Die literarische Welt (Berlin), 128, 179
Litterära Magasin, 257
Litzmann, Berthold, 64, 95, 104–5, 110, 111, 117, 123
Litzmann, Grete, 95, 104–5, 110, 111, 117, 123, 207
Lives of a Bengal Lancer (film), 237

Lloyd George, David, 23
Loeb, Dr. Albert, 3, 5, 6, 32, 33, 65
Loeb, Frau, 219
Löhr, Eva-Marie, 52, 53, 55–56, 59, 103
Löhr, Ilse-Marie, 59
Löhr, Josef ("Jof"), 9, 12, 43, 52, 53,
    55–56, 59, 61, 65, 78, 98, 99, 104,
    105, 120, 123; 357
Löhr, Julia ("Lula") Mann, 7, 8, 9, 31,
    33, 52, 53, 55–56, 61, 63, 65, 66, 78,
    83, 98, 104, 105, 120, 123. Ill. A1
Löwe, Ferdinand, 41
Löwenfeld, Philipp, 306
Löwenstein, Prince Hubertus zu, 269,
    318; 374
Löwenstein, Karl, 127, 139, 144, 145,
    146, 153, 219, 319
Löwy, Siegfried, 71, 74, 75
Lokal-Anzeiger. See Berliner Lokal-Anzeiger
Long, John, 327, 328, 341
Long, Lucy, 299
Lorrain, Claude, 4
Louis, Joe, 301; 380
Lowe, Elias, 343, 344
Lowe-Porter, Helen, 141, 161, 167, 311,
    320, 343, 344; 377, 385
Lubbe, Marinus van der, 137, 174, 179,
    181; 363
Lubitsch, Ernst. Ill. C6
Ludwig III of Bavaria, 19
Ludwig, Alois, 47, 48, 60, 75, 89, 90
Ludwig, Emil, 150, 256
Ludwig, Gustav, 45
Lüttwitz, Baron Walter von, 89, 91
Lukács, Georg, 282
Luther, Martin, 5, 143, 202, 220, 222
Luxemburg, Rosa, 31, 32

M

McDonald, James Grover, 381
MacDonald, James Ramsay, 238, 253
Mack family, 326
Maenner, Emil, 54
Magg, Alfons, 264
Mahler-Werfel, Alma, 127, 135, 258,
    259, 272
Mahler, Gustav, 71, 104, 279; 421, 423,
    426. Das Lied von der Erde, 110. Second
    Symphony, 104

Mahrholz, Werner.
    Deutsche Selbstbekenntnisse, 116; 360
Maier, 312
Majer, Herr, 32
Manchester Guardian, 217
Mann, Carla. Ill. A1
Mann-Borgese, Elisabeth Veronika
    ("Lisa," "Medi"), 3–123 passim, 128,
    146–49 passim, 182, 263, 270, 283,
    310, 312. TM's special affection for, 4,
    10, 16, 50, 52, 65, 127. Return to
    school in Munich, 129–45 passim.
    Schooling in Zurich, 147, 152, 175,
    208, 214, 246. Schwegerle head of,
    276; 351, 425. Marriage, 320, 325–26,
    344. Ills. B6, 7, 8, 9, 15
Mann-Auden, Erika Julia Hedwig, 10, 46,
    51, 52, 98, 101, 114, 129, 130, 214,
    225, 253, 255, 308, 311, 330–41
    passim; 356. As actress, 31, 77, 109
    (see also The Peppermill). Rescues Joseph
    ms. from Munich, 127, 128; 362.
    Finds house in Zurich for TM, 141,
    169. Writing of, 146, 297, 337, 340;
    382. Advisor and interpreter for TM,
    165–66, 276, 295–97 passim, 327.
    Marriage to Auden, 242, 278, 317–18;
    371. Escape to Life, 304; 380. Muck, der
    Zauberonkel, 164; 364. School for
    Barbarians, 299, 319; 379. Ills. B1, 6,
    10, 15, 16, C2
Mann, Golo, 3, 53, 58, 77, 99, 118, 144,
    161, 162, 215, 279, 285, 293, 302,
    317, 319, 328. Represents TM in
    Munich, 129, 132, 133, 137, 138,
    142, 147, 153, 154, 155, 158, 171.
    Searches for teaching position, 145,
    150, 152, 270; 375. In Rennes, 248.
    Editorial work on Mass und Wert,
    282, 299, 332, 333, 334; 374.
    Ills. B1, 6
Mann, Gret, née Moser, 283, 293, 311,
    317, 319, 320
Mann, (Luiz) Heinrich, 27, 37, 38, 41,
    57, 62, 76, 88, 89, 159–70 passim,
    218, 240, 241, 304; 363, 365, 368,
    372, 374, 376, 382. TM's
    estrangement from, 5, 10, 11, 32, 44,
    69, 86, 95, 114. Correspondence with,
    238, 249, 286, 291, 320. Brabach, 49,
    69. Es kommt der Tag, 258; 372. Der
    Hass, 365. Henry, King of France, 282,
    319. Madame Legros, 15, 49; 351.
459

The Patrioteer, 25, 45, 48, 49, 87; *351.*
Der Weg zur Macht, 49. Ills. A1, C6
Mann, Julia, née da Silva-Bruhns, 3, 34,
    51, 58, 69, 71, 77, 85, 87, 89, 94,
    117, 118, 240. Ill. A2
Mann, Katia (Katharina), née Pringsheim,
    3–345 *passim; 349, 350, 356, 357,*
    362, 374. Ills. B7, 8, 11, 13, 15, C3
Mann, Klaus Heinrich Thomas ("Eissi"),
    7, 25, 46, 51–58 *passim,* 66, 78, 92,
    96, 98–103 *passim,* 112, 139, 157,
    162, 213, 240–41, 249, 253, 278,
    307, 318, 330, 344; *362, 371, 372,*
    384. Writing of, 100; *358, 378, 382.*
    As editor of *Die Sammlung,* 170, 176;
    365, 366. Correspondence with, 256,
    292, 299, 324; *379. Kind dieser Zeit,*
    352. Mephisto, 263. *Der Vulkan,* 319;
    382. Ills. B1, 6, 10, 15
Mann, (Henriette Marie) Leonie
    ("Goschi"), 57, 89, 271
Mann, Magdalena ("Nelly"), née Kilian,
    78, 85, 98
Mann, Maria ("Mimi"), née Kanova, 57,
    85, 89, 260, 271; *357*
Mann, Michael Thomas ("Mischa,"
    "Bibi"), 51–52, 55, 59, 151, 152, 182,
    214, 276, 285, 286–87, 294, 311,
    337, 338, 341; *357.* Musical training,
    156, 175, 194, 208, 300; *395.*
    Marriage, 293, 317, 320. Ills. B7, 8, 15
Mann-Lányi, Monika, 33, 58, 64, 78, 89,
    98, 100, 117, 158, 191, 223, 253,
    304, 334, 335. Ills. B1, 6
Mann, Nelly, née Kröger, 165, 241. Ill. C6
Mann, Thomas, illustrations of: A1; B6,
    7, 8, 9, 12, 13, 14, 15, 16; C3, 4, 5,
    6, 7, 8
Mann, Thomas Johann Heinrich, 57; *361.*
    Ill. A3
Mann, Viktor ("Vicco"), 11, 19, 26, 78,
    98, 143, 144, 148, 177
Mannheimer, Viktor, 66, 101
Marchesani, Lisa, 161, 179
The March of Time, 329
Marck, Siegfried, 264, 269, 311
Marcks, Erich, 32, 34, 58, 76, 77, 92,
    99, 109, 114, 122. *Männer und Zeiten,*
    14
Marcks, Erich, Jr., 58, 99
Marcks, Friederike, 32, 34, 58, 77, 92,
    99
460   Marcks, Gerta, 99, 114

Marcks, Otto, 52
Margolies, 317
Maril, Konrad, 133
Marilaun, Karl, 73
Martens, Armin, 63, 210
Martens, Kurt, 8, 15, 22, 26, 34, 36, 39,
    48, 55, 58, 112, 116, 122. As editor,
    3, 25, 49, 75–76, 117, 120. *Scho-*
    nungslose Lebenschronik, 120, 122; *361*
Martin, 32
Marx brothers, 309
Masaryk, Jan, 322–23
Masaryk, Tomáš Garrigue, 280; *377*
Massary, Fritzi, 137, 143, 152
Mass und Wert, 269, 273–74, 276, 277,
    282, 284, 286, 292, 294, 296, 318,
    320, 328, 332; *374, 376, 377, 378,*
    379, 384. Ill., 281
Matuschka, Count, 112
Maupassant, Guy de, 92, 185
Maurach, Johannes, 104
Maury, Geneviève, 117
Max, prince of Baden, 11, 12, 18, 20
Maync, Harry, 109
Mayrisch de Saint-Hubert, Aline, 269,
    273, 334; *374*
Mazzucchetti, Lavinia, 132, 134, 148,
    149, 304, 334
Medicus, Fritz, 248
Meier, Oskar, 208
Meier-Graefe, Anne Marie, 156, 163,
    164, 165, 167, 168, 170, 272
Meier-Graefe, Julius, 155, 156, 157, 163,
    164, 165, 167, 168, 170
Meisel, Hans, 312, 313, 317, 318, 319,
    320, 324, 327, 328, 329, 330, 341,
    342, 343
Meisinger, 192
Meissinger, Karl August.
    Helena, 303
Melantrich, publishers, Prague, 201
Melba, Nellie, 84
Mencken, H. L., 212
Mendel, Alfred O., 292
Mendelssohn, Felix Manuel, 156; *365*
Mendelssohn, Gerda von, 85
Mendelssohn-Bartholdy, Albrecht, 58
Meng, Dr. Heinrich, 255
Menuhin, Yaltah, *415*
Menuhin, Yehudi, 186
Meredith, George.
    Lord Ormont and His Aminta, 54
Merezhkovsky, Dmitri, 12, 32, 110

Mérimée, Prosper, 328
Merkur. See *Der Neue Merkur*
Merrem-Nikisch, Grete, 127
Merz, Georg, 86; *357*
Messersmith, George S., 311
Meyer, Agnes E., 286, 301, 302, 303, 307, 313, 320, 326, 334, 336, 340, 342, 344. Writings on TM, 292, 312; *378, 383*. Part in TM's appointment to Princeton, 296, 299, 301; *379*. Financial support of *Mass und Wert*, 318, 328
Meyer, Camilla Elisabeth, 122, 185
Meyer, Conrad Ferdinand, 12, 122, 185. *Ein Briefwechsel*, 12; *350*
Meyer, Eduard. *Die Israeliten und ihre Nachbarstämme*, 225; *369*
Meyer, Elizabeth, 297, 326
Meyer, Eugene, 301, 312, 313, 326
Meyer, Georg Heinrich, 102; *359*
Meyer, Lieutenant, 111
de Meyier, Fenna, 273
Mhe, Herbert, 38
Michalski, Heinrich, 47
Michelangelo, 63, 269
Milstein, Nathan, 283
Mironas, Vladas, 325; *382*
Mitford, Rupert and Flora, 302
Die moderne Welt (Vienna), 14; *351*
Möhl, General Arnold von, 55, 56, 90
Moellendorf, Wilhelm von, 256
Mohr, Johann, 272
Mohr, Max, 153, 256
Moissi, Alexander, 70, 94, 237
Molière. *The Miser*, 123
Molnár, Ferenc, 294
Molotov, Vyacheslav Mikhailovich, 339
Mombert, Alfred, 157
Der Monat, 167
Mondadori, Editore, Milan, 149
Montagsblatt. See *Prager Montagsblatt*
Monternach, 136, 139
Montgomery, Robert, 297, 341
Morazzi, 211
Morena, Erna, 20; *351*
Morgen, Ruth von, 130, 134, 135
Der Morgen (Berlin), 208; *368*
Der Morgen (Vienna), 70
Morgenstern, Christian, 94
Móricz, Zsigmond. *Sárarany*, 120; *361*

Moritz, Karl Philipp, 198
Motta, Giuseppe, 146, 149, 150, 151
Moy, Count Max von, 34, 55
Mozart, Wolfgang Amadeus, 42, 109, 186, 256, 343
Muckle, Friedrich. *Goethe's Frömmigkeit*, 264; *373*
Mühll, Hans von der, 155
Mühll, Theodora von der, 155
Mühsam, Erich, 19, 22, 39, 63
Mühsam, Kreszentia, 261
Müller, Adolph, 150, 151
Müller-Hofmann, Eva, 39
Müller, Dr. Friedrich von, 6, 9, 11
Müller, Hans. *Die Sterne*, 74; *356*
Müller, Karl Eugen, 26
Müller-Hofmann, Wilhelm, 39, 71, 73
München-Augsburger Abendzeitung, 15, 53
Münchener Zeitung, 15, 48
Münchner Blätter für Dichtung und Graphik, 353
Münchner Neueste Nachrichten, 18, 20, 22, 24, 25, 34, 38, 39, 40, 45, 49, 58, 69, 76, 84, 87, 90, 105, 116, 151, 153; *357, 359, 365*
Münzenberg, Willi, *382*
Mummenhoff family, 104
The Mummy (film), 248
Muncker, Franz, 85
Munich Political Society 1918, 25; *351*
Muret, Maurice, 39, 40
Murray, Gilbert, 148, 150, 152, 335
Murray, Mrs., 152
Musarion Verlag, Munich, 102, 114, 117; *360*
Muschg, Walter, 274
Musil, Robert, 70, 71, 72, 75, 94, 247, 248, 272; *378. Vereinigungen*, 72, 85
Mussolini, Benito, 157, 206, 238–39, 243, 244, 247, 308, 309, 324, 325, 327, 338, 344; *383*. On TM, 149. Meetings with Hitler, 239, 299, 340
Mutius, Gerhard von, *352*
Muto, Anthony, 243–44

N

Nachrichten. See *Münchner Neueste Nachrichten*
Nadoleczny, Dr. Max, 31, 42, 104

461

Näf, Hans, 225
Nägel, 243, 276
Nahys von Eugen, Alice, 333; *384*
Nansen, Fridtjof, *364*
Napoleon, 170
The Nation (New York), *377*
National Socialist German Workers'
  (Nazi) party (NSDAP), 131–32, 134,
  136–37, 138, 141, 148, 149, 151,
  153, 160–61, 164, 169–70, 171–73,
  199, 215–17, 218, 220–21, 222, 225,
  227, 254, 260, 262; *363*
National-Zeitung (Basel), 139, 204, 237,
  248, 255, 282, 283, 334; *376, 381*
Natonek, Hans, 271
Naumann, Hans, 110, 111
Neppach, Robert, 334; *384*
Das neue Deutschland, 317
Neue Freie Presse (Vienna), 72, 74, 83,
  152, 176
Der Neue Merkur (Munich), 24, 40, 46,
  49, 66, 76, 87, 99, 102, 115, 120,
  123; *353, 361*
Die Neue Rundschau (Berlin), 10, 11, 16,
  19, 44, 57, 76, 83, 85, 88, 100, 128,
  130, 145, 146, 154, 165, 168, 169,
  184, 209, 226, 254, 260, 261; *362,
  364, 365*
Das Neue Tage-Buch (Paris), 138, 164,
  177, 181, 195, 219, 234, 249, 286,
  292, 298, 318, 319, 326, 328, 329,
  330, 333, 343; *356, 377, 379, 380,
  381*
Neue Volkszeitung (New York), 309
Die Neue Weltbühne (Prague), 258, 262,
  286, 302, 318, 319; *363, 372, 378,
  379*
Neues Wiener Journal, 41; *370*
Neues Wiener Tagblatt, 74
Neue Zeitung (Munich), 110
Neue Zürcher Zeitung, 62, 122, 128, 133,
  141, 150, 176, 177, 178, 180, 185,
  197, 201, 202, 237, 254, 256, 260,
  261, 303, 344; *354, 357, 361, 368,
  372, 373*
Neueste. See *Münchner Neueste Nachrichten*
Neumann, Alfred, 161, 177; *374*
Neumann, Johann Martin Andreas, 119
Neurath, Baron Konstantin von, 223
The New Republic (New York), 294
New School for Social Research, New
  York, 269, 276; *374, 376, 406*
News Chronicle (London), 306

Newton, Caroline, 299, 300, 304, 309,
  330, 341, 345; *385*
New York Herald Tribune, 181, 311; *368,
  376, 381*
The New York Times, 176, 195, 212, 243,
  299, 300, 307, 310
New York World's Fair 1939, 317, 318,
  328, 343; *382, 385*
Nicolson, Harold, 180, 335; *378*
Niderlechner, Max, 61, 84
Niebuhr, Reinhold, 317
Niedermann, Max, 193
Niemöller, Martin, 236
Nietzsche. See Bertram, Ernst
Nietzsche, Friedrich, 5, 6, 52, 102, 110,
  150, 178, 201, 204, 205, 226,
  234–35, 242, 246, 254–55, 260–61,
  280, 284, 303. *Also sprach Zarathustra*,
  5, 261. *The Birth of Tragedy*, 280. *The
  Case of Wagner*, 280. *Gesammelte Werke*
  (Musarion edition), 114
Nikisch, Arthur Philipp, 127
Noelle, 104
Nolde, Emil, 119
Norddeutsche Allgemeine Zeitung (Berlin),
  21; *351*
Noske, Gustav, 89
Nouvelles Littéraires (Paris), 145, 184
Nouvelle Revue Française (Paris), 120; *361*
Novak, Arne, 259
Novalis, 100, 269

O

O'Brien, Father John A., 298
Odeon (proposed journal), 85; *357*
Öhler, Adalbert, 110
Østergaard, Carl V., 129, 131
Oestvig, Karl Ägaard, 69, 73
L'Oeuvre (Paris), 335
Olden, Rudolf, 334–35.
  *Hindenburg oder der Geist der preussischen
  Armee*, 240
Oldenbourg, Rudolf, 47
Onegin, Sigrid, 175
Onno, Ferdinand, 70, 72, 73, 75
Opitz, Walter, 4, 8
Oppenheimer, Carl, 26
Oppenheimer, Franz, 26
Oppenheimer, Friedrich, 312
Oppenheimer, Max, 272, 312

Oprecht, Emil, 227, 264–65, 278, 282, 283–84, 291, 292, 304, 318, 320, 332, 333. Ill. C7
Oprecht, Emmie, 227, 264–65, 278, 283–84
Oprecht, Verlag, Zurich, 258, 259, 264, 270, 273, 308; *373, 374*
Oprescu, Georges, 270
Orchard, Thomas, 329
Ortega y Gasset, José.
Revolt of the Masses, 218; *369*
Osborn, Dr., 299
Osel, Heinrich, 34, 37
Ossietzky, Carl von, 196, 208, 247, 248; *363, 371*
Otte, Sara Catharina ("Rini"), 340
Otto, Walter F.
The Gods of Greece, 204

P

Pacurariu, Aurelian, *374–75*
Padisha, 335, 336
Pallenberg, Max, 94, 214
Pannwitz, Rudolf, 76, 86, 87, 102, 157; *352, 357. Einführung in Nietzsche*, 102
Panofsky, Erwin, 328
Papen, Franz von, 129, 132–33, 140, 214, 216, 218, 336, 343
Paquet, Alfons, 32
Pariser Tageblatt, 385
Pariser Tageszeitung, 344; *385*
Patzak, Julius, *259*
Paul, Elliot, *385*
Paulsen, Wolfgang, 293
Pavlova, Claudia, 118; *360*
Payer, Friedrich von, 4, *5*
Peat, Harold, 292, 296, 297, 298, 309, 317
Péguy, Charles, *255*
Péladan, Joséphin.
La Panthée, 58, 59. La Rondache, 93, 94
PEN Club, 131, 185, 194, 204, 212, 273, 327; *363, 367, 384.* Stockholm Congress 1939, 335; *383*
Penzoldt, Dr. Fritz, 175
People's party, German (DVP), 98
The Peppermill, 139, 146, 175, 191, 207, 232, 233; *363, 377, 400*
Perl, Walter H., 207

Perrault, Charles.
"The Ass's Skin," 48, 50. "Fairy," 101. Fairy tales, *369*
Pester Lloyd (Budapest), 36, 238; *372*
Peterson, Houston, 148
Le Petit Parisien, 182
Petri, Egon, 212
Petru, Sietcu, *374*
Pfaehler, Albert, 109
Pfitzner, Hans, 7, 11, 14, 17, 26, 57, 84, 86, 91, 99, 164, 174, 198; *354, 357, 365. Der arme Heinrich, 59; 354. Palestrina*, 8, 87, 120; *350, 355*
Pfitzner, Maria, 9, 26, *59*, 86
Pfitzner, Paul, 17, 26
Pfordten, Baron Hermann Ludwig von der.
Deutsche Musik, 9; *350*
Phantasus-Verlag, Munich, 86; *353*
Philip II, king of Spain, 14; *378*
Philippe, Charles-Louis, 91.
Marie Donadieu, 85, 92
Philipson, Ivar, 337
Piccaver, Alfred, 97
Pidoll, Carl von, 65, 105
Pidoll, Baroness Ester von, 269
Piétri, François, 243
Pilar, princess of Bavaria, 104, 117
Piloty, Melanie von, 26
Pinder, Wilhelm, 159
Pinkus, Klaus, 162, 197, 207, *253*
Piokarska, Frau, 67, 84, 97
Piper, R., & Co., publishers, Munich, 248
Pius XI, *366*
Pius XII, 324, 344
Pixis, Erwin, *59*
Planck, Max, 161, 180, 186, 233
Platen Hallermund, Count August von, 65, 197–98; *350, 366, 367*
Plato, 171
Platzer, Martin, 109–10, 204, 248
Pniower, Otto, 96, 97; *358*
Podach, Erich F., 204
Podbielski, 191
Poincaré, Raymond, 22
Political Council of Intellectual Workers, 25, 26, 37
Politiken (Copenhagen), 122, 179
Ponten, Josef, 32, 41, 56, 58, 67, 95, 104, 111–12, 114, 115, 116, 122, 202, 233. *Der babylonische Turm*, 21, 22. *Der Bockreiter*, 67. "Die Fahrt nach Aachen," 95. *Griechische Landschaften,*

57; *354*. *Die Insel,* 42. *Jungfräulichkeit,* 67

Pontoppidan, Henrik.
  Kingdom of the Dead, 105
Poschingerstrasse house, Munich. Ills. A7–8
Die Post, 38, 88
Prager Mittag, 170
Prager Montagsblatt, 271
Prager Presse, 123, 216, 218, 310; *362, 377*
Prager Tagblatt, 232, 271
Prantl, 78
Preetorius, Emil, 15, 22, 32, 34, 44, 47, 69, 92, 153; *350*
Prince, Conseiller, 203; *367*
Princeton house. Ill. C4
Princeton University, 296, 299, 301, 328; *379, 380, 382, 383, 385*
Pringsheim, Alfred, 6, 19, 47, 55, 57, 58, 99, 129, 159, 182, 214, 215, 247, 258, 302, 329–30; *349, 350, 370, 383–84.* Majolica collection of, 100–101, 141, 298; *358.* Ill. B7
Pringsheim, Emilie ("Milka"), 62, 260, 271
Pringsheim, Erik, 84; *357*
Pringsheim, Hedwig, 14, 16, 18, 33, 39, 40, 48, 49–58 *passim,* 76, 84, 86, 88, 90, 92, 99–105 *passim,* 114, 129, 134, 137, 138, 141, 159, 163, 182, 185, 214, 215, 245, 258, 302, 329–30; *349, 370, 383–84.* Ill. B7
Pringsheim, Heinz, 111; *359*
Pringsheim, Klara ("Lala"), née Koszler, 62, 111; *359*
Pringsheim, Klaus, 51, 62, 87, 104, 111, 120; *359*
Pringsheim, Olga, née Markowa Meerson, 111; *359*
Pringsheim, Peter, 64, 65, 67, 77, 78, 104, 111, 120, 155, 184, 213, 238
Prinz, Robert, 83
Prittwitz, Maria Luise von, 93
Progress (stenographic bureau), 76, 92, 102; *356*
"Protest by Munich, the Wagner City," 151, 152, 153, 161, 163, 164, 172, 174, 217; *365, 366*
The Protocols of the Elders of Zion, 254; *372*
Proust, Marcel, 102, 185.
  Swann's Way, 286, 291; *378*

Prussian Academy of Arts, 62, 130, 131, 136, 143, 157, 159, 163, 195; *363, 365*
Puccini, Giacomo, 93.
  La Bohème, 84, 86
Pulver, Max, 219, 221
Pushkin, Alexander, 9.
  The Captain's Daughter, 233. *Dubrovsky,* 233
Putz, Arnold, 110

Q

Querido, Emanuel, 165, 333
Querido Verlag, Amsterdam, 176, 178, 258, 280, 286; *365, 375, 384*
Quidde, Ludwig, 24

R

Rabener, Johann, 207, 226, 264.
  Condemned to Live, 178
Radek, Karl, 31
Raff, Helene, 85
Raimund, Ferdinand.
  Alpenkönig und Menschenfeind, 207; *368*
Random House, publishers, 336; *386*
Rascher, Albert, 246
Rascher, Hans, 206, 236
Rascher, Max, 206, 226, 236, 246
Rascher & Cie., Verlag, Zurich, 226, 246
Rastede, Hans Gerhard, 319, 341, 343
Rathenau, Walther, 7, 12, 13, 32, 39, 96, 157. *Zeitliches,* 7
Rauch, Dora, 10
Rauschning, Hermann, 328, 332, 333, 344. *The Revolution of Nihilism,* 312; *381*
Rebal, Amica Savic, 292
Reclam, Philipp, Jr., publishers, Leipzig, 140, 204, 234, 299
Reich Central Office for National Service, 33; *352*
Reich Literature Chamber, 221, 237; *362, 369, 370*
Reichner Verlag, Vienna, 285
Reichstag fire, 137, 151, 199, 215, 218, 226. *See also* Leipzig trial

Reiff, Hermann, 109, 122, 174, 175,
182, 184, 209, 215, 283, 303
Reiff-Sertorius, Lilly, 109, 122, 174, 175,
182, 209, 215, 283
Reinacher, Eduard, 8, 99
Reinhardt, Delia, 46, 117
Reinhardt, Karl, 218.
Sophokles, 218
Reinhardt, Max, 215, 297; *364*. Ill. C6
Reisiger, Hans, 63, 104, 127, 128, 181,
185, 186, 191, 192, 194, 195, 196,
221, 226, 227, 234, 241, 253, 264,
265, 280, 282. As translator, 116; *360*.
As reviewer of TM, 184. TM's special
fondness for, 225, 246, 254, 269, 270.
Desperation of under Nazis, 221, 299;
379. Correspondence with, 131, 133,
145, 150, 160, 201, 212, 248, 273,
276. Ills. B6, 8
Remarque, Erich Maria, 150, 156; *365*.
Three Comrades (film), 306
Rembrandt, 333
Renn, Ludwig, 133
Renner, Paul, 26
Republic of Germany, 20, 23, 24, 25, 38,
50, 53, 54–55, 68, 89, 90, 93, 157,
161, 195, 202, 220, 221, 223
Requadt, Paul, 26
Die Rettung (Hellerau), 76
Reuss, Crown Prince Heinrich XXV, 110
Reventlow, Count Ernst von, 76
Revue de Genève, 105, 117
Reynaud, Paul, 343
Rheinhardt, Emil Alphons, 95, 102, 117,
158; *358*
Rheinhardt, Gerty, 102, 117
Rheinstrom, Heinrich, 179
Ribbentrop, Joachim von, 334, 342
Richter, Dr., 129, 255, 291, 293
Richter, Georg Martin, 31, 41, 46, 57,
60, 67, 68, 84, 85, 89, 92, 93–94, 96,
97, 101, 102; *353, 355, 357*
Richthofen, Elsa von, *406*
Rieder, Hermann, 96
Riemer, Friedrich Wilhelm, *375*
Rieser, Marianne, 233
Riess, Curt, 276, 301, 308, 311, 317,
326
Rikola-Verlag, Vienna, 116, 117; *360*
Rilke, Rainer Maria, 26, 27, 78, 237; *370*
Rimsky-Korsakov, Nikolai, 291
Ritchie, Frank, 309

Robert, Paul Anton.
Der missbrauchte Mensch, 242
Robespierre, 216
Rockefeller Foundation, 301
Rodenberg, Julius–Meyer, Conrad
Ferdinand.
Ein Briefwechsel, 12; *350*
Röhm, Ernst, 170, 216, 317
Rohan, Prince Karl Anton, 169–70; *366*
Rohrscheidt, Dietrich von, 110
Rohrscheidt, Marta von, 122
Rolland, Romain, 36, 105, 162, 275;
376, 389. Danton, 104. *Jean Christophe*,
21
Romains, Jules, 344
Roosevelt, Eleanor, 244, 309; *381*
Roosevelt, Franklin Delano, 244, 253,
318, 326–27, 336; *383*
Rosar, Anni, 71, 74
Rosé, Alfred, 72
Rosé, Arnold, 72
Rosé, Justine, 72
Rosenbaum, 178
Rosenberg, Alfred, *366*
Rosenberg, Else, 63, 104, 110, 111; *361*
Rosenberg, Hans, 111
Rosenberg, Käthe, 110, 119, 131, 205,
237, 335; *370, 371*
Rosenthal, Friedrich, 70–75 *passim*, 102;
356
Rossbach, Gerhard, 220
Rosshaupter, Albert, 34
Rossini, Gioacchino, 309
Rostovtzeff, Michael Ivanovich.
*The Social and Economic History of the
Roman Empire*, 313
Rotary Club, Munich, 131, 146, 147,
149
Roth, Joseph, 170, 332; *365*
Roth, Sergeant, 44; *353*
Rothbart, Margaret, 304
Rowohlt, Ernst, *353, 356*
Ruffo, Titta, 84
Rummel, Baron Gustav von. *See* Waldau,
Gustav
Rundschau. See Die Neue Rundschau
Rupprechts-Presse, Munich, *356*
Russell, Henry Norris, 319
Rust, Bernhard, 159, 233
Rutgers University, New Brunswick, New
Jersey, 327
Rychner, Max, 178, 202

S

Saenger, Samuel, 168, 169
Saint-Saëns, Camille, 248
Salisbury, Marquis of, 34
Salten, Felix, 74, 75; *356*
Saltykov. *See* Shchedrin, N.
Salzer, Dr. Fritz, 102
Die Sammlung (Amsterdam), 168, 170,
    171, 176, 178, 195, 223, 241; *365–66*
Sarraut, Albert, 257
Saturday Review, 212
Satz, Frau, 64
Satz, "Hanni," 63
Satz, Herr, 63
Sauber, Fritz, 36
Sauerbruch, Ferdinand, 36
Saunders, Arthur Percy, 149
Saxl, Fritz, 334
Schacht, Hjalmar, 203, 205, 285
Scharff, Alexander, 208, 247
Scharnagl, Karl, 127
Scheidemann, Philipp, 17, 18
Schellong, 63, 64, 65
Schenk, Baron, 63
Schertel, Max, *325*
Schickele, Anna, 159, 163, 165, 167,
    168, 170, 192, 241
Schickele, Hans, 157, 158, 159, 160, 241
Schickele, René, 152, 156–70 *passim*,
    176, 192, 227, 241, 285; *366, 374.*
    Correspondence with, 151, 181, 214,
    216, 278, 284, 293. *Die Flaschenpost*,
    274; *376. Witwe Bosca, 376*
Schildkraut, Rudolf, 94
Schiller, Friedrich von, 284.
    Ballads, 319. *The Maid of Orleans*, 32,
    111; *352. The Piccolomini*, 284; *377.*
    Wallenstein's Camp, 284; *377*
Schillings, Max von, 130, 131; *363*
Schipper, Zacharias Emil, 74
Schlageter, Albert Leo, 254
Schlamm, Willi, 232, 235
Schlegel, Friedrich, 178
Schleicher, Kurt von, 216, 218, 222
Schloss, Sibylle, 248
Schlumberger, Jean, 192, 269, 273
Schmalenbach, Hermann, 155
Schmeling, Max, 301
Schmid, Karl, *389*

Schmid-Bloss, Karl, 284
Schmidt, 104
Schmidt, Josef, 276
Schneider, 185
Schneider, Anne Marie, 186; *367*
Schneider, Walther.
    Schopenhauer, 274
Schnitzler, Arthur, 72, 74, 75; *378*
Schnitzler, Heinrich, 74
Schnitzler, Lili, 74
Schnitzler, Lily von, 26–27
Schnitzler, Olga, 74, 75
Schoch, Paula von, 26
Schöll, Else, 16, 22, 40, 86, 105
Schöll, Hedwig, 22, 105, 118
Schöne, 116
Schönherr, Karl, 272
Schoeps, Hans-Joachim.
    Gestalten an der Zeitwende, 284; *377*
Scholl, 280
Schopenhauer, Adele, *376*
Schopenhauer, Arthur, 68, 226, 293, 299.
    The World as Will and Idea, 61, 277,
    286; *354, 376, 378*
Schott, Werner, 74
Schrempf, Claus, 168
Schrenck, Edith von, 69
Schubert, Franz, 99, 269, 338
Schuh, Willi, 256
Schulthess-Reimann, Paula, 204
Schumann, Robert, 17, 26, 40, 256.
    Piano Concerto, 248
Schuschnigg, Kurt von, 258, 259, 260,
    294, 339
Schwabe, Rudolf, 203–4
Schwarzenbach, Annemarie, 157, 214,
    221, 231, 247–48, 249, 279, 303,
    304. Ill. B12
Schwarzschild, Leopold, 138, 161, 162,
    164, 176, 234, 320, 328; *356, 376–77.*
    Das Ende der Illusionen, 207; *368*
Schwegerle, Frau, 117
Schwegerle, Hans, 26, 32, 36, 45, 53,
    112; *351, 361*
Schweizer Monatshefte (Zurich), 265
Secker, Martin, Ltd., publishers, London,
    214
Seger, Gerhart.
    Oranienburg, 195; *367*
Seidel, Willy, 98, 100, 112
Seidl, Walter, 260
Seif, Dr. Leonard, 69
Seitz, Karl, 151, 217

Selbstwehr (Prague), 214
Serkin, Rudolf, 208, 248
Servicen, Louise, 216, 332; *369*
Sessions, Roger, 344
Severing, Karl, 140
Shakespeare, William, 285, 304.
  Anthony and Cleopatra, 256. *As You Like It*, 109. *Hamlet*, 311; *381*. *Romeo and Juliet* (film), 275; *376*. *Troilus and Cressida*, 304
Shaw, George Bernard, 274.
  The Adventures of the Black Girl in Her Search for God, 160. *Peace Conference Hints*, 57. *Pygmalion* (film), 323
Shchedrin, N.
  The Messieurs Golovlev, 83; *357*
Shearer, Norma, *376*
Shenstone, Allen, 344
Shenstone, Molly, 319, 330, 332, 341, 344
Sibelius, Jean, 212, 218, 279
Sieburg, Friedrich, 196, 202
Sieveking, Heinrich, 109, 122
Silone, Ignazio.
  Fascism, 233. *Fontamara*, 279
Silver, Rabbi Abba Hillel, 298
Simmel, Georg, 10
Simon, Heinrich, 120, 327
Simon, Hugo, 168; *380*
Simon, Sir John, 236, 238
Simons, Hans, 311
Simplicissimus (Munich), 57, 100; *358*
Sinclair, Emil. *See* Hesse, Hermann
Sinsheimer, Hermann, 116
Skuhra, Alexander, 116, 120
Smith, Bernard, 341
Social Democratic party (SPD), 11, 12, 17, 18, 36, 38, 44, 45, 90, 91, 98, 132, 133; *349*
Sologub, Fëdor.
  "In the Crowd," 52. *The Kiss of the Unborn*, 46. *Light and Shadows*, 46, 47, 49. *The Little Demon*, 94
Sommerfeld, Martin.
  Goethe in Umwelt und Folgezeit, 286; *378*
Sonnemann, Emmy, 238
Sonn- und Montagszeitung (Vienna), 233
Sophie, grand duchess of Saxony, *375*
Sorel, Georges, 254, 255
Späth, Frau, 278
Spaet, Frau, 239
Spartakists, 21, 33, 34, 36, 39, 41

Specht, Richard, 72, 73.
  Richard Strauss und sein Werk, 105
Spengler, Oswald, 61, 68, 69, 83, 117, 217, 226, 260, 261; *352*. *Decline of the West*, 61, 62, 63, 64, 261; *354*. *Preussentum und Sozialismus*, 77
Speyer, Wilhelm, 96, 139, 147, 149, 152
Spiecker, Karl, 320; *379*
Der Spiegel (Charlottenburg), 56
Spiegler, Albert, 71, 73
Spiegler, Nina, 71, 73
Spinoza, 322
Staats-Zeitung (New York), 243, 309
Stäheli, Kurt, 270
Stahel, Dr. Jakob, 249, 279
Stahlhelm, 150, 163; *364*
Stalin, Joseph, 335; *385*
Stampfer, Friedrich, 309
Starhemberg, Prince Ernst Rüdiger von, 260
Staudinger, Hans, 328
Steegemann, Paul, 59
Stein, Baron Friedrich vom und zum, 202
Stein, Leo, 74
Steinböck, Felix, 71, 72, 73
Steiner, Herbert, 131, 246; *362*
Steinicke, Georg, 103
Steinrück, Albert, 49
Stengel, Paul, 163
Sterne, Laurence.
  Tristram Shandy, 215; *369*
Sterns, 275
Stevens, George, 311
Stevens, Miss, 320
Stickelberger, Emanuel, 194, 201; *367*
Stickelberger, Rudolf Emanuel, 204
Stifter, Adalbert, 8, 178.
  Indian Summer, 8; *350*. *Witiko*, 166; *365*
Stokowski, Leopold, 212
Strasser, Otto, 273
Strasser, Stefan, 88
Stratz, Rudolf, 208
Strauss, Johann, 274
Strauss, Richard, 105, 134, 174, 209, 300, 332; *363, 365, 384*. *Die Ägyptische Helena*, 238. *Die Frau ohne Schatten*, 356. *Friedenstag*, 332; *384*. *Der Rosenkavalier*, 271. *Salomé*, 209; *368*. *Die schweigsame Frau*, 220; *369*
Strauss, Dr. Richard, 71, 85
Straussmann, Dezsö, 270; *375*

Strauss und Torney, Lulu von. *See* Diederichs, Frau
Strecker, Karl, 48, 49, 51
Streicher, Julius, *368*
Strich, Fritz, 236, 274
Strindberg, August.
   Black Flags, 55; *354. By the Open Sea,* 67
Stroh, Heinz, 233
Stuck, Franz von, 55
Studer-Guyer, Lux, 180, 334
Der Stürmer (Nuremberg), 209; *368*
Stybel, A. Y., publishers, Tel Aviv, 170
Suarès, André, 203
Süddeutsche Monatshefte (Munich), 57, 76, 87, 105, 116; *354, 359*
Süskind, W. E., 186
Suhrkamp, Peter, 127, 131, 169, 208; *365, 391*
Sulzbach, Ernst, 238
Suppé, Franz von.
   Boccaccio, 259; *373*
Survey Graphic (New York), 313, 317; *381*
Svenska Dagbladet (Stockholm), 85
Swarzenski, Georg, 328
Swift, Jonathan, 258
Swing, Raymond Gram, 343

T

Tägliche Rundschau (Berlin), 49, 51
Tageblatt, Paris. See *Pariser Tageblatt*
Das Tage-Buch (Berlin), 76, 87, 88, 94, 130; *356*
Tagore, Rabindranath, 117
Taine, Hippolyte, 223; *369*
Tardieu, André, 193
Tchaikovsky, Peter Ilyich, 197, 216, 218.
   Fifth Symphony, 196. Violin Concerto, 217, 283
Le Temps (Paris), 114, 163, 182, 216
Tennenbaum, Richard, 153, 154, 163, 172, 178, 181, 236, 258, 285
Térey, Edith von, 13, 24, 36, 66
Thälmann, Ernst, 133
Theilhaber, Felix A.
   Goethe, Sexus und Eros, 237; *370*
Thiers, Adolphe.
   History of the French Revolution, 236
Thiersch, Friedrich, 99

Thomas, Adrienne, 150
Thomas, George, 296
Thomas, Otto, 47
Thomas Mann Archive, Zurich, *367, 389, 404*
Thomas Mann Collection, Yale University, *378, 389*
Thomas Mann Fund, Prague, 272, 297; *375*
Thomas Mann Fund, Zurich, 297
Thomas Mann Society, Prague, *376, 394, 410*
Thompson, Dorothy, 213, 243, 276, 307, 310, 311, 324; *368, 382*
Thurn und Taxis, Prince Gustav Franz von, 55
Thyssen, Amélie, 214
Thyssen, Fritz, 167
Tillich, Paul, 317
Time, 212
The Times (London), 197, 257, 305; *380*
Timm, Johannes, 37
Timpe, Willri, 210, 245
Tirso de Molina.
   Don Gil of the Green Trousers, 94; *358*
Tisza, Count István, 16
Törring, Count, 54
Toller, Ernst, 45, 48, 49, 53, 54, 59, 150, 329, 332. *Die Wandlung,* 61; *354*
Tolstoy, Count Alexei, 97
Tolstoy, Count Leo, 59, 105, 116, 117, 185, 270, 276, 303; *360. Anna Karenina,* 257 (film); 329; *383. The Cossacks,* 301. *The Death of Ivan Ilyich,* 8; *350. Diaries,* 27. Folk tales, 38. "Khodynka," 10, 52. *Master and Man,* 51; *354. War and Peace,* 132, 133, 138–48 *passim,* 157, 158
Torgler, Ernst, 179, 185, 186; *363*
Toscanini, Arturo, 262, 286, 300
Tragi, 109
Trebitsch, Siegfried, 70, 71, 75, 259, 272; *356*
Treviranus, Gottfried, 216
Trog, Hans, 109
Trotsky, Leon, 139, 166
Trübner, Wilhelm, 53
Trummler, 41, 57, 112
Tschudi, Dr., 197
Tucholsky, Kurt, 143
Tucker, Henry St. George, 329; *383*
Türk, Werner, 292, 303
Turel, Adrien, 260; *373*

Turgenev, Ivan, 122.
  The Family Charge, 123; *361. Faust,* 97.
  "Jakov Pazynkov," 54, 55. *Virgin Soil,*
  57; *354*
Turner, Joseph Mallord William, 322
Twice a Year, 317; *381*

U

Uexküll, Baron Jakob Johann von.
  Theoretische Biologie, 112
Uhde-Bernays, Hermann, 67, 97
Ulmann, Fräulein, 299
Ulrich, Dr. Konrad, 256, 262
Unger, Hermann, 114.
  Knaben und Mörder, 360
Union of German Scholars and Artists,
  20, 56, 88
University of Illinois, Urbana, 298; *379*
Unruh, Fritz von, 269; *374*
Unterleitner, Hans, 26

V

Vaihinger, Hans, 110, 112
Valéry, Paul, 159; *378*
Van Aken, 139, 144
Van Gogh, Vincent, 333
Van Loon, Hendrik Willem, 242, 243,
  319
Vansittart, Sir Robert, 282, 341
Veit, Otto, 226
Velázquez, 73
Velhagen und Klasings Monatshefte, 48, 51
Verdi, Giuseppe, 93.
  Aïda, 84, 86. Requiem, 76, 286, 310
Vermehren, Julius, 119
Versailles, Treaty of, 56, 60, 91, 130,
  167, 234, 308, 324
Viereck, George Sylvester, 69
Viereck, Peter, *385*
Vilhelm, Prince of Sweden, 340
Vitzthum von Eckstädt, Count Hermann,
  38, 118
Vivaldi, Antonio, 161
Völkischer Beobachter (Munich and Berlin),
  141, 150, 159, 179, 182, 199, 248,
  262, 284; *364*
Volkszeitung. See *Neue Volkszeitung*

Vollmoeller, Karl Gustav, 155, 156
Vorwärts (Berlin), 11, 24, 87; *350*
Voss, Johann Heinrich.
  Luise, 16; *351*
Vossische Zeitung (Berlin), 97, 99, 100,
  101, 102, 105, 116, 132, 138, 140,
  152, 184, 195; *358, 359, 360*
Vossler, Karl, 156, 191, 231

W

Wälterlin, Oskar, 305
Der Wagenlenker (Munich), 57
Wagner, Cosima, 280
Wagner, Erika, 70, 71, 72
Wagner, Richard, 8, 38, 58, 69, 93, 95,
  105, 201, 202, 223, 278, 280–82,
  283; *362, 377. Die Meistersinger,* 40,
  65, 134, 226, 262, 283, 300; *369.*
  Parsifal, 7–8, 66–67, 93, 115, 262. *Der
  Ring des Nibelungen,* 95, 283: *Die
  Walküre,* 97, 264, 269, 282; *Die
  Götterdämmerung,* 194, 231, 310;
  "Rhine Journey," 286. *Siegfried Idyll,*
  278, 280. *Tannhäuser,* 84, 253, 303.
  Tristan und Isolde, 90, 97, 99, 278, 303
Wagner, Siegfried, 280; *377*
Wagner, Winifred, 223
Wahl, Rudolf, *255*
Das wahre Deutschland, 293; *379*
Waldau, Gustav, 34
Waldsanatorium, Davos. Ill. A6
Waldstetter, Ruth, 204
Wallace, Henry, 242
Walser, Karl, 197, 203
Walser, Robert, 94
Walter, Bruno, 13, 17–20 *passim,* 36, 40,
  41, *58–59,* 70–74 *passim,* 98, 99, 112,
  116, 123, 135, 214, 259, 303; *379.*
  Performances by, 8–9, 42, 59, 72, 76,
  86, 90, 98, 104, 115, 300, 343.
  Mahler and, 104. Nazi ban on, 131,
  134; *363, 364.* Correspondence with,
  5, 64, 161, 166, 337. Ill. B16
Walter, Elsa, 17, 34, 40, 59, 70–74
  passim, 86, 90, 98, 104, 115, 123, 214,
  259, 272, 303, 343
Walter, Frau, 153, 154, 245
Walter, Grete, 98, 334, 343; *352, 384*
Walter, Lotte, 46, 115, 116, 296, 343;
  352, 379

Walz, John Albrecht, 242
Wandrey, Conrad, 69, 83, 117.
    Theodor Fontane, 69; *355, 356*
Warburg family, 212
Warburg Institute, 334; *384*
Warner, Jack L., 297
The Washington Post, 292, 303, 326; *378*
Washington Star, 244
Wassermann, Jakob, 52, 54, 103, 115,
    116, 122–23, 130, 146, 186, 191,
    192; *364, 365*. Correspondence with,
    24, 36, 93, 152. *The World's Illusion*,
    32, 33, 36; *352*
Wassermann-Speyer, Julie, 146; *364*
Wassermann-Karlweis, Marta, 115, 116,
    122, 123, 186, 191, 246, 293, 303.
    Jakob Wassermann, 234, 246; *370, 371*
Wassermann, Oskar, 142
Wassmann, Hans, 94
Waterboer, Heinz.
    Das Tagebuch des Dr. Sarraut, 246; *371*
Weber, Alfred, 200, 203
Weber, Carl Maria, 100
Weber, Carl Maria von.
    Oberon, 17, 98, 210
Weber, Hans von, 21, 55
Weber, Max, 58, 84
Wedekind, Frank, 49, 92, 94, 278; *376*.
    Der Liebestrank, 122; *361*
Weese, Arthur, 109
Wegener, Paul, 94
Weigand, Hermann, 214, 292, 300.
    Thomas Mann's Novel "Der Zauberberg,"
    178
Weigel, Helene, 339; *393*
Weigl, Franz.
    Die Schweizerfamilie, 13; *350*
Weil, Prof., 327
Weingartner, Felix von, 204, 274
Weiss, Julian, 238
Weitbrecht, Günther, 57, 60
Wells, H. G., 274, 339, 340
Wels, Otto, 142
Welsh, M. H., *383*
Die Weltbühne (Berlin), 130; *363*
Welti, Jakob, 305
Weltliteratur (Munich), 100
Weltmann, Lutz, 184
Werfel, Franz, 127, 258; *378, 381, 405*
Werkbund, 41, 112; *353*
Wertham, Fredric, 329
Wertheim, Maurice, 276

Wertheimer, Martha, 221
Wessel, Horst, 238, 254; *363*
Wessely, Paula, 277
Whitman, Walt, 116; *360*
Wickihalder, Hans, 185
Wiegand, Heinrich, 135, 138, 160
Wieland, Christoph Martin.
    Agathon, 211; *368*
Wiener Journal. See *Neues Wiener Journal*
Wiener Kunstwanderer, 366
Wilde, Oscar, *368*
Wildgans, Anton, 110
Wilhelm II, Kaiser, 3, 5, 15, 17, 18, 20,
    21, 23, 56, 63, 74, 174, 221; *349*
Willer, Luise, 117
Williams, Emlyn.
    Night Must Fall (film), 297; *379*
Willich, Charlotte, 33, 34, 38
Wilson, Woodrow, 6, 12–16 *passim*, 24,
    25, 33, 40, 51, 53, 57, 87, 88, 90
Winder, Ludwig, 324
Winter, Sophus, 325
Winterfeldt, Joachim von, 60
Winterstein, 91
Witkop, Philipp, 3, 4, 31, 56, 152.
    Heinrich von Kleist, 123
Wittgenstein, Paul, 71
Wittkowski, Viktor, 253, 254
Wölfflin, Heinrich, 102, 109, 180, 181,
    283
Wolf, Hugo, 40, 64, 248, 278.
    Der Corregidor, 98, 259; *358*
Wolfe, Thomas.
    Look Homeward, Angel, 276
Wolfer, Rudolf Hans, 110
Wolff, Elisabeth, 104
Wolff, Hans, 207, 247
Wolff, Kurt, 104, 114, 117, 166
Wolff-Verlag, Kurt, 43; *351, 353*
Wolff, Theodor, 198
Wolff-Metternich, Count Paul, 150
Wolfskehl, Karl, 47, 217, 218
Wolynski, Akim L.
    Das Reich der Karamasoff, 85
Workers' and Soldiers' Councils, 18, 19,
    20, 21, 38, 221
Das Wort (Moscow), 259; *372*
Writers' League, Munich, 22, 25, 127,
    133, 134; *350, 362*
Writers' League, Prague, 286
Wüterich, Dr., 150
Wurm, Mathilde, 238; *370*

Y

Yale University, 285, 292, 293, 300; *380*

Z

Zarek, Otto, 10, 40, 41.
 Die Flucht, 10; *350*
Zech, Countess Isa von, 120
Zech, Count Julius von, 120

Zechbauer, Max, 76
Zeitschrift für freie deutsche Forschung (Paris),
 313
Zemlinksy, Alexander von, 117
Zillmann, Friedrich, 97
Zimmer, Heinrich, *385, 405*
Zuckerkandl, Viktor, 272
Zuckmayer, Carl, *378, 405*
Die Zukunft (Berlin), 17, 32; *351*
Die Zukunft (Paris), 318, 319, 329; *382*
Zweig, Stefan, 85, 102, 149, 152, 209,
 220; *351, 366. Drei Meister*, 102; *359.*
 Erasmus of Rotterdam, 220, 221, 222.
 Romain Rolland, 105

Photo Credits

Gottfried Bermann Fischer: B 7 bottom, 9, C 7 bottom; Mann family: B 7 top, 11; Princeton University Library: C 4 bottom, 5; Stadtbibliothek, Munich (Handschriften-Abteilung): B 1, 6 top, 8, 13, 15; Thomas Mann Archiv, Zurich: A 1–5, 7, 8, B 2–5, 10, 12, 14, 16, C 1–4 top, 6, 7 top, 8; Universitätsbibliothek, Düsseldorf (Thomas Mann-Sammlung "Dr. Hans-Otto Mayer"): A 6, B 6 bottom.

In-Text Illustration Credits

Beinecke Rare Book and Manuscript Library, Yale University: pages 121, 183, 281, 331; Thomas Mann Archiv, Zurich: page 35; Universitätsbibliothek, Düsseldorf (Thomas Mann-Sammlung "Dr. Hans-Otto Mayer"): page 113.

The diaries themselves are housed in the Thomas Mann Archiv, Zurich.

Mittwoch den 11. September.